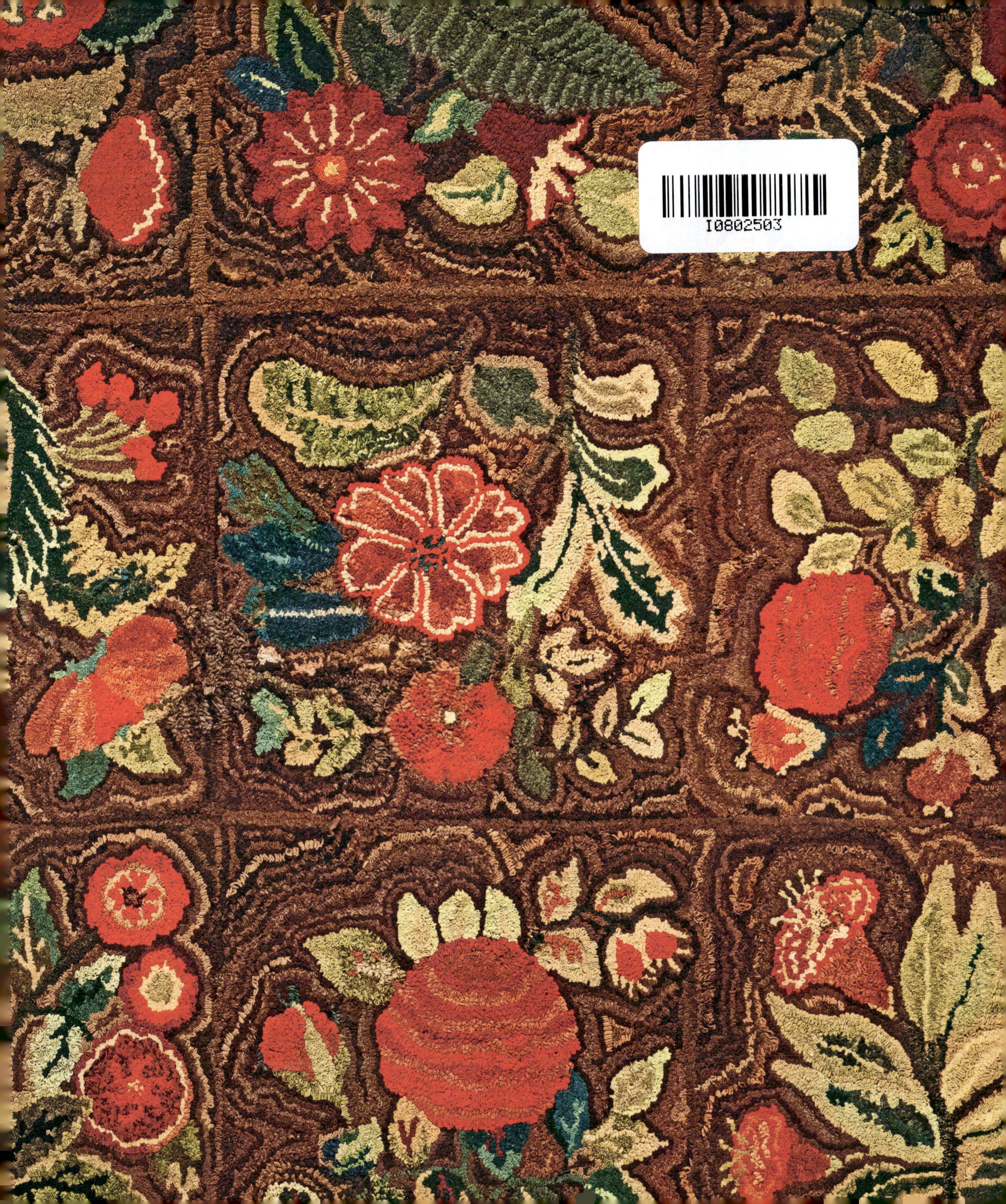

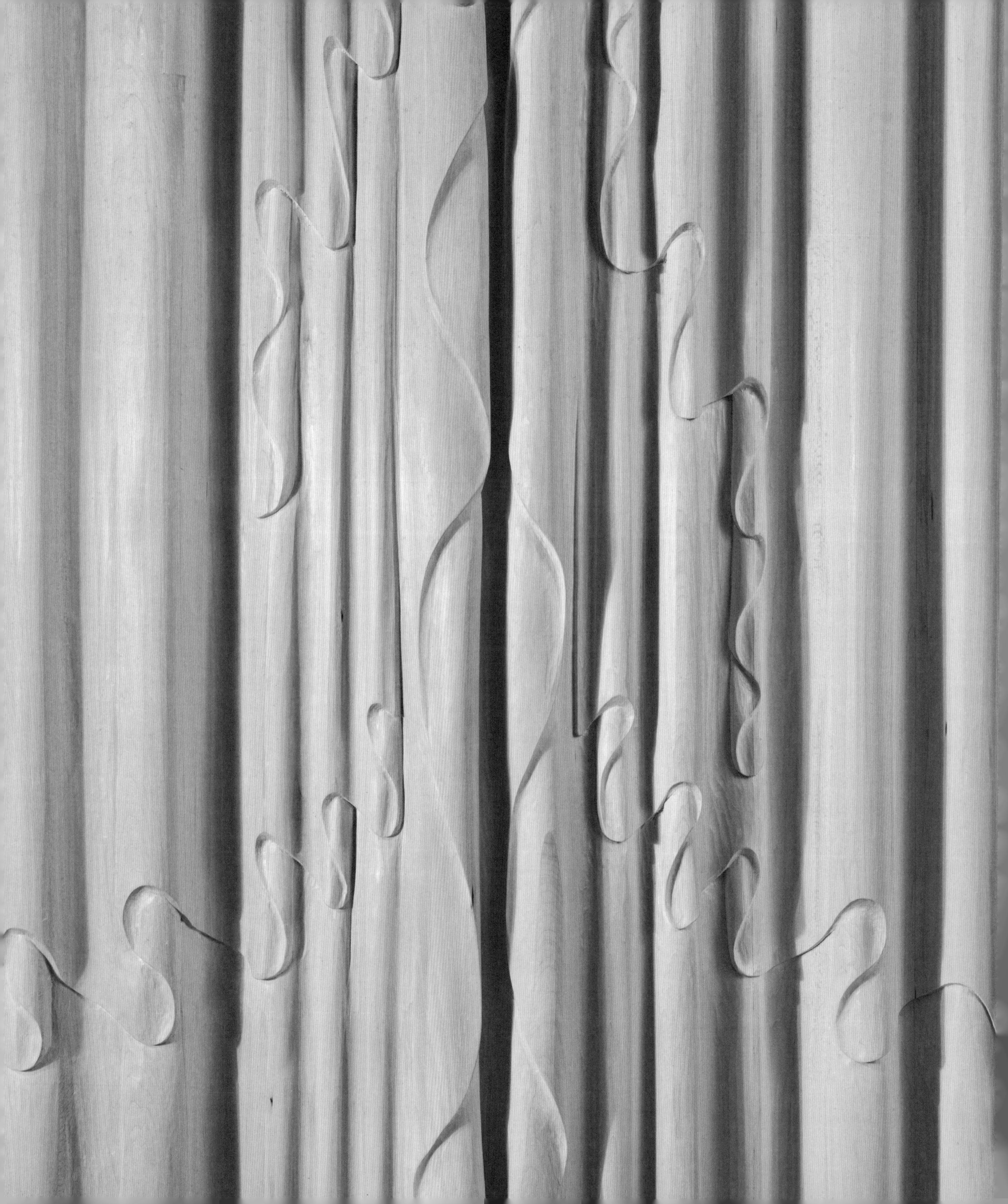

HANDWORK

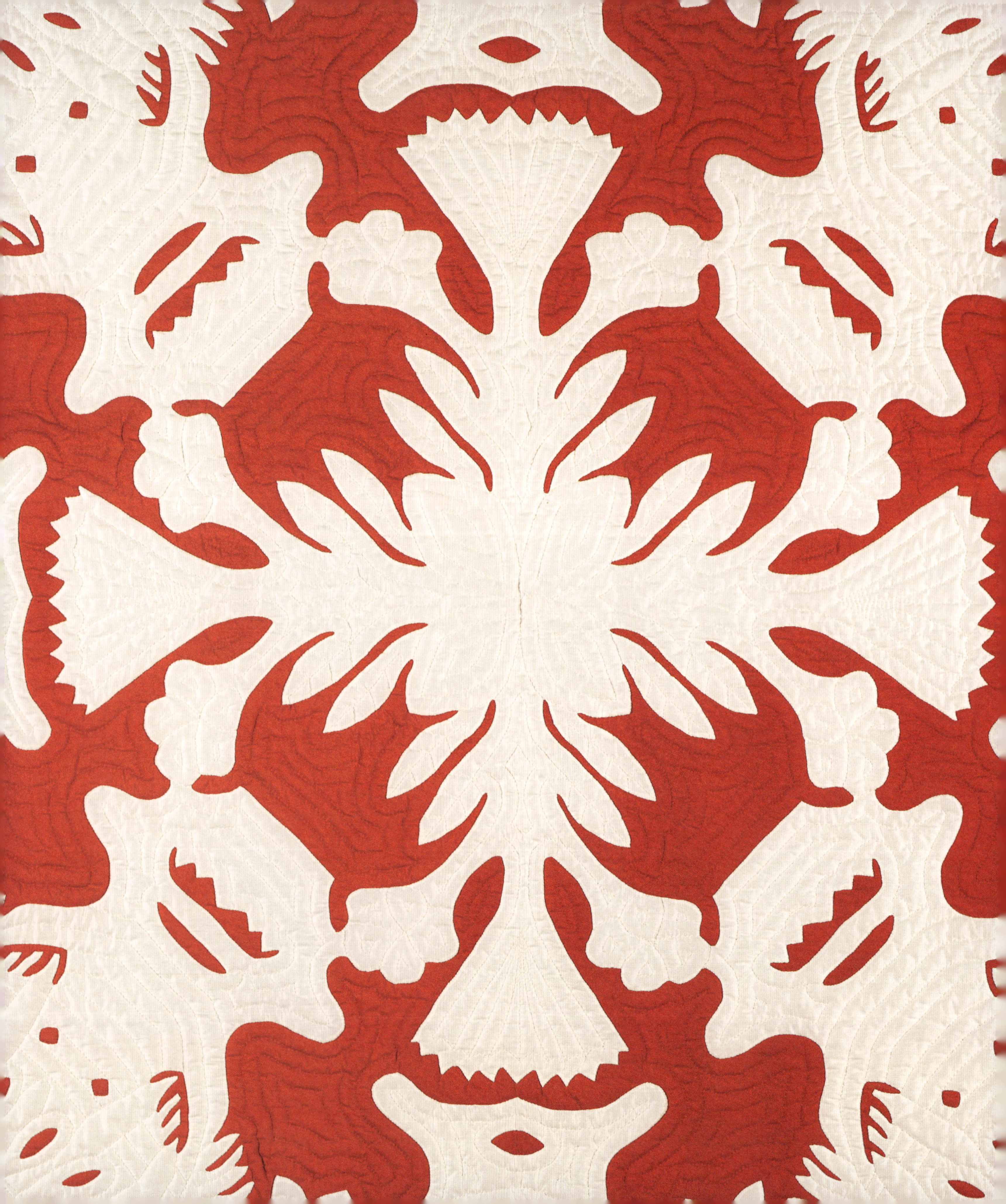

HANDCRAFTED OBJECTS

HAND WORK

THAT MADE AMERICA

Foreword by
CAROL SAUVION

Edited by
EMILY ZAIDEN

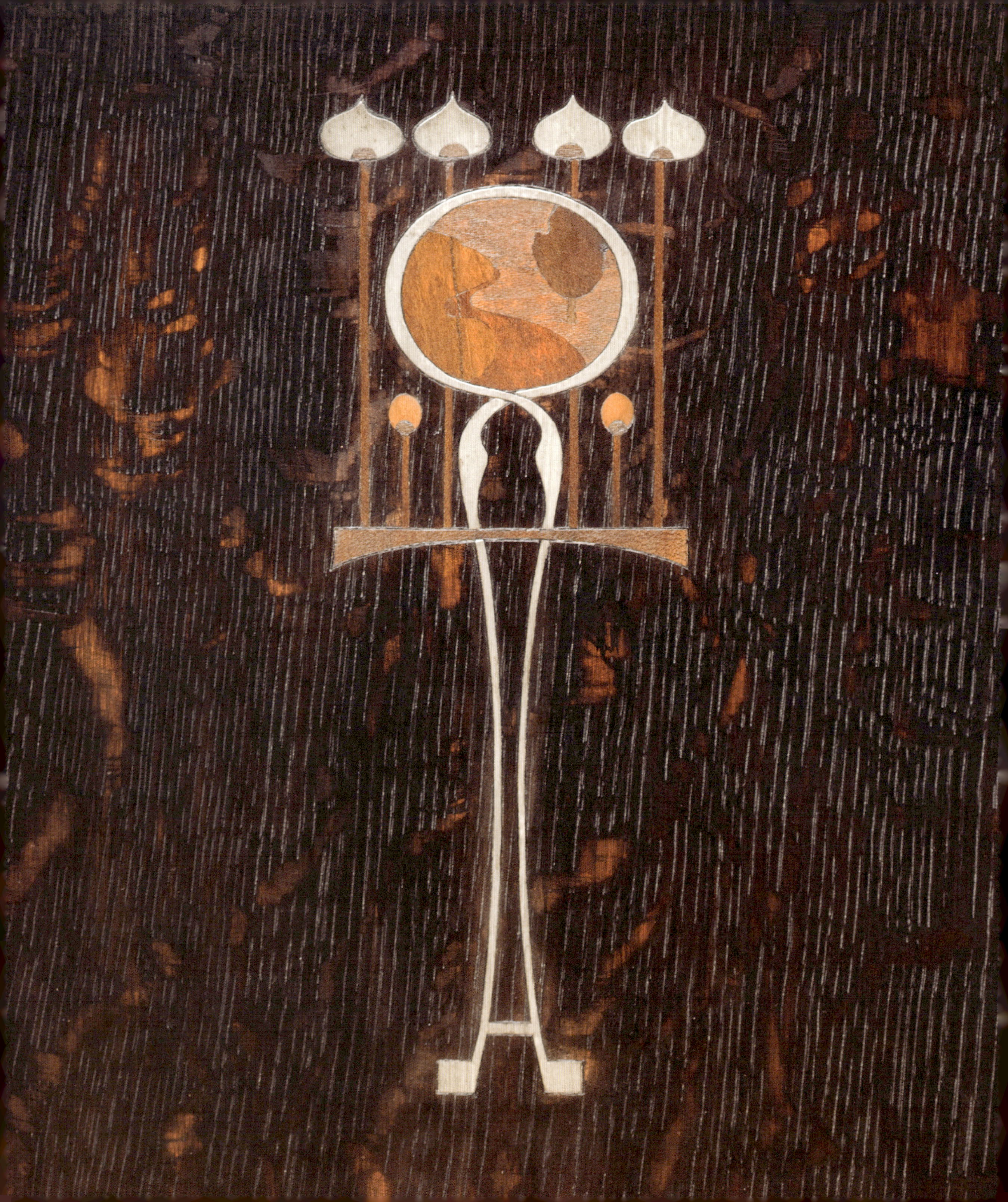

7
FOREWORD
Carol Sauvion

9
Acknowledgments

11
THE OBJECTS THAT DEFINE US
Emily Zaiden

DWELL

20 The Light: To Illuminate
30 The Basket: To Collect
40 The Container: To Keep
50 The Gate: To Greet
54 The Tool: To Work
64 The Lure: To Provide
72 The Toy: To Play
84 The Instrument: To Resonate
96 The Carrier: To Transport

FEED

114 The Cup: To Drink
126 The Plate: To Serve
136 The Bowl: To Contain
150 The Pot: To Pour
160 The Utensil: To Dine

FURNISH

174 The Chair: To Sit
184 The Table: To Set
198 The Cabinet: To Store
214 The Rug: To Cover
224 The Quilt: To Warm

ADORN

244 The Vase: To Decorate
252 The Necklace: To Frame
268 The Garment: To Wear
284 The Accessory: To Enhance
294 The Shoe: To Walk

305 Notes
309 Selected Bibliography
313 Contributors
315 Credits
316 Index

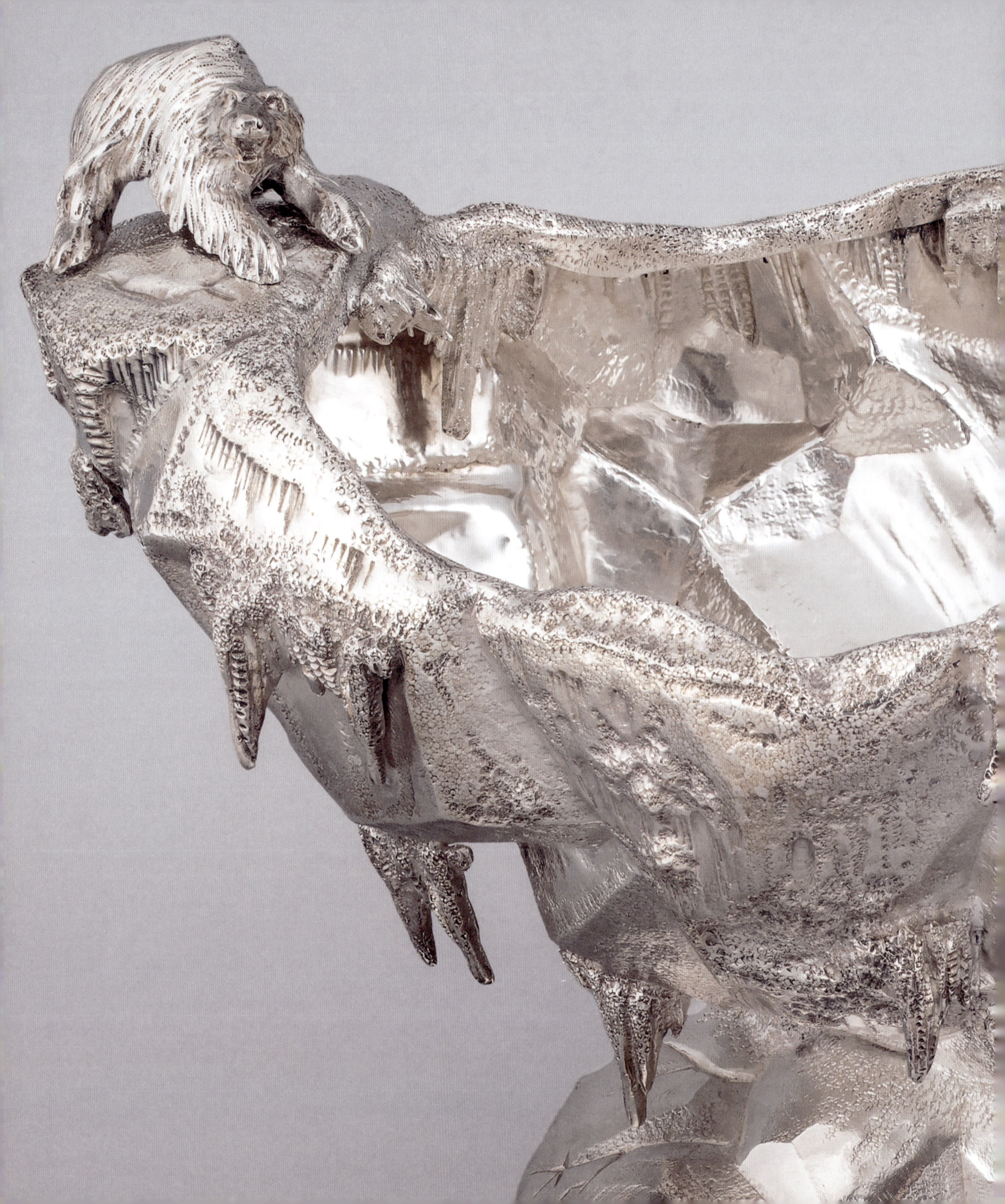

FOREWORD

This book was created as part of *Handwork: Celebrating American Craft 2026*, an initiative to honor the crafts during our Semiquincentennial, the 250th anniversary of the founding of the United States. It tells the stories of the handmade objects that we surround ourselves with and how they have evolved throughout our national history. It documents the meaning of these objects and contributions of their makers. It is a keepsake, a measure of our promise and our progress as a nation.

What is *craft*? In the words of potter and teacher Frances Senska: "You design it and make it yourself." Craft is all around us, of course, and almost everyone has a craft story. Collectively, the essays in this book demonstrate the myriad craft stories that have existed, sometimes on parallel paths, sometimes following long traditions, and often on journeys of self-expression that reflect the skill of the maker, uniting the disparate cultures within our country. These essays also cause me to think about our place and our time in the history of America. Why craft now, in the midst of a technological revolution? Is there still a basic human need to create, and does making things by hand give them added meaning? Certainly, a hand-pieced quilt and a hand-thrown pot hold the energy of their makers.

Some of the objects in this book are old friends; some are new to me. All are as familiar as their forms and functions require them to be but yet as unique as the artists who made them, which is always the way with things made by hand. How remarkable that a spoon or a bowl or a cup could be so universal an object as to last and be reinvented through centuries.

It has been fifty years since our last national celebration, the 1976 Bicentennial. Handwork 2026 includes craftspeople who may have been omitted during that jubilee, giving them and their craft heritages a chance to be recognized. For the first time, through the objects contained in this book, I feel a connection to many kinds of crafts that I didn't know enough about, many evolving over generations and centuries, all in our country.

I thank Emily Zaiden, who took on the monumental task of structuring and editing the Handwork book. I thank the writers, craft lovers all, who have taken the time to explain the place of these special objects, both in our history and in our moment. With their essays, they help us to understand the importance of each piece and each maker, whether known or anonymous. And I thank the generous supporters of the book, who made this unique view of our handmade heritage possible.

This book is more than a souvenir: it is a compendium of objects handcrafted in our American history, examples of our finest handwork, the products of our culture. We have so much to treasure and to be thankful for.

Carol Sauvion
Founder and former Executive Director,
Craft in America
Los Angeles, California, 2025

PAGE 2: Detail, *Umeke O Kamehameha*, 2025, see pages 238–39.
PAGE 4: Detail, Armchair, c. 1903, see pages 180–81.
OPPOSITE: Detail, Ice bowl, 1871, see pages 142–43.

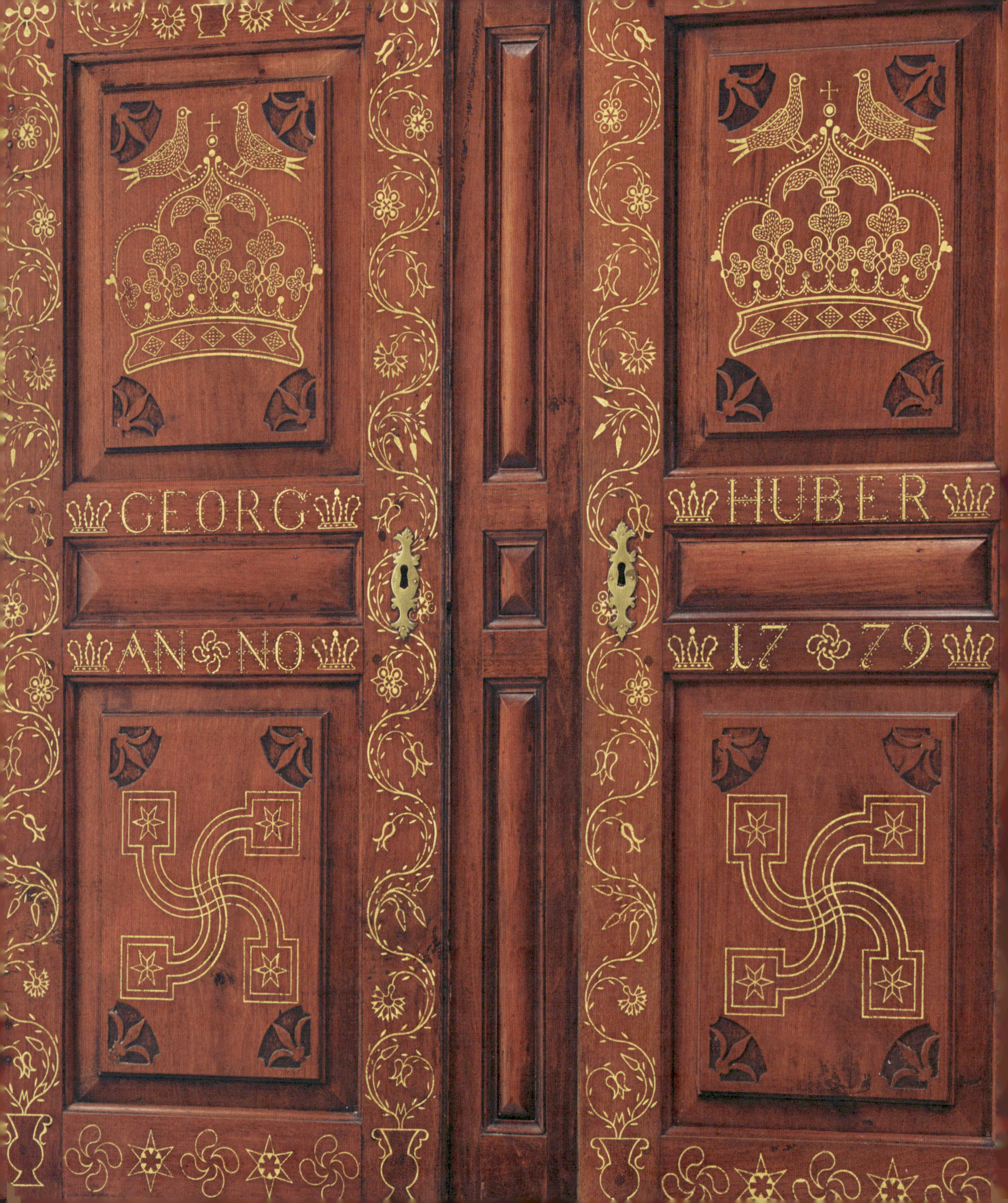
GEORG
HUBER
ANNO
1779

ACKNOWLEDGMENTS

This book would not have been possible without the generous support of individuals who are tireless advocates for advancing the examination of craft and its role in shaping American society. Todd Wingate provided support from day one and a steady stream of wisdom throughout the process. Susan Steinhauser, a lifelong patron of craft, immediately jumped in to build a strong base for this publication. This book was able to move forward because of the generosity of the Americana Foundation, Boardman Family Foundation, Steven Cason, Corinna Cotsen, Cynthia Lovelace Sears, Barbara Waldman, and other anonymous individuals.

The unwavering vision and passion of Craft in America's founder and executive director Carol Sauvion have changed how we understand craft in the United States, and this book is one of the many products of her efforts. Carol conceptualized and guided plans for Handwork 2026 along with a planning committee—which included Harriett Green, Lois Jecklin, Jean McLaughlin, Ann Pifer, Lynn Pollard, and Consuelo Jimenez Underwood—that has gathered organizations, museums, and many individuals all collaborating to celebrate our nation's craft heritage.

The book took shape thanks to Shaye Areheart, who brought our ideas to Monacelli. It has been an absolute joy to work with Monacelli senior editor Jenny Florence, who has made the entire process smooth and seamless. Monacelli editorial assistant Jenny Mutch brought her editorial eagle eye to the book, and production director Michael Vagnetti ensured the quality of the final product. Jessica Fleischmann interpreted the content beautifully with her strong design perspective. Karen Ehrmann worked with dedication to obtain and organize the images. We are grateful to all the institutions, collections, photographers, and gallerists who shared their photography with us. The additional project assistance from Katrina Reynolds was a tremendous boost. Denise Kang, Victoria May, and Michelle Starks, along with the staff of both Craft in America and Freehand, helped to realize the book through their dedicated work.

We are indebted to the contributing writers and artists, who lent their thoughtful perspectives and vast knowledge to the book. They include Glenn Adamson, Elisabeth Agro, Barry Bergey, Alexandra Cade, Lauren Cross, Christina De León, Jeannine Falino, Nonie Gadsden, Christine Garnier, Steve Grafe, Katherine Gray, Leslie King Hammond, Carla Hemlock, Suzanne Isken, Mary Jackson, Alexandra Kirtley, Debra Krol, Jo Lauria, Colette Lemmon, Robert Liu, Roberto Lugo, Tess Lukey, Wendy Maruyama, Marques Hanalei Marzan, Jane Milosch, Mira Nakashima, Monica Obniski, Joyce Scott, Julie Silber, Therman Statom, Lowery Stokes Sims, Matt Thurlow, Einar and Jamex de la Torre, Ehren Tool, Consuelo Jimenez Underwood, Lynne Zacek Bassett, and Zac Zetterberg.

We additionally thank the following people who aided with the research of the book in myriad ways: Dick Boak, Owen Duncan, Michael Grauer, Thomas Gleason, the late Bernie Herman, Todd Huber, Allison Jaqua, Lois Jecklin, Jo Lauria, Justin Lemberg, George McDaniel, Forrest Merrill, Farrol Mertes, Jane Milosch, Dru Muscovin, Diana Pardue, Jamie L. Swartz, Sarah Walcott, and Edward Wright.

We are deeply grateful to all of the institutions, museums, galleries, and individuals who allowed us to include objects from their collections in this book and who facilitated the process.

Without the encouragement, patience, and input of family and friends, this book would not exist. Thank you all, with infinite gratitude.

OPPOSITE: Detail, Kleiderschrank (clothes press), 1779, see pages 198–99.
OVERLEAF: Detail, *Paired Box* (one of a set), c. 1990s, see pages 46–47.

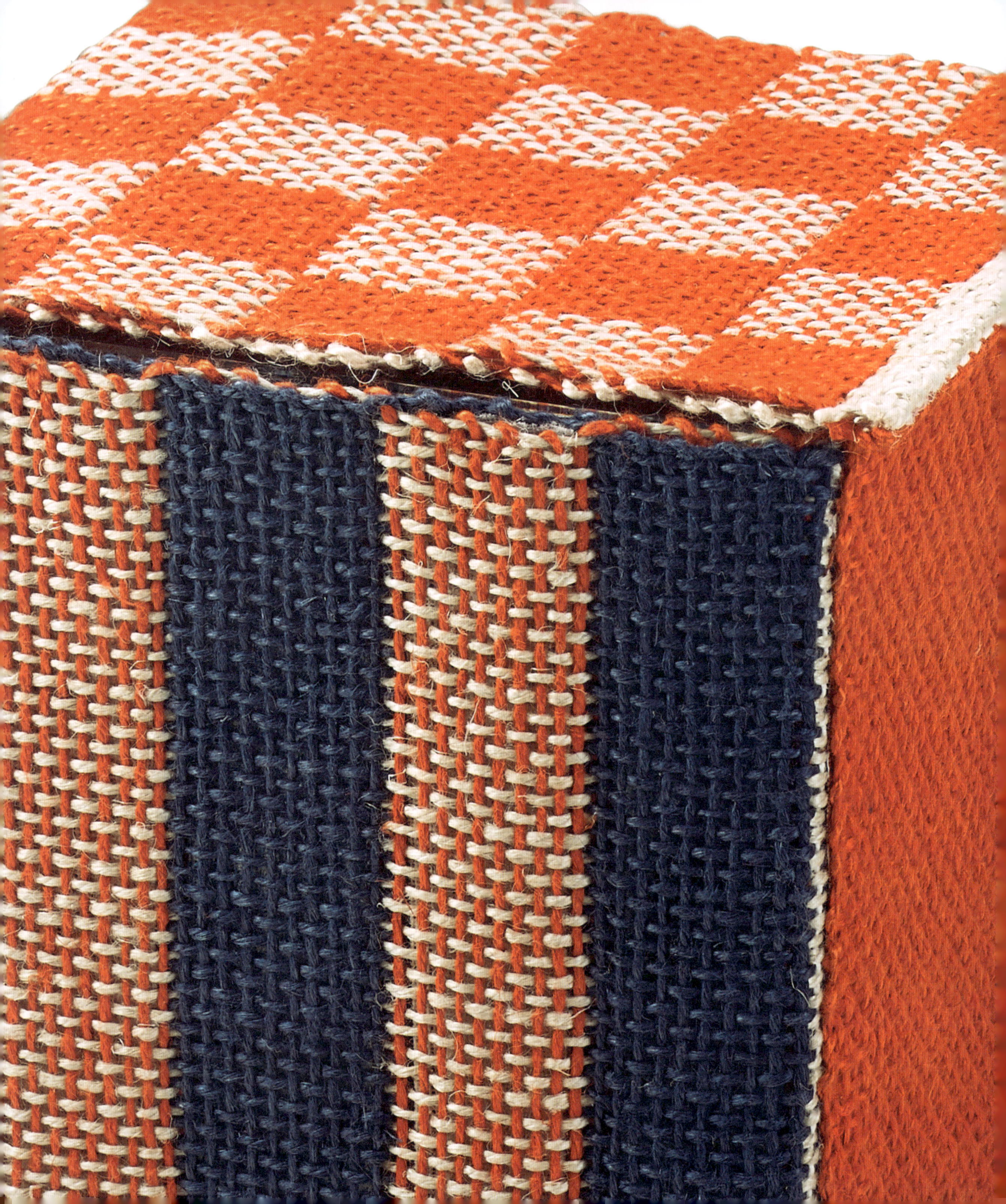

THE OBJECTS THAT DEFINE US

Emily Zaiden

"It is dearness only that gives everything its value."
—Thomas Paine, *The American Crisis*, No. 1, 1776

Objects tell stories. Each object is formed by thoughts before it is shaped by hands. Each object is a record of the moment when it was made, a reflection of the social and environmental circumstances around its origin. Each object is tied not only to the story of a maker, but to the story of its owner or user, and the stories of when it was purchased, gifted, inherited, preserved, and enjoyed over time. Each object in this book, handmade in America and spanning from centuries before the country's founding to the present, contains a unique story originating in personal history, ideas, values, and expression.

The story of craft in America begins with an obvious truth: At first, everything, everywhere, was handmade. Handwork was the only way of life prior to 1776. Craft traditions practiced by the Indigenous people who inhabit this land defined its objects for millennia. Understanding, respecting, and using raw materials from the landscape was and is fundamental to Native American life. As colonists arrived from Europe and sought to build a world for themselves, they took from Native practices and tapped into their cultures of origin to form a new material culture. And as others arrived from across Europe, as well as from Africa, other parts of the Americas, and Asia in the decades following the Declaration of Independence, various forms of craft helped forge early America. At its inception, the country was viewed by many Americans as a blank slate. The knowledge and traditions of Indigenous peoples, settlers, and enslaved people shaped the new country. There were sacrifices, human and environmental costs, and undeniable violations made all along the way. Those tragedies, long disregarded, are at the forefront of our consciousness now.

Ingenuity and individualism are ideals that have long inspired Americans to make the objects we surround ourselves with. In the nascent nation, handwork was not only inevitable, but also an antidote to the reliance on imported goods—a political and economic rejection from which this country itself was born. Things, from cloth to beads, were crafted for personal use but as commodities and currency they were also the backbone of our earliest economy (in addition to being infused with many other layers of meaning). Craft has always been more than the means to an end, the fulfilment of a need; making things was, and is, often a practice of self-reliance and an expression of independence—ideals that have been at the very core of this country since before its birth.

Even prior to the founding of the United States, cottage industry was synonymous with craft production and gave its makers financial and, therefore, political freedom. Craft was also an act of autonomy that fed patriotism and pride, and the things that were made reflected the formation of a national identity. Craft translated the country's wealth of raw materials, skills, and vision into physical form.

The reliance on handcraft changed as industrialization swept the United States during the late nineteenth and early twentieth centuries. It played a continued but more nuanced part in homes as well as in shops and factories. The repositioning of handwork's role in the production of objects was the impetus for the Arts and Crafts movement that developed at the turn of the twentieth century, and it established the ideals for what became the Studio Craft movement a few decades later. Then, with roots planted in Studio Craft, handwork in the form of contemporary craft emerged and spilled over into the domains of art, activism, cultural practice, ritual, and functional design. Craft thrives in new forms in the twenty-first century.

Despite negotiating shared and enduring concerns such as process, material, design, tradition, and utility, the trajectory of craft in America has rarely been viewed as beginning with Indigenous peoples, continuing into early and modern America, and persisting to the present. But craft is a bridge across history, a chain of countless hands, and this book aims to recast the narrative. This book highlights more than one hundred exquisite, richly storied objects made over the course of American history in order to explore the what, the how, and, most importantly, the why of American handcraft, then and now. This collection of essays unites historic examples of craft, decorative arts, and traditional cultural practices with the most recent craft innovations. It is not a comprehensive, sweeping history of American craft. However, the selected handcrafted objects together present a more inclusive way of approaching that legacy across time and across geography, cultures, and identities. Collectively, the gathered objects form a vibrant and diverse portrait of American history and life.

The making of this book was a colossal shared effort involving forty contributors, all experts in their respective fields. Among them are art historians, historians, folklorists, cultural practitioners, artists, and more. Each of them was tasked with selecting a handmade object and considering its physical features as keys to unlock revelations about our history.[1] Through their texts, craft is explored from a broad range of perspectives. This multiplicity of voices helps give a democratic account of the handmade throughout American history.

The contributors' essays demonstrate the layering of stories within each handmade object. At the moment of an object's creation, there is first the story told by the maker. Then, later, there is the story that we can discern about that maker, traced in the object itself. Often that story can lead us to an understanding of the context in which the maker produced the object. When a maker is living, we are fortunate that their voice can be present; ten artist statements are included in this book, in which an object's creator tells us its story in their own words.

When examined closely from dozens of perspectives, both with and without direct insight into the makers' intentions, and when taken as a whole, the scores of objects in this book raise important questions: What does American handwork look like? Which craft forms have endured and why? How have American craft processes changed over time? What makes an object American? How are American craft objects distinguished from handmade things elsewhere in the world? The essays herein explore the ideas that shape objects, how objects distinctly embody our history, and what objects say about who we are.

The 110 objects in the book are organized by a loose taxonomy. They are first grouped into four principal sections based on how they are used within our daily lives—Dwell, Feed, Furnish, and Adorn. Dwell and Feed include objects that are actively engaged to perform tasks. Furnish and Adorn include more passive objects, those that are worn and those that remain stationary. Within these sections, subsections classify handmade objects by the appearance of their form and function—the Bowl, to Collect; the Cup, to Drink; the Quilt, to Warm—and are arranged chronologically, beginning with the earliest and ending with the most contemporary. For each type of object, there are examples from the intervening centuries that demonstrate how the role of craft ebbs and flows in society. Each object is a lens for understanding our culture across time. Throughout our history, the one constant is that the world is constantly changing, sometimes radically. But however much the world shifts, objects remain largely the same. In the words of anthropologist Sidney Mintz, "Everyday substances may help us to clarify both how the world changes from what it was to what it may become, and how it manages at the same time to stay in certain regards very much the same."[2] Familiar things create ties between the past and the present.

We know that objects can tell us about people and places, moments in history, circumstances of daily life, and value and belief systems that are sometimes lost in the preserved papers we traditionally rely upon to learn our history. Material things speak to us with an immediacy and can be understood instantaneously by the eye. Each familiar object form, from the ladder to the spoon to the candlestick, is part of a common language spoken across cultures and time. The continuity of familiar objects imbues the past into the present; the kinds of objects that came before still play a part in our lives, even if their purposes shift. For example, before electricity was commonplace, the candlestick was fundamental to extending life into the nighttime. Now, while no longer strictly utilitarian, we still keep candlesticks on our tables as nostalgic nods, decorative pieces only used to create ambiance.[3]

As their utility and meaning have changed over time, many objects could easily shift between—or even overlap—multiple categories. For instance, any vessel is also a container; they share certain attributes even when their forms or roles are so different. This book aims to stretch definitions of archetypal forms and types by looking at objects from new perspectives, challenging how we normally see them.[4] A container, whether a jug or a sack, can literally contain things such as water or clothing, or it may metaphorically contain familial ties, or the story of an individual's life. A treaty belt is an accessory in form, and more importantly, a symbol of the bolstering of diplomatic relations.

Additionally, objects can fulfill a function, *and* they can provide a multisensory experience. Objects have always operated on multiple levels when designed and crafted with beauty in mind, and none of the things in this book would be considered purely utilitarian. Made by skilled artists and makers, they operate on visual, tactile, auditory, and sometimes additional levels. A piano is played to please the ear with music and its surface is adorned with inlay that pleases the eye. A pair of silver tongs helps grasp a cube of sugar while providing sparkle to a tea table. A beaded cradleboard protects a baby and provides a vibrant cocoon that represents the identity of its precious cargo. At each step, the choices of the maker appeal to the senses through shape, color, form, decoration, material, technique, and much more.

The featured objects range widely, from showstopping craft triumphs to humble workhorses comforting in their familiarity. There are feats of exceptional technical bravado and complexity. They are the objects that catch the eye, providing a visual spectacle and perceived tactile or multisensory stimulation that makes it difficult to look away. They are testament to American artistry and the desire to amaze, to enchant, to lure with indulgent splendor. Those objects are juxtaposed with more modest pieces, the outcome of necessity and circumstance. While early craft was aimed at usefulness, that by no means limited beauty, intricacy, and representation of human ability. Some of the more visually understated objects in the book tell the most complicated, sentimental, and multilayered stories. Simplicity to the eye might lead to a multifaceted world and significant insight into a pivotal chapter of American history. This book places on equal footing the everyday and ordinary, the overlooked and disregarded, and the exceptional and acclaimed.

Finally, while objects are anchored within the framework of the book by their physically manifested purpose, many works of craft produced today use their implied function, and all the meaning that has accrued over time, as the starting point for cultural critique or exploration. For example, a bowl has a cavity for containing things—but it may not be used as such. Most craft made in the twenty-first century references the notion of an object type but takes it in a conceptual direction away from pure function. This book places early functional examples next to contemporary interpretations with artist statements that make their ideational approach clear.

While a conceptual approach to craft may be said to typify contemporary practice, it is a fallacy that the intentions of earlier makers were aimed strictly at ornament and serviceability. All too often mischaracterized, craft has always been a communicative channel for giving material form to concepts. Craft has always been expressive. Chairmakers never carved ball-and-claw feet out of pure necessity. Potters deliberately depicted specific flowers, animals, and imagery that embodied ethnic identity on chargers and bowls. A beaded moccasin expresses the identity of its maker as part of a culture that uses beadwork in their clothing. A mug made and decorated by a young immigrant girl can voice her ambitions and optimism for her new life. The construct that a function somehow overrides the craftsperson's ability to articulate ideas and narratives is limited. This body of essays breaks down the traditional hierarchies associated with craft. Art has a function: most often, to make people think and feel, and to convey the ideas of the artist. Objects perform certain tasks—providing a surface for sitting or the means to pick up food—and they additionally provide visual, tactile, intellectual, and emotional stimulation.

This book is also about new, expansive definitions of craft and the many modes of making. The objects it explores are not just the products of a solitary individual working from start to finish, from material cultivation through final touch-ups. Some were made by the shop of a craftsperson who oversaw a small group of other makers. Others were created by those who worked with family or their community at kitchen tables or on the ground. Craft reaches into the most revolutionized factories, in which teams of proficient laborers and artisans played their differentiable parts in the steps of object formation. It stretches into the realm of modern production, in which craft is integral to prototyping and finishing. These are the inclusive declarations of how craft suffuses American production. Craft is more widespread, and enduring than we acknowledge.

With that said, the book does not, nor can it, include everything. These objects were selected to give an expansive view of the creativity of American craftspeople, makers, and artisans. Craft is boundless and multifaceted. And in that spirit, understanding and summarizing American craft is equally complex. The objects do not fit one singular characterization of what handcrafted means. They are as divergent as American culture.

Objects are finite entities that have an undeniable physical existence, but they are so much more. Objects transfer history and encapsulate human experience.[5] American handcrafted objects perpetually reflect the struggle to form identity, to define beauty, and to confront crisis. The kinds of objects that are made, their forms, and their ornamentation, through surface and shape, echo these themes. Objects can be more than what we are as humans. They are what we can control. They can speak even when the maker or user's voice is muted. They can get closer to the perfection we seek. They are our ambitions. As a verb, "to object" means to challenge. Many of the stories in this book describe how handmade things can shake up the status quo, promote new ways of living, facilitate daily life, or express societal shifts in tangible packages. As art historian Margaretta Lovell states, "The art object is the quintessential expression and the agent of that will to order, a bulwark against the infinitude of possibilities and instabilities the flow of time creates."[6]

The idea of handcraft making things seem more "real" and honest was crucial to the Arts and Crafts movement, when theorist Charles Keeler stated, "People are growing weary of shams and are longing for reality. They will never get it till they learn that the ideal is the real, that beauty is truth . . ."[7] Keeler's message and the movement of his peers have renewed relevance today, as we are immersed in amorphous and intangible digital worlds that pervade our modern lives. Now more than ever, handmade objects provide evidence of reality. Objects may be the only truth we have.

DWELL

THE LIGHT: TO ILLUMINATE

THE BASKET: TO COLLECT

THE CONTAINER: TO KEEP

THE GATE: TO GREET

THE TOOL: TO WORK

THE LURE: TO PROVIDE

THE TOY: TO PLAY

THE INSTRUMENT: TO RESONATE

THE CARRIER: TO TRANSPORT

TO DWELL IS TO LIVE OR RESIDE, and sometimes, to linger. The word relates to the physical occupation of space, and it pertains to the relationship between place and life. Additionally, and importantly, it is tied to the psychological and emotional aspects of inhabitation. The things featured in the following pages have appeared in Indigenous and American homes for centuries. The objects in this chapter are diverse in form and purpose. Some are ancient, many are fundamental to cultures worldwide, enabling us to dwell, to exist on the earth. Many of these objects are tied to survival and subsistence, and have become, over millennia, replete with meaning. First peoples, colonists, early Americans, and contemporary artists have all formed their own interpretations of these objects. Several, from baskets to saddles, result from the passing of traditional knowledge between generations or the transmittal of specialized craft techniques via apprenticeship, practices that continue to flourish in America today.

Dwell opens with an object type that has become essential to facilitating daily life: the light. Whether emitted via fire, wick, or bulb, light on demand transforms our experience of time by allowing for activity after dark. This first chapter brings together objects that expand time, such as candlesticks, with those that save time, such as the spinning wheel. It also includes items that make passing time more pleasurable, that are anchors for creativity and communion, such as the chess set, the doll, and the piano.

Many of these objects are nomads: designed to move with people and small or light enough that they are easily transported, such as the fishhook and the basket. Others are designed to be people movers, carrying humans across the American landscape, such as the cradleboard and skateboard.

Several objects are vessels, intended to contain a variety of substances. Jugs are obviously vessels; a pouch or pocket is too, and what they hold can be both corporeal and conceptual.

Throughout this book, objects function on multiple levels. Their purposes shift and expand over time. Whether an object was ever used as it was intended, or treasured, guarded, preserved, and displayed as a work of art, is another question. Objects consistently take on additional roles—as gifts, heirlooms, signs of wealth or prestige, even as products of artistic expression and centerpieces of conversation. And even though many of the objects presented here are no longer critical to our existence, they are both so commonplace and so ripe with significance that artists continue to borrow their typologies in the creation of art. The contemporary function of handmade objects is often purely artistic. Today, these pieces are collected and prized as craft achievements.

Each of the objects here can teach, communicate, inspire interaction, and bring joy. —EZ

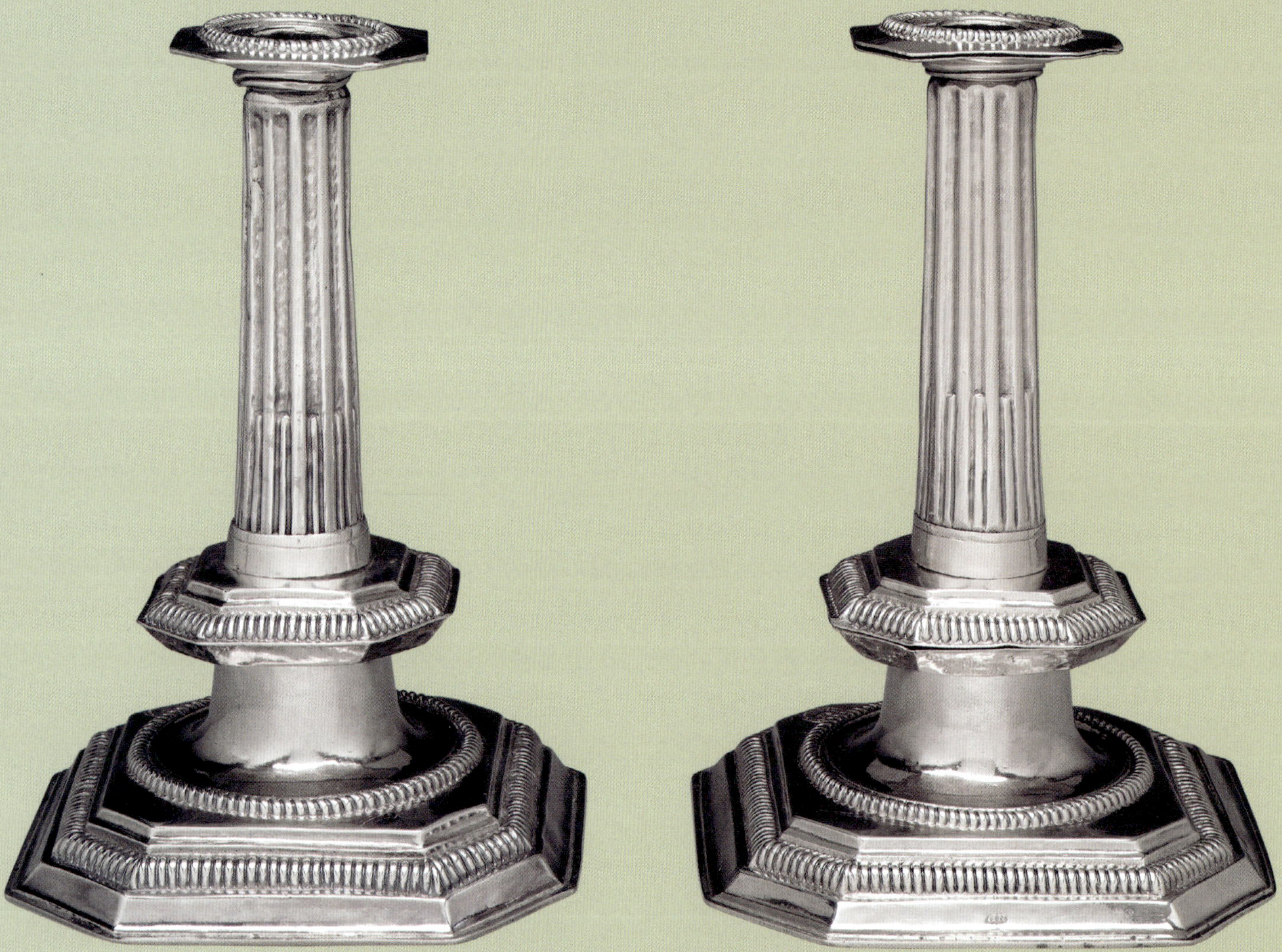

PAIR OF CANDLESTICKS

c. 1695–1700, **John Noyes** (1674–1749),
Silver, 9 ¼ × 6 ⅜ in. (23.5 × 16.2 cm), Museum of Fine Arts, Boston,
Gift of Miss Clara Bowdoin Winthrop, 1954, 54.595.

The functioning of daily life in the North American colonies, like all preindustrial cultures, was highly dependent upon the sun. When day gave way to night, pine knot torches, candles, oil lamps, and fires offered limited sources of light for reading and detailed tasks like needlework. Many early American households owned candlesticks made of base metals such as wrought iron, brass, and pewter, or ceramic. However, nearly a third of the colonial population had few to none of these; they lived in darkness once the sun set.

Silver candlesticks, by virtue of their valuable material, were small in number. They were the preserve of the wealthy, and especially rare in the seventeenth century. (This is one of only two pairs known to survive.) This fashionable set was executed in an architectural style similar to Dutch, French, and English examples made from the mid- to late seventeenth century, with notable features that include fluted and reeded columns supported by a broad square base having a stepped foot and cut corners. The silver is mostly constructed, rather than cast, which required considerable skills from the silversmith to manipulate the metal.

Executed in a baroque style that favored a dramatic method of presentation, they feature high and low areas creating heightened regions of light and shadow, an effect amplified by candlelight. This was especially true of decorative treatments like the narrowly spaced gadroons, curved, bead-like forms that here make up three narrow bands across the lower portion of the candlesticks, as well as the removable bobeche at the top, used to catch candle drippings. Features like these added to the visual experience of living by candlelight and were especially prized in a world where so little light was available after sundown.

As in the ancient world, candles were made of beeswax or tallow. When set into silver candlesticks in the dining room of a prosperous colonist, their light multiplied as it glanced off the polished, multifaceted metal surfaces and scattered in all directions. Silver particularly magnified the effect of candlelight, piercing the dark and enlivening the surfaces of the polished wooden table, dishes, and other table accessories, as well as the garments worn by those in attendance.

The silversmith John Noyes was born in Boston. Around the age of thirteen, he was apprenticed to Jeremiah Dummer, the first native-born silversmith. Apprenticeships were a typical means of craft training for centuries, allowing young people to learn their particular skills over about seven years. By the age of twenty-one, apprentices were considered to have gained enough knowledge to work as journeymen for other craftsmen or as masters of their own shop.

We can sometimes trace who apprenticed with whom by looking at legal documents. Noyes appears in the account book of the Salem, Massachusetts, judge Samuel Sewall, who sold borax to Dummer in 1691, delivering it to "Jno" Noyes. Borax is a cleaning agent for metals, and it is also used as a flux that enables solder to flow freely while also preventing surface oxidation.

It appears that Noyes went on to work independently. Shortly after his apprenticeship, he fashioned these candlesticks for Pierre Baudouin (later anglicized to Bowdoin), a Huguenot merchant and physician who fled France for the American colonies due to religious persecution. Although Baudouin had suffered losses in leaving his country, he was nevertheless wealthy enough to order these very fine candlesticks within a decade of his arrival in Massachusetts. —JF

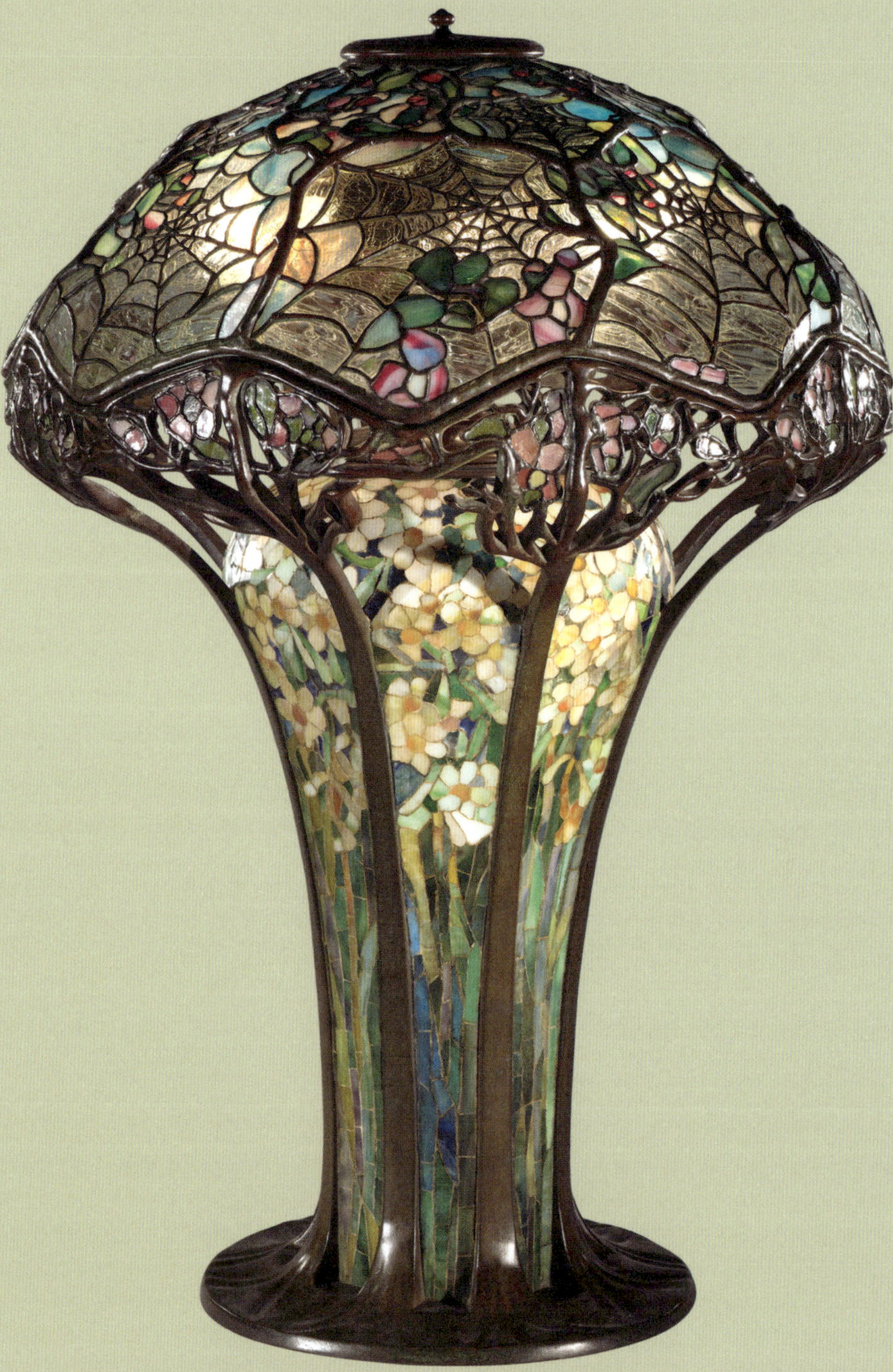

THE LIGHT

COBWEB LAMP

c. 1902, **Clara Driscoll** (1861–1944) for **Tiffany Studios** (active 1894–1932),
Leaded glass, bronze, mosaic glass tiles, 29½ × 20 in. (74.9 × 50.8 cm),
Virginia Museum of Fine Arts, Richmond, Gift of Sydney and Frances Lewis, 85.164.a-c.

While many of the beautiful lamps produced by Tiffany Studios were once believed to have been designed by the firm's founder, Louis Comfort Tiffany, today they are recognized as work by women in his employ known as the Tiffany Girls. This tall and rather mysterious lamp, with its Cobweb shade floating like a scarf over its mosaic base, has been attributed to Clara Driscoll, now considered one of Tiffany's most prominent designers.

Thanks to a near-miraculous surviving body of correspondence, the names of many of the women who worked at the firm in the late nineteenth and early twentieth century have survived. The letters were written by Driscoll, head of the Tiffany Girls, and passed among family members living at some distance from each other. Driscoll wrote of her experiences working for Mr. Tiffany, the projects that they produced, and the young women who were under her charge.

The Tiffany Girls were instrumental in developing large windows for the 1893 World's Columbian Exposition in Chicago and for the 1900 Exposition Universelle in Paris, but their chief contribution was in the realm of lamps, which were an important profit center for the firm. It is now known that Driscoll, who is believed to have designed the magnificent work seen here, designed some of the most iconic Tiffany lamps, including the Dragonfly, Wisteria, and Poppy, among many others, as well as being first to successfully experiment with mosaic decoration on the bronze bases, as seen in this example.

Educated at the Western Reserve School of Design for Women, now known as the Cleveland Institute of Art, Driscoll was ambitious, and soon after graduation she moved to New York, where she enrolled in the Metropolitan Museum of Art's short-lived art school. She joined Mr. Tiffany at what was then the Tiffany Glass Company in 1888 and focused on designs for lamps and various other products while supervising the Women's Glass Cutting Department, which produced windows as well as mosaic designs. Tiffany was supportive of the department's work developing sketches, presentation drawings, and full-size preparatory designs, as well as selecting glass for the windows, cutting them, and wrapping their edges with foil for attachment to the lead cames (the metallic pieces that connect the colored glass). The male staff did similar work, in addition to the more physical tasks of creating molds and leaded shapes in which the glass would be situated.

In 1907, Tiffany arranged a three-month trip to Brittany for himself, Driscoll, fellow Tiffany Girl Agnes Northrop, and Dr. Parker McIlhiney, a chemist who worked on creating colored glass. Their luxurious excursion was to gather inspiration through photography and sketches. Such a remarkable trip speaks volumes about Tiffany's high regard for his talented female staff. And thanks to Clara Driscoll's letters, we now know their names.

—JF

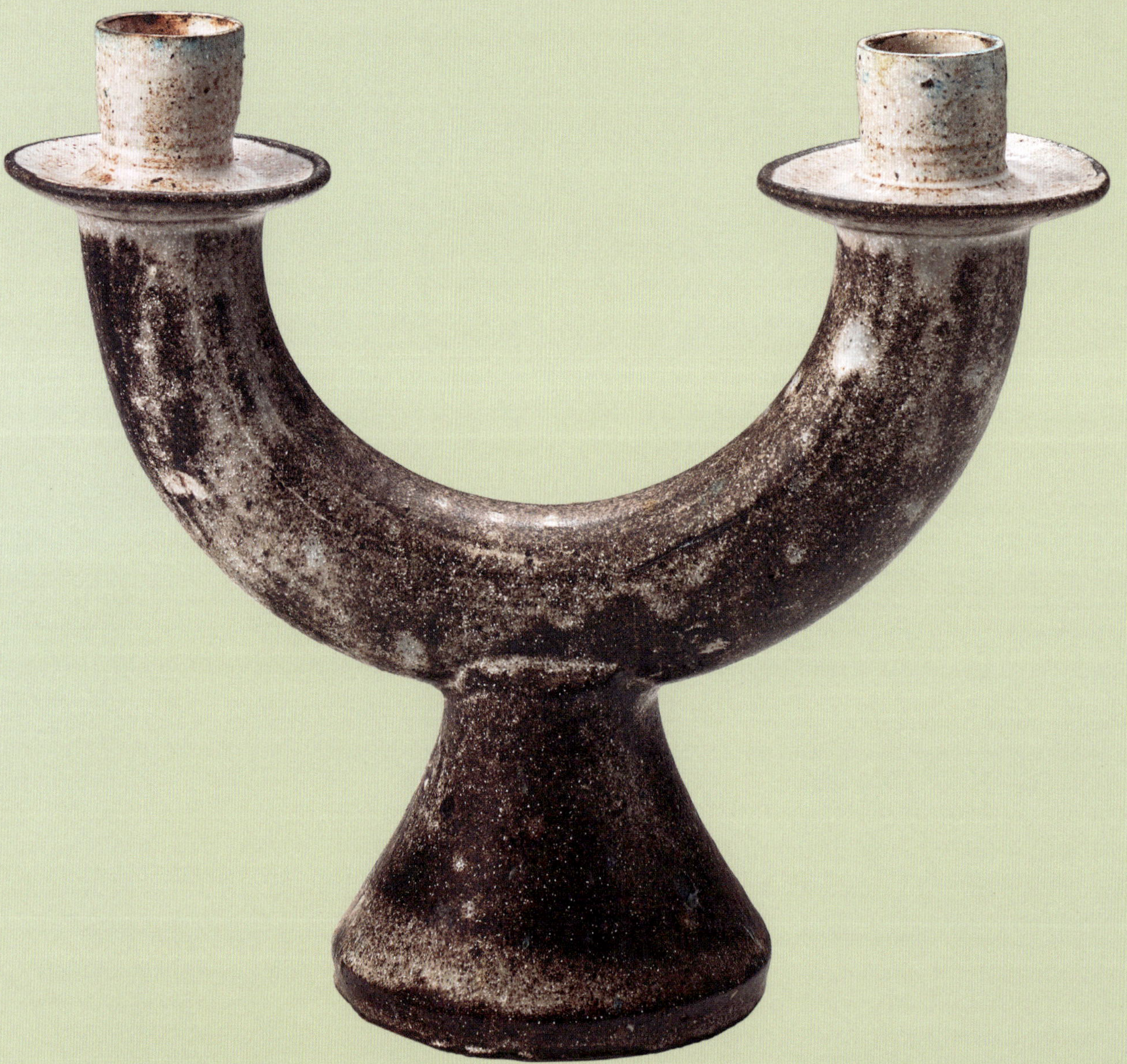

THE LIGHT

CANDELABRA

1950s, **Marguerite Wildenhain** (1896–1985),
Glazed stoneware, 8½ × 10 × 3⅛ in. (21.6 × 25.4 × 7.9 cm),
Forrest L. Merrill Collection.

Candlesticks are the kinds of objects that became entirely nonessential once electricity entered the picture. Yet as object forms, they endure. We light candles to set the mood. They bring romantic nostalgia blended with mystique, formality, and festivity to the table and into a room. They link us to the past. It would be hard to argue that they are strictly decorative, considering the intangible sensory impact that they can make.

This candelabra straddles history in a perfectly modern way with its simple components and widely outstretched arms. Harmonious and balanced, the rounded core structure allows for two candles to be paired together. The piece is an exercise in circularity, and the construction is an assemblage of the various circular forms that vessels can take. From the footprint of the tapered base, a curved and elongated cylinder rests above and is topped by two small bobeches—saucer-like surfaces meant to collect dripping wax—with diminutive cups for containing candles. The piece shows the profound and encyclopedic ceramic knowledge of its maker, the twentieth-century sculptor, designer, master potter, and educator Marguerite Wildenhain.

The pure geometry of this candelabra is indicative of Wildenhain's Bauhaus training and perspective. Born in France, she joined the Bauhaus at its beginning in 1919 as one of very few women. She was mesmerized by the school founder Walter Gropius's idea of returning to craftsmanship and erasing the boundaries between artist and artisan. These Bauhaus ideas were foundational for Wildenhain, who was instrumental in transferring them to the burgeoning American Studio Craft movement.

Wildenhain, who was Jewish, was living in Germany in 1933 when the rising Nazi regime led her to flee to Holland. She eventually moved to California in 1940 and started teaching at the California College of Arts and Crafts. Upon the invitation of patrons Jane and Gordon Herr, she helped form the art community of Pond Farm in Guerneville, California, in 1942. There, she mentored hundreds of students and lived until her death in 1985.[1] Amid the turmoil and destruction of World War II, she saw the constructive, regenerative power of craft and played an indelible role in forming the discipline of American studio ceramics.

Known for her exceptional skills at the kick wheel and her rigorous approach to technique, Wildenhain adhered to the traditional apprenticeship system that she had learned in Europe. She taught her students not just how to make the pots, but also how to see their nuances with attentiveness. Most significantly, she saw the pursuit of craft as an entire philosophical pursuit. In her words, "It's not only that we learn pottery. We learn something about life and how to live."[2]

In the case of this candelabra, illumination is both its utilitarian purpose and its symbolic significance. It is reflective of how Wildenhain enlightened Americans on the potential of craft and ceramics through her work and life. She will also be known for passing her torch to the next generation of ceramists and lighting a pathway for this medium. —EZ

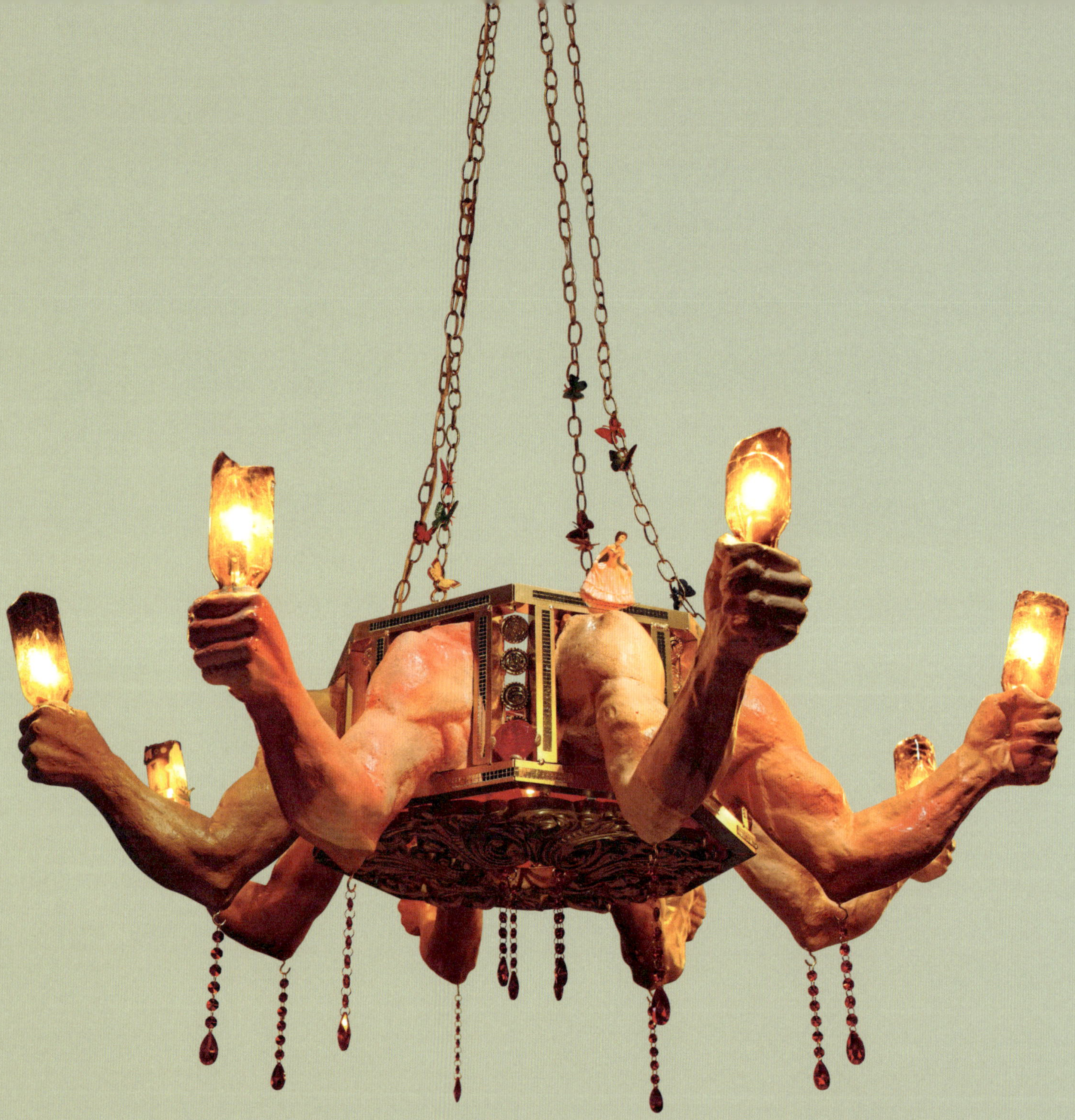

THE LIGHT

DE LA TORRE BROTHERS on THE LIGHT

Le Point de Bascule (The Tipping Point) **(detail of chandelier)**, 2024,
Einar de la Torre (b. 1963) and **Jamex de la Torre** (b. 1960),
Mixed media installation *Upward Mobility*, March 1–September 15, 2024,
McNay Art Museum, San Antonio.

What happens when you integrate light into glass? It glows, like watery biology, and it glows again, seemingly alive. Light makes other materials seem static by comparison. It's a kind of Frankensteinian experiment, a spark that animates a glob of minerals that mimic life so well—perhaps because life itself is often watery, translucent, and luminous. Primordial soup, indeed.

Our foray into integrated lighting began years ago, with wired lamps and rope lights—experiments with mixed results. Today, we're surrounded by a dizzying array of lighting technologies: full-spectrum LEDs, wireless systems, interlocking panels that can stretch a video across the face of a building. . . . This is a thrilling time to be an artist working with light.

About fifteen years ago, we began using LED panels to illuminate our lenticular work. These panels are engineered to produce an even pool of light—no hot spots. When lit correctly, lenticular images exhibit astonishing depth and dimensionality. We quickly learned it was worth the investment to use the highest-quality lighting available.

In 2024, we were invited to exhibit at the McNay Art Museum in San Antonio, Texas, within the soaring Tobin Exhibition Galleries. The space—a daunting 45-by-60-foot rectangle—threatened to swallow even our 24-foot banquet table. We envisioned a lush, decadent banquet scene: elaborate wallpaper, looming taxidermy heads, and a table teeming with blown-glass characters. These figures would also appear on chandeliers hanging above, bridging the space and extending the narrative into the air. The museum wanted to add a platform to dissuade the viewers from touching the works, so we decided to cover the platform with mirror and added an "underbelly," with the scene reflected on the mirrored surface to reveal the ugly guts of the spectacle above—a kind of peek into what it takes to provide such a display of conspicuous consumption.

The chandeliers, reminiscent of traditional baroque glass bouquets found in palaces and grand homes, became central to the installation. But unlike their historical counterparts, ours carried not just beauty, but contemporary commentary. Chandeliers conjure complicated histories: opulence, excess, labor, and class. They are exquisite symbols of the extreme accumulation of wealth—a perfect emblem of our times. At once seductive and grotesque, they illuminate not just the space, but all the once-hidden faces at the bacchanal.

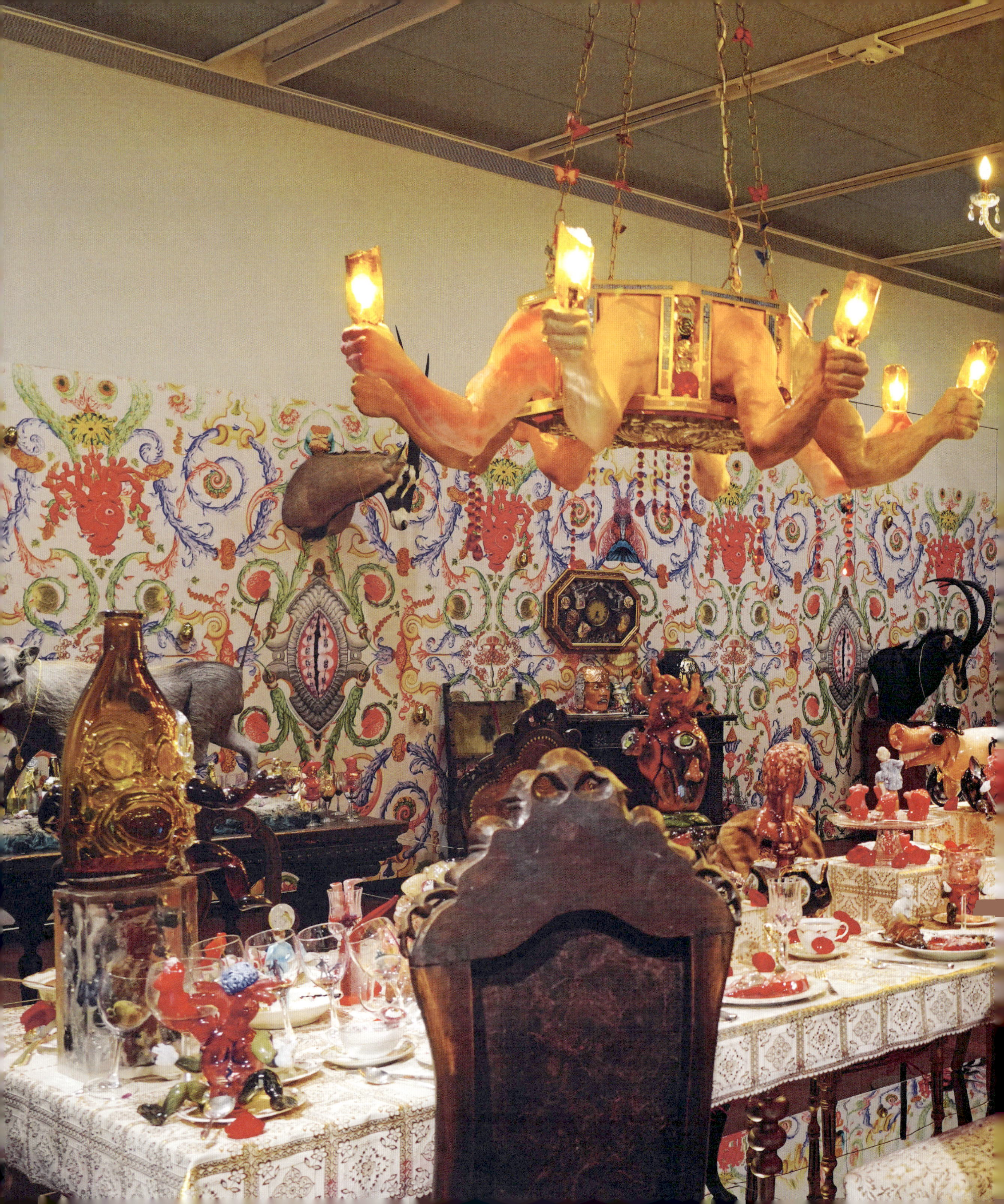

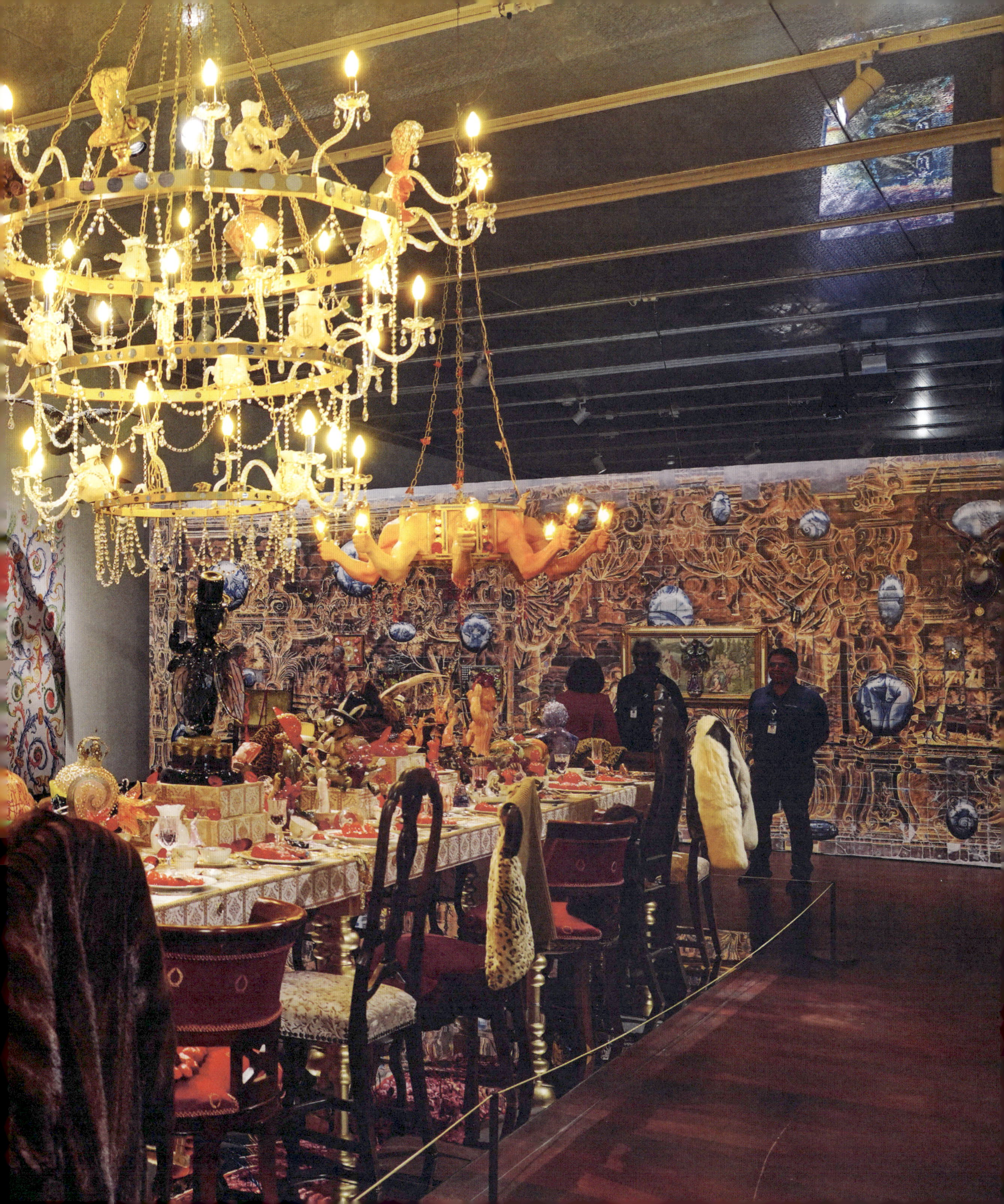

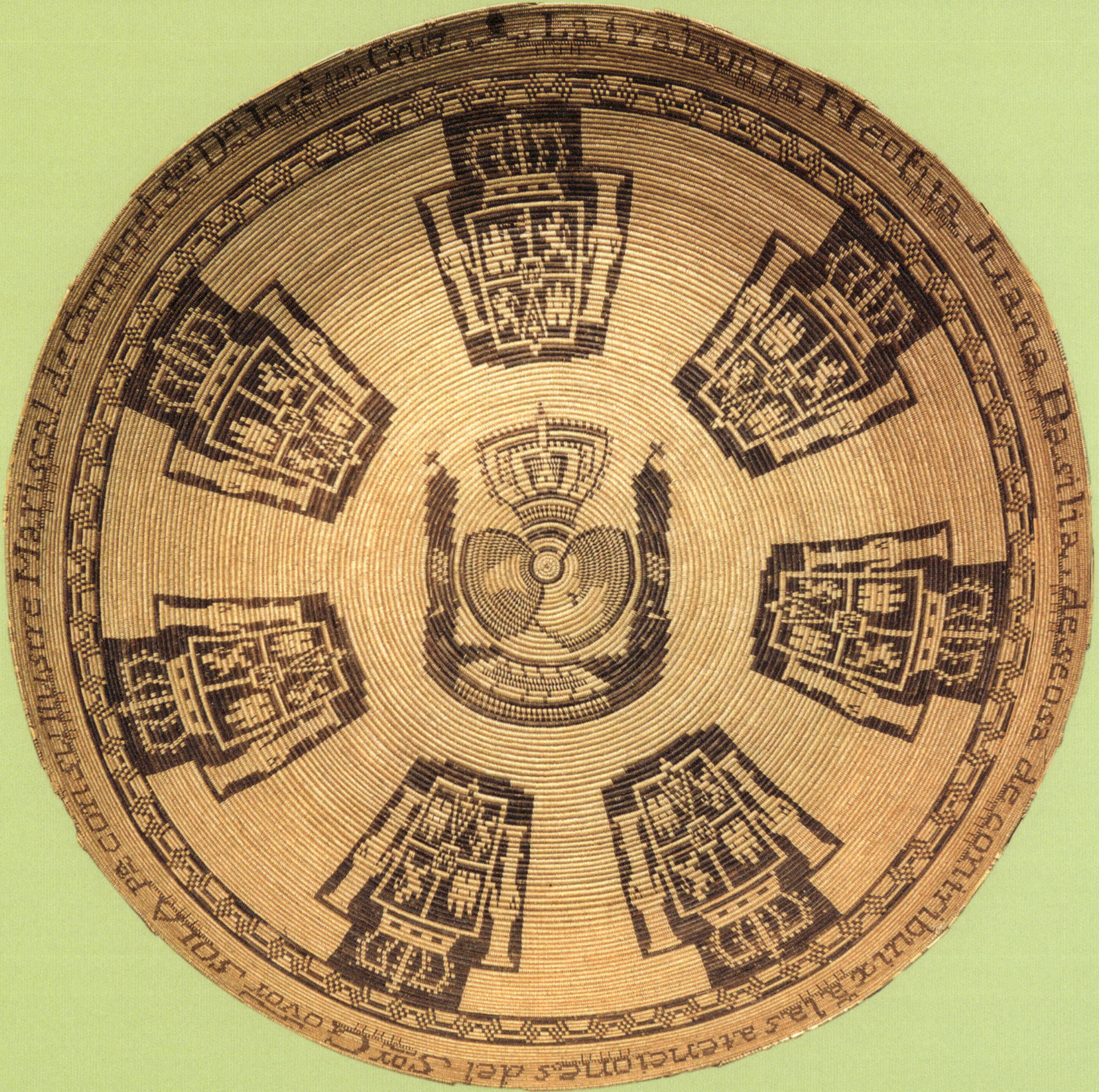

THE BASKET

COIN BASKET

c. 1815–22, **Juana Basilia Sitmelelene** (Chumash, 1782–1838),
Sumac, *Juncus textilis*, mud dye,
4 × 24½ in. (10.2 × 62.3 cm), Santa Barbara Museum of Natural History, Cat No. NA-CA-CH-4F-3.

"I made it, Neophyte Juana Basilia, desirous of contributing to the attentions of Sr. Governor Solá toward his illustrious Field Marshal Sr. Don José de la Cruz." This pictorial basket is emblazoned with the Spanish coat of arms, a decorative rim, and the weaver's inscription. Signing baskets was not a common practice in the nineteenth century; however, some Chumash master weavers such as Juana Basilia Sitmelelene were proud of their intricate works and were encouraged to weave their names into them.

Sitmelelene was acclaimed for creating artistic basketry. Born around 1782 in Sumuawawa, a Chumash community in the Santa Monica Mountains of California, she was baptized at Mission San Buenaventura—now Ventura—in 1806, at about age twenty-six.

Transforming humble materials like juncus, sumac, willow, deer grass, and hazel sticks into stunning designs, Indigenous California basketry is an art form admired and even beloved around the world. To make this basket, Sitmelelene painstakingly wove natural and mud-dyed juncus rods and sewed them tightly with split strands of more juncus in an outward spiral, alternating between natural and dyed juncus. Baskets, products of the weavers' hands, hearts, and traditions, were an integral part of everyday life in Indigenous communities from time immemorial; before European colonization, these woven works were also offered for trade or sale at regional gatherings of Native peoples known as Big Times. The tradition of making baskets for commercial purposes, such as this coin basket by Sitmelelene, continued in colonial times.

Only after yearslong preparation could basket weaving begin. Basket weavers first stewarded stands of juncus, willow, and other plants. They harvested these materials at the proper time for each, then stored and processed them. Some shoots were dyed using walnut shells, ocher, mud, or other natural dyes to make rich russet or nightside black. Weavers needed a fine sense of geometry and keen math skills to create their designs. Some of Sitmelelene's surviving coiled baskets have more than two hundred stitches per square inch. A basket such as this could feel almost as smooth as a finely woven blanket.

The skills and knowledge to craft basketry were lovingly passed from mothers to daughters in lines stretching back hundreds of generations. But life changed for many Native people when Spanish missionaries and settlers arrived along the California coast in the eighteenth century. Many Indians were taken to one of twenty-one missions. As the Franciscan missionaries converted Indians to Catholicism and forced them to adopt Spanish culture, many Natives continued their ancestral practices. Baskets became more important as products of Native commerce than objects of everyday utility as they were increasingly coveted by the Spaniards who colonized California. Basket weavers responded by creating specially designed baskets on commission. The coin basket here, bearing the Spanish coat of arms, was a "presentation basket" commissioned by Governor Pablo Vicente de Solá, the last Spanish governor of California, for one of his officers, Field Marshal Don José de la Cruz.

Only seven of these presentation baskets are known to have survived. —DUK

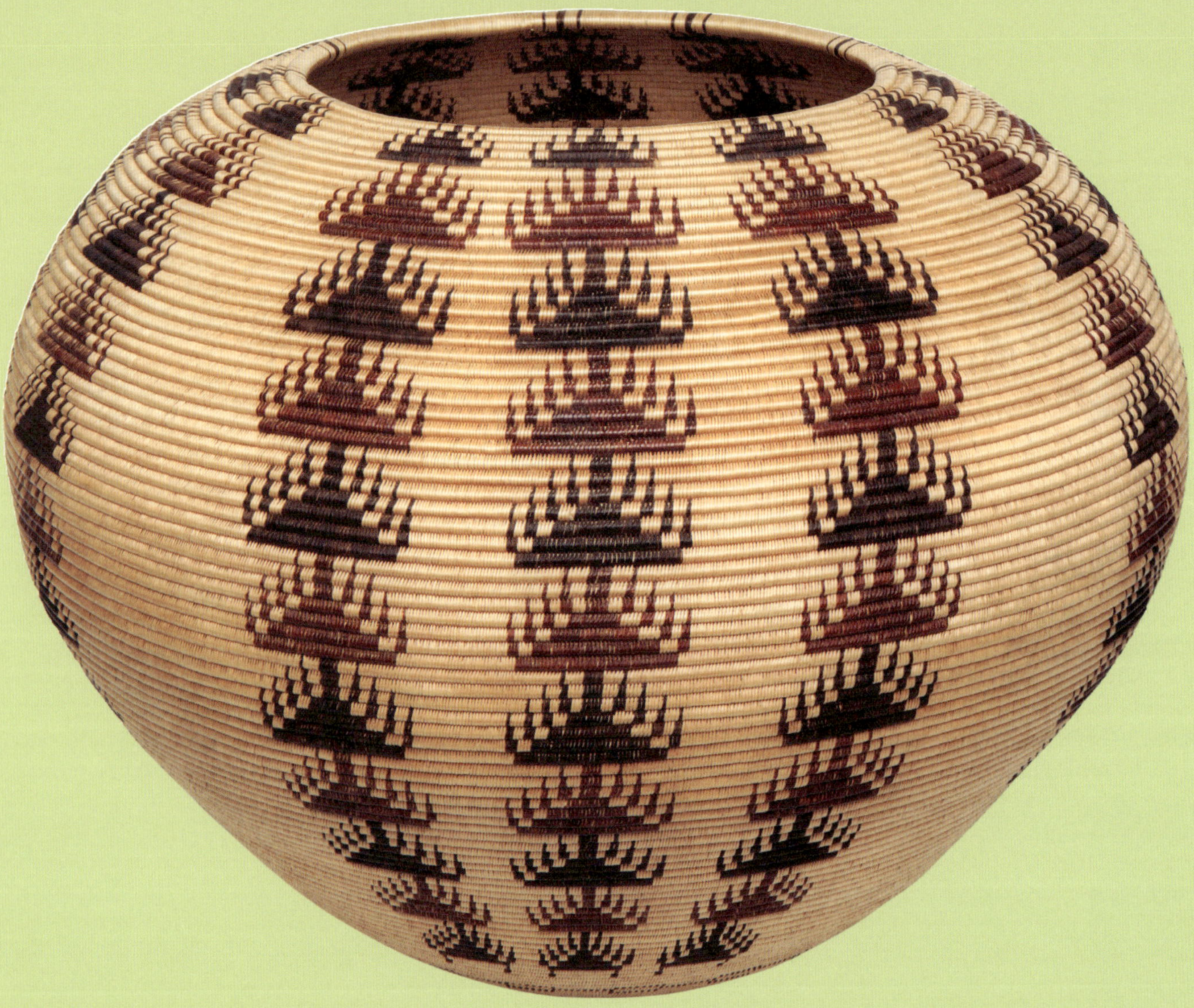

DEGIKUP

1917–18, **Louisa Keyser (Dat So La Lee)** (Washoe, 1829–1925),
Willow, redbud, bracken fern root, 12¼ × 16⅜ in. (31.1 × 41.6 cm),
Philbrook Museum of Art, Tulsa, Gift of Clark Field, 1942.14.1909.

In her time and today, the Wá·šiw (or Washoe) weaver Louisa Keyser was revered for her degikups, coiled spheroid baskets with an incurving rim. In this beautiful example, each light brown willow thread builds upon another, as Keyser tightly packed approximately thirty stitches into every circular inch. Strands of black bracken fern root and bright redbud create a balanced geometric design out of a repeating shape known as Keyser's "bearpaw" design.

Keyser was one of the most celebrated Indigenous weavers of the early twentieth century, creating around three hundred baskets known to date. Native basketry became popular among Euro-American patrons during the Arts and Crafts movement, and dealers organized to patronize, purchase, and sell Native-made baskets through curio shops, catalogs, and department stores. California Native weavers produced significantly more baskets during this period, and many museums throughout the world acquired these works for their fine arts collections.

This "Basket Craze," as it was known, coincided with a period of rapid transformation around Lake Tahoe due to the mining, logging, and tourism industries. Wá·šiw homelands straddle the western edge of the Great Basin into the Sierra Nevada Mountains, with the sacred lake of Dá'aw (Lake Tahoe) at the heart. Euro-American miners and ranchers rushed to this region after the discovery of silver on the Comstock Lode in 1858, bringing livestock that overran grasslands, clear-cutting trees, and rerouting waterways connected to plant cultivation for basket materials. Under duress, many Wá·šiw families worked low-wage jobs to survive and others turned to weaving baskets for the curio industry.

In Carson City, Nevada, Keyser worked as a laundress for white families, including Abe and Amy Cohn, who operated a local emporium. Recognizing her skills in basketry, the Cohns became the exclusive promoters of her baskets to collectors. Like many curio dealers, they constructed a romantic image around Keyser's life and work, while also closely tabulating the hours expended for each basket in their ledgers. For example, Keyser spent eleven months, from March 26, 1917, to February 16, 1918, weaving this degikup now in the Philbrook's collection.[1]

Focusing just on the design of this basket overlooks the continual practice of Indigenous science, often referred to as Traditional Ecological Knowledge, required to bring this artwork into being. Weavers are not only exceptional mathematicians in planning and executing their designs; they are also expert botanists. Willow, a principal fiber in Washoe basketry, grows along the main waterways and in floodplains, including along the Carson River, where Keyser lived.[2] If tended to properly and not overharvested, willows can provide long, straight shoots foundational to creating sturdy threads for coiling. For Keyser to achieve the tight weave on this basket, she had to harvest the material, strip the outside bark from the shoots, and allow it to dry before she could start weaving. This degikup is emblematic of Keyser's ingenuity, as well as the greater Wá·šiw community's stewardship of these plants years before Keyser sat down to weave the Philbrook degikup. —CG

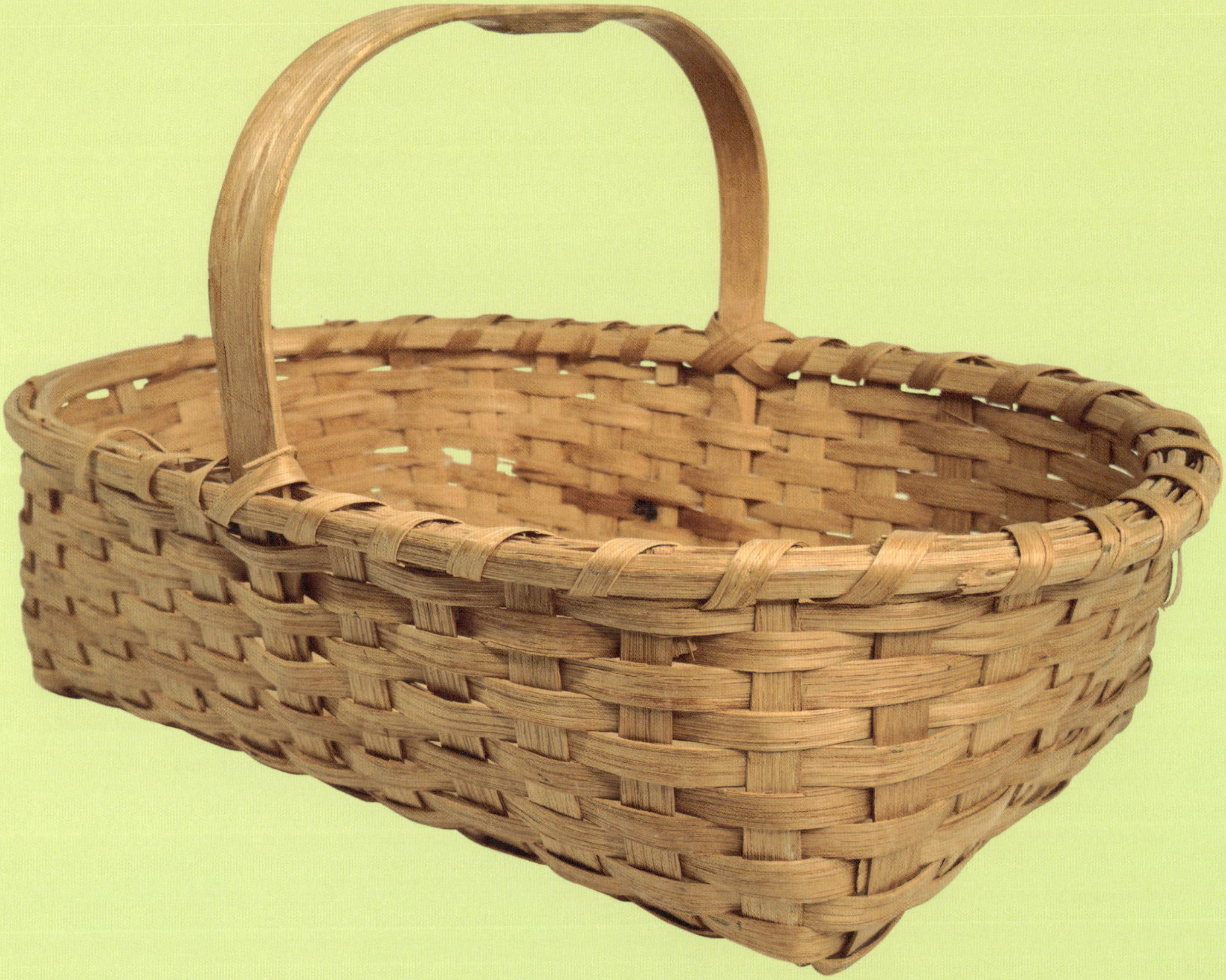

THE BASKET

DOUBLE PIE BASKET

1984, **Roger Curry** (1945–1994) and **Betty Curry** (1940–2018),
Split oak, 12½ × 20¾ × 10 in. (31.8 × 52.7 × 25.4 cm).

The Currys' split-oak double pie basket represents three elements of handwork tradition: family, region, and function. Its makers, Roger and Betty Curry, married in 1973, joining two basketmaking genealogical lines: the Gibson family of northwest Arkansas (Roger's family) and the Derryberry family of the Missouri Ozarks (Betty's). Roger's great-great-grandfather, Christopher Columbus "Lum" Gibson was weaving split-oak baskets as early as the 1840s. Family lore asserts that when walking to the general store, he would cut down a tree, split and shave off splints, and weave a basket before reaching his destination so that he could trade the basket for goods.

The Derryberry family lived in Shannon County, Missouri. Betty's great-grandmother Melinda Derryberry twined buckbrush baskets while her great-grandfather Bob wove white oak baskets. Interviewed in the early 1940s, Bob Derryberry said: "I am eighty-two years old and have spent my life in the jungles of the Ozarks, workin' makin' baskets, diggin' roots, an' doin' a little of this and a little of that, to get by on and raise my family."

For Roger and Betty Curry, basketmaking became a partnership melding process and product. Roger would select and cut the oak tree, split and shave off the splints, and carve the handle. Betty wove the bottom of the basket in a plaited twill pattern and the sides with an over-and-under weave. Stylistically this basket echoes the Gibson family tradition, particularly in the notched handle attached to the rim and the distinctive thicker top of the handle for strength and comfortable carrying. A stylized R/B/C brand at the bottom of the basket signified both their pride in the work and an acknowledgment of their teamwork in the execution.

Betty's grandfather described the family's baskets as "a beauty and a durability." Durability applied to both the baskets and the knowledge and skills in making them. In the late 1970s, the Currys began teaching basketry classes at Shannondale, a church mission in the Ozarks, and they did so for nearly twenty years. Later the couple taught basketry in the Missouri Traditional Arts Apprenticeship Program. The Missouri Basketweavers Guild created a scholarship to their annual conference as a memorial to the Currys' service.

This double pie basket, which I acquired from the Currys forty years ago, has lived up to its reputation for durability—although it has held more magazines than homemade pies to be carried to community socials. When our daughter was born more than thirty years ago, I placed her in the Curry basket for a photo just after returning home. The basket carried hope for the future of our family. Little did I realize at the time that more than a hundred years earlier, Lum Gibson had been photographed standing next to his young grandson nestled inside one of his Gibson family baskets. —**BB**

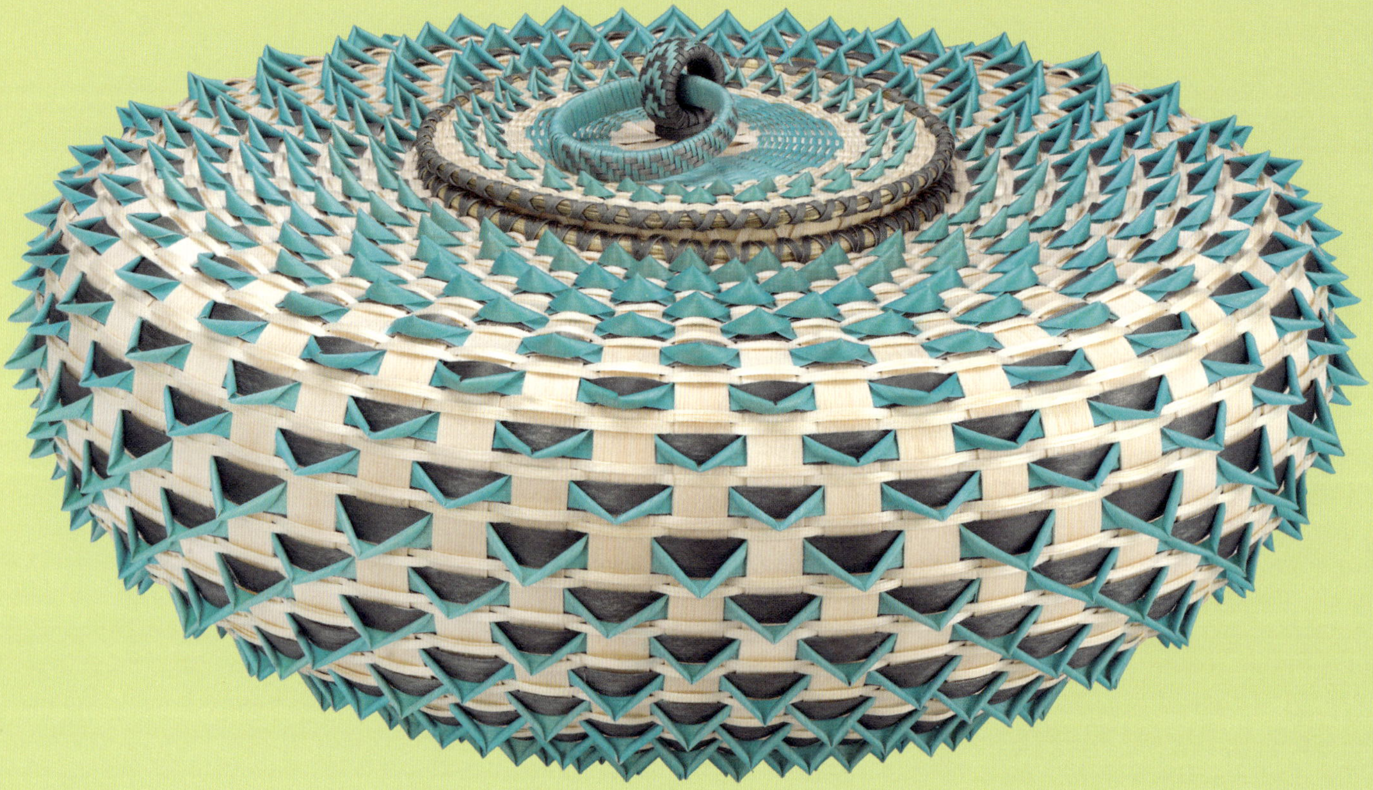

THE BASKET

LARGE TURQUOISE URCHIN BASKET

2019, **Jeremy Frey** (Passamaquoddy, b. 1978), Brown ash, sweetgrass, dye, 5¼ × 11½ in. (13.3 × 29.2 cm), Smithsonian American Art Museum, Washington, DC, Museum purchase through the Kenneth R. Trapp Acquisition Fund, 2020.55.

It would be sufficient to look at this Jeremy Frey (Passamaquoddy) basket and let its visual impact speak for itself. The pleasingly sculptural shape inspired by sea urchins, the intricacy of the precisely cut and interwoven strips of brown ash, and the textured surface animated with projecting turquoise points make for a stunning artistic statement. However, as with so many creative endeavors, the story behind the artistry is just as complex and awe-inspiring. This urchin basket represents not only a significant achievement for the maker but also a landmark for the revitalization of the people's cultural and artistic heritage.

The Wabanaki peoples (Maliseet, Penobscot, Micmac, and Passamaquoddy) have been transforming trees into baskets for generations. In fact, the Wabanaki literally trace their lineage to a tree, believing that they emerged when their ancestor Glooskap pierced an ash tree's bark with his arrow. Toward the end of the twentieth century, however, Maine Indian basket makers were experiencing threats to their traditional practice: the average age of the fewer than fifty remaining makers was sixty-three; the market for their wares was not strong enough to provide a livelihood; and their access to suitable trees was becoming increasingly limited, mainly due to environmental changes brought on by climate conditions.

In 1993, the Maine Indian Basketmakers Alliance (MIBA) was formed and its founding director, Theresa Secord, a Penobscot basket maker, became a driving force behind efforts to revitalize the artistic and cultural tradition. At a 2002 basketry workshop, sixth-generation basket maker Francis "Gal" Frey (Passamaquoddy) asked Theresa if her son Jeremy, then in his twenties, could help prepare wood for a workshop. Theresa agreed. Jeremy credits this opportunity as his first encouragement in the art world. Soon he was harvesting his own wood using ancestral knowledge and tackling more complex basketmaking techniques taught by his mother.

With MIBA's support, Jeremy's basketmaking career took off, and through the years his work has become more and more innovative. The use of wooden puzzle molds, pieced forms that baskets such as this one are woven around, is traditional among Wabanaki weavers, but Jeremy created customized molds for unique shapes and larger sizes. With Secord's encouragement, he began showing baskets at the storied Santa Fe Indian Market, where he won top prize and sold a basket for an astounding $15,000 in 2011. Today, Jeremy's baskets are collected and widely exhibited.

The conversation between tradition and innovation continues. Jeremy points out that ash tree selection and harvesting are critical to his ability to construct his finely woven baskets in new and complex shapes. He learned that lesson as a boy, when his uncle Fred "Moose" Moore took him into the woods and taught him about the brown ash tree. One of the lessons of the ash is that as you pound the harvested tree to separate the concentric rings, you move through time getting closer and closer to the heartwood. As you travel through lean and lush seasons, reflected in narrow and wide bands of growth, you learn the unique characteristics and potential of that tree. The woven basket becomes a manifestation of that environmental and cultural history. —BB

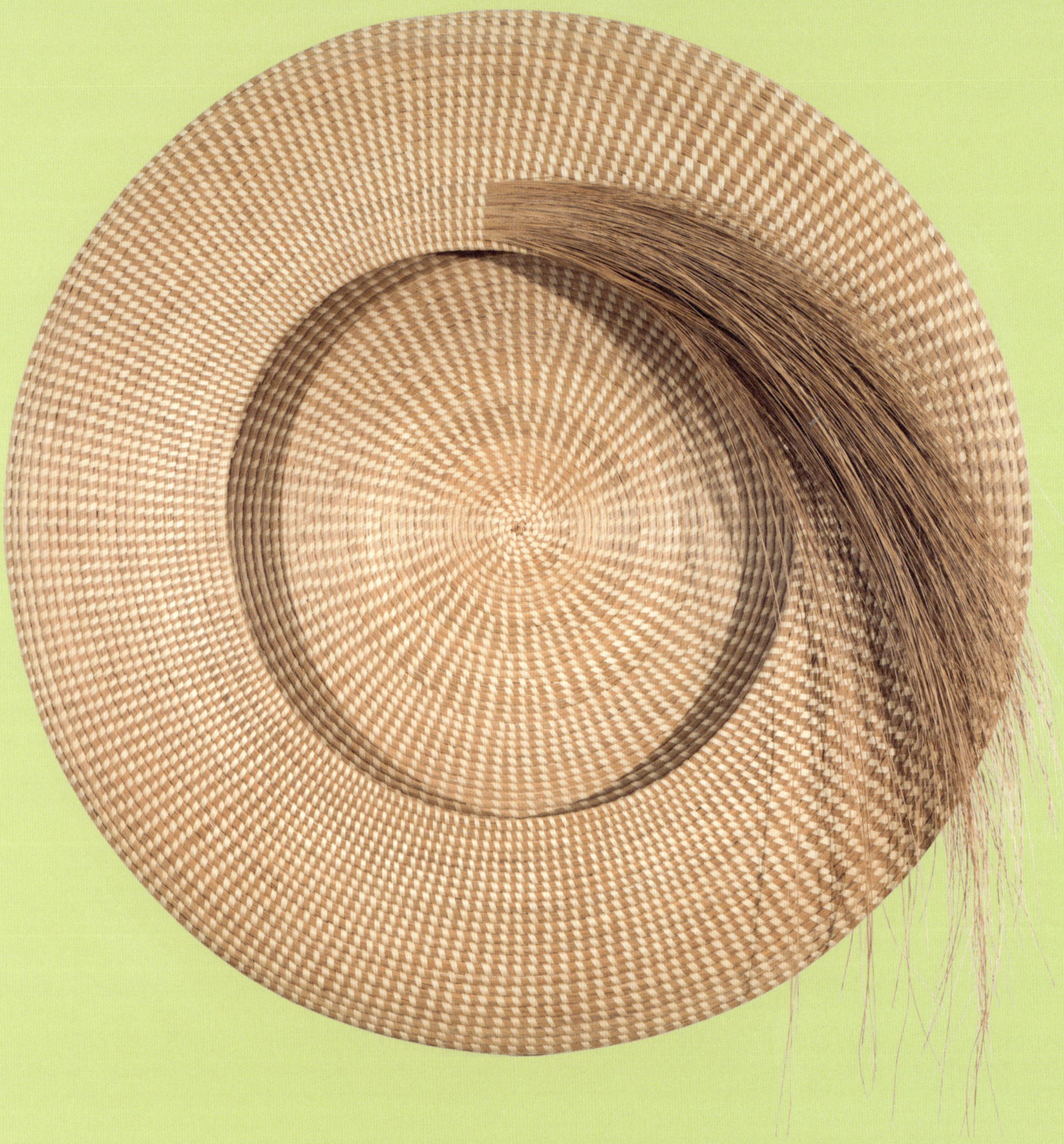

THE BASKET

MARY JACKSON on THE BASKET

Never Again, 2007, **Mary Jackson** (b. 1945),
Sweetgrass and palmetto, 42 × 2 in. (106.7 × 5.1 cm),
The Gibbes Museum of Art, Charleston, The Braithwaite Family, 2017.005.

The art form of basketry originated in West Africa. It was brought West by my ancestors, who came as slaves from Africa. The baskets that they made were for everyday, utilitarian use, and basketmaking was a lifestyle that they always had. My ancestors were brought to my area, here in South Carolina, by the plantation owners because they had the skill of rice cultivation and they could work the fields for cotton and indigo. These crops were staples here and the plantation owners needed people to work the fields; basketry was a bonus.

When I'm making a basket, I am actually locking each coil of sweetgrass to the other with palmetto or other plant fibers, sewing row upon row. In modern terminology, people refer to it as weaving or coiling. But the local term for me, in this tradition, is always "sewing a basket," because I'm actually feeding into the coil, attaching each coil to the other.

This type of sewing is unique to this basketry. It is only practiced for this art form. It is considered one of the oldest crafts of African origin in America. It's the only basket of its kind in the entire United States, and these baskets are only made in this area where I live, passed down from generation to generation, from mother to daughter to granddaughter.

I use sabal palmetto, which is native to the area where I live. It produces a very strong frond, so I'm able to pull very tight. Sweetgrass has a long life, it's very durable, it doesn't get brittle or decay. It makes these baskets very long-lasting for functional use every day. I also use dark pine needles laid over sweetgrass because they give a beautiful color for a pattern. I also use grass that's native to the area here where I live: a marsh grass called bulrush. Bulrush is a coarse, stiff grass, but it gives a beautiful color. Grasses are indigenous to the area where I live—and they resemble what my ancestors used in Africa. We've used these grasses here for more than three hundred years.

My ancestors made large agricultural baskets for field work, harvesting cotton and rice and different kinds of grain. And the women made household baskets for everyday living—for bread, for storage, for laundry. These baskets were made throughout the plantation era. After the plantation system was over, my ancestors kept this tradition with them because they felt that it was something that we would have in hand and that we would identify with, and that the future generation would identify with, as their heritage. These baskets would symbolize how and why they came, and future generations would know that we should never allow our history to be repeated. So, for more than three hundred years, this art form has been in continuous production in a community right outside of Charleston: Mount Pleasant, where I grew up.

When I'm sewing a basket, there's always a feeling of being close to my ancestors and how proud they would be. They had this beautiful art form that they kept and mastered and shared with me. I have just a wonderful feeling about making every stitch. I have a commitment to carry on this tradition. My real goal is to carry on what they have given me. It's tough work, but I have a really strong feeling about doing this.

—As told to Nigel Noble during the filming of the *Craft in America* documentary series episode "MEMORY."

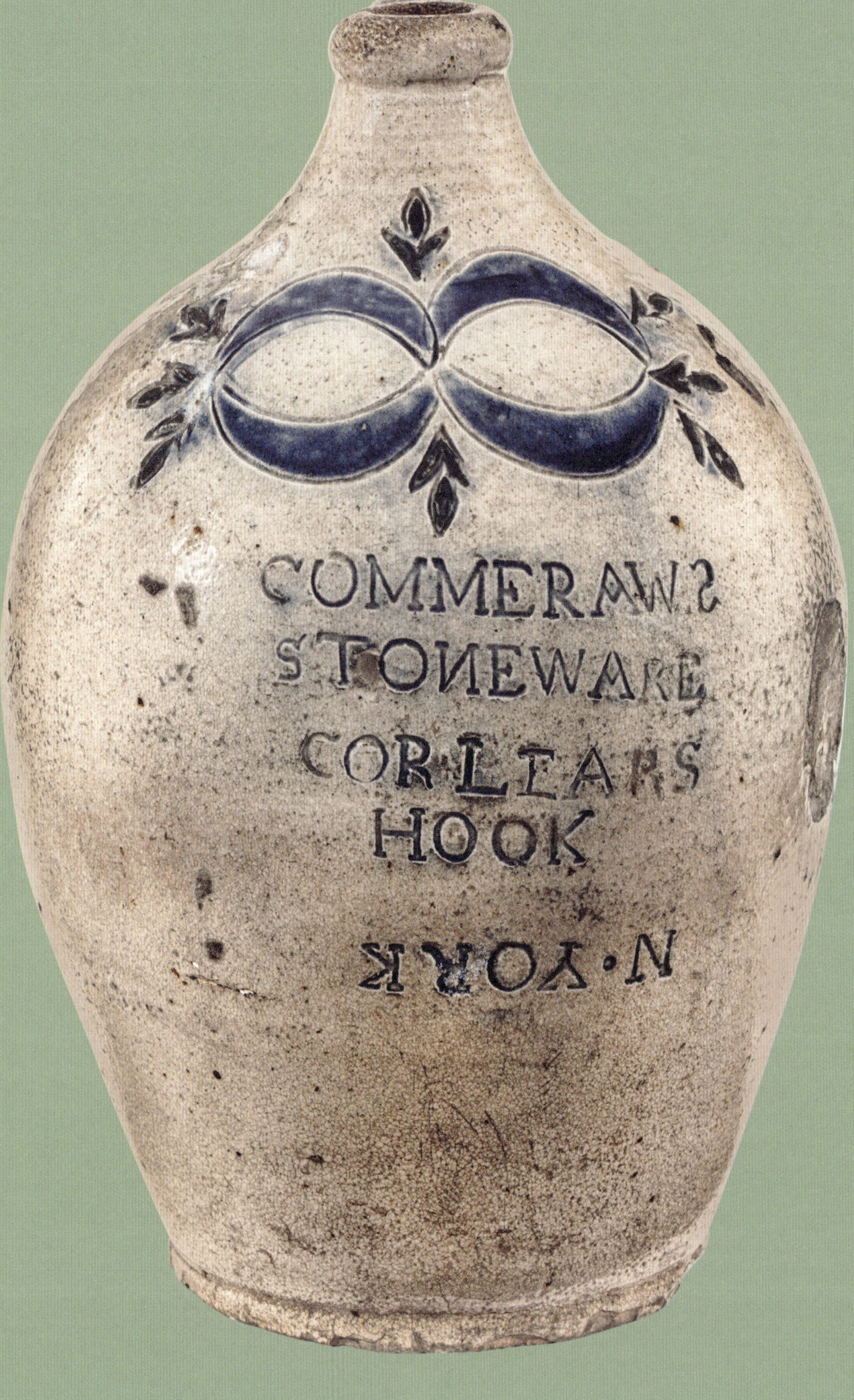
COMMERAWS
STONEWARE
CORLEARS
HOOK
N·YORK

JUG

c. 1797–1819, **Thomas W. Commeraw** (c. 1771–1823),
Salt-glazed stoneware, cobalt oxide, 12 × 7¾ in. (30.5 × 19.7 cm),
The New York Historical, Purchased from Elie Nadelman, Gift of Samuel V. Hoffman, 1937.820.

In 2010, the historian A. Brandt Zipp made a surprising discovery: a certain Thomas Commeraw, who founded a stoneware manufactory in New York City's Seventh Ward in 1797, was African American. This came as quite a revelation, not because he was unknown—pots bearing his name in cobalt-blue lettering had long been sitting in plain sight—but because no one had previously identified him as the same Thomas Commeraw who was a prominent leader of the city's Free Black community. (He eventually went to Sierra Leone, one of the first to seek a so-called return to Africa in the colonization movement.)[1] He was immediately added to an all-too-brief list of celebrated Black artisans who achieved extraordinary things in their trades despite facing brutal racism, including such figures as fellow ceramist David Drake (aka "Dave the Potter"), cabinetmakers Thomas Gross Jr. and Thomas Day, seamstress Elizabeth Keckley, and quilter Harriet Powers.

In the years since this discovery, scholars have conducted extensive and intrepid archival work, unearthing records of many other Black craftspeople: barbers and blacksmiths, coopers and coffinmakers, shoemakers and stonemasons.[2] Nonetheless, it remains extremely challenging to associate specific objects with Black makers. American museums are full of artifacts made by their hands—but which ones are they? We know that silversmithing shops, for example, often had highly skilled enslaved workers, but they left no hallmark to identify their work. Conversely, vernacular objects like face vessels, which were perhaps intended as ritual implements, and "memory jugs," thickly encrusted with found objects and possibly used as grave markers, are rarely attributable to a specific person.[3] It's a fact of craft history that we simply have to accept. In one way or another, functional objects of the past were to some extent generic, lying outside the domain of explicit authorship.

Craft today? That is another matter. Confronting this situation is one of the great tasks that contemporary makers are taking upon themselves. Their efforts are inflected, to be sure, by the identity politics that are so pervasive in the art world, and society at large. But craft disciplines are a bit different; relatively "understated," perhaps, in the literal sense of that word. Pottery, in particular, seems to encourage a thoughtful interiority through which past erasure can be acknowledged, absorbed, and then, quietly but powerfully, refused.

The strategy is perfectly embodied in the works of artist Woody De Othello. Othello's haunting sculpture *Secrets Safe* (2022) has the accumulative composition of a memory jug; it is liberally supplied with ears, eternally vigilant. These remarkably affecting works invite us not to look at them—they seem to deflect any objectifying gaze—but rather *through* them. They are in communion with ancestors otherwise invisible: not just the exceptional cases like Commeraw as well as Dave the Potter—whose majestic inscribed jars have been the subject of a recent restitution agreement between the Museum of Fine Arts, Boston, and his heirs—but also all those whose names we will never know, in all their numbers, who left us all their unheralded achievements. That is the true revelation. —**GA**

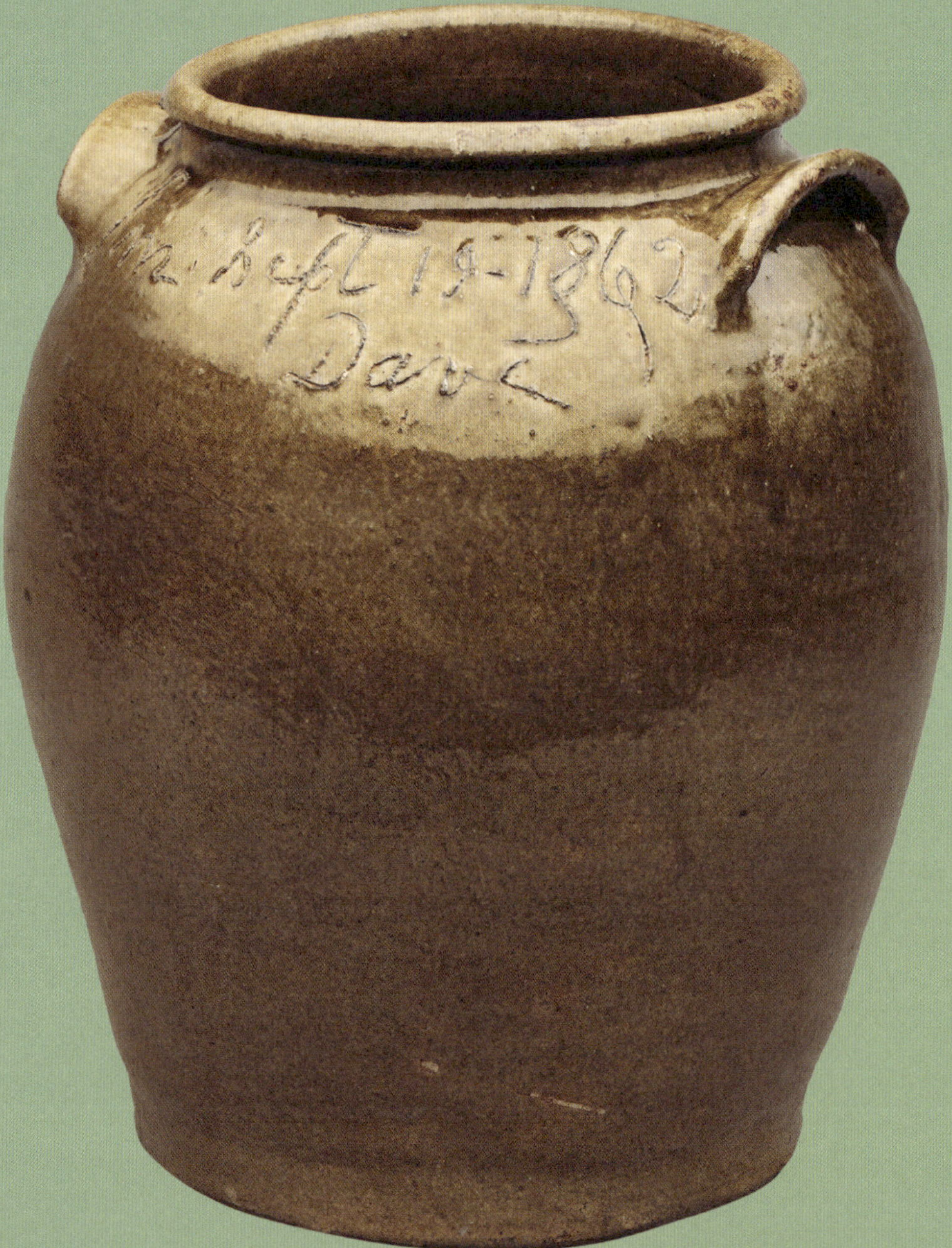

Storage Jar, 1862, **David Drake** (c. 1800–1870s), **Lewis Miles Factory**, Alkaline-glazed stoneware, 15 × 12 in. (38.1 × 30.5 cm), Collection of Kenneth Fechtner, L2020.1401.009.

THE CONTAINER

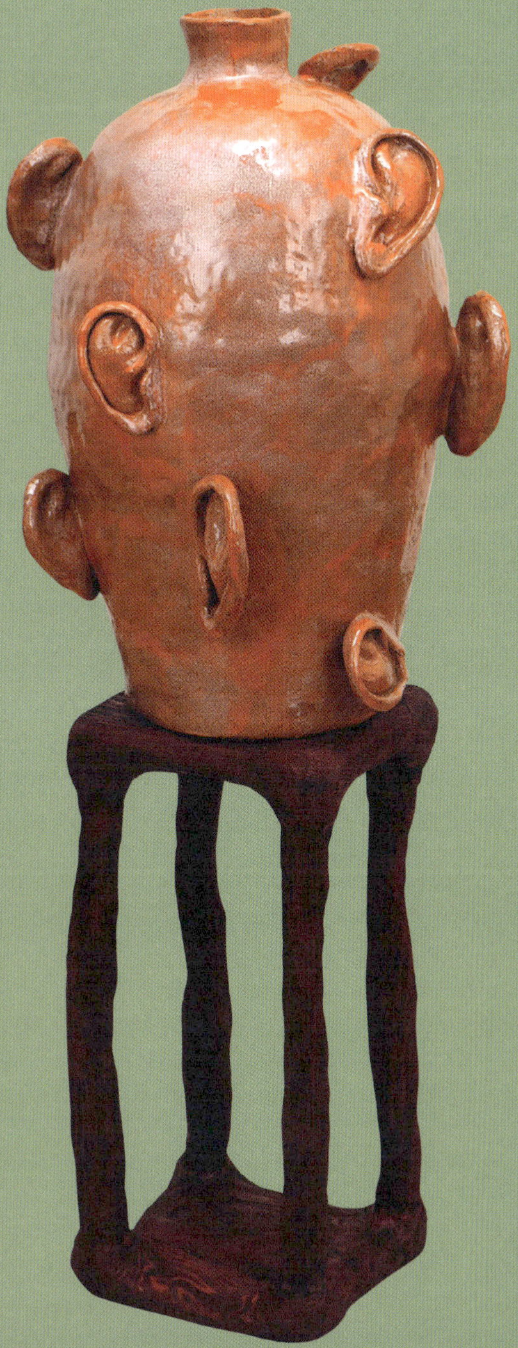

Secrets Safe, 2022, **Woody De Othello** (b. 1991),
Ceramic, glaze, wood, 58½ × 22 × 22 in. (148.6 × 55.9 × 55.9 cm),
High Museum of Art, Atlanta, Purchase with funds from Dwayne Majors and Belinda Stanley-Majors,
the Decorative Arts Acquisition Endowment, Gregor Turk and Murphy Townsend,
Jane and Clay Jackson, and Friends of African American Art. 2023.8.

TO KEEP

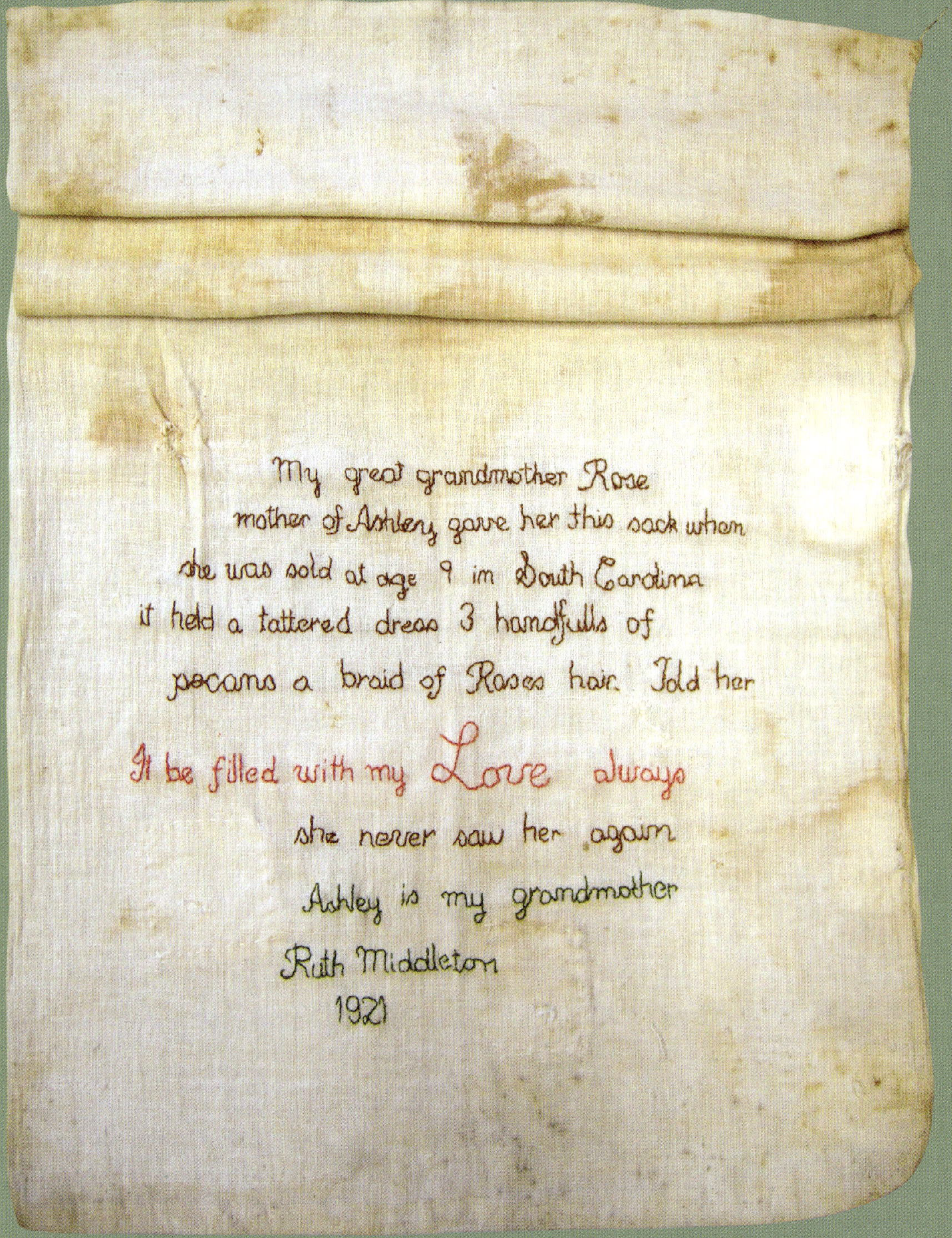

THE CONTAINER

ASHLEY'S SACK

1921, **Ruth Middleton** (c. 1903–1942),
Cotton, 33 × 15 in. (83.8 × 38.1 cm),
Middleton Place Foundation, Charleston.

Ashley's Sack suggests an extraordinary American story of one family's resistance, resilience, and survival in the face of unfathomable horrors experienced by enslaved Africans. It also tells a profound and intimate story of compassion, pain, and a mother's love for her daughter.

During the seventeenth and eighteenth centuries, at the height of the Middle Passage, when enslaved Africans were brought across the Atlantic Ocean to the Americas, people of African descent had no control over their own fate or their family's. Many enslaved people were kidnapped from Africa; survived a monthslong journey, full of unspeakable horrors, across the vast ocean; and were auctioned to a plantation. Enslaved Africans endured constant abuses to their bodies—long hours of arduous work, violence, injuries, malnutrition, diseases, and the threat of imminent death at the will of the dominant class for any slight provocation or whim. Africans were treated as subhuman, as purchased property with no rights to citizenship, no freedom from bondage.

The embroidered inscription on what has become known as Ashley's Sack tells a tale that speaks to this legacy of terror—and the multigenerational love that eclipsed it. In 1921, Ruth Middleton embroidered these words on what she identified as the cotton sack that her enslaved great-grandmother, Rose, had packed for her daughter Ashley's journey when the nine-year-old girl was sold away from her:

> My great grandmother Rose / mother of Ashley gave her this sack when / she was sold at age 9 in South Carolina / it held a tattered dress, 3 handfulls of / pecans a braid of Rose's hair. Told her / It be filled with my Love always / she never saw her again / Ashley is my grandmother / Ruth Middleton / 1921

The recorded contents of the bag can be read as a powerful, loving tribute of a mother under severe duress and trauma, the last act of care she could provide for her beloved child.

The continuum of the oral and storytelling traditions in African culture and the African diaspora has prevailed in powerful and remarkable ways. The descendants of Rose's family held this precious history close and kept it sacred and alive. The earliest "herstories" of women have been underrepresented, disregarded, dismissed, and too often, invisible. Using needle and thread in colors, images, and texts, women recorded visual narratives in fiber, still yet to be recognized as crucial to the documentation of America's cultural heritage. The poignancy and ubiquitousness of a sack—a utilitarian object traditionally used to contain grain, seeds, rice, or flour—metaphorically signified and resonated new meanings for lives lived in difficult times. In Ashley's Sack, the unwavering love of a mother for her daughter transcended the horrors of slavery to defiantly state their agency and personhood as African descendant people. This is a resounding testament to the historical fragility of African American families, which enslavement sought to dismantle by every means possible. Ashley's Sack radiates with the power of pride, survival, humanity, and the remarkable resilience of Black family kinships in America today. —LKH

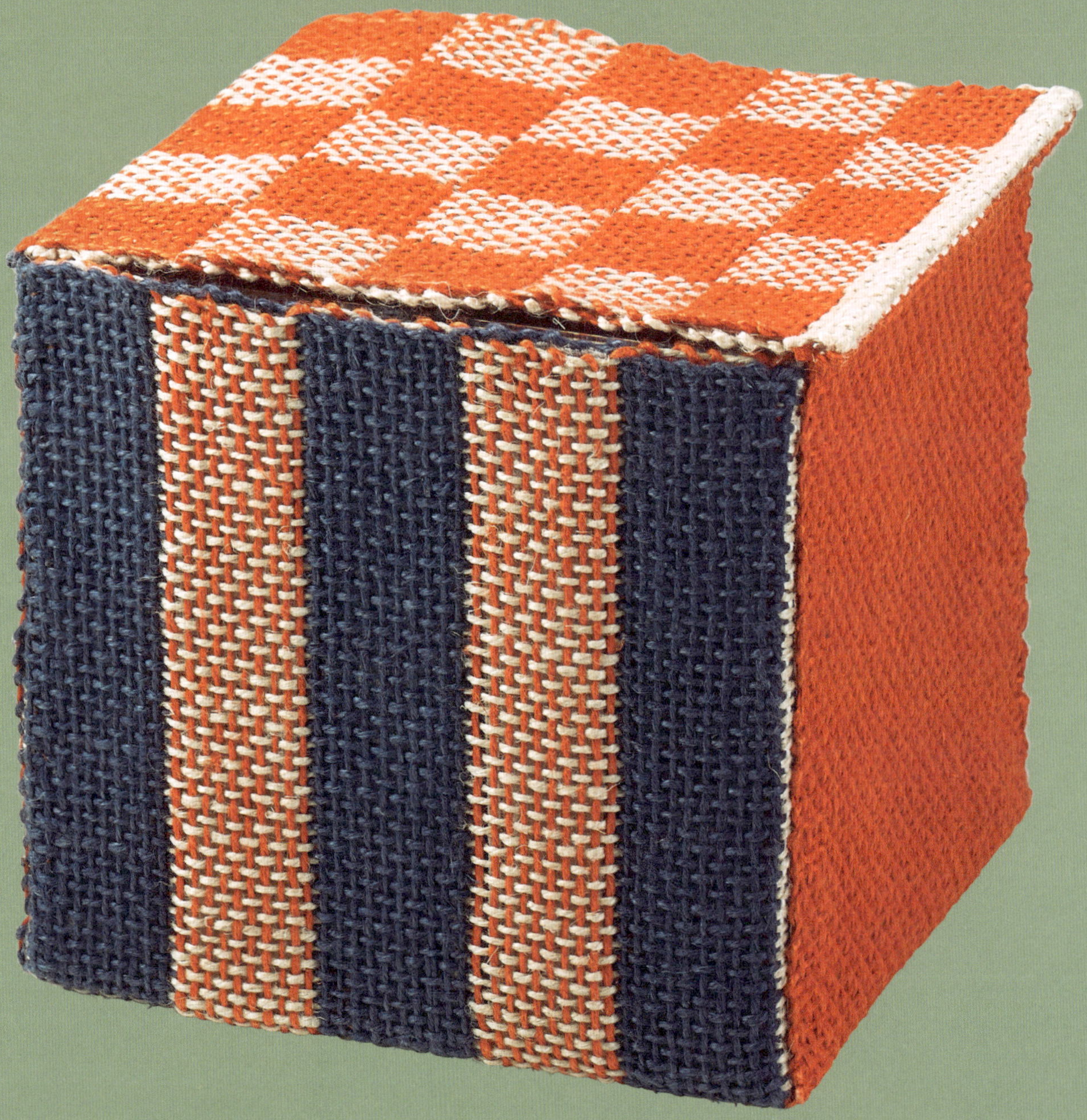

THE CONTAINER

PAIRED BOX (ONE OF A SET)

c. 1990s, **Kay Sekimachi** (b. 1926), Natural and dyed linen, 4 × 4 × 4 in. (10.2 × 10.2 × 10.2 cm), Forrest L. Merrill Collection.

When you look at Kay Sekimachi's weavings, you wonder, *How did she do that?* And no matter how well or how often Sekimachi's techniques are explained, they still remain a mystery. This box, one of a pair that are magically woven in two dimensions and come off the loom ready to become three-dimensional, is one such enigmatic object (see detail, page 10).

The artist was born in San Francisco in 1926. When she was a teenager, in 1942, she, her sisters, and their mother, who were Japanese American, were interned at the Topaz internment camp in Utah as a result of Executive Order 9066. "The first time, when we lined up for meals, carrying a tin dish and a tin cup," Sekimachi has said, "I thought, *Are we going to survive this?*" They remained there for three years.

When the war ended, Sekimachi and her family returned to California and she enrolled at the California College of Arts and Crafts in Oakland, where she discovered weaving—and found her calling. "It's so interesting that I didn't know that my mother was a weaver until I got my loom. And she said, 'Oh, I wove.' Then she told me that her mother used to say to her that to be a good weaver you had to feel like a thread," the artist says.

For Sekimachi, her skill on the loom was her entrée to her work as an artist. She took humble materials—shells, leaves, as well as monofilament, which is commonly used as fishing line—to weave and build sculptural objects of beauty and technical mastery. Her exploration of both form and material makes her a pioneer of the modern craft movement.

For thirty years, Sekimachi was married to the celebrated woodturner Bob Stocksdale. "He helped me by making anything and everything I needed for my work," she says. "He put blocks on my treadles on my twelve-harness looms, so that I could reach the treadles with my feet. He made my card weaving boards. He made molds for me. . . . I couldn't have done some of the things I did without his help."

Stocksdale was born in Indiana in 1913. He began working with wood as a child, first whittling, then learning the essentials of wood turning on a lathe. When America joined World War II, Stocksdale was a conscientious objector and spent three years in a Civilian Public Service camp. While there, he worked for the forest service and honed his skills as a woodturner, making bowls for food and teaching others to turn wood. At the end of the war, Stocksdale moved to Berkeley, California, and set up his lathe.

Stocksdale's skill as a woodworker evolved in his Berkeley studio. He was among the best turners in the world, pioneering the use of the lathe in turning rare hardwoods into graceful, expertly thin bowls that glowed with grain and form.

When he and Sekimachi married in 1972, it was the beginning of a three-decade partnership in art as well as life. Their *Marriage in Form* bowls, created when Sekimachi used Stocksdale's turned bowls as forms to create her paper bowls, were a true creative breakthrough. The bowls were displayed, side by side, in exhibitions throughout the country. —**CS**

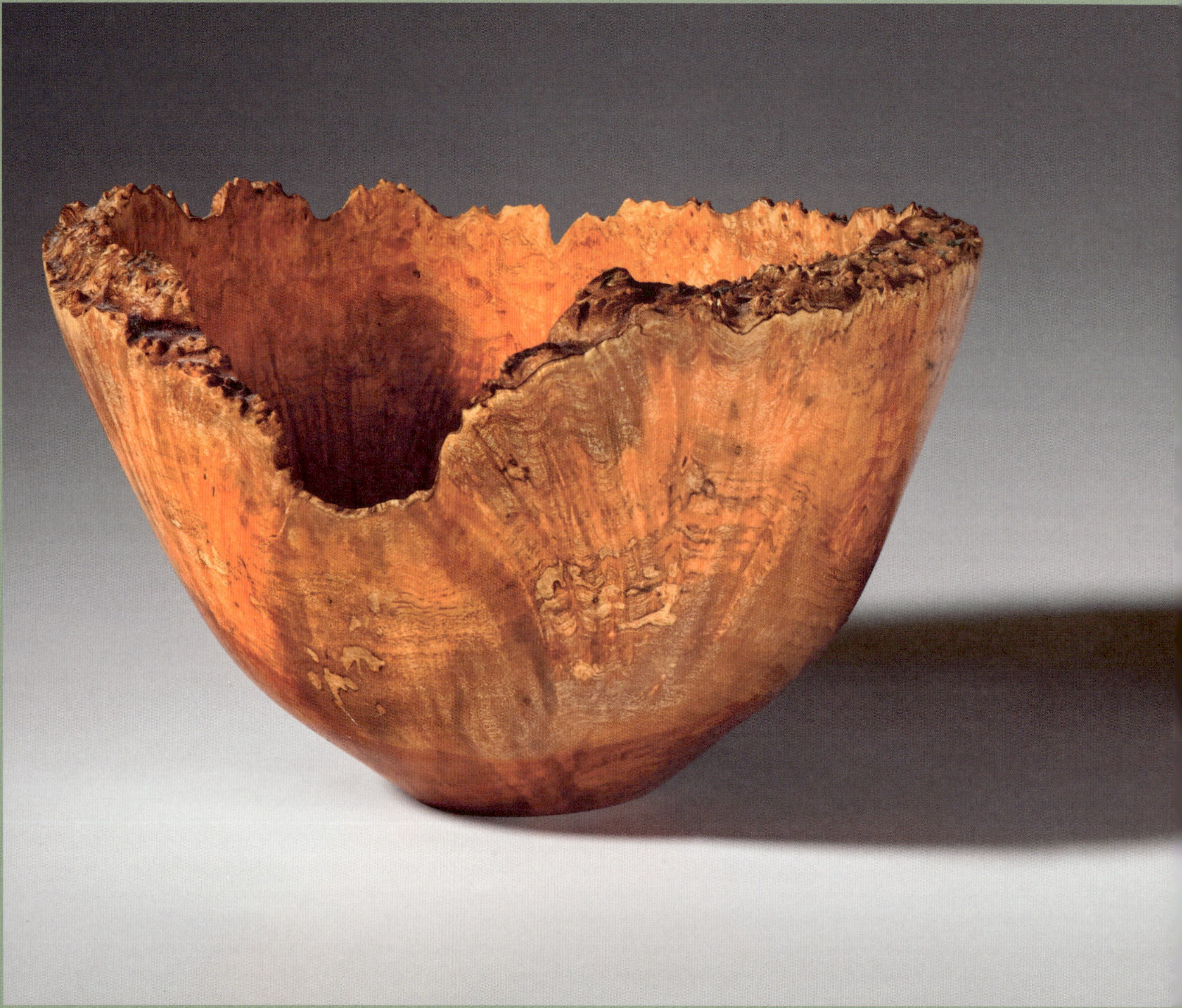

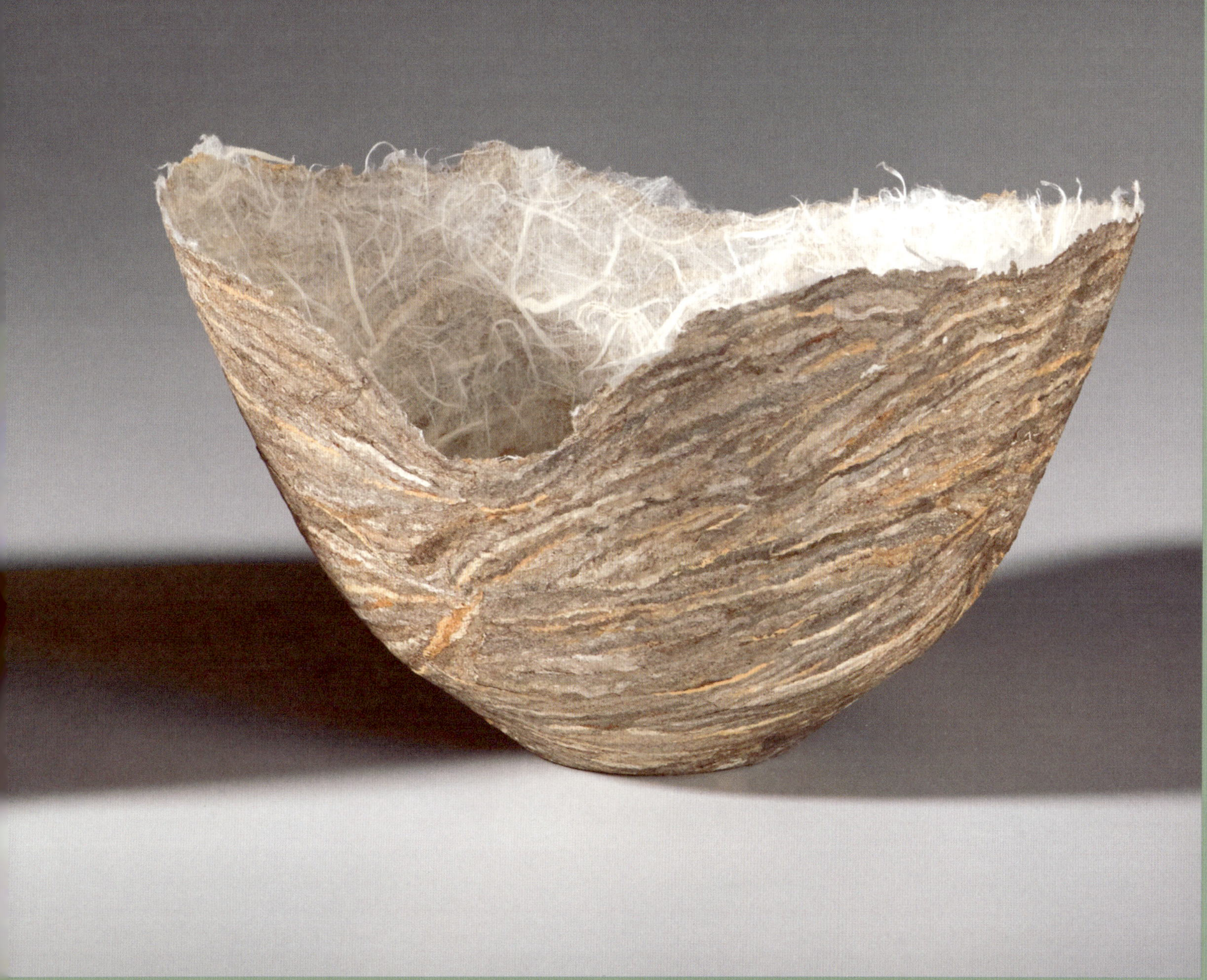

Marriage in Form, 1999, **Bob Stocksdale and Kay Sekimachi,**
Left: Mexican Chechen wood, Right: Hornet's nest paper, handmade Japanese Kozo paper,
Each: 4⅜ × 4⅜ in. (11.1 × 11.1 cm), Forrest L. Merrill Collection.

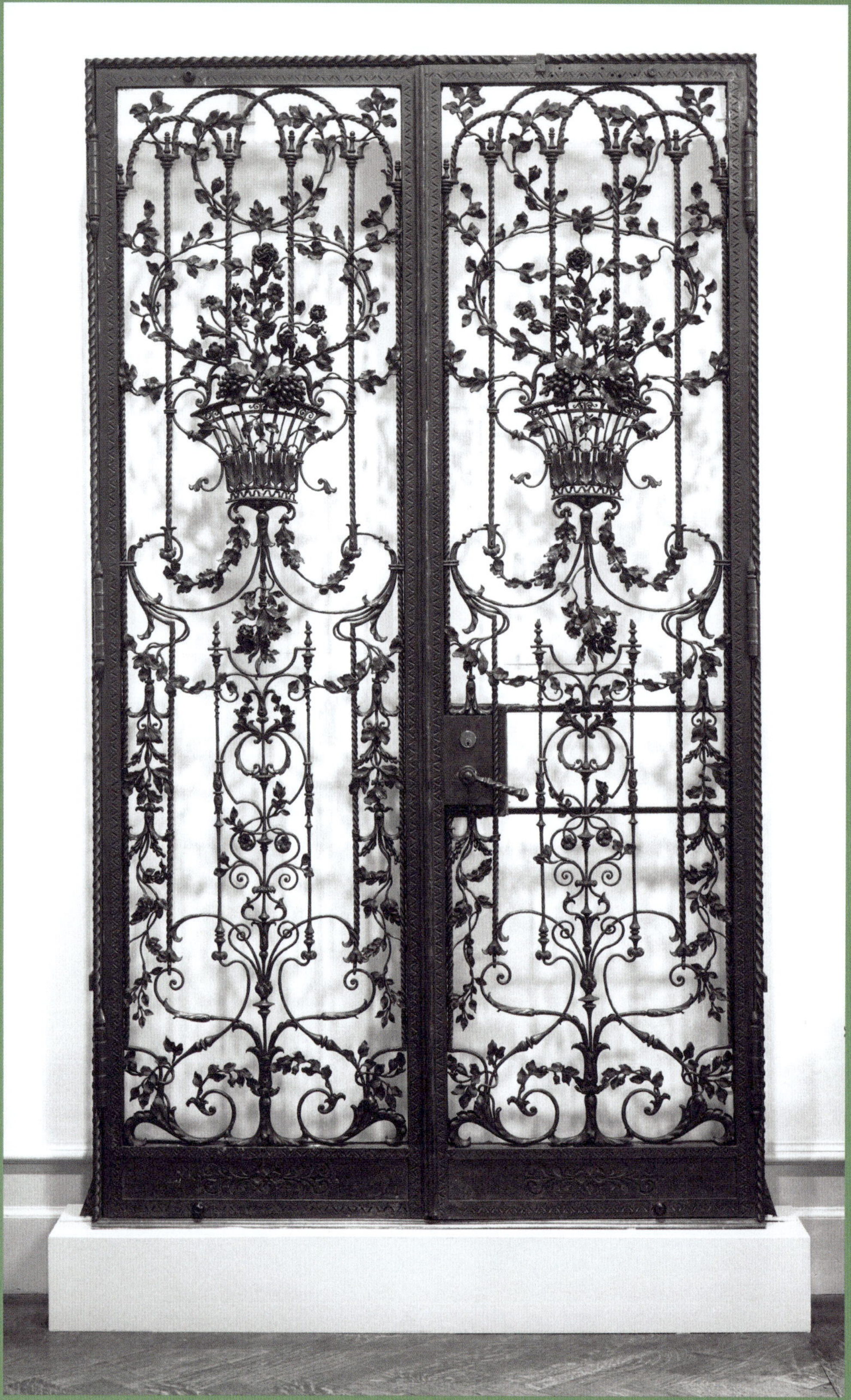

THE GATE

DOORS

1915, **Samuel Yellin** (1884–1940),
Iron, 91⅜ × 53½ in. (232.1 × 135.9 cm),
Metropolitan Museum of Art, New York, Gift of Manuel Pollack and Morris Baris, 1965. Inst.65.1.1a–j.

Providing the bare canvas of a plaster or concrete facade with a pop of ornamentation, gates and doors can be focal moments of decorative flourish at a building's entrance. Those created by early twentieth-century blacksmith Samuel Yellin are among the most exuberant and rich with detail. They are proof of the fluidity of iron. Yellin used his material to highlight its surprising organic, curvilinear potential, forging and hammering the metal into unlikely, mind-bending shapes, from flora to fauna to mythical creatures to abstract forms. In the case of these vestibule doors for the residence of New York socialite Elvira Brokaw McNair, Yellin transformed iron into climbing roses, grapes, and acorns.[1] He brought metal to life and planted bursts of stylized nature in the urban cityscape.

Gates, doors, window grilles, and fences signal points of access just as much as they provide barriers to entry. They welcome, but they also exclude and protect. To Yellin, they were the bridges between interior and exterior worlds.

In the early twentieth century, the Arts and Crafts movement in America developed a philosophy and approach to creating objects with careful consideration of materials, processes, function, and precedent. It was an innovative new way of making artful and meaningful things. Yellin was a main proponent of these ideals and transferred them to the realm of metalwork. During the phase of revivalist architecture that was widespread in the first decades of the 1900s through the World Wars, gates and grilles were key elements in setting the tone and style of a building. They were prominent features that supplied high ornamental contrast to large, sweeping walls, providing accents of pattern and detail.

Yellin emigrated to the United States in 1900 from Mogilev, Russia, after apprenticing in blacksmithing and building his foundation in European techniques and aesthetics.[2] In addition to teaching at the Pennsylvania Museum and School of Industrial Art (later the University of the Arts), he established a shop in Philadelphia in 1909, where he produced wrought iron for various architectural elements, hardware, lighting, and more. He rapidly found success, and by 1928 he had a team of more than two hundred craftsmen who worked with him and in unison to craft his designs as though they had been made by the hand of one person.

Yellin's clients and projects were scattered throughout the East and beyond. He created his historically infused iron adornments for banks, universities, public buildings, and private residences alike. His metalwork, which he called the "salt and pepper of architecture,"[3] brought natural elements and a playfulness and delicacy to urban architecture, balancing the monolithic qualities of buildings typical of the era. Each and every detail was executed with perfection, as Yellin viewed even the smallest component as essential to the quality of the total piece. It is no wonder that he made many framing devices for architectural openings; he saw iron as the "stuff of which the frame of the earth is made."[4] —EZ

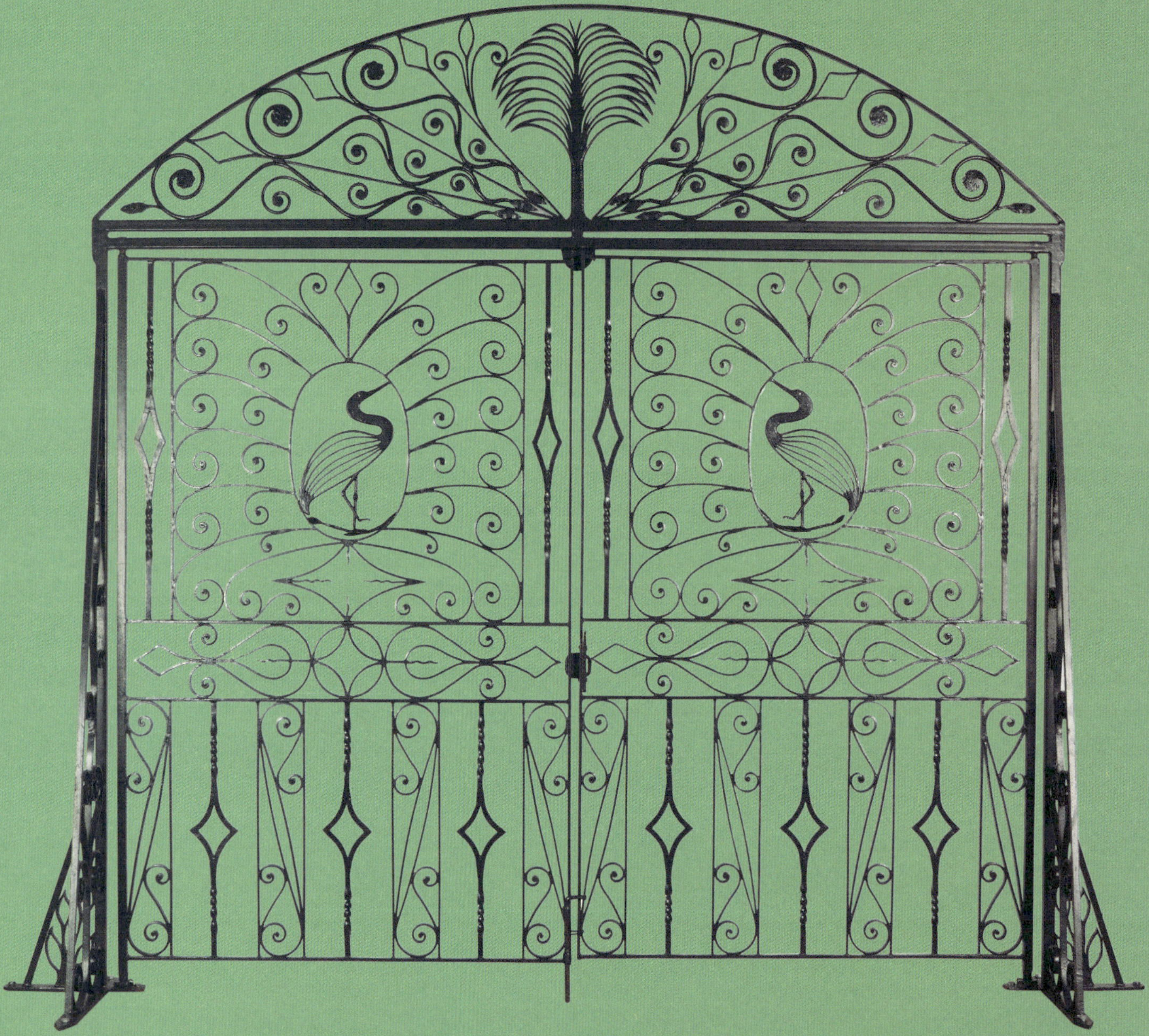

THE GATE

THE PHILIP SIMMONS GATE

1987, **Philip Simmons** (1912–2009),
Wrought iron, 135 × 129 × 24 in. (342.9 × 326.4 × 61 cm),
South Carolina State Museum, Columbia.

Places such as Charleston carry a long legacy of Black blacksmiths who created the beautiful ironwork featured throughout those urban landscapes. Beginning in the South Carolina Lowcountry, among the Gullah Geechee culture, early enslaved and free Black craftsmen created the iconic decorative ironwork—the black gates and railings—that adorns many of the city's houses. Most of those skilled artisans continue to go unnamed and their contributions remain unrecognized, but there is no finer contemporary example of this tradition than the ironwork of master blacksmith Philip Simmons, whose portfolio of more than one thousand works throughout Charleston translates early ironwork customs passed down from both British craftsmen and the enslaved.

Simmons began working as a blacksmith at a young age, serving as an apprentice to another master blacksmith in Charleston named Peter Simmons (no relation), who was taught the trade of his enslaved ancestors. After Peter Simmons retired from the business in the 1930s, Philip Simmons took over his shop and continued to serve Charleston by repairing and creating new wrought iron.

Most of Philip Simmons's commissions were for private clients and were designed to complement historic architecture. To complete these commissions, he would build on eighteenth-century ironwork designs introduced to the region by British makers, bringing his own twist to the motifs common in Charleston. However, a 1987 commission by the South Carolina State Museum allowed Simmons the opportunity to more freely express his unique ideas. The resulting gate here is a sculptural interpretation of a typical driveway gate that unites early Charleston ironwork traditions with icons that pay special tribute to South Carolina. The gate features motifs including the Charleston green palmetto tree, low-country egrets, scrolls, twists, diamonds, and running vine. Simmons was able to fully experiment and perfect the forms in the work and create the type of gate that suited his own interests.

In turn, Simmons trained his cousin Joseph Pringle and nephew Carlton Simmons as apprentices to his blacksmith workshop, allowing them to contribute to some of his later commissions in Charleston. After his death in 2009, Pringle and the younger Simmons would continue the family tradition of blacksmithing in the Simmons shop. Pringle died in 2021, and just a few years later, in 2024, Carlton Simmons died. Though these important keepers of the tradition have passed on, their legacies live through the Philip Simmons Foundation, the Philip Simmons Collection at the Avery Research Center, and in the collection of the National Museum of African American History and Culture at the Smithsonian Institution. —LC

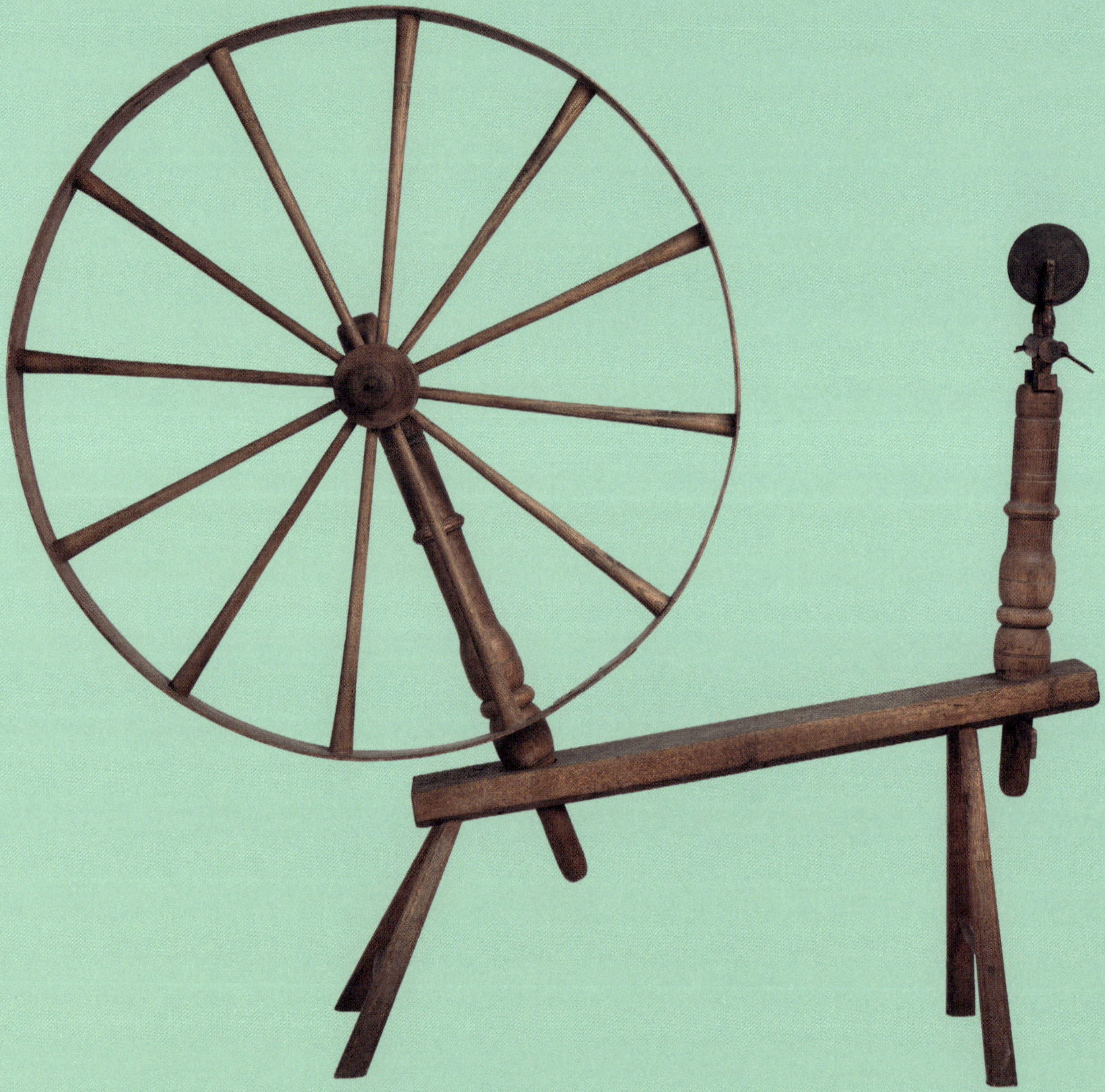

THE TOOL

SPINNING WHEEL

Early 18th century, **Unidentified artist (likely Massachusetts)**, Wood and paint, 68 7⁄8 × 64 × 18 in. (174.9 × 162.2 × 45.7 cm), The Huntington Library, Art Museum, and Botanical Gardens, San Marino, CA, Gift of Jonathan and Karin Fielding, 2016.25.145.

Originating in India during the eleventh century, spinning wheels would appear later in Europe and America as a common tool for textile production. In early American households, equipment such as spinning wheels and niddy noddies (tools used to wind yarn) was critical to the process of transforming wool and cotton into the thread and yarn to make textiles. Large walking wheels or "great wheels," like the one shown here, were used for spinning wool or cotton, while small spinning wheels were used for making linen from flax. This spinning wheel produced cotton yarn that was used for weaving or for making cloth to create other items such as clothing, quilts, samplers, and rugs.

Prior to the growth of the American textile industry later in the nineteenth century, the high cost of imported goods and garments led many early Americans to make their own clothes, requiring them to create their own yarn, textiles, and even the tools needed to produce them. Spinning wheels were often made by craftspeople or carpenters who fashioned furniture and other household items out of wood. Research into the woodwork, tension devices, and frequently found maker's marks for eighteenth- and nineteenth-century American spinning wheels has made it possible to identify makers and regions of origin. This spinning wheel is inscribed with the initials "J. C.," a mark that has been linked to other spinning wheels originating in New England.[1] Spinning wheel collector, researcher, and restorer Brenda Page identified a similar great wheel and smaller flax wheels marked "J. C." near Westerly, Rhode Island.[2] The fact that this spinning wheel was also found in New England suggests that it was a household item that was likely passed down across generations locally, especially in rural areas that relied on homespun textiles. The equipment was later updated or repaired by installing a nineteenth-century spindle to enhance the wheel's speed and increase the level of textile production.

In the eighteenth century, homespun textiles and handmade clothes were needed in order for Americans to be self-sustaining and less reliant on goods with foreign tariffs. Women's groups such as the Daughters of Liberty hosted spinning bees, creating large volumes of yarn to support this effort. Popular imagination typically casts the women of the household—wives and daughters—as operating the spinning wheel. However, spinning was a very labor-intensive practice that may also have been delegated to enslaved and free Black women,[3] who were often charged with making the textiles and clothing for the wealthier households as well as for other enslaved people. — LC

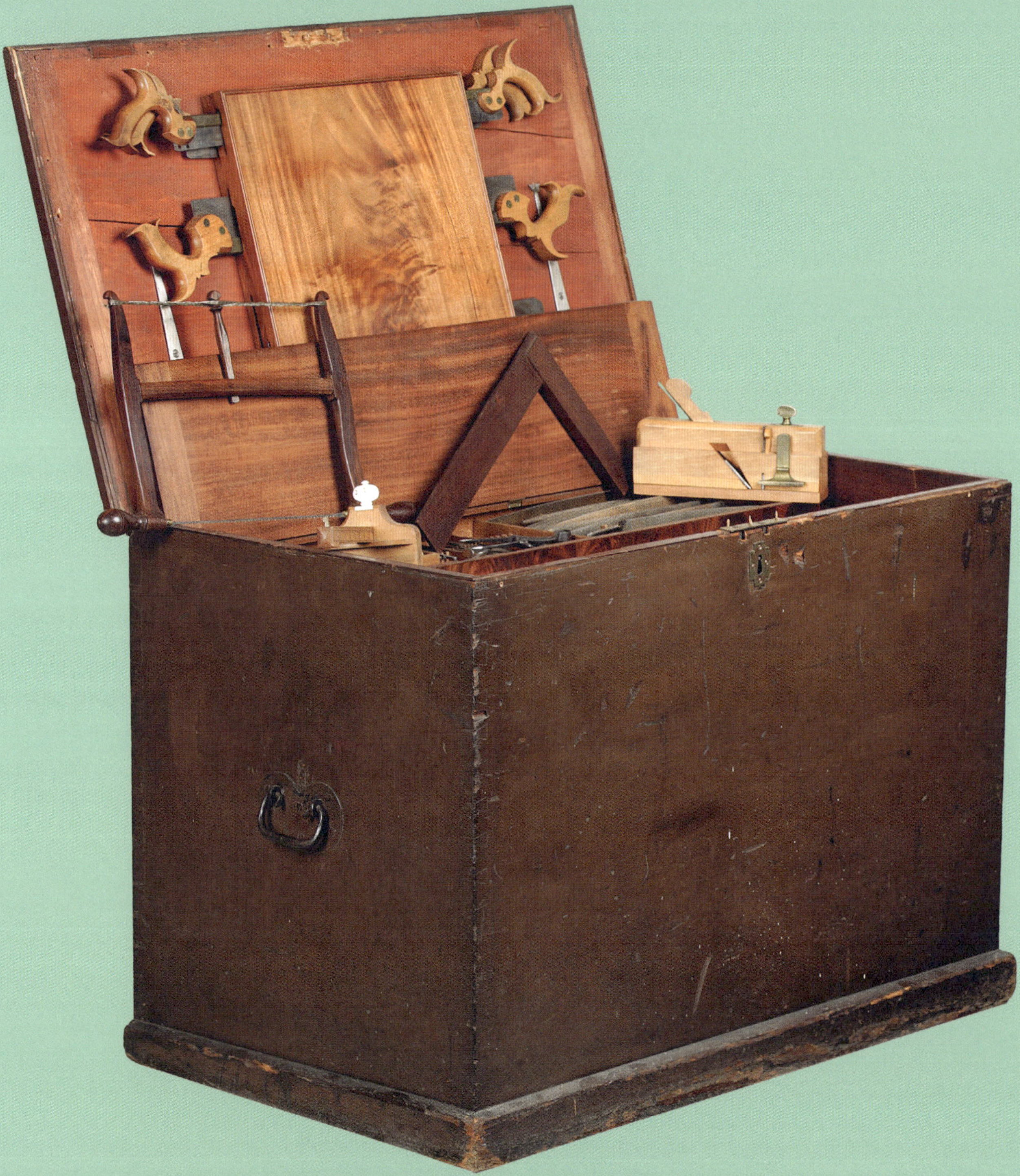

THE TOOL

TOOL CHEST

c. 1790 with later additions, **Duncan Phyfe** (1770–1854),
Pine with mahogany, paint, brass, ivory, 21¾ × 26½ × 38 in. (55.3 × 67.3 × 96.5 cm),
The New York Historical, Loaned by the families of Henry Pinkney Phyfe and Churchill B. Phyfe, L.1927.1.

What does your household toolbox look like? Mine is the size of a large shoebox and is made of molded plastic. It was mass-produced in China but is well designed, with compartments for hardware, a removable tray, and a storage area below. Purchased during college from a national retailer, the toolbox has moved with me a dozen times. Many of the tools within are hand-me-downs from my father, contributing to countless household projects of no artistic significance whatsoever.

Now consider the toolbox shown here. The chipped paint on the plain exterior belies the beauty and extravagance that lies within. What looks to be a utilitarian blanket chest from the outside is in fact a furniture maker's pride and joy on the inside. The till is fitted out with neat rows of drawers joined with finely cut dovetails, covered in thin sheets of mahogany veneer of the utmost quality, and adorned with delicately turned ivory pulls. The chest holds nearly three hundred tools, the handles of many of which are rendered from costly exotic woods, such as ebony and rosewood, emphasizing their significance to the owner. There are only a handful of surviving eighteenth-century tool chests known, in spite of the tens of thousands of craftsmen who undoubtedly owned them. Side handles suggest the need for mobility; most furniture makers in this era were called journeymen, untethered free agents working on behalf of master shop owners, who traveled to where their skills were needed. And the quality of the chest they owned was indicative of their skills as an artisan and employee.

This chest was built by the legendary New York cabinetmaker Duncan Phyfe and accompanied him for more than six decades as he charted his course from unknown Scottish immigrant apprentice to internationally renowned artisan. Phyfe is arguably the best-known American cabinetmaker. He was once known as the "United States rage" in reference to his immense stature in the trade.[1] According to family legend, he remained an active woodworker even when his business had expanded, transitioning his role from artisan at the bench to shop master overseeing dozens of craftsmen. He kept a small workshop behind his house, which sat across Fulton Street in Lower Manhattan from his impressive manufactory and wareroom.

Tool chests are static vessels for dynamic contents. Over the course of a lifetime, new tools are acquired for specific purposes or as technology evolves, hence the need for a dozen varieties of saws for cutting, planes for molding, gauges for marking, rasps for filing, and gouges for carving. The manufacture dates of the tools contained within Phyfe's chest suggest that he continued to purchase them throughout his lifetime.

This tool chest was passed down through the descendants of Phyfe's son, James D. Phyfe, who worked alongside his father until the family business closed in 1847, and was clearly a cherished heirloom. It is a powerful artifact of this celebrity cabinetmaker. Tool chests and their contents, today as in the nineteenth century, are more than practical; they are vessels of intimacy, memory, and assets, passed down between generations. —MT

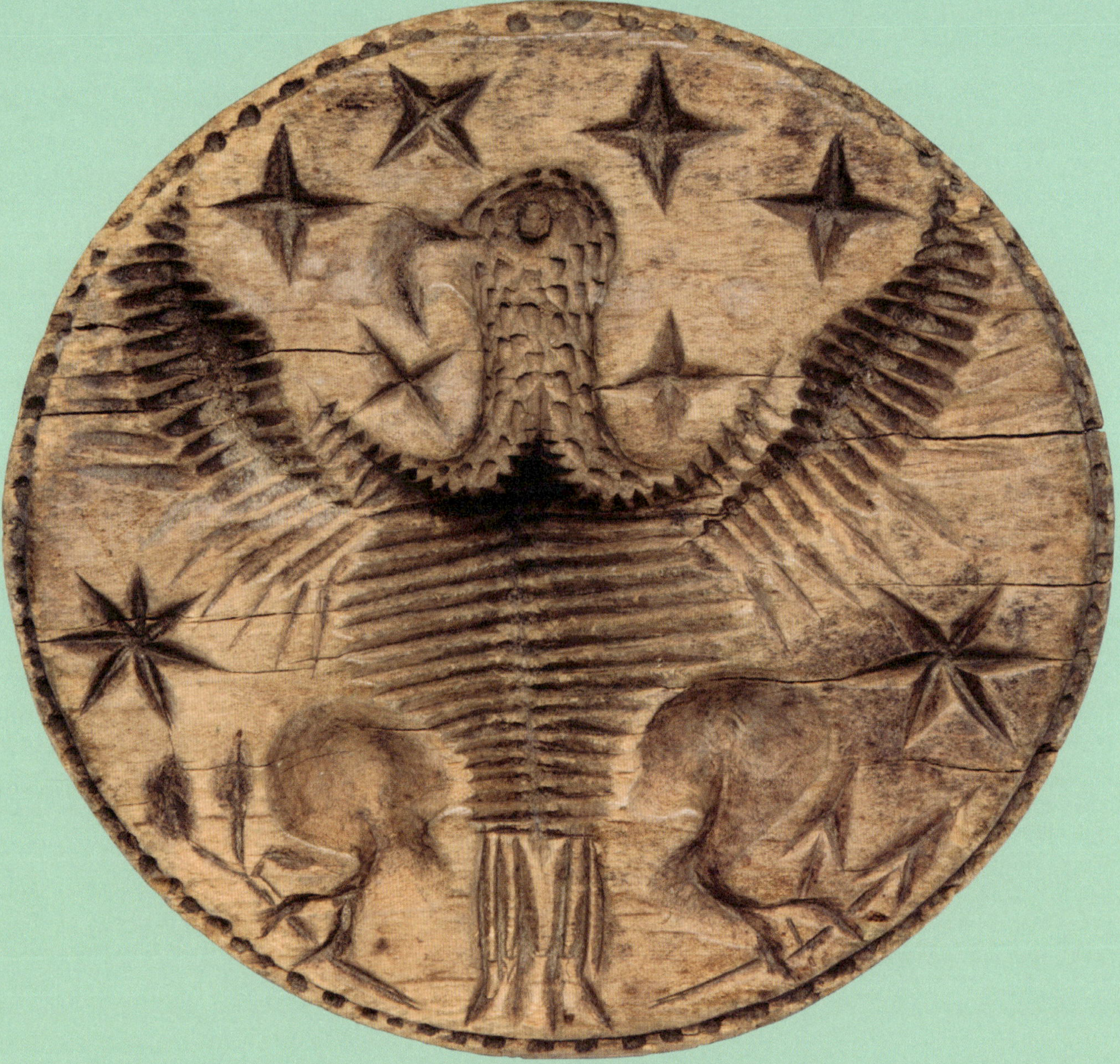

THE TOOL

BUTTER PRINT

1800–1840, **Unidentified artist (Pennsylvania)**,
Maple, 1 × 5⅛ in. (2.5 × 13 cm),
Philadelphia Museum of Art, Titus C. Geesey Collection, 1955 (1955-94-24).

The desire of rural Pennsylvanians of the eighteenth and nineteenth centuries to ornament everyday objects to make their world less mundane provides today's world with insight into theirs. This butter print, for example, tells us something of the cultural background, ambition, economy, physical work, and social lives of entrepreneurial women living in the agricultural Eden of the lands north and west of Philadelphia.

Butter prints were used by women to mark the butter they made and sold. Making butter was both time-consuming and physically demanding, and almost exclusively done by the women on farms. As butter became a more popular ingredient and condiment in the nineteenth century, women seized the opportunity to make more than their family needed and sell the excess to generate income. These Pennsylvania farming women—mostly members of the numerous German immigrant groups—packaged their butter in small wooden boxes by the pound or half-pound, then used a tool like this one to brand their wares. This distinguished the butter's maker, giving purchasers in market towns such as Lancaster and Philadelphia confidence in what they were buying and the ability to seek that product again. In this way, women could take pride in their product and build a thriving business for themselves.

Butter prints were made by woodworkers who specialized in producing implements from turned discs of woods including tulip poplar, pine, and maple. A knob handle was affixed to the reverse of the disc, while the face of the butter print was chip-carved. The specialist makers, who often signed the butter print, used chisels and gouges to create compositions centering on geometric designs; plants such as corn, wheat, and flowers; and animals such as cows and eagles. The motifs were part of the visual lexicon that recurred in Pennsylvania German textiles, ironwork, Fraktur drawings, ceramics, and as painted decoration on furniture. The face of this butter print still has its finely carved decoration; surrounded by eight stars, a spread-winged eagle spans the center with lines delineating its overall plumage, round chips articulating the individual feathers, and its claws grasping arrows and a laurel branch.

Butter prints that were specially commissioned became, in effect, the signature for butter made by an entrepreneurial woman; the design of the butter print became her brand, her label. The practice of women making excess butter and selling it with their own label paralleled a shift in the economy of the early industrial years of the mid-nineteenth century, when this one was made. Not only had foodways changed to embrace butter on bread and in soups and sauces, but improved transportation made it easier for butter to get to the markets for sale.

The wear on butter prints is a strong reminder of the work of women who gained a foothold in the burgeoning economy of the nineteenth century. While this finely wrought and well-preserved butter print has no history of ownership, others were passed down through the generations from woman to woman, a further suggestion that these humble craft objects—small in stature but highly ornamented—represented a source of pride for countless women. —**AK**

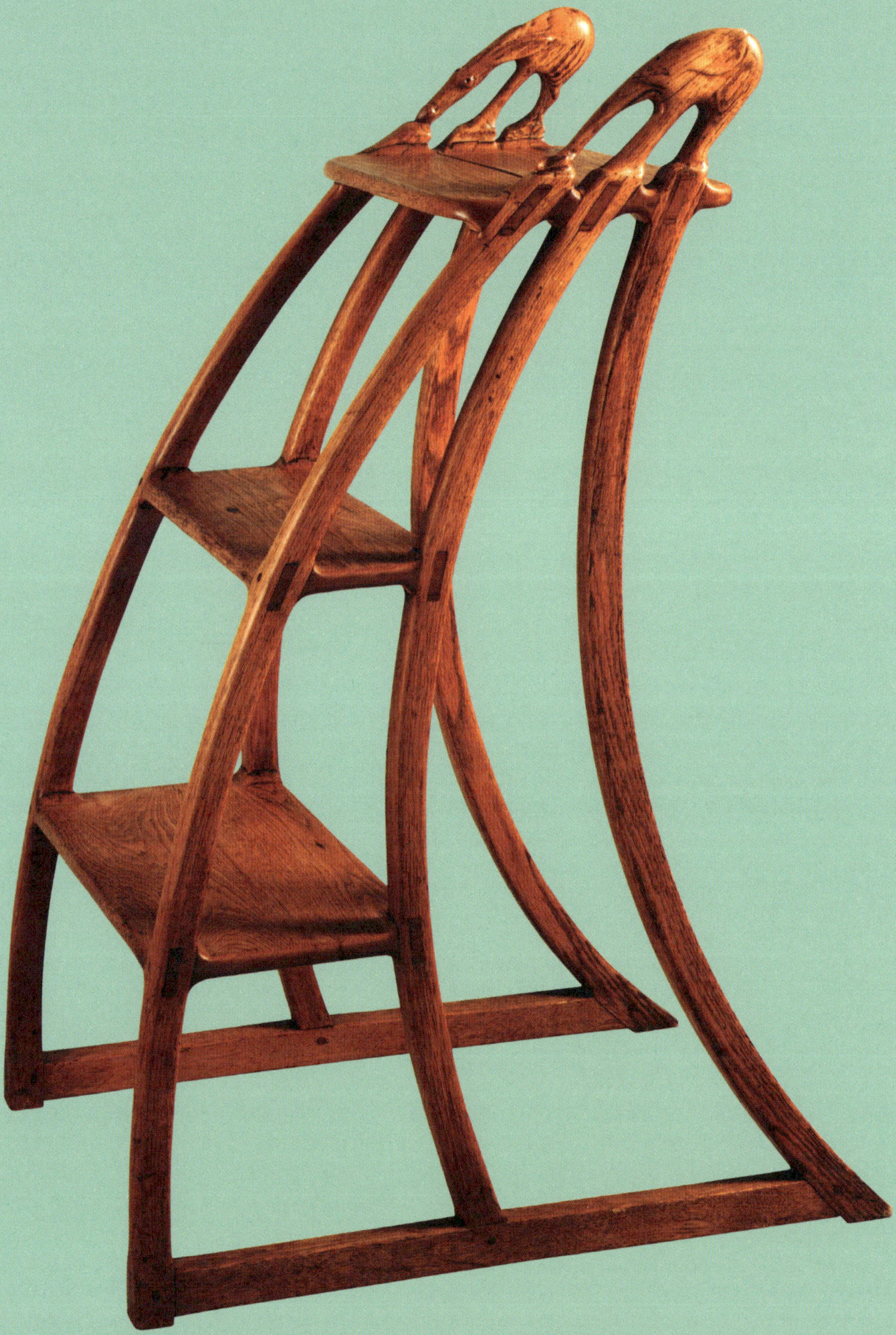

THE TOOL

LIBRARY LADDER

1935, **Wharton H. Esherick** (1887–1970), Hickory, oak,
34¾ × 18 × 23¼ in. (88.3 × 45.7 × 59.1 cm), Philadelphia Museum of Art,
125th Anniversary Acquisition, Gift of Rachel Bok Goldman and Allen S. Goldman, M.D., 2001-14-1.

A ladder is a ubiquitous object that most people use without much thought. Often out of sight until pulled into service, it is fundamentally elemental in both its design and purpose. As a practical household object, a ladder is an inelegant workhorse, a tool.

Philadelphia artist Wharton Esherick crafted this unique library ladder in 1935.[1] Trained as a painter at the Pennsylvania Academy of Fine Arts, Esherick's interest in three-dimensional forms evolved from carving wooden frames for his canvases and woodblocks for printmaking. Commissioned by Judge William Curtis Bok and his wife, Nellie Lee, as part of Esherick's renovation of their Philadelphia Main Line home in Gulph Mills, this remarkable ladder was made for a law library and its floor-to-ceiling bookshelves.[2] Although definitively a stepladder, and in essence a tool to reach books on those uppermost shelves, like many things designed by Esherick, this object falls somewhere between function and sculpture.

Made during the Great Depression, this ladder reflects how Esherick, like many others, rationed materials and creatively used or reused what was available to him. Esherick was known for his particularly inventive use of existing materials, not wanting anything to go to waste. He purchased wagon wheels from a local shop that was selling an overstock in varying sizes, creatively utilizing them in several of his designs.[3] Here, he skillfully repurposed felloes—curved pieces used to make the outer frame of wooden wheels—for the vertical rails of this ladder. The ladder's shapely, organic, bowed composition is informed by the inherent curves of these three arched frames. Projecting above the top step on both sides, the frames converge to form handholds, which Esherick carved into a donkey on the left and an elephant on the right, representing the Democratic and Republican political parties—ingenious details communicating the impartiality of the judicial branch. Made for Judge Bok's personal law library, where he reviewed cases and appeals, the ladder became, essentially, a powerful tool as a symbol for justness.[4] —**EA**

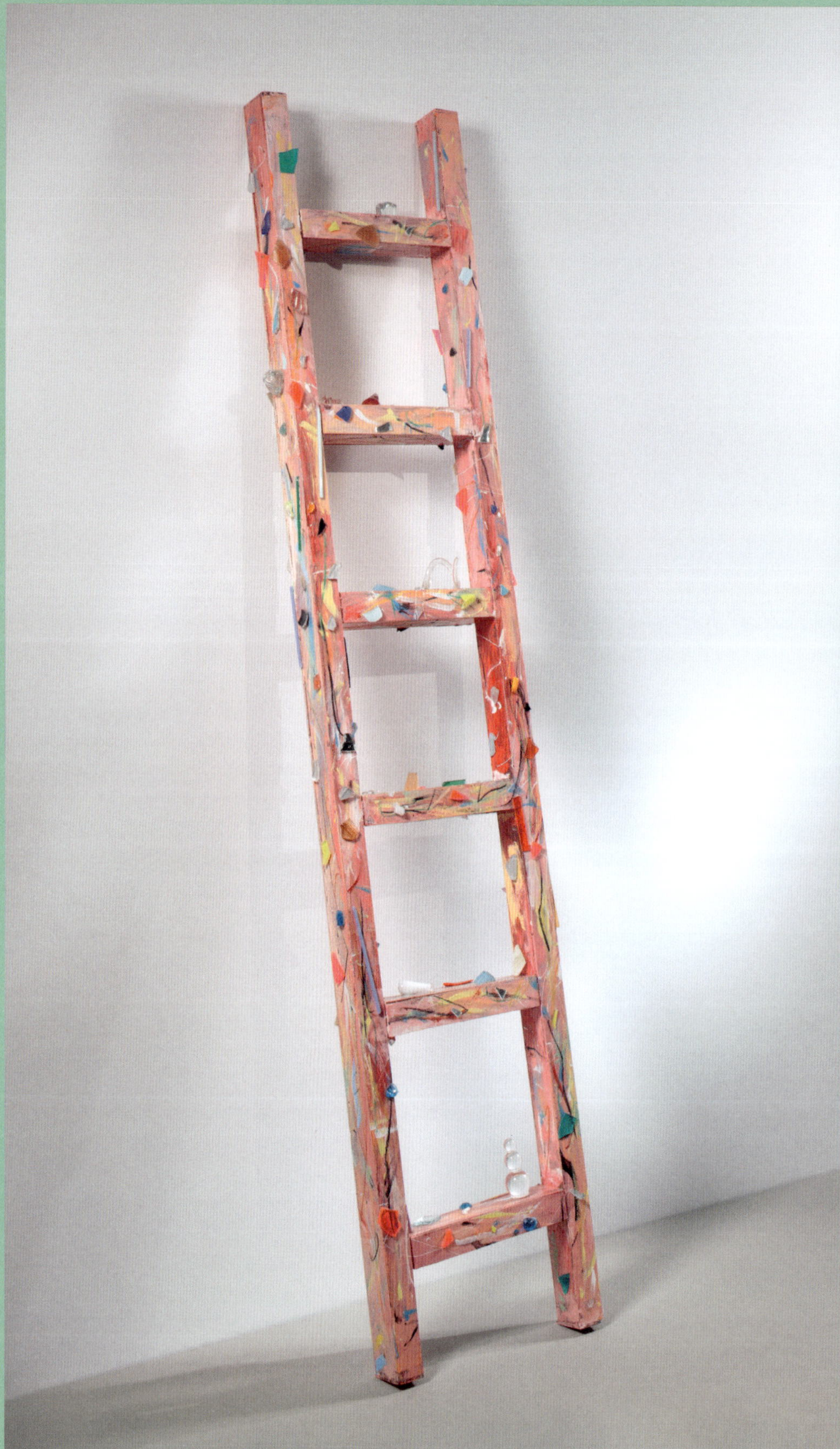

THE TOOL

THERMAN STATOM on THE LADDER

Pink Ladder, 1986, **Therman Statom** (b. 1953),
Sheet glass, blown glass, paint, adhesive tape, colored pencils, found objects,
84½ × 18½ × 4¼ in. (214.6 × 47 × 10.8 cm), Toledo Museum of Art, Gift of Dorothy and George Saxe, 1991.103.

As an artist/craftsman, for me one of the most important elements in the making of art is the process of becoming. One of the successes I search for in the realization of an artwork is the catalytic energy that exists in the process of making art out of materials that can speak, such as clay, fire, or glass. This energy promotes personal artistic growth, regardless of the end product. The ladder, being one of my primary formats, is so much about change and growth.

The use of tools in my work has always been a challenge. When I initially learned glassblowing, I was challenged by the equipment and techniques in terms of how my personal vision developed. Tools, if used from a visionary point of view, become an extension of our creative forces. Early in my career, and even now, I am constantly changing the tools that I use in my work.

I've always been intrigued by decision-making and how it's structured and influenced in the making of an artwork. A ladder is a functional tool, but has a very instinctive process of feel, memory, and texture and strong symbolism. This became clear to me when I was creating a site-specific artwork and using a ladder. I noticed that the installation was more successful with the ladder present. When the installation was completed, I rebuilt the ladder out of glass.

Glass implies a certain level of fragility and impermanence; the work can be broken (it doesn't last forever). Things change. Working with glass is very much about working with light and is as close as possible to giving light a material presence without using film. Much of the art I do is glass that is then painted, and I picture it as being painted with light.

A ladder is very much about becoming, and there is an emotional synchronicity. In the end, the glass ladder is more of a question—of growth, fragility, and transformation. It holds light, memory, and instinct, becoming something more than a tool. By turning a functional object into a site of emotional and symbolic meaning, I invite the viewer to reconsider how we see the everyday. The ladder, in its delicate transparency, becomes a quiet gesture toward change, possibility, and the beauty of becoming.

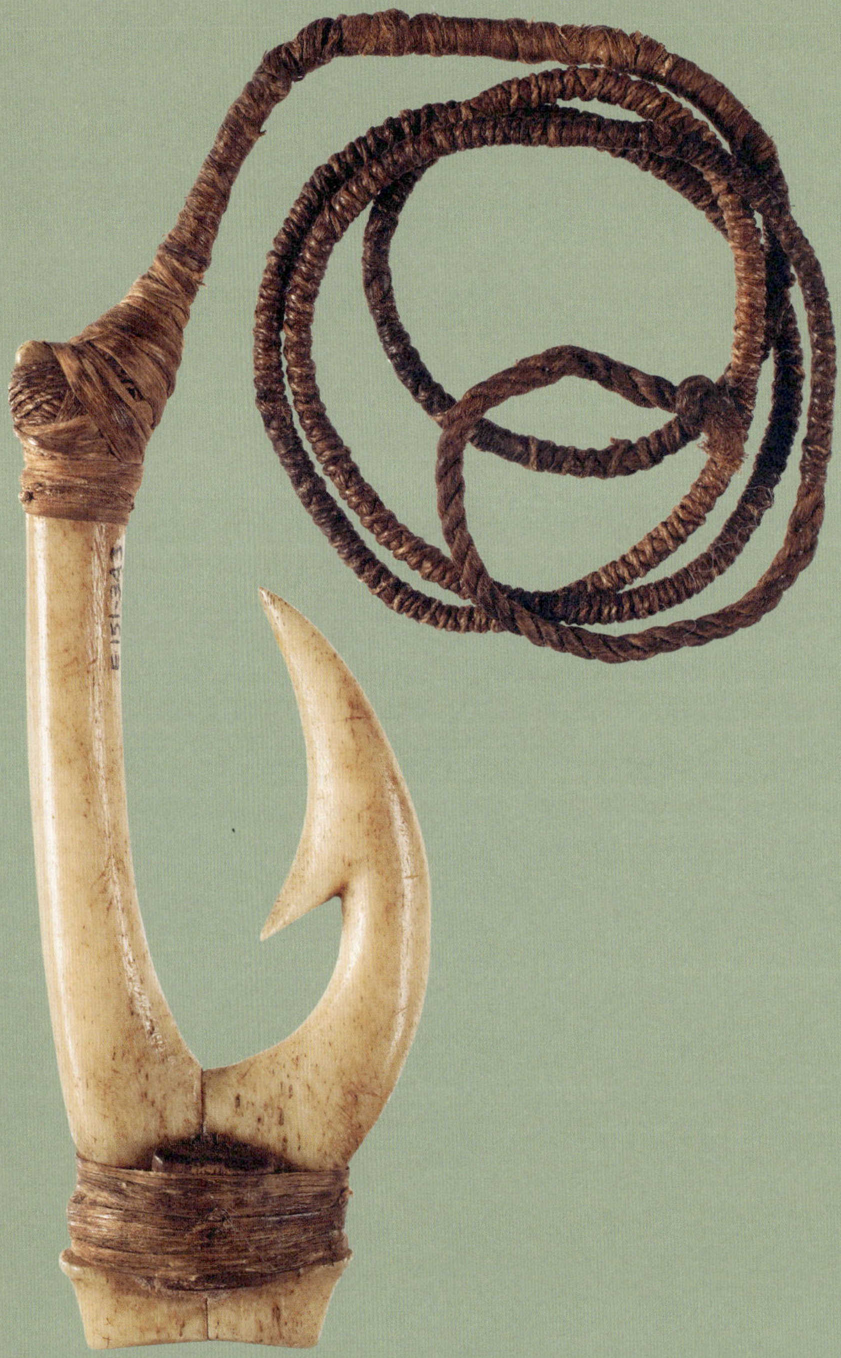

THE LURE

MĀKAU (FISHHOOK)

1800s, Mākau (fishhook), **Unidentified artist (Hawai'i)**,
Bone and 'olonā (*Touchardia latifolia*), 3 15⁄16 × 1½ in. (10 × 4 cm),
Bishop Museum, Honolulu, Ethnology Collection, item no. D.00389.

Hawaiian culture pays deep respect and reverence to the natural world, and that ethos is embodied in this fishhook. The materials used to make Hawaiian fishhooks such as this regularly brought together elements of both the sea and the upland forest, as well as the byproducts of daily life.

Fishing in Hawai'i was not a gendered responsibility. Women customarily fished using methods that were shoreline-based, including hand nets and traps. Men typically fished from wa'a (canoes) with fishhooks and large drift and bag nets and used multipronged spears when fishing along the shore. Each fishhook was designed to attract and catch a specific species of fish. They were commonly fashioned from materials that were remnants of food sources from the sea and of land-based necessities for daily life—wood, bone, pearl shell, and turtle shell. (Utilizing materials to their fullest was a practice and mindset passed down through the generations and is fundamental to Hawaiian culture.) *Mākau* is the Hawaiian word for fishhook. A modifier identifies its material composition or function, such as in makau pāpaua (mother-of-pearl shell hook) and makau manō (shark-catching hook).

Fishhooks were fashioned using traditional pump drills, abrasive rocks, and fine-grained corals to outline and grind the materials into their desired shapes. Hooks could be as small as one-eighth of an inch in width and height to larger than six inches in width and twelve inches in height. Bone was a durable and desirable material for fishhooks, but most animal bones were not big enough to make fishhooks from a single piece, so smaller fragments were combined to produce larger hooks. Some of the most precious hooks used and passed down through generations were made from the bones of expert fishermen themselves; these hooks were believed to be imbued with the mana or spiritual power and skill of those individuals.

The fishhook here is a makau ho'onoho, a two-piece composite bone hook lashed together at the base of the shank with cordage. The intentional placement of wooden slats between the bone surface and the lashing secured the join further as the wood would expand when submerged in water, thereby tightening the lashing. This style of hook was dragged behind a wa'a in deep water to catch larger fish.

The lashing and fishing line on every Hawaiian fishhook was made from the fibers of the olonā plant. Olonā is an endemic member of the nettle family in Hawai'i and among the strongest natural plant fibers on the planet. It has never been domesticated and grown in fields in the lowlands; rather, it is a plant cultivated in its upland forest habitat. The material is in high demand in fishing communities.

Cultural items such as makau, besides being tools of survival, are visual reminders to communities to never overexploit nature. Our collective prosperity is dependent on the balance we maintain with our environment; if that equilibrium is preserved, we can support each other for generations to come. —MHM

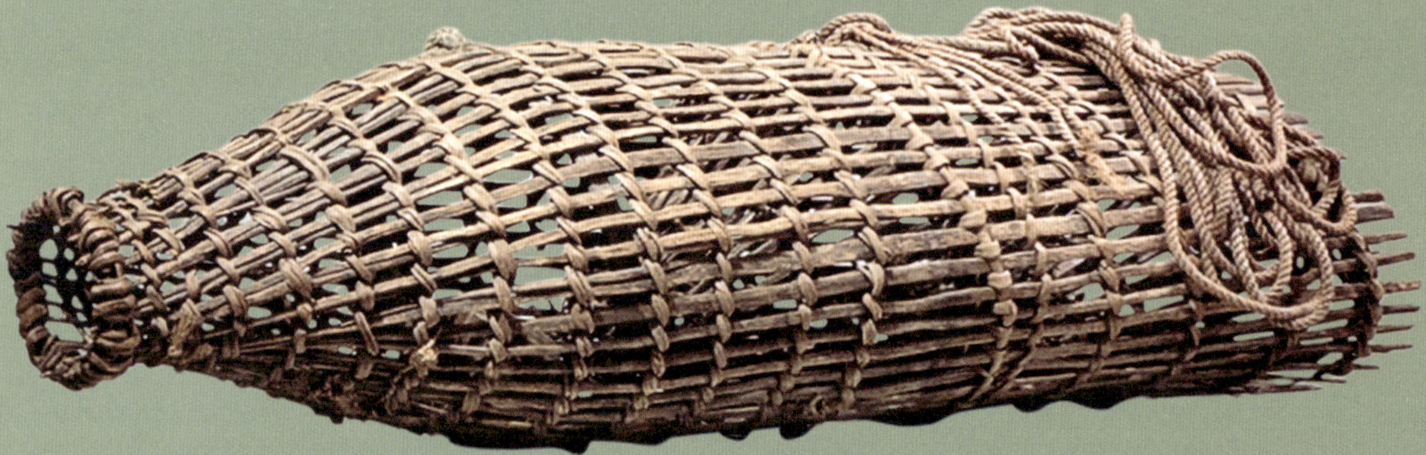

THE LURE

EEL TRAP

c. 1900, **Unidentified artist (Aquinnah Wampanoag),**
Wood, bast, and iron, 12¼ × 47 in. (31.1 × 119.4 cm),
Peabody Essex Museum, Salem, MA, Museum purchase, 1931, E20884.

The three-chambered wicker eel trap is a powerful example of traditional ecological knowledge and craftsmanship passed down through generations of the Aquinnah Wampanoag. This trap would have been vital for the harvesting of eels—a critical source of sustenance for Indigenous communities across the Northeast. While it may appear to be a simple object, its design reflects centuries of knowledge, environmental adaptation, and cultural continuity.

Martha's Vineyard, known to the Aquinnah Wampanoag people as Noepe, has long been home to deeply rooted and historical eel fishing practices. The name of Quansoo, now a private beach near Tisbury Great Pond in Chilmark, Massachusetts, is believed to translate from the Wampanoag language as "a place where the long fish is caught." For the Aquinnah Wampanoag people, eel fishing was more than a means of nourishment—it was a lifeway for sustaining communities, embedded in seasonal rhythms and respectful interactions with the environment.

Weaving, inherent to the construction of eel traps, is itself a core part of Wampanoag identity. The technique used to create such traps has been perfected over centuries—long before the arrival of European settlers. Traditionally, traps like this would be woven from pine splints, which were prized for their durability and flexibility. The lacing holding the weave together was often made from split pine roots, another example of the resourcefulness and sustainable methods employed by Indigenous artisans. Weaving is not only a technical skill but a cultural expression, symbolizing the interconnectedness of land, water, and people.

Ideal fishing spots—where tides, currents, and terrain favored eel movement—often guided the placement of Indigenous villages, anchoring communities in deep relationships with the land and waters. Eel traps, typically used alongside fishing weirs made from stone or wooden stakes driven into the waterbed, embody a sophisticated balance of form and function. The weirs funneled fish, especially eels, into the trap's conical chambers, engineered to prevent escape. The three interior cones that narrow toward the center are more than clever design; they are a testament to an intimate understanding of animal behavior and the natural world. For the Aquinnah Wampanoag and other Indigenous peoples, tools like these are not relics, but living links to a worldview grounded in sustainability, respect, and interdependence with the land—a reminder that utility and reverence are not at odds, but rather one and the same.

This fusion of tradition and innovation echoes powerfully in the work of artist Joe Feddersen, a member of the Colville Confederated Tribes of Washington State. His glass sculpture *Fish Trap,* created with Carly Feddersen, draws directly from the traditional fish traps of Native communities, like the Aquinnah trap. Shaped in the same conical form—broad and inviting at one end, narrow and secure at the other—Feddersen's work becomes a vessel of both memory and transformation. Crafted from glass and aluminum, *Fish Trap* honors the ingenuity of Native peoples while incorporating bold colors and visual language drawn from contemporary culture. Through this synthesis, Feddersen celebrates the enduring significance of fisheries and the salmon that sustain his people, affirming that Indigenous art—as the traps shown here reflect—is not frozen in the past; it is vital, adaptive, and alive. —TL

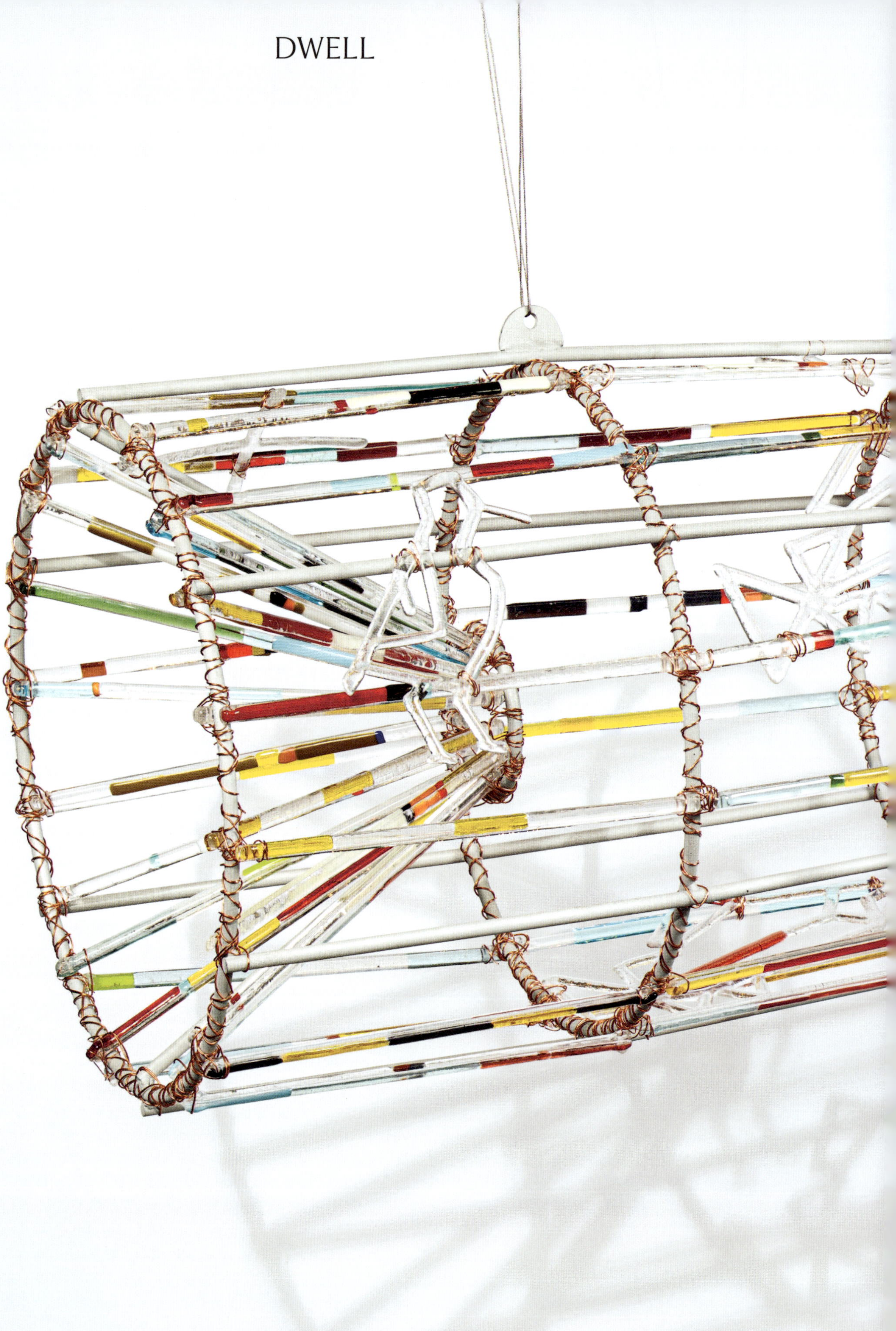

THE LURE

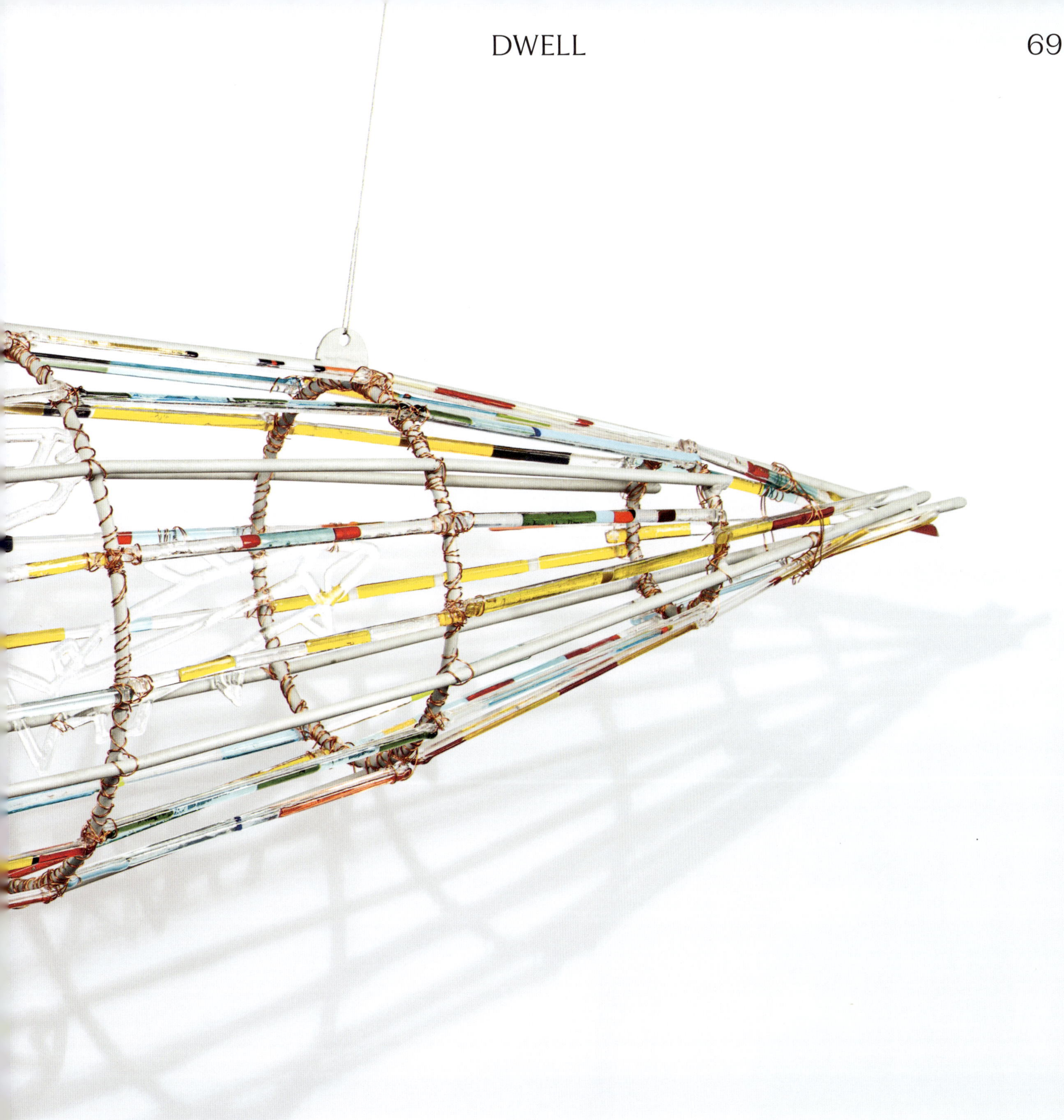

Fish Trap: Coyote Frees the Salmon, 2025
Carly Feddersen (b. 1982) and **Joe Feddersen** (b. 1953),
24 × 72 in. (61 × 182.9 × cm), Fused glass and metal.

TO PROVIDE

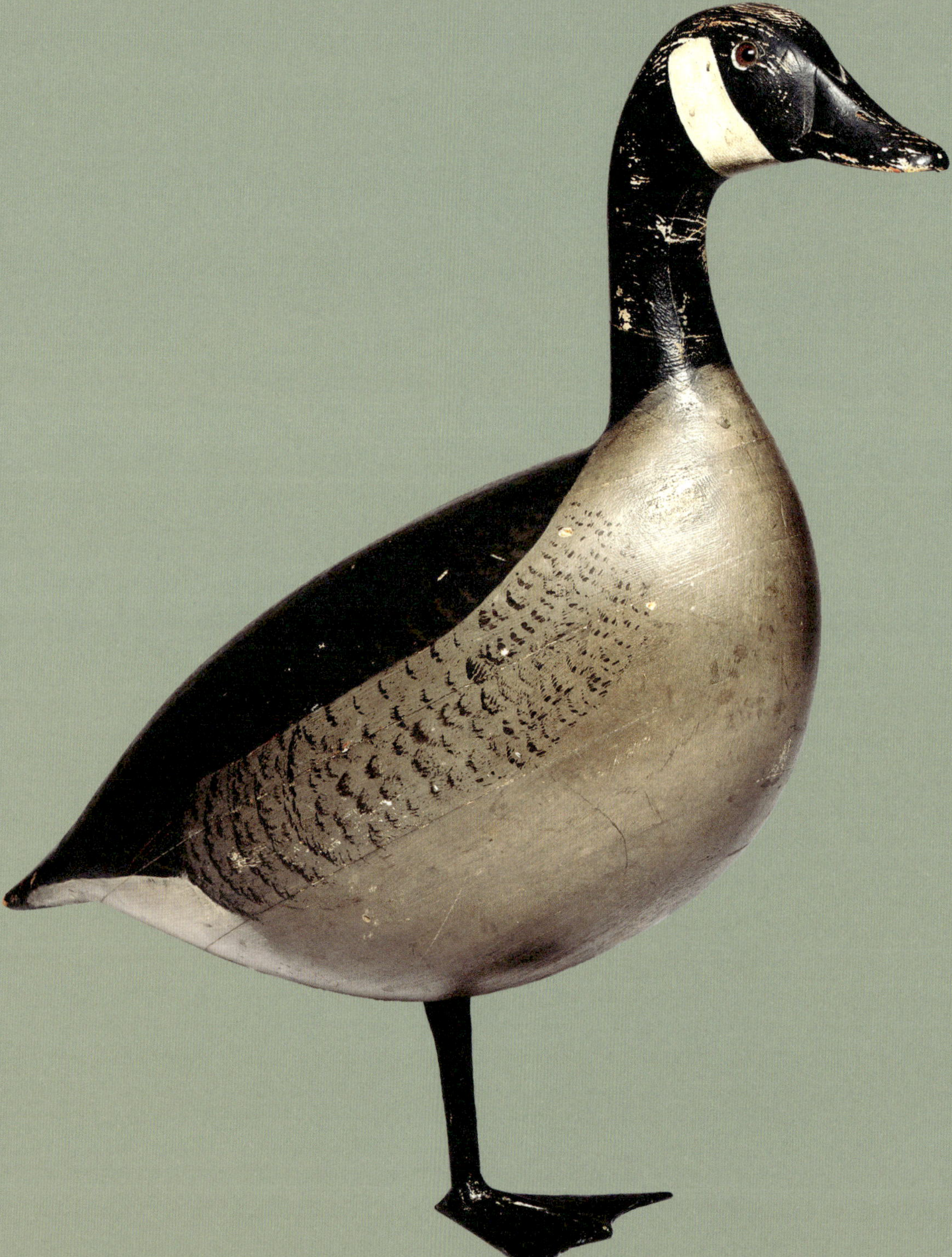

STANDING GOOSE DECOY

c. 1918–20, **Charles S. Schoenheider Sr.** (1856–1924),
Wood, paint, glass, iron, 22 × 6 × 21 in. (55.9 × 15.2 × 52.3 cm),
Promised gift of Thomas K. Figge to Peoria Riverfront Museum.

Charles Schoenheider's ten standing goose decoys, each delicately balanced on a single cast-iron foot and hand-carved from multiple laminated layers of pine, are among the most iconic decoys in American history. They were originally created as practical hunting tools and are now celebrated as exceptional examples of American folk art. Each uniquely carved goose stands in an alert position. They feature glass eyes and feathers painted in monochromatic tones reminiscent of those employed by James Whistler in his famous portrait of his mother, *Arrangement in Grey and Black No. 1*. Today, these decoys are revered for their modern and sophisticated style and survive as the only standing geese the artist ever produced. Their origin story is a classic among decoy collectors and folk art enthusiasts.

As the story goes, in 1918 a wealthy sporting hunter, Daniel W. Vorhees, commissioned well-known decoy maker Charles Schoenheider to create a unique rig, or set, of standing goose decoys. After spending a year carving and painting the birds, Schoenheider sought his $125 fee, but Vorhees refused to pay. Frustrated and disappointed, Schoenheider stored the decoys at his home, where they remained unused for nearly fifty years. In 1966, legendary St. Louis decoy collector Joe French discovered the rig. Ultimately, the decoys—of which ten standing geese and one floater are known today—found their way into some of the most respected museums and private collections in the country.

The development of the wooden decoy is closely linked to the era of the market hunter, a professional gunner who made a living by selling game to the growing metropolitan populations. However, hunting decoys were originally created by Native Americans more than two thousand years ago. They simulated waterfowl by shaping mud and stacking rocks in shallow water, mounting bird heads and bodies on sticks, and by stuffing bird skins with dried grasses. In 1924, a cache of eleven handmade duck decoys fashioned from tule rush and feathers was discovered in a cave in Lovelock, Nevada; they are today known as the oldest surviving examples.

The years from 1840 to 1918 are considered by many to be the golden era of wildfowl hunting, when resources seemed limitless and hunters enjoyed hunting seasons with no restrictions. As industry and urbanization expanded westward beyond the Mississippi River, hunting waterfowl for survival became a thing of the past, while hunting for pleasure and profit grew to become the custom. By 1918, market hunting had so severely impacted migratory bird populations that the federal government took action. Congress passed the Migratory Bird Treaty Act, which established federal limitations on hunting privileges, ending market hunting and establishing a new era that catered to wealthy sporting hunters.

The Illinois River Valley, once home to hundreds of decoy makers, including market hunter Schoenheider, was one of the decoy-making centers of the country. Schoenheider's distinct and innovative single-foot design made him one of the most significant carvers from the region. A carpenter by trade and the father of fourteen children, he ingeniously supplemented his meager income by hunting and used his woodworking skills to produce decoys for himself and others. Today, his wooden duck decoys and famous standing geese are testaments to the alluring artistry of early American material culture and symbols of humanity's constantly evolving relationship with nature. —ZZ

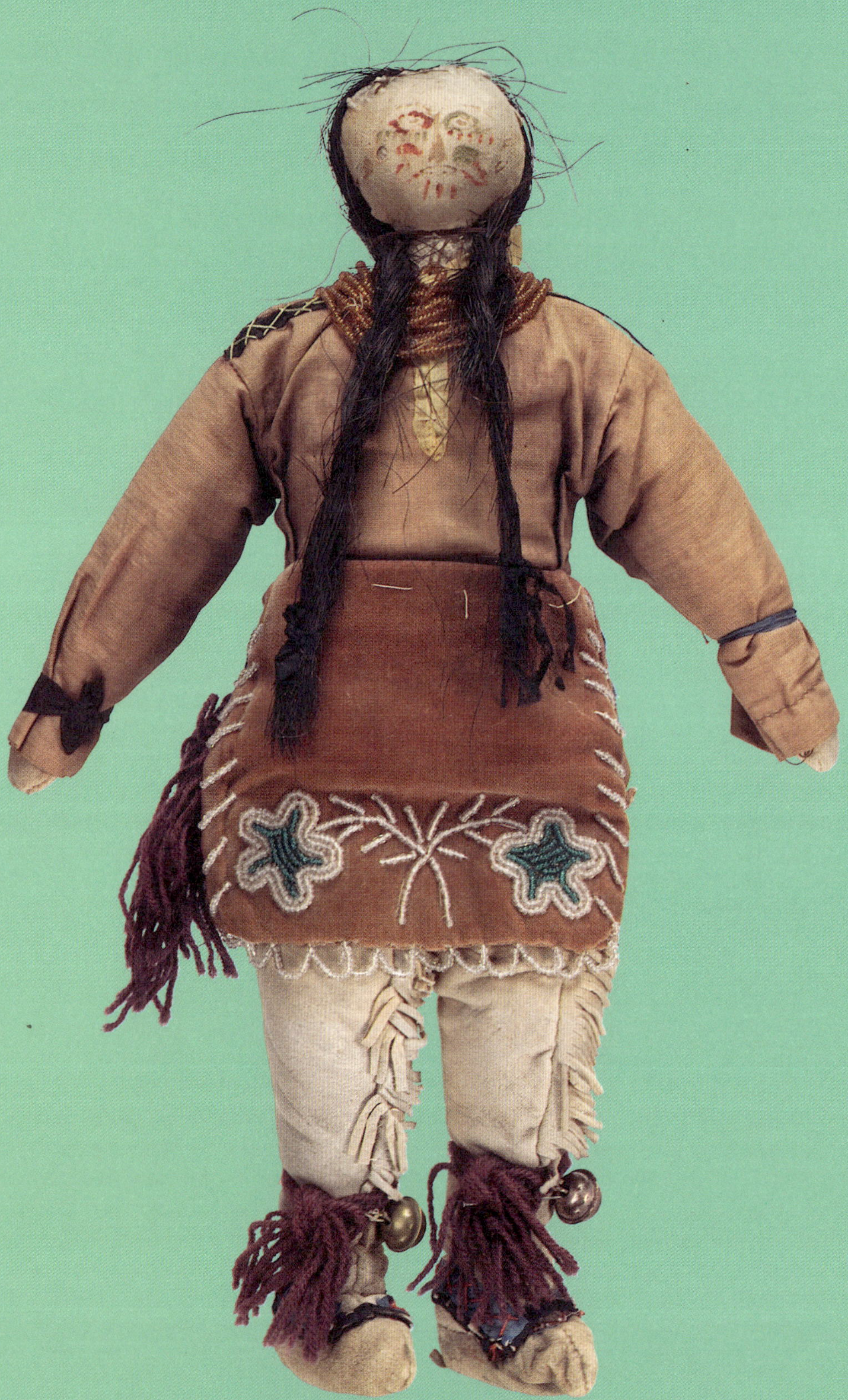

THE TOY

DOLL

1850–80, **Sarah Marie Arnold Cisco** (Nipmuc, 1818–1891), Hide, wool yarn, velveteen, cotton cloth, horsehair, brass bells, glass beads, thread, unknown stuffing, ink, ribbon, 13 ¼ × 8 ¼ × 2 ¾ in. (33.5 × 21 × 7 cm), National Museum of the American Indian, Smithsonian Institution, Washington, DC, 25/7213.

Dolls have always been beloved for their engaging nature and capacity to teach children around the globe about their own culture through play. This intricately crafted male doll is dressed in the traditional regalia of Northeastern Native communities, particularly in the post-contact period. The doll features an outfit consisting of full-length fringed hide leggings and a velvet breechcloth decorated with green and white beaded leaf motifs, both of which are foundational components of a man's regalia. However, this design also reflects the evolving nature of Native dress following European contact, incorporating a cotton shirt—a new piece of clothing introduced through trade. The shirt is embellished with subtle ribbon accents, showcasing the maker's creative ability to integrate new materials using Northeastern Native aesthetics.

The doll's garments include numerous additional elements: strings of brown or golden beaded necklaces, silk yarn leg bands with bells, a yarn belt, and hide moccasins with a ribbon and beaded design. The figure's face is painted and framed by two long braids made of horsehair. All the doll's attributes emphasize Nipmuc cultural identity, personal adornment, and tribal sovereignty.

This doll was made by Sarah Marie Arnold Cisco, the sonksq (female leader or chief) of the Hassanamisco Nipmuc. Born in 1818 in Hassanamesit, located in current-day Grafton, Massachusetts, she was the daughter of Harry Arnold and Lucy Gimby. Her mother, descended from Moses Printer, lived on her ancestral family's last remaining parcel of tribal land her whole life. The homestead she was raised in and that was built for her mother in 1802 remains an important historic site for the current-day Hassanamisco Nipmuc Nation. She later married Samuel Cisco, a prominent member of the Narragansett tribe. After her father's death in 1851, she assumed the role of matriarch, guiding her family and community through a period of great adversity. As tribal lands dwindled under external pressures, she ensured that her parcel would never be sold, passing on this responsibility and determination to her descendants.

Known for her work as a basket maker, Cisco's artistry extended beyond utilitarian objects. Her creation of this doll likely had deep personal and political significance, as she gifted it to Cornelia Antoinette Brigham, the daughter of Charles Brigham, the Indian agent who was working with the Nipmuc at a time when their reservation lands were being taken or sold. This present, given during a time of upheaval, may have been a gesture of diplomacy, trust, or goodwill. In gifting such an object, Cisco was not only offering a token of friendship but also preserving and asserting her people's traditions in a time when their very survival was under threat. —TL

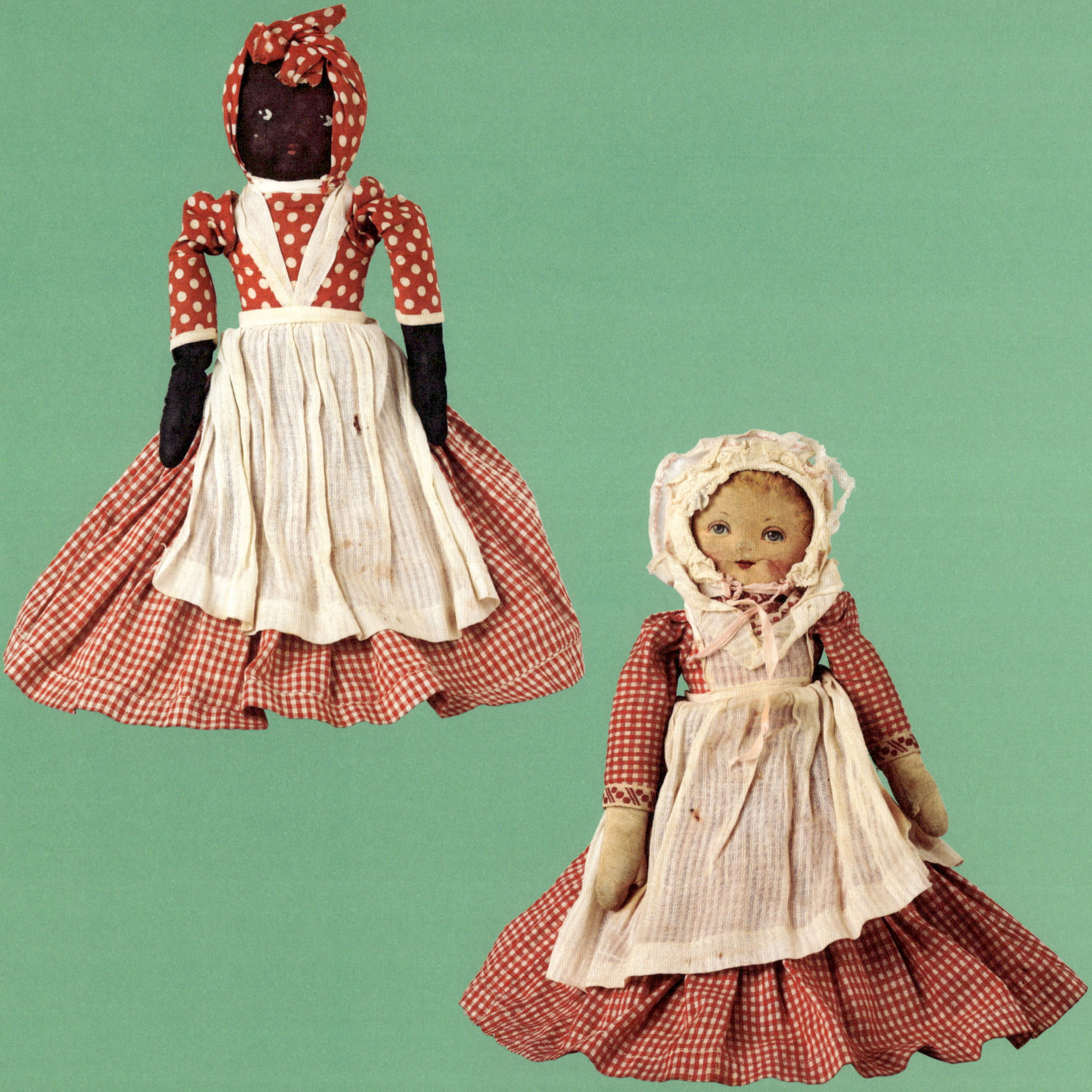

THE TOY

TOPSY-TURVY DOLL (ALTERNATE VIEWS)

c. 1926, **Albert Bruckner's Sons** (active 1901–1930),
Cotton and ink, 12½ × 13 in. (31.8 × 33 cm),
Winterthur Museum, Garden, and Library, Winterthur, DE, Gift of Margaret H. Prince, 2014.0026.

She is a doll. No, she is two dolls—two dolls in one. She is the anatomical anomaly that is the Topsy-Turvy doll: two half figures joined together—one white, the other Black, each to be experienced one at a time. Given the doll's origins in mid-nineteenth-century America, it is not surprising that often the attire of the white half was finer than the dress of the Black half. Here, the headwear of each side of the doll also marks the class distinction, with the white doll wearing a bonnet and the Black a headwrap familiar from depictions of the "mammy" archetype. The conventional wisdom is that the doll may have been inspired by the characters of Little Eva and Topsy in Harriet Beecher Stowe's sensationally abolitionist novel *Uncle Tom's Cabin*. This example was produced in the 1920s by Albert Bruckner's Sons, which claimed to be one of the oldest doll manufacturers in the United States.

But what are the origins of these dolls, and for whom were they created? These dolls were widely handmade in the beginning, but by the twentieth century versions had been created in ceramic and even plastic. In the last century and a half, the basic form of the Topsy-Turvy doll has remained consistent, with infinitesimal variations. The features and anatomical details have been embroidered, hand-painted, or lithographed, as they were by the late nineteenth century (and as they are on this doll).[1] By the 1940s, there were even sewing patterns produced for the dolls; McCall's version was called the Upside Down Doll.[2]

And what was their purpose, if any? The dolls may have first been created to reinforce the social hierarchies of antebellum America.[3] They may also have been sewn for Black children, who would typically have been forbidden from possessing a white doll; with a quick flip, they could hide one half of the doll and preserve their secret.[4] It has also been theorized that Topsy-Turvy dolls were a way of preparing Black girls to become caregivers of white charges, in addition to their own children.[5]

Writer Julian K. Jarboe observed that "long past their prime as playthings, topsy-turvy dolls continue to ignite discussion in large part because they resist being squarely fixed to one meaning—instead, they flip back and forth between ideas that conflict even as they coexist."[6] —LSS

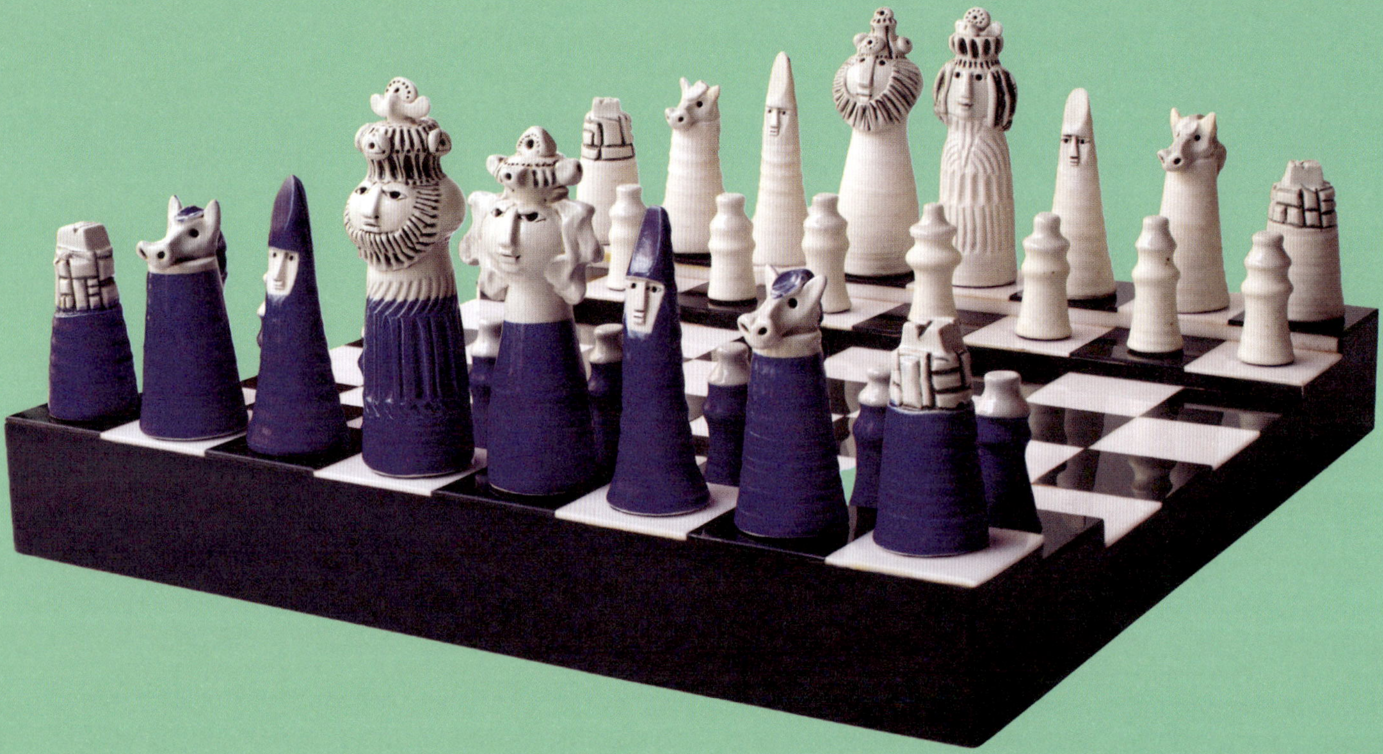

THE TOY

CHESS SET

c. 1970, **Dora De Larios** (1933–2018),
Glazed porcelain, Board: 3¼ × 24 × 23⅞ in. (8.26 × 60.96 × 60.64 cm),
Los Angeles County Museum of Art, Gift of Drs. Alan Grinnell and Feelie Lee, M.2015.96.1-.33.

The royal court is poised to receive guests. Lined up in proper order, these chess set pieces, commissioned by a collector, led Dora De Larios to join a legion of artists and designers—among them Isamu Noguchi, Man Ray, Yayoi Kusama, and Frank Gehry—who have created chess sets. This set aptly demonstrates how De Larios animated her clay objects with whimsy and a multiplicity of influences drawn from her own life experiences.

De Larios's chess set features animal and human forms that combine her often-used references to pre-Columbian, Greek, and Japanese clay works, and is one example of her aim to "harmonize the animal and the spiritual, the earthly with the divine." Depictions of royalty, wild horses, and abstract architectural forms represent the essential game pieces. The handsome, bearded blue king is sculpted with a bird-shaped crown, while the lionlike white king smiles serenely with his similarly amused queen. Two droll, straight-backed bishops align themselves with spirited horses whose nostrils flare with energy. De Larios developed several vibrant glazes, among them the bright indigo blue seen here. Her application of blue and white to the chess set reflects a timelessness that harkens variously to ancient Assyria, where the bright cobalt tin glazes were first used; the blue and white of classical Chinese porcelain; and the lively shades of Italian and Moorish ceramics.

The unusual blend of influences that De Larios brought to her work reflected the artist's experience growing up in multicultural Los Angeles, as well as her travels around the world. She was born in Boyle Heights (now a largely Hispanic community) to parents of Mexican descent. De Larios cited as a formative childhood experience a trip to the Museo Nacional de Antropología in Mexico City, where she was mesmerized by a carved Aztec calendar. She grew up alongside the Japanese American community in Boyle Heights and was long inspired by an interest in Japanese art and culture.

While many of her artistic peers eagerly embraced modernism and abstract expressionist ceramic forms, Dora De Larios's clay work consistently reflected her own vision, to which she remained forever true. Her means of expression combined figurative and functional ceramics with references to her Latinx heritage, her feminism, and her spiritual beliefs. Her 2009 artist's statement read, "My joyful purpose in life has been to create beauty. . . . Through my work, I hope to express the unique beauty of the planet." She went on to list her interests as the divine, symbolism, and mythology.

After earning her college degree in ceramics from the University of Southern California in 1957, De Larios took a yearlong trip around the world, where her studies of world religions and ancient art coalesced into a multicultural artistic vision. She remarked that the similarities between global myths and cultural practices could be reduced to positive or destructive forces. Her travel further helped her to contextualize the opposing forces she experienced abroad and at home between poverty and wealth, temporality and eternity, and rigidity and freedom of belief. De Larios's chess set is both ancient and modern, reflecting the cultures of Los Angeles as well as the worlds of flora and fauna that were intrinsic to her worldview. —**SI**

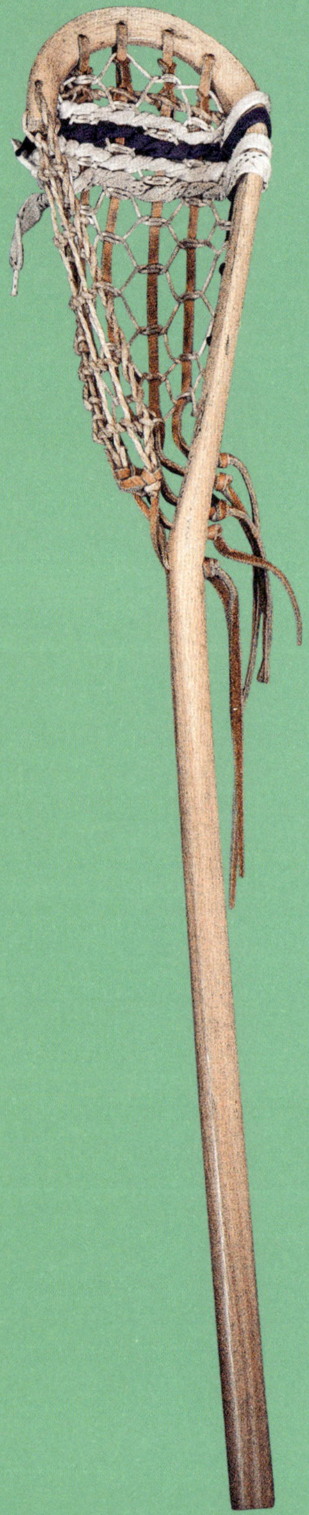

THE TOY

LACROSSE STICK

c. 2013, **Alfred Jacques** (Onondaga, 1949–2023), Hickory, leather, catgut, nylon cord, cotton, 43 × 6 in. (109.2 × 15.2 cm), Private collection of Koltin Huff (Seneca Nation Hawk Clan).

Trees hold a physical memory of their experience—years of drought and plenty, storms weathered, and a lifetime anchored in the protective or restrictive shadow of their kin. That individuality and exceptional resilience are honored and celebrated in the lacrosse sticks made by Alfred "Alf" Jacques.

This stick was selected for a young lacrosse player named Koltin Huff and is constructed from hickory, chosen for its strength and flexibility. Handhewn wooden sticks dating as early as the 1840s can be found in museum collections throughout North America. The techniques embraced by Jacques have changed little since.

The nearly yearlong process of this stick's creation began in the winter, when a mature specimen was selected and felled. The bottom eight feet of the fallen giant was split lengthwise and reserved for sticks. The head or curved end of the stick was fashioned from the section of the tree nearest to the earth, where the wood had become stronger and more rigid in response to wind stress. In Jacques's accomplished hands, the excess, in graceful wooden curls, was rapidly parted from its core with a drawknife, achieving an impeccable balance exclusively by feel. Jacques's intent as a craftsman, and a legendary player, was to honor and distill the energy and strength of the once-living tree into each of his sticks, imparting it to both the individual and the power of the game.

Jacques's intimate relationship to his material was founded in his traditions as a member of the Onondaga Nation, one of the six nations of the Haudenosaunee Confederacy. The game of lacrosse or Dehoñtjihgwa'és ("they bump hips") is as intricately intertwined with Haudenosaunee culture as the lacing on his sticks. Lacrosse is played throughout the world today, but at Jacques's home at Onondaga Nation, it retains its traditional significance as a medicine game requested for healing and played exclusively with wooden sticks. The sticks function as vital components in an enduring set of cultural practices that fortify and unite the Haudenosaunee. Boys are often gifted miniature sticks at birth. Full-size sticks accompany Haudenosaunee men to the grave; they will play for the Creator in the next world.

Koltin's stick is one of eighty thousand that have been handcrafted in a small shop on Jacques's mother's land at Onondaga Nation. The first of these was a collaboration between Jacques and his father, Louis. Driven by the family's economic limitations and a twelve-year-old's desire to play, this fledgling endeavor would ignite a lifelong passion and develop into an immense responsibility. From 1968 to 1974, together with coach and player Eli Cornelius, the three would produce 11,500 sticks annually out of the Onondaga shop. In the years that followed, Jacques revised and refined the foundational techniques, acquiring a painstaking precision that would launch his legacy as a true master.

Two years after his passing in 2023, a small hickory tree has quietly taken root in my side yard—a single individual on a seven-acre wooded lot. Alf often brought gifts to his visits—a carved kitchen tool, dogbane to make cordage, and more than once, a pocketful of hickory nuts for planting. Like the artist himself, that small tree is fulfilling its purpose, generously sharing its gifts and reminding us of the Haudenosaunee principle of reciprocity. —**CL**

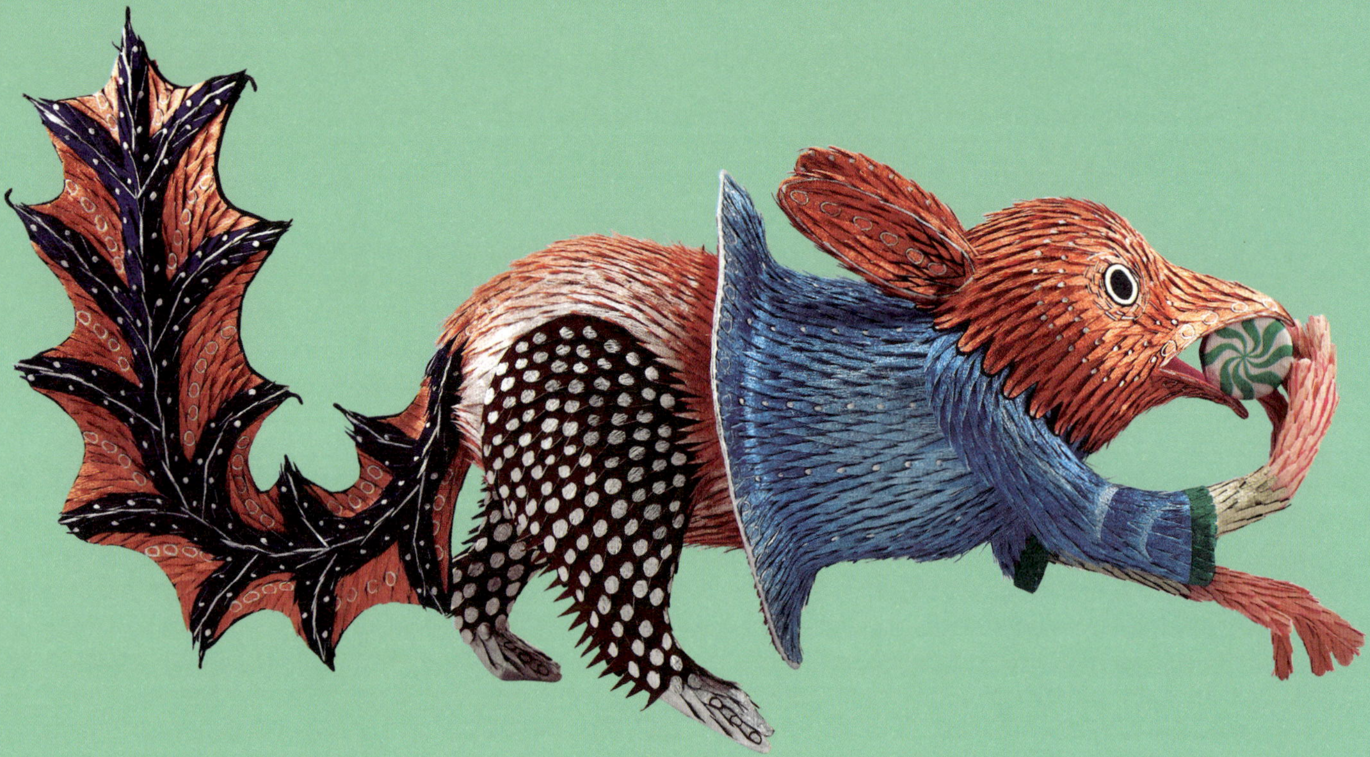

THE TOY

ILLUMINATED PIÑATA NO. 21

2024, **Roberto Benavidez** (b. 1973), Paper, paperboard, tape, glue, wire, crepe paper, 19 ¾ × 37 ½ × 9 ⅛ in. (50.2 × 95.3 × 23.2 cm), Smithsonian American Art Museum, Washington, DC, Gift of Cynthia Lovelace Sears in honor of *Handwork: Celebrating American Craft 2026*, 2024.28.2.

Deeply rooted in Mexican culture, the piñata has reached new artistic heights in the hands of American artists like Roberto Benavidez. Most Americans know the piñata as a ubiquitous fixture at birthday parties, wedding showers, and celebrations of all kinds. Yet one would never think about bashing and smashing the vivid, meticulously constructed paper sculptures of Benavidez. Stepping out of a fantastical world that melds illuminated medieval manuscripts with Dr. Seuss, a new species of magical and mysterious paper beings come to life in Benavidez's hands. His beguiling creatures—such as this one, which was inspired by an illustration in a fourteenth-century manuscript known as the Luttrell Psalter—explore dualities of permanence and ephemerality, fragility and stability, and more. Benavidez defies hierarchical artistic categorization through his imaginative reinvention of material and tradition.

Many believe the piñata spanned centuries and several continents before flourishing in Mexico. It is theorized that between the late thirteenth and early fourteenth centuries, Marco Polo and early traders witnessed an ancient Chinese spring ritual in which a clay ox, filled with seed, was shattered by officials to inaugurate the start of the laborious farming season. This Dachunniu ("hitting the spring ox") custom may have been imported by the explorers to Northern Italy, where it eventually became known as the "pignatta," referring to the Italian name of a clay pot in the shape of a pine cone, or "pigna."[1] Simple ceramic vessels filled with candies and fruit were broken during festivities around the time of Lent in Italy and Spain in the fourteenth century. Spanish Catholic missionaries transferred this tradition to the Americas in the sixteenth century; there they continued using breakable, treat-filled vessels for religious celebrations that were part of an indoctrination process for Indigenous peoples.

Folklore suggests that missionaries likely built upon the Native precedent of games and practices involving the shattering of clay pots. The classic seven-pointed star piñata is another reflection of this colonial history. The points are said to signify the seven deadly sins, while the act of destroying the piñata when blindfolded represented unquestioned faith and the triumph of good over evil. Until just a few decades ago, when paper and cardboard became more commonplace, piñatas in Mexico were commonly made with ceramic cores that would send shards flying when shattered.

The impermanence, informality, whimsicality, and popularity of piñatas are all potential reasons for their omission in art history. The cultural marginalization of those who have predominantly made piñatas also factors into this overlooked artistic format. Yet piñateros have always shown how piñatas are shape-shifters that can take any form, be that of plant, animal, object, or idea. Benavidez melds all of these together, attentively building cardboard skeletons and trimming feathers and fur, all the while tearing down the misperception that piñatas are inherently delicate. Paper is a material that is entirely accessible, versatile, and surprisingly durable. His otherworldly designs are neither fragile nor throwaway objects. By inverting the common perception of piñatas as fleeting objects for playful destruction, Benavidez highlights the possibilities of humble materials, fine craftsmanship, and cultural innovation to endure and evolve. —EZ

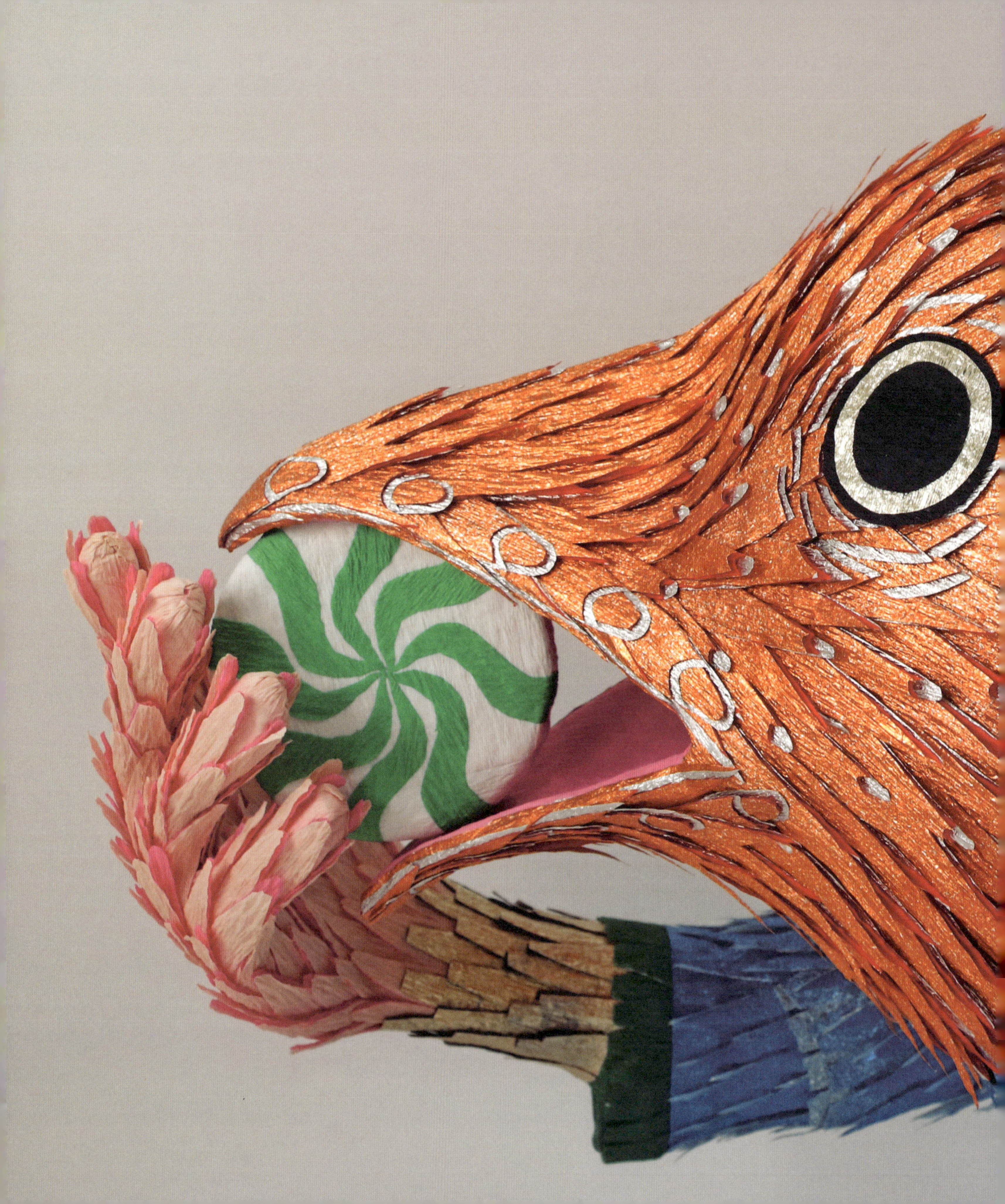

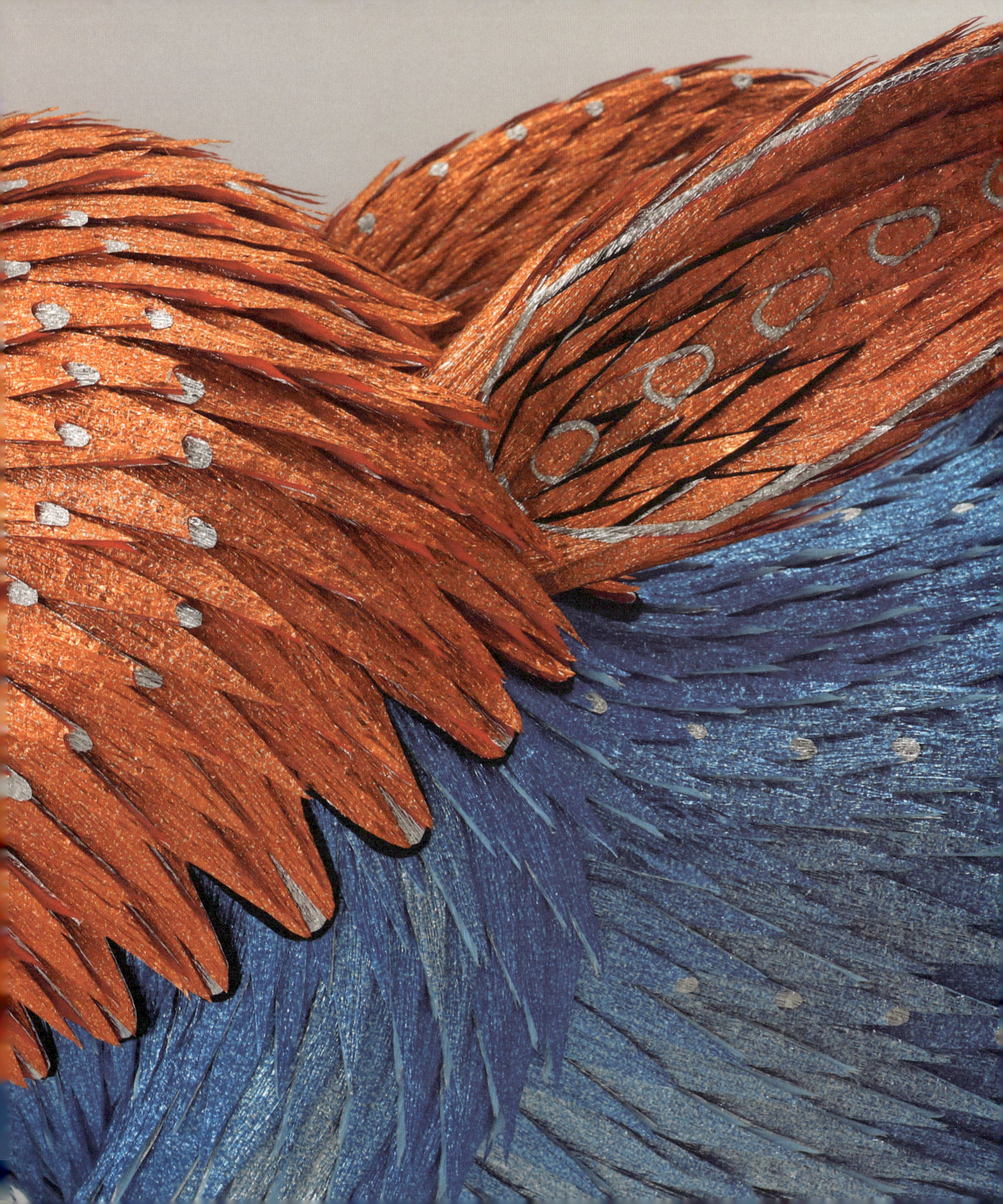

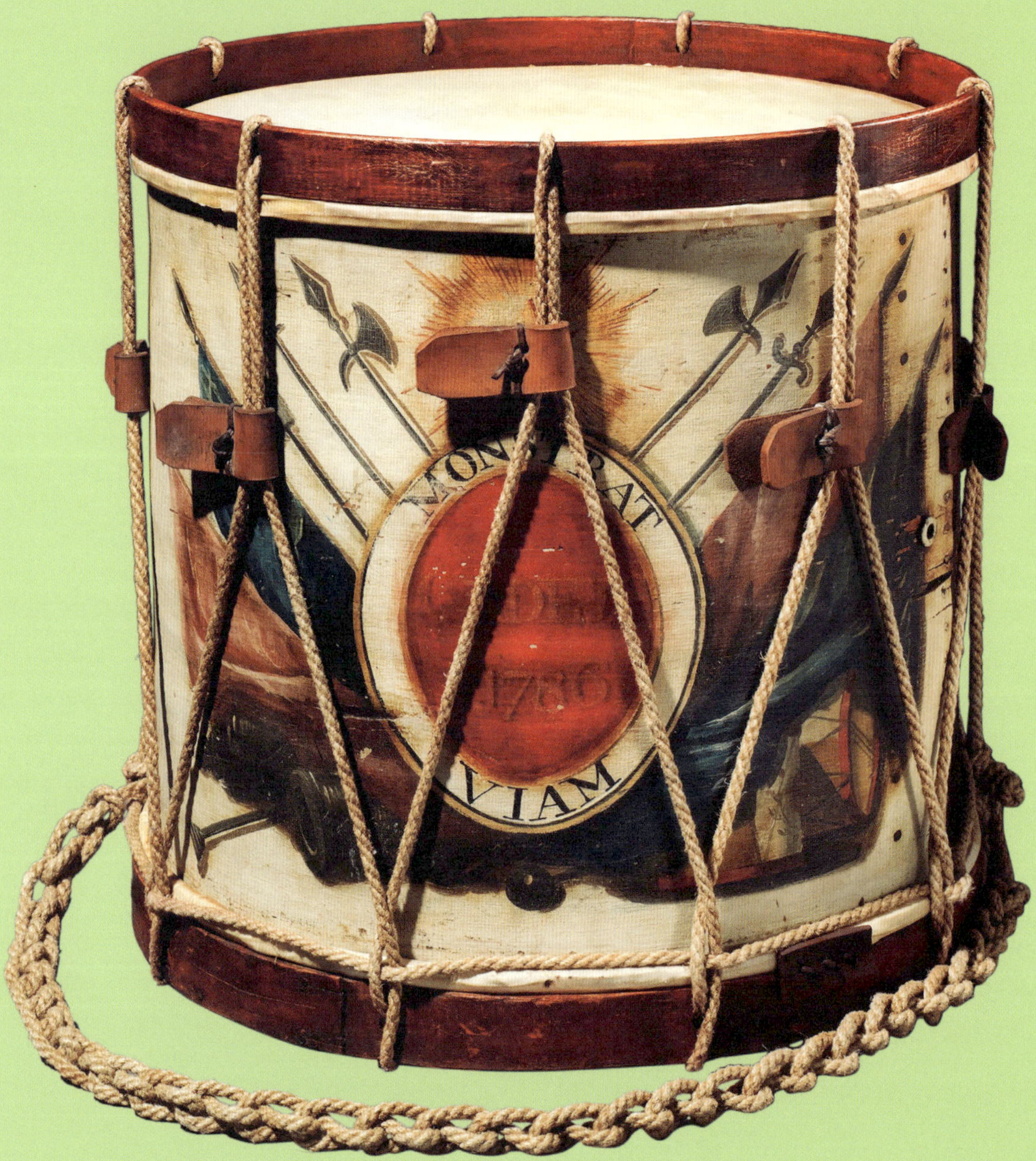

THE INSTRUMENT

SIDE DRUM

c. 1840, **Henry H. Prentiss** (1801–1860),
Wood, paint, rope, leather, skin, 18 × 17 in. (45.7 × 43.2 cm),
Metropolitan Museum of Art, New York, Purchase, Amati Gifts, 2008, 2008.239.

Marching to the sound of your own drummer—what a good description of a life in craft. The regular beat of a hammer or a loom, the pace of a day in the studio, the orchestration of a product line, the succession of seasonal tasks: craft is all about keeping time. When a skilled maker creates a drum, it's hard not to see it as a self-portrait.

At the same time, drums bring people together. They lay down the firm foundation on which musical architectures of melody and harmony, call and response, can be built. We often find them anchoring common cause. The sheer sonic force of a military drum could help direct troop movements even across a loud battlefield. An early American example now in the Metropolitan Museum of Art, made by Boston instrument maker Henry Prentiss, bears the Latin slogan *monstrat viam*: showing the way.

In providing such service, drums correspond to another side of skilled making: not just its well-disciplined individualism, but the way it can become the armature of community. Craft establishes a steady cadence that propels us forward. It is, we might say, the percussion section of cultural production. All of this and more is present in Cheryl Riley's *World History I (Drum)*, a recent commission for the Brooklyn Museum. It is a supremely elegant design: a great bowl ornamented with gold leaf, elevated on carved legs. Where the head of a functional drum would be, we instead find a tabletop inset with photographs of prominent historical figures and containers filled with found objects.

The work is replete with symbolism. The gold pattern, for example, refers both to the pinwheel designs of African American quilts and to the triangular trade of enslavement. The legs, sculpted in emulation of Zulu spoons, are intended, in Riley's words, to "honor the strength of the gender—the givers of life—and our beauty." They are made of ebony, an allusion to the magazine founded in 1945 "to provide positive images for Blacks in a world of negative images and non-images."[1] From the underside of the table hangs a cluster of slender brass pendants, ending in shovellike forms that allude to agricultural labor; Riley also intends this passage as a commemoration of the thousands of victims of lynching in America.

The artist was intrigued by talking drums, which are played to match the rhythms and tones of spoken language, transmitting messages through association. This was the earliest long-distance instantaneous communication technology that humans conceived, predating telecommunications by many centuries.[2]

This underappreciated bit of world history, too, is conjured in Riley's table. One can so easily imagine children gathering around it in the museum, having its features pointed out to them, shouting out their own ideas about what this or that might signify. Eventually they might be told about the talking drums of Africa and the many stories that they could tell. "I too am sharing information through the distance of time," Riley comments. And so, the beat goes on. —**GA**

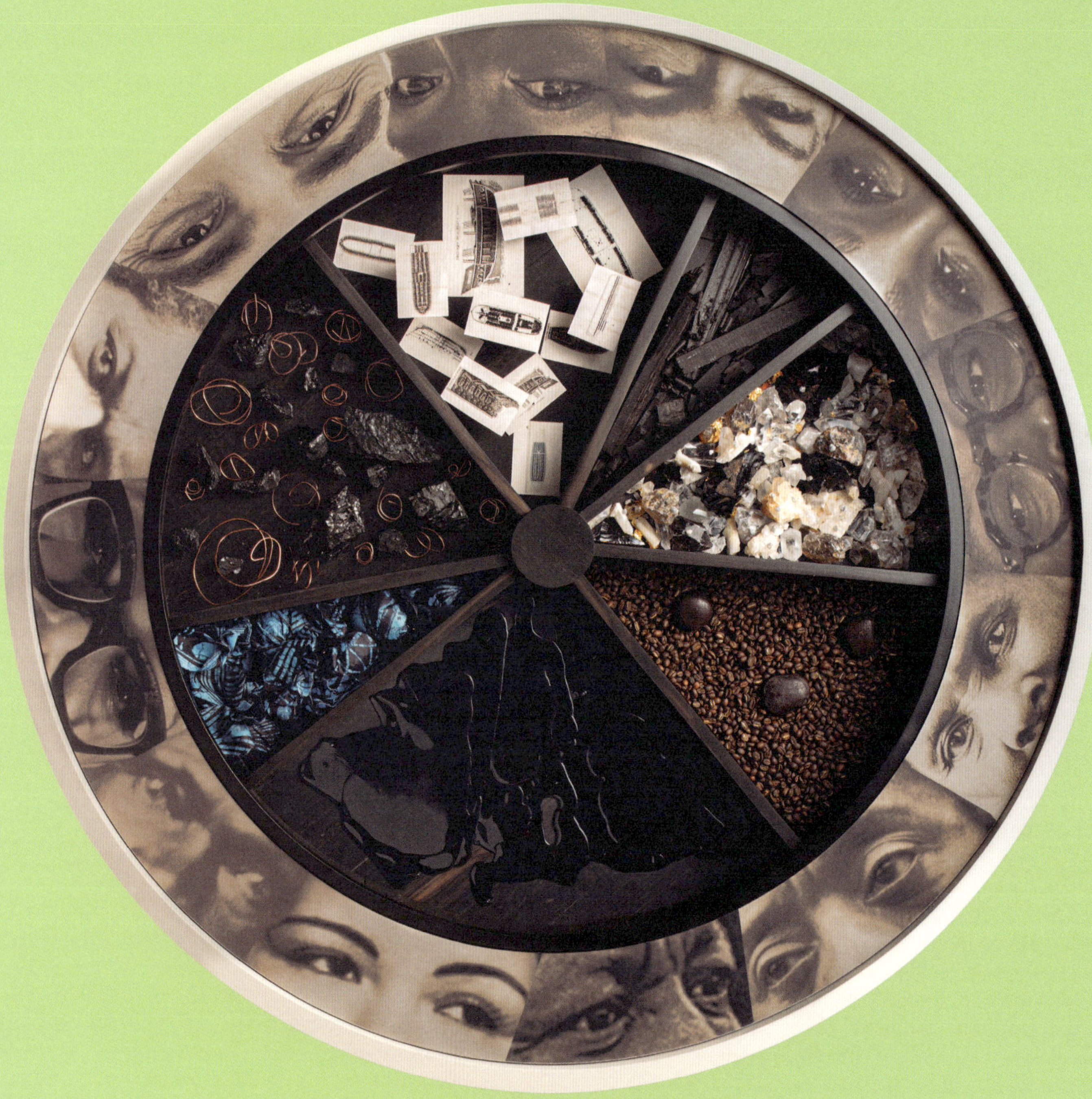

THE INSTRUMENT

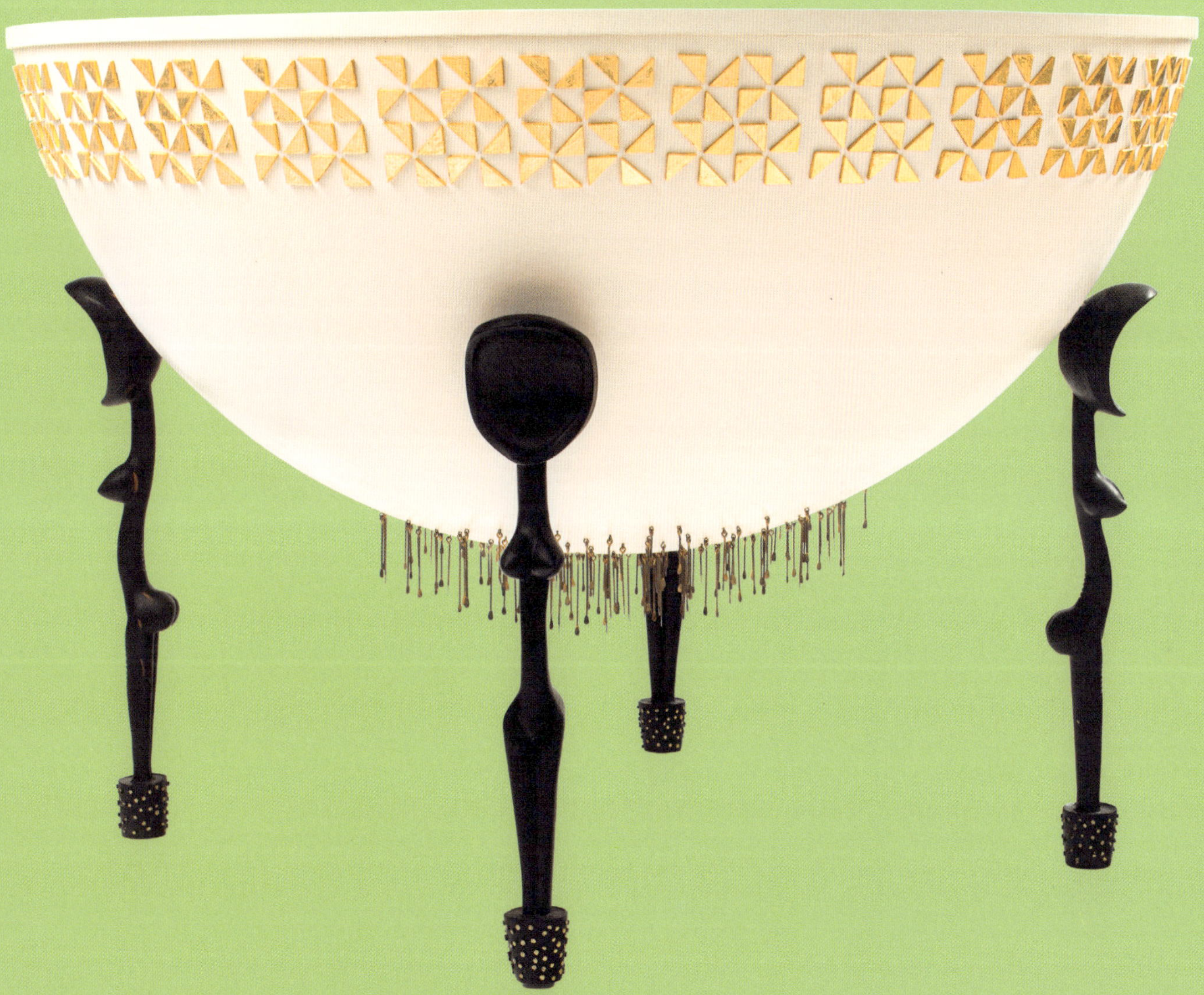

World History I (Drum), 2023, **Cheryl Riley** (b. 1952), Plywood, ebony, wood chips, paint, glass, industrial diamonds, quartz, 24kt gold leaf, ink, textile, DIBOND, StyroCoat, 30 × 42 in. (76.2 × 106.7 cm), Brooklyn Museum, Purchased through the generous support of Tracey and Phillip Riese, Larry Satterfield and Sabir Ward, Rough Diamond World, Spur Jewelry, Urte Tylaite, Marc Neal Simon, Bisa Butler, and Friends of the Artist; with additional support from the H. Randolph Lever Fund, 2023.57.

TO RESONATE

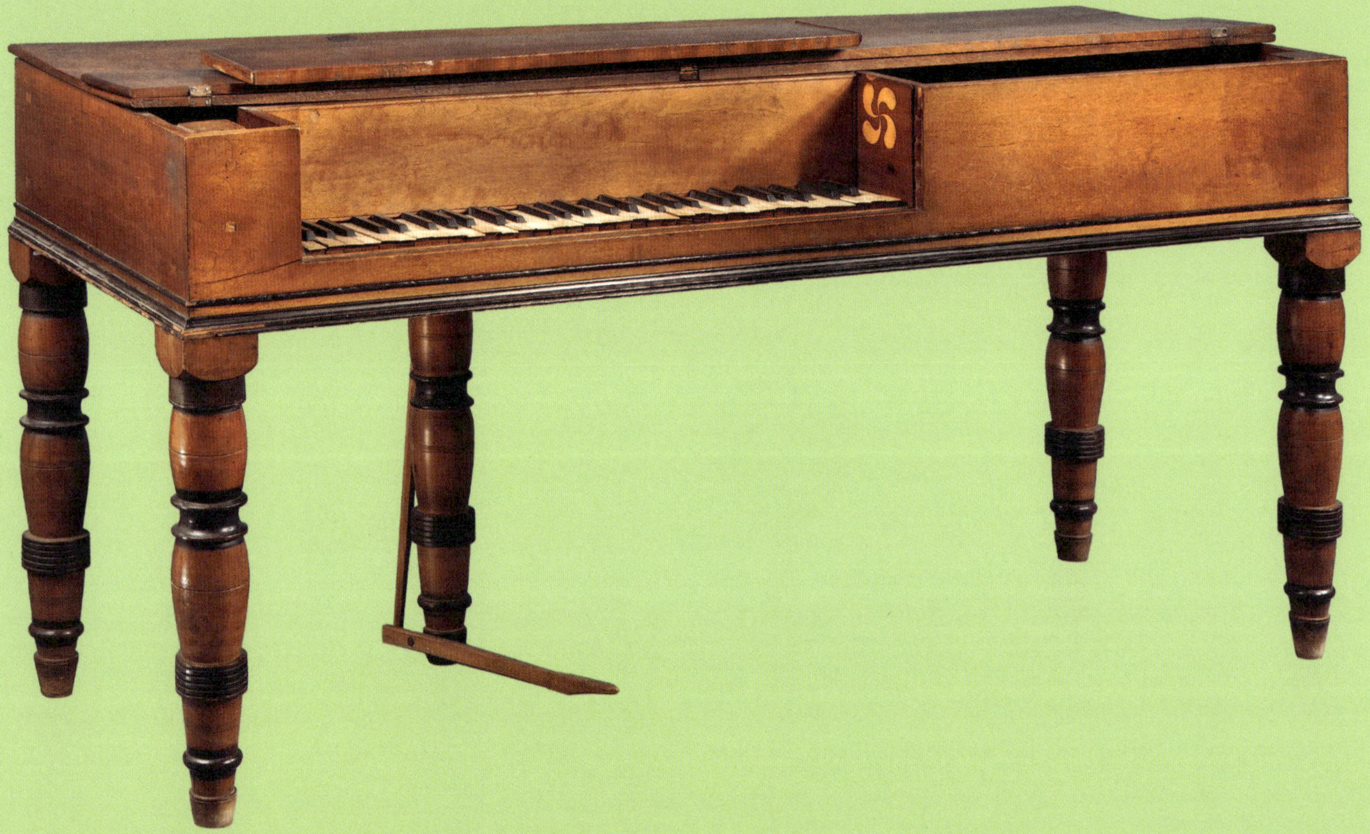

THE INSTRUMENT

SQUARE PIANO

c. 1835–40, **David Prichard** (1798–1884),
Cherry, yellow pine, fruitwood, bone, 32 5⁄8 × 64 × 24 1⁄8 in. (82.9 × 162.6 × 61.3 cm),
The Museum of Early Southern Decorative Arts, Winston-Salem, Accession No. 5736.

Forget apple pie—there's nothing more American than the square piano. Flip through any nineteenth-century American newspaper, and you'll quickly come across an advertisement for the now-forgotten instrument that defined domestic music-making and performative womahood for almost a century. Invented in England during the 1760s as a compact, inexpensive alternative to full-sized keyboard instruments, the square piano took on a new life in the United States. Over the course of the nineteenth century, American piano makers technologically transformed the instrument and made it more powerful, expressive, and affordable. It was the people's piano; parlors across America were united as access to the instrument was increasingly democratized.

This particular square piano was a fixture in the central North Carolina parlor of a young woman named Sophia Correll. The instrument embodied the white, middle-class femininity demanded of women like Sophia, whose skills on the piano were simultaneously a socially prescribed accomplishment *and* a vehicle for agency and personal expression. Yet the Correll family didn't purchase or rent the piano from a professional firm or acquire it secondhand, as was typical even in their rural milieu. Instead, Sophia's father sourced it from a member of their extended kinship network, a local cabinetmaker and self-taught piano maker named David Prichard.

Musical instruments, and specifically keyboard instruments, were some of the most complex objects in the pre-industrial age and their construction posed many challenges. The basic form was ubiquitous to consumers at the time; a rectangular case supported by five or more legs, and a keyboard tucked into the left side, with strings inside running to the right. Prichard infused the case of his piano with design features found on the furniture from the North Carolina Piedmont, including ebonized rings on the turned legs and contrasting inlaid fylfots on the cheeks abutting the keyboard. Wrought in cherry and pine, adorned with bone and stained fruitwood key covers, the exterior of this piano presented a devoutly regional yet conventional appearance.

With hundreds of parts and tight tolerances, the production of a piano did not easily lend itself to attempts by untrained makers. Though Prichard was able to employ construction skills that overlapped with his work as a cabinetmaker, it was a tall order to create an object that not only had a pleasing appearance but could also produce music. In the instrument he built for Sophia, he navigated the unknowns of piano production by creating a much-reduced action, swapping out individual dampers linked to each key for one large single damper operated by a foot pedal. This shift created a profound difference from a typical square piano, fundamentally changing how a player interacted with the instrument.

Though this technical curiosity is invisible from the exterior, hearing the piano would quickly reveal the impact of Prichard's alternative approach: a muddy sound with unclear distinction between pitches. Yet in the age before recorded sound, the capabilities of what a piano *can* and *should* be able to do were less standardized as makers across America continued to innovate. Rural and resourceful craftspeople like Prichard were inspired by conventional keyboard instruments, but competing in markets far from urban centers freed their work from conventional comparisons. Evident from its survival as it passed between generations, Sophia's square piano was beloved. The instrument—a complex object in every sense—embodied the ingenuity that flourished in nineteenth-century America's inland South. —AC

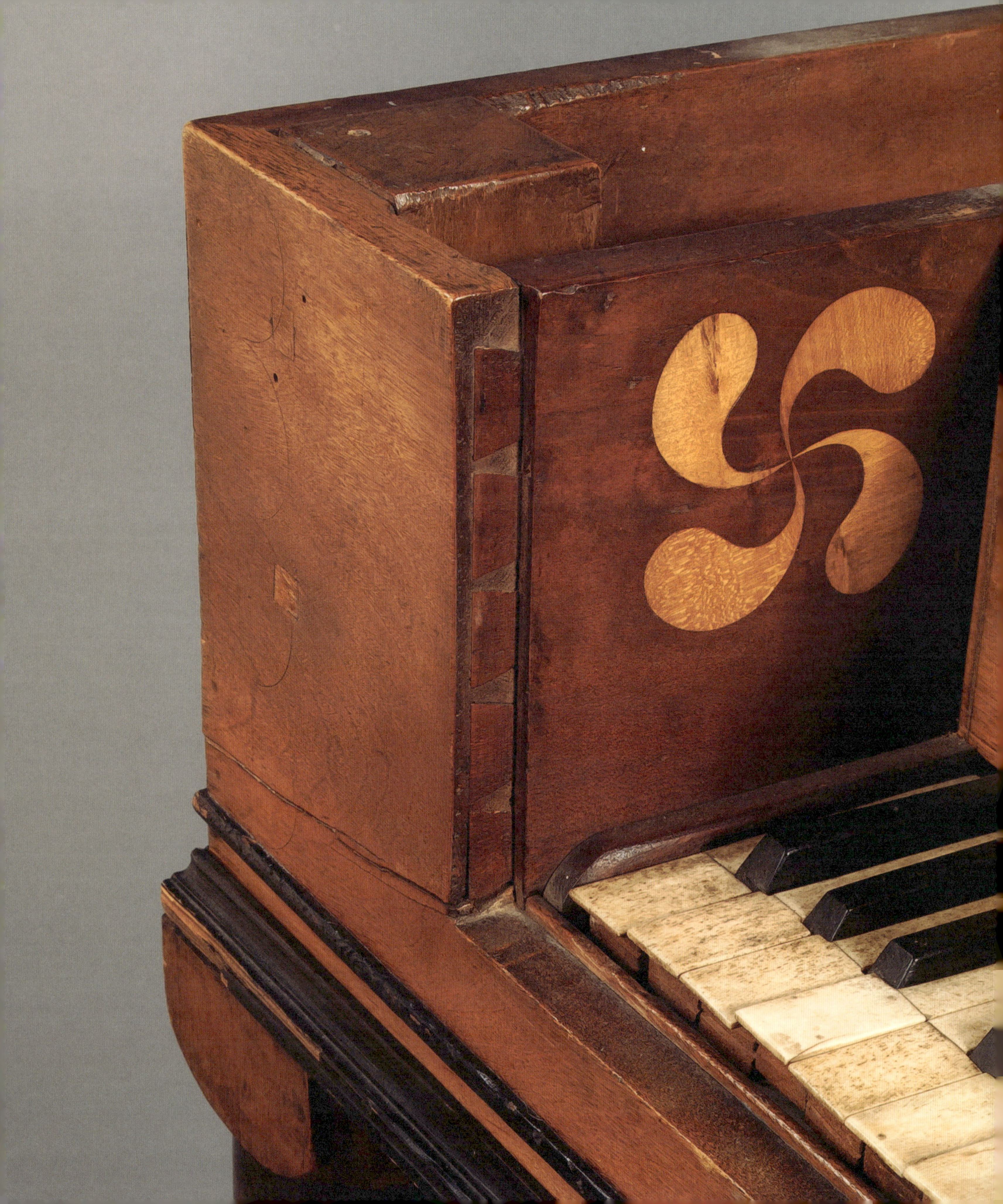

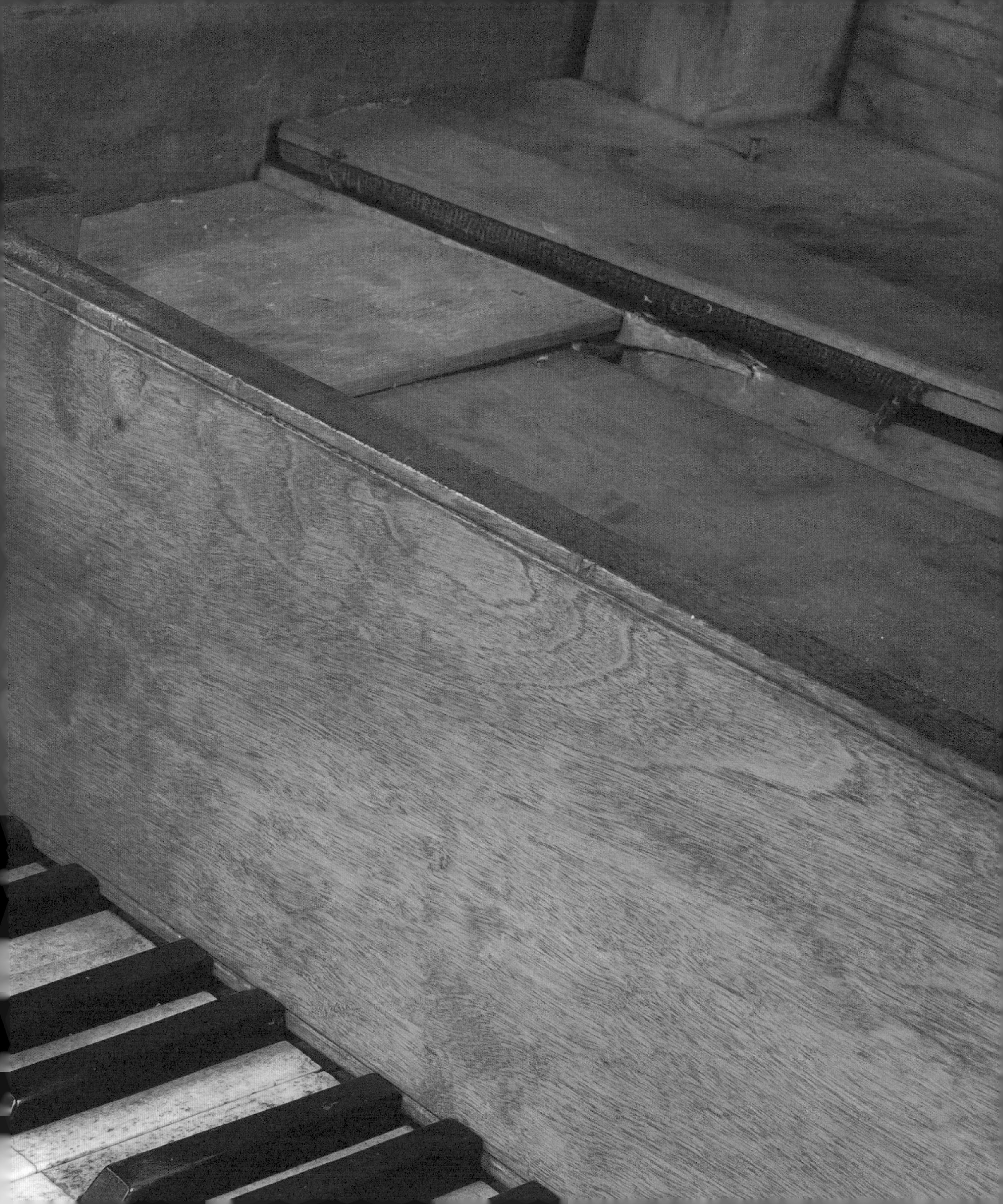

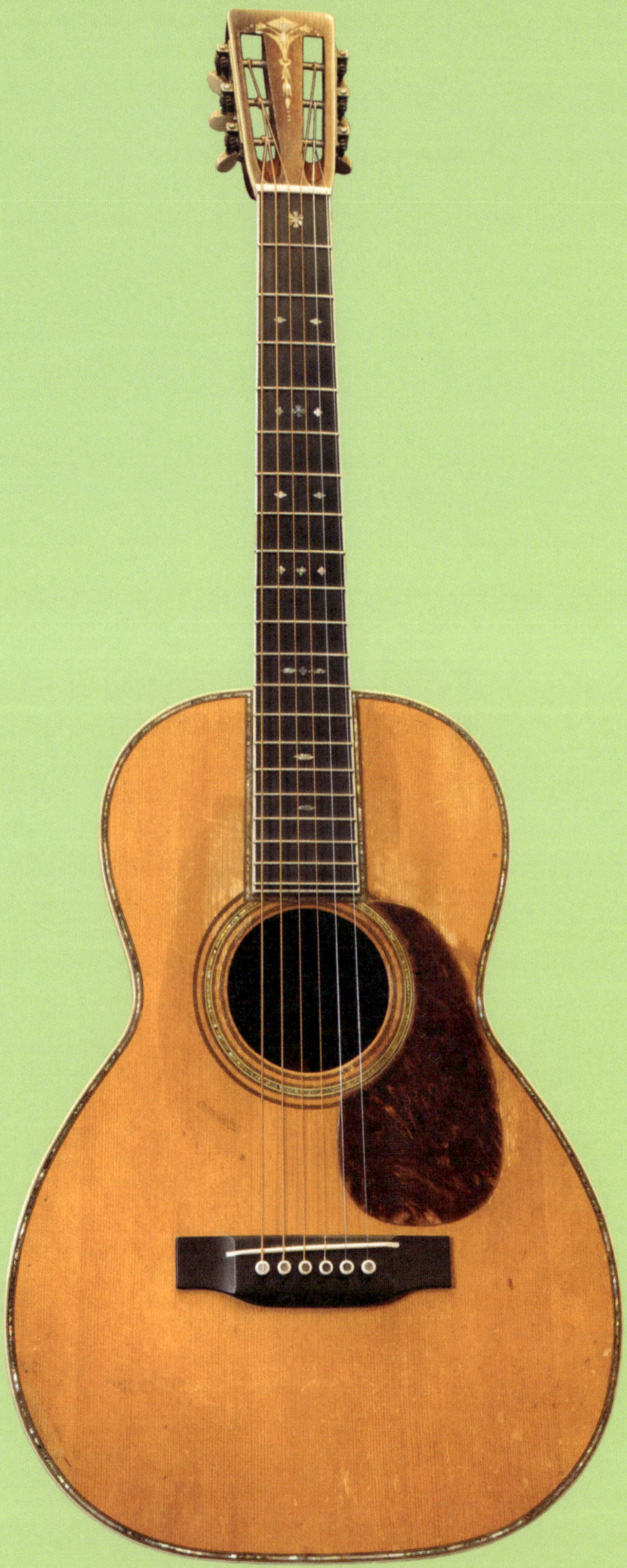

THE INSTRUMENT

JOAN BAEZ'S MARTIN GUITAR

1929, **C. F. Martin & Co.** (est. 1833),
Brazilian rosewood, Adirondack spruce, African black ebony, mahogany, Ivoroid, ivory, abalone, and metal,
37 3/4 × 13 1/2 × 4 3/16 in. (95.9 × 34.3 × 10.6 cm), Private collection.

[The Martin] was my first serious folk guitar. I had a Goya with gut strings and I also had a gigantic Gibson, which hung down around my knees. I've never been able to deal with a really large guitar, so this one just felt like home, you know? Over the years it has been everywhere with me. I retired it from the road at some point because I didn't want to risk damage by traveling with it anymore.

So it's been mostly sitting quietly, though it has done a stint at the Musical Instrument Museum and has been featured in various exhibitions. A funny story about this guitar surfaced when Martin produced a special limited edition in my honor, the 0-45JB. It's fashioned exactly after this one, except that I asked that Brazilian rosewood not be used because it's an endangered tree, and without it, there's a certain nuanced tone that's missing. In order to make the new ones, they had to inspect the inside of this one to see the structure and so on. I mean, I can't imagine how they did it. But when they went in there, they found, written on the inside, on one of the pieces of wood, "Too bad you're a Communist." Evidently, whoever worked on it previously was not a fan of my politics and had apparently written "too bad you're a Communist" in there. So when [Martin] made the special edition, they wrote it in every guitar and included a little dentist mirror so you could put the mirror inside and read it. That's a wonderful story.

The first really dangerous situation involving the guitar that I remember was a Sane [National Committee for Sane Nuclear Policy] rally, an antinuclear rally, with Pete Seeger, and people started pelting us with tomatoes and eggs, and I took the guitar and put it behind me, 'cause I didn't care what happened to me, but I didn't want the guitar to get hurt.

Why is music important? You don't have to have any explanations for anything. It doesn't have to be political if it moves the soul. And without it, I really can't imagine . . . I can't imagine life.

—**Joan Baez** as told to Carol Sauvion during the filming of the *Craft in America* documentary series episode "MUSIC."

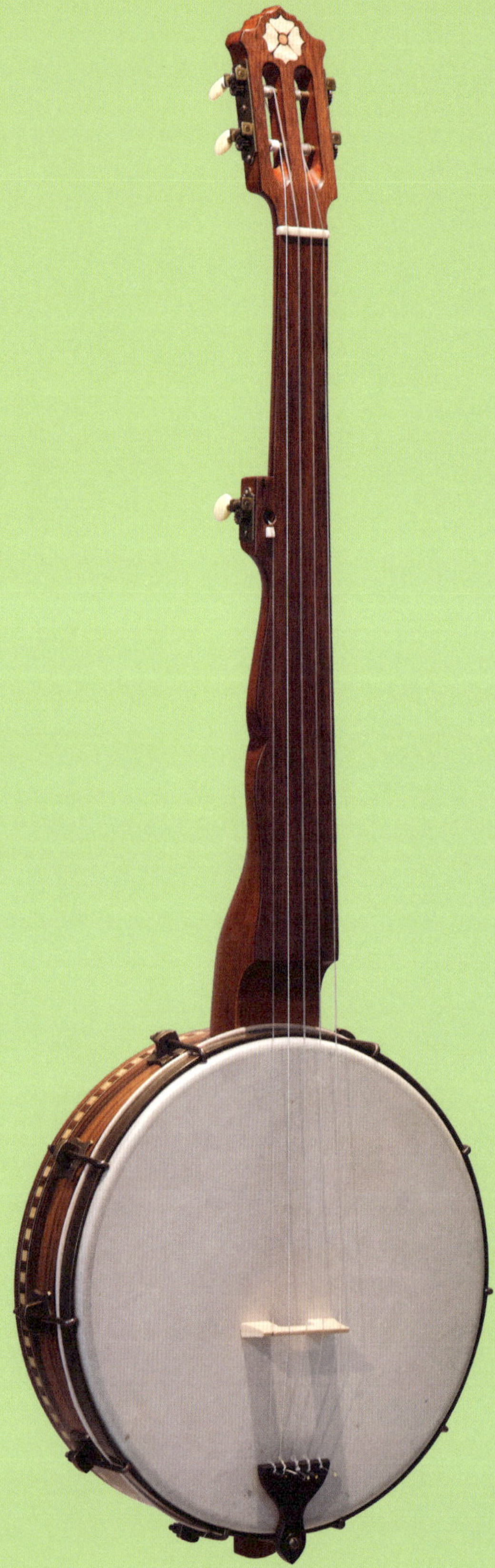

THE INSTRUMENT

RHIANNON GIDDENS'S BANJO

2013, **James J. Hartel** (b. 1947), reproduction of c. 1858 Levi Brown banjo,
Maple rim with rosewood veneer and ladder binding, cherry neck with rosewood fingerboard and peghead overlay, maple inlay on peghead, calfskin head on rim, 37 × 13 3/8 × 4 5/16 in. (94 × 34 × 11 cm).

One of the things that I love about this banjo is that it's a triple threat: it's historically accurate; it's beautifully made; and it sounds amazing.

I met Jim Hartel and his banjos at Harpers Ferry, [West Virginia]. He brought this one in. I didn't want to let it go and he wanted to put a new skin on it. But it was like one of those things when you pick up an instrument and you start playing it and you're just like, "How much is this? I don't care. Here's my bank account, just clear it out." And this was the one that I've written songs on. I brought it into *The New Basement Tapes* session. The very first that I led was on this banjo and it's become a part of my songwriting, which I never expected, so it's cool. And everywhere I go, people are like, "Who made that? What is that?" As soon as I start to play it, other musicians are just like, "That is the coolest thing ever."

One of the reasons I love having this as my primary banjo, this minstrel banjo, is that you can tell people that the banjo's an African American instrument and that its antecedents are in Africa. But when you tell them this is the first commercial-style banjo in the United States, and you play it, that connection is more visceral. You hear the depth of it. You can hear the connection to the gourd banjo that it replaced. This is the beginning of our music. American music is right here. That pulled me in, but the history, you know, keeps me there. American history is not all bad and it's not all good. It's a mixture of things and that's what minstrelsy is.

Minstrelsy is a very broad term that covers the music of America's earliest, real American music. People were doing minstrel music back in the 1820s and '30s. Banjo comes into it in the 1840s and '50s, but it continued on into the 1900s. It still reverberates today in American culture—I mean, it was the most popular form of entertainment for a long, long time.

And it started off with one guy singing, and then [became] one guy singing and playing the banjo at the turn of the century, then [turned into] these huge extravaganzas of dancers and musicians. Minstrelsy was all done in blackface. And so, it's a very problematic time period for us to look back on because we do not have a very good way of talking about race in this country. It's a very difficult thing to get into, but the banjo led me there. The more that I've gotten into it, the more that I have realized that it's a really important time to dig into because it's what sets up the American character. It's some of the earliest cultural interactions between Black people and white people that we have notation of. And then of course there's just beautiful music in it. Music is important because you can say things with music that you can't in any other way.

— **Rhiannon Giddens** as told to Carol Sauvion during the filming of the *Craft in America* documentary series episode "MUSIC."

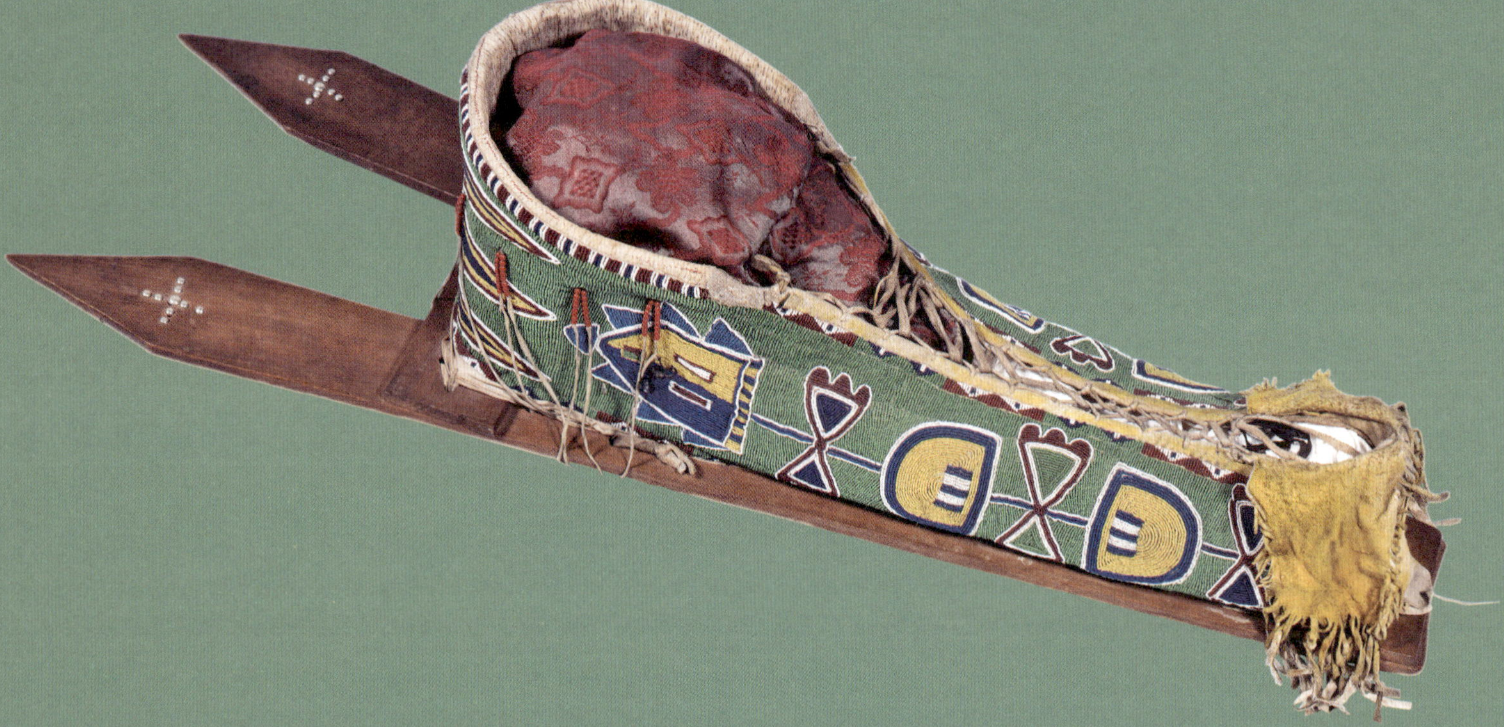

THE CARRIER

KIOWA CRADLEBOARD

c. 1890, **Unidentified artist (Kiowa)**, Glass beads, wood, buckskin, brass tacks, cloth, sinew, brass miniatures, thimbles, 46 × 14 × 9½ in. (116.8 × 35.6 × 24.1 cm), Heard Museum, Phoenix, Fred Harvey Fine Arts Collection, 81BE.

Over the centuries, mothers, grandmothers, aunts, and other women in Indigenous communities created cradleboards, cradle baskets, and carriers to protect their most precious hopes for the future: their children. Cradleboards kept infants swaddled and safe while their parents carried out everyday chores. Babies were propped upright so they could see their new world and mothers could keep a careful eye on their children. The carriers could be strapped to the mother's back for easy transport.

Each functional and decorative component of an infant carrier carried significance. Some cradleboards had semicircular wooden bands at the top to protect the infant's fragile head while others featured a hood made from buckskin or a miniature basket cap. Here, a buckskin outer layer has a wire-reinforced hood to protect baby's soft spot. The buckskin is attached to the frame with sinew; the interior is lined with soft cloth.

Some cradleboards were decorated with beads handcrafted from bone, shell, copper, and stone, with different motifs and colors for male or female children. Other bead designs reflected their culture or cultural region, the child's family lines, or animals and stories important to the artist or a family member. More elaborate beading or higher-quality materials could also showcase the family's wealth or standing within the community.

Although glass beads have largely replaced traditional beads, the techniques to create intricate designs, bead by bead, to decorate a carrier or cradleboard cover are the same used for millennia. Some cradleboard covers are completely covered with beads, affixed using lazy stitch, overlay, or by sewing long strings of beads onto the cloth. In other cases, a loom is used to weave beads in intricate geometric patterns, which are then sewn in strips to the covering. As Kiowa bead artist Teri Greeves once said, the wee ones are "encased in glass beads."[1] And, as with all other beadwork, artists incorporate one mistake in their work. The idea is that nothing in life is perfect.

This cradleboard is lovingly beaded in geometric patterns using the commercial glass beads that Native beadworkers came to treasure. Thimbles and miniature lanterns also decorate the cradleboard's sides. The frame is made from two long pieces of wood chiseled to points at the top and two shorter crosspieces. The cradleboard pictured sports brass-tack decoration in a cross pattern.

Kiowa artist Vanessa Jennings calls cradleboards "living beings."[2] Like many endeavors in Indian Country, the final steps in the process are prayer, offering tobacco, and laying the cradleboard down at the roots of a bois d'arc tree, the traditional cradleboard wood. Jennings says that at the beginning of the process, before harvesting the wood for the frame, you tell the tree, "There's a little Kiowa coming along that Milky Way road, and we want to prepare a cradle for him."

These works of art are still made and used throughout Indian Country. Moms proudly display their babies enjoying the view, or napping, swaddled and secure. —**DUK**

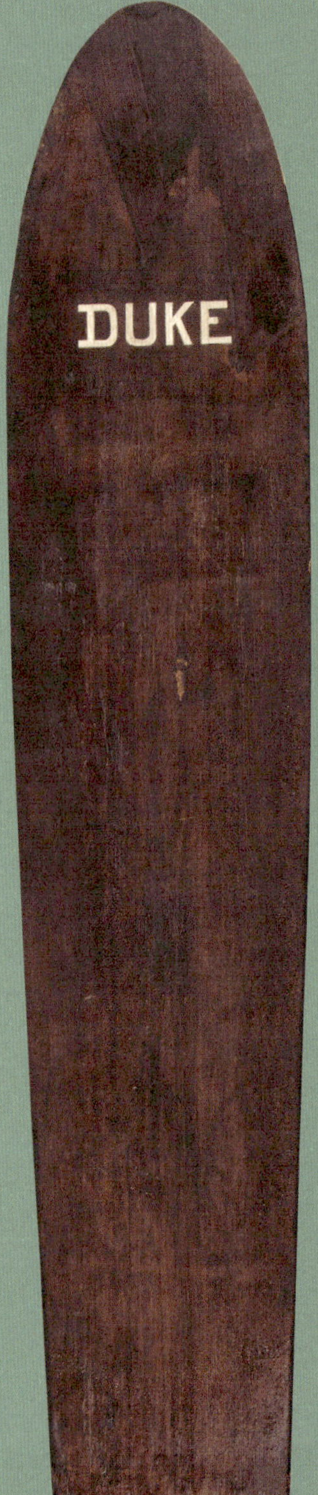

THE CARRIER

PAPA HEʻENALU (SURFBOARD)

c. 1915, **Duke Paoa Kahanamoku** (1890–1968), California redwood, paint, 118 ⅛ × 23 ¼ × 2 ¾ in. (300 × 59 × 7 cm), Bishop Museum, Honolulu, Ethnology Collection, item no. C.04385.

The mesmerizing ebb and flow of the ocean and the sound of crashing waves on the shore have drawn people to the sea for generations. The ocean's call inspired early Hawaiians to invent papa heʻenalu: surfboards. "Heʻenalu" means "to slide on waves." It was a sport accessible to all members of Hawaiian society but particularly enjoyed by the chiefly ranks. Two styles of papa heʻenalu developed, the olo and alaia, with the latter being comparably shorter, thinner, and plank-like in contrast to the longer and thicker olo boards. Alaia boards were designed to catch smaller waves and offer greater maneuverability, whereas the olo provided more stability and speed in catching larger waves. These remained the only two board forms well into the early 1900s, when the first significant evolution of surfboard design developed with the help of innovative papa heʻenalu shapers.

Duke Paoa Kahanamoku was the eldest son of Duke Halapu Kahanamoku and Julia Paʻakonia Lonokahikina Paoa. He grew up on the shores of Kālia, Waikīkī, where he learned to be an avid waterman. Kahanamoku later became an Olympic medalist in swimming in the 1912, 1920, and 1924 games. In the 1910s, he introduced the world to the Hawaiian sport of heʻenalu through surfing exhibitions first in Southern California and then later in Sydney, Australia. Kahanamoku had many surfboards during his lifetime, including this longboard. The iconic board is carved with his name, "DUKE," at its nose and infilled with white paint, making it easily identifiable from a distance.

Because of Duke's love for the ocean, he was able to share the culture and history of Hawaiʻi with the world. With his rise in popularity following Olympic successes, he was offered roles in movies and television programs. He traveled the globe sharing his gifts and stories about surfing and the sea. In 1959 he was appointed Ambassador of Aloha by the state of Hawaiʻi. His contributions to the surfing and swimming worlds paved the way and inspired many Hawaiians, including athletes such as Carissa Moore, who was the 2020 Olympic gold medalist in surfing.

Surfing has become a sport loved by many around the world. The ocean continues to call people to its shores and dares them to experience its awe-inspiring surf breaks. The gift that Hawaiʻi has shared with the world is the ability to find oneself dropping into a break, shooting the barrel of a wave, and emerging cleanly at the other end. The intensity and exhilaration a surfer feels after catching a wave is adrenaline pumping. When Hawaiians developed the sport of heʻenalu, it became a sign of skill, courage, and bravery to overcome the raw power of the sea—something that continues to hold true today. Heʻenalu will be practiced as long as the waves roll into its shores. —MHM

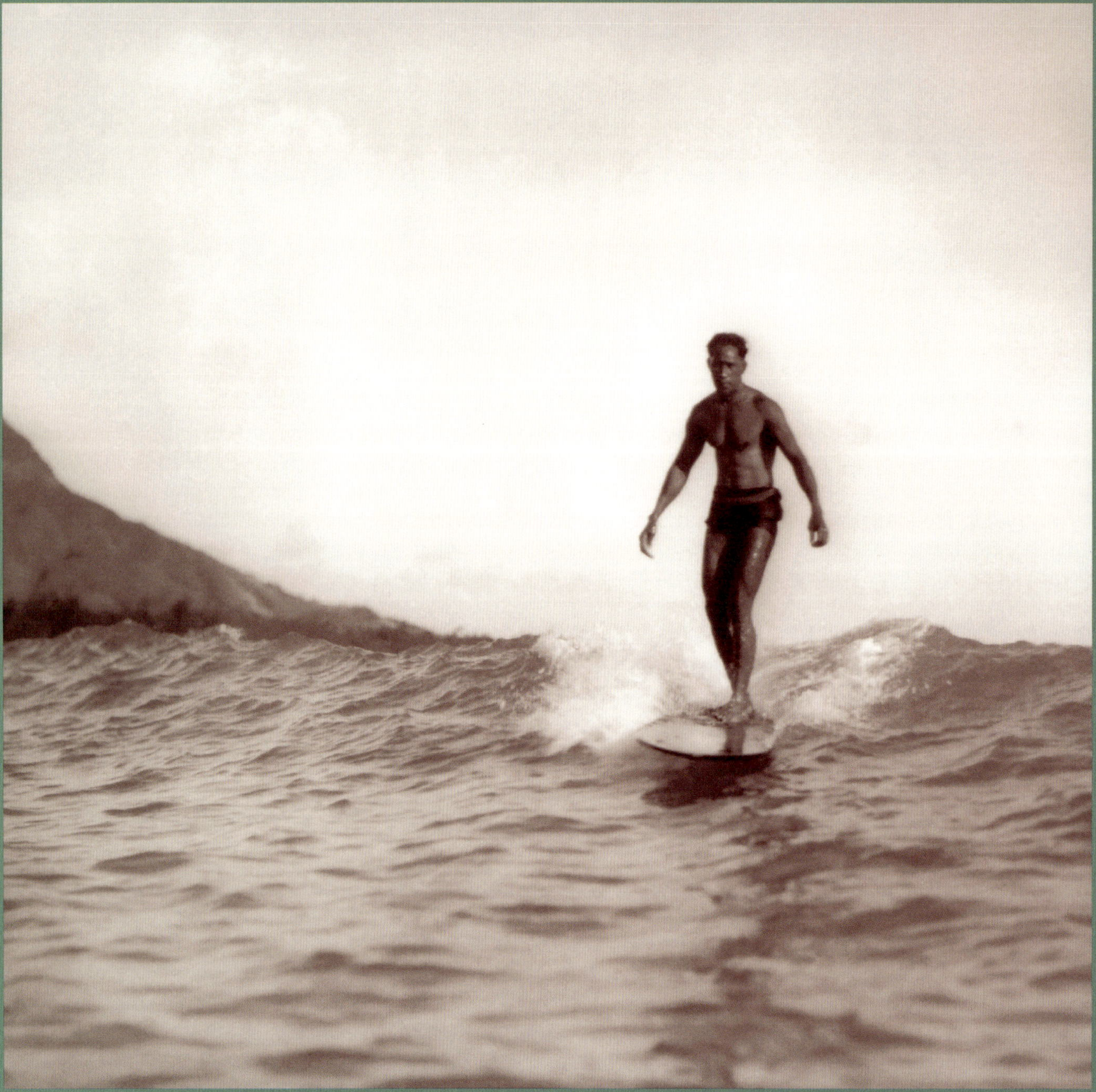

ABOVE
Duke Kahanamoku riding a wave on a wooden surfboard in Waikiki, Hawai'i, with Diamond Head in the background, 1928.

OPPOSITE
Duke Kahanamoku in front of his surfboard, c. 1912.

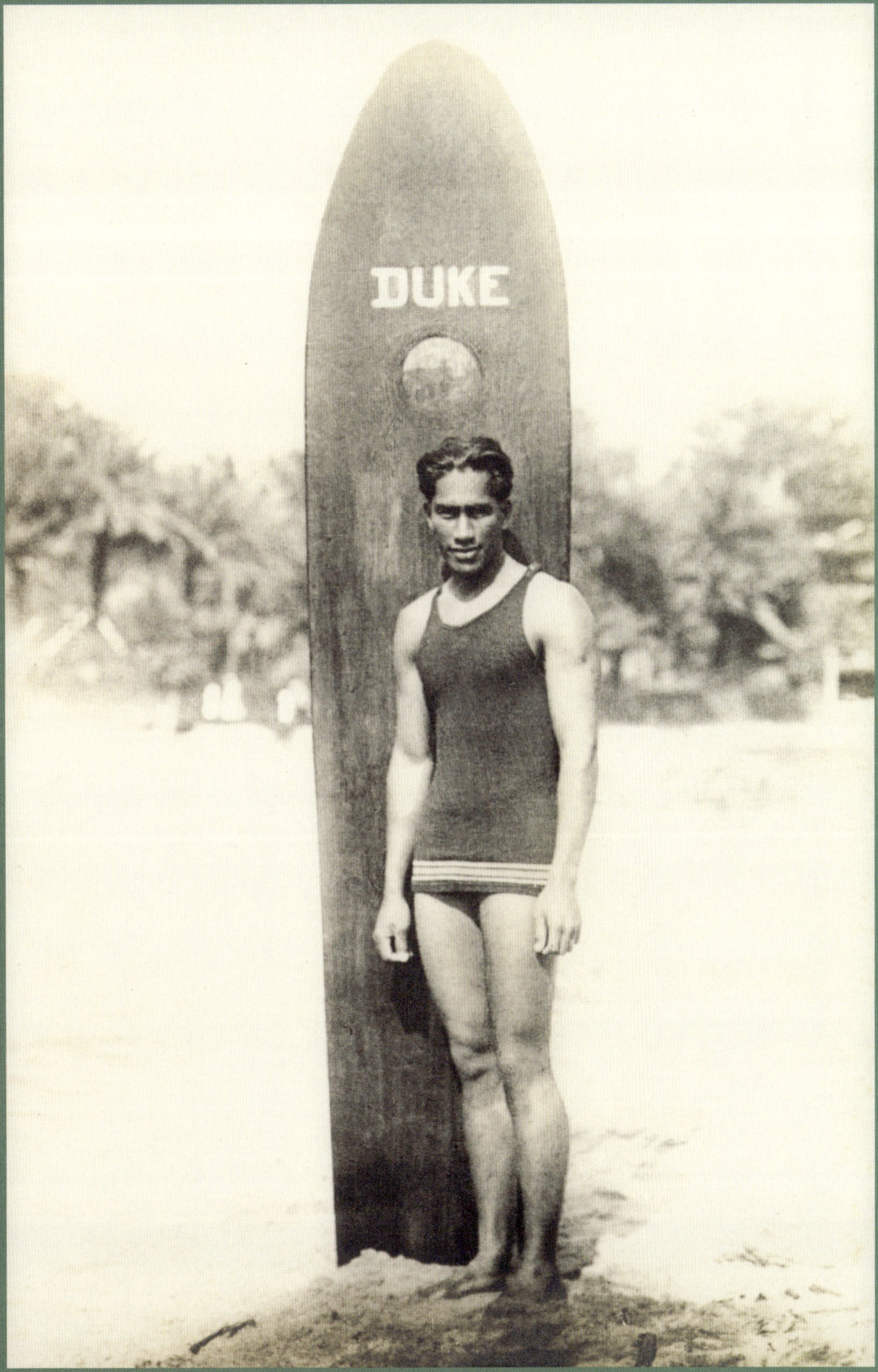

TO TRANSPORT

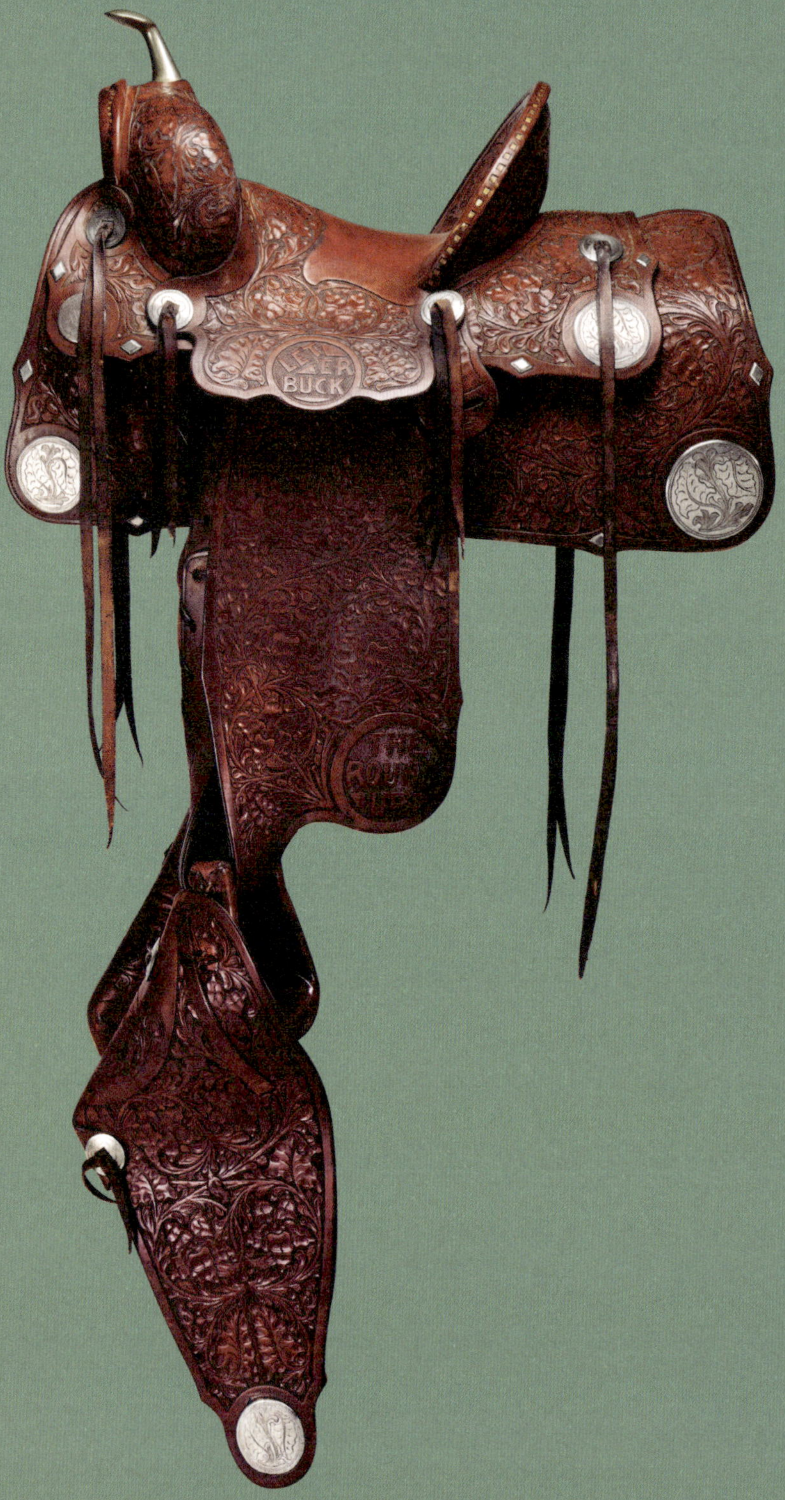

THE CARRIER

PENDLETON ROUND-UP TROPHY SADDLE

1916, **Hamley & Company** (est. 1883),
Leather, silver medallions, sheepskin, metal horn and buckles, 40½ × 30½ × 17 in. (102.9 × 77.5 × 43.2 cm),
Oregon Historical Society Museum, Portland, 94-94.1.1-.3.

Produced by Hamley & Company for the Pendleton Round-Up rodeo in 1916, this trophy saddle was awarded to Nimiipuu (or Nez Perce) cowboy Jackson Sundown, who won that year's saddle bronc competition and was honored as the Round-Up's All-Around Cowboy.

John James "J. J." Hamley arrived in Pendleton, Oregon, in 1905 and there established a custom saddle and tack business. Hamley's was not an assembly-line shop; he employed a talented group of saddle-makers who worked together on the production of every saddle. After 1910, the company supplied to the fledgling Pendleton Round-Up trophy saddles that were presented to the winners of the event's competitions. Hamley's was given this honor because they were known for the quality of their saddles, the skillful approach to their craft, and for the beauty of their completed works, including the excellent design and tooling of their leather surfaces.

This saddle leather is decorated with finely tooled leaf motifs. On the back of the pommel, the year of the rodeo, 1916, appears within a surrounding circle. "Let 'Er Buck" and "The Round Up"—also within circles—are tooled on the jockey seat and near the bottom of the fenders. Tooled leather tapaderos cover the stirrups. Engraved sterling silver conchos appear at the corners of the skirts and jockeys and at the bottom of the tapaderos. A large, engraved silver plaque—now missing—once graced the back of the cantle. According to period accounts, Sundown asked that his wife's name be engraved on it.

Jackson Sundown (Waaya-Tonah-Toesits-Kahn, "Earth Left by the Setting Sun" or "Blanket of Sun") was born in about 1863. He was a member of the Wallowa Band Nez Perce and was a nephew of Chief Joseph. In 1877, the Wallowa people fled their ancestral homeland in northeast Oregon, preferring refuge in Canada to forced relocation to an Idaho reservation. Although still in his early teens, Sundown was skilled enough with horses to be counted among the young men who cared for the two to three thousand animals that accompanied the exiles during their flight.

The Nez Perce were pursued by the U.S. Army and, trying to avoid capture as his compatriots surrendered in northern Montana, Sundown and others slipped away from the final battle site. Suffering from minor bullet wounds, he escaped by riding on the side of a horse—a ruse that kept him from being seen by soldiers. The refugees soon reached Canada and found shelter in Sitting Bull's camp.

Sundown moved to Montana's Flathead Reservation in about 1880 and there built a reputation as a horseman. Relocating to Idaho's Nez Perce Reservation in 1910, he continued working as a horse trainer and enjoyed success as a regional rodeo competitor. He was a seminal performer during the first decade of the Pendleton Round-Up and figured prominently in celebrated 1911 and 1915 bucking horse contests. He then considered retiring from rodeo but was encouraged by the artist Alexander Phimister Proctor, who had used him as a model for several sculptures, to enter the 1916 event. After Proctor paid his entry fee, Sundown entered and won the 1916 saddle bronc competition and the Round-Up's All-Around Cowboy honors. He was fifty-three years old. —SG

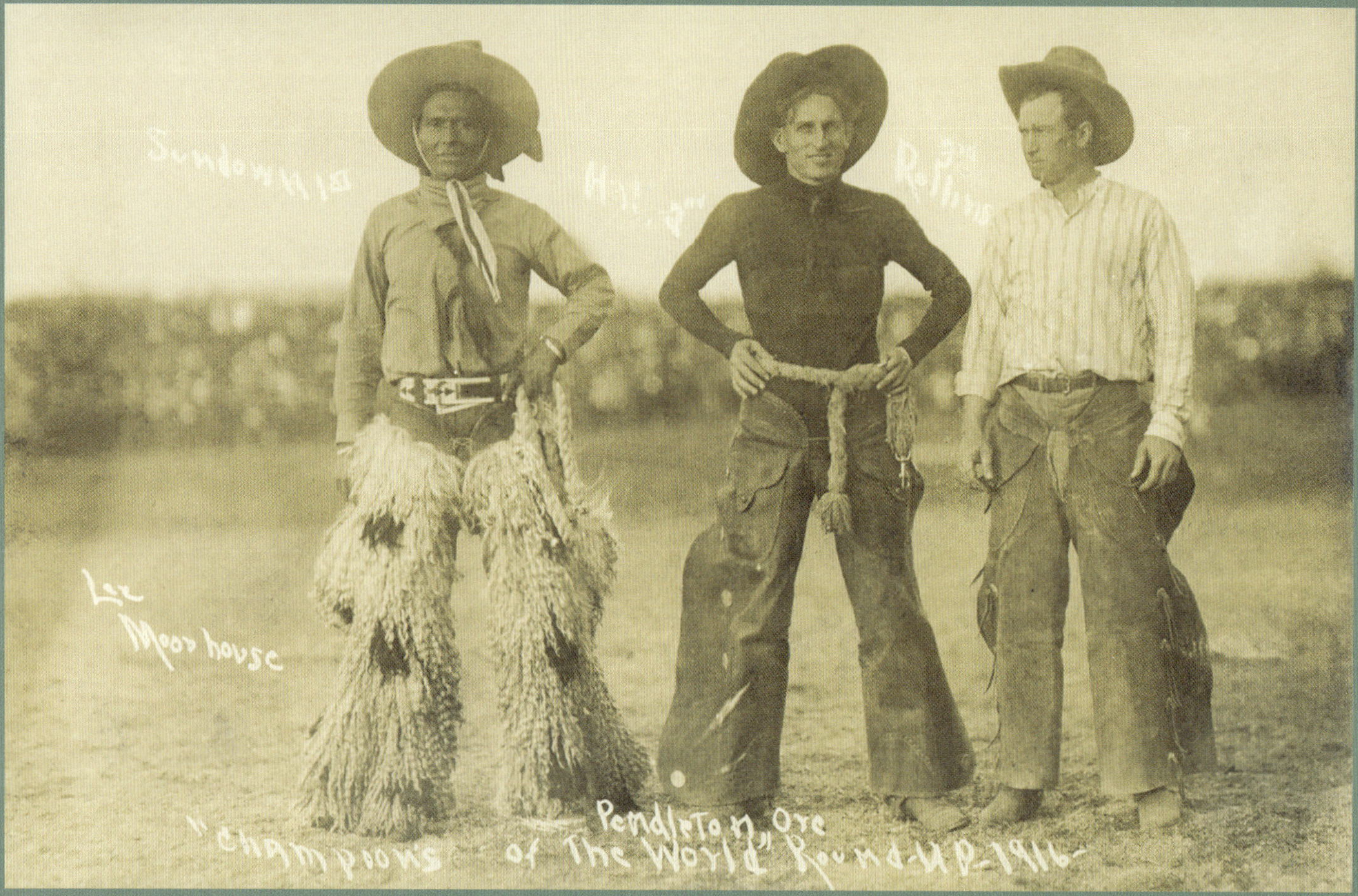

1916 Pendleton Oregon Round-Up "Champions of the World,"
from left: Jackson Sundown, Bob Hall, and Rufus Rollins,
Bruce McCarroll Collection of the Bonnie & Frank McCarroll Rodeo Archives,
Dickinson Research Center, National Cowboy & Western Heritage Museum, Oklahoma City,
RC2006.076.360.

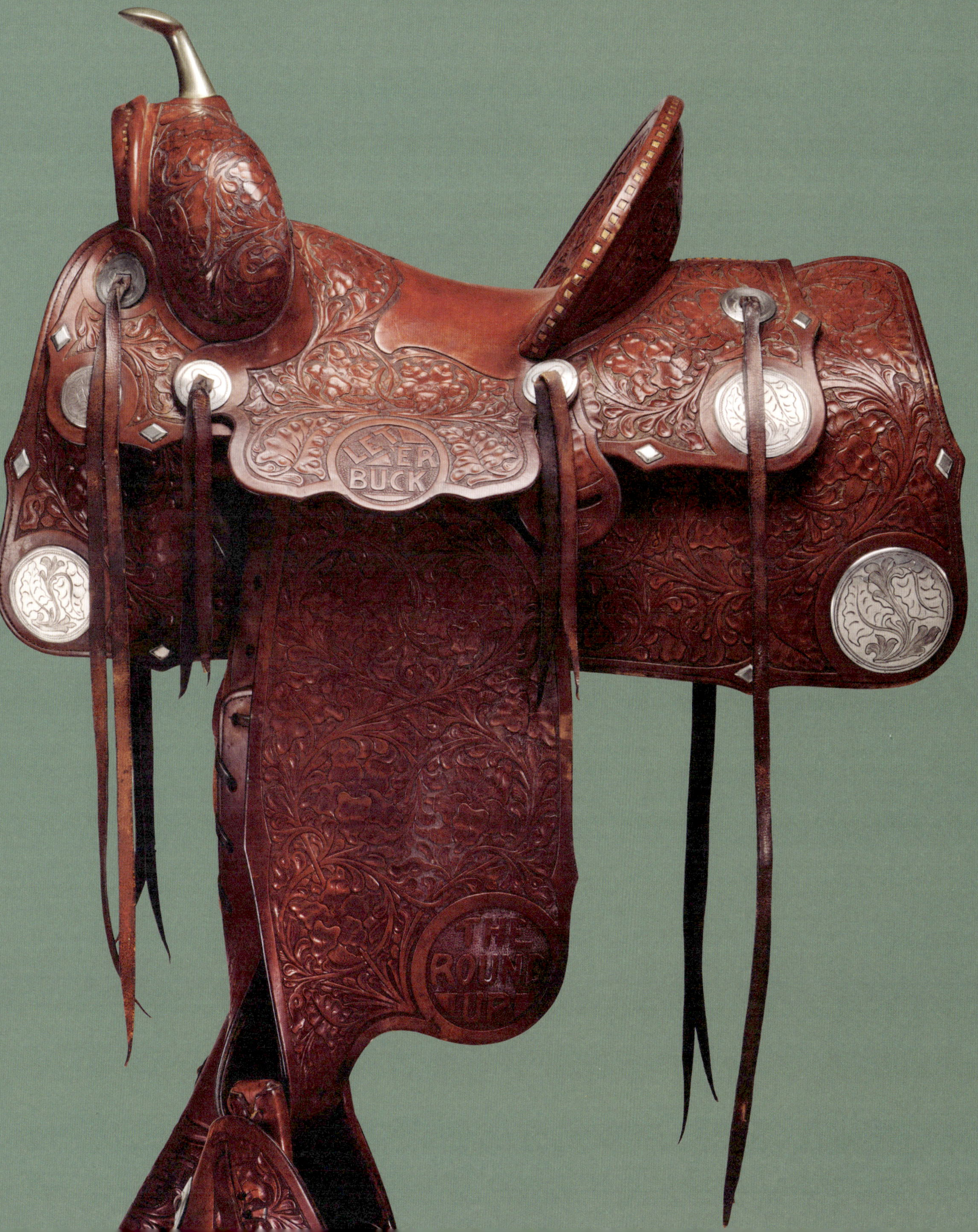
LET ER
BUCK
ROUND

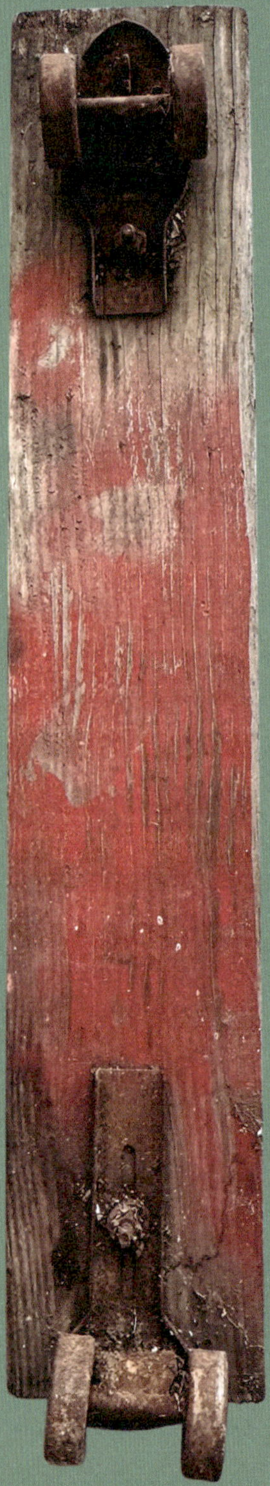

THE CARRIER

SKATEBOARD

1961–62, **Don and Bill Diehl**, Repurposed wood, metal roller skate wheels, paint, 5 × 21 in. (12.7 × 53.3 cm), Todd Huber, Skateboarding Hall of Fame, Simi Valley, CA.

As early as the 1910s, American kids started making a precursor to the skateboard from modified scooters, roller skates, and repurposed wood. A 1913 *Woman's Home Companion* article described the "New Roller Skatemobile" as a zippy toy on wheels that could be built from converted scooters by the "boy craftsman."[1] The beauty of the original skateboard, as described by some of the first skateboarders, was that anyone could make one. With old roller skates, part of a wooden milk or fruit crate, or a plank and some nails, voilà, a skateboard was born. All kinds of homespun versions of what would become the skateboard popped up. By the 1950s, the concept had spread and taken root in California, where surfers adopted skateboarding as a dry-land parallel to catching waves. They brought a new spin to the skateboard as the sport of "sidewalk surfing" took flight.[2]

What was first creatively cobbled for play became the seed of an industry. After all, anything this irresistible was naturally going to lure in manufacturers, who found ways to produce aerodynamic boards of beauty in all shapes and sizes.

Pinpointing the first modern skateboard is contentious among aficionados. It was not until the 1959 Roller Derby Skateboard and into the early 1960s that the first skateboards were made and sold commercially. In 1962, Bill Richards is credited with attaching Chicago Roller Skate Company wheels to a wooden board and launching skateboards at the famed surf shop Val Surf in Los Angeles. Larry Stevenson, a surfer who recognized the skateboard's potential, founded Makaha Skateboards in 1963. Stevenson's designs took boards to the next level, incorporating clay wheels instead of the crude metal wheels, which were difficult to ride and harder to control. This innovation was a crucial step toward skateboards and skateboarding achieving widespread popularity by 1965.

Over time, skateboarding bloomed to become an entire community and culture—and a bona fide Olympic sport. Boards became increasingly complex. Numerous advances were made in wheel materials, including urethane thanks to Frank Nasworthy's Cadillac Wheels, introduced in 1973. Decks that were first shaped like scaled-down surfboards and made of old planks or metal gave way, in the 1970s, to decks made of plastic, fiberglass, and polypropylene. Engineering became more nuanced and sophisticated, as did the sport itself. Board design and aesthetics also became a realm for visual and artistic appeal. Today, decks are displayed on walls as artworks, treated as canvases by blue-chip artists, and collected and coveted as objects in and of themselves. Keeping skateboarding's countercultural origins at the forefront, many of the pioneers tell stories of making their first boards as a rite of passage and entry into a whole new world that they crafted.

Like many forms of craft, a culture emerged around the object. Skateboarding became a way of connecting and even a lifestyle. It is a form of expression through movement with global appeal. The American-born skateboard became one of the country's most popular twentieth-century exports on an international scale, and remains an indelible part of our culture today.
—**EZ**

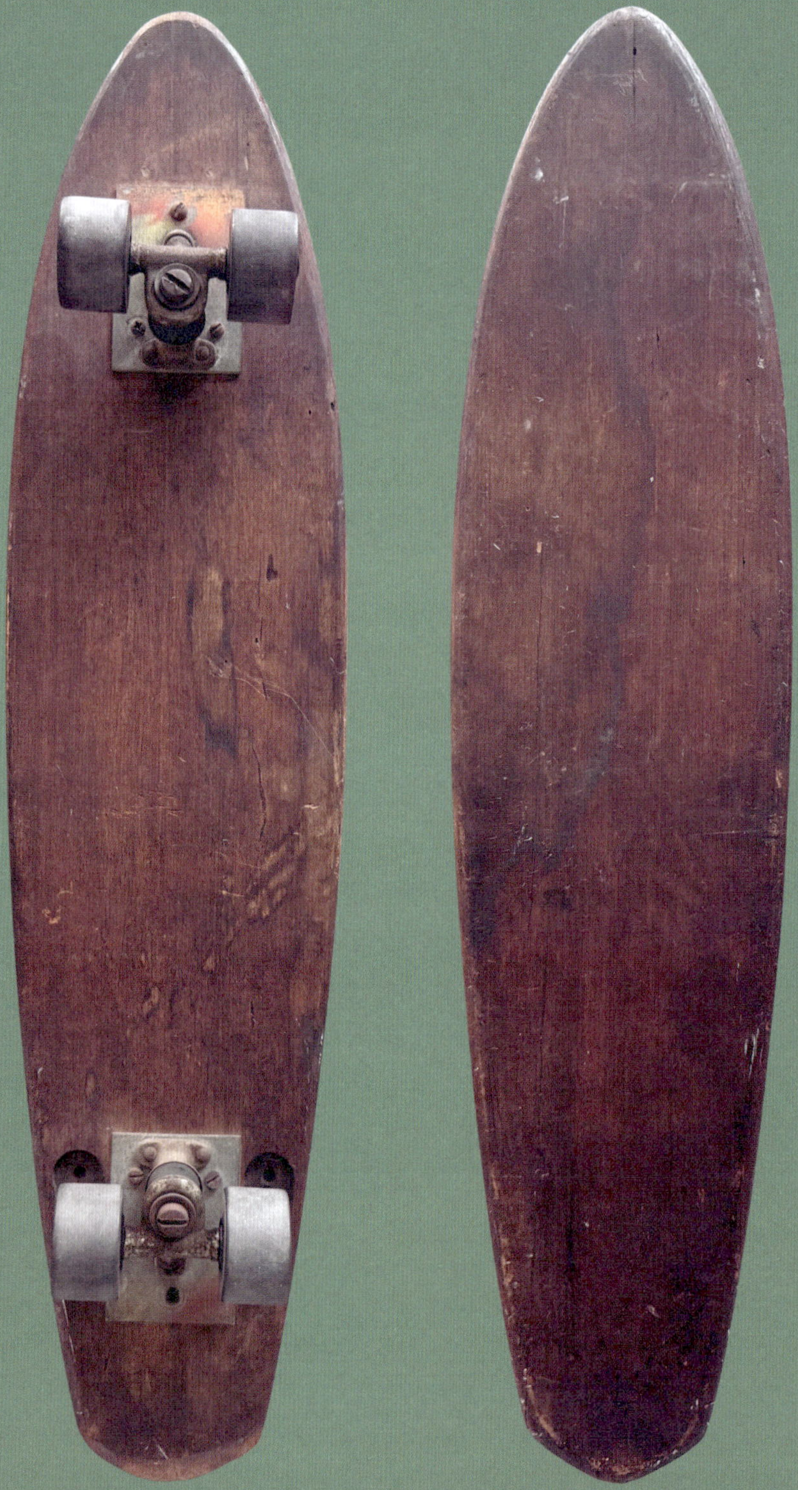

Handmade skateboard, c. 1973, Unknown maker,
Wood with early urethane "Cadillac Wheels," 5 × 21 in. (12.7 × 53.3 cm),
Todd Huber, Skateboarding Hall of Fame.

THE CARRIER

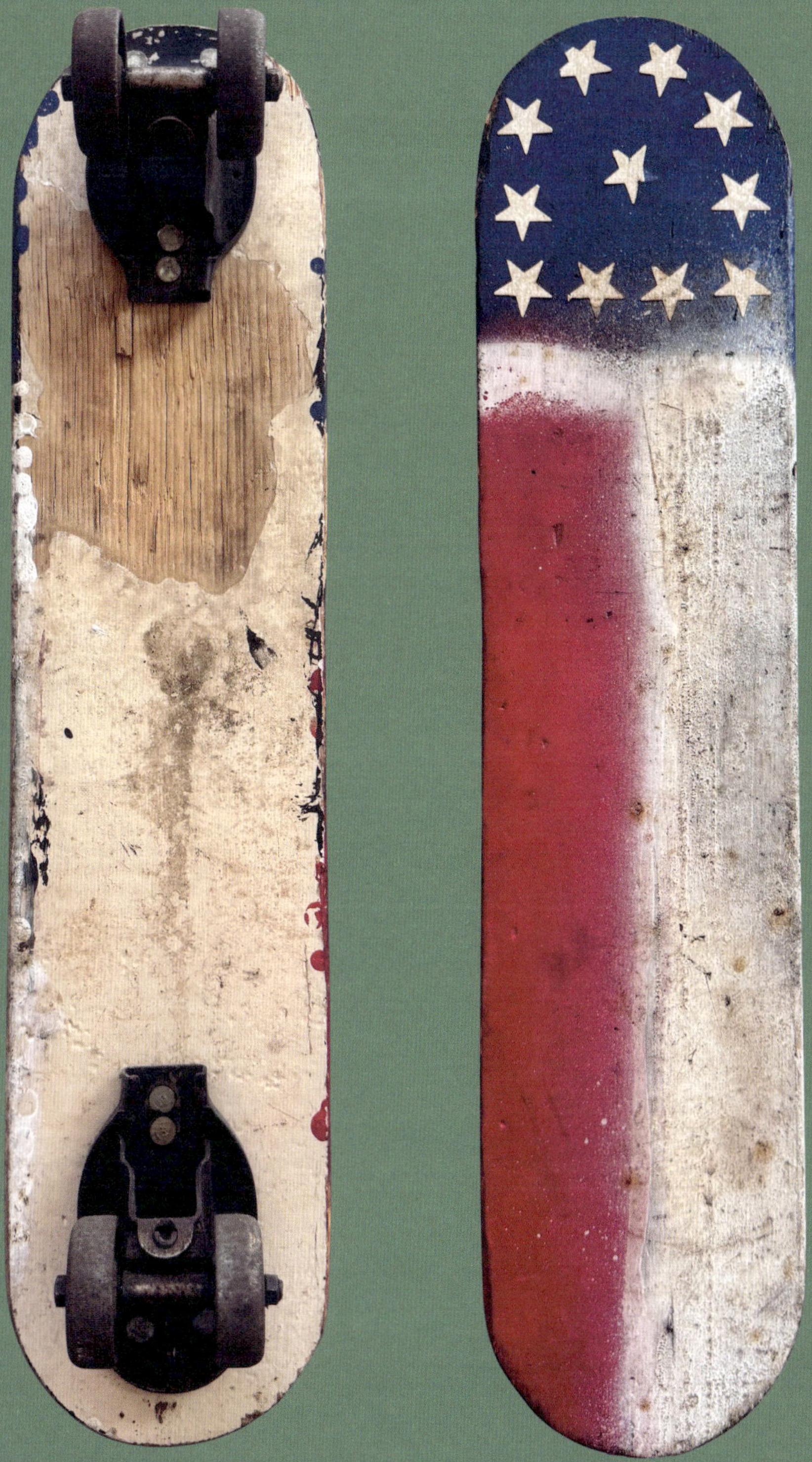

Handmade Americana skateboard, c. 1970, Unknown maker, Wood, paint, clay wheels, stickers, 5 × 21 in. (12.7 × 53.3 cm), Todd Huber, Skateboarding Hall of Fame.

FEED

THE CUP: TO DRINK

THE PLATE: TO SERVE

THE BOWL: TO CONTAIN

THE POT: TO POUR

THE UTENSIL: TO DINE

WHILE THE WORD *FEED* TODAY has an entirely new, intangible definition related to the digestion of digital content, the handmade objects in this chapter pertain to the fundamentals for consuming food and drink. They are also things that provide sustenance on other levels. As handcrafted items, they are carefully designed and constructed to nourish and gratify the eye, hand, body, mind, and soul simultaneously. Feed implies a sense of hunger, a yearning for satisfaction beyond subsistence, and many of these objects were created with that desire in mind. Those that are utilitarian can make the act of consumption more fulfilling and meaningful through their craftsmanship, while the contemporary works memorialize notions of dining and drinking and use them as a conceptual impetus.

These objects are a harmonious group. They are almost entirely made of one of three materials: clay, glass, or silver. Considering them for their pure geometry, the circle or cylinder predominates. We describe many of their components anatomically, almost intimately: the lip of a glass, the foot of a bowl. Although they are inanimate objects, they are enlivened with such features by the potter, silversmith, or the glassblower, and they then have close contact with the hand or mouth of their user.

Our interaction with these objects is dictated by longstanding standards and rituals of civility and etiquette. According to these codes, they are placed at specific positions on a table, where they "belong," and their roles are clearly delineated. Each of these things delivers food or drink from one location to another, be it from kitchen to dining room, hand to hand, or table to mouth.

Bowls are among the most ancient of objects, whether used for eating or passed around ceremoniously to symbolize the sharing of resources and the importance of collaboration and community. Most of the objects in this chapter are tied to ritual and celebration as food and drink are inextricably intertwined with both. For modern craft, the form of the bowl is "the content" in and of itself, in the words of ceramist Gertrud Natzler.

Utensils are the tools of the table. Handheld, they allow us to slice, stir, scoop, toss, serve, spread, cut, and lift our food, and much else. Plates usually exist in unison with utensils. The plate is a surface, usually the largest on a table, and it anchors a meal. As objects, they are flat and open with possibility. A plate is an ideal canvas for artwork; when covered by food, it then becomes a decorative frame.

Material can guide formality and set the tone at the table. Silver, one of the most historically coveted materials for drink pots and utensils of all kinds, has today become almost obsolete. Along with porcelain, it was a signifier for luxury and privilege at the table. Sets of silver and dishware were included in doweries or given as wedding gifts to mark the creation of new families. They symbolized prosperity, based on European standards, throughout much of American history. Whereas earthenware, with much deeper heritage among Indigenous cultures, was typically associated with informality, comfort, and ease.

Formal or humble, these are among the objects that we utilize and touch the most on a daily basis. —EZ

INTRODUCTION

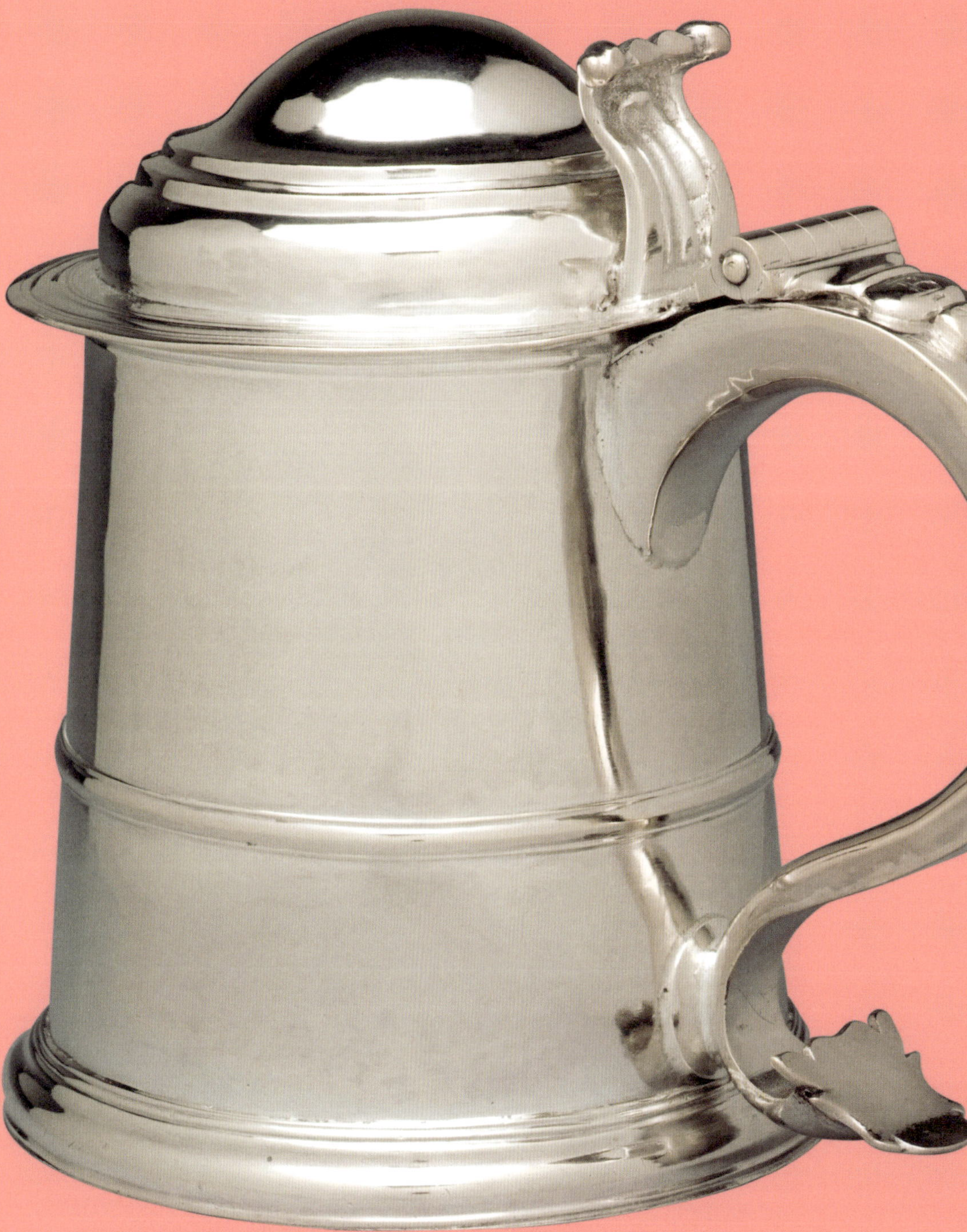

THE CUP

TANKARD

1709–15, **Francis Richardson Sr.** (1681–1729), Silver,
7 × 7⅞ × 5½ in. (17.8 × 20 × 14 cm), Philadelphia Museum of Art, 125th Anniversary Acquisition,
Gift of Mr. and Mrs. Harold P. Starr, 1999, 1999-142-1.

This tankard may be the earliest surviving example of silver made by renowned silversmith Francis Richardson. It was created for William Branson, a prosperous advisor to the family of William Penn, founder of Pennsylvania. In 1701, Penn recorded the purchase from Richardson of shoe buckles for his daughter Letitia, and this connection, along with the prominence of the silversmith's family, may have led to Branson's purchase of the tankard.[1]

The Richardson family provided Philadelphia and surrounding areas with three generations of talented silversmiths. First among them was Francis Richardson, the maker of this vessel, who may have apprenticed in London, or locally with Cesar Ghiselin or Johannis Nys. Due to his widowed mother's marriage to Edward Shippen, the city's mayor and one of its wealthiest people, Richardson had the means to purchase the necessary tools to establish himself as an independent silversmith.

Tankards have been in use since the fifteenth century as drinking vessels for ale or beer, and were popular in Northern Europe, the British Isles, and colonial America. Having one handle, tankards were originally fashioned like barrels, using wooden staves bound with metal hoops. Since those early days, they have been made of various materials, including leather, pewter, clay, and silver. The broad, domed lid of this vessel is characteristic of Philadelphia silversmithing. (Flat lids were typically found in Boston during the same era.) The prominent cast baluster decoration on the seamed handle is also more characteristic of Middle Atlantic silver. The tall, curved, cast thumbpiece and the shield-shaped terminus at the base of the handle are features that were found throughout the colonies. So is the applied midband decoration, which serves no practical purpose and is thought to be an echo of the early wooden stave and hoop-bound tankards.

Like many colonial silversmiths, Richardson lightly scratched the weight of the tankard on its base: "30 ounces 2 dwt" in troy ounces, the unit of measurement for precious metals. Beyond its weight, the number indicates the value of the silver used to make the finished object. Because of the lack of standardized currency in colonial America, precious metals were considered especially valuable. Affluent individuals purchased silver hollowware as a means of preserving their wealth while also enjoying its use. A 1688 quote by the Virginia planter William Fitzhugh, who owned a large quantity of silver, sums up its importance in colonial life: "I esteem it as well politic as reputable to furnish myself with an handsome cupboard of plate which gives myself the present use and credit, is a sure friend at a dead lift without much loss or is a certain portion for a child after my decease."[2]
—JF

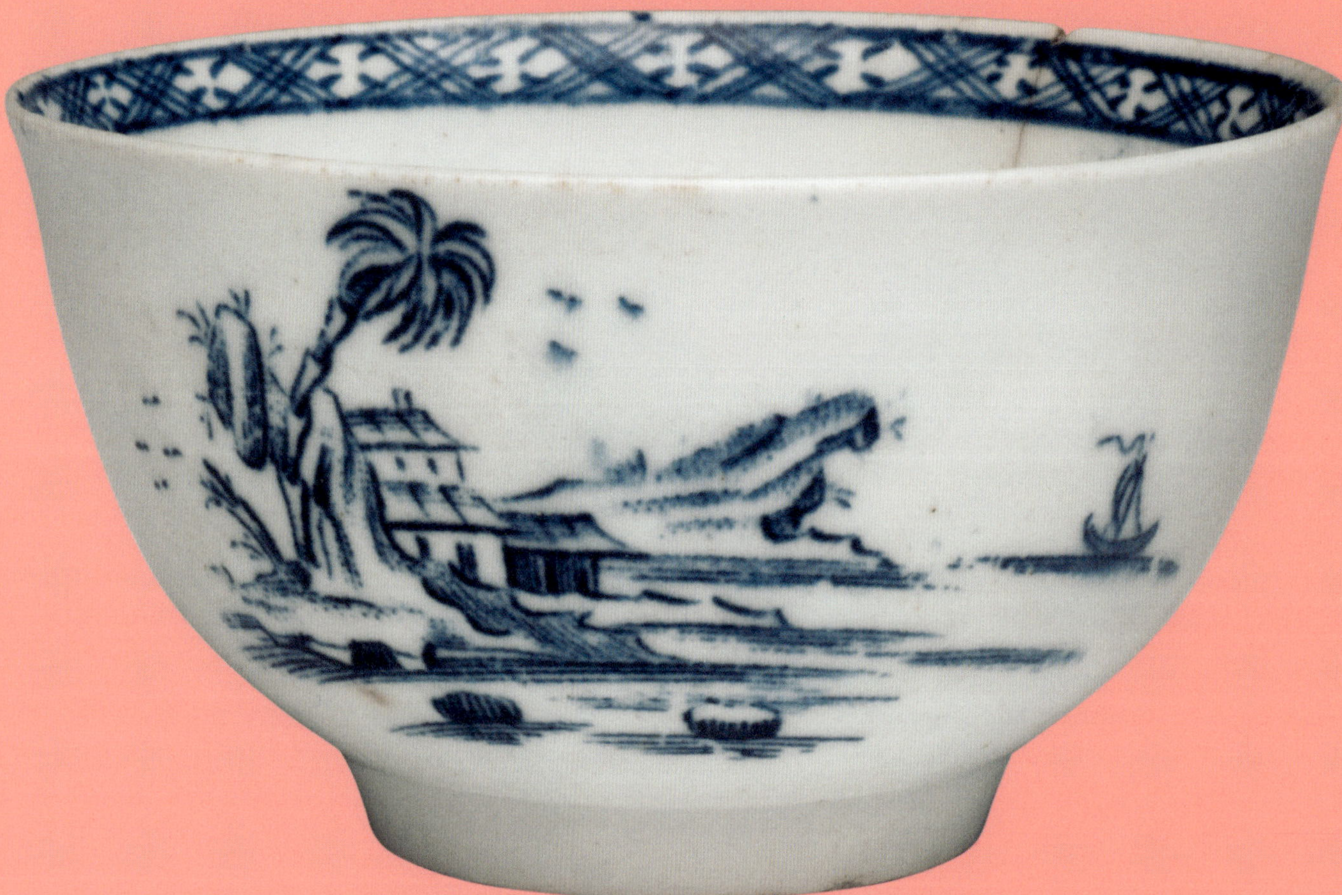

THE CUP

TEABOWL

1765–70, **John Bartlam Manufactory** (1765–1769),
Soft-paste porcelain with underglaze blue hand-painted (interior) and transfer-printed (exterior) decoration,
1⅝ × 3 in. (4.1 × 7.6 cm), Philadelphia Museum of Art, Purchased with the Baugh-Barber Fund, 2012. 2012-77-1.

This teabowl's petite size and finely executed cobalt-blue decoration belie its remarkable significance in the history of American ceramics or, more specifically, porcelain. Porcelain's main ingredient is the white clay known as kaolin, or gaoling, meaning "high ridge," and referring to the location of the material in the province of Jiangxi, China. Combined with a flux such as a feldspathic stone (and later quartz and bone ash), kaolin was potted into fine vessels, decorated with cobalt blue and glazed. Once fired at incredibly high temperatures, it produced a hard, strikingly white ceramic that was translucent, resonant, and durable. The mystical ceramic mesmerized fourteenth-century European traders, and when they returned to Italy, it was given the name for a cowrie shell, porcellana, because of its shell-like texture.

With that, the race to make porcelain was on. Europeans spent nearly four centuries attempting to unlock the secret. Finally, the Germans found kaolin in Saxony and began producing porcelain in 1708. With limited supplies of kaolin in Cornwall, the British relied on the natural resources of their North American colonies, where kaolin was discovered in New Castle County, Pennsylvania (now Delaware), and in copious amounts throughout the South. In Georgia, the colonists found that the Cherokee nations had identified and long admired the qualities of firing kaolin, which they referred to as unaker, meaning "white." In fact, it was the export of North American kaolin that allowed the Brits to patent porcelain in 1748.

Entrepreneurial-minded potters saw opportunity in manufacturing porcelain in the Southern Colonies of North America—close to the major sources of kaolin. Born and trained as a potter in Staffordshire, England, John Bartlam arrived in South Carolina in 1763 and had established his pottery in Cain Hoy—about nine miles north of Charleston—by 1765. Demand was high, but the process of making porcelain was both exacting and expensive, requiring materials, molds, wheels, kilns, and fuel, as well as highly skilled artisans.

This teabowl's thin, translucent walls, crisply painted decoration, and evenly applied glaze reveal the skills of Bartlam's porcelain artisans—at least two of whom were enslaved Africans named Fortune and Hector. The decoration wrapping around the exterior of the teabowl relates to landscapes found on Chinese porcelain pieces but was designed specifically for the Bartlam manufactory. The hill and river scenes—with local palmettos along Cain Hoy's Wando River—were engraved on copperplates in Charleston and then transferred onto the porcelain wares with paper dipped in pigment. This technique made the decoration on Bartlam's wares uniform, and for a manufactory that produced wares for many years, it would have reduced the labor required to decorate. Notably, the flourish on the inside of the teabowl is hand painted.

One of only a handful of surviving works from the Bartlam manufactory, this teabowl represents the ability of colonial Americans to make elegant and delicate yet sturdy porcelain that rivaled not only European and British porcelains but also Chinese wares. The manufactory of such a high-grade porcelain ware beginning in 1765 inspired the likes of leaders including Benjamin Franklin, Dr. Benjamin Rush, and many others who were mulling the idea of independence and plotting the potential for the economic success of a new nation. After all, if Americans could make such a luxury ware, they believed that surely they had the potential to out-manufacture Britain. —AK

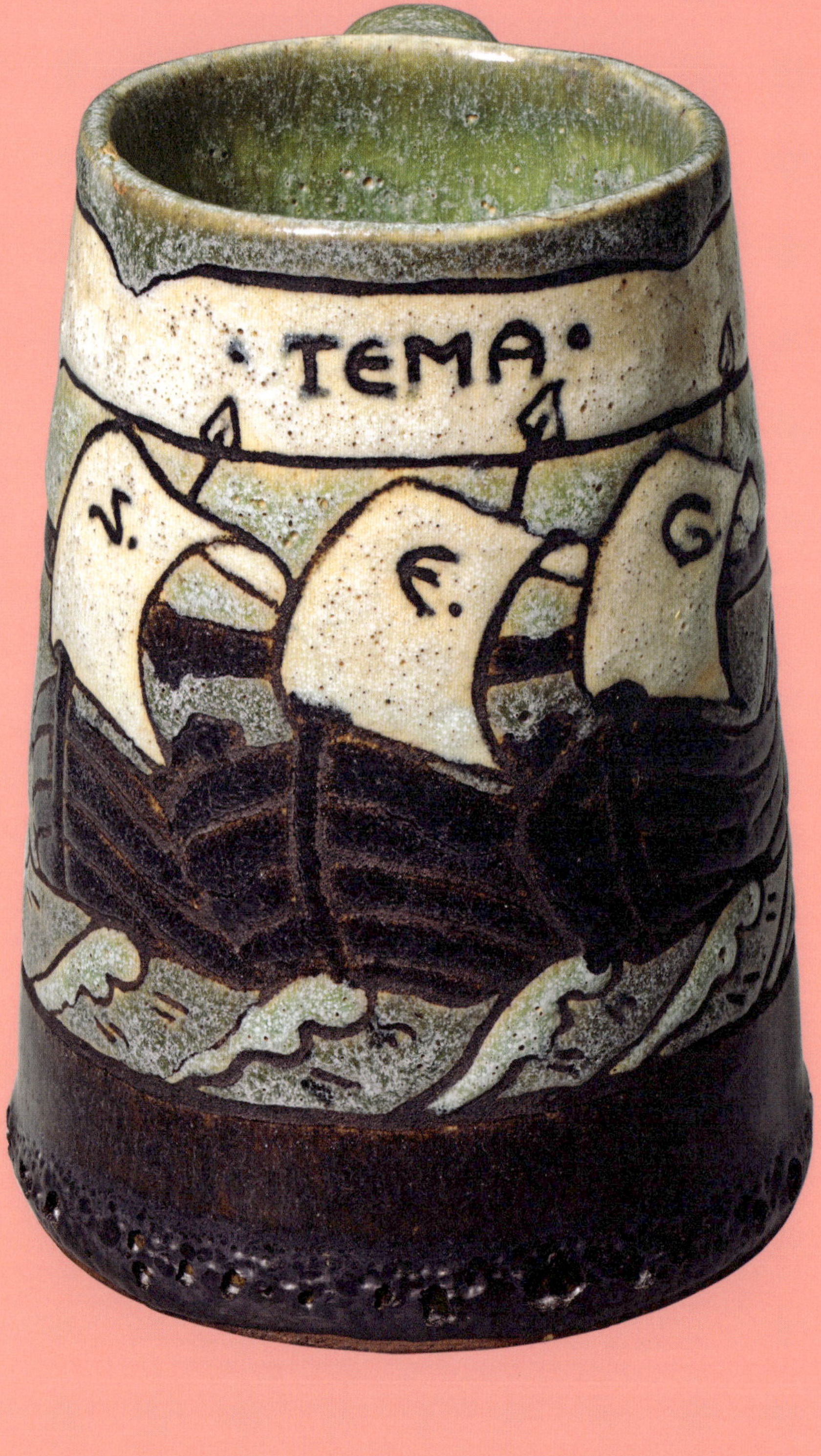

THE CUP

MUG

1909, **Matilda "Tillie" Block** (1894–1970), **Paul Revere Pottery of the Saturday Evening Girls club** (active 1908–1942), Glazed earthenware, 4 × 3¾ × 3 in. (10.2 × 9.5 × 7.6 cm), Museum of Fine Arts, Boston, Gift from Elizabeth, Peter, and Barry Wald in memory of our grandmother, Tillie Block Wald, 2016, 2016.770.

Tillie Block was only fifteen years old when she decorated this mug in July 1909. She worked for the Paul Revere Pottery, a recently established workshop in the middle of Boston's bustling North End. While she painted, Tillie was surrounded by a dozen other teenagers, all daughters of Italian and Jewish immigrants. The girls had originally met through a library club established by Edith Guerrier, the head of the Girls Reading Room at the North Bennet Street Industrial School, a neighborhood settlement house and educational institution. Club members called themselves the Saturday Evening Girls and organized their weekly gatherings to include a story or lecture, business meeting, singing and dancing, and games. The club provided the SEGs (as they referred to themselves) not only with camaraderie and friendship across ethnic lines, but also with unusual access to a liberal arts education through lectures and programs.

The success of the club attracted the attention of Helen Osborne Storrow, a Boston philanthropist interested in the education and empowerment of girls. Storrow provided the SEGs with a summer camp on Wingaersheek Beach in West Gloucester, where, for ten dollars, each girl could enjoy a two-week vacation in nature, far from the crowded tenements of the North End. But many members could not afford the camp dues, so, in response, Guerrier and her friend Edith Brown, a children's book illustrator, established a pottery as a way for the girls to earn their camp dues, as well as to help provide for their families. They named it the Paul Revere Pottery, inspired by its historic North End location near the famous patriot's home, but also to emphasize the American nature of its products, and, by association, its workers.

In purpose and in product the Paul Revere Pottery embodied the progressive social and aesthetic goals of the Arts and Crafts movement of that time. Arts and Crafts principles encouraged handcraftsmanship, the integration of art into everyday life, and healthy working conditions to combat the negative social effects of industrialization. The pottery offered a sunny workroom full of flowers, eight-hour days with a half day on Saturday and Sundays off, and two weeks of paid vacation. Employees were encouraged to sign their initials, along with the date, and "SEG" to the bottom of their works. The girls decorated the pottery with playful stylized designs provided by Brown, using the ancient cuerda seca (Spanish for "dry cord") technique of applying thin strips of black wax (tinted with manganese) to create the outlines of their designs. The wax formed a barrier that separated the glazes and then burned off in the kiln.

Block was one of the first to join the pottery full time. Her family had emigrated from Russia over a decade before to escape its dangerous anti-Jewish pogroms. Perhaps she thought of that long journey when she painted the three ships on the surface of this mug. In the sails, she proudly proclaimed her association with her new American family, the SEGs. But she also held on to her heritage, incorporating her Hebrew name, Tema, in the clouds above the ships. Tema means "perfect," or "complete." Perhaps at the Paul Revere Pottery, Tillie had finally found comfort and safety in her new home.
—NG

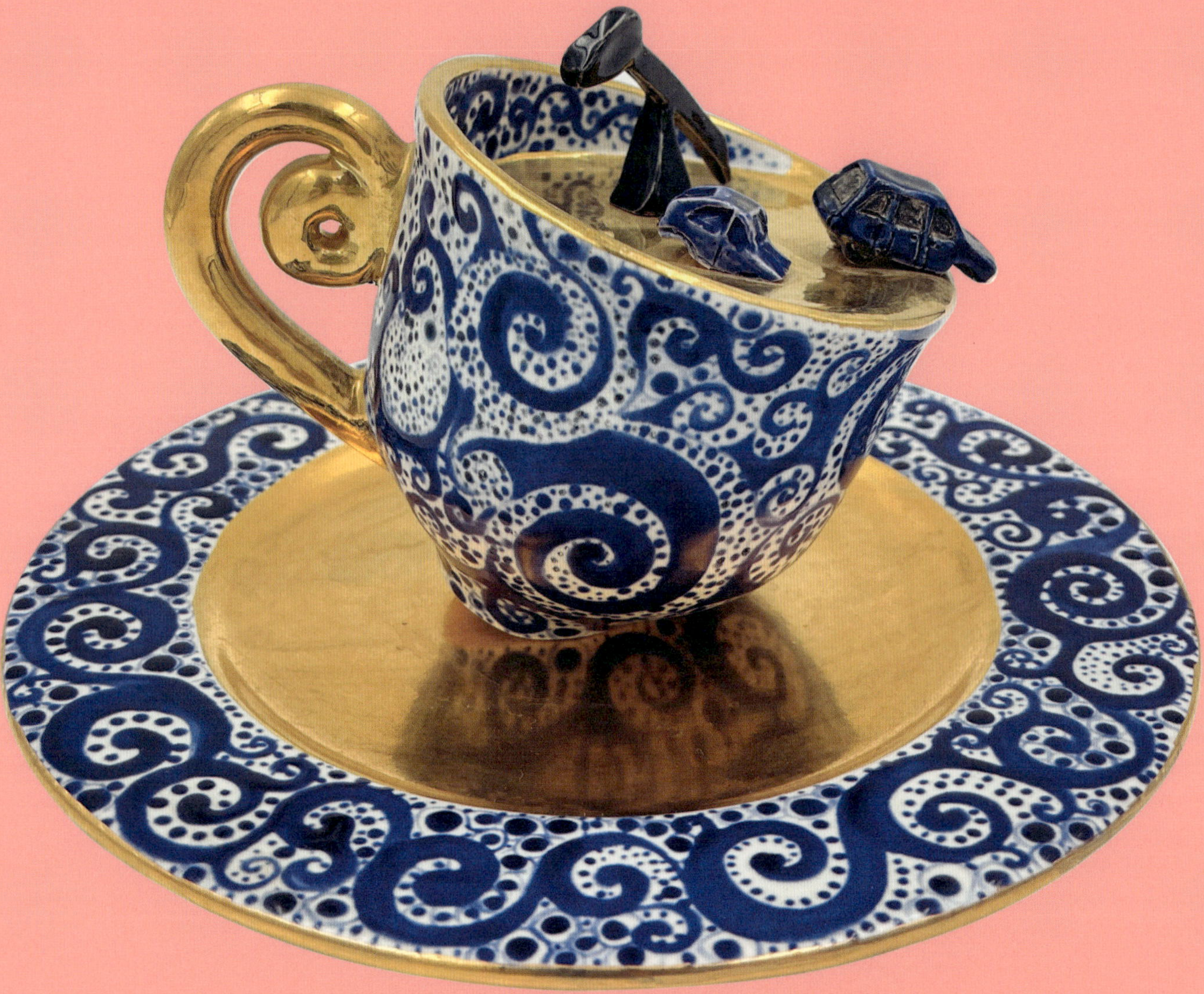

THE CUP

SUVS, FROM THE TIPPING POINT SERIES

2008, **Joan Takayama-Ogawa** (b. 1955),
Glazed earthenware and gold luster, 5 × 8 in. (12.7 × 20.32 cm).

In colonial America, tea was a vital import that had a critical impact on cultural, economic, and political life. Ceramic artist Joan Takayama-Ogawa's twenty-first-century teacup echoes this history to address an essential modern-day commodity—petroleum—whose overexploitation has the potential to topple society on a global scale. In this work, a precariously tilted cup is filled to the brim with liquid gold, captured, as though it were frozen in time, a split second from spilling over. A pumpjack emerges from the "liquid" and two tiny SUVs are in danger of washing over the lip of the cup. Takayama-Ogawa's ceramic sculpture is a multilayered visual pun about our dangerous reliance on this non-renewable resource. She uses glazed surfaces and unexpected forms to push the envelope for American ceramics, balancing beauty with dark humor.

Takayama-Ogawa makes teapots, cups and saucers, and other tableware, but they are rarely intended for drinking or eating. Instead, the vessels are meant to convey her views on sustainability, overconsumption, injustice, and social change. One could say that clay is in Takayama-Ogawa's DNA: teaware has its own familial and cultural associations for the artist, whose family history with ceramics dates to the sixteenth century in Tokoname, Aichi Prefecture, the location of one of Japan's Six Ancient Kilns. Her choice of ornamentation—the cobalt swirls—is a nod to the prized blue and white porcelain of China, which was traded in Europe in the sixteenth century and later widely imitated. Chinese export porcelain was brought to the colonies and considered a staple for privileged, fashionable eighteenth-century households.

When it came to her own education in ceramics, Takayama-Ogawa was mentored during the late 1980s by Ralph Bacerra at Otis College of Art and Design, where she learned technique, pattern, decoration, and glaze chemistry. She became notorious for filling her tableware forms with political messages delivered under the veil of playfulness.

When the subprime mortgage crisis reared its head across the United States in 2008, Takayama-Ogawa was already thinking about the additional factors driving socioeconomic instability. The advancing climate crisis had been on her mind since the 1970s, when she first learned about it as an undergraduate. After reading Malcolm Gladwell's book elucidating his concept of the tipping point, she made a teacup to visually articulate her take on one of the most powerful factors driving political and environmental disaster: fossil fuels.

The ramifications of our dependency on fossil fuels were acutely exacerbated by the increase of SUVs that were then flooding the auto market. The artist shaped her toylike miniatures to ironically distill some of the most ominous issues into a small scale. For this tempest in a teacup, a nod to her frustration over the dismissive and deliberate minimization of some of the most serious global threats, the swirls and swells that decorate the cup and saucer also form the golden handle. As a critic who often sounds alarms well before others pick up on the issues, Takayama-Ogawa uses tableware to serve up the messages that are hardest to swallow. —EZ

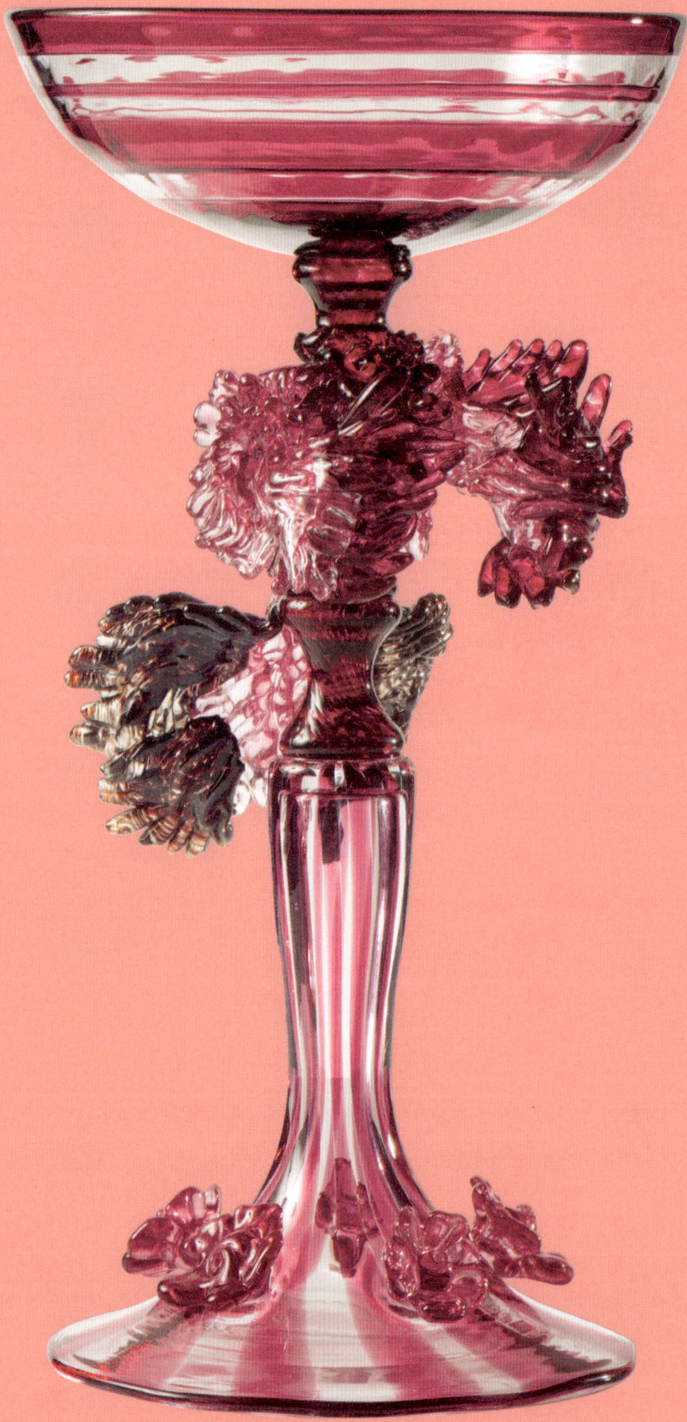

THE CUP

RUBY STRIPE

2022, **Kazuki Takizawa** (b. 1986),
Blown glass, 13½ × 7½ × 7 in. (34.3 × 19 × 17.8 cm).

Artist Kazuki Takizawa gives a new spin to the traditional Venetian-style blown-glass goblet by breathing personality into his stately forms. His expressive, oversized goblets stand tall and seem to strike poses on their elongated stems. Alongside flawless flourishes, they usually bear features that are offbeat, imperfect, and unexpected. Their bowls are sometimes bulbous, other times they are overly shallow tazzas. They can even be somewhat askew. In Takizawa's deft hands, the glass goblet is nearly a figurative sculpture.

Takizawa has said that he felt like an outsider during his early life. Born and raised by Japanese parents in Hong Kong, he attended high school in Bangkok. He went on to study glass at the University of Hawai'i at Mānoa, drawn to the duality of the material's inherent strength and fragility as well as its ability to change rapidly from liquid to solid states. For Takizawa, who experienced mood disorders and was diagnosed as bipolar, the rich metaphorical potential of glass became a focal point of his practice.

Takizawa has operated his own shop in Los Angeles, KT Glassworks, since 2018. He tells stories through his work and gives physical form to topics that are often stigmatized and therefore go unspoken, such as mental health. He makes the ugly and the dark beautiful and vibrant, expressing through his art his experiences with depression and exploring through his work color's capacity to heal, a notion central to chromotherapy. Realized in a vivid and varied palette ranging from ruby and violet to gold, each goblet he produces is a vessel that holds and reflects colored light like a bolt of energy.

He infuses Japanese cultural philosophy and Shintoism into much of his work. The artist considers the belief that deities reside within nature and objects that surround us. For instance, the idea of growing roots into the ground is reflected in his works' strong bases. Balanced on elaborate stems, he forms vessels that bulge, swell, and lean. Some take on postures of humility and bow or curtsy. Others appear as though something inside is straining to get out or stretching its arms or wings for an embrace. A vessel can be also a metaphor for emotional capacity. Those who are large vessels can take in a lot, while those who are little can only hold so much.

In the series of vessel sculptures of which this is part, the *Container* series, Takizawa morphs new elements inspired by nature with forms seen in Venetian glassware. He began the series in 2016 by shaping his stems into vines, leaves, branches, and coral. He titles each vessel after colors, gems, minerals, birds, and flowers. Some of his goblets resemble creatures with wings, tails, and feathers.

The fragility of glass is central to Takizawa's work. He plays with the idea that glass can be shattered easily and instantaneously. It is a precious material that requires delicate care and handling. Yet at the same time, ancient glass survives in our world today. The material itself has resilience, permanence, and strength that continues to fascinate and captivate. —EZ

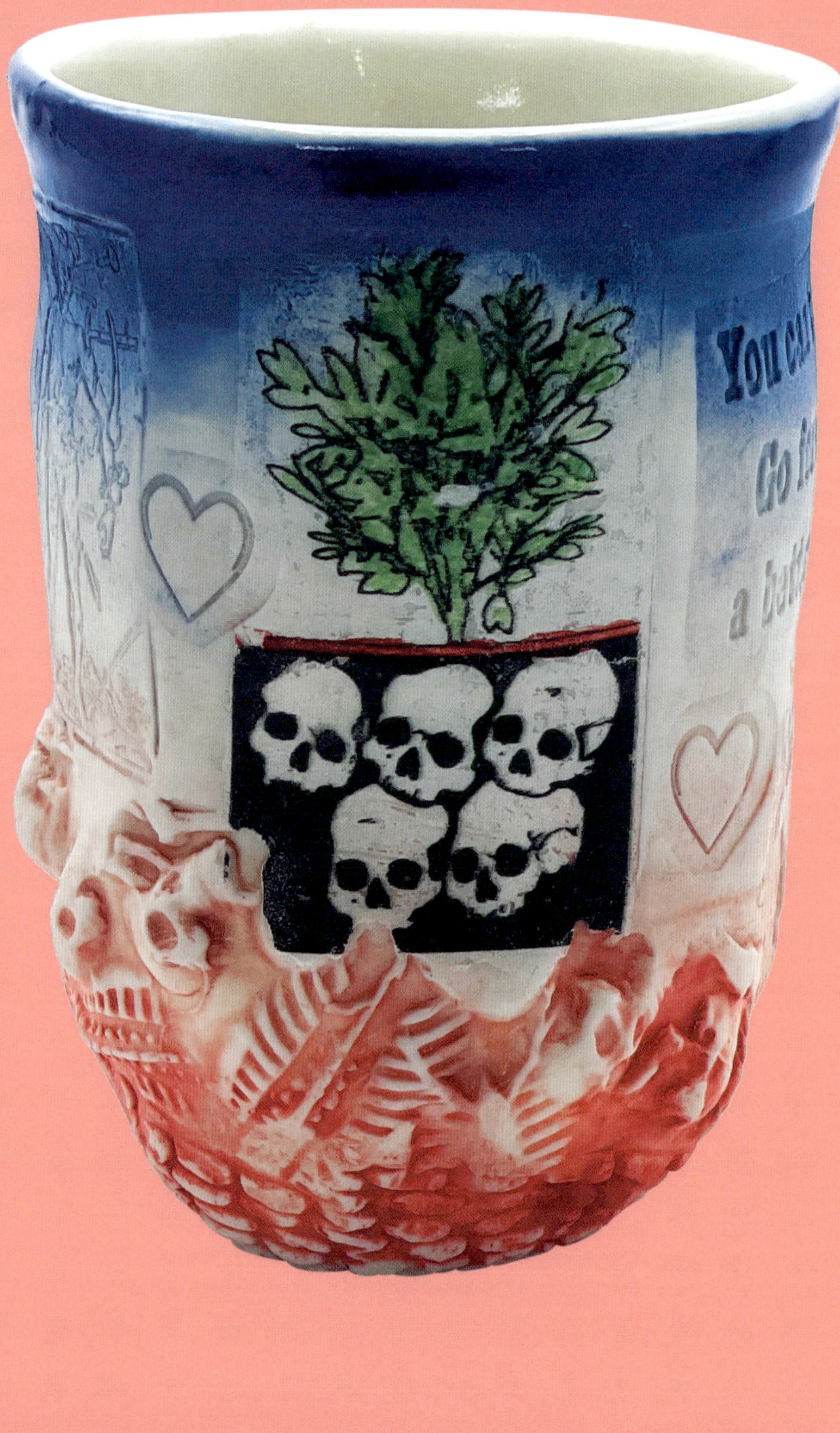

EHREN TOOL on THE CUP

one of thousands (untitled), 2024, **Ehren Tool** (b. 1970),
Glazed porcelain, 5½ × 4 in. (12.5 × 10.2 cm).

I just make cups. Why cups? For me, peace is the only adequate war memorial. My cups are a small but appropriate scale to deal with immense and complicated issues from my hand to your hand to some hand hundreds of thousands of years in the future. Most of the work I make is considered dark. Many of the images on the cups are very disturbing. But as dark and disturbing as some of them are, there is an optimism in my making them. Making cups implies there will be people to drink from them and something to drink. My hope is that my cups can be touchstones to speak about unspeakable things. War is murder and military sexual trauma is rape. Here is the appropriate place to speak about these things. My hope is that it will be with a trusted or new friend over a beverage. Another artist once said, "Art is the possibility of love between strangers." I love the idea of putting a cup down and someone picking it up thousands of years later and enjoying the cup and the beverage as if I had poured the drink and handed the cup to them myself.

My cups are flawed and heavy, like me. I'm not sure that objects have auras. I'm not sure what the empirical difference is between a machine-made and a handmade cup, but it is important to me that my cups are made by me for the hands of others.

Returning to the civilian world after serving in the Marine Corps and taking part in Operation Desert Storm was difficult for me. Using the GI Bill, I staggered into college and eventually ceramics. I didn't want to talk, but I definitely had some things to work through. Ceramics seemed like the right material and cups the appropriate objects to make. Clay is very immediate. Clay records the compressions, the cuts, tears, scratches, marks, and impressions. Once clay goes through the fire, it can last hundreds of thousands of years. Likewise, war is immediate and what is done in war echoes through eternity. I hate the quote "one death is a tragedy, a million is a statistic." The war dead are an incalculable tragedy. There is no way to describe, explain, or encompass the impact of war. But my cups seem like the correct scale to talk about war.

All of my cups and the images on them mean something to me. What I think is more important is the feeling they will evoke when they are in the hands of someone you already know, love, and trust. Maybe in that person's hands a conversation may come up that had not before. To be demonized or idolized for something you did or didn't do in a context you find difficult to explain is painful. It often seems easier not to talk, but that also has a cost. My hope is that my cups will travel through time, hand to hand, bringing people together for stories and beverages that relieve regrets and remorse and inspire relief and positivity.

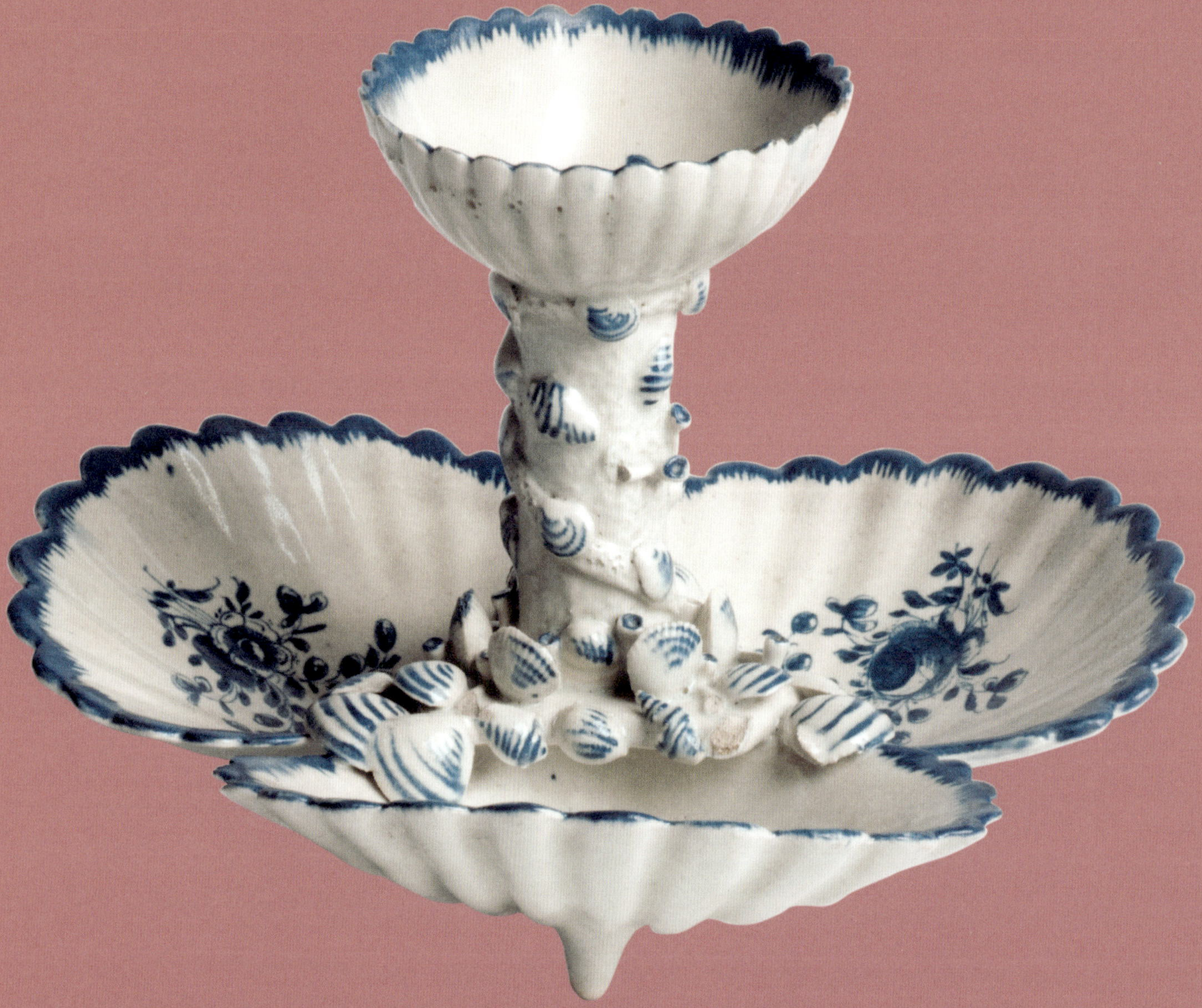

THE PLATE

PICKLE STAND

1770–72, **American China Manufactory** (active 1770–1772),
Soft-paste porcelain with underglaze blue decoration, 5⅛ × 7 in. (13 × 17.8 cm),
Philadelphia Museum of Art, Gift of a seventh-generation Philadelphian, 2014, 2014-166-1.

Maybe it's the diminutive stature or maybe it's the intricate shells and other bits encrusted on the stalk. Whatever it is, this pickle stand beckons for a closer, more serious inspection. Made in Philadelphia just before the American Revolution, it is composed of seventy-two individual elements carefully arranged on a structure just over five inches high. It was likely a pair with another, which is in the collection of the Brooklyn Museum.

Today, the form is not familiar—and quite curious. The scallop shells and top bowl were intended to be filled with pickled and sugared comfits—nuts and fruit such as cucumbers and watermelon rind—for the dessert course of a midday meal. The two-tiered design and its marine-themed decoration were closely modeled after those made in England. Such intricate ornament was best conceived in porcelain, the most refined ceramic material known and one that could hold detail.

The Staffordshire, England–born potter Gousse Bonnin and Philadelphian George Anthony Morris partnered in 1769 to open a porcelain manufactory in Philadelphia, which they named the American China Manufactory. Their announcement followed on the identification of kaolin clay specimens from New Castle County, Pennsylvania (now Delaware). They advertised in March 1770 in *The South-Carolina Gazette*, announcing that "Workmen skilled in the different Branches of Throwing, Turning, Moulding, Pressing, and Handling . . . [and] served their Apprenticeships in England, France, or Germany" should apply for "Passages to Philadelphia," where they would find immediate employ. The high-level skills demanded of the workmen—and perhaps some women—can account for the array the enterprise produced: wares for the table and dressing in a variety of shapes, surface treatments (including molded floral and quilted patterns), and painted decoration.

Almost two centuries later, in the 1960s, interest in Bonnin and Morris's enterprise expanded. An excavation of the manufactory site unearthed sherds, kiln furniture, and saggers (ceramic containers used to protect pottery in the kiln) that tell an even deeper story. By 2001, nineteen intact wares were known, including six pickle stands. For a 2008 exhibition at the Philadelphia Museum of Art, ceramic artist Michelle Erickson reproduced the pickle stand. That process confirmed that the three shell dishes on the bottom tier were slip cast—not molded—from an actual scallop shell, *Pecten maximus*. The smaller cockle and scallop shells were press molded—also from natural examples—while the tube shells were hand rolled.

Shells are somewhat of a double entendre as the central ornament on porcelain, which takes its name from having the same texture of the Italian cowrie shell or porcellana. And though the Philadelphia porcelain-making enterprise succeeded for less than two years, the extraordinary skill of many artisans is packed into this diminutive pickle stand—a most ambitious undertaking for this early manufactory. —AK

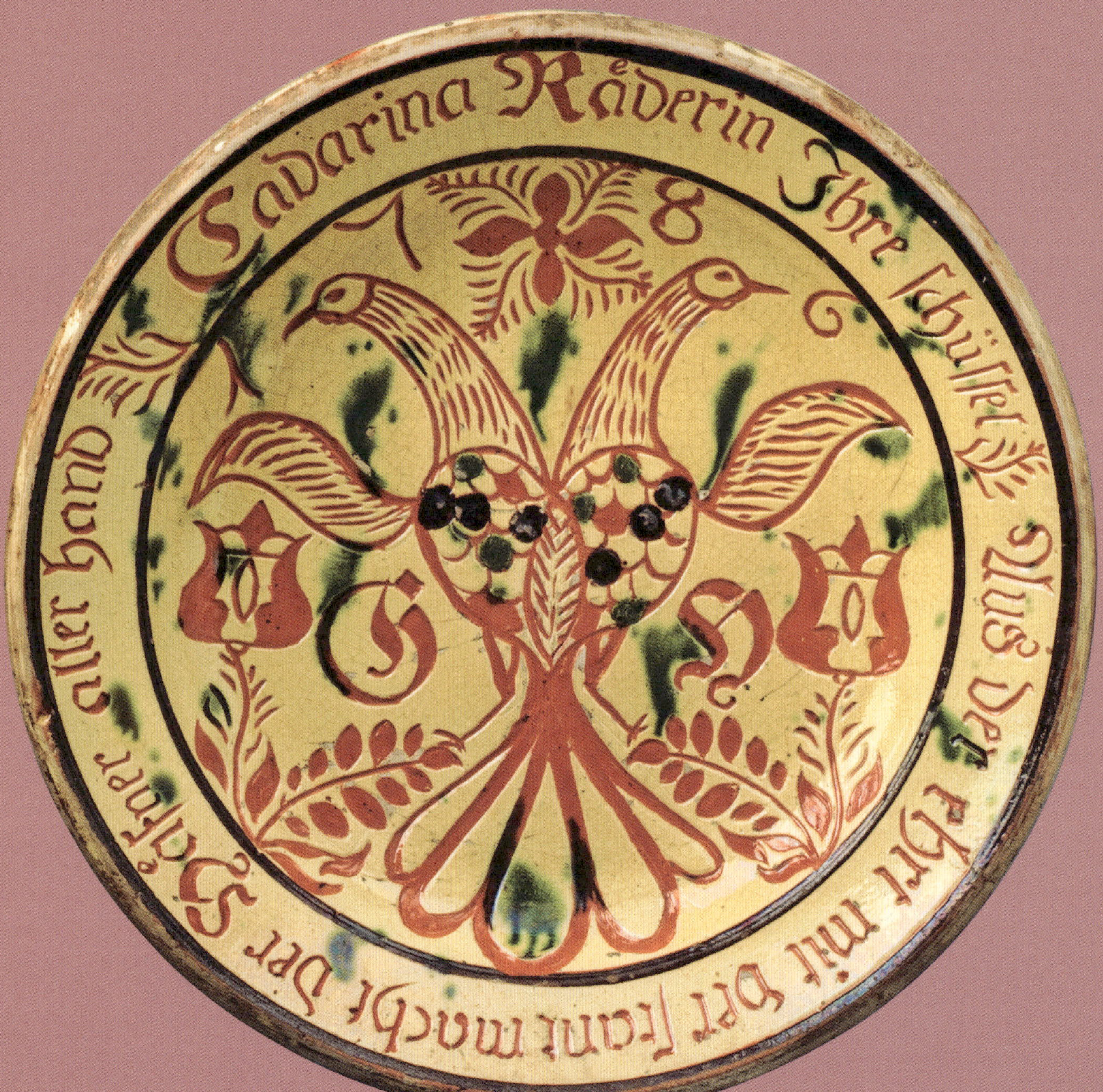

THE PLATE

DISH

1786, **Georg Hübner** (1757–1828),
Lead-glazed red earthenware with slip, copper oxide, manganese dioxide, and sgraffito decoration,
2⅛ × 12⅝ in. (5.4 × 32.1 cm), Philadelphia Museum of Art, Gift of John T. Morris, 1900. 1900-21.

Far from being just any old dish, this is among the earliest and most elaborate works by Pennsylvania's Germanic potters, who transformed red earthenware plates into canvases for folk imagery and witticisms.

Pennsylvania was ripe for the blossoming of this tradition. The colony's British, Irish, and European colonists found that the soil of the Delaware River Valley was rich in white and red clay. The more plentiful red clay (which achieved its color from iron in the soil) was fired at low temperatures to make sturdy, utilitarian wares. White clay (also called kaolin) was fired at high temperatures to produce thinly potted, translucent porcelain and is the main ingredient of the viscous clay called slip that covers the surface of this dish. By the early 1700s, Philadelphia's potters—both English- and German-speaking—made red earthenware vessels for storing and serving food. When Pennsylvania's colonists rallied around the concept of American independence in the 1770s, those who hailed from Germanic regions began to reinforce their cultural identity. They broadened their impact by moving outside of the city and using language, religion, and iconography—such as the intricate folk ornament on this dish—to keep their culture relevant and flourishing.

The charger-sized dish started life humbly—as a ball of dense, damp red clay. A potter vigorously kneaded and batted it, adding water, powdered clay (grog), and sand to improve the texture and workability and to mitigate shrinkage during firing. Once flattened into a slab, the potter laid it over a wooden mold to give the dish its shape—in this case, a wide rim around a shallow well. The edge was trimmed or shaped and the face of the dish was then covered with the slurry slip made from a mixture of kaolin, feldspar, and other materials that gave it color and consistency.

The decoration was either drawn and traced onto the slip-covered surface with a stylus or drawn directly onto the slip with a bladderlike pouch of charcoal. Proving that artisanal techniques were shared not only from one generation to the next but also across cultures, the Pennsylvania German potters used the ancient technique of sgraffito, exposing the red clay by removing the coating of white slip with any number of blunt-ended tools. Dabs of metallic oxides of copper (green) and manganese (purple) added more color to the design.

Slip-decorated dishes made by Georg Hübner in Montgomery and later Chester counties show him to be the finest potter in southeastern Pennsylvania in the 1700s. Hübner's compositions on these dishes, made for display only, combine accomplished versions of Germanic iconography with writing executed in the familiarly Germanic fraktur (or broken) font.

The date "1786" is inscribed at the top of the well, and Hübner boldly signed this dish with the elegantly formed "GH" framing the eagles. The verse inscribed around the rim exalts the skill of the potter, translating to "From the earth with sense the potter makes everything. Cadarina Raeder, her dish." Hübner's choice of German for this verse attests to his devotion to language as a means to provide the community with its ethnic identity.
—AK

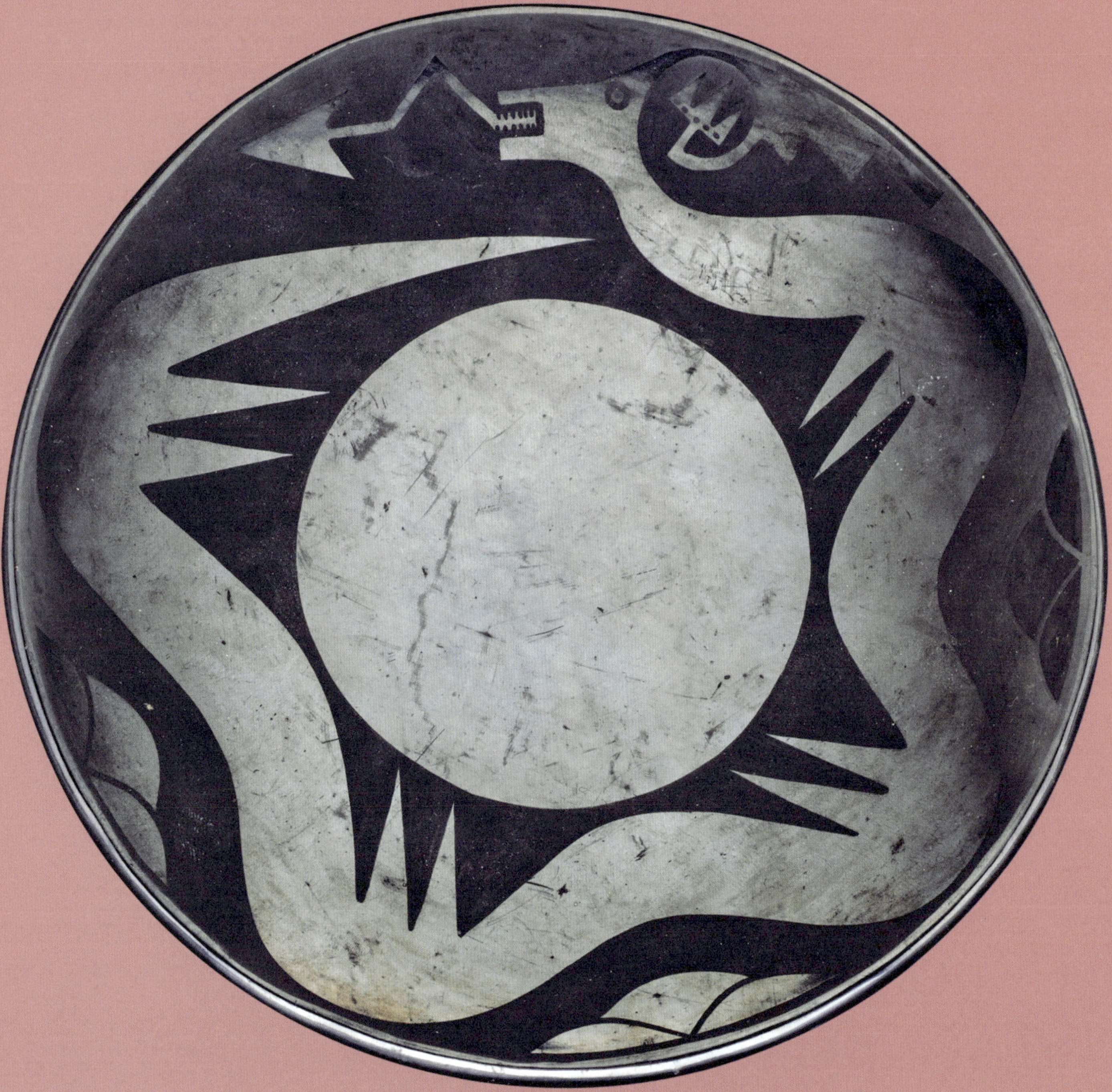

THE PLATE

PLATE WITH AVANYU DESIGN

1954, **Maria Poveka Martinez** (Po-Woh-Geh-Owingeh/San Ildefonso Pueblo, 1887–1980) and **Santana Roybal Martinez** (Po-Woh-Geh-Owingeh/San Ildefonso Pueblo, 1910–2002), Black-on-black ceramic, 1⅛ × 9⅞ in. (3 × 25 cm), National Museum of the American Indian, Smithsonian Institution, Washington, DC, 26/4234.

By the 1950s, black-on-black pottery was synonymous with the name Maria Martinez. The famed San Ildefonso ceramist, who began creating this style of pottery in the 1910s, mobilized the ancient method of hand coiling clay to create intricate forms, and her husband, Julian Martinez, painted them until his death in 1943. Together, the Martinezes developed this style of burnished blackware, a marked departure from traditional, polychrome pottery of San Ildefonso Pueblo. Matte paint covers the highly polished base, articulating a duality—positive and negative forms—not through color but finish.

Avanyu, the Tewa guardian of water, rings this plate's circumference, its body composed of soft curves with spikes jutting toward the center, referencing the deity's plumes. An arrow of lightning is released from behind clenched teeth as a plea to the ancestors to send rain from the sky. Water is life. It nourishes plants, encouraging them to grow, be harvested, and served on such a plate, only to repeat the cycle each season. Water also sustains bodies, animal and human alike. A being of transition, the serpent traverses along waterways and between the earth's surface and its depths. This water serpent was a motif that the Martinezes returned to many times to adorn their black-on-black pottery.

Maria Martinez was a leader in the development of Pueblo pottery through sharing knowledge about ceramics within her family, community, and other kinship networks, which helped revitalize the market for Native craft in the Pueblos. The plate is a collaboration between Maria and her daughter-in-law, Santana Roybal Martinez, who painted its surface. Maria and Julian Martinez had trained their oldest son, Adam, in ceramics. Then Adam married Santana, a woman from another prominent family in the San Ildefonso Pueblo. Santana had learned traditional pottery skills from her maternal grandmother, Pino Martinez; her mother, Alfonsita; and her aunt Tonita Roybal. During the early years of Adam and Santana's marriage, Julian trained Santana in the art of pottery painting. After Julian passed away in 1943, Santana painted for Maria, working with her on commissions that include this plate, which was purchased by the Indian Arts and Crafts Board in 1955 during the Pueblo Indian Arts and Crafts Market.

Ceramic plates and vessels provide critical points of connection between all things, as Avanyu's presence reminds us. Inspired by this idea, the artist Rose B. Simpson reimagined her 1985 El Camino as a vessel painted in black-on-black. Raised in Española, New Mexico, the "Lowrider Capital of the World," located just outside of the Santa Clara Pueblo, Simpson combined her knowledge of custom lowriders and ceramics—two modes of craftsmanship that might seem estranged at first—to design a car named in honor of Maria Martinez as a driving force behind Pueblo art in the twentieth century. Like jars and plates that hold and move food, Simpson uses her El Camino to help harvest and transport squash, corn, and beans—the "Three Sisters." Painted with designs that evoke the history of Española as a landscape and storied place, Simpson reminds us that we build identity through many types of vessels often individuated by handwork. —CG

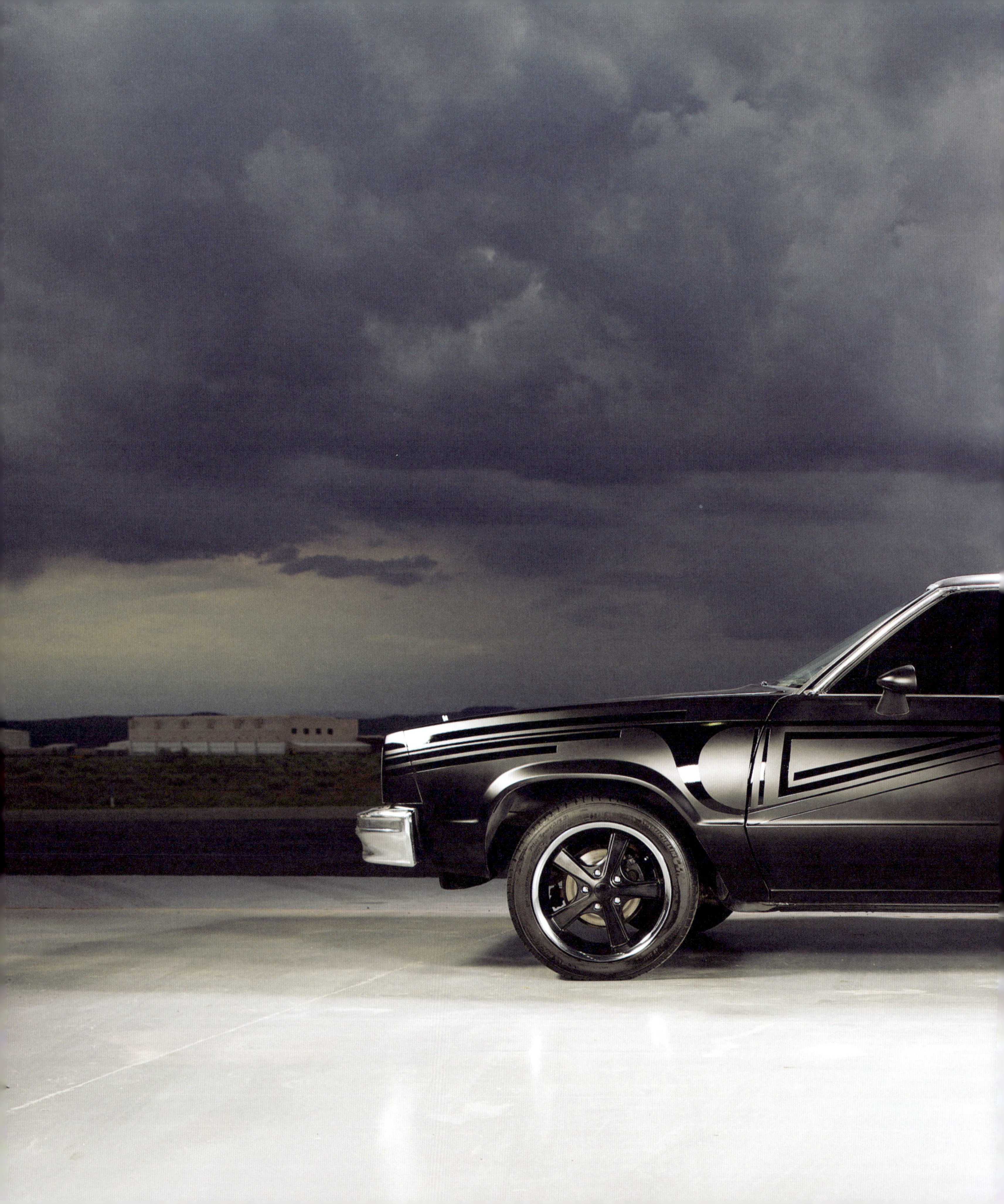

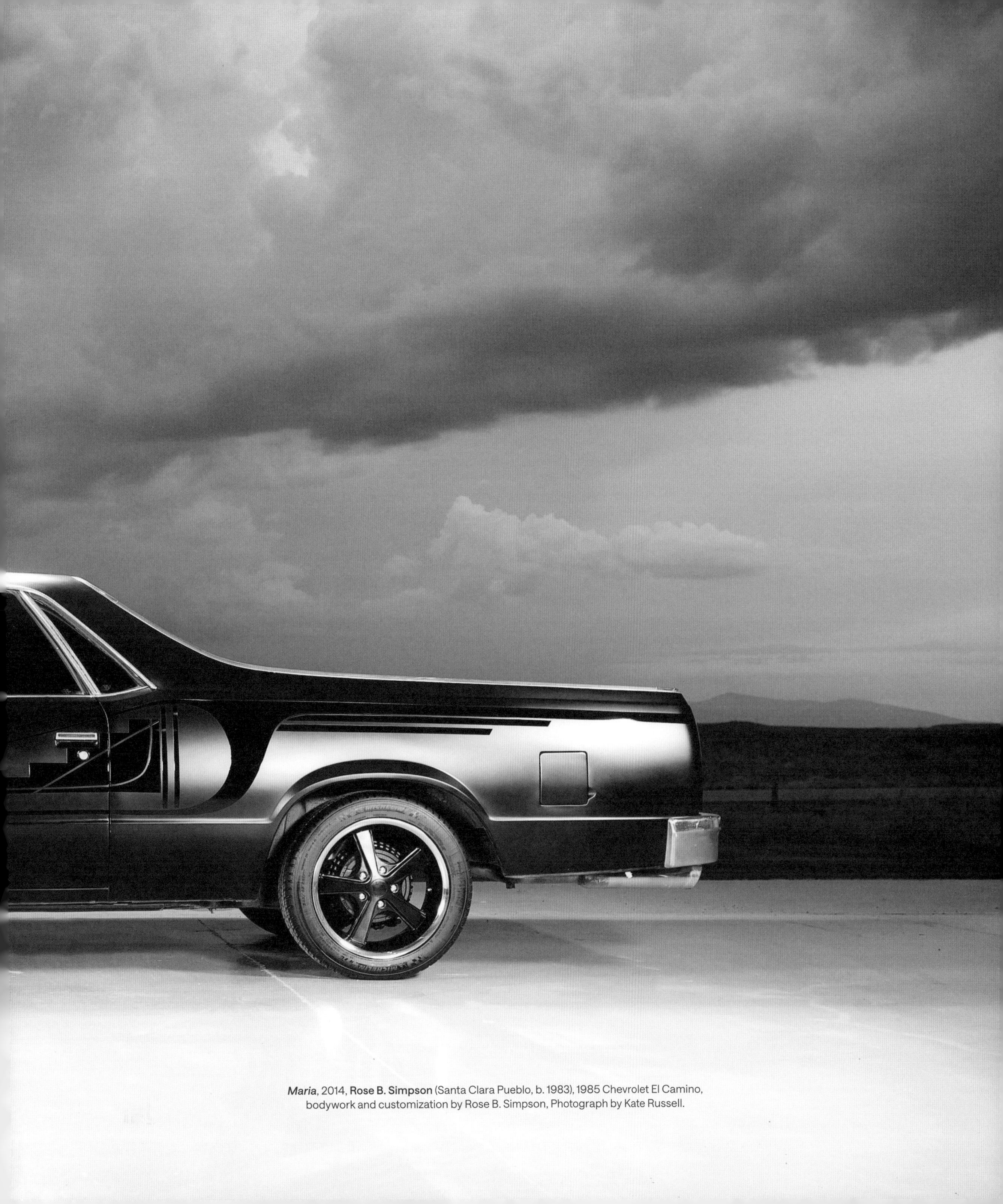

Maria, 2014, **Rose B. Simpson** (Santa Clara Pueblo, b. 1983), 1985 Chevrolet El Camino, bodywork and customization by Rose B. Simpson, Photograph by Kate Russell.

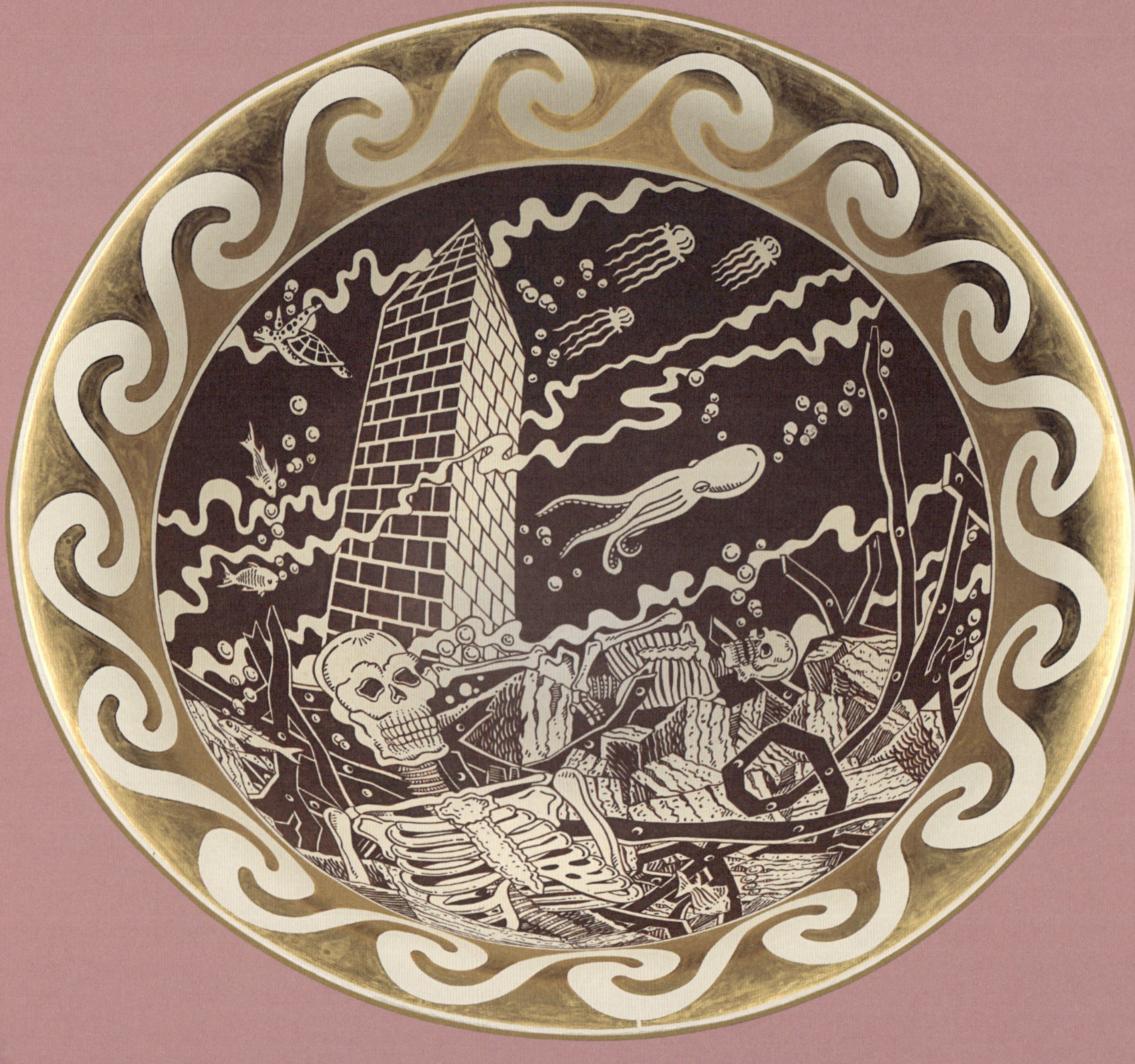

THE PLATE

NEW GENESIS

2025, **Diego Romero** (Cochiti Pueblo, b. 1964),
Ceramic with gold luster, 5⅛ × 16¾ in. (12.7 × 42.6 cm),
Smithsonian American Art Museum, Washington, DC, Gift of Todd Wingate and Steven Cason
in honor of *Handwork: Celebrating American Craft 2026*, 2025.29.

New Genesis, a charger by ceramist Diego Romero, depicts a postapocalyptic world where civilization has collapsed underwater and marine species reclaim the planet. The Washington Monument is toppled alongside skeletons entangled in twisted metal—remnants of a deconstructed and destroyed society. Romero summarizes: "Sharks, jellyfish, squid, and turtles continue life swimming around; they are the reemerging of life after a catastrophic extinction event, now followed by this rebirth. Hubris is the word that comes to mind."[1] All neatly served on a plate. *New Genesis* represents the continuation of a series about postapocalyptic landscapes that Romero revisited from an earlier vessel, *Apocalypto,* which featured a half-submerged Statue of Liberty as an iconic symbol of a civilization in ruin.

If Romero's goal is to be recognized as a provocateur in the ceramics field, then he has succeeded dramatically. His pottery—in the form of domestic items that evoke comfort and nourishment, such as bowls, plates, and cups—seduces viewers into confronting what they'd rather ignore. His hand-formed vessels depict scenes of violence, colonialism, cultural trauma, and apocalypse rendered in such exquisite detail that the beauty forces audiences to linger over images they might otherwise reject. This is Romero's artistic gambit: using masterful technique to mask bitter truths about indigeneity, environmental destruction, and colonial legacy, creating a sublimity and a sensory assault that operates on both global and tribal scales.

As a young boy, Romero and his brother collected comic books, spending hours studying their pages. Diego taught himself to draw heroes and villains in the brisk, boldly graphic style of their illustrators. These superheroes would later resurface on his vessels, often with Indigenous features. Comfortable with his dual identity—descending from a Cochiti Pueblo father and German Irish mother—Romero enrolled at the Institute of American Indian Arts in Santa Fe to explore his "half-Indian" heritage. There he learned traditional pottery making from distinguished Hopi master Otellie Loloma, who taught him the hand-coiling technique he continues to use today.

As a graduate student at UCLA, Romero began to create narratives rich in intellectual content. Although he draws from his ancestral past for method and motifs, frequently borrowing decorative elements from prehistoric Mimbres and Anasazi pottery, he emphasizes that his updated themes address contemporary issues of "colonialism, resilience, and social and environmental justice from an indigenous perspective, and the broader narrative of the human condition and our shared humanity. . . . Because, as artists, we have to use our voice."[2]

Developing his professional career in Santa Fe as a member of the Cochiti Pueblo, Romero's narratives have evolved over the last decade, digesting and reinventing traditions that inform his practice. The narratives providing the greatest emotional punch depict violence against Indigenous peoples by various villains operating across time and territory: Spanish conquistadores as the first colonizers, missionary fathers as converters through enslavement and torture, and the military and government claiming Manifest Destiny and forcing tribes onto reservations, condemning them to lives of poverty, disease, and alcohol abuse.

Through his provocative vessels, Romero transforms ceramic tradition into a cultural reckoning, proving that the most beautiful art can carry the heaviest truths.
—JL

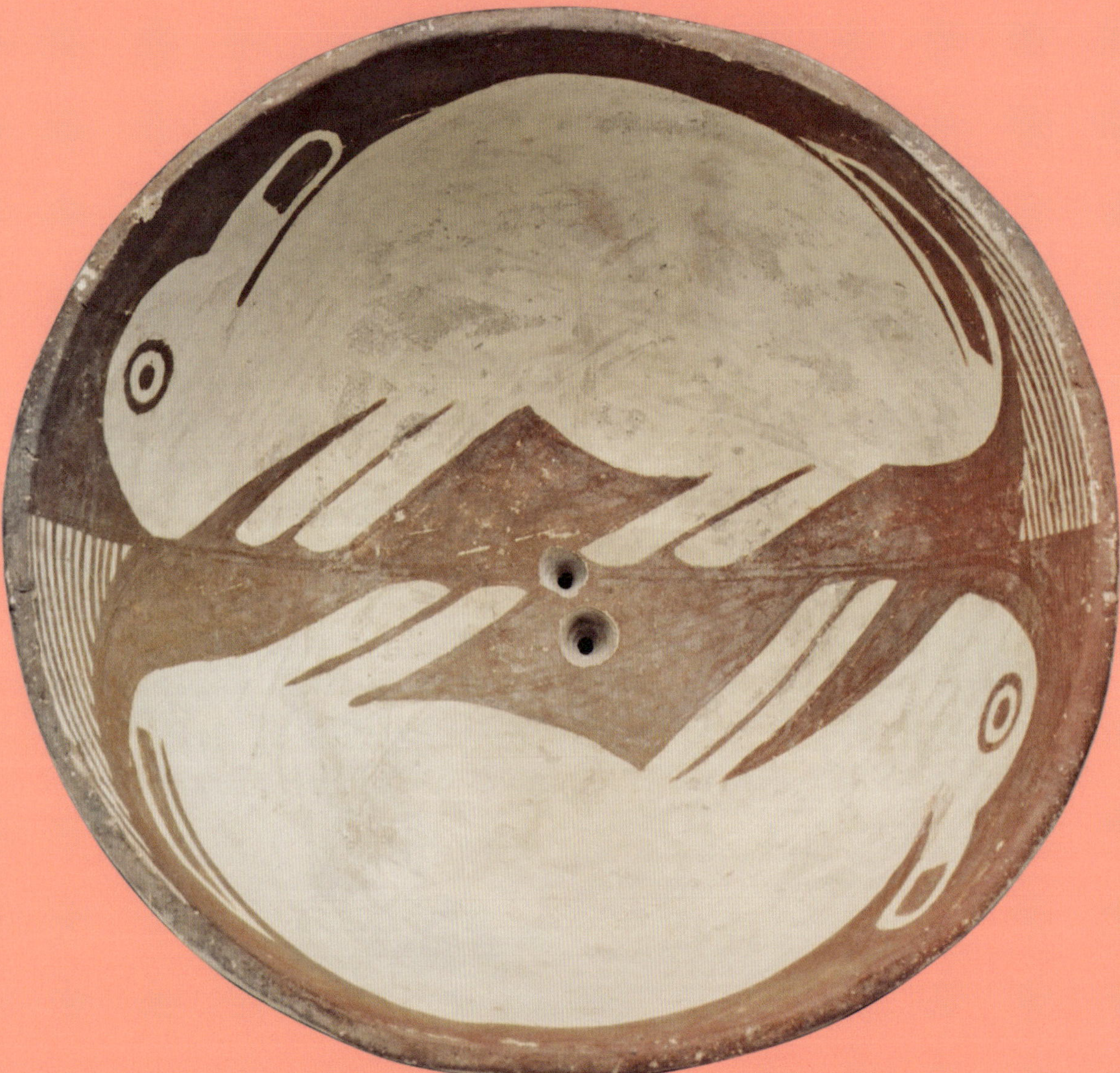

THE BOWL

BOWL WITH TWO RABBITS

Mid 9th–12th century, **Unidentified artist (Mimbres, New Mexico)**,
Clay and slip, 2½ × 5⅜ in. (6.4 × 13.7 cm), Metropolitan Museum of Art, New York,
the Michael C. Rockefeller Memorial Collection, Purchase, Nelson A. Rockefeller Gift, 1964. 1978.412.118.

This distinctive bowl originates from the Mimbres Valley of New Mexico, where artisans lived and produced these striking ceramic works between 1000 and 1150. Like most ceramics from the Southwest, this piece was crafted from clay and slip, likely harvested from the natural landscape of the region. However, what makes this particular bowl unusual for the Mimbres people is the use of brown and white slip instead of the traditional black-and-white palette for which the Mimbres are best known. This variation sets it apart from the majority of Mimbres pottery and speaks to the artistic diversity within their tradition.

A common practice for artists, both ancestral and contemporary, is to depict the environment around them, and this round-bottomed bowl is no exception. Painted on the interior of this vessel are two jackrabbits. These creatures are easily identifiable by their long legs and black-tipped ears and tails. Rabbits have been significant animals among Pueblo communities for millennia, appearing in petroglyphs, oral traditions, and even modern-day regalia. For the Mimbres people, these animals were not only a vital food source but also an important symbol in their artistic and cultural expressions.

The depiction of animals in Mimbres pottery often follows a distinct visual convention. In this case, the two jackrabbits are positioned in a circular fashion, seemingly chasing each other around the bowl's interior. This parallel arrangement is intentional, emphasizing the importance of balance. It was a common artistic strategy among Mimbres potters to place large, dynamic animal figures in such a way that they split the design space evenly.

Because of jackrabbits' wide territory, they appear as cultural heroes, omens, and signs in various tribal traditions, not just those of the Mimbres. Among Pueblo communities, jackrabbits are particularly noted for their family-oriented behavior. This characteristic may also have contributed to their frequent representation on Mimbres bowls, which were often used by multiple generations within a household. The significance of rabbits extends into contemporary traditions as well, as seen in Katishtya (or San Felipe Pueblo), where annual rabbit hunts and dances continue to take place. These practices underscore the enduring relationship between Pueblo peoples and the natural world, reinforcing the historical continuity of their traditions.

A notable feature of this bowl is the pair of drilled holes at its base. These perforations were likely not part of the original design. Instead, they were probably made later, possibly to facilitate mounting the piece for display. This suggests that the bowl, at some point in its history, transitioned from a functional object into a piece meant for exhibition. —TL

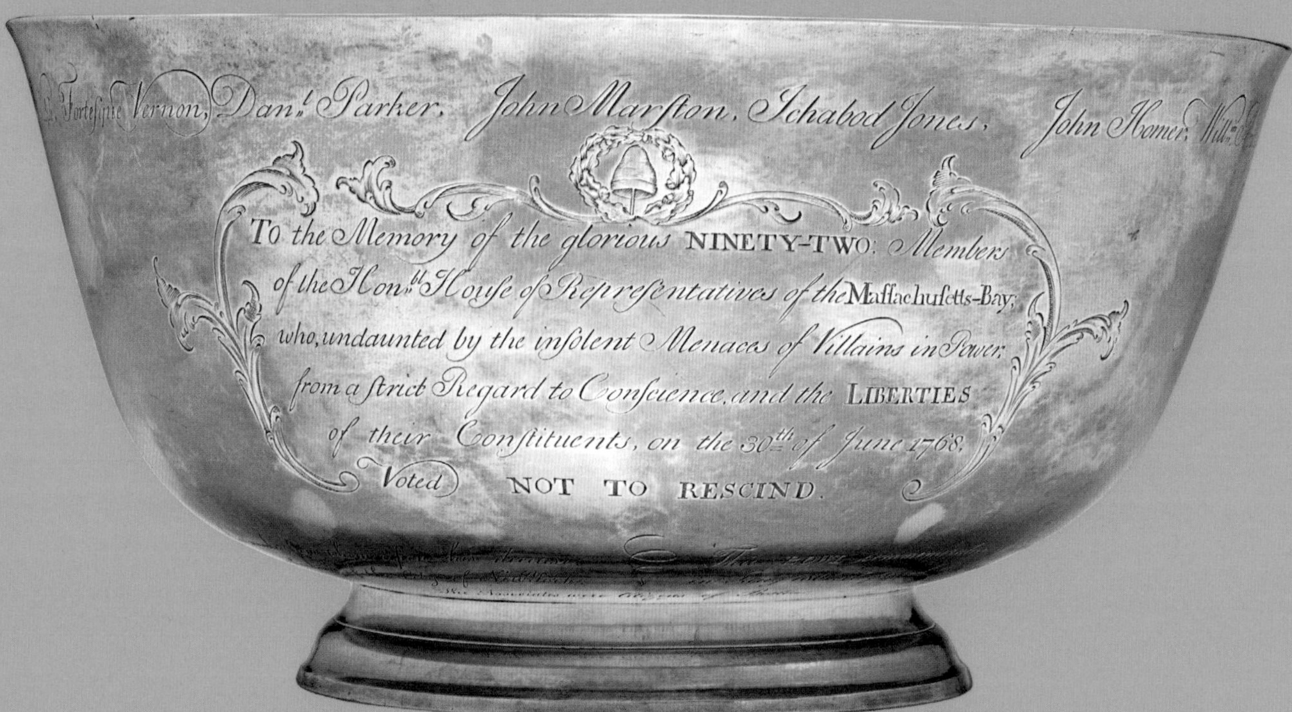
Dan.l Parker, John Marston, Ichabod Jones, John Homer,
To the Memory of the glorious NINETY-TWO: Members
of the Hon.ble House of Representatives of the Massachusetts-Bay;
who, undaunted by the insolent Menaces of Villains in Power,
from a strict Regard to Conscience, and the LIBERTIES
of their Constituents, on the 30th of June 1768.
Voted NOT TO RESCIND.

THE BOWL

SONS OF LIBERTY BOWL

1768, **Paul Revere Jr.** (1734–1818), Silver, 5½ × 11 in. (14 × 28 cm), Museum of Fine Arts, Boston, Museum purchase with funds donated by contribution and the Francis Bartlett Donation of 1912, 49.45.

This silver punch bowl of royal size immediately sparks images of conviviality. But in fact, the bowl was commissioned by the Sons of Liberty to memorialize an act of cunning disobedience against King George III less than a decade before the start of the War of Independence.

In 1767, British Parliament passed the Townshend Acts, placing high taxes on lead, paper, glass, tea, and other commodities imported to the American colonies from England. Speaker Thomas Cushing, on behalf of the Massachusetts House, issued an official letter to the other colonies declaring these taxes to be "infringements of their natural and constitutional rights" due to the colonies' lack of representation in the British Parliament.[1] Pressed by British politicians to retract the letter, the Massachusetts House took a vote. The outcome was celebrated on the bowl. Framed by scrollwork topped with a liberty cap, the famed silversmith Paul Revere Jr. inscribed a dedication to these representatives "who, undaunted by the insolent Menaces of Villains of Power from a Strict Regard to Conscious, and the LIBERTIES of their Constituents, on the 30th of June 1768 voted NOT TO RESCIND."

The Sons of Liberty, the secret organization to which Revere and the patrons of the bowl belonged, was devoted to the protection of personal liberties and central to the American Revolution. The Boston-based group adopted the views of British politician John Wilkes, whose radical writings about natural liberties inspired political change among many of the group's members, including John Hancock and Samuel Adams. Wilkes's most inflammatory writing criticizing the king was published in 1763 as essay "No. 45" in *The North Briton*, leading to an arrest but failed conviction. The number forty-five then became a symbol of revolt against the government and was adopted as a sacred number within the Sons of Liberty's ceremonies. The bowl's engraving features the phrase "No. 45 Wilkes & Liberty" within a round cartouche, along with flags referencing the Magna Carta and Bill of Rights and a paper with "general warrents," torn in an act of refusal.

Fifteen Boston merchants and craftsmen, all members of the Sons of Liberty, commissioned Revere to create the punch bowl in honor of this event. He was one of the most celebrated metalsmiths in the region, and an active church member, soldier, Freemason, and member of the group. Over the course of a month, Revere hand-raised the bowl and engraved its passage and other ornamental emblems, including the clear references to liberty and political freedom. In an act of superior craftsmanship, Revere formed the bowl to weigh exactly forty-five ounces and hold forty-five gills of liquid,[2] aligning with the organization's secret number. While punch bowls were rare in Boston at this time, one can imagine this one's use among gatherings as the Sons of Liberty plotted protests and devised political actions leading to the war. Alongside the Declaration of Independence and the Constitution, the Sons of Liberty bowl is one of the nation's three most important historical documents. —CG

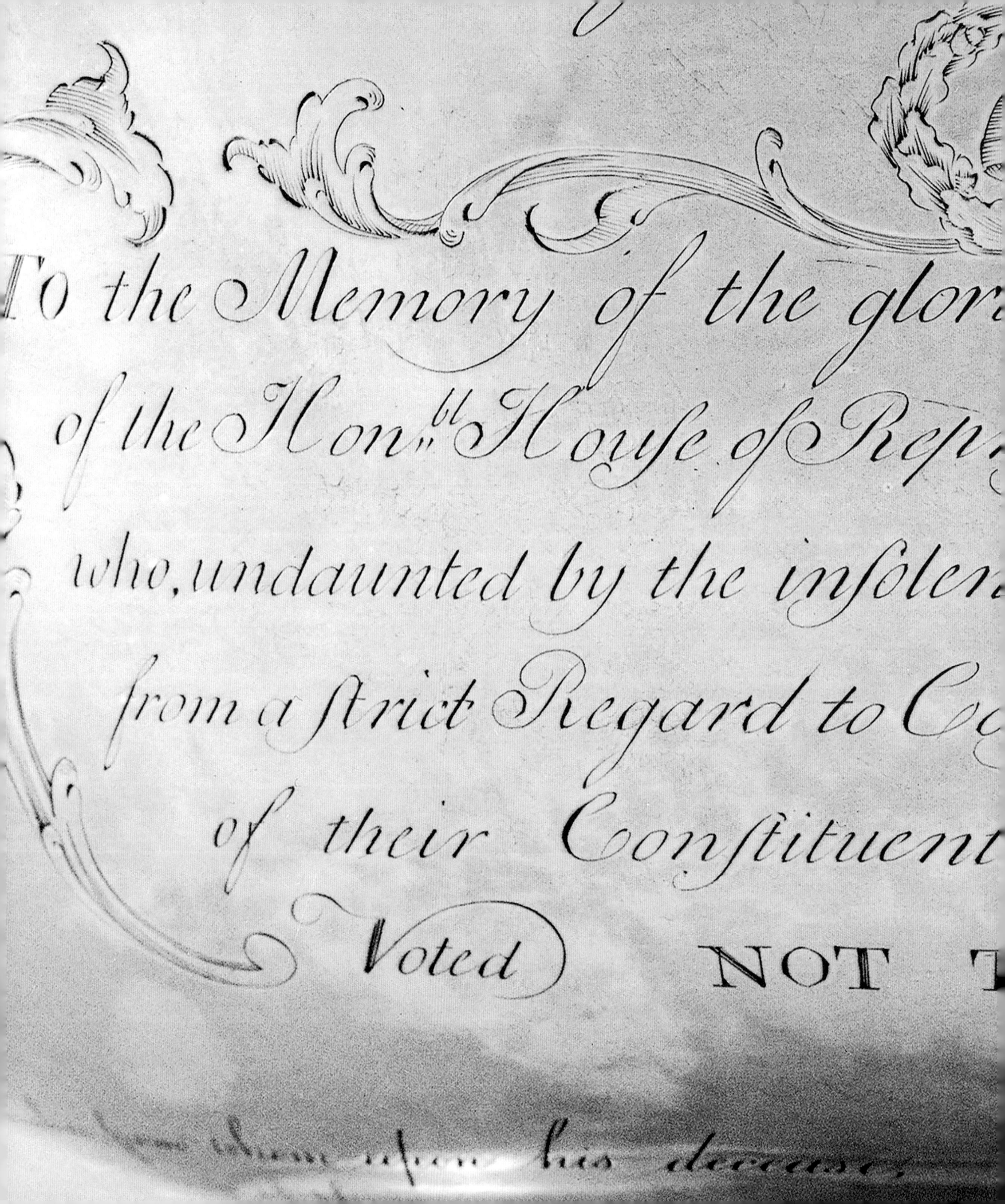
To the Memory of the glori
of the Hon.ble House of Rep
who, undaunted by the insolen
from a Strict Regard to Co
of their Constituent
Voted
NOT T
upon his decease

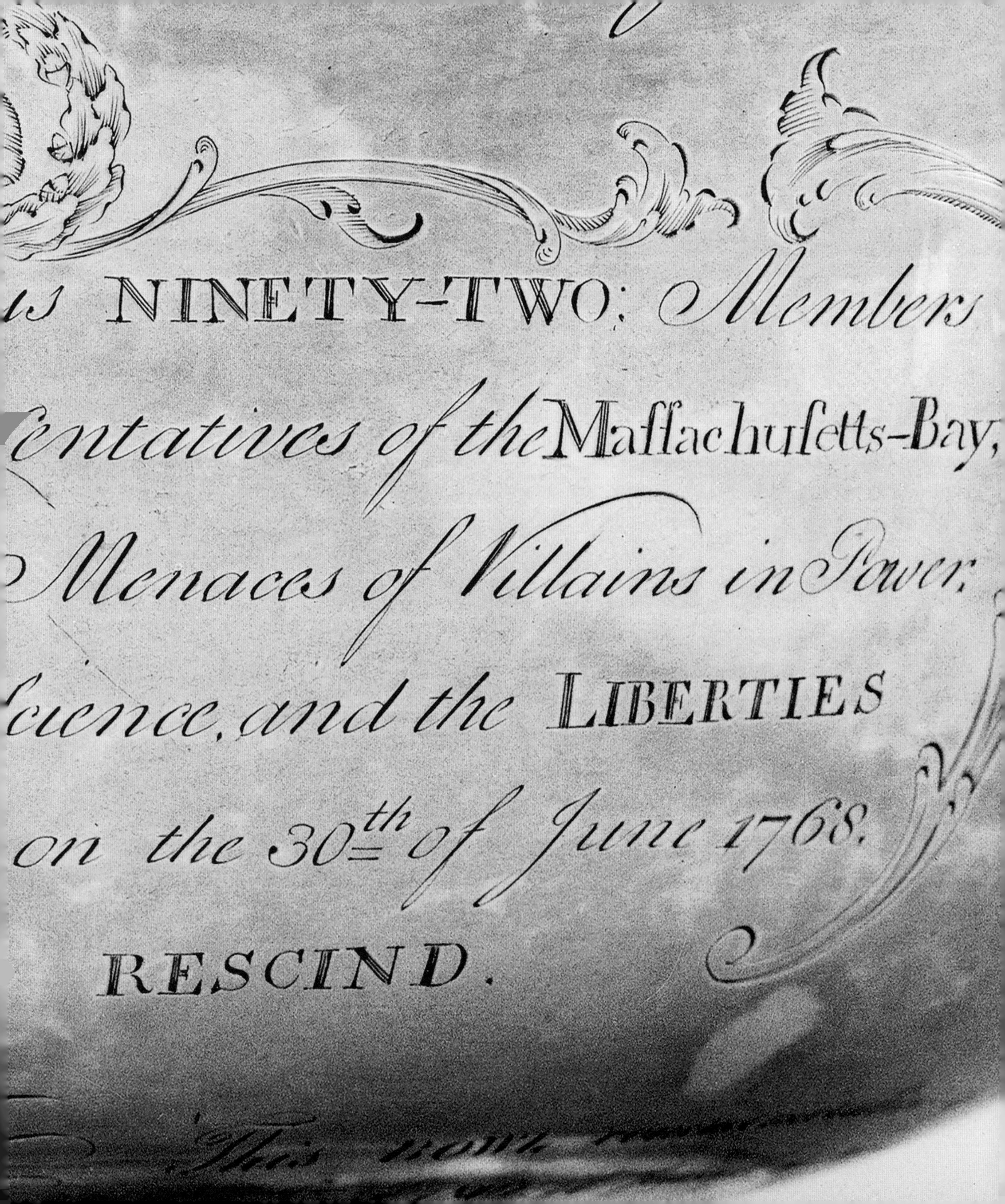
s NINETY-TWO: Members
entatives of the Maſſachuſetts-Bay,
Menaces of Villains in Power.
cience, and the LIBERTIES
on the 30th of June 1768.
RESCIND.

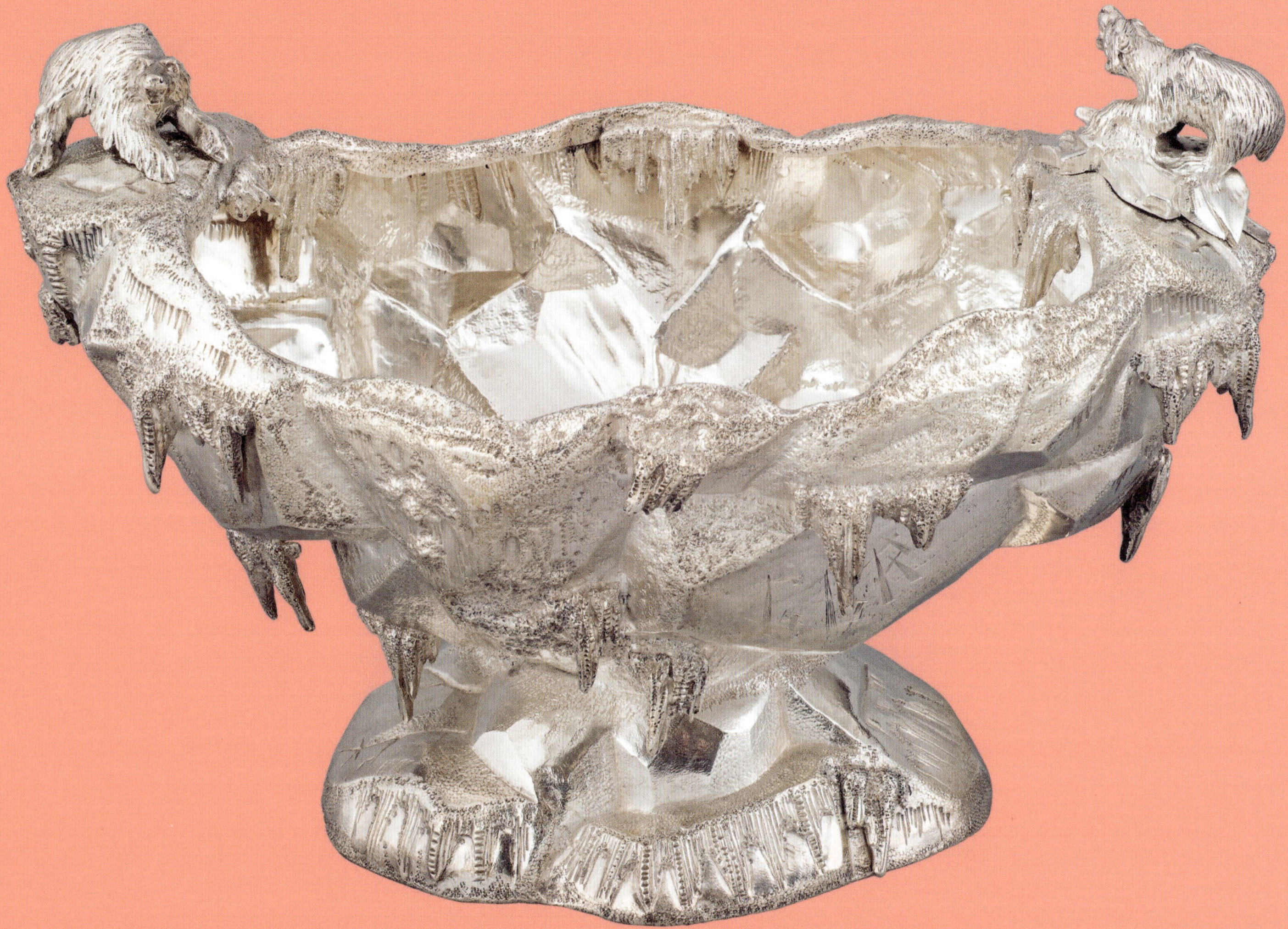

THE BOWL

ICE BOWL

1871, **Gorham Manufacturing Company** (est. 1831), Silver, 6 ¾ × 10 ¾ in. (17.2 × 27.3 cm), High Museum of Art, Atlanta, Virginia Carroll Crawford Collection, 1990.85.

Two polar bears crouch and growl as they cling to sheets of floating ice, completing an iconic Arctic tableau (see detail, page 6). Imagine this bowl piled high with cubes and chips of ice, transforming a dining table into a miniaturized iceberg. As ice melts inside the bowl and chills the silver, a film of frost forms on the outside, exaggerating the smooth, hand-polished planes of the silvered iceberg and its jagged clusters of icicles, which were chased by hand. Water droplets concentrate at these points, dripping down the icicles and onto the table, creating an exotic spectacle when illuminated by candlelight. Accompanying this bowl was a spoon designed to look like a harpoon, with a polar bear entangled in rope along the handle. Conceived under the direction of lead designer Thomas J. Pairpoint, this theatrical ice bowl was one of the most popular items created by Gorham Manufacturing Company in the 1870s.

Ice harvesting was an important industry across North America in the nineteenth century. Workers cut sheets from rivers that were so clean, the ice shavings could be put directly into drinking water. At the start of the century, a Bostonian named Frederic Tudor developed technology to harvest, transport, market, and sell ice to affluent clients as far-flung as England and India, initiating the international ice trade and the development of iceboxes as a form of early refrigeration. Ice pitchers, buckets, bowls, tongs, and platters made from a range of materials—particularly frosted glass and silver—became popular toward the end of the nineteenth century. To serve ice or ice cream, the newest fashion, at one's table was a sign of prestige and wealth.

Indigenous communities of the Arctic region navigated the landscape by hunting seals, walrus, whales, and polar bears. Those same animals frequently appeared in their artistic work, whose motifs directly inspired the era's decorative wares by makers like Gorham. Iñupiaq artists from the Bering Sea Islands carved polar bear forms into rests for harpoons—the vital tool with which the artist or family member would hunt such an animal for meat, hide, and fur. One example made in the 1880s and now in the collection of the National Museum of the American Indian depicts two bears back-to-back with narrow eyes, snarling teeth, and pulled-back ears to reveal the artist's acute knowledge of animal behavior.[1] Nonindigenous artists of this period, while increasingly drawn to Arctic themes, romanticized the polar landscape and often incorrectly depicted it as unpopulated.

Early nineteenth-century British and American expeditions to find the Northwest Passage captured the imagination of the public, inspiring artists such as Frederic Edwin Church to envision exotic landscapes of icebergs. The U.S. government, led by Secretary of State William H. Seward for President Andrew Johnson's administration, purchased Alaska, which included Iñupiaq homelands, from Russia for $7.2 million in 1867. While politicians argued that the purchase would support trade, critics decried the space as uninhabitable for Euro-American lifestyles. The press mocked the purchase, calling Alaska "Seward's icebox" and "Johnson's polar bear garden." Gorham's ice bowl picks up on both this romanticization and criticism, transforming the image of an iceberg into a bowl adorned only with polar bears. —CG

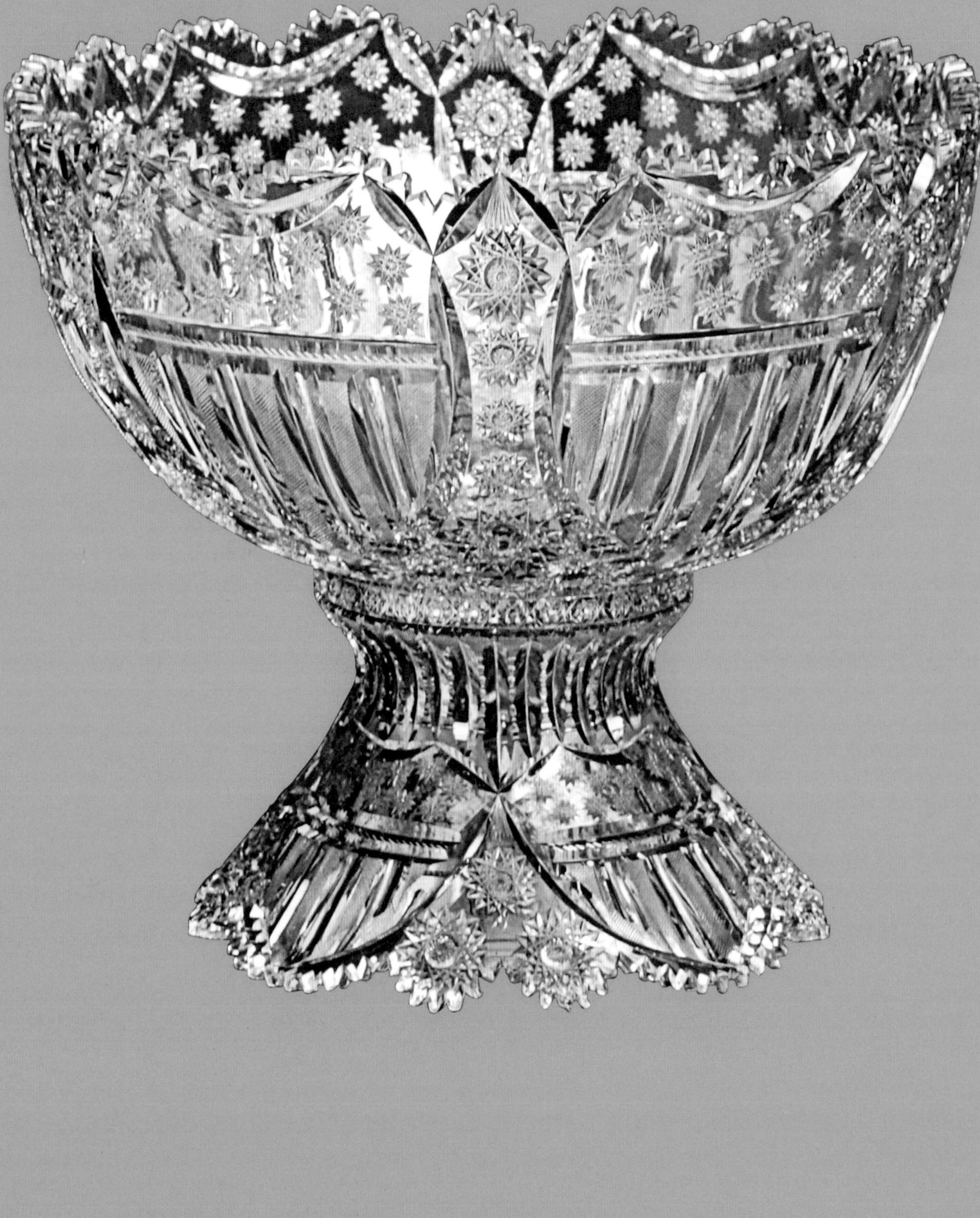

THE BOWL

PUNCH BOWL

1898, Designed by **William Marrett** (1859–1921) for the **Libbey Glass Company** (est. 1818),
Lead glass with cut and engraved decoration, 17 × 18 in. (42.3 × 45.7 cm),
High Museum of Art, Atlanta, Purchase with funds from the Decorative Arts Acquisition Endowment, 1985.51.1.

This seventy-five-pound behemoth, at the time widely considered the largest cut glass punch bowl ever made,[1] featured shields of thirteen stars and stripes circling the bowl and the base, with additional shimmering stars of various sizes nestled between them to represent the thirteen original states of the Union. As an object of American craft, it demonstrates the mastery of materials, skills, and techniques that made America a leader in the cut glass industry during the late nineteenth century.

The punch bowl was covered extensively in press of the period. In the late nineteenth century, Americans were captivated by cut glass—glass, with its roots in translucence, made intricate through the creation of three-dimensional decorative patterns—the result of a labor-intensive, multistage process that produced a sparkling, faceted object for the home.

While modern glass cutting originated outside of the United States, many domestic manufacturers displayed dizzying examples at the 1876 Centennial Exposition in Philadelphia. By the 1890s, Libbey Glass Company, which originated in the New England Glass Works of East Cambridge, Massachusetts, emerged as one of the United States' leaders in cut glass. After some initial economic challenges (the economic depression of 1873, labor strikes, and expensive fuel and materials), this new arena for glass production found favor due to a surprising tactic that has once again become relevant today: tariffs placed on foreign goods.[2] In 1890, the McKinley Tariff became law. William McKinley was at the time a congressman from Ohio, and the Toledo-based Libbey Glass Company was grateful to him for making inexpensive European cut glass imports *more* costly than their American counterparts through protectionist measures.[3] After McKinley became president, representatives from Libbey traveled to Washington, DC, in 1898 to give McKinley a "purely personal" gift, which he admired for its excellent workmanship, American iconography, and provenance from his home State of Ohio. The punch bowl and cups in the High Museum of Art's collection are the twin set—an explicitly made second set that could function as a backup for damages—to the prized original that the McKinley administration used to serve punch at White House functions in an elegant and genteel fashion.

The complicated design of the McKinley set would have enlisted the help of many hands. The rougher followed the pattern of the design to make initial guiding cuts with a metal wheel. The smoother softened the edges of this first pass and added smaller detailed cuts with a stone wheel. Other workers would have polished the glass using various techniques (by hand with brush, wooden wheel, or chemical assistance). Given the large size of the bowl and base and the complicated design, this set promoted the ingenuity and industry of the United States using iconography. —MO

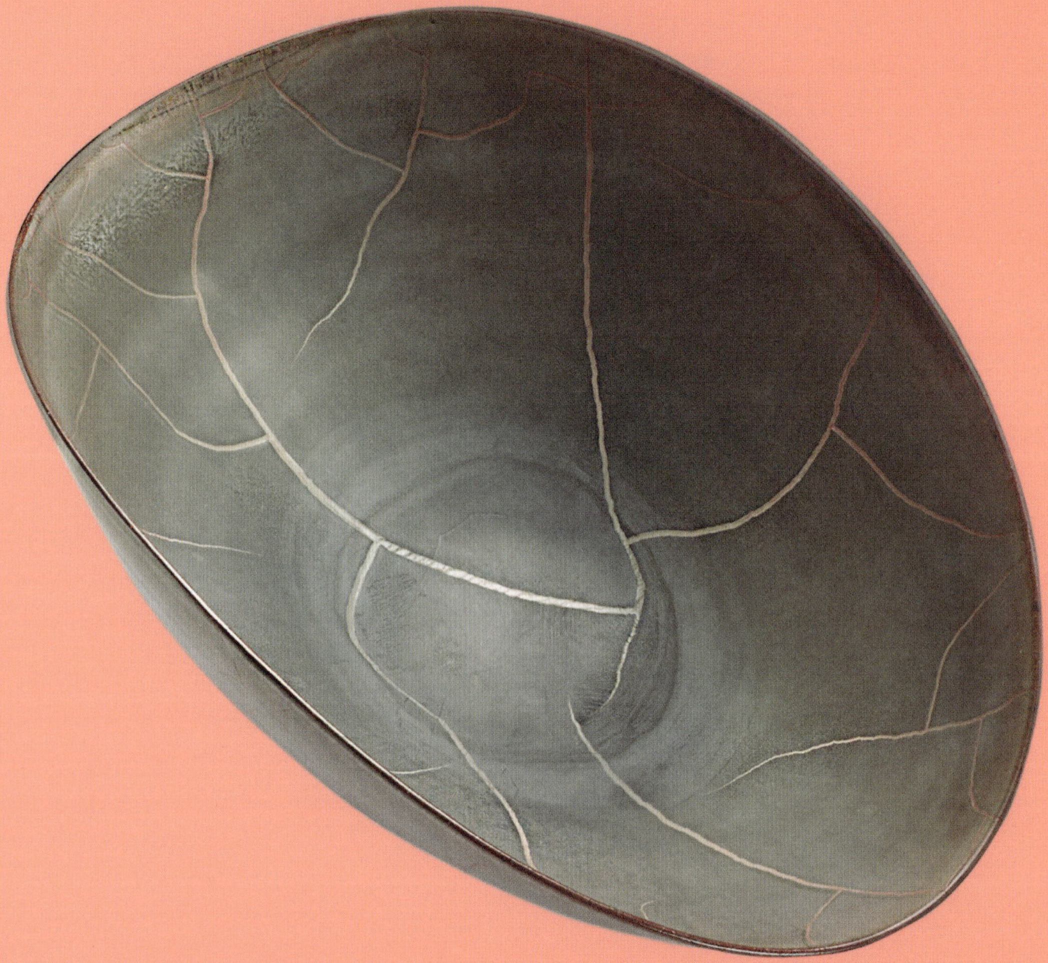

THE BOWL

OVAL BOWL

1942, **Gertrud Natzler** (1908–1971) and **Otto Natzler** (1908–2007),
Earthenware, gray celadon reduction glaze with melt fissures, 4⅛ × 10¼ in. (10.5 × 26 cm),
Collection of Forrest L. Merrill.

The fractured appearance of the interior of this crisp, ovular bowl is indicative of what Viennese émigré couple Gertrud and Otto Natzler achieved through form and glaze in their collaborative ceramics. With subtlety and restraint, it speaks to a new interpretation of both clay—which they helped usher in during the mid-twentieth century—and the bowl, the most common and ancient of crafted items. This quietly mesmerizing piece inspires meditation in the viewer, a characteristic of modernist tendencies toward simplicity. It was crafted a few years ahead of the color field paintings by Mark Rothko and it parallels other manifestations of contemplative abstract expressionist art in response to, and following, World War II. It conveys what ceramics can become in skilled, thoughtful hands and also how they mirror the society in which they are created.

The Natzlers' artistic and personal partnership began when the pair met in Vienna in Gertrud's brother's bookstore in July 1933. It was kismet. Largely self-taught artists, they embarked on a lifelong exploration of clay together. After Adolf Hitler annexed Austria in 1938, the Jewish couple was forced to flee and landed in Los Angeles, where they established their studio. Over the following decades, Gertrud gave shape to their perfectly proportioned, eggshell-thin vessels and Otto developed the textures, applications, and tones of their glazes. They consistently achieved pottery in which form and glaze were indivisibly wedded. The two always worked in sync, harmoniously fusing concept and vision to mutually create each of their purist vessels together, producing work until Gertrud's death in 1971.[1]

The transformative and unexpected results of the firing process brought elements of improvisation and spontaneity into the Natzlers' modern approach to ceramics. Otto was a master of chemistry who embraced the calculated accidents that were inherent to the elusive, uncertain qualities of his medium. For this early bowl he stated that "every aspect of the glaze—color, texture, melt fissures—came as a surprise for which we had no explanation. My fascination with reduction firing began with this piece, which emerged from the second reduction fire."[2]

Echoing nature and organically absorbing features and qualities of their adoptive home landscape, including Californian clays, the bowl is also like a curled leaf in color, shape, and pattern. "Perhaps we are creating for those who still look for serenity and respite from the turbulent life of the twentieth century," Otto explained in 1971 of their practice.[3] This is one of very few examples of their early work that remains, made only a couple of years after their emigration. The elongated bowl was the result of Gertrud's misshaping and bending one of her flawless circular vessels out of line so that it begins turning inward on itself. The melt fissures mar the surface and animate it with unexpected visual interest, like lightning tightly contained within the interior. The fissures can be read as the outcome of a world at war. The bowl conveys the fragile nature of ceramics and life. Understated and poetic, it takes on a new life as a perfect metaphor for the violent and shattered society that surrounded the Natzlers at the time. —EZ

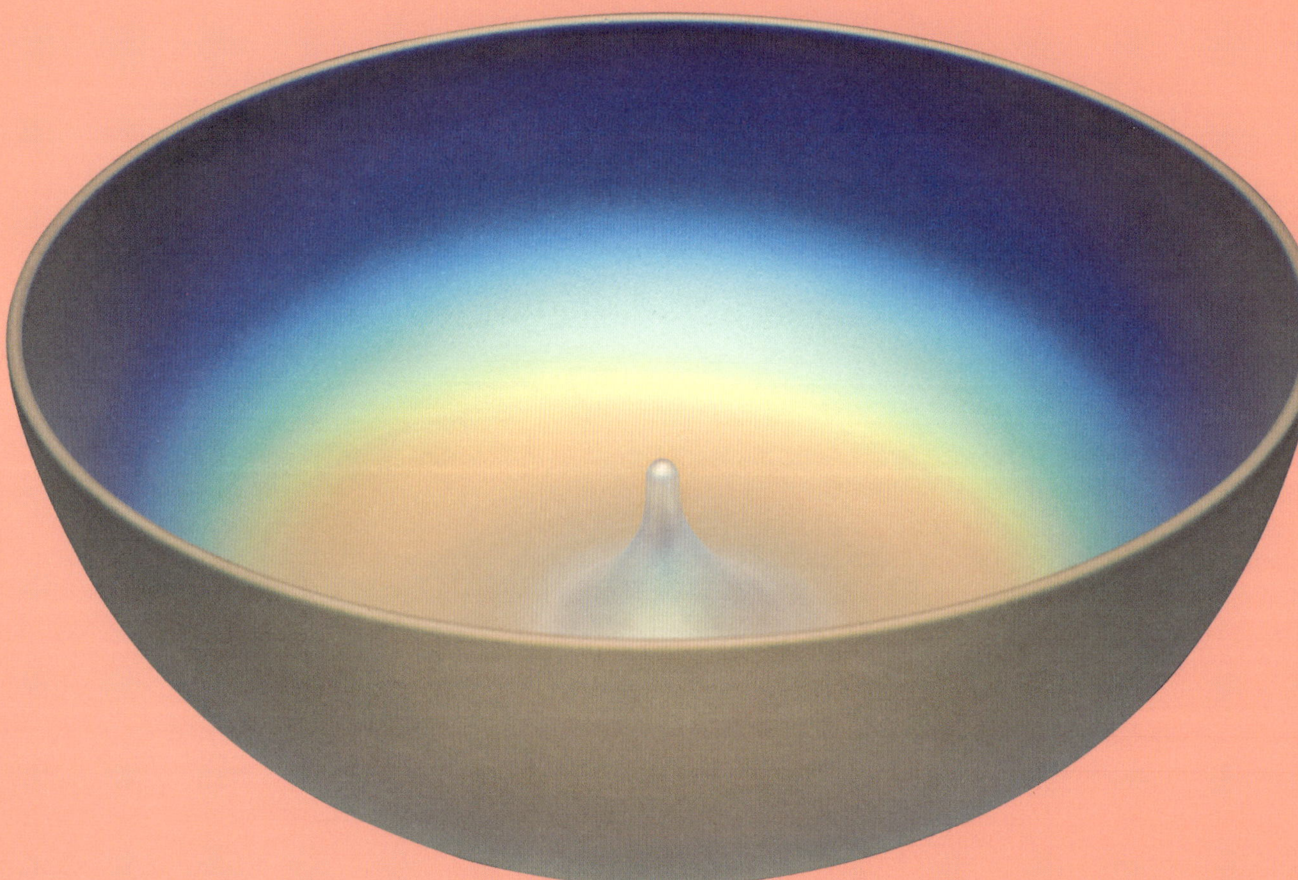

THE BOWL

KATHERINE GRAY on THE BOWL

Spectral Bowl, 2016, **Katherine Gray** (b. 1965), Iridized blown glass, 4 × 11 in. (10.2 × 27.9 cm).

Bowls can be great catchalls, and yet my bowls are all about being caught. When making bowls in glass, the gathering of the glass is of paramount importance. Your gathers have to be even and symmetrical. If you have to pick an air bubble out of the glass or if your gather is wonky, you may as well try to make a different shape from it. It will be a struggle every step of the way if you are trying to make a classic, refined bowl shape. However, if the very first steps of the process are done well and you don't make any mistakes along the way, then the very last steps of opening up the bowl are so satisfying. The heat and the spinning conspire so that all you have to do is "catch" the bowl—or more specifically its lip—with your tools, whether that is newspapers, jacks (tools resembling giant tweezers), or parchoffis (wooden jacks). You have to set the bottom, ample but subtle, allow the walls to widen and shorten with a luscious curve (almost any curve will do as long as it is fluid and continuous), and then, at last, the lip. That last step sounds as if it could be easy, and as long as you have surmounted and mastered all the difficult steps that came before, it can be. I don't know if there is anything more satisfying than returning to sit at the bench, with the perfect heat, spinning fast and using centrifugal force to let the lip spin open into your waiting tool. It's a magnificent feeling.

Bowls are, in fact, great catchalls. They can be where you leave your keys as you arrive home, where you display fruit, or they can catch and reflect the ambience of a room. Their openness makes it easy to add things and easy to grab things out of them. They are almost like children, soaking up what is imparted to them and guileless in returning the favor.

There are so many conundrums and contradictions inherent in the idea of a bowl. It can be as simple as your cupped hands, or it can be an exquisitely crafted confection that fits oh-so-elegantly into your hands. A bowl can be ceremonial yet functional, blandly utilitarian or aesthetically pleasing. You can use it with cutlery or chopsticks or your fingers, or without all of the above as you sip from its lip. Unlike a plate, it can contain both liquids and solids, adding to its versatility. They can be used for and by an individual, or they can be used by a group of people, to be the font from which its contents are shared. Its capaciousness can indicate a gathering, or a family, or a community. There's an implicit invitation to partake when you see a large, overly filled bowl.

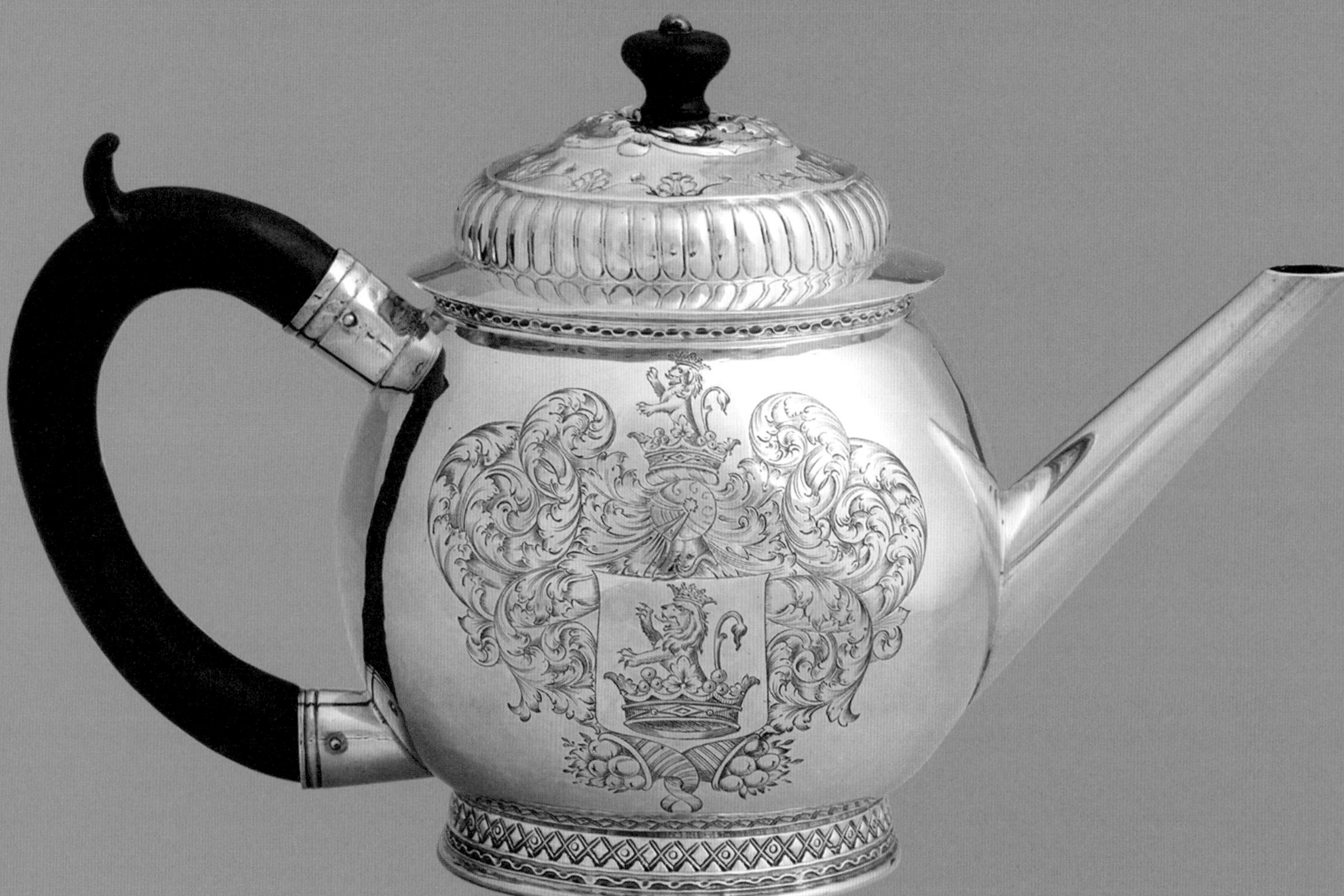

THE POT

TEAPOT

1690–1700, **Jacob Boelen** (c.1657–1729),
Silver, 6 7⁄16 × 10 3⁄8 × 5 1⁄16 in. (16.4 × 26.4 × 12.9 cm), Metropolitan Museum of Art, New York,
Gift of Mrs. Lloyd K. Garrison, in memory of her father, Pierre Jay 1961. 61.246a, b.

This silver teapot by New York silversmith Jacob Boelen is one of the first made in North America with this precious metal. The teapot was ordered by the merchant Frederick Philipse, whose family were wealthy landowners and prominent in New Amsterdam society (today's New York City). It is thought that the teapot was a wedding gift to his daughter, Eva, upon her marriage to Jacobus van Cortlandt. Such bridal gifts allowed parents to give valuable objects to their daughters in a world where women had little legal status.

Tea drinking in the West began sometime in the late sixteenth century, when Portuguese priests and merchants visiting China took up the practice and returned home with this new beverage. Originally valued for its medicinal properties, tea soon became a fashionable staple of English life, complete with its own etiquette for service. Colonists brought the drink to America, along with accoutrements that by the eighteenth century became a standard feature of a handsome table. These included teapots, tea stands, and sugar bowls, sugar tongs, teaspoons, and pierced mote spoons—spoons with small holes punched into them—to lift errant tea leaves from the cup. In the late seventeenth century, when this teapot was made, there were few accessories and a greater emphasis on the teapot itself.

Having short, rounded sides probably inspired by Dutch silversmiths or Chinese forms, this teapot has a removable lid and an oilcan-style spout, which is often found in Dutch ceramics of the same period. The body and lid are raised, and the lid chased with decoration. Its narrow foot is die-stamped. A wide wooden handle with a delicately curled thumbpiece, and a button-shaped (or capstan) wooden finial are essential for use, insulating fingers from the intense heat of the tea-filled silver pot.

Its most remarkable aspect is the exuberant engraving, featuring heraldic imagery, motifs used since antiquity as symbolic language to distinguish compatriots from enemies on the battlefield. Codified during the Middle Ages, by the late seventeenth century coats of arms were engraved on silver for wealthy Americans proud of their ancestral status—and sometimes created out of thin air for Americans with social-climbing aspirations. Here, amid the leafy scrolls that rise up like clouds, is a shield carrying the elements of traditional heraldry: a combination of symbols used by the family that ordered the teapot, in this case, a crowned lion emerging from a crown.

As there were then no silver mines in the colonies, craftsmen typically recycled old, unfashionable, or badly damaged silver articles; they were provided by the patron to be melted down and fashioned anew. Foreign coinage was also an important source of silver. Because American currency was then in its infancy, a vast range of coins circulated widely in the colonies, including silver Spanish reales, or royal currency, that was mined and minted in South America.

Silver was widely mined in South America and Mexico by the Spanish, who colonized those regions. It is thought that a high proportion of the silver found today in museums, as well as at home in the form of tableware and jewelry, was mined in the town of Potosí, in present-day Bolivia, which was in the sixteenth century colonized by Spain. The mining and processing of the ore into silver was hard and especially dangerous, and the Spanish used forced Indigenous labor to extract the silver. Thus the lustrous surface of silver also reflects this hidden story of conquest and struggle. —JF

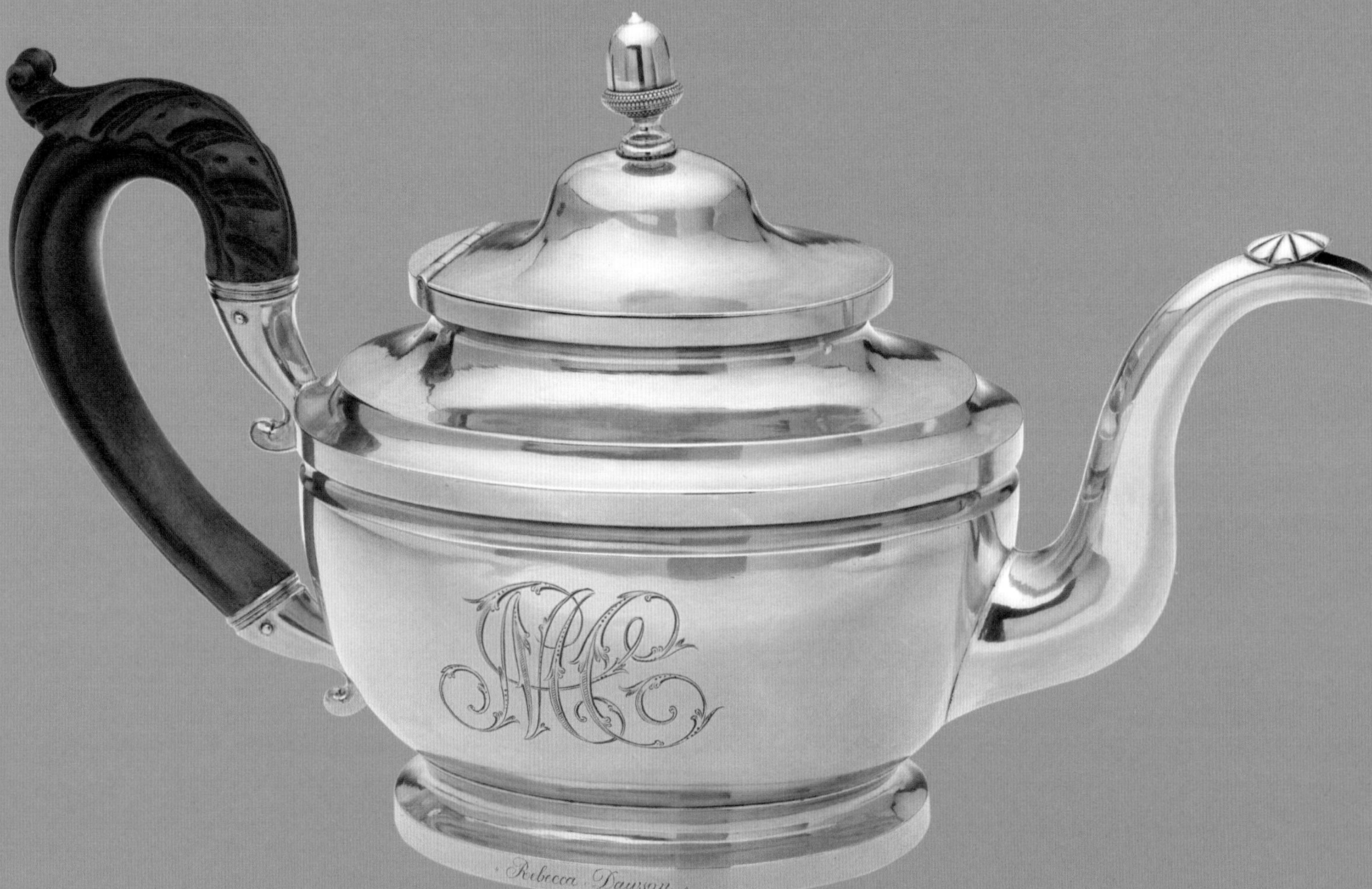

THE POT

TEAPOT

c. 1817–29, **Peter Bentzon** (c. 1783–after 1850),
Silver and wood, 7 × 12 × 5 in. (17.8 × 30.5 × 12.7 cm),
National Museum of African American History and Culture, Smithsonian Institution, Washington, DC, 2010.14.

Topped with an acorn finial, the elegant oval profile of this neoclassical-style teapot by Peter Bentzon, the first silversmith of African descent living in the United States to be identified by his own hallmark, is exemplary of Philadelphia-style hollowware (containers for the table) in the early years of the Republic. The wooden handle's singular acanthus curve is balanced by the graceful bend of the spout. Most silversmiths started to assemble teapots from this period with industrial-produced flattened silver sheet, resulting in boxy forms. In contrast, Bentzon used a hammer to form the pot's soft shape.

Bentzon was born into a free, racially mixed family on the island of St. Croix in the Danish West Indies. His father, a judge, likely used his connections to secure an apprenticeship for his son in Philadelphia at the age of eight. After training and living in the city for a decade, Bentzon returned to his hometown of Christiansted, St. Croix, to open his own business as a silversmith and merchant. In 1816, he relocated his family to Philadelphia after the Danish reoccupation of St. Croix. Listed as a jeweler, goldsmith, and silversmith in census records, Bentzon likely created everyday objects—everything from shoe buckles to teaspoons. He rented a property in the commercial district of Market Street from the Quaker merchant Robert Dawson, whose family was associated with the Pennsylvania Society for the Abolition of Slavery. In this part of the city, the Bentzon family intersected with both African American and Cruzan diaspora populations coming and going from the port city. Bentzon traveled between Philadelphia and Christiansted for most of his life, which exemplifies the historical networks of craft and artisanal knowledge between the United States and the Caribbean.

Two identical teapots survive in public collections, this one at the National Museum of African American History and Culture and one at the Saint Louis Art Museum. The name Rebecca Dawson is inscribed on the base of both teapots; she likely commissioned these pieces of hollowware from Bentzon shortly after he started to rent his workshop from her father. The teapots were later engraved with "MC" in elaborate scrollwork. This monogram likely references one of several Mary Coateses related to the Dawson family tree. Rebecca may have gifted these silverworks to mark the birth of her second cousin, Mary Coates, who was named after Mary Morrison Coates, the aunt of Rebecca.[1] Bentzon's teapots not only tell the story of one of the first named Black silversmiths working in the United States, but of the complex familial histories traced through the commissioning and gifting of silver objects. —CG

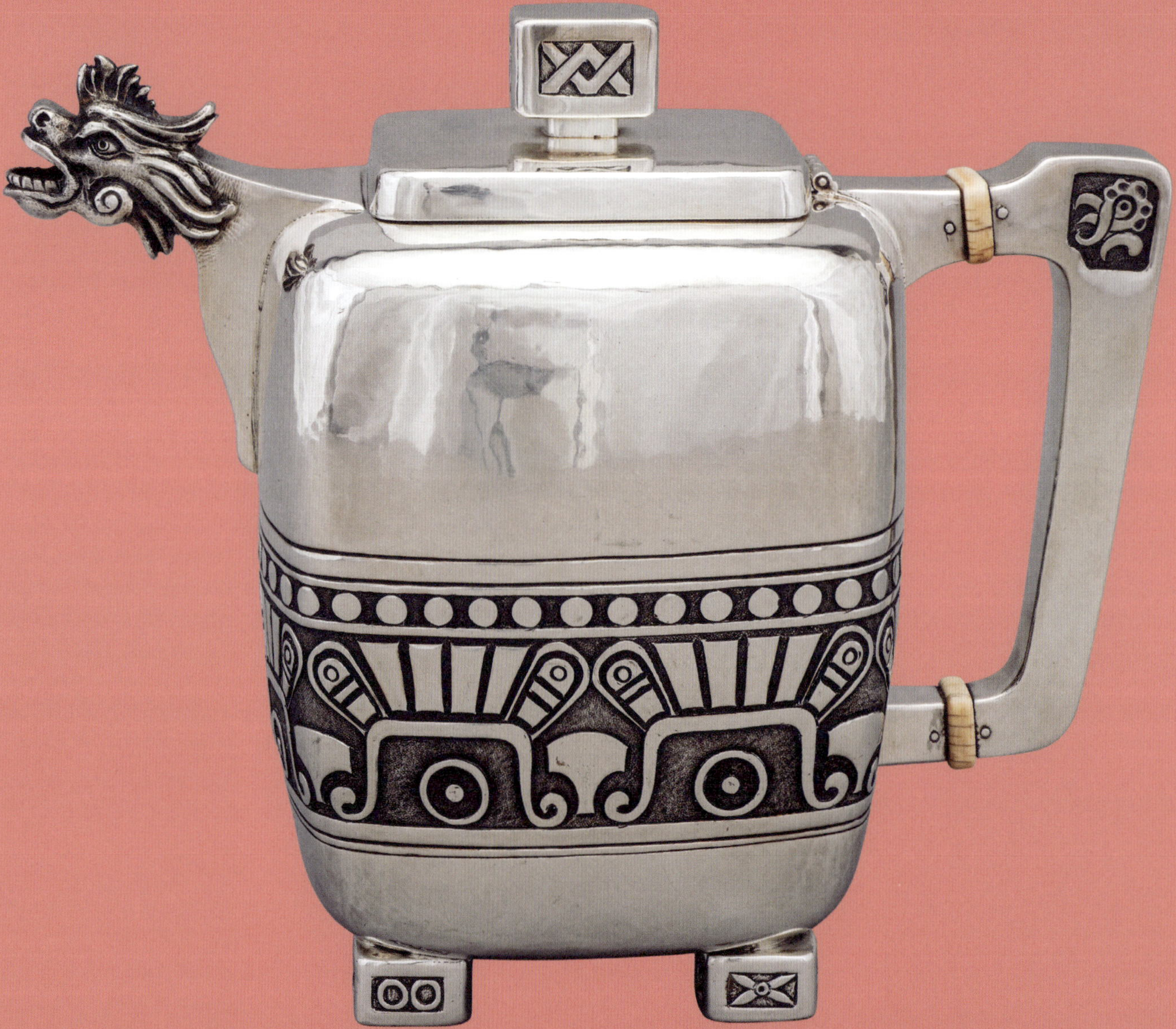

THE POT

CHOCOLATE POT

1936, **Clemens Friedell** (1872–1963), Silver and insulators, 8 × 9½ × 4½ in. (20.3 × 24.1 × 11.4 cm), The Huntington Library, Art Museum, and Botanical Gardens, San Marino, CA, Gift of Charles Briscoe in memory of Pearl Knapp Briscoe, 89.23.2.

An eye-catching band of repeating geometric forms encircles this chocolate pot: a box with scroll ends is seen from the side; four solid rays representing zacate grass extend from its top, flanked by two stylized awls or lancets. Together, this image suggests a symbol of self-sacrifice from the Aztec world. The band of repeating solid circles above it suggests the precious metal it is formed from as well as the liquid chocolate held within.[1]

In 1936, Clemens Friedell crafted this pot for hot chocolate—a drink originally developed for the Mayan and Aztec elite—to accompany a matching service for his patron, Dr. Pearl Gilliland Knapp Briscoe. Friedell trained as a silversmith in Vienna before moving to the United States to work for Gorham Manufacturing Company in 1901 as a chaser for the Martelé division, a premier line of handwrought silver. In 1910, he would become an independent artist, eventually setting up a studio in Pasadena, California, a popular wintering spot for wealthy Easterners. These patrons invested in Arts and Crafts artistry and developed cohesive themes for their retreats' interiors, including in the Mayan or Aztec revival style. Briscoe, who would become chief psychologist at Cedars-Sinai Medical Center, commissioned this chocolate pot for her hacienda-style home in the foothills of the San Gabriel Mountains. It was part of a service that also included a coffeepot, a teapot, a lemonade pitcher, a dinner bell, and a sugar bowl.

Briscoe's commission coincided with the end of a ten-year excavation program at Chichén Itzá, run by the Carnegie Institution. This project, as well as excavations at Teotihuacan and Tenochtitlan (modern-day Mexico City), reinvigorated the interest of the American public in the Mesoamerican past, resulting in the republication of ancient codices and archaeological studies, as well as a proliferation of films, novels, and artworks, including the murals of Diego Rivera. Briscoe's commission follows a broader trend for Aztec- and Mayan-inspired architecture and design across Los Angeles at the time.

Contemporaneous with Friedell, the U.S. architect–turned-silversmith William Spratling traveled to Mexico in the 1930s to reestablish a silver industry in Taxco, working with local artisans to design silver based on pre-Columbian motifs, including the iconography of Quetzalcóatl, the Aztec deity known as the feathered serpent. For example, in Spratling's design for a brooch, now in the collection of LACMA,[2] Quetzalcóatl is shown with an open mouth baring teeth, a curled snout, a tight spiral to articulate the jaw, and plumed feathers at the crown of the head. We see these same features of Quetzalcóatl, particularly a comb of feathers and gaping mouth, on the spout of Friedell's chocolate pot.

The Friedell service is a reminder of how American artisans continuously looked to Mexico for a deeper understanding of what it meant to create an "American" design as part of an undivided continent. —**CG**

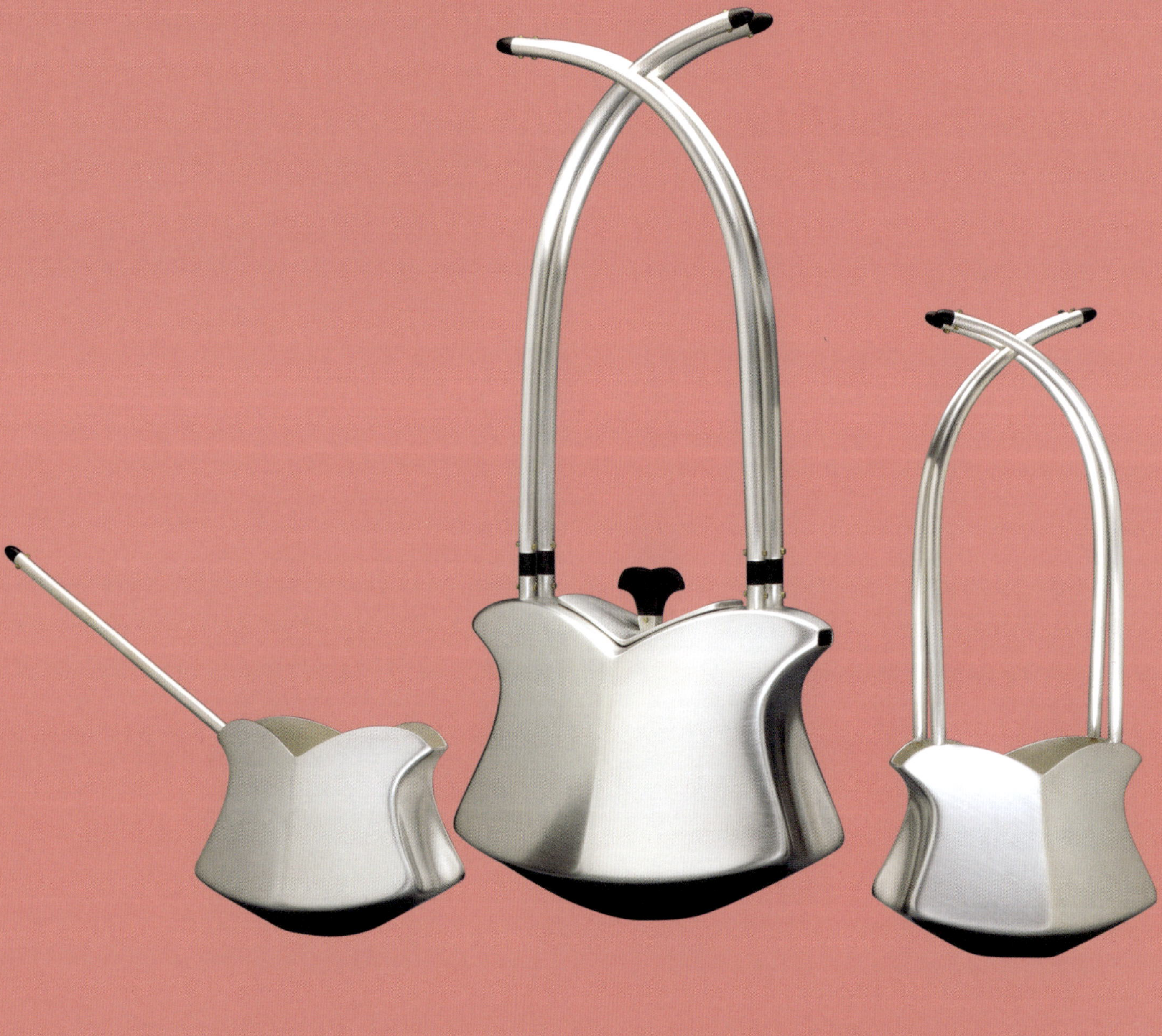

THE POT

TEA SERVICE

1987, **Chunghi Choo** (b. 1938), Electroformed and silver-plated copper; carved ebony fittings and brass rivets, Teapot: 17½ × 5½ × 8¼ in. (44.5 × 14 × 21 cm), Creamer: 12 × 5¼ × 4 in. (30.5 × 13 × 10.2 cm), Sugar bowl: 4¼ × 5½ × 4 in. (10.8 × 12.5 × 10.2 cm), Figge Art Museum, Davenport, IA, City of Davenport Art Collection, Friends of Art Acquisition Fund (1997.4).

Tea Service is a testament to the formal mastery and innovative techniques of Korean American artist and metalsmith Chunghi Choo. The electroformed copper- and silver-plated set—which includes a teapot, creamer, sugar bowl, and spoon—is a symphony of organic forms and decorative, functional elements that include hand-carved ebony fittings and tiny brass rivets. Arranged together, the teapot takes center stage, its form suggestive of a handbag or even a ballerina with gracefully raised arms. This interplay between form and function, stasis and movement, imbues Choo's designs with a timeless quality that is both classic and contemporary.

Choo's artistic philosophy emphasizes essential elements. Her background in brush calligraphy, considered the pinnacle of artistic expression in East Asia, profoundly shaped her diverse artistic practice. Like a master calligrapher who distills complex meaning into essential strokes, Choo distills her ideas into gestural, abstracted metal forms that achieve a similar economy. She describes her process as "mind-matter," drawing upon the concept of qi, the concentrated energy fueling creative expression. *Tea Service*, with its curving forms, flowing lines, and upward-sweeping handles, embodies the energy, elegance, and pleasure of serving tea.

Choo revolutionized metalsmithing by adapting industrial electroforming for studio use. Instead of traditional casting or raising, she modeled her vessels in wax, applied a conductive silver lacquer, and immersed them in an electrically charged copper solution, melting out the wax once the desired thickness was achieved. After filing, sanding, and polishing, she plated the surface with sterling silver. This innovative process allowed her to create lighter, more fluid and organic metal forms not easily achieved with other conventional methods.

Through her combination of innovative and traditional techniques, Choo can create multiple iterations of a form, each capable of individual modification. For instance, the creamer and sugar bowl share the same body, yet their tubular components—the spoon and handle—are suggestive of a male and a female form, respectively. The teapot's hand-carved ebony fittings and brass rivets serve both decorative and functional purposes by preventing heat transfer. Its spout merges seamlessly with its shapely body. The highly polished silver surface creates a constantly shifting interplay of light and reflection. The ebony tips at the ends of the armlike handles subtly suggest painted fingernails, making *Tea Service* a functional, sculptural ensemble. The tulip-like shapes of the three vessels appear to float yet remain grounded, creating a dynamic and visually engaging trio.

After earning her MFA in metalsmithing from Cranbrook Academy of Art in 1965, Choo became a professor and established a renowned metalsmithing and jewelry program at the University of Iowa. Her impact on the American Studio Craft movement extends beyond her own significant body of work to the generations of metalsmiths she mentored over five decades of teaching.[1] *Tea Service* stands as a testament to her pioneering vision in contemporary craft. —JM

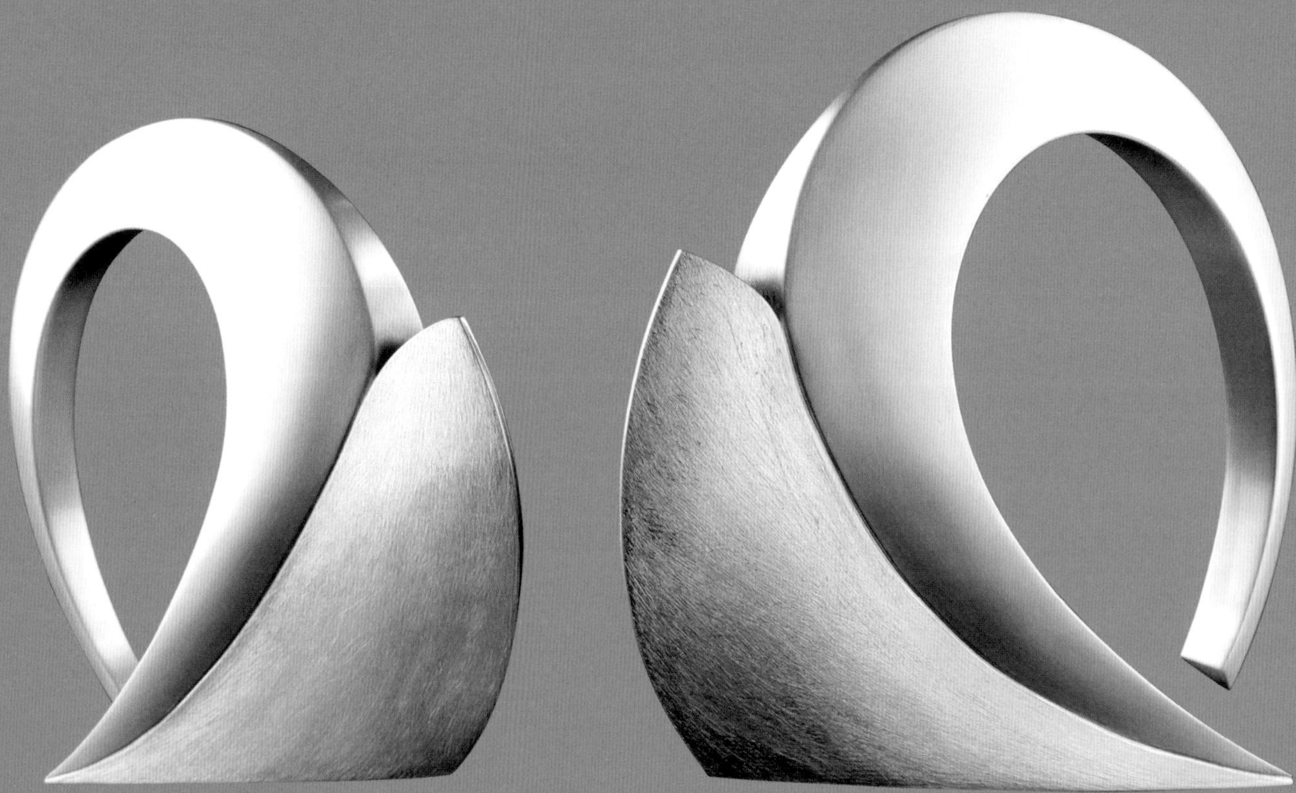

THE POT

SWAN VESSELS

2019, **Randy Stromsoe** (b. 1951), Pewter,
Left: 6 × 6¾ × 2½ (15.2 × 17.2 × 6.4 cm). Right: 7 × 8 × 2¾ in. (17.8 × 20.3 × 7 cm).

Swans have captured our imaginations for centuries, inspiring ballads, ballets, and fashion trends. Even writer Truman Capote borrowed their mystique, referring to the elegant society women around him as his "swans." The bird's distinctive S-line shape, symbolizing grace and sensuality, has long been a motif in art and design. It was this elegant form that inspired California metalsmith Randy Stromsoe when he sought to elevate common serving pieces—a teapot and creamer—into sculptural objects.

The resulting *Swan Vessels*, which appear to be gliding effortlessly on the water, guided by their swooping necks and balanced by the shapely volume of their bodies, demonstrate a masterful command of geometry and curvilinear arcs. Stromsoe developed his expertise through an apprenticeship with Porter Blanchard at his silversmithing studio in Los Angeles from 1970 to 1973. Working hand in hand with his mentor, he received classical training in the Arts and Crafts tradition, learning all facets of silver and pewter work. Beyond technique, Stromsoe absorbed Blanchard's ethos: a commitment to technical excellence and intellectual rigor, an emphasis on hammer skills, and a reverence for the handmade. After Blanchard's death in 1973, Stromsoe continued at Porter Blanchard Silversmiths Inc. until 1980, when he established his own studio. He built a combined workshop and home in Templeton, on California's Central Coast, where he houses the metalsmithing tools that belonged to his mentor. Stromsoe felt strongly about "preserving the history of the tools," including the hammer and anvil that belonged to Blanchard's father, George Porter Blanchard, also a distinguished Arts and Crafts silversmith. He feels "humbled and appreciative" working with these same handcrafted tools that shaped his mentor's legacy.[1]

Blanchard's drive to experiment and innovate became core to Stromsoe's practice, fueling his "natural curiosity to explore alternative forms and techniques." In *Swan Vessels,* Stromsoe challenged himself to design and solve a puzzle: "I set out to create a consistent, fluid, curvilinear arc from a single pewter disc with no breaks or additions . . . making a shape, deconstructing it, and then reconstructing it without adding anything. The Swans are a departure from how one would go about making a teapot and creamer, although they function quite nicely."[2] True to his Arts and Crafts training, Stromsoe's swan design is based on function, constructed with consideration of ergonomics, balance, and weight distribution: tea and cream flow easily from the pots' perfectly angled spouts, and the hand finds an easy grip at the arc of their handles. Functional and sculptural, the result elevates traditional holloware forms through a flowing arrangement of mass and void, floating gracefully in space like swans gliding on water.
—JL

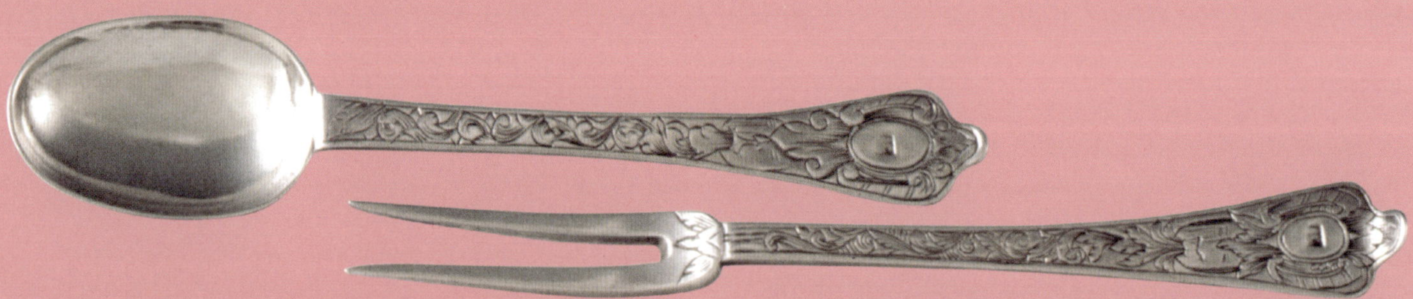

THE UTENSIL

MINIATURE FORK AND SPOON SET

c. 1700, **John Coney** (c. 1655/56–1722),
Silver, Each: 4 5⁄16 in. (11 cm), Museum of Fine Arts, Boston,
Gift of Mr. and Mrs. Dudley Leavitt Pickman, 1931, 31.222-223.

Now a common kitchen tool, forks were highly unusual in colonial North American homes. Most colonists brought food to their mouths with their fingers or a spoon. In fact, Massachusetts governor John Winthrop caused a scandal in 1633 when he ate dinner with a fork, then seen as a decadent luxury by many in the Puritan community. Although forks slowly gained acceptance in England in the mid- to late 1600s (Charles I decreed forks "decent to use" in 1633), the utensil remained uncommon in America until well after the Revolution.[1]

The fork of this miniature travel set is exceedingly rare, one of only a handful of colonial American forks known today. The two-tined silver form possesses a handle lavishly engraved on both sides with sinuous decoration emanating from the mouth of a human face, or foliate head, a common decorative symbol of rebirth. The matching spoon shares the same handle decoration. This set may have originally been accompanied by a knife and carrying case. Such miniature travel sets were fashionable among European and colonial elite, as hosts then were not expected to provide utensils for guests.[2]

An oval cartouche at the end of the handle frames an undecorated medallion that bears the maker's mark, IC in a rectangle, on the front and the owner's initials "MW" engraved on the back. This set was made around 1700 by John Coney, Boston's leading silversmith of the era. Coney was known for introducing new forms and styles to his wealthy clientele, as well as for his skill as an engraver, as evidenced here on the fork and spoon. Of the 225 works by Coney known to survive, this is the only fork.[3] Rather than add his maker's mark to the bowl of the spoon or the back of the handle, as was conventional at the time, Coney prominently marked this set on the front of both handles, boldly asserting his craftsmanship.

Coney made this miniature fork and spoon set for Mary Willoughby, the daughter of a wealthy and politically influential family in Salem, Massachusetts. She presumably carried these implements with her as she visited friends and family in Salem, Charlestown, and throughout the Boston area. At the late age of thirty-four, Mary wed Dr. Thomas Drummond Barton, a physician and apothecary in Salem, and the couple had two children. After his death in 1751, Barton bequeathed "unto my Dearly beloved wife . . . All her Maiden Plate [silver] as a tankard, Spoons etc. and as much More as she may want to be Useful for her."[4] Silversmith ledgers and estate inventories indicate that more silver forks existed in the colonies than what survives today, as silver was regularly recycled, or melted down, to create something new, in the latest fashion. —**NG**

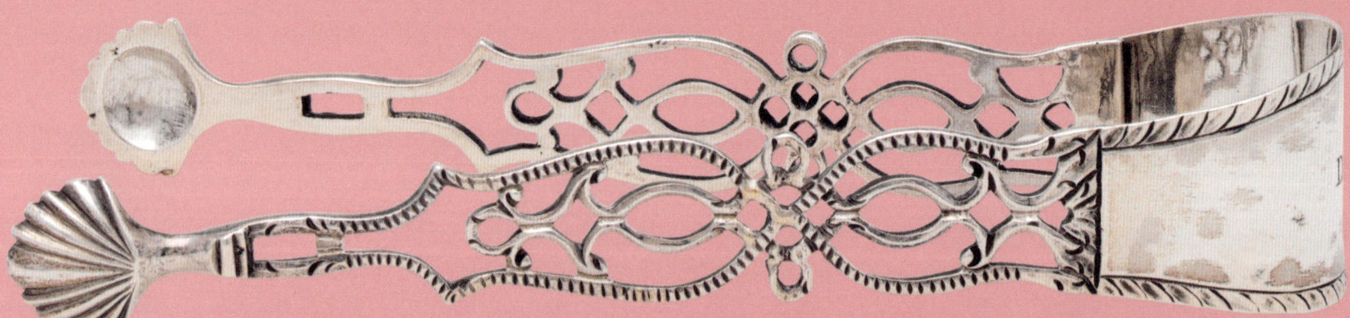

THE UTENSIL

SUGAR TONGS

c. 1772, **Attributed to Myer Myers** (1723–1795),
Silver, 15⁄16 × 5 1⁄4 in. (2.4 × 13.3 cm), Metropolitan Museum of Art, New York,
Purchase, Mr. and Mrs. Robert G. Goelet Gift, 2012, 2012.244.4.

These silver tongs are as light and airy as the sugar they are meant to hold. Made by the famed New York silversmith Myer Myers, the pierced scrollwork of the arms was first cast then soldered to a spring arch to operate as a hinge. One's fingers would have to press against these delicate passages to pick up a lump of refined sugar between its shell-shaped tips. An icon of rococo design, such shells were a common flourish on sugar tongs—a utensil that emerged among elite patrons during the late eighteenth century.

Myers was one of the first practicing Jewish metalsmiths not only in eighteenth-century New York, but throughout the British Empire. Most European countries had maintained laws prohibiting Jewish residents from working with precious metals or joining guilds, yet Myers carved out a niche for maintaining an active retail business for both domestic and religious silver. As an elder of the Shearith Israel congregation (founded in 1654) and reader of the Torah, Myers produced bespoke finials to adorn the sacred scroll—a central symbol for community and the source of Jewish law. The symbolism behind the elements of the finials, from crowns at the top to three rows of bell extensions, reflected passages of the Torah's text.[1] Jewish patrons commissioned silver finials for both synagogue- and privately owned Torah scrolls, alongside Myers's broad selection of domestic silver.

The New York merchant Abraham Brinckerhoff commissioned these sugar tongs for his wife, Dorothy Remsen, whose initials are engraved on the hinge. He presented Myers with a British rococo coffeepot for design guidance and commissioned the accompanying objects that would complete a full coffee service. This was a common practice in colonial America that allowed established artists to closely study the latest styles imported from Europe. The C- and S-scroll work and floral chasing across the set are typical of the rococo style, yet the ornamental repoussé, or relief, for this set is more two-dimensional than the coffeepot, as well as earlier designs produced by Myers and his workshop. Members of the Brinckerhoff family and their guests would use these tongs (also known as "nips") to move sugar cubes from bowl to cup as part of a broader performance of gentility and status connected to a world of commerce that often remained hidden, linking the silver mine and the sugar plantation through a single object.

Myers, and members of his workshop, crafted these bowed sugar tongs in a moment of social and political transition, on the eve of the War of Independence. Brinckerhoff was a member of the Committee of One Hundred, a patriot organization of New York merchants akin to Boston's Sons of Liberty that organized resistance campaigns against British rule starting in 1775. This included the disruption of Loyalist trade networks and seizure of ships and weaponry in advance of battles. One wonders if the Brinckerhoffs discussed the intricacies of trade and personal liberties throughout the British Empire while offering their guests coffee, cream, and sugar in silver hollowware. —CG

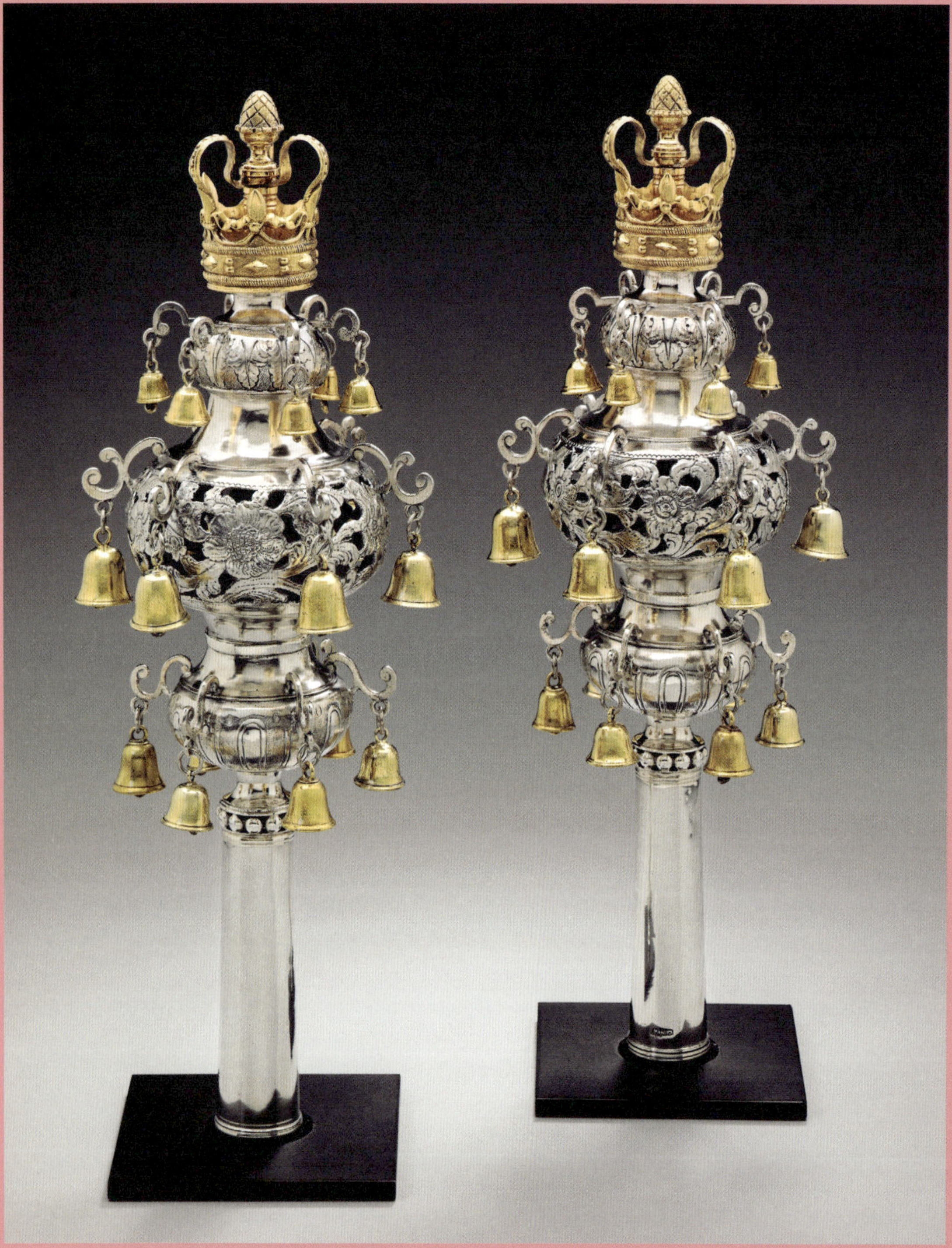

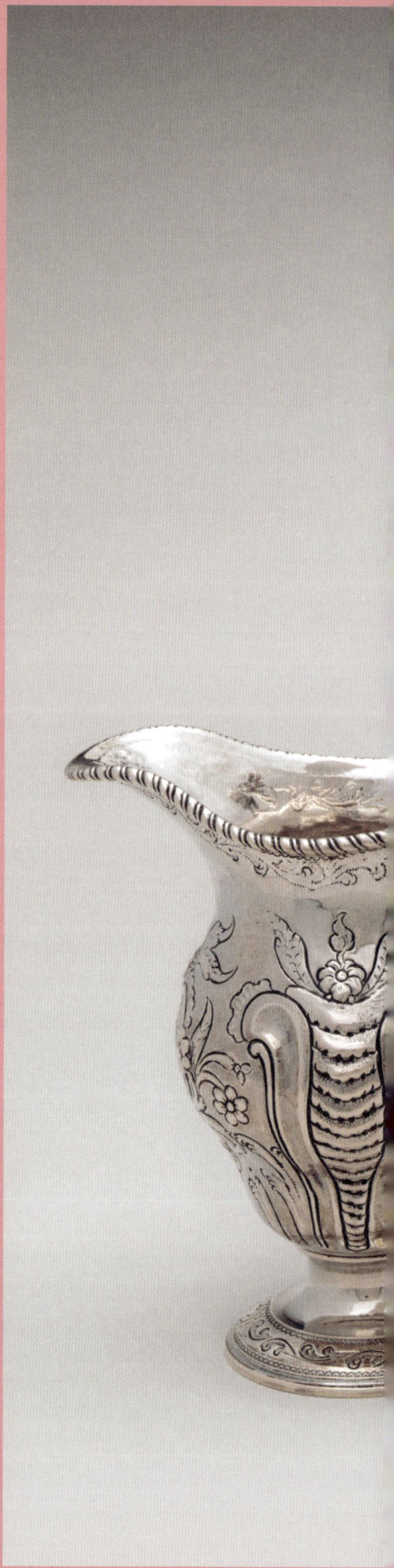

ABOVE
Pair of Torah Finials, 1766–76, **Myer Myers** (1723–1795), Silver and brass with parcel gilding
14½ in. (36.8 cm), From the Touro Synagogue, Newport, RI,
Collection of Congregation Shearith Israel, New York, L-R 44.2019.1-2. Museum of Fine Arts, Boston.

OPPOSITE
Complete set with sugar tongs, creamer, and sugar bowl, Myer Myers, with coffeepot by British silversmiths William and Robert Peaston,
Metropolitan Museum of Art, New York, Creampot: 2012.244.2. Sugar bowl: 2012.244.1.

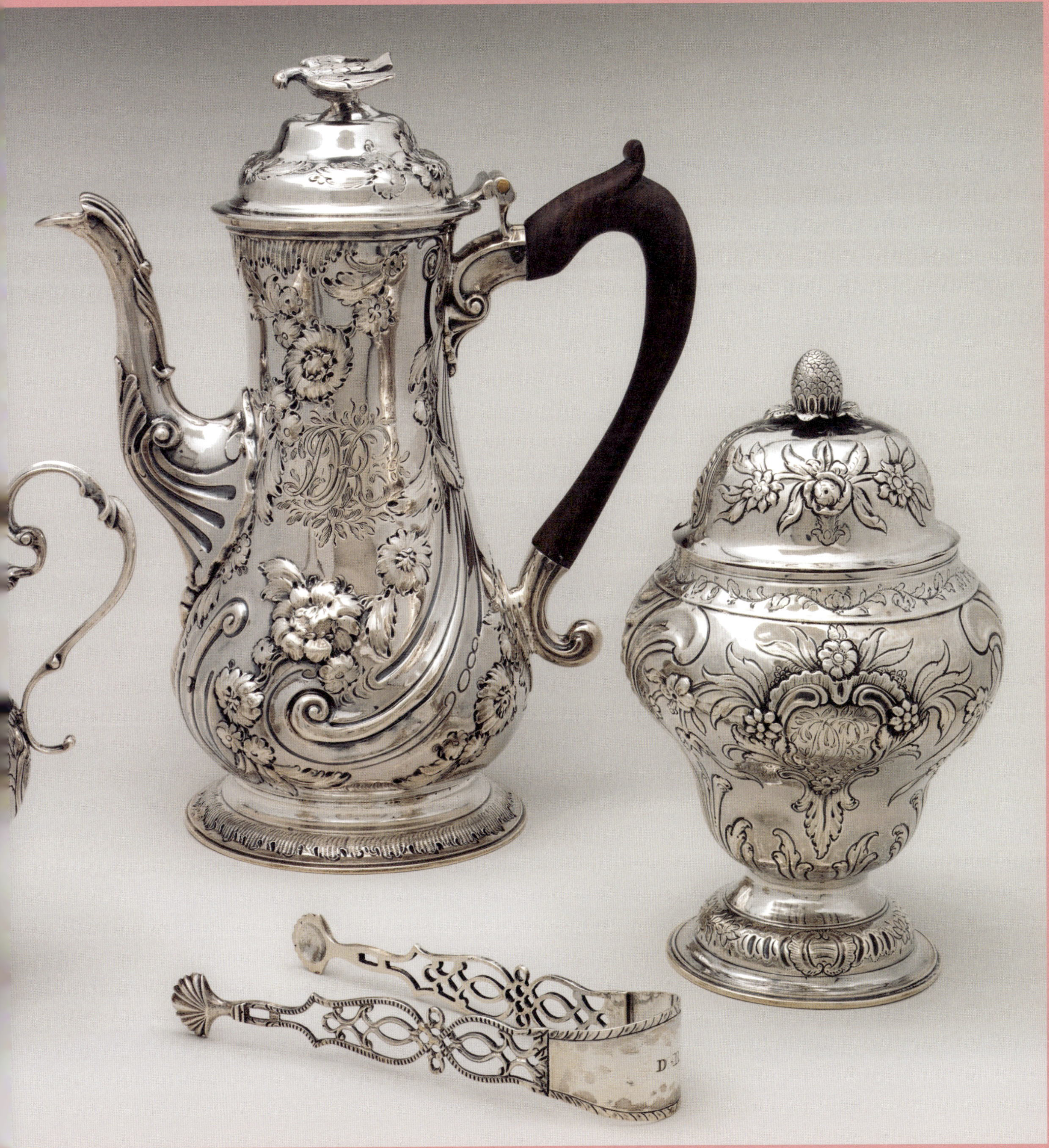

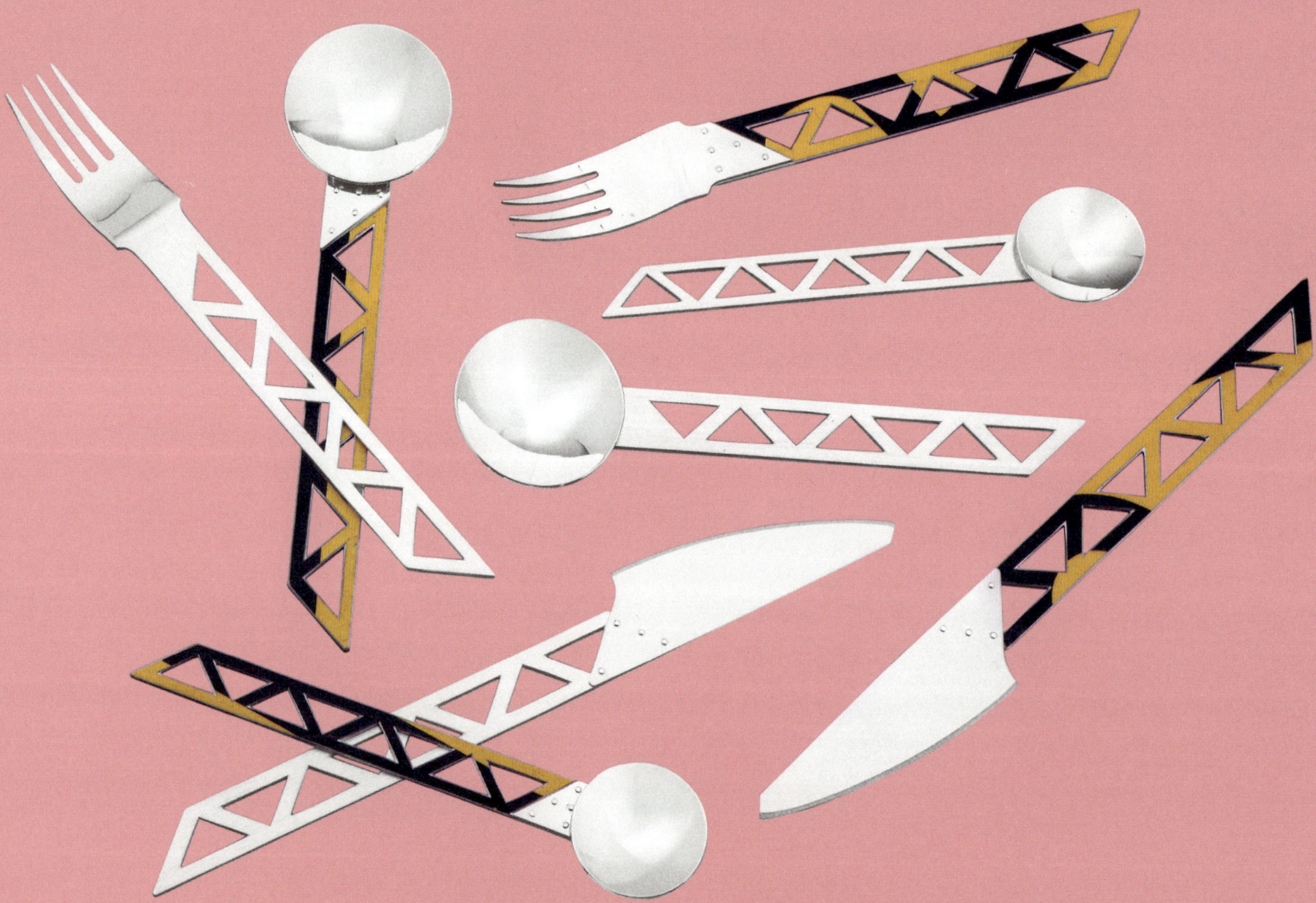

THE UTENSIL

PIERCED TRUSS TWO

2001, **Boris Bally** (b. 1961),
Silver, repurposed traffic signs,
9⅝ × 2⅛ × ½ in. (24.5 × 5.4 × 1.3 cm).

After Boris Bally graduated from high school in a suburb of Pittsburgh, he spent time in Basel, Switzerland, apprenticing with metalsmith Alexander Schaffner Goldschmied. There, he took part in the custom of enjoying long, elaborate lunches at home. These meals featured heirloom place settings and in-depth discussions about design that reminded Bally of home. His parents were Swiss, an industrial designer and a weaver; it was their European traditions and professions that inspired him to begin working with metals and jewelry as a teenager.

In 1985 Bally founded his studio business, giving it the humorous and humble name Humanufactured. Culinary design felt like a logical hybrid of three key elements of his practice—art, design, and craft—and continues to be a focus. For centuries, silverware has been both functional and symbolic, often associated with wealth and aristocracy, a marker of high social status. Bally's work, while rooted in the tradition of silversmithing, challenges the ideals that once associated silver with privilege and social hierarchy, and often includes political messages.

In creating a set of flatware, Bally often applies large-scale construction techniques to the production of these small-scale pieces.[1] He loves that they are useful and calls them "jewelry for the table." Each year, he chooses a theme that informs all his design iterations. One year featured a perforation theme, another an I beam theme. The influence of urban high-rise construction can be seen in forks, knives, and spoons that feature open grid works, bent pipes, and solid constructions.

The artist has mined industry for scrap metal to make furniture, using his leftover fragments to create increasingly smaller works such as jewelry and silverware. Sustainability through the reuse of cast-off objects has become central to the work of many contemporary makers, and in Bally's case, the use of scrap metal in silverware production inspired a practical joke. In 2001, he and his students at Haystack Mountain School of Crafts "borrowed" cafeteria cutlery and returned altered versions. After he was "caught," Bally provided students with scrap tableware to improve upon and donate to Haystack's end-of-session auctions.

While the first iteration of *Trussware* (1993) did not include scrap metal, *Pierced Truss Two* follows the contemporary trend of using unorthodox materials to create traditional handcrafted objects. Here, Bally uses silver and discarded metal road signs. He makes all of his flatware by hand; each piece of *Pierced Truss Two* was hand-constructed without using a laser cutter or other mechanisms that would speed up the process. A tableware commission might take months to complete, and always starts with drawings and paper mockups. This pattern was inspired by designs from bridges, overpasses, and structural steel bridges. With *Pierced Truss Two,* combining silver and found metal speaks to the juxtaposition of luxury and construction, showing us the dazzle of a city filled with cranes, high-rises, and elevated structures as well as the industrial reality it takes to bring them to life. —SI

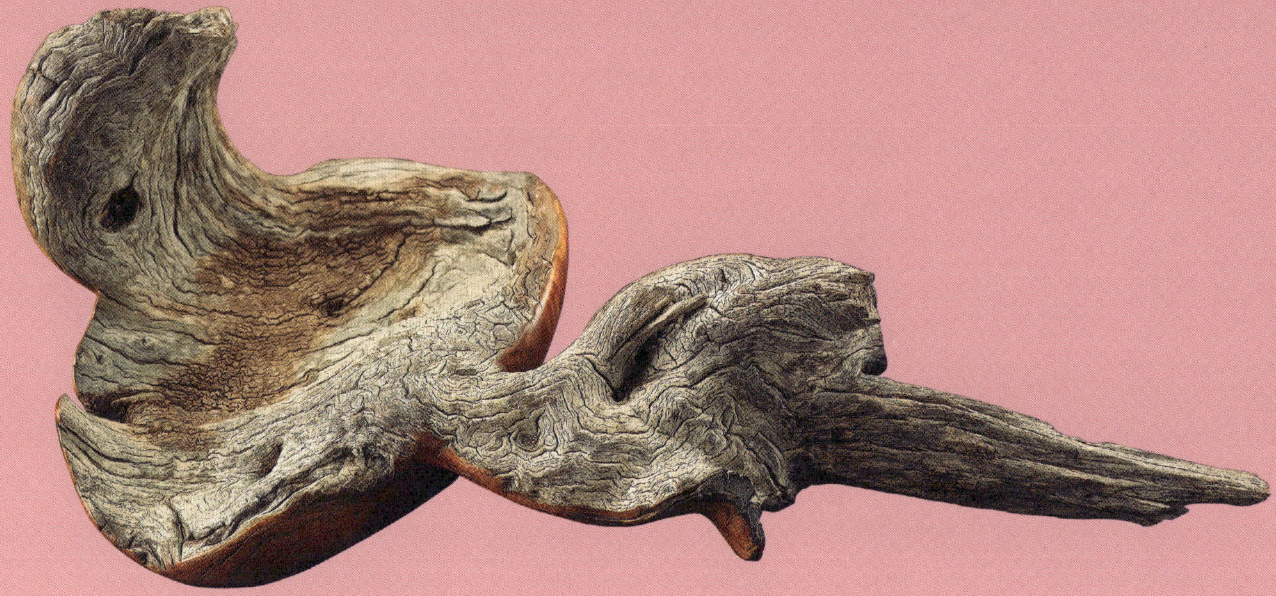

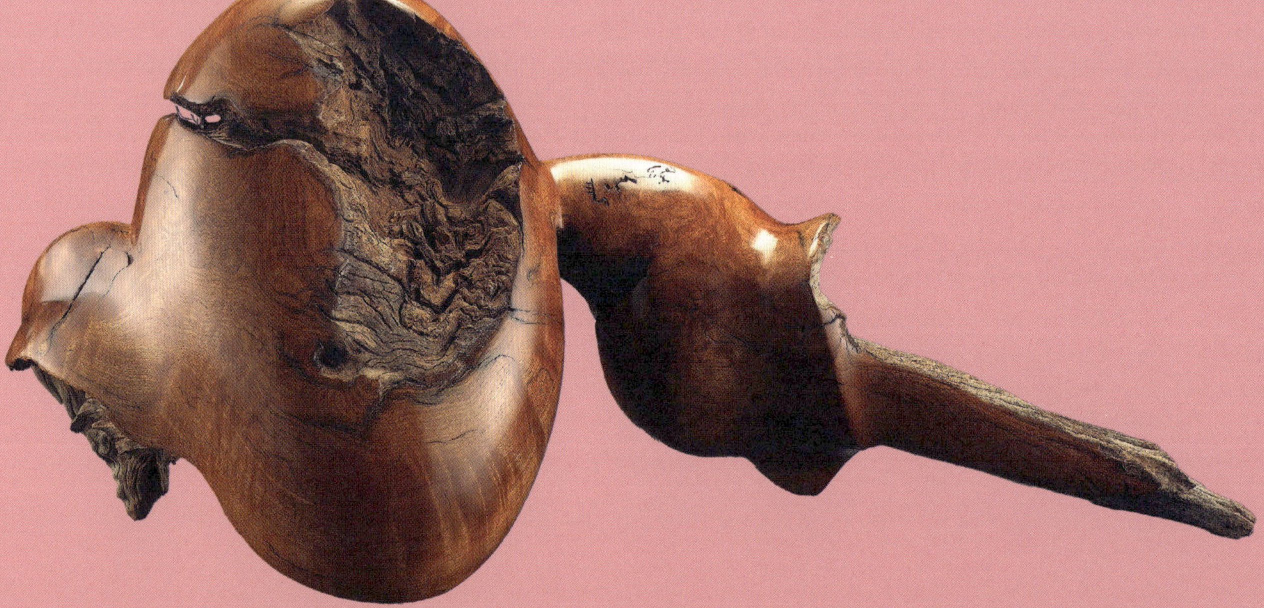

THE UTENSIL

OLD AND IN THE WAY (ALTERNATE VIEWS)

2006, **Norm Sartorius** (b. 1947),
Creosote bush, 13½ × 6½ × 5 in. (34.5 × 16.5 × 12.7 cm),
Crystal Bridges Museum of American Art, Bentonville, AK, Donated by Fleur Bresler.

Gnarly, unrefined, and primitive could describe Norm Sartorius's nonfunctional spoon, titled *Old and In the Way*—until the other side of the spoon is revealed. Here, the artist's hand is apparent in the shape, finish, and signature attention to the transition from bowl to handle. He created this work after a serious illness and convalescence during which he found himself feeling old and unproductive, much like the block of wood that sat on his table, unused, for a very long time. His psychological struggle with aging and the reality of his physical limitations and mortality prompted him to take up this previously ignored, twisted piece of wood and deal creatively with its limitations.

Using his vast knowledge of spoon making and sculptural influences gleaned from museum visits, Sartorius's unconscious guides him in his intuitive and sometimes autobiographical sculpting. Sartorius explores the ubiquitous wooden spoon as a sculpture because it is a relatable art form that provides infinite variation and inspiration. He uses rare and unusual woods, shaping each nonfunctional spoon into a unique artistic composition of color, form, and texture. The wood grain, knots, and the impact of weathering, along with his observations of other natural objects such as seashells, animal horns, or plants, and global spoon-making traditions all influence his shaping. His spoons vary in size and shape, each intuitively created, many in wild and wonderful forms reminiscent of a Dr. Seuss illustration. In this way, Sartorius participates in the contemporary trend of using craft processes and materials to create nonfunctional art forms.

Sartorius feels that each piece of wood dictates the first cut, a decision that determines the ultimate size and shape of the spoon. Wood blocks sit untouched on his workbench as he studies the many directions he could pursue with them. Once he visualizes the spoon, he acts to capture his creative inspiration. Sartorius then determines the outside shape, beginning with band saw cuts, and further subtraction via a sanding drum. He later mechanically removes a mass from the concave interior of the bowl, then uses small cutters, carving knives, and a grinder to refine the interior surface, forming abstract and expressive shapes and ornately carved handles.

In this piece, the interesting striations in the wood's exterior are intentionally brought forth, whereas the grain, color, and distressed surface of the interior remain largely untouched. The inner and outer design disparities recall the story of Dorian Gray, or the human clash between our interior and exterior selves. Sartorius turns the idea of a spoon on its head. The Platonic ideal of a spoon surpasses the possibility of actual functionality; he creates a piece that expresses the concept of a spoon without necessarily demonstrating the balance and precision necessary to carry liquid or mass in the bowl. *Old and In the Way* illustrates the principles of Sartorius's work: it speaks to his own experience with illness and aging, and represents his collaboration with nature and the raw qualities of the materials he works with. —**SI**

FURNISH

THE CHAIR: TO SIT

THE TABLE: TO SET

THE CABINET: TO STORE

THE RUG: TO COVER

THE QUILT: TO WARM

THIS CHAPTER FOCUSES ON THINGS that anchor a space. Compared with many other objects in the book, the things in this chapter convey a sense of stability; most of them endure, are more permanent. Figuring prominently within interiors—these are, for the most part, the objects with the largest footprints and mass—they can be primarily functional but may also operate as signals of sophistication and luxury. Fixed in position within a room, they encourage a set of interactions and become the center of an orbit of activity. Although there are five categories of furnishings included here—seating, tables, cabinetry, rugs, and quilts—there are numerous examples within each, from rockers to armchairs, writing tables to altars, hooked rugs to woven mats.

Chairs are engineered to support the human form. And, like us, they have arms, legs, and feet. Chairs must offer surfaces for sitting and also often for draping or storing other objects—but as long as they fulfill this basic function, chairs can take nearly infinite forms. Some are the most static fixtures in a room. Others are intended to be flexible and mobile; they can be stored at the periphery and slide into place when they are called to service.

Many kinds of tables are the nucleus of a room. They are seen in profile when approached, and from overhead once one is seated. These differing viewpoints are often reflected in the positioning of design features. The surface of the table can be a working canvas and the base can become a sculptural element.

INTRODUCTION

Cabinets provide order and safeguard our belongings. They can be considered markers of status in and of themselves, as they would not exist without the need to protect valued items. Often, the importance and nature of their contents are signified by their outward appearance. These pieces have a large presence within the home. The early Pennsylvania German Kleiderschrank, a distinct cultural form of cabinetwork, demonstrates that furniture can also establish and articulate a familial legacy.

Quilts can also convey a legacy. Many have been made as multigenerational collaborations. They are often passed between family members, sometimes on the occasion of a birth or a wedding. They are also cocoons for the human body, wrapping a person with warmth. As the other soft, fiber objects in this chapter, rugs also provide warmth and they act as cushions under feet. Rugs and quilts are normally placed in unchanging locations and cover large areas. Their two-dimensional surfaces are slates for imagery, color, pattern, and expression.

The primary materials for this group of objects are plant-based—various kinds of wood, in addition to cotton and makaloa. Second to the plant materials are animal-based materials, from leather and wool to mother-of-pearl. Metal fittings, inlay, and hardware are the additional elements. All of these pieces were therefore made with a set of media-specific craft techniques in weaving, joinery, cabinetmaking, and upholstery, paired with techniques for creating decorative flourishes. —EZ

INTRODUCTION

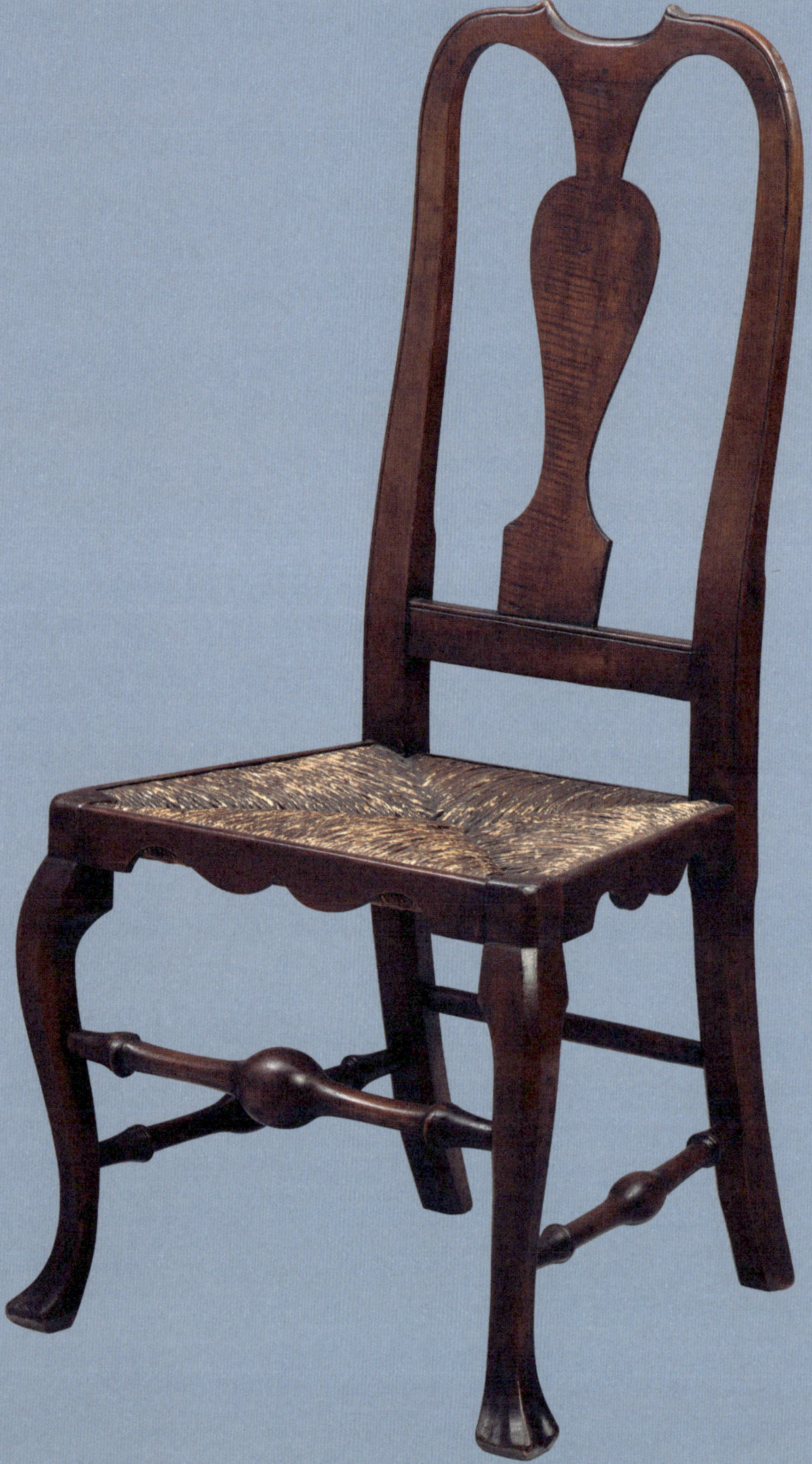

THE CHAIR

RUSH-BOTTOMED CHAIR

c. 1740, Possibly made by **Solomon Fussell** (c. 1704–1762) or **William Savery** (c. 1721–1787), Stained maple, replacement rush seat, 40 × 21 × 19 in. (101.6 × 53.3 × 48.3 cm), Philadelphia Museum of Art, Purchased with the proceeds from the sale of deaccessioned works of art, 2019. 2019-106-1.

A chair like this one is as essential an item today as it was in 1740s Philadelphia, where it was made. Small and light, it was highly functional and heavily used. It survives today because it incorporates many elements that cue it as being consciously designed. The yoke crest rail with rounded ends, vase-shaped banister back, trapezoidal seat, scroll-cut applied rails, and abstracted cabriole legs nod toward fashionable seating, while the materials and portable, sturdy construction suggest its functionality—a functionality that appealed to early Philadelphians across social classes.

Chairs like this one were known as rush-bottomed chairs. Their seats were woven with the stiff stems of dried rush, often in a pattern of four pennant-like triangles. They emerged in the early part of the eighteenth century, and by the 1730s were commonly listed in probate inventories.[1] The popularity of rush-bottomed chairs such as this one exploded in the 1730s because of their accessibility—and they were accessible because of the ingenuity of their manufacture. Philadelphia Quaker chairmaker Solomon Fussell, who was born in York, England, took advantage of highly skilled and diversified artisans in Philadelphia to make these chairs in an assembly-line style. Fussell stockpiled the various elements needed to make them from other specialist artisans: crest rails, banisters (or slats, depending on the type of chairback), stretchers, horse bone–shaped cabriole legs (also known as crookt foot), rush, and more. Fellow Quaker William Savery apprenticed with Fussell and continued this efficient method of making rush-bottomed chairs, which often came to be owned in multiples.

Locally abundant maple was the wood of choice for these chairs, though variations were certainly made. In the inventories, their status ranged from being described as "pretty good" to "ordinary."[2] This specific chair would be considered extraordinary because of its incredibly rare ball-turned side stretchers and the fine pattern of striped maple on its banister back. Like others, it was covered with an iron oxide wash and then coated in a varnish to make the maple look like walnut or mahogany—a desirable effect, considering it likely would have stood alongside finer walnut and mahogany chairs as extra seating in the house of a wealthy Philadelphian.

What makes rush-bottomed chairs like this one remarkable—and is a testament to their enduring appeal—is their incredible design. Despite being assembled from parts and made in multiples, the elements are perfectly proportioned and finely wrought, making such chairs look upscale in grand and humble houses alike. From any angle, the modest rush-bottomed chair has a superbly sculptural presence. —**AK**

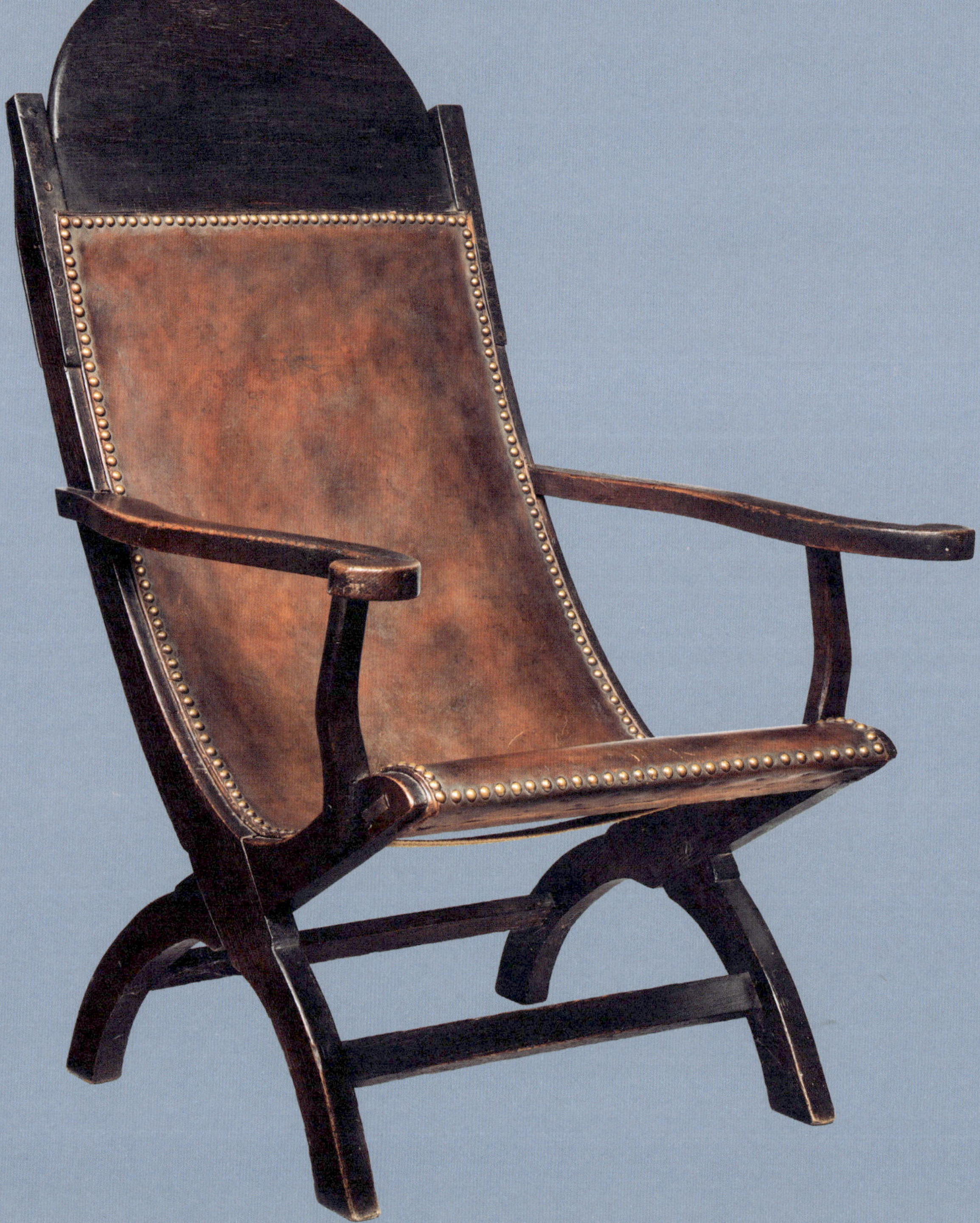

THE CHAIR

BUTACA (CAMPEACHY CHAIR)

1819–20, **John Hemings** (1776–1833),
Oak, leather, brass, 43 × 29¼ × 28½ in. (109.2 × 74.3 × 72.4 cm),
Chipstone Foundation, Milwaukee, 2012.7.

Designed for optimal comfort and repose, the butaca (from the Spanish for "easy chair") is a low-sitting chair with an inclined seat and back attached to a wooden frame, forming a characteristic J or L shape. While variations of the butaca spread to parts of the Americas, Asia, and Europe, the chair originated in the Circum-Caribbean region, where artisans blended Indigenous and European furniture traditions.

The origins of the butaca can be traced to the duho, a revered ritual seat used by high-ranking members of Indigenous society in the Antilles. Duhos were carved from one solid piece of wood, sat low to the ground, and featured a sloped seat and back—characteristics still found in modern butacas. The arrival of European joiners to the Americas in the sixteenth century—tradesmen responsible for maintaining and repairing ships—introduced new iron tools, serrated saws, and techniques such as the use of nails to the region.

By the late eighteenth century, the production and trade of butacas was flourishing. In Campeche, Mexico, artisans crafted elaborately decorated butacas featuring tooled leather seats and ornate carving or marquetry. The spread of the butaca was further facilitated by Charles III of Spain's 1778 decree allowing free trade among Spanish American ports, which expanded its reach to cities such as New Orleans. From the late eighteenth to the mid-nineteenth century, Louisiana merchants and craftsmen played a crucial role in disseminating butacas throughout the southern United States, where they became known as campeachy chairs, an anglicization of Campeche.

At the time, the act of sitting low to the ground in a reclined posture was neither reflected in contemporary seating designs nor an acceptable posture in public settings. The butaca's design, which demanded the sitter position their body in deep recline, was curious and novel. By the nineteenth century, cabinetmakers across the Eastern Seaboard had adopted the design, introducing further stylistic modifications that omitted many of the decorative details found in Mexican examples, and in some cases included cushioned upholstered seats, presumably to conform to a local clientele that preferred a more conservative aesthetic.

The butaca was famously favored by former president Thomas Jefferson. He was gifted a New Orleans–made example, which was part of a pair, split between him and his close friend Elizabeth House Trist. His chair was primarily made from cherrywood and included a circle of stars inlaid at the crest—possibly a reference to the first United States flag—with tufted red leather upholstery. The chair served as a prototype for John Hemings, an enslaved carpenter at Jefferson's Monticello estate, who produced several more examples for the property. Hemings made a few adjustments to the chair's design and production, such as using metal screws, oak, and a heavy cowhide seat.

Despite its successive adaptations, the butaca remains deeply rooted in the historical and cultural exchanges of the Circum-Caribbean and the United States, emerging as a distinctly American chair type. Its design embodies the convergence of Indigenous and European craftsmanship, and its trade history underscores the interconnected nature of colonial economies throughout the Americas. —CDL

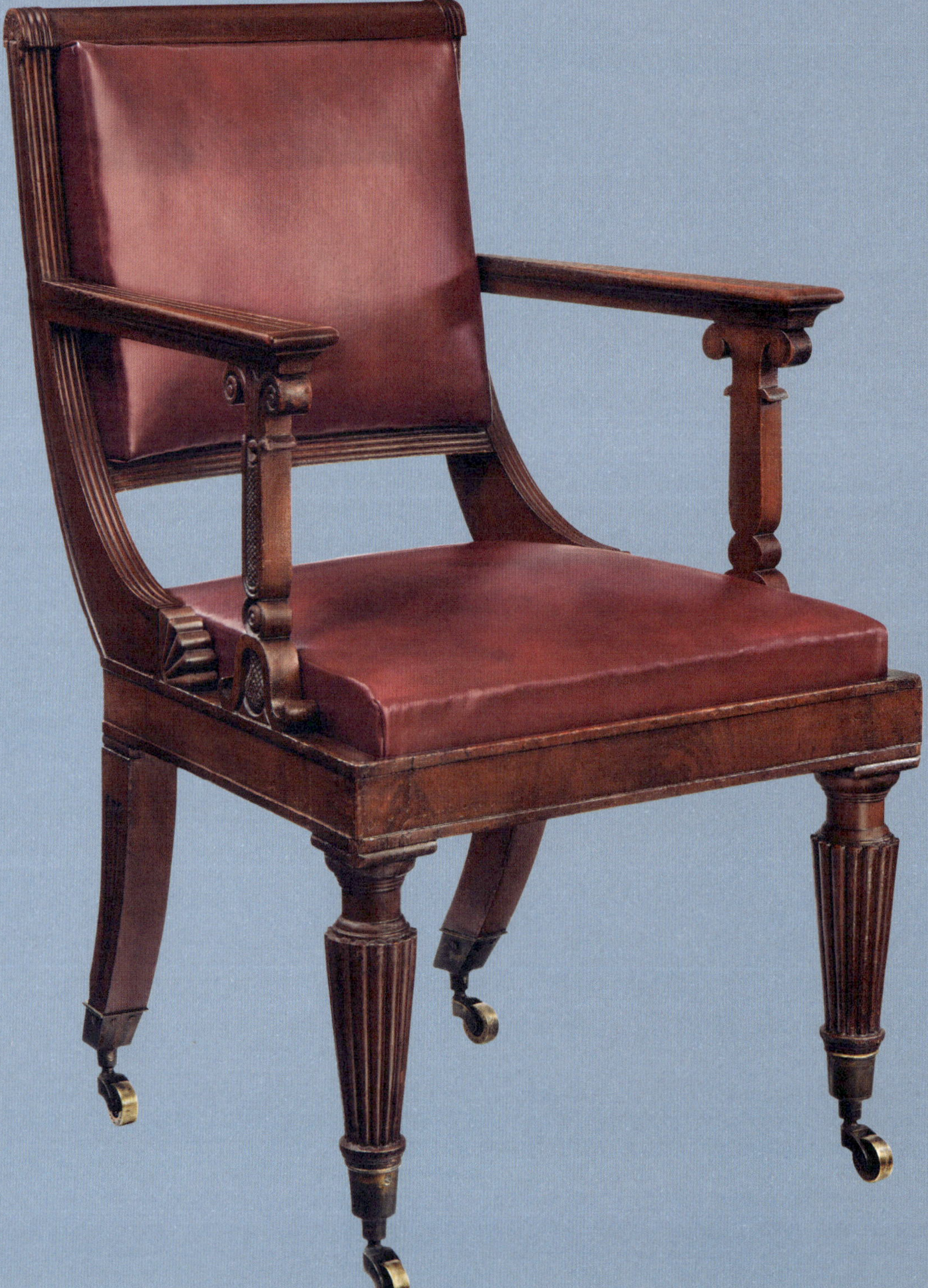

THE CHAIR

ARMCHAIR

1819, **Thomas Constantine & Co.** (active 1815–1826),
Mahogany, mahogany veneer, maple, brass, replacement castors, replacement leather upholstery,
38⅜ × 23¼ × 19½ in. (97.5 × 59 × 49.5 cm), Private collection.

A nation's capital in ruins. The assembly building and the presidential palace are burnt-out shells, the elegant furniture they once contained used as kindling to start the inferno. This desolate scene could describe any number of cities impacted by revolution or civil war, but Americans often forget that the British torched Washington, DC, during the War of 1812. The Capitol and president's house were both gutted as a rebuttal to the destruction American soldiers wrought on York (now Toronto) in Canada. Once the fires were extinguished, rebuilding took more than five years.

Heading the rebuilding process, ironically, was English architect Benjamin Henry Latrobe. His style was drawn from ancient Greece and Rome and therefore deemed suitable for the Capitol. Likewise, the design for this armchair, which would furnish the rebuilt Senate, was pulled almost directly from a plate in an English design book, Thomas Hope's 1807 *Household Furniture and Interior Decoration*.

When the Senate returned to the Capitol at the end of 1819, members were welcomed into a richly furnished chamber with crimson fabric draped along the walls and forming a canopy overhanging the vice president and secretary of the Senate's desks. A handsome crimson carpet was underfoot, and each senator was provided with an armchair covered in crimson leather and a mahogany desk, also likely designed after furniture in Hope's volume. The chairs were stately but sturdy, with a heavy seat frame made from maple, a robust native hardwood often used by early nineteenth-century cabinetmakers.

Since the first United States Congress gathered in New York in 1789, the Senate and the House of Representatives have always been separated by the appearance of their furnishings: the senators sitting on the more regal red, and the representatives on the more democratic black. In the newly reconstructed Capitol, the House furniture was likewise less impressive, and they sat in small groups at communal desks.

Despite the markedly different appearance of the two suites of furniture, the manufacturer was the same: the relatively unknown New York City firm of T. Constantine & Co. Constantine was sufficiently proud of his work to order bespoke casters for the rear legs of the Senate chairs, which are marked "T. Constantine N. York." Although casters are an essential element of the modern office chair, this feature was still quite novel for seating furniture in the early nineteenth century, and their inclusion here speaks to the vital need to move chairs around the chamber when the body was in session.

All forty-eight desks that T. Constantine & Co. produced for the Senate are still in use in the Capitol today. The chairs, however, scattered to the wind beginning in the late nineteenth century, when senators were permitted to take theirs home as a souvenir at the end of their term. The whereabouts of only three of them are known today. This example was removed from the Capitol in 1881 by Hannibal Hamlin, a Republican from Maine, and descended in his family as a treasured heirloom until it was sold at auction in 2010. —**MT**

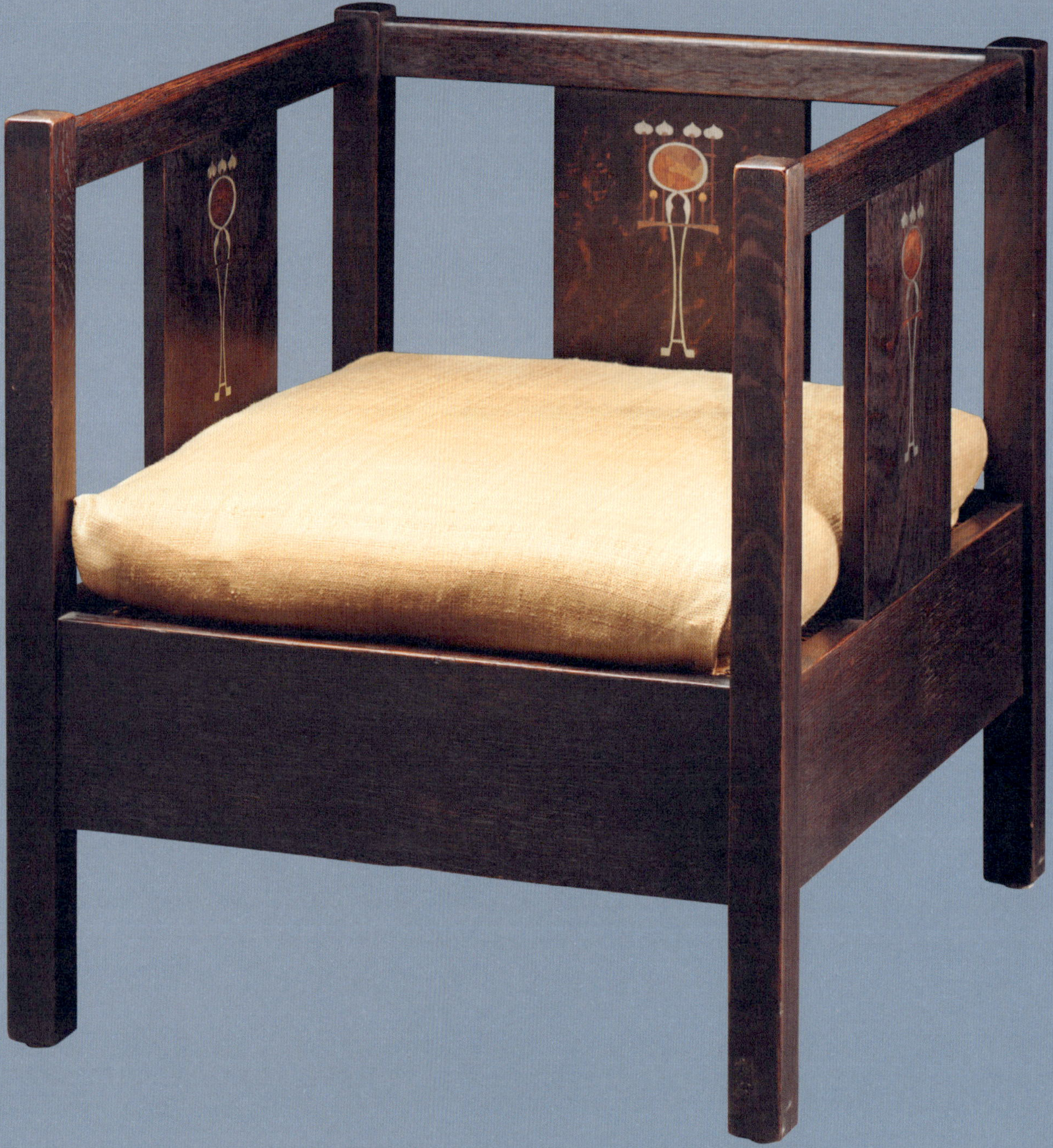

ARMCHAIR

c. 1903, **United Crafts/The Craftsman Workshops** (active 1898–1916) of **Gustav Stickley** (1858–1942), Oak, pewter, copper, various woods, replacement upholstery, 28 ½ × 26 × 27 ¾ in. (72.4 × 66 × 70.5 cm), Crab Tree Farm Collection, ACF.178.94.

In its heft and spartan form, this cube chair is an architectonic landing spot, enclosing the sitter in its simple geometry and play of positive and negative space. Its restraint and rectilinearity marked a stark departure from the curvaceous, overstuffed opulence of Victorian furniture into a new realm of design. The chair was a leap toward modernism and a new aesthetic for a new century as conceived by Gustav Stickley and his workshop. Instilled with the values of the Arts and Crafts movement, objects and furniture like this chair conveyed a philosophical and artistic stance that embraced practicality in form, straightforwardness in the treatment of materials, and the joy of handwork, as exemplified by joinery and detail. This chair is not for slouchers and loungers; it encourages a straight back and honest morals.

Craft as we know it today is part of a trajectory embedded in the Arts and Crafts movement that began in the late nineteenth century. The parallels in ideology are remarkably fresh 125 years later. Stickley founded his furniture company near Syracuse, New York, in 1898 after trips to Europe that deepened his interest in the ideology and aesthetics of the Arts and Crafts movement as it was sprouting up in pockets of the United States. Design was no doubt essential to the appeal of the movement, as much as what it posited as a more redemptive way of making meaningful objects. These were the roots of what was further embraced and achieved by countless artists who led the Studio Craft movement in the years after World War II and through the latter half of the twentieth century.

The notion of finding value in the handmade and uplifting the craftsman-designer spoke to Stickley, whose father was a stonemason and whose uncle owned a chair manufacturing business. Stickley built a small and relatively short-lived empire in United Crafts, renamed the Craftsman Workshops in 1903,[1] and *The Craftsman* magazine, in which he marketed an entire approach to domestic design and life. Through both ventures, he translated the concepts of John Ruskin, William Morris, and other European decorative arts theorists into an American idiom.

One of the standout designers who helped define Stickley's product line and aesthetic at the time this chair was made was architect Harvey Ellis, who worked at the company for less than a year before his untimely death in January 1904. During Ellis's short period with the Stickley team, inlay and a nuanced shift in proportions introduced a more refined look. Stickley saw the metal and wood inlay as injecting a delicate element of color through the imagery of abstract plant forms. In the case of this chair, roundels also feature miniature inlaid landscape scenes (see detail, page 4). LaMont A. Warner and Claude Bragdon were also working with Stickley at the time and creating designs in this vein.[2] Today, we are beginning to recognize that furniture, like many kinds of craft, was rarely the work of a sole auteur but often a collaborative effort between designers and many skilled makers. To design is one part of the puzzle. Having the technical ability to execute is the other. —EZ

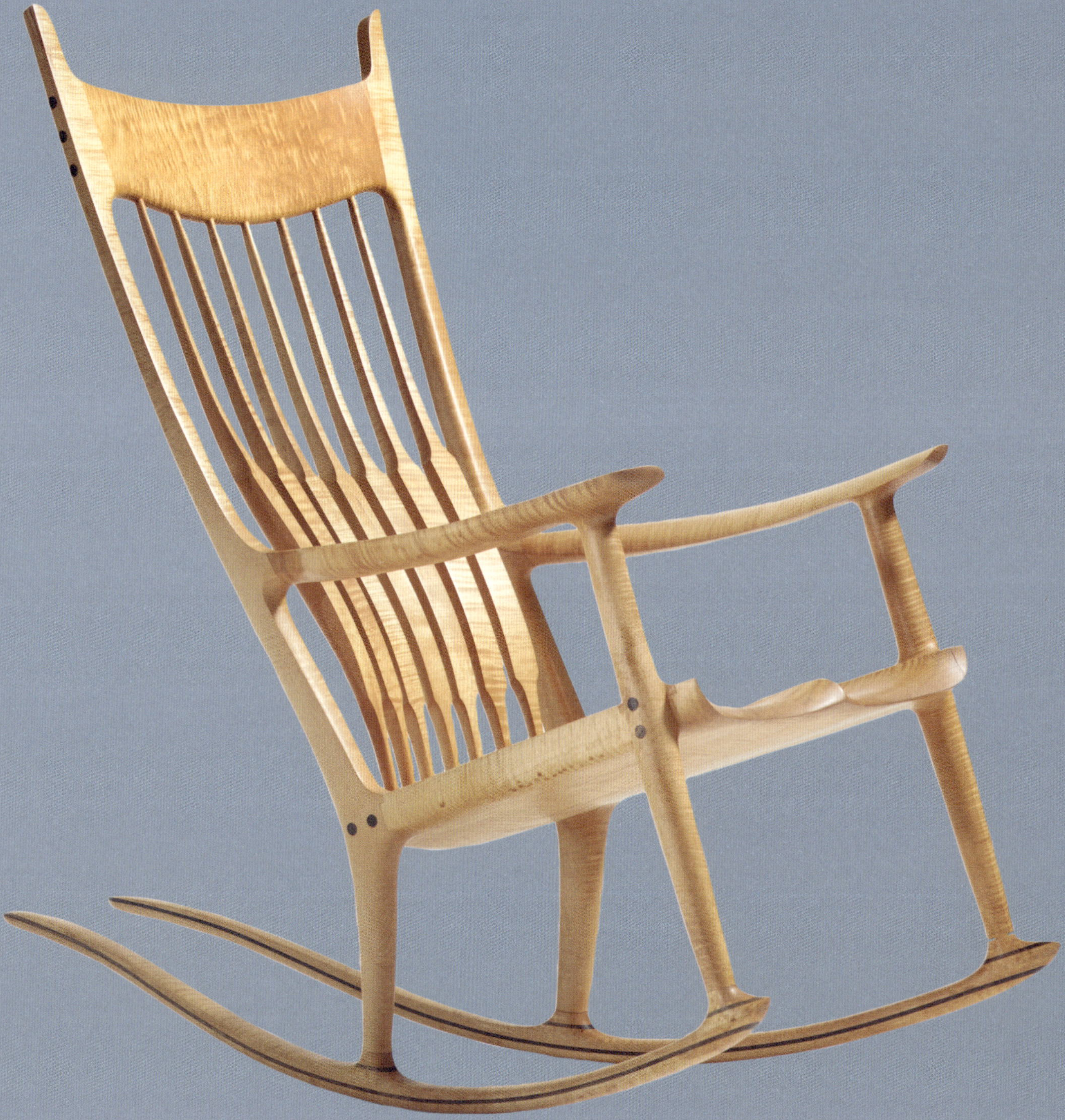

THE CHAIR

ROCKER

1990, **Sam Maloof** (1916–2009),
Fiddleback maple, ebony, 45½ × 26¾ × 45 in. (116 × 68 × 114 cm),
Private collection.

"My simple rule of thumb is this: when you cut down a tree, what you make of it should be at least as miraculous as what you cut down." So says one of the characters in Richard Powers's 2018 novel *The Overstory*, a persuasive literary case for forest preservation and the revelation that trees are in constant communication with one another, rivalry and collaboration in one single, sprawling intelligence. The provocation of this "simple rule of thumb," of course, is that it seems impossible to satisfy.

Making wood better than it was in a living tree? Good luck with that. But if anything comes close it's a Sam Maloof rocking chair. Although the rocking chair first appeared in England in the eighteenth century, it has since developed into arguably the most American of chairs, and Maloof's were owned by presidents Jimmy Carter and Ronald Reagan alike, installed on the Truman Balcony of the White House. Throughout his long career, Maloof was the nation's leading furniture maker, both by popular acclaim and professional reputation. And among the designs he developed and perfected, his rockers were his most celebrated. He made so many of them that a few of his peers indulged in mild carping about his lack of adventurousness, as if he were a one-man oldies band, wearing out his biggest hit. In fact, the chairs just got better and better, their taut curves that much more expressive, their silky surfaces that much more sublime.

When Maloof had beautiful wood in his hands, the results could indeed be miraculous. The late, great rockers he made in tiger maple, one of several timbers that naturally exhibit the property of chatoyance—from the French for "cat's eye"—an inner shine produced by light reflecting off an undulating grain pattern. Maloof clearly loved this quality of animation, which is only seen when the timber is shaped, smoothed, and finished. It actually *is* better than it was in the tree, at least visually. He then enhanced the effect, sculpting the chair's seat, spindles, crest, and arms into a perfectly coordinated composition. The lines of the chair are sleek, potent, their latent kinetic energy emphasized by long curves of ebony laminated into the runners.

When he made these masterworks, then, Maloof was not so much an aging rocker as a teenager pinstriping a hot rod (and I do vividly remember him turning up at a Furniture Society conference in the late 1990s driving a brand-new black Porsche). Studio furniture makers of his generation are most often praised for the organicism of their work, the faith that they had in the beauty of unadorned timber. That quality is certainly present in Maloof's work; nobody ever did more to showcase the rippling grain of walnut or maple. Yet he always balanced this naturalism with an intensely artificial, quintessentially man-made orchestration of form. To recapture wood's innate beauty took more than humble craft; it also took bold artistry. —**GA**

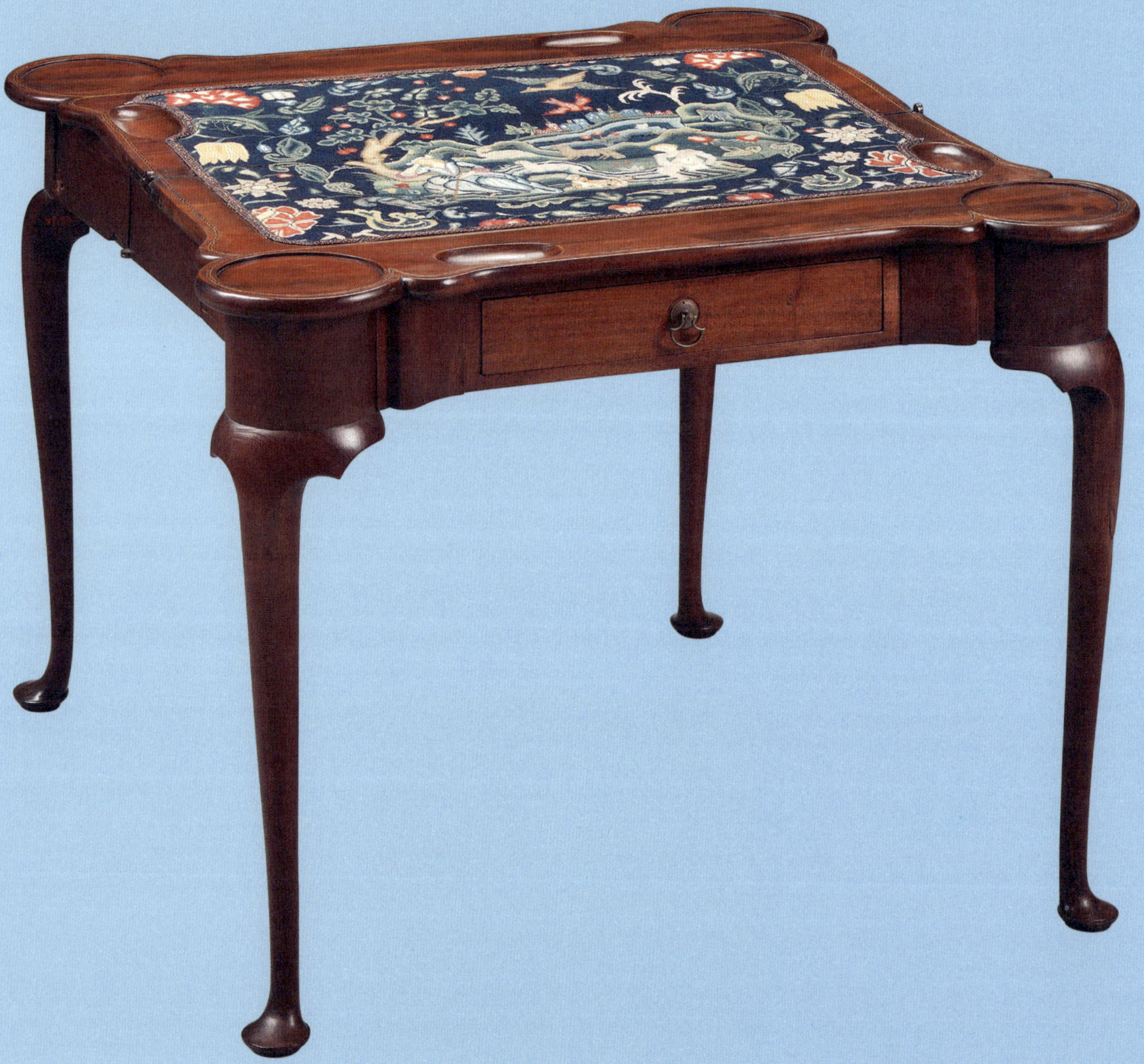

THE TABLE

CARD TABLE

c. 1730–50, **Unidentified artist (Boston)**, Mahogany, chestnut, eastern white pine, original needlework top, 27 × 35⅝ × 35⅛ in. (68.6 × 90.5 × 89.2 cm), Museum of Fine Arts, Boston, Museum purchase with funds donated anonymously and William E. Nickerson Fund, 1949, 49.330.

The card table was still a relatively new form when this example was made in the mid-eighteenth century. While it became more common in British households after Parliament passed the 1710 Gaming Act, which cracked down on public gambling houses, card tables were still a rarity in Boston homes. The once-Puritan city maintained strict laws against social vices such as card playing well into the eighteenth century. Yet the survival of this table and a small group of related examples signals the shifts happening in Boston as the city became a more secular society. It also embodies the handwork skills of two very different Boston craftspeople: a cabinetmaker and an embroiderer, both unidentified, who contributed to that societal change.

The table was likely made by a recently arrived English-trained craftsman who immigrated for the financial opportunities of the colonies rather than for religious freedom. He brought with him the latest English fashions and techniques to share with his colonial patrons, such as the sophisticated mechanism incorporated into this card table to support the two-leaf top when open. Instead of a hinged gate leg that rotates ninety degrees to support the top, both side rails are hinged and able to extend, secured by an iron hook. The benefit of this construction method (a technique often called a "concertina action" due to its accordion-like movement) is that all the legs remain at the corners, stabilizing the surface and eliminating the need for one card player to straddle an obtrusive gate leg. However, the concertina mechanism was not only significantly more expensive due to its need for extra labor and imported hinges, but all those moving parts also made it more fragile and susceptible to breakage. Therefore, even though it was more stylish, the construction method was not regularly requested by more frugal colonial patrons.

The needlework surface was probably embroidered by a young woman hailing from a prosperous New England family while attending one of the city's elite finishing schools. These schools taught genteel manners, needlework, and dancing—a move away from an earlier emphasis on religious instruction. A teacher would have drawn or traced the image onto canvas, then the student chose the threads and colors for its execution. The central image features a pastoral scene, derived from contemporary prints. A shepherdess sits beneath a cherry tree, resting her head on her elbow, as if daydreaming. A dog lies near her feet, and a male figure, possibly a cupid holding a lamb, is seated nearby. The grouping is surrounded by rolling green hills populated with additional sheep and colorful birds above, with a cityscape in the distance. The central image is framed by a border of oversized flowers and leaves, including carnations and tulips. Many of these motifs symbolize love, renewal, and hope, stereotypical secular desires of its young maker. Such a large-scale project would have represented the culmination of a young woman's schooling and would have been proudly displayed on the wall of the family home, or, in this case, adorning the morally tainted card table.[1] —NG

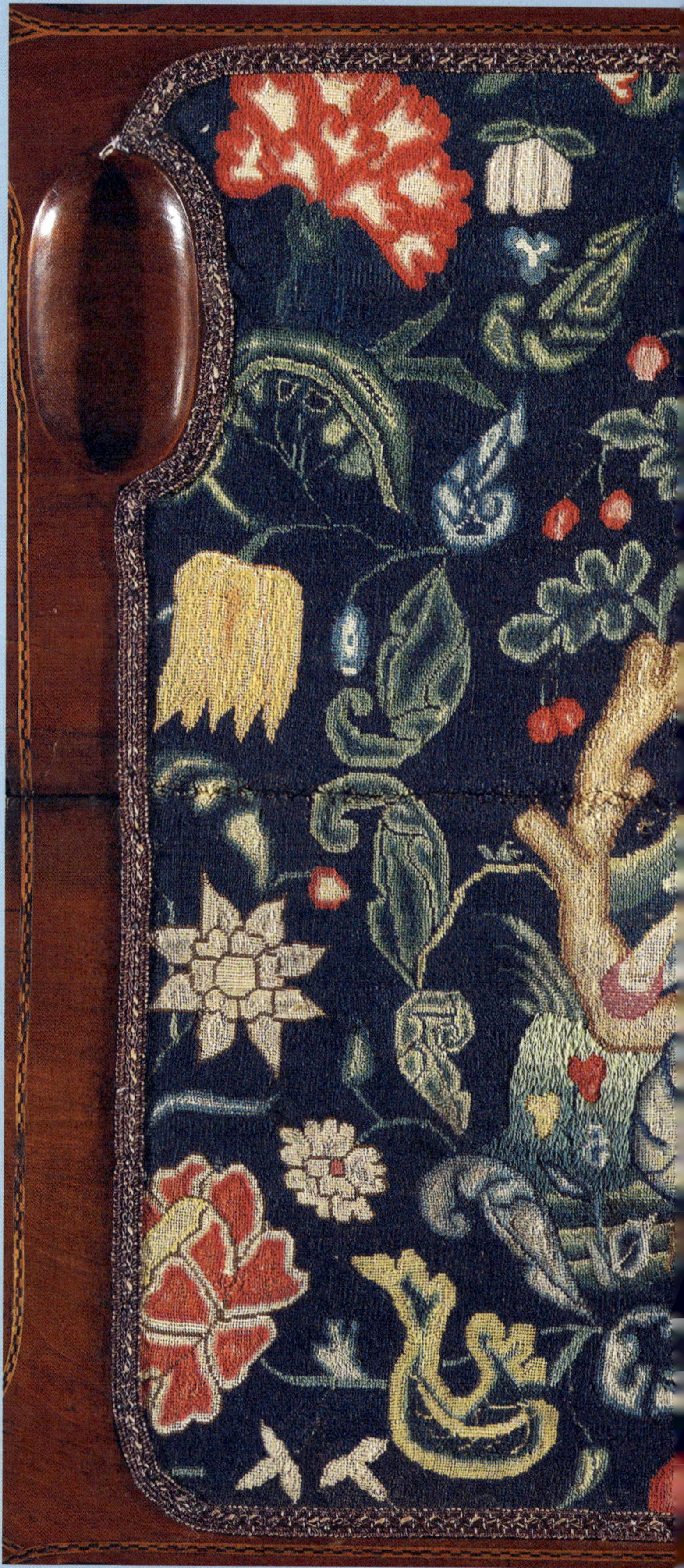

THE TABLE

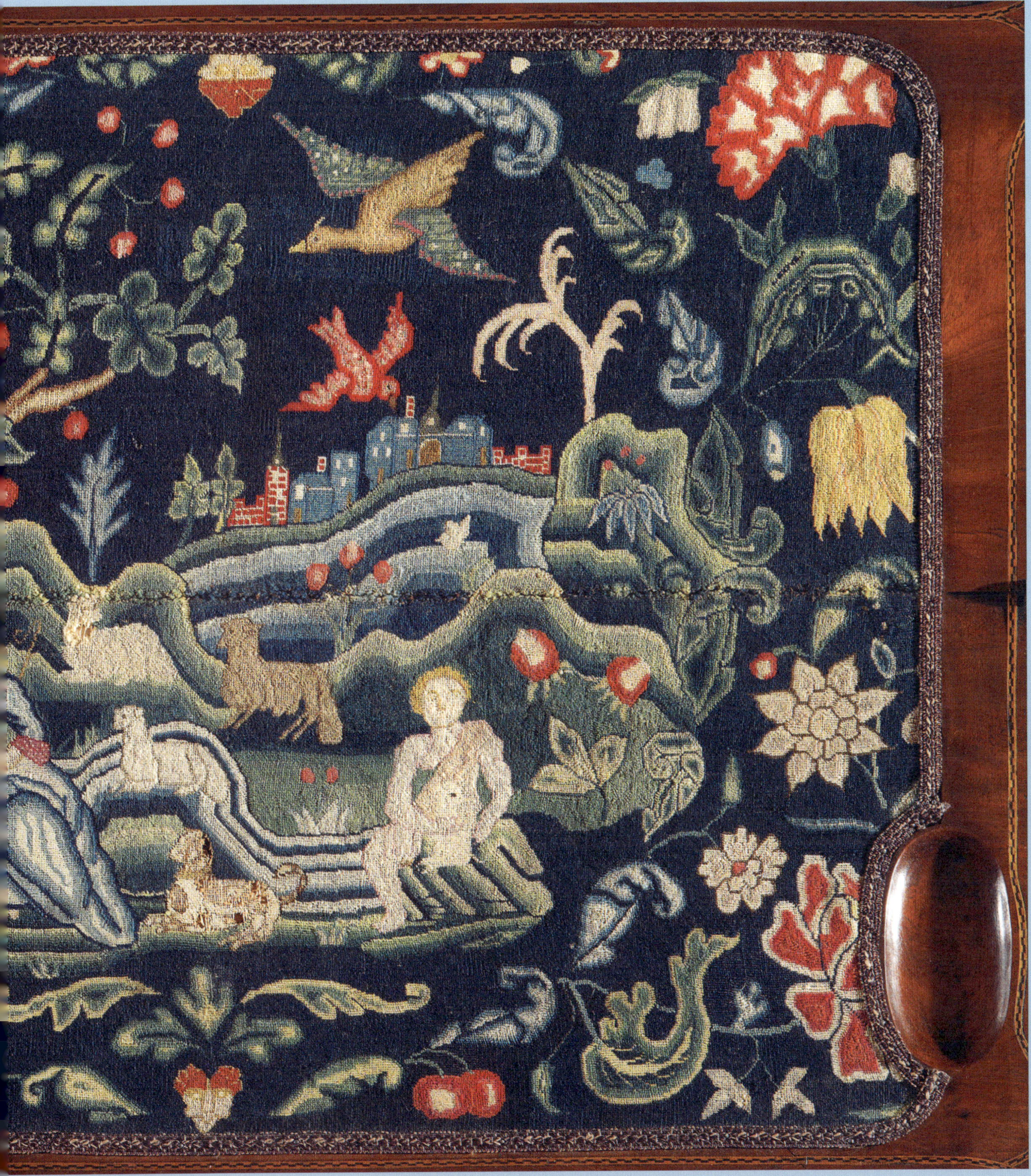

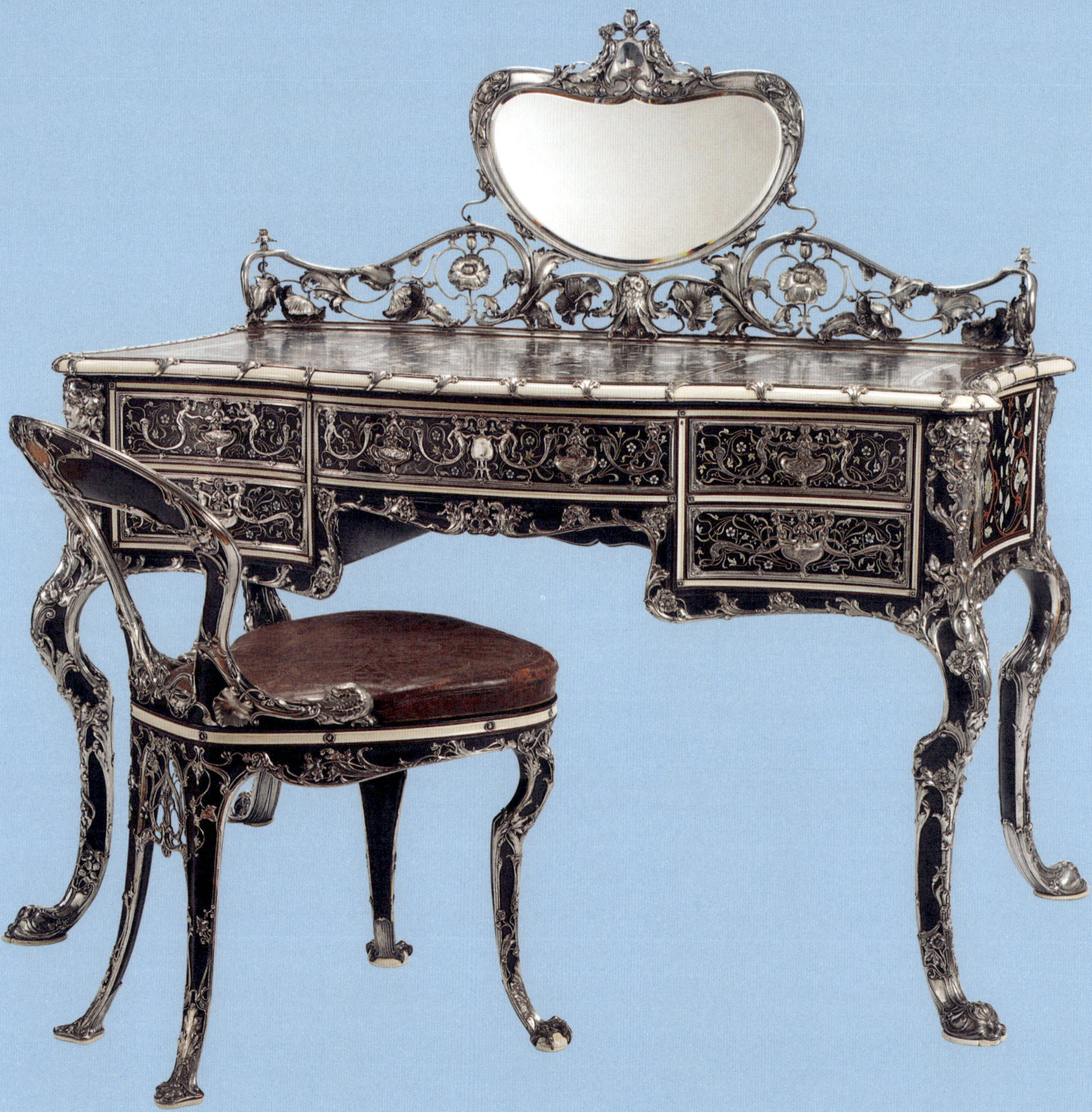

THE TABLE

MARTELÉ WRITING TABLE

1903, Designed by **William Christmas Codman** (1839–1921), modeled by **Franz Ziegler**, silverwork by **Joseph Edward Straker**, and cabinetry by **Potter and Company, Gorham Manufacturing Company** (est. 1831), Ebony, mahogany, boxwood, redwood, thuya wood, ivory, mother-of-pearl, silver, mirrored glass, gilded tooled leather, Table: 48 13⁄16 × 53 3⁄4 × 29 15⁄16 in. (124 × 136.5 × 76 cm), Rhode Island School of Design Museum, Providence, Gift of Mr. and Mrs. Frederick B. Thurber, 58.095ab.

Silver vines twist along and ensnare the legs and edges of this desk and chair. One can imagine sitting on the embossed leather cushion, looking into the semicircular mirror crowned with two figures sitting in contemplative thought, one's gaze returned by the wide eyes of an owl sculpted at the base, imparting wisdom and inspiration. Interlocking florals repeat across the top and sides of the desk, each individually carved and inlaid, made from exotic materials including ebony, mahogany, ivory, and mother-of-pearl. Four fantastical female faces emerge from the desk's corners, allegorizing the seasons: Spring, by the incorporation of lilies at her temples; Summer with wild rose; Fall with chrysanthemum; and Winter with pine cones. Encrusted with fifty pounds of wrought silver, this desk brings together several different specialties to form one of the most stunning Art Nouveau pieces made in the United States.

This desk set is part of the famed Gorham Martelé line, Art Nouveau handmade silver produced in Providence, Rhode Island, from 1896 to 1917. The chief designer for Gorham Manufacturing Company, William C. Codman brought a historicist impulse to the business, developed through his previous work for an English architectural firm and the British silver firm Elkington & Co., an international rival of Gorham. Codman was committed to the design reform tenets of the Arts and Crafts movement, which prioritized handcraftsmanship, restrained design, and the amplification of a material's truth. Codman proved that these Arts and Crafts principles could thrive within the corporate structures of Gilded Age decorative arts firms with the successful Martelé line.

The Martelé line was a selection of high-end objects produced as a collaboration between designers and craftsmen who were trained by and reported directly to Codman. The name of the line comes from the French verb *marteler*, "to hammer." While silversmiths had historically been able to artfully cast, hammer, stretch, and chase metals to take any form or style, by the late nineteenth century, decorative arts firms across the United States and Europe had applied industrial technologies such as electroplating and sheet rolling to streamline the silversmith's work, enabling them to focus their skills on decorative details. Gorham, like most silver firms from the period, hired an entire department of chasers who worked with chisel and hammer to create works of art. Martelé artists were encouraged to embrace self-expression in each object, intentionally incorporating hammer marks and chasing lines that previously would have been polished or buffed out.

Martelé objects were designed and crafted to be unique works of art. This desk set embodies silver's fluid nature, with rarely a sharp angle or straight line to be found. To achieve this look, Gorham used a softer silver (95/100 parts of silver instead of sterling's 92/100) that was easier for silversmiths to work with hand tools. Because of the specialized labor required of Martelé objects, such pieces were often the most expensive on the market. Gorham employees and outside specialists contributed more than 10,000 hours of labor to create this desk set, which cost $25,000 in 1904 (more than $800,000 today). Gorham executives exhibited this specific desk at the 1904 Louisiana Purchase Exposition (St. Louis World's Fair), and again at the 1915 Panama-Pacific International Exposition in San Francisco. —CG

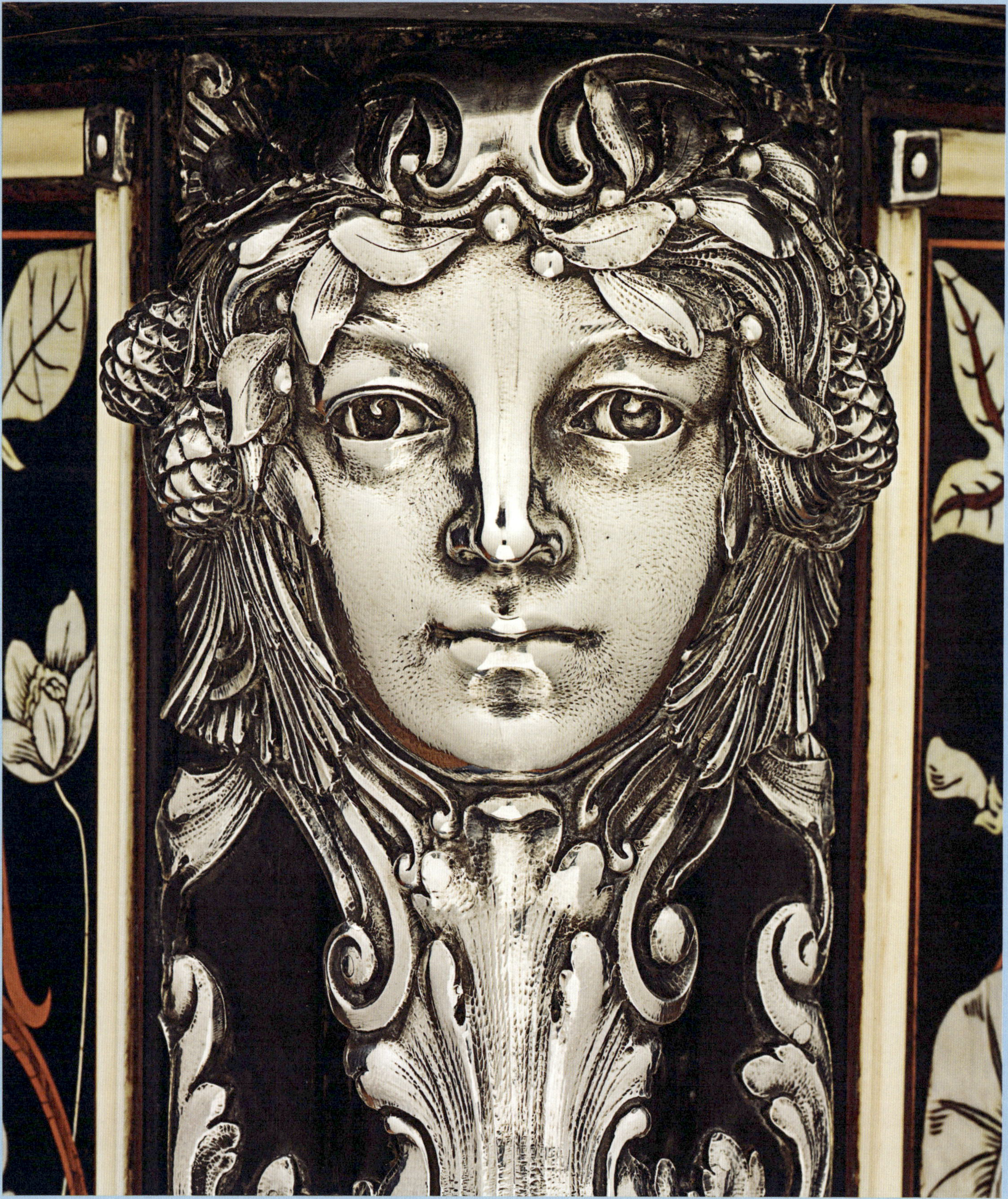

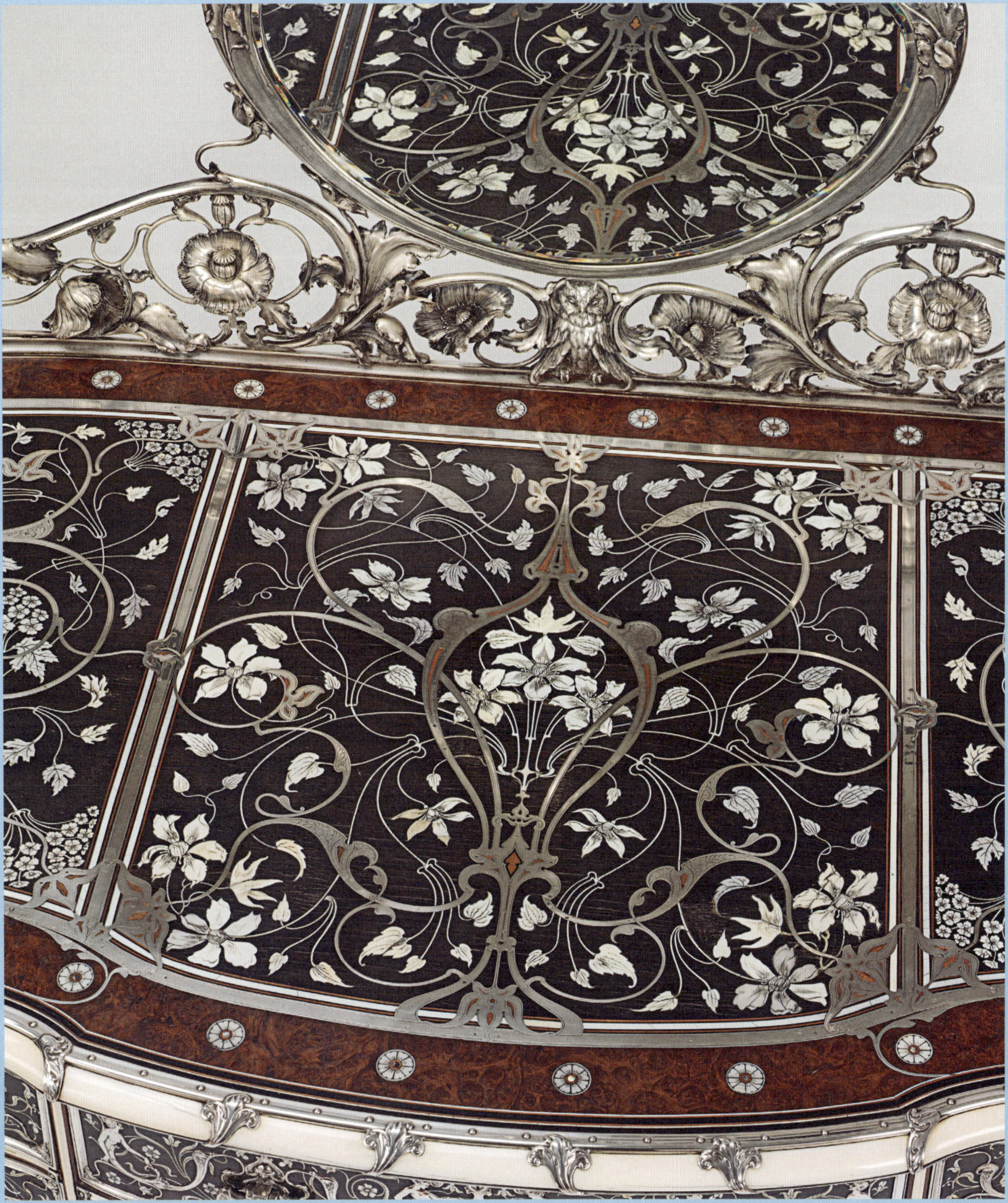

TO SET

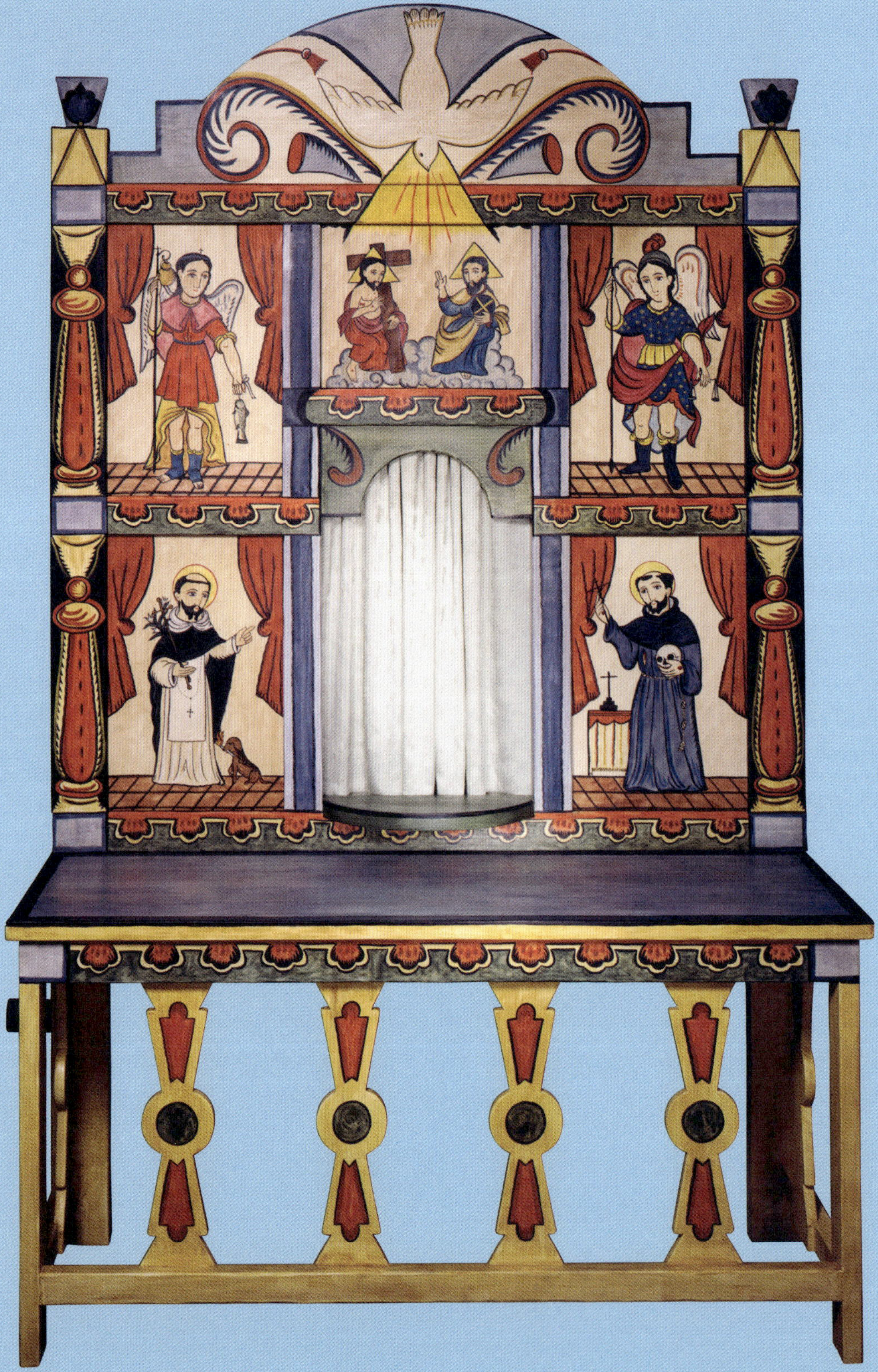

THE TABLE

DEVOCIÓN DE NUEVO MÉXICO (DEVOTION OF NEW MEXICO)

1998, **Charles M. Carrillo** (b. 1956),
Gesso and natural pigments on pine, 96½ x 60 × 21¾ in. (245.1 × 152.4 × 55.3 cm),
Smithsonian American Art Museum, Washington, DC, Museum purchase made possible by
William T. Evans and the Smithsonian Institution Collections Acquisition Program, 998.94A-D.

For more than 425 years, carved and painted wooden objects have played a significant role in spiritual life in what is now the southwestern United States. As early as 1598, Franciscan friars accompanied soldiers and settlers into the territory known as New Spain. As settlement continued and missions were established, altares (altars or altar screens), bultos (sculptures), and retablos (paintings on wood) accompanied religious practice, both in the chapel and at home. While imbued with sacred qualities, the images applied to these objects also served as mediums for devotion, storytelling, and healing.

Charles M. Carrillo, commonly known as Charlie, holds a PhD in archaeology and has written scholarly works on New Mexico art and history; yet he has drawn national and international attention as a santero, a maker of religious images. While directing an archaeological project in the late 1970s in the community of Abiquiú, New Mexico, he became engaged with the local morada (chapel) of the Penitente Brotherhood. Out of this experience came a concerted study and eventual artistic commitment to create religious images using historically accurate natural pigments and techniques.

The *Devoción de Nuevo México* altarpiece (altar mayor, or side altar) commissioned by the Smithsonian American Art Museum in 1998 demonstrates Carrillo's attention to both artistic detail and the history of the form. Carrillo employed a mortise and tenon construction instead of nails and used paints made from local plants, insects, and minerals. The right and left sides of the altar feature retablos depicting four saints. On the upper left, Saint Rafael holds a staff with a flask and carries a fish, a native trout. Saint Rafael is the patron saint of, among other things, medicine, good health, doctors, and fishermen. Below is Saint Antonio of Padua (a popular subject of santeros in northern New Mexico), the patron saint of lost objects and happy marriages. He wears a blue robe associated with the Conceptionist Franciscans, the primary missionaries in the region, and carries a white lily, a sign of purity. Saint Michael, on the upper right, is known as a defender of faith and a protector from enemies, an attribute that was perhaps frequently desired in the early settlements. He is also said to play a role in the Last Judgement, weighing souls, so he is often shown carrying a scale. Below is Saint Francis of Assisi, the patron saint of animals and the poor. He too wears the blue robe of the Conceptionist Franciscans and around his waist is a belt with three knots symbolizing the triad of Franciscan vows: poverty, chastity, and obedience. His hands bear the stigmata, and he clutches a skull, a memento mori, typically indicating that he is meditating on mortality. Centered at the top of the altar are images of the Holy Trinity: the Father, Son, and—depicted as a white dove with rays of light emanating from its head—the Holy Spirit. The retablos surround a platform that could support a carved religious sculpture.

This work is a manifestation of the artist's head, heart, and hand. Literally and figuratively, the altar screen is an article of faith. Carrillo has observed, "In most cases santos and images were created to act as 'windows' to the divine."[1] When making his retablos, he paints the eyes and mouths of his saints last to prevent them from staring at or talking back to him. When the image is finished, it has been given a soul. —BB

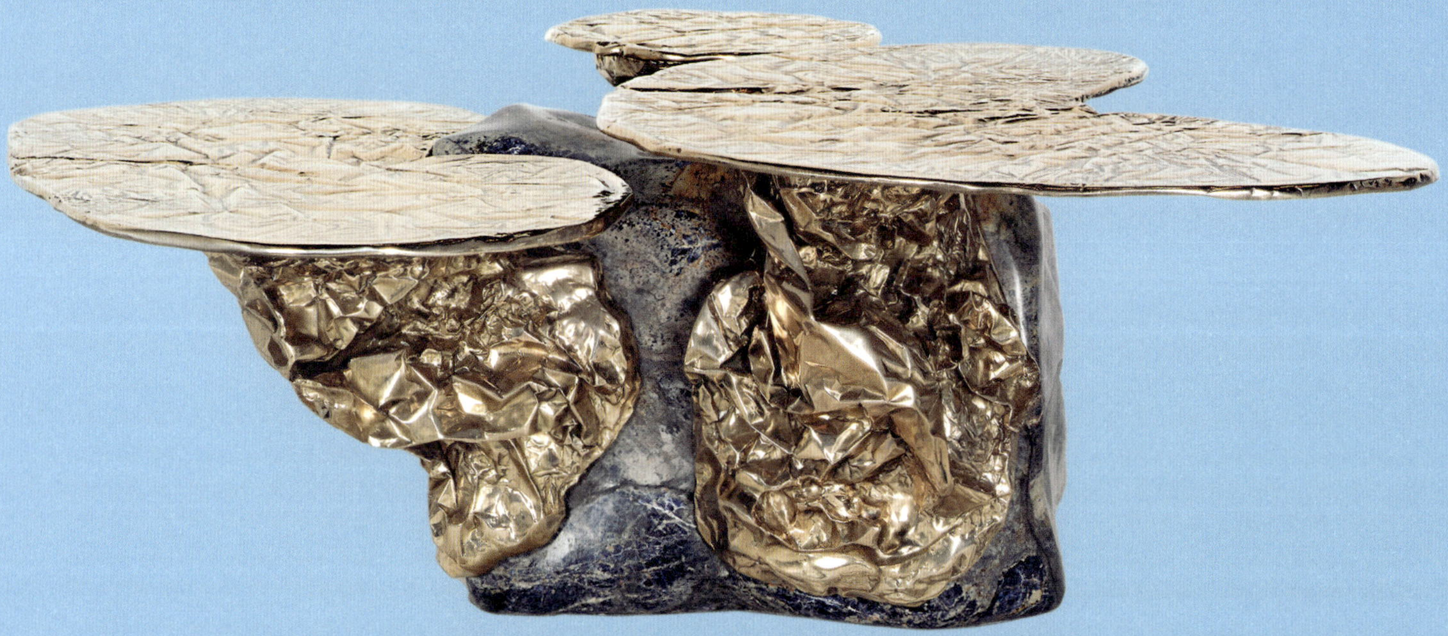

THE TABLE

ENHANCING SELF TRUST

2022, **Misha Kahn** (b. 1989),
Sodalite, bronze, 19½ × 57½ × 49¼ in. (49.5 × 146.1 × 125.1 cm).

Before the 1920s, there was no such thing as a coffee table. Tea tables, yes; that form had developed more than two hundred years earlier in tandem with the mass importation of tea leaves from China and India and a whole range of other accompanying apparatus—teapots, teabowls, tea caddies. The phenomenon was a quintessential expression of what scholars call the "consumer revolution" of the eighteenth century.

Tea drinking was also an opportunity to socialize in a new way, with women taking an unprecedentedly significant role in the parlor discussions that it engendered. Such gatherings were still rather formal affairs, however, and historic tables reflect this. Their tops look a bit like silver trays, and their legs are often richly carved. They are not very large, as they were only meant to accommodate just one tea set, from which the host or hostess would serve.

Coffee tables, when they finally came along, put things on a whole new level—literally. They are significantly lower to the ground than tea tables, announcing a more relaxed approach to conviviality. Once again, they arrived as part of an ensemble of other forms, including low-slung sofas and other seating furniture, as well as entertainingly exuberant Art Deco coffee services. Eighteenth-century tea drinkers sat bolt upright and handled their tiny teabowls with care. Modern coffee drinkers were free to slouch, put up their feet, and serve themselves.

Interestingly, the company that first introduced "coffee tables" to the American market in 1925—the Imperial Furniture Company of Grand Rapids, Michigan—was firmly traditional, specializing in the then-popular colonial revival style. Soon enough, though, modernist designers had made it their own. Unlike tea tables, which usually had folding tops and were light enough to be easily moved out of the way, coffee tables tended to be a more or less fixed, central feature of a room. They also had few functional requirements; any flat surface would do. This made the coffee table an obvious and unprecedented opportunity for sculptural invention, and figures such as Paul Frankl, Isamu Noguchi, and T. H. Robsjohn-Gibbings took full advantage. Studio furniture makers soon followed suit.

Fast-forward yet another century, and the coffee table is still in action. For those who follow Misha Kahn, the young designer phenom based in New York City, it is no surprise that he would alight on the form. Talk about fast-forward; Kahn is wildly inventive, generating whole design idioms at a dizzying rate. The coffee table was a sitting duck for his restless energies, and he has made quite a few of them. The one shown on these pages is from his Krinkle Cast series. In this technique, he simply crushes foil over an existing shape—here, an impressive chunk of bluestone—then casts the foil in bronze, and finally attaches that where the foil had been. An impromptu composition is thus made monumental, the innumerable happenstance folds and creases transmuted into a gorgeous, gleaming crush of metal. What kind of conversation might be had around such a table? One can only imagine, but it might well involve something stronger than caffeine. —GA

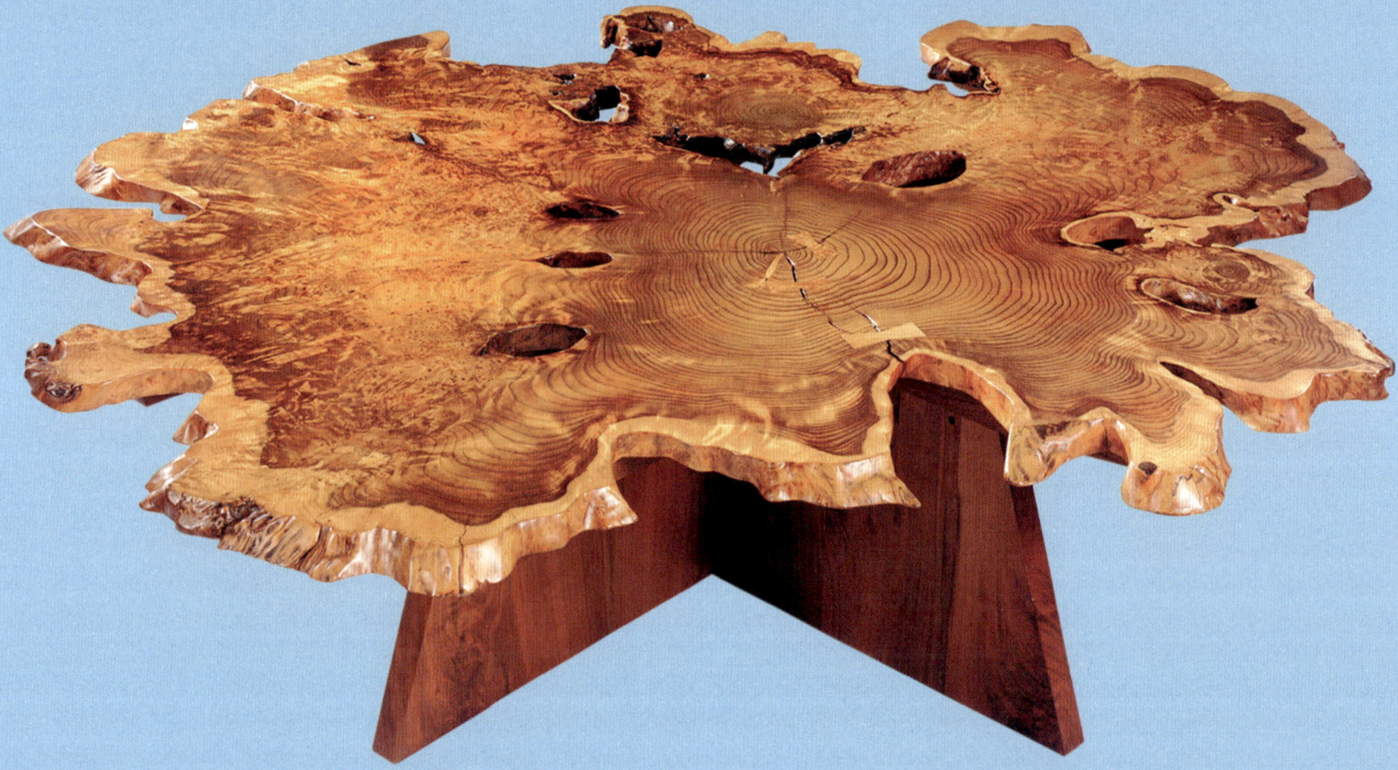

THE TABLE

MIRA NAKASHIMA on THE TABLE

Arlyn table, 1988, **George Nakashima** (1905–1990),
Redwood root burl, black walnut, East Indian laurel, madrona burl, hickory, 26 × 89 × 91 in. (66 × 226 × 231 cm),
From the Collection of the Two Red Roses Foundation, Florida.

I imagine the first table might have been a rock or a tree stump, where food was placed or prepared before it was eaten. Later, it became somewhere offerings were placed, where sacrifices were made to the Divine, and offering tables became altars.

As housing and architecture developed over the centuries, so did furnishings and table forms. Early farm tables were heavy and thick, multipurpose, strong enough to shoulder vegetables, fruit, or meat as it was harvested, processed, cooked, and consumed. These tables, through constant use, became the center of the family, the offering place of people's lives.

As urban populations grew, tables evolved within domestic architecture to suit different spaces and uses. Some dining tables were designed to expand and contract according to the number of people invited to dinner. In living rooms, low, upholstered seating called for small tables on which people could place their drinks during social gatherings. Then of course, there were tables for bridge, pool and ping-pong, so people could play games indoors during leisure hours.

My father first started his furniture business in the mid-twentieth century, when people were beginning to recognize furniture as an important form of art and design. He was introduced to Hans and Florence Knoll, who hired artists to design furniture with the aim that innovative modern design would be affordable to the masses. Among these designers were Isamu Noguchi, Harry Bertoia, and my father, George Nakashima, who produced for Knoll two chair designs, two table designs, and a chest of drawers. The prototypes were created by each artist and then adapted for mass production as necessary. It was through their work with Knoll that my father and his friends not only survived but gained recognition in the design world.

Later, when my father tried to start his own business, he found the "good" straight-grained lumber was too expensive. He learned to scavenge the outside cuts discarded by the lumberyard, offcuts that retained the natural shape of the tree as well as cracks, wormholes, lightning scars, and knots of all kinds. My father embraced these flaws and designed each piece around them, often securing cracks with butterflies, using a technique he had learned in Japan. At first people were often puzzled by the imperfections, but later cherished them as beauty marks. From these humble beginnings, we still make tables in all shapes and sizes, mostly cut from logs salvaged by a local arborist. Sometimes they are "practical" rectangular forms, but they usually retain the free (natural) edges of the tree.

In his later years, my father purchased an extraordinarily large and beautiful walnut log and dreamed that he would make Altars for Peace for each continent from it—a discrete offering toward world peace. He built and installed the first one at the Cathedral of St. John the Divine in New York City and was trying to find a place for one in Russia when he passed in 1990. We built and placed one in Auroville, India, in 1996; another went to the Russian Academy of Arts in 2001.

I believe that all tables have the potential to be sacred places of offering and should be used as such. A small end table in my house has become an altar. My father insisted that his furniture not be considered overly precious—that it be used daily and oiled occasionally, ensuring those dents and scratches would become part of the patina of life.

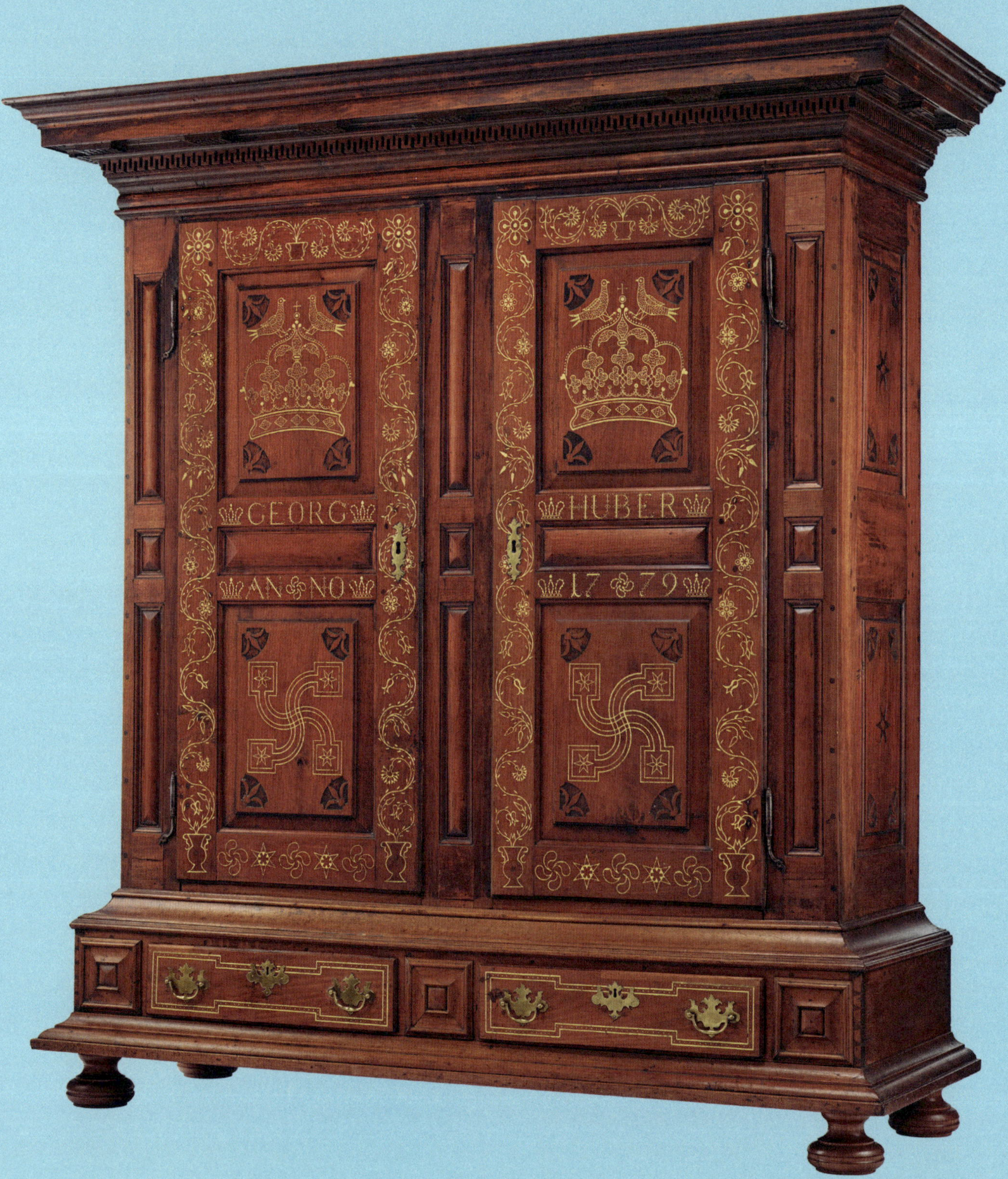

THE CABINET

KLEIDERSCHRANK (CLOTHES PRESS)

1779, **Unidentified artist (Lancaster, Pennsylvania)**,
Walnut, yellow pine, oak, sulfur inlay, iron, replacement brass, 6 ft. 10 ¼ in. × 6 ft. 6 in. × 27 ½ in. (2.1 × 2 × 0.7 m),
Philadelphia Museum of Art, Purchased with Museum funds, 1957. 1957-30-1.

While British style predominated in the Lenapehoking (lands of the Lenape people) of colonial Pennsylvania, German-speaking artisans maintained their cultural traditions in a way that deeply shaped the visual expression in the region. These Pennsylvania Germans—who primarily hailed from the Palatinate (present-day southern Germany) and Switzerland—marked one's passage into adulthood by gifting sets of household textiles such as napkins, tablecloths, towels, bedsheets, and pillowcases; more prosperous families presented these textiles in a lift-top chest or a Kleiderschrank (clothes press) like this one, profusely decorated in patterns that connected them to their Germanic roots.

The Pennsylvania Germans' distinctive pegged mortise and tenon joinery was used throughout such furniture, but it was the imagery pervading the broad surfaces that delighted and urged people to save these works of art. Decoration was commonly painted, but this monumental Lancaster-made clothes press is one of a small group that has applied molten sulfur to shallow valleys carefully carved in the wood (see detail, page 8). The pale yellow sulfur strikingly contrasts the deep brown walnut, and the regularity of the inlay brings light and pattern to the piece's wide expanses in a way that carving and wood inlay do not. Over time, the color of the sulfur—which referenced exotic materials like ivory and orpiment—has deepened from the effects of oil varnish.

Kleiderschranken are typically composed of multiple interlocking sections: in this case, a top cornice, a central cabinet with two doors, and a base with two drawers. The cornice secures the cabinets together in a Jenga-like fashion. Architectural in its conception, the design borrows elements from the Doric order of classical Greek architecture, such as the projecting cornice above ornamental protrusions. This, along with the carved fleurs-de-lis at the corners of the four door panels, is found in the same combination in M. Jacopo Barozzio da Vignola's 1562 work *The Five Orders of Architecture* (*Regola delli cinque ordini d'architettura*), an influential design source in baroque and early neoclassical Europe and extending, as this clothes press suggests, to the Americas. (Notably, a translation of the book was published in German in 1759.)

The crowns topped with pairs of birds are familiar references to wedding traditions that Swiss and German immigrants brought with them to Pennsylvania in the early 1700s. The X-shaped fylfots and stars are also part of the common lexicon of the Swiss Germans. The curved "rattail" hinges on the cabinet doors are found in the Lancaster area but not on related furniture. The meandering flowering vines running up the sides and across the tops of the doors are a familiar framing element drawn from textiles—a fitting choice for Georg Huber, the man for whom the clothes press was made, as he was listed as a weaver in the 1779 tax exoneration.

Several different artisans have been proposed as the maker, including Georg's brother Jonas Huber, a joiner, but none has been verified. While Georg's death in 1785 meant that he did not enjoy it for long, the remarkable artisanry of the many involved in making this clothes press and its plethora of design influences have secured the piece's position as a premier example of the arts of the Pennsylvania Germans. —**AK**

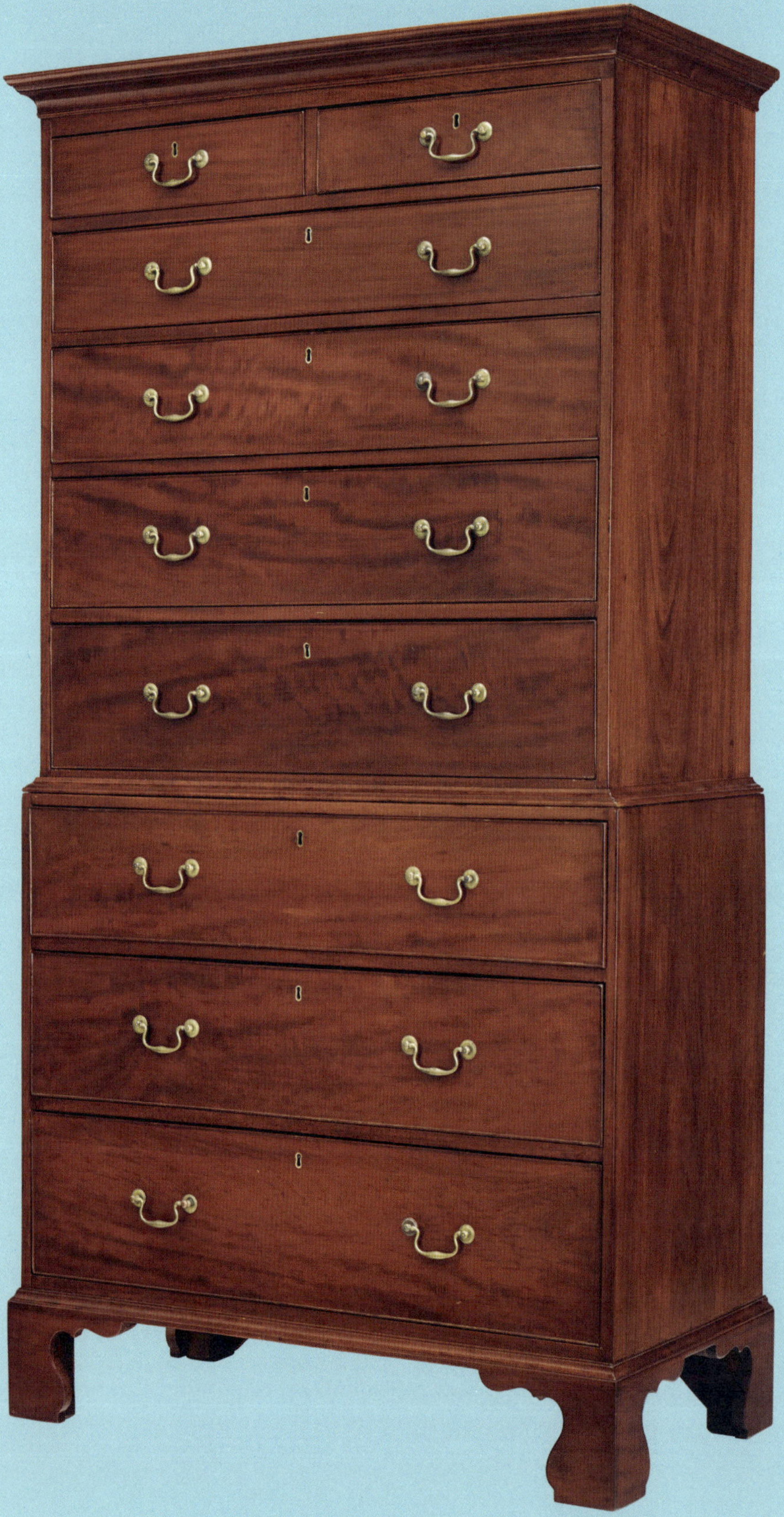

THE CABINET

DOUBLE CHEST

1805–10, **Thomas Gross Jr.** (1775–1839),
Mahogany, tulip poplar, yellow pine, brass, 6 ft. 10¾ in. × 43¼ in. × 22½ in. (2.1 × 1.1 × 0.6 m),
Philadelphia Museum of Art, Gift of Mrs. Leslie Legum, 1983, 1983-167-1a,b.

In a sure hand and expressive script, Thomas Gross signed not just his name on the underside of the bottom drawer of this double chest but also his connection to it: *maker*. That he included his role as the maker could suggest that Gross realized how anonymous he and his fellow Black artisans were in Philadelphia, then the most competitive cabinetmaking landscape in the United States. We will never be certain what inspired Gross to identify himself as maker, but his flourish makes this the only known documented furniture piece from Philadelphia's robust community of free African American woodworkers whose work, often anonymous and conscripted, was certainly more substantial than is credited.

Gross was born in Philadelphia at a time when people of African descent were newly able to acquire freedom from their enslavers—though they were surely not immune to racial injustices. Learning an artisanal trade gave Black Philadelphians economic opportunity. Thomas Gross's father was a carpenter, perhaps at the behest of an enslaver, who would have reaped his wages. His father's trade likely influenced Gross to pursue cabinetmaking, which he understood required greater skill than carpentry and was therefore more lucrative.

The design of this chest—two chests of drawers framed by moldings with applied beaded edges outlining each drawer—speaks to the enduring taste for a simple yet elegant cabinet to satisfy the need for storage. The design was a perennial favorite, originally appearing in design and pattern books from the late eighteenth century.[1] The pronounced height of the upper case in relation to the lower case and the high rise and bold profile of the bracket feet are subtle clues that it was created in the early 1800s. Gross applied the waist molding to the upper case instead of the lower case, a wise engineering choice found in the best furniture from Rhode Island, but not Philadelphia. The swirling mahogany grain adds interest to the drawer fronts, which are punctuated by simple bail handles and all have keyholes outlined in brass.

Gross lived and worked in the racially diverse Cedar Ward,[2] and like most cabinetmakers, also had a thriving business as an undertaker. The area was also home to Old St. Paul's Church, a Roman Catholic parish where it is registered that Gross married Eliza Mills in 1798. Throughout his life, Gross's name appears in documents of other free Black people who lived in this corner of Philadelphia, such as testifying in 1810 to his eighteen-year acquaintance with Benjamin Jasper, who was seeking naturalization rights. Gross also served as witness to the will of the Black brass founder Matthew Black, and it is tempting to think that he acquired the brass elements of this chest from Black.

By signing his name, Gross left the double chest as a tribute not only to his artistry as a free Black cabinetmaker but also to the many whose names appear in inventories or directories but whose talents remain unrecognized: enslaved and free people of African descent who made, carved, painted, ornamented, upholstered, or otherwise contributed to furniture making in colonial North America and in the early years of the United States. —AK

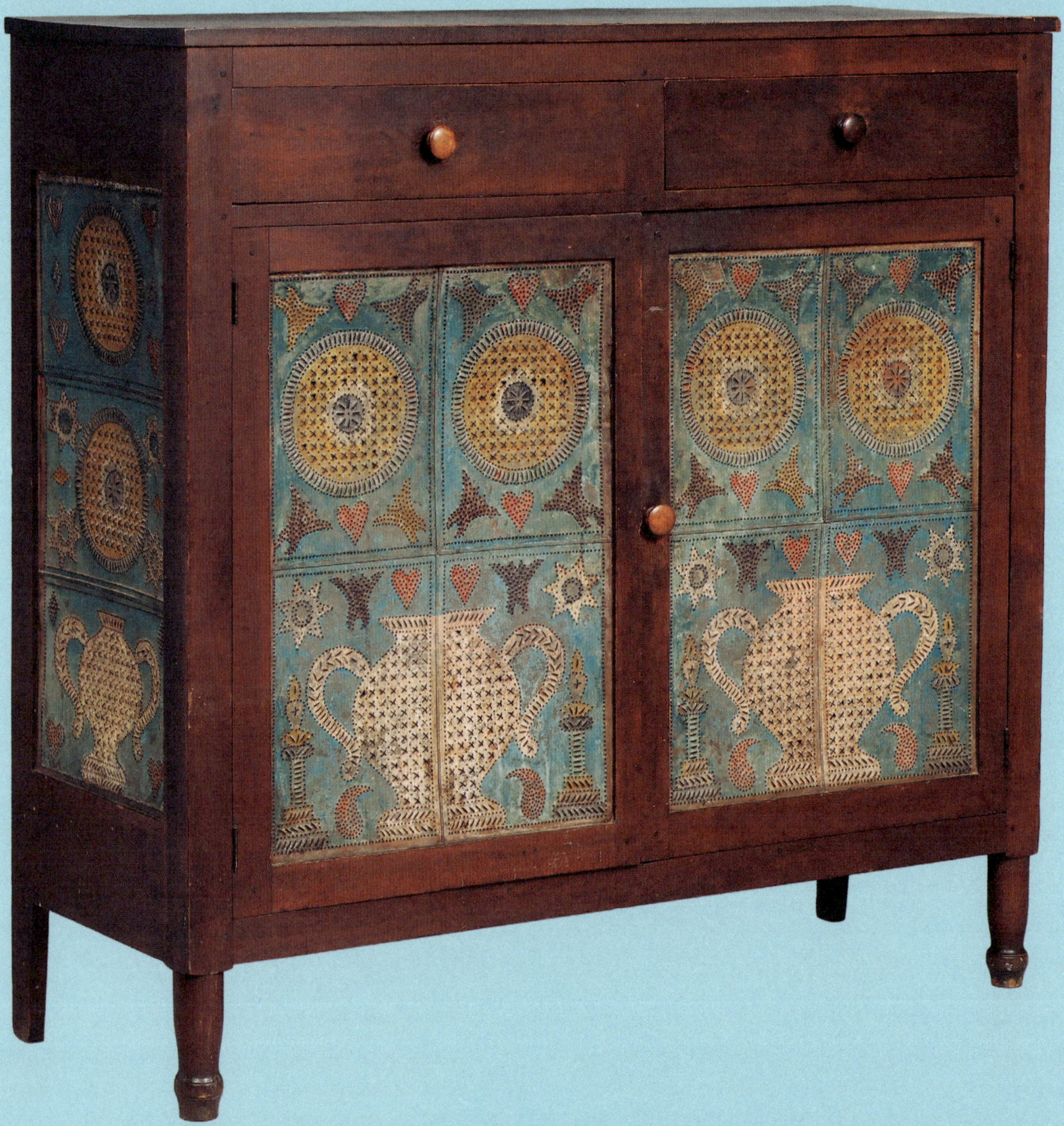

THE CABINET

PIE SAFE

c. 1830–60, **Unidentified artist (East Tennessee)**, Walnut, tulip poplar, tin, paint, 47½ × 48½ × 17½ in. (120.7 × 123.2 × 44.5 cm), High Museum of Art, Atlanta, Purchase with funds from the Fraser-Parker Foundation in memory of Nancy Fraser Parker who loved the decorative arts, 2016.6.

An almost exclusively American furniture form, used widely during the eighteenth and nineteenth centuries, the tin-paneled food storage unit, or pie safe, served a critical function: to hold perishable foodstuffs. Most likely made in Greene County, Tennessee, this pie safe is composed of walnut and tulip poplar, and its decorative punched-tin panels retain their cheerfully painted surfaces today.[1]

Punched-tin panels became a popular facing material in the southeastern United States in the 1830s. (Prior to then, linen had been used, which allowed air to circulate while also keeping unwanted pests at bay.) The punched-tin panels here are suggestive of the type made in Wytheville, Virginia, at the shop of Fleming K. Rich, who made larger panels that were crimped together, necessitating larger-scale pie safes to accommodate them.[2] It is known that Rich's shop provided delivery to customers in southwestern Virginia, where his shop was located, and East Tennessee, where this pie safe originated. However, this safe was likely made by a woodworker in East Tennessee's Sullivan, Washington, or Greene Counties, where other pie safes with large, punched-tin panels with similar decoration have surfaced. Taken together, these pie safes suggest that local makers were creating a regional pie safe variety influenced by various cultures and craft traditions.

The decorations on this piece—an arrangement of urns, candlesticks, compasses, hearts, sunbursts, and organic shapes—are reminiscent of decorations on blanket chests that developed out of the Pennsylvania Dutch tradition in Wythe County, southwestern Virginia. German immigrants and others moving south from Pennsylvania began arriving in this part of Virginia in the early eighteenth century. The designs are multicolored, awash in symbols composed of hues of blue, yellow, and pink. At the time, viewers would have been able to decode the symbols, which often had specific meanings. The urn and candlestick, for example, may recall a loved one who has passed away; further, the hearts, starbursts, and teardrops support the notion that this work memorialized a family member.

This pie safe was passed down to members of the Bowers family of Greene County, Tennessee. The family was German in origin, and after first arriving in Pennsylvania, they migrated to Virginia. Jacob Bowers, born in a Germanic settlement in southwestern Virginia, relocated to Tennessee at some point in the mid-nineteenth century. While the exact details surrounding the construction of this pie safe may never be fully confirmed, the work deftly demonstrates the movement of symbols, people, and furniture technologies across artificial boundaries (such as nations and states), affirming the shared experiences across humanity and through craft over which no one group or locale may claim ownership. —MO

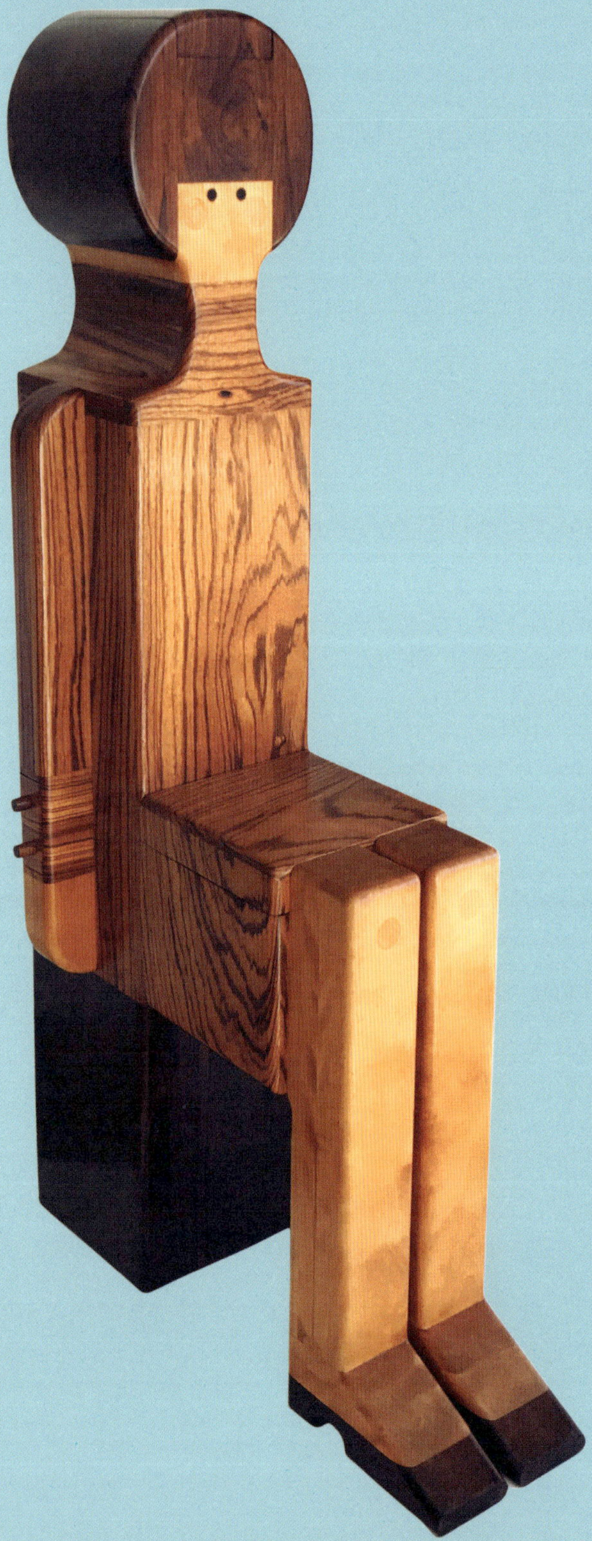

THE CABINET

GEORGY GIRL

1969, **Pamela Weir-Quiton** (b. 1944),
Zebrawood, rosewood, birch, ebony, 57½ × 18 × 31 in. (146.1 × 45.7 × 78.7 cm),
Collection of Alice and Ted Fong.

Fashionably fitted in a swath of swirling wood grain, the mod-chic *Georgy Girl* chest sits cheerfully at your beck and call. Inlaid circles serve as the only facial features on her rounded head. Who knew that the placement and repetition of one simple shape could subtly convey so much personality? Curiously, *Georgy* has no mouth.

This three-dimensional cutout doll is at rest but always ready for service. Like her mid-twentieth-century counterpart Barbie, *Georgy*'s limbs are stiff; her shoulders are strong; and her posture erect, frozen at attention. Fulfilling her prescribed gender norms, she is attractive and demure. She sits, taking in the world with her blank stare. At first glance a chair, she comes with a surprise twist: she is also a sculptural cabinet built to open, receive, store, and hold.

Georgy was brought to life at a time of political tumult, feminist theorizing, and cultural transformation. Dapper as any 1960s "it girl," she was the creation of student sculptor Pamela Weir (now Pamela Weir-Quiton) at a pivotal turning point in the women's rights movement. Titled after a 1966 movie and theme song of the same name, it was not intended as direct commentary on feminist ideology, though *Georgy* is indeed a product of that moment.

As a craft student at California State University, Northridge in the mid-1960s, the budding artist and designer listened to the advice of her counselor to ditch the ceramics studio and head into the woodshop with the boys. Her first woodworking assignment was to make a toy; she created a small wooden doll that captured her fashion-forward aesthetic. Seeing the infinite design possibilities that existed by tapping into the colors and strong patterns of laminated hardwoods, she could create an entire array of fashionista dolls. A semester later, when she was instructed to make a piece of furniture, her wooden dolls became the inspiration for a cabinet that was equal parts functional and sculptural. She was visited by influential craft and design patron Eudorah Moore while working on campus soon after. Moore saw her work and invited her to be part of the groundbreaking *California Design X* exhibition in 1968. Weir was plucked out of school and quickly on her way to a woodworking life.

Cabinets have long been interpreted with anthropomorphic features, from their legs to feet: Salvador Dalí famously toyed with a Freudian take on these ideas in 1936 in his *Anthropomorphic Cabinet*. Hidden compartments were prized in casework from the mid-eighteenth century, providing clever security features for colonial homes and early American residences. In Weir-Quiton's take, *Georgy*'s head opens up as an inviting spot for holding personal items. Her spine is a tower of drawers that can safely hold jewelry or lingerie. Her dual-purpose lap flips open as an additional container for small objects and also serves as a seat. With irony and optimism, it embodies the irreverent spirit of an era in which women were breaking from traditional gender roles, defying expectations and limitations. *Georgy* playfully shows the world that she's the kind of girl who can do it all—and make it look easy. —EZ

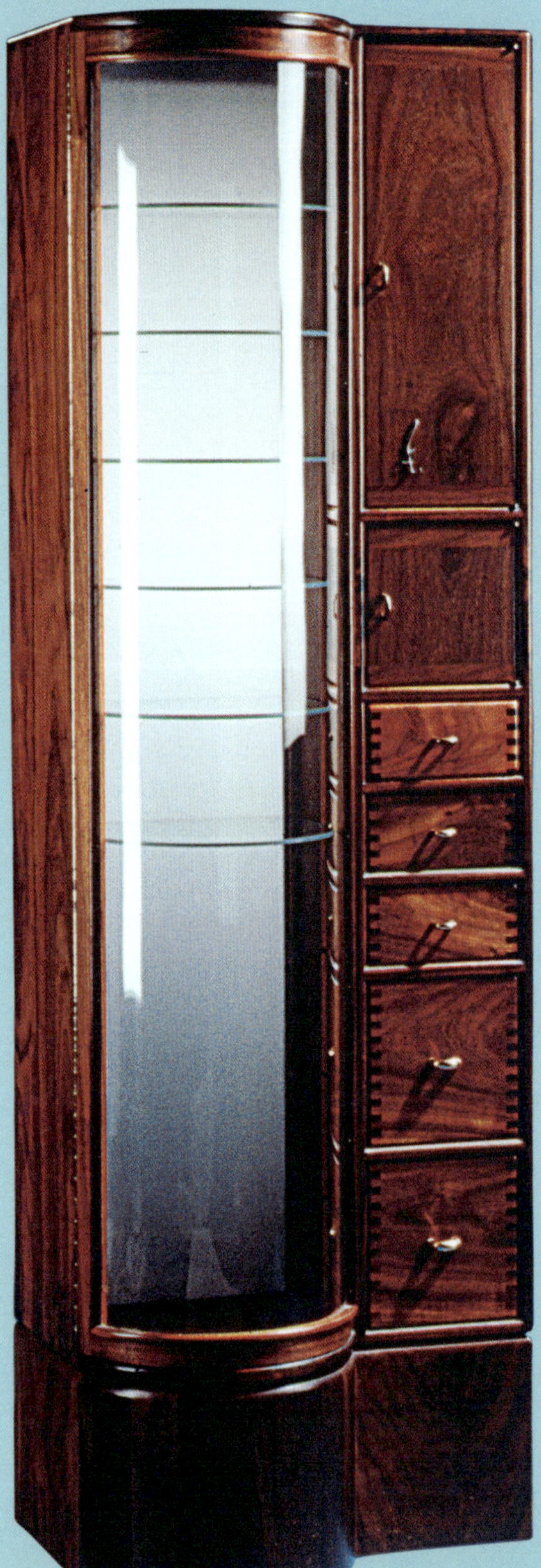

THE CABINET

NAIL CABINET

1979, **Garry Knox Bennett** (1934–2022),
Padauk, glass, lamp parts, copper, nail, 74 × 24 × 17 in. (188 × 61 × 43.2 cm),
Collection of Garry Knox and Sylvia Bennett Estate.

Garry Knox Bennett's 1979 *Nail Cabinet* sparked a craft revolution with a single, provocative act: driving a cheap nail into a six-foot-tall, richly grained padauk wood cabinet. It was his most technically advanced and controversial work to date.

Bennett aimed to challenge the woodworking world's obsession with fancy woods, exposed dovetails, and what he called "trick joinery." "I wanted to make a statement that I thought people were getting a little too goddamn precious with their technique," he explained. "I think tricky joinery is just to show, in most instances, you can do tricky joinery."[1] The resulting piece showcased the very techniques he critiqued. *Nail Cabinet* featured imported padauk wood in the California roundover style, a curved glass door sourced from a defunct barbershop pole, secret latches, and a dovetailed carcass. Then, in the upper door of this finely crafted cabinet, Bennett drove a sixteen-penny nail into the surface, bent at an expressive angle in the style of a novice, and surrounded it with a circle of hammer marks on the polished wood.

In traditional woodcraft, value and skill are measured by construction without nails. By creating something immaculate and then driving a nail through it, Bennett demonstrated the death of the purist aesthetic. This purposeful vandalism, intended to reduce the cabinet's "traditional" value, generated unexpected controversy and changed the course of woodworking as an artistic field. Some viewed it as desecration, canceling their *Woodworking Magazine* subscriptions when it appeared on the back cover. Others saw it as a sacrifice, a perfect specimen offered to the gods, while some appreciated the humor mocking overly precious creators. "To understand my art," Bennett wrote in 1986, "the viewer has to understand jokes. . . . I have the punch line in my mind, and I just have to bring all of the elements together."[2]

Born in Alameda, California, Bennett attended the California College of Arts and Crafts, training as a metal sculptor. His successful businesses—including Squirken-works, which became the largest manufacturer of roach clips in the United States—and his invention of electroprinting provided the financial freedom to pursue his craftwork. He turned to wood when he sought to make larger pieces, such as furniture, that could incorporate his electroprinting techniques.

Nail Cabinet became such a popular piece that it was frequently on loan. (Someone even stole the original nail, which was later replaced and wired down.) Eventually, Bennett decided to keep it crated, to be unpacked only after his death by the highest museum bidder. Bennett's approach to furniture-making was always evolving. He sketched directly on materials, letting shapes emerge as he worked. His pieces were described as alive, demanding attention through playful color, unique shapes, and contrasting textures. They first drew in viewers with craftsmanship, then charmed them with wit. As Bennett intended, his pieces commanded every room they occupied, impossible to ignore and delightful to experience. —JL

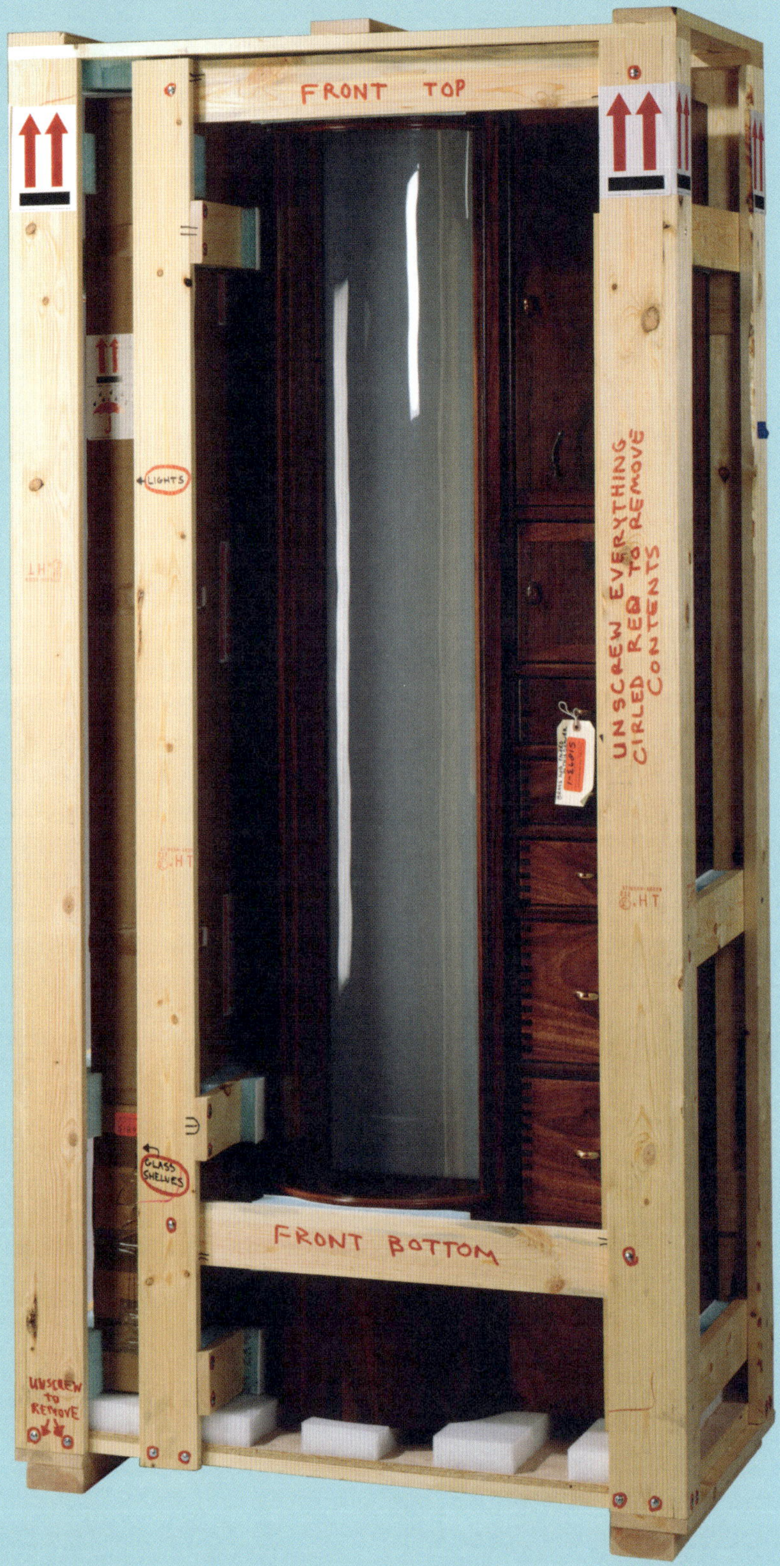

Nail Cabinet Encased (crated),
Collection of the Garry Knox and Sylvia Bennett Estate.

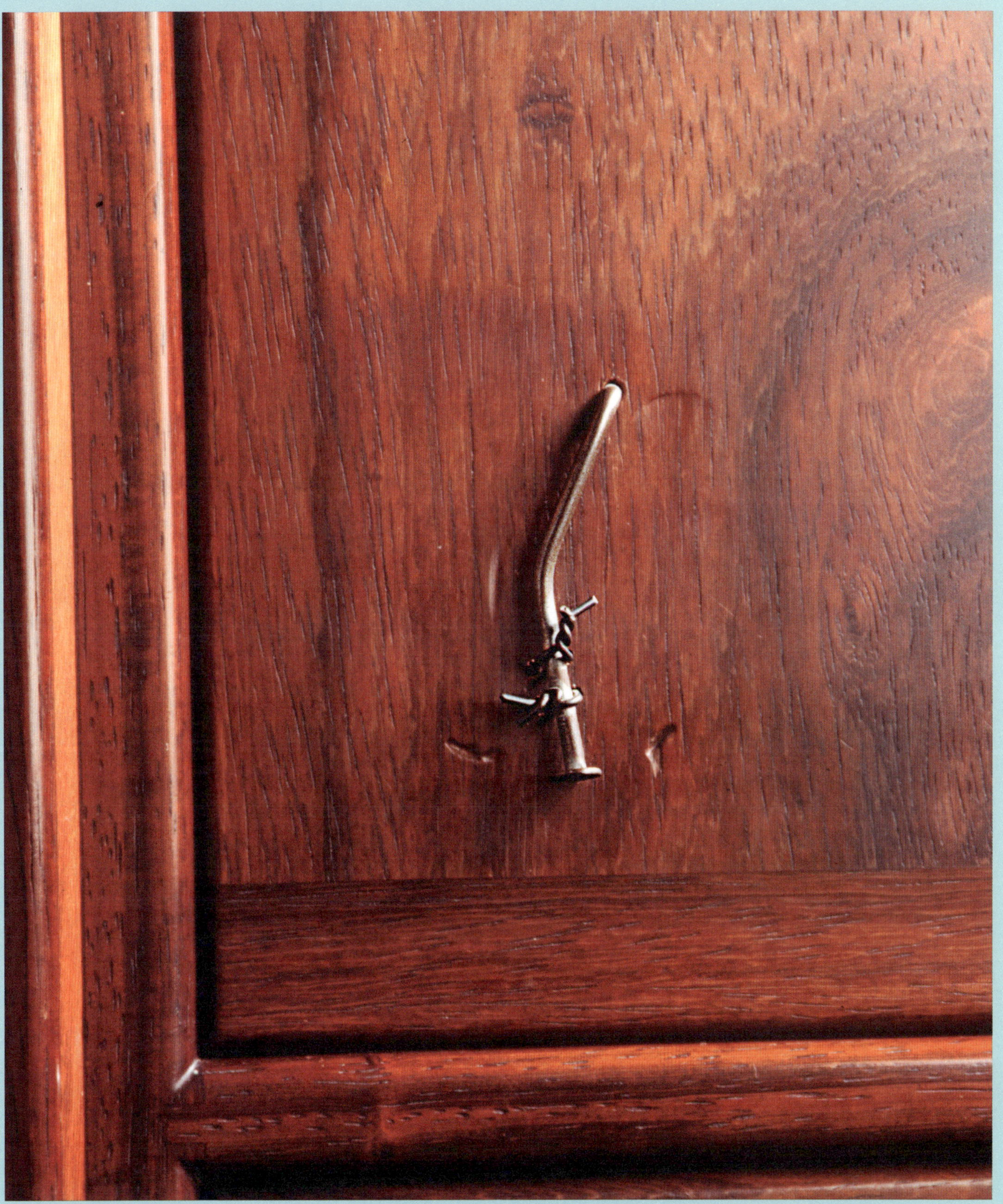

TO STORE

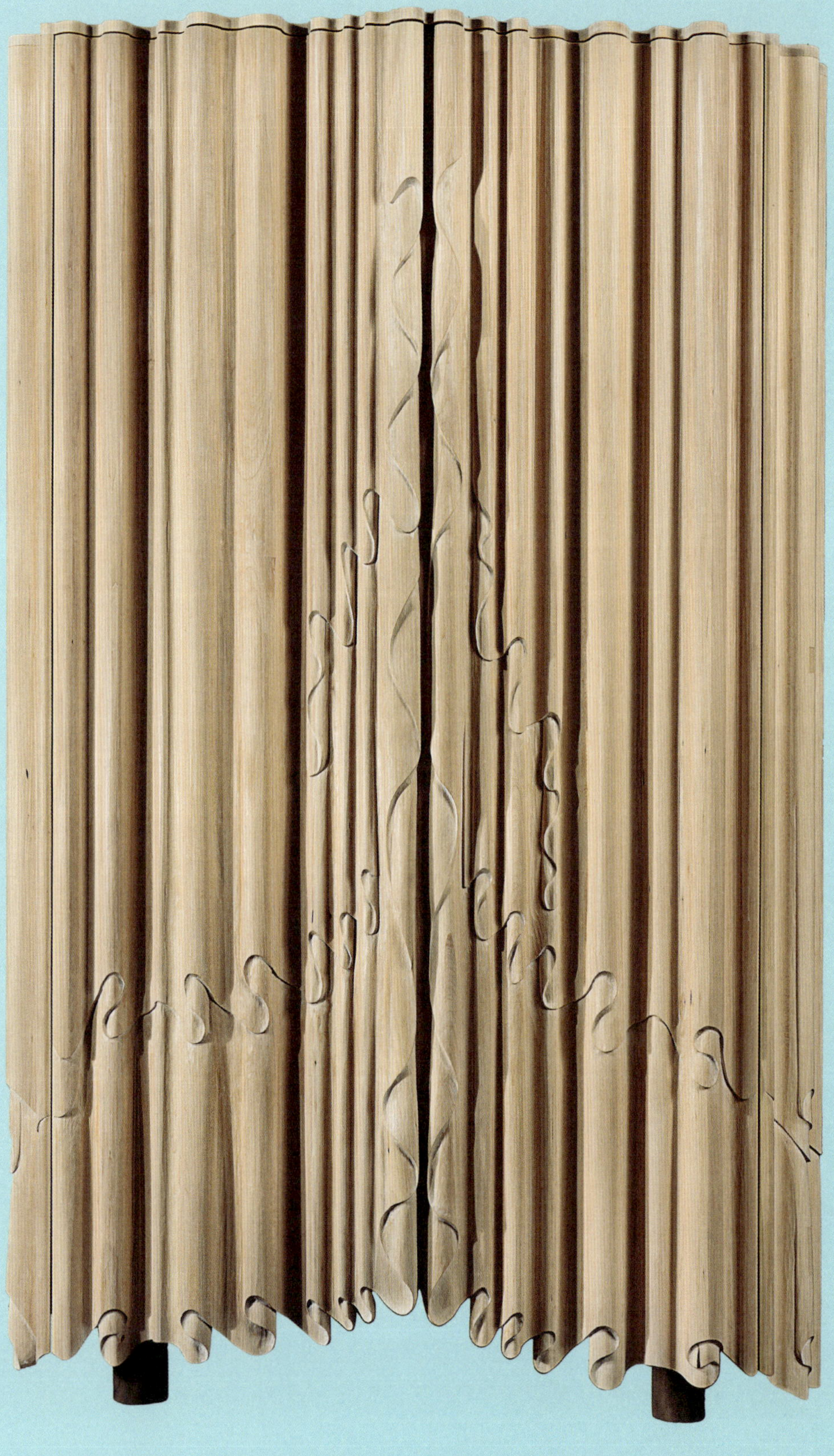

THE CABINET

LINENFOLD ARMOIRE (PERPENDICULAR STYLE)

2020, **Christopher Kurtz** (b. 1975),
Basswood, milk paint, walnut burl, bronze, 76 × 49 × 31 in. (193 × 124.5 × 78.7 cm).

On the hunt for a lion or a witch? The Hudson Valley–based maker Christopher Kurtz has fashioned the perfect place to look. He calls it his *Linenfold Armoire*, but it might just as well be described as a wardrobe, for the terms are more or less interchangeable. Either way, it is an imposingly tall piece of case furniture, with an interior volume big enough to hang full-length garments . . . or, perhaps, find a portal to another world.

That is what Kurtz seems to have done. Taking his cue from Gaston Bachelard's book *The Poetics of Space*—"Does there exist a single dreamer of words who does not respond to the word wardrobe?"—he has made a piece of furniture in the guise of draped fabric.[1] One can so easily imagine it being whisked open like a set of stage curtains to reveal a domain of further imagination beyond. In fact, the doors open to a warm golden glow of milk paint, and a silver leaf–lined interior cabinet. The top of the piece is made from a slab of beautifully figured burl walnut. Little hints of paradise.

The wardrobe also transports us in time, for the linenfold carving that graces the piece is inspired by architectural paneling and furnishings of the late Middle Ages—the era of the Gothic, or Perpendicular, style.[2] The idiom itself was likely inspired by the folds of classical togas and other garments; churches of the same era sometimes have columnar figures or "jamb statues" guarding their doors, garbed in highly stylized robes. Yet linenfold also expresses inherent craft logic. A simple version can be executed readily with chisels, by carving a series of long straight grooves and then a tightly orchestrated series of gouge cuts. Kurtz's version is unusually delicate, having been executed in basswood rather than the oak favored by medieval joiners. Ribbonlike lines arc across the facade of the piece; they do suggest the edges of lightweight fabric, but also sound waves rippling in sinuous rhythm. It's a piece of design you can almost hear.

And what would it sound like? A requiem. Kurtz was interested to learn, while developing the design, that linenfold carving reached its height in the wake of the Black Death. The relative austerity of the style may actually have reflected a shortage of available labor; so many craftspeople had died. But it also expressed a need, as Kurtz puts it, for "pure expression of form, confronting the gravity of mortality and loss."[3] It is no coincidence that the work was completed in 2020, in the depths of the COVID-19 pandemic. There was something strangely medieval about that time: the scale of the loss, the terror, the superstition, the monkish isolation. Kurtz's wardrobe stands as a monument to that tragic time, while also transcending it. Best to see it as a spiritual diagram: a sheaf of lines, all pointing upward to heaven. —**GA**

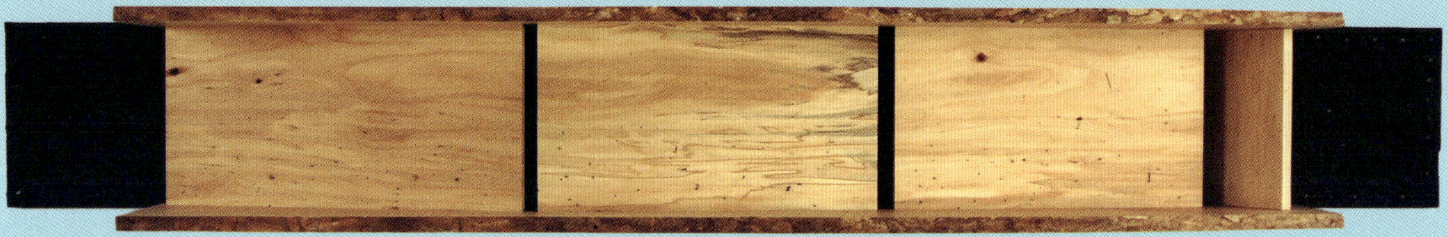

THE CABINET

WENDY MARUYAMA on THE CABINET

Fractured, 2010, **Wendy Maruyama** (b. 1952),
Elm, tar paper, nails, 6 × 48 × 8 in. (15.2 × 121.9 × 20.3 cm).

Of all the furniture I have made over the past fifty-plus years, I still find case furniture the most interesting category to work with. As an artist and craftsperson, the potential for storytelling, for tricks and surprises, for hidden messages is endless. As a woodworker, the considerations when designing a case piece are much like a miniature piece of architecture or a study in anatomy: There are structural considerations, both internal and external. There is the selection of skins that would go over the structure, as well as small compartments supported by the internal skeleton. There is also the potential for surprise—is the outside of the work a signifier of what lies behind the doors? Last, but not least, is the function of the piece, the size and type of objects to be stored, and their meaning (or not). Are there hidden spaces? Who uses this piece of furniture?

Historically, the study of furniture has revealed the lifestyles of the societies who owned the objects. Initially, casework was used to organize essential and domestic possessions: blankets, clothing, tools. Often, vernacular furniture reflected the culture from which it was made. A story I loved told by an English furniture tutor referenced a sixteenth-century cupboard from Scotland. They were puzzled by the bottom shelf, which was an open wire structure. It was later discovered that the cabinet was used to house the family chickens overnight to protect them from predators or the elements. Typically, large case pieces evolved into status symbols, a way to show off and display collections of silver, glass, or souvenirs from travel. Casework also became, and to a degree is still, a vehicle of class and style.

My own work has been able to take full advantage of what a casework's design can offer as a narrative object. For my exhibition *Executive Order 9066* I made long, horizontal case pieces influenced by many elements: the bleak desertlike landscapes of the U.S.'s ten Japanese incarceration camps during World War II, sliding doors often seen in Japanese houses, and the spirit of gaman (a Japanese term from Zen Buddhism that means "enduring the seemingly unbearable with patience and dignity") in Japanese Americans during their forced imprisonment.

These cabinets are very simple compared with the many elaborate case pieces I have made. The absence of hardware placed the focus on the materials used, which were mostly plain, sometimes wormy woods like pine, ash, and elm. For me, it was a move away from the highly decorated and embellished work I am known for to a focus almost exclusively on content. Of the ten case pieces I made for this exhibit, one stands out for me despite its relative simplicity and homeliness: *Fractured*. The back of the piece is torn tar paper nailed down to its substrate, and the sliding doors are set haphazardly at angles, causing them to collide with each other, disrupting the expected harmony and tranquility associated with smooth-sliding doors. The piece was made of wood salvaged from a fallen elm tree at Monticello, the former estate of Thomas Jefferson. This cabinet does not organize possessions or reflect status. Through the Monticello wood it contains the darker moments of American history; it consciously carries the weight of more than four hundred enslaved lives—a reminder that democracy was built on profound contradictions. By joining this material with the memory of Japanese American incarceration, I built upon those layers of injustice and endurance that shape our nation—then, in World War II, and still today.

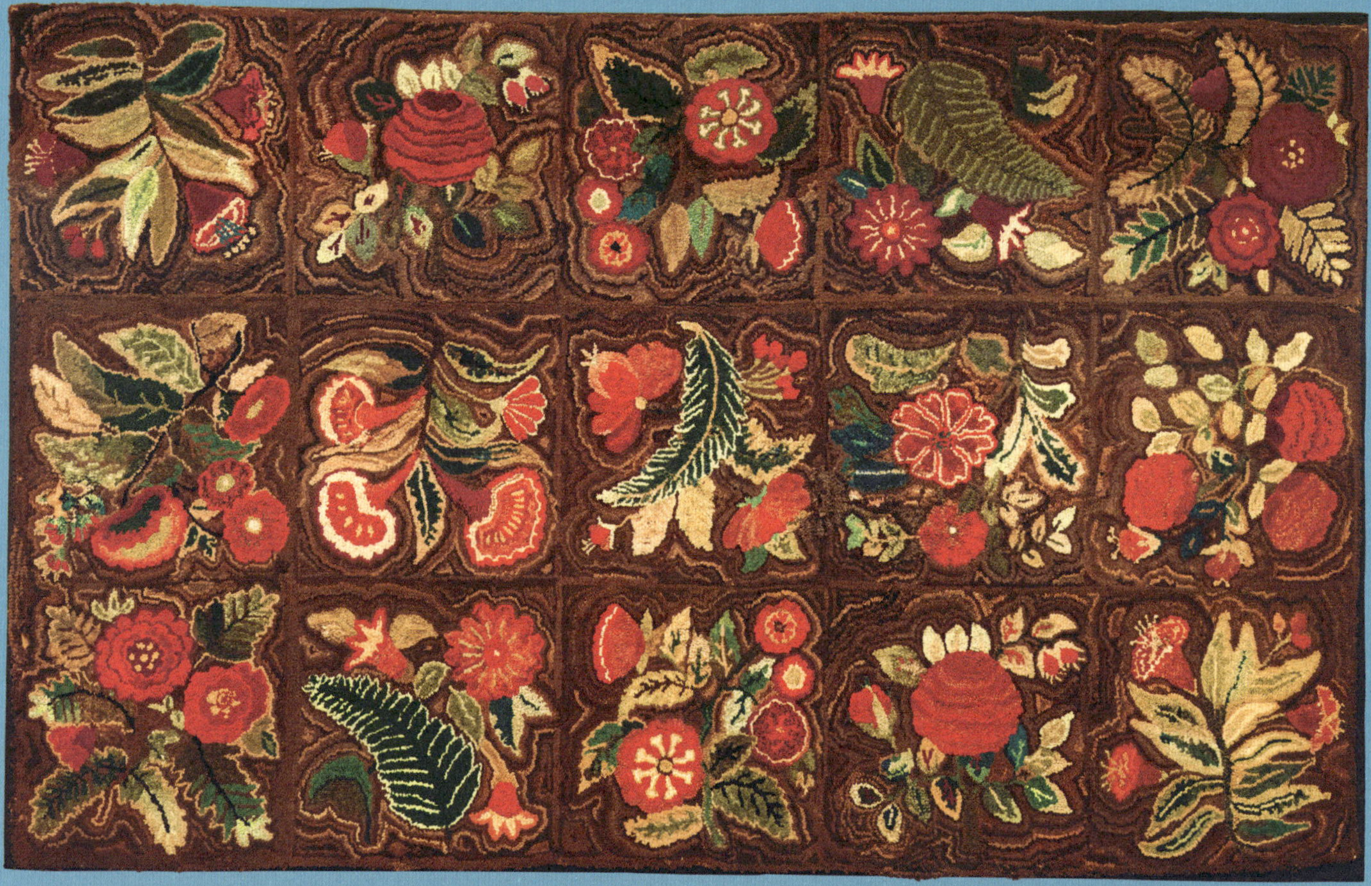

THE RUG

LARGE FLORAL HOOKED RUG

Late 19th century, **Unidentified artist (Maine)**, Dyed wool and burlap, 55 × 88 in. (139.7 × 223.5 cm), The Huntington Library, Art Museum, and Botanical Gardens, San Marino, CA, Gift of Jonathan and Karin Fielding, 2022.25.22.

In colonial America, the import of foreign-made rugs as a decorative defense against colder climates was common practice, though the rugs were highly expensive due to high trade costs and limited to the very wealthy. In the post-colonial period, as textile industries in New England increased production and made materials more accessible, early American women began using leftover fabric and yarn to make their own handmade rugs, keeping their floors warm and providing colorful decoration at a low cost. In the early nineteenth century, rug making was especially popular in states such as Maine and Massachusetts, where there was a history of yarn production and textile mills. The practice of hooked rug making would eventually expand throughout New England and to other parts of the country, making early rug making one of the first folk art traditions in America.

The earliest rugs were yarn-sewn and could be used for both the bed and the floor. Other rugs were made by shirring, a technique that involved manipulating fabric with gathered thread and hand-sewing it to a foundation. After the mid-nineteenth century, hooked rugs became much more popular. To make a hooked rug, loops of wool and yarn were pulled through burlap sacks or a woven backing using a hooked tool. The most common motifs on these rugs were florals, leaves, landscapes, animals, and geometric patterns. Early makers often used preexisting scraps of wool and yarn that were bold and colorful, producing designs that were expressive but less detailed. By the turn of the century, hooked rugs became much more elaborate and representational as rug makers honed their skills and gained access to a wider range of colors.

Floral and leaf motifs like the ones in this rug from Maine were especially popular during this time because they were both easy to design and beautiful to look at. The contrasting colors and outlines used to create this pattern suggest that the maker had both technical skills and a sense of design that exceeded many of their contemporary makers. Additionally, in places like Maine, it was not uncommon for groups of women to gather in community to work in rug-making circles, especially later in the twentieth century. If this maker began rug hooking at an early age or within a community of makers, it is possible that the rug might be not only informed by a variety of design influences but also collaboratively made.

While hooked rugs declined in popularity in the first half of the twentieth century, interest renewed in the 1970s, when early American traditions became increasingly valuable and scholars and institutions began to more widely recognize the creative practices of women and folk art traditions. Contemporary craft artists are now learning the hooked-rug tradition and expanding on it with higher-quality materials and modern technology. As a result, early American hooked rugs and the history of the makers who created them are being celebrated as a critical expression of the country's earliest folk traditions. —LC

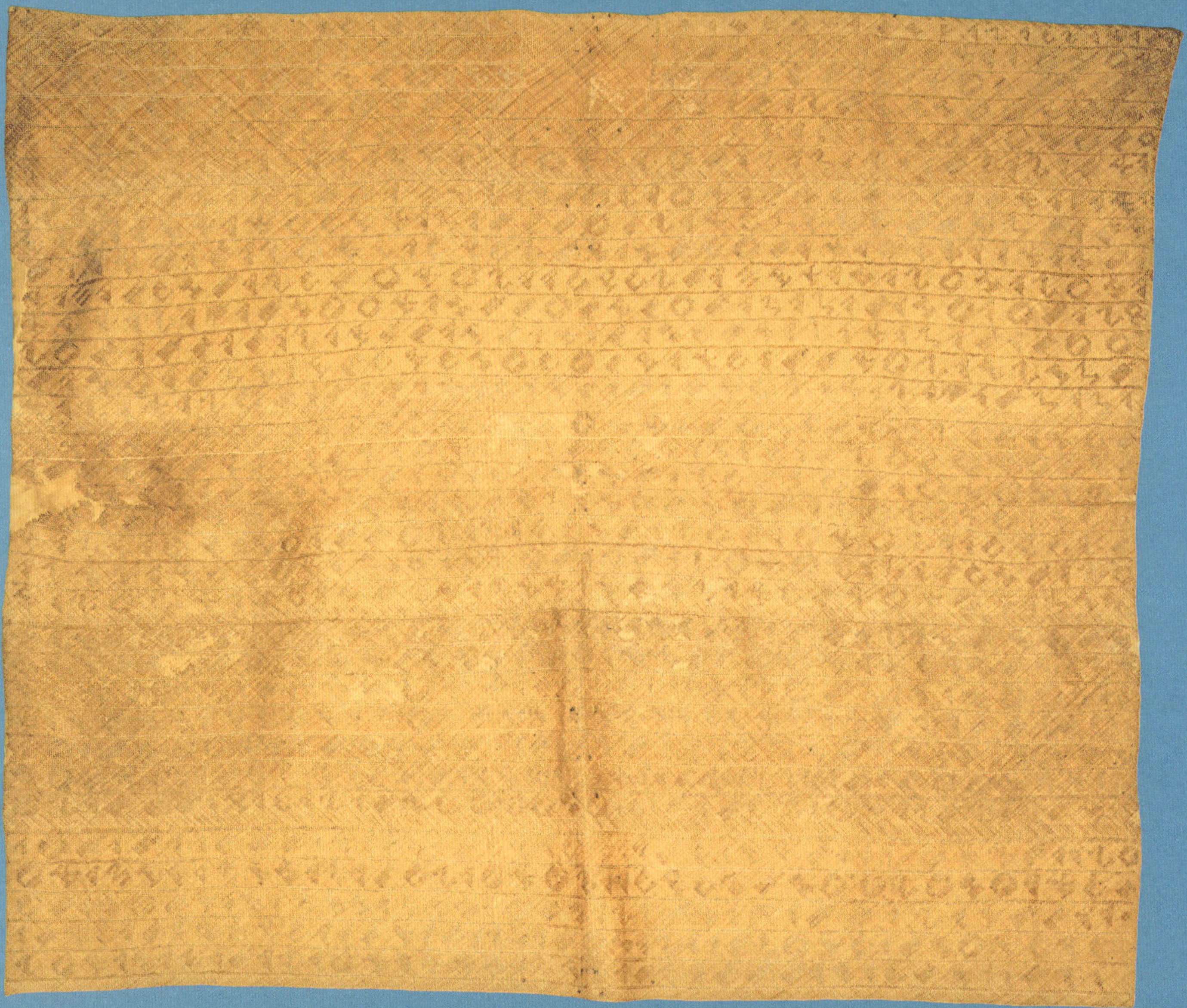

THE RUG

MOENA PĀWEHE (MAKALOA MAT)

c. 1873, **Kalaiokamalino** (c. 1795–1880),
Plaited makaloa (*Cyperus laevigatus*), 72 × 83 15⁄16 in. (183 × 213 cm),
Bishop Museum, Honolulu, Ethnology Collection, item no. 02570.

Plaited sails used on double-hulled voyaging canoes traversed the uncharted waters of the Pacific for thousands of years, bringing the first Polynesians to the shores of the Hawaiian Islands as early as 400 CE. These adventurous and skilled knowledge-keepers established a vibrant plaiting legacy in Hawaiʻi that continues to flourish. Ulana, the practice of Hawaiian plaiting, reached a milestone of excellence and skill in the nineteenth century through the creation of moena pāwehe, decorated fine mats, by weavers of the island of Niʻihau. This westernmost inhabited island of the main Hawaiian archipelago is home to thirteen seasonal ponds, ideal habitats for an indigenous sedge known as makaloa (*Cyperus laevigatus*). Niʻihau families, the only ones to practice ulana using makaloa, shared the tradition when they intermarried and settled on neighboring islands.

This special moena pāwehe, made from makaloa, was created around 1873 by a weaver named Kalaiokamalino. Upon its finely plaited surface, she overlaid a letter intended for King William Lunalilo, Hawaiʻi's first elected constitutional monarch. Moena pāwehe were among the most precious gifts one could offer and were rare commodities, especially since only a handful of experts were still practicing the art by the 1870s. The contents of the letter shared the hardships the citizens of Hawaiʻi were experiencing due to an imposed cash tax on animals and requested reprieve from this burden. The moena was made over the course of eleven months with thousands of two-millimeter-wide strips. No tools other than the weaver's hands were used, and Kalaiokamalino is believed to have been eighty years old at the time of its completion. At that age, she would have lived through the establishment of the Hawaiian Kingdom under King Kamehameha in 1810 and all the positive actions the successive monarchs of the Kamehameha dynasty provided to the Hawaiian people.

Kalaiokamalino's message spoke to her proficient grasp of both Western and Hawaiian thought. She began by eloquently addressing the king with all the proper honorifics and salutations one would afford members of the chiefly ranks. She also made the distinction that the prosperity and success of the kingdom were built upon the actions of the preceding Kamehameha dynasty, not his own. That allowed her to address her concern in a way that reminded the king of his responsibilities to his people that his predecessors established. She also intentionally used only a portion of her name in signing her humble request: "KALA." Kala has multiple meanings, all completely different from that of her full name, such as "to release, unburden, absolve, or forgive." It also is a noun for money. Even through her name, she reinforced her request for relief while asking for forgiveness.

Ulana continues to uplift cultural frameworks for sustainability, preservation, and innovation with examples like this one serving as anchors that connect generations together. Many Hawaiian elders and culturally grounded experts teach younger generations the importance of caring for the natural world and valuing proper material harvesting and preparation practices. This becomes the foundation on which plaiting techniques and the stories that preserve the art's history are built. Ulana, the physical act of interweaving individual elements into one piece, reminds us that we are stronger together. —MHM

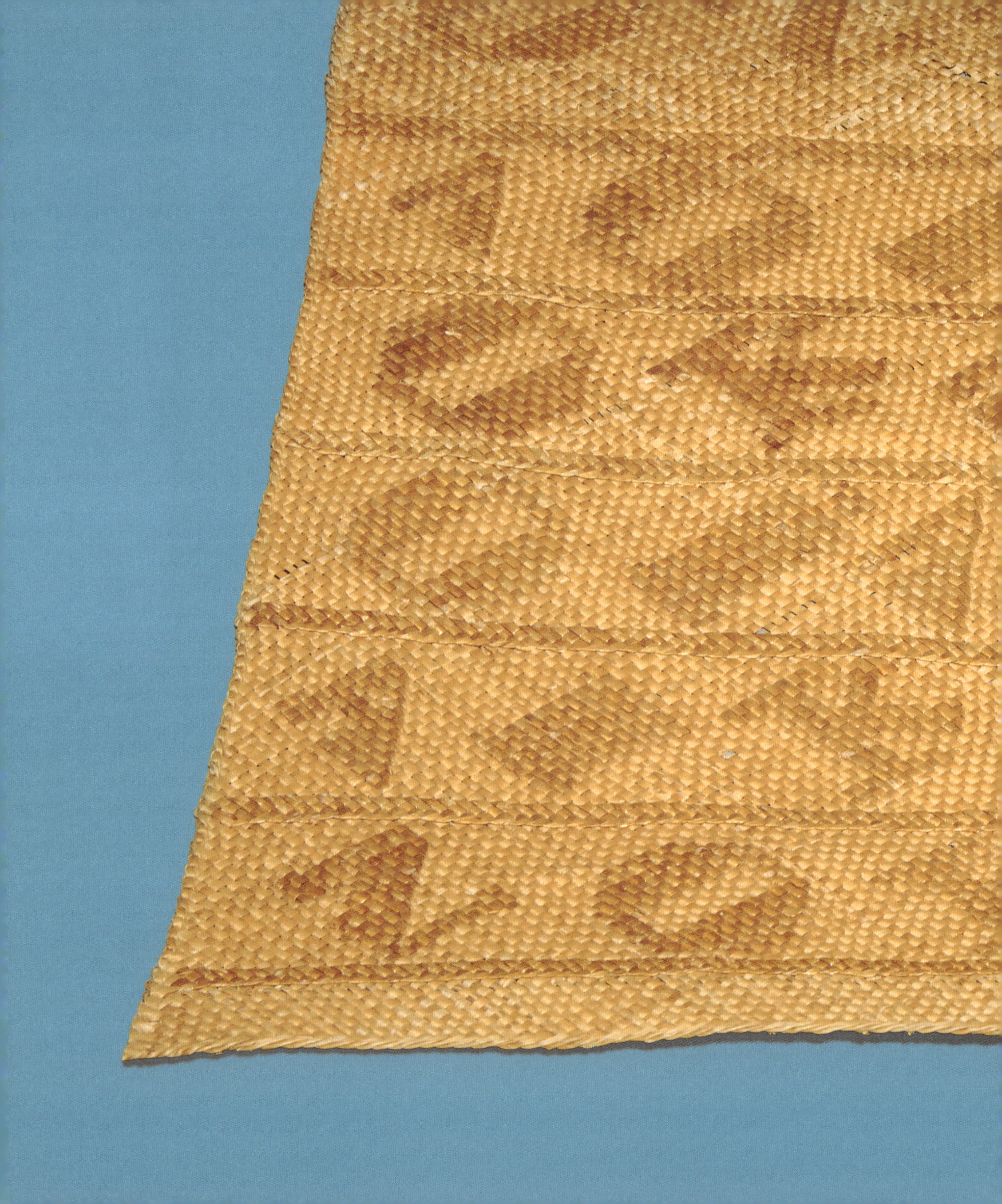

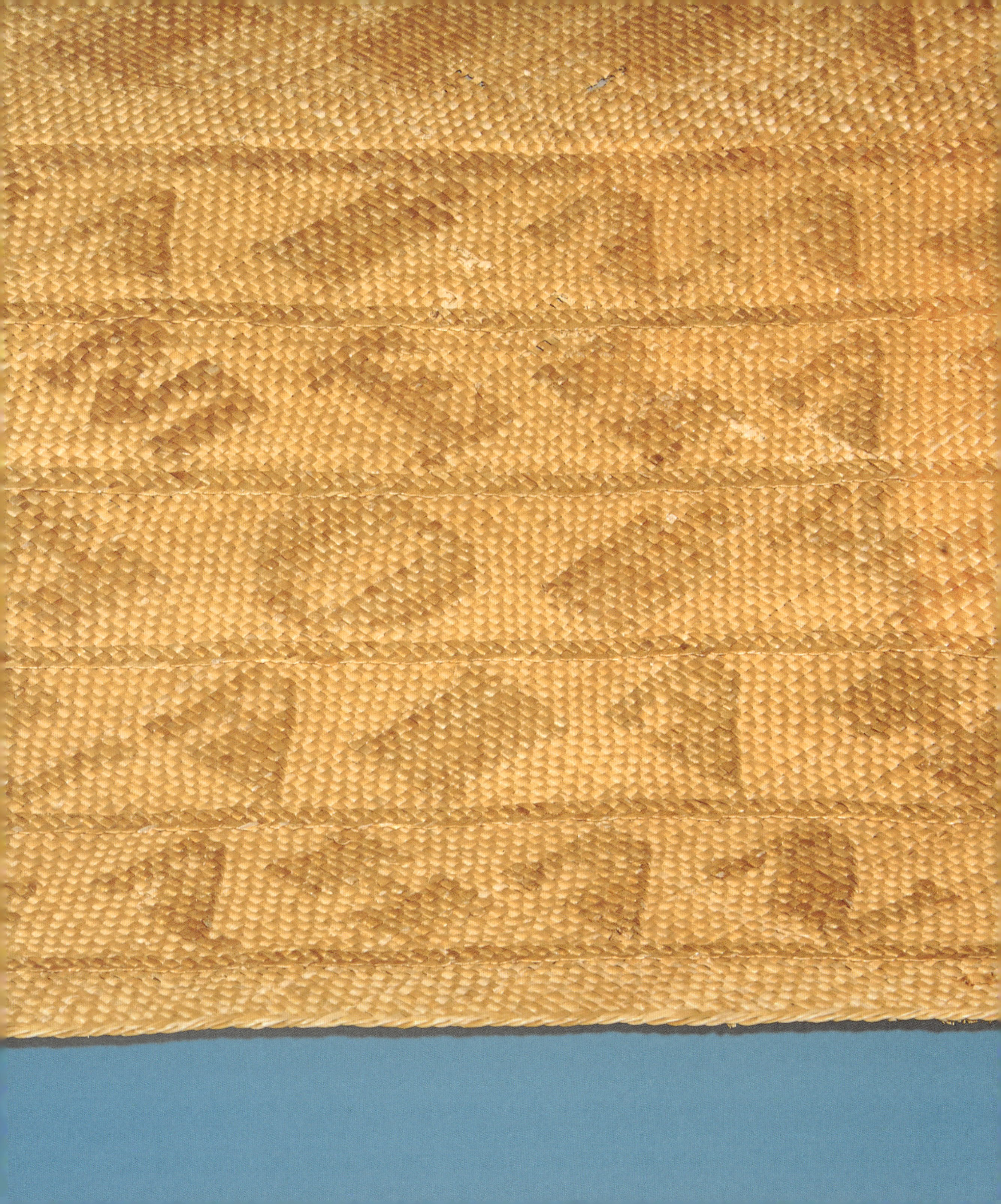

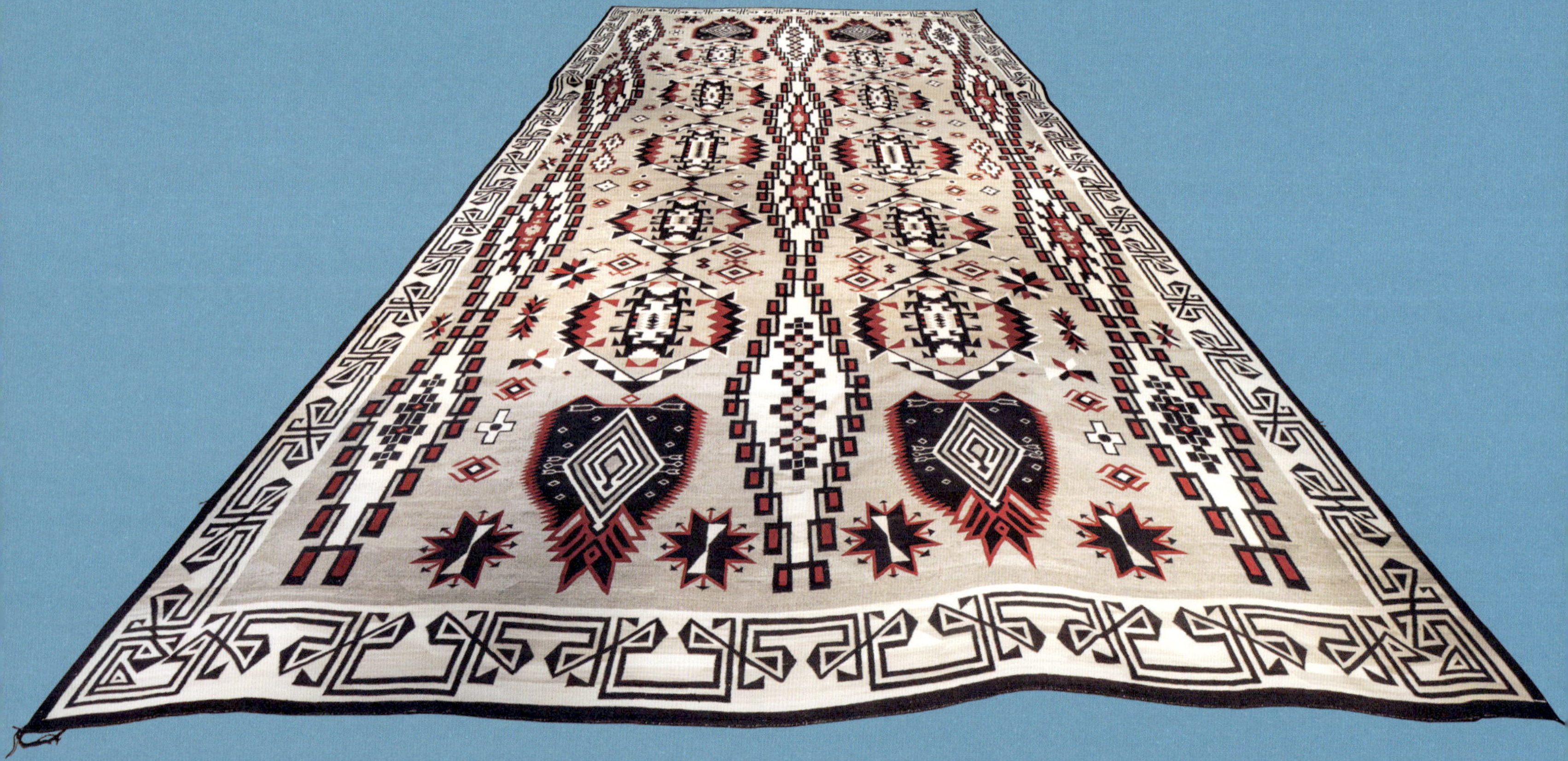

THE RUG

DIYOGÍ TSOH (THE BIG RUG)

c. 1937, **Julia Joe** (Diné/Navajo, 1875–1974) and **Lillie Joe Hill** (Diné/Navajo, 1913–1992),
Hand-carded, dyed, and spun wool, 21 ft. 4 in. × 32 ft. 7 in. (6.5 × 9.9 m),
Collection of Affeldt Mion Museum, Winslow, AZ.

Tourists are often the intended audience for handcrafted objects. Although the original attractions of the southwestern United States might have been canyons, mesas, and deserts, its silver jewelry, Pueblo pottery, and Navajo weaving became equally alluring. In this case, handwork was intended as the primary motivation for tourism, not the by-product. Lorenzo Hubbell Jr., son of the Hubbell Trading Post scion, decided to commission the "World's Largest Navajo Rug" to address the area's decline in tourism caused by the Great Depression. In 1932 he enlisted Julia Joe, a skilled Navajo (Diné) weaver of the Red House Clan, to create this rug to display at his Winslow, Arizona, trading post.

Julia's husband, Sam, built a structure on their Greasewood, Arizona, land to house a giant loom made of metal pipes constructed specifically for the project. Family members and friends sheared hundreds of Churro sheep and spent nearly two years carding, dyeing, and spinning the wool. Julia and her daughter Lillie Joe Hill worked, as she described it, from dawn to midnight for three years and three weeks weaving the massive rug. In 1937, it was displayed at the Hubbell Trading Post and in 1939 at the Gallup Inter-Tribal Indian Ceremonial. It also traveled to New York and Chicago until Lorenzo Hubbell Jr., went bankrupt in 1949 and the rug was put into storage.

Aside from its scale, the rug is a masterpiece of design and execution. The color palette includes grays (achieved by combining wool from eighteen black and sixty white sheep sheared for the project), black, and Ganado red (a deeper, more traditional color as opposed to the brighter chemical dyes that had become popular at the turn of the century). Stars and horned toads, said to be protective talismans for Joe family members, figure prominently in the pattern. The rug is bordered by designs taken from potsherds found near the family home. Borders were uncommon in Navajo blanket weaving until outside customers began using them as "rugs" requiring larger and thicker textiles with a framing outline.

In September 2023 the Hubbell-Joe rug, as museum personnel called it, was again put on permanent display at the Affeldt Mion Museum in Winslow, Arizona, in a room specifically designed for the work. Many descendants of Julia Joe attended the opening. Most likely, few visitors who view the rug today will notice the thin line transversing the solid black border at the lower right corner. This single strand, the ch'ihónit'l, or split line, appeared in Navajo weaving after 1900 and is thought to be crucial to the survival of the cultural tradition. The weaver's spirit is said to become entwined in the wool of the weaving and must be given a path to escape and remain within the maker and the community. Whether the deliberate "imperfection" is a subtle statement of resistance to the demands of the market, as exemplified by the innovation of borders for the "rugs," or a deep-felt cultural belief, the spirit line is a clear indication of the weaver's intention to assure the survival of their artistic traditions. —BB

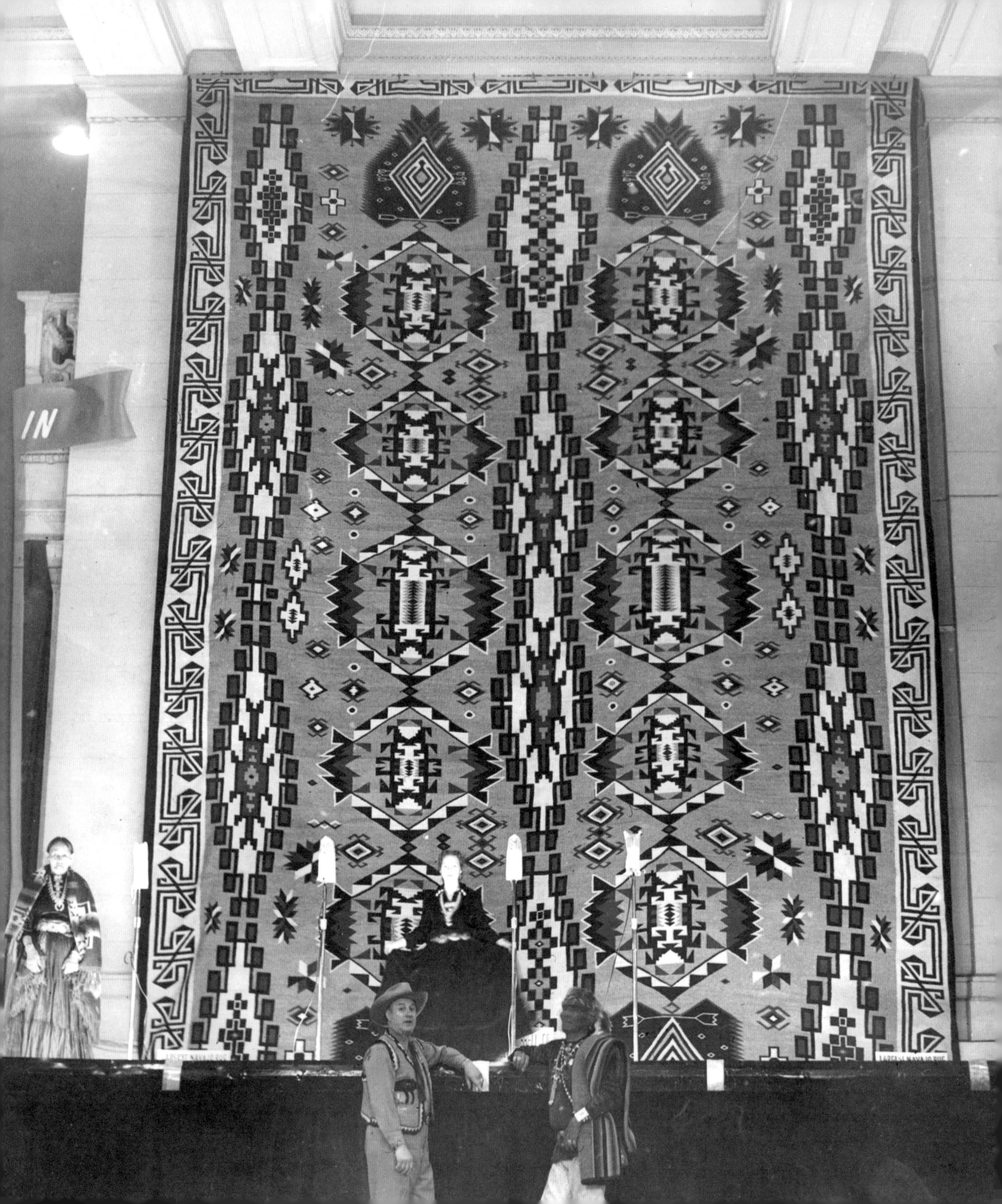
IN

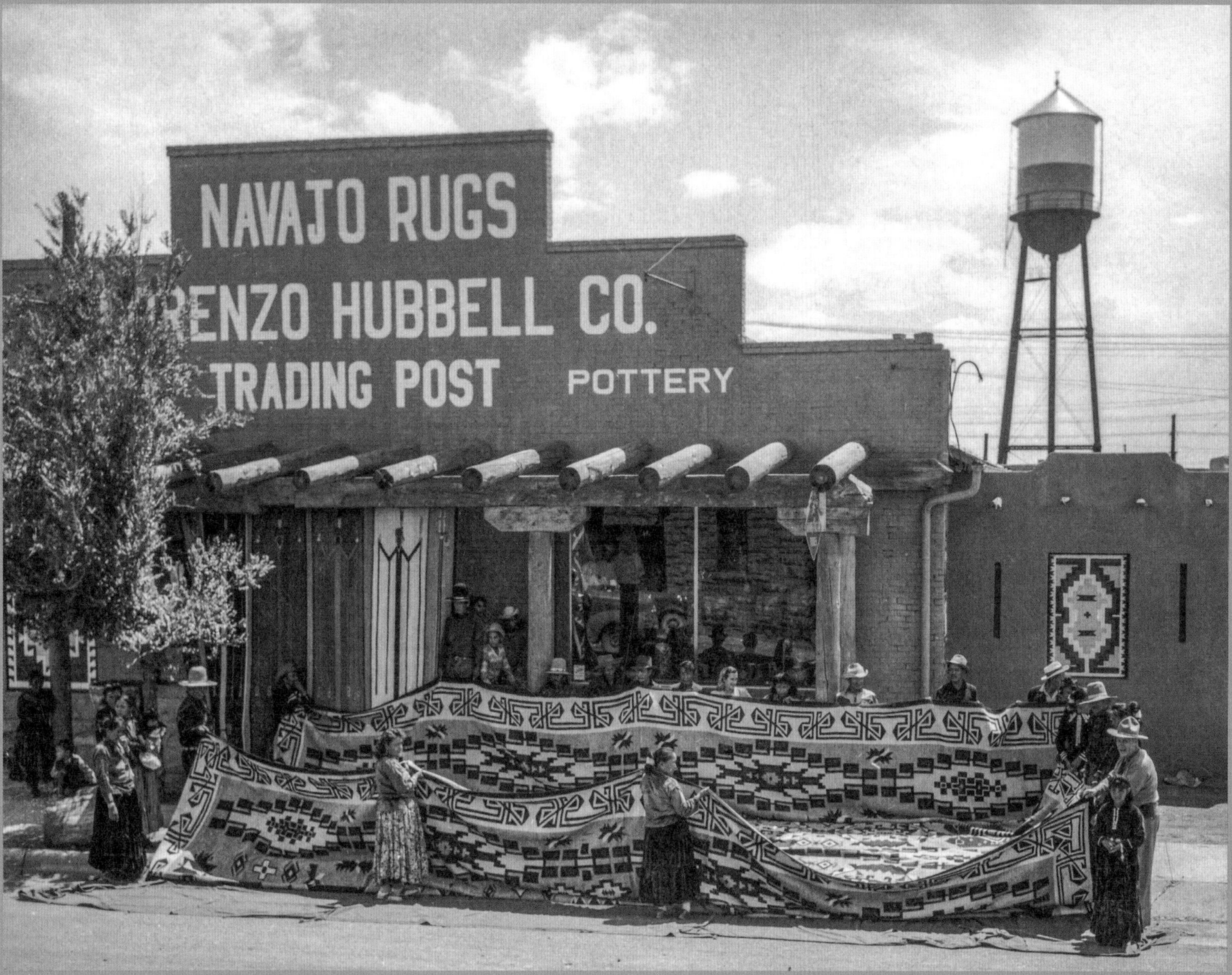

OPPOSITE
Winslow Chamber exhibit at the International Travel Show, Grand Central Palace, New York City, 1948.

ABOVE
Diyogí Tsoh (The Big Rug) is spread in front of the trading post.

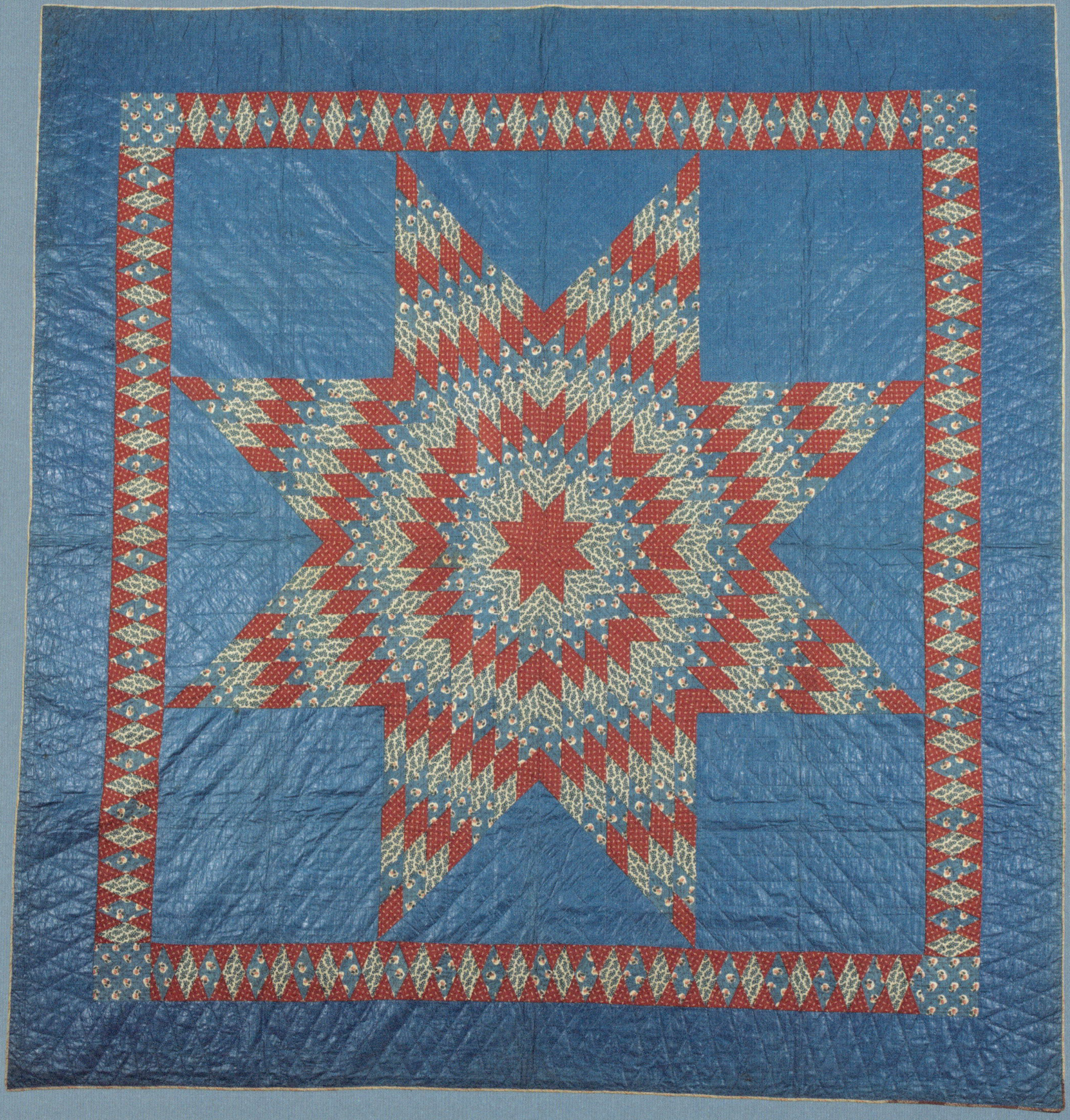

THE QUILT

LONE STAR QUILT

c. 1850, **Unidentified artist**, Cotton, 96½ × 94 in. (245.1 × 238.8 cm), The Huntington Library, Art Museum, and Botanical Gardens, San Marino, CA, Gift of Jonathan and Karin Fielding, 2016.25.58.

This spectacular quilt represents a type that has become iconic in the history of American craft: the Lone Star quilt. The success of this Lone Star quilt design lies particularly in the unusual choice of a glossy blue cotton (an effect produced by a combination of pressure, heat, and starch) that makes a stunning backdrop for the rusty red, cerulean blue, and creamy white and green calico prints of the piecing. Polished solid-color cottons such as this background fabric were common linings used in nineteenth-century dresses. The prints of the pieced star and border represent fashionable dress fabrics of the 1840s.

Beginning in the eighteenth century, the industrial revolution shifted textile production from human to waterpower, dramatically reducing the cost of fabrics, especially cottons, by the early nineteenth century. This affordability meant that families could increase their wardrobes substantially, making recycled scraps as well as new fabrics readily available for quiltmaking. Early colonial women are often incorrectly credited with the development of pieced quilts; the truth is that pieced cotton quilts did not become common until the second quarter of the nineteenth century. Because quiltmakers often reused the fabrics of worn-out clothing for their pieced designs, by the time this extraordinary quilt was stitched, the authors of needlework instruction and household advice books had declared calico patchwork quilts to be "old-fashioned," and only "good enough for servants' beds."[1] (Only template-pieced quilts made of silk or whole-cloth quilts made of a fashionable furnishing chintz were deemed by them worthy of a woman's time to make.) Fortunately, as evidenced by the abundance of surviving calico quilts from this period, little heed was paid to such advice. American women enthusiastically adopted this textile technique and made it a cultural icon.

The earliest published reference to this pattern appeared in *Graham's Magazine* in 1844, where it was called Rising Sun.[2] Many other names have been associated with the design, including Star of Bethlehem, Blazing Sun, Setting Sun, Morning Star, and Sunburst Star. This pattern is typically pieced as a large, central, eight-pointed star (though other numbers of points have been produced), with diamond-shaped pieces of various colored calicoes or silks making up the points. Traditionally, the quiltmaker organizes the pieces of the star points in rows of the same fabric (patterned or solid), so that the gradation of colors visually radiates.

The earliest Lone Star design appearing in an American quilt was made by Catharine Collins of Smyrna, Delaware, who cross-stitched her name and the date "Aug the 7 1806" on the back.[3] This large-scale star pattern gained popularity in the 1820s and 1830s and remains a popular choice for showing off piecing skill today. Texas, the "Lone Star State," claims a particular affinity for this quilt design, while the Lakota and Assiniboine Native American tribes in the Dakotas and Montana have adopted the pattern, which they call the Bethlehem Star, and imbued it with great cultural meaning, taking the place of earlier buffalo robes painted with star designs.[4]

As the stars at night have inspired many great works of art, science, and literature, so they have inspired great quilts. For more than two hundred years, the Lone Star (or Bethlehem Star) design has inspired ambitious quiltmakers to create radiant bedcovers and special ceremonial gifts embedded with personal and cultural meaning. —LZB

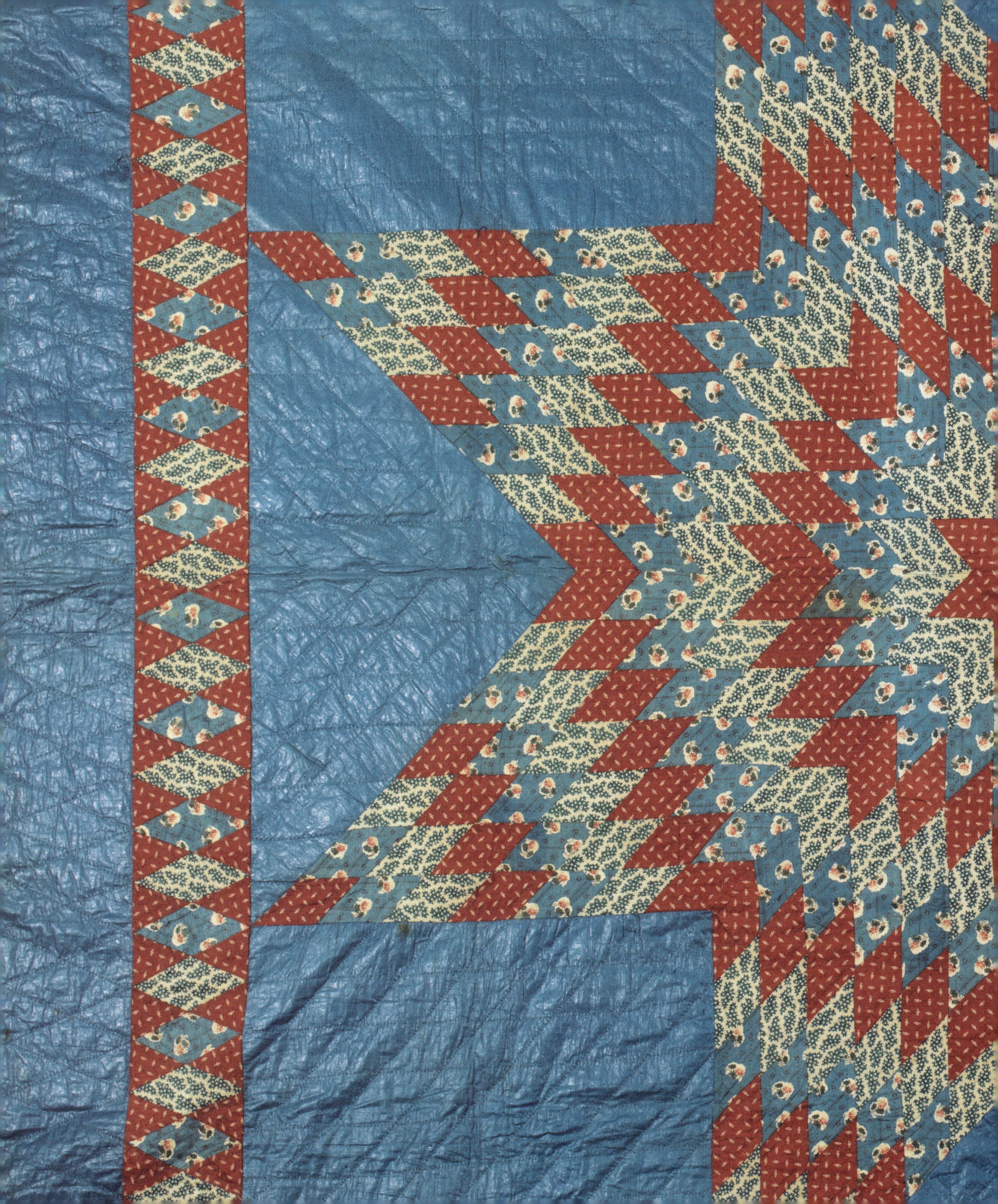

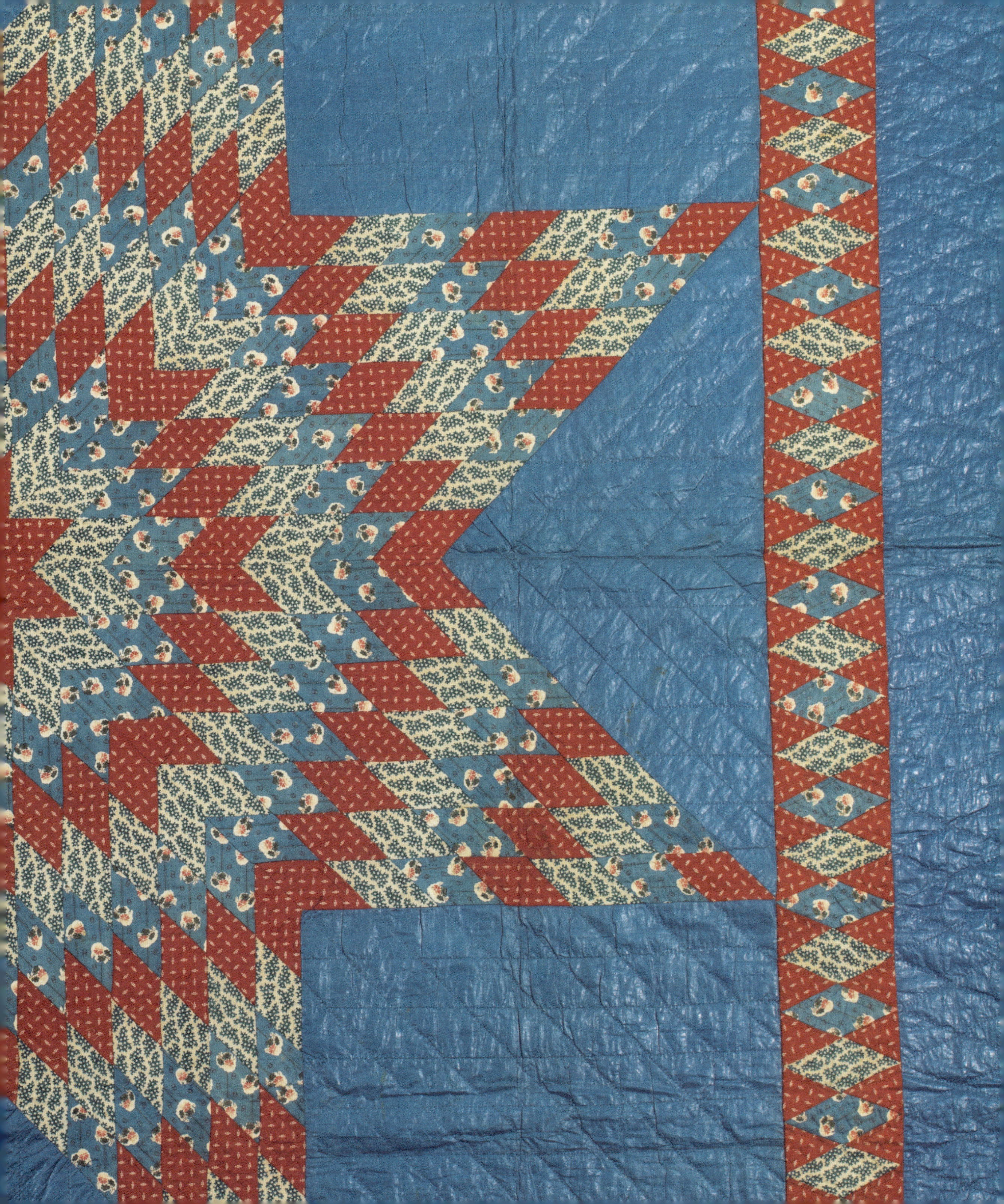

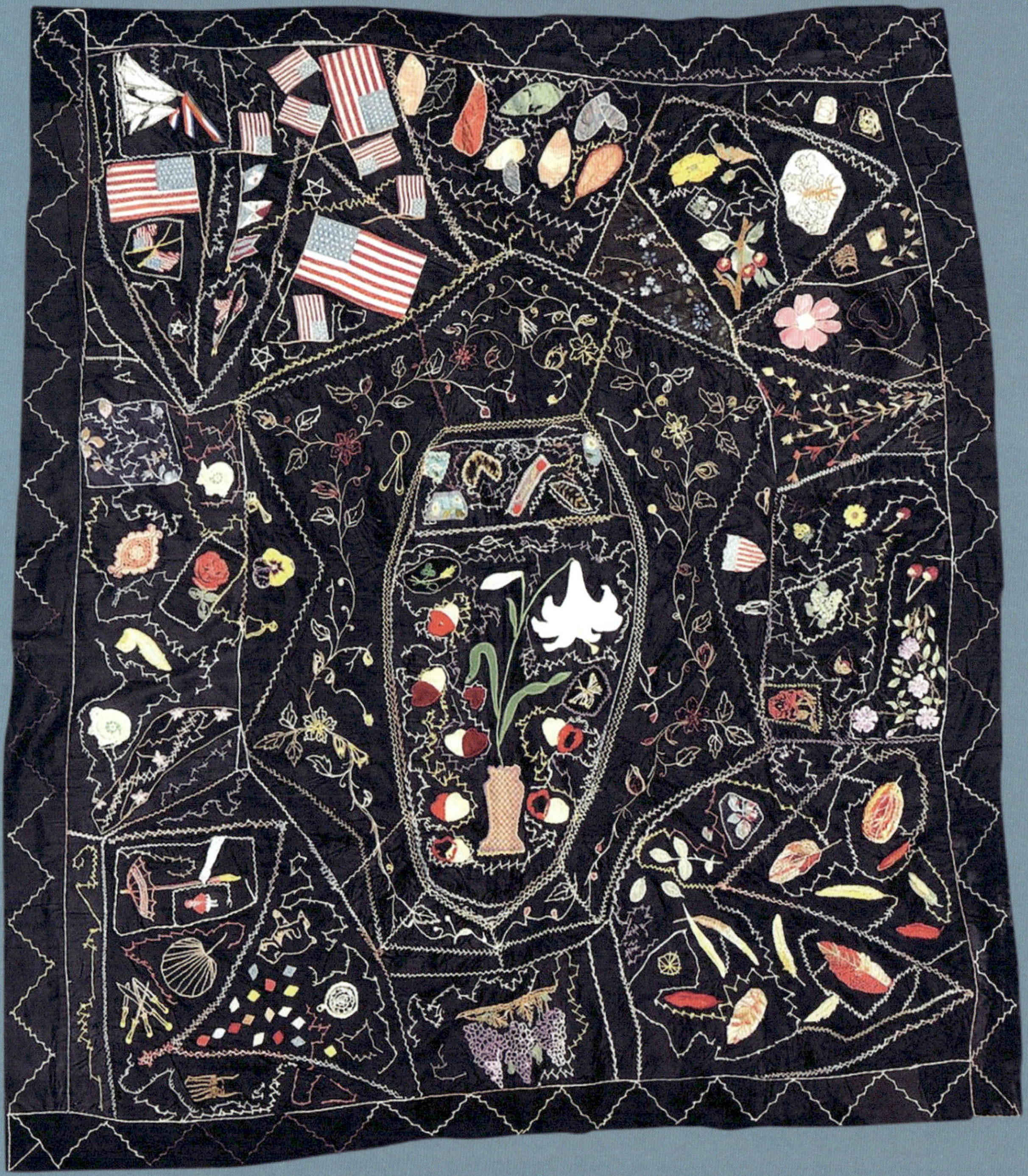

THE QUILT

MOURNING CRAZY QUILT

c. 1900, **Unidentified artist**,
Silk, cotton embroidery thread, velvet, lace, 68 × 64 in. (172.7 × 162.6 cm),
Private collection.

In the last decades of the nineteenth century, American women became captivated by the seemingly sudden arrival of a new kind of quilt: the so-called crazy quilt. Makers of fancy crazy quilts commonly embellished scores of irregularly shaped pieces of luxury fabrics with elaborate embroidery, sometimes adding small trinkets, metallic threads, or even oil painting. Fragile and impractical, crazy quilts were intended as showpieces, not as warm bedcoverings.

Previously, American quilts had been either appliqué designs, often inspired by the natural world, or composed of geometric, pieced designs. Quiltmakers typically laid out repeating designs in a grid or oriented around a center medallion. Usually made of sturdy materials such as cotton or wool, most quilts were expected to withstand use. Of course, even within these conventions, nineteenth-century women left us an astonishing body of personalized and inventive variations. By contrast, in their crazy quilts women could ignore practicality and let their artistic visions run wild.

Crazy quilting eventually developed its own set of conventions, and many extant examples have a rather generic appearance. However, some makers working within this style created quilts of singularly memorable design, expressing a unique personal vision. Such is the case with this quilt, a tour de force of design and imagery. Crazy quilt fashion clearly inspired the meandering lines of embroidery around each piece, but the random-shaped background pieces all appear to be the same material. Could those black background shapes be pieces of a disassembled garment? The maker's mourning dress perhaps? In the center, a coffin-like form floats within a shape resembling a star. Inside the "coffin," a vase holds a single drooping white lily. And surrounding the lily are numerous pairs of overlapping hearts. The maker appliquéd and embroidered a lone red heart closest to the vase. Other embroidered and appliquéd embellishments appear on the quilt, but not the usual butterflies, horseshoes, owls, and fans that we see repeatedly in classic crazies. Instead, there are American and naval flags, grapes, a tiny man outlined in white, and a girl in a red dress protected by an umbrella. The combination of motifs seems to tell a story—but what is that story?

Is the quilt what it seems—a mourning quilt, perhaps made by a widow? Are the appliqués and embroideries personal images unique to this family's life? As the quilt's history is unknown, we can only ascertain so much. But we can often learn a lot by studying a quilt: its age, the skill of its maker, sometimes its geographic or ethnic origin. What we cannot know is what was in the heart of its creator. We can only know how it touches ours. —JS

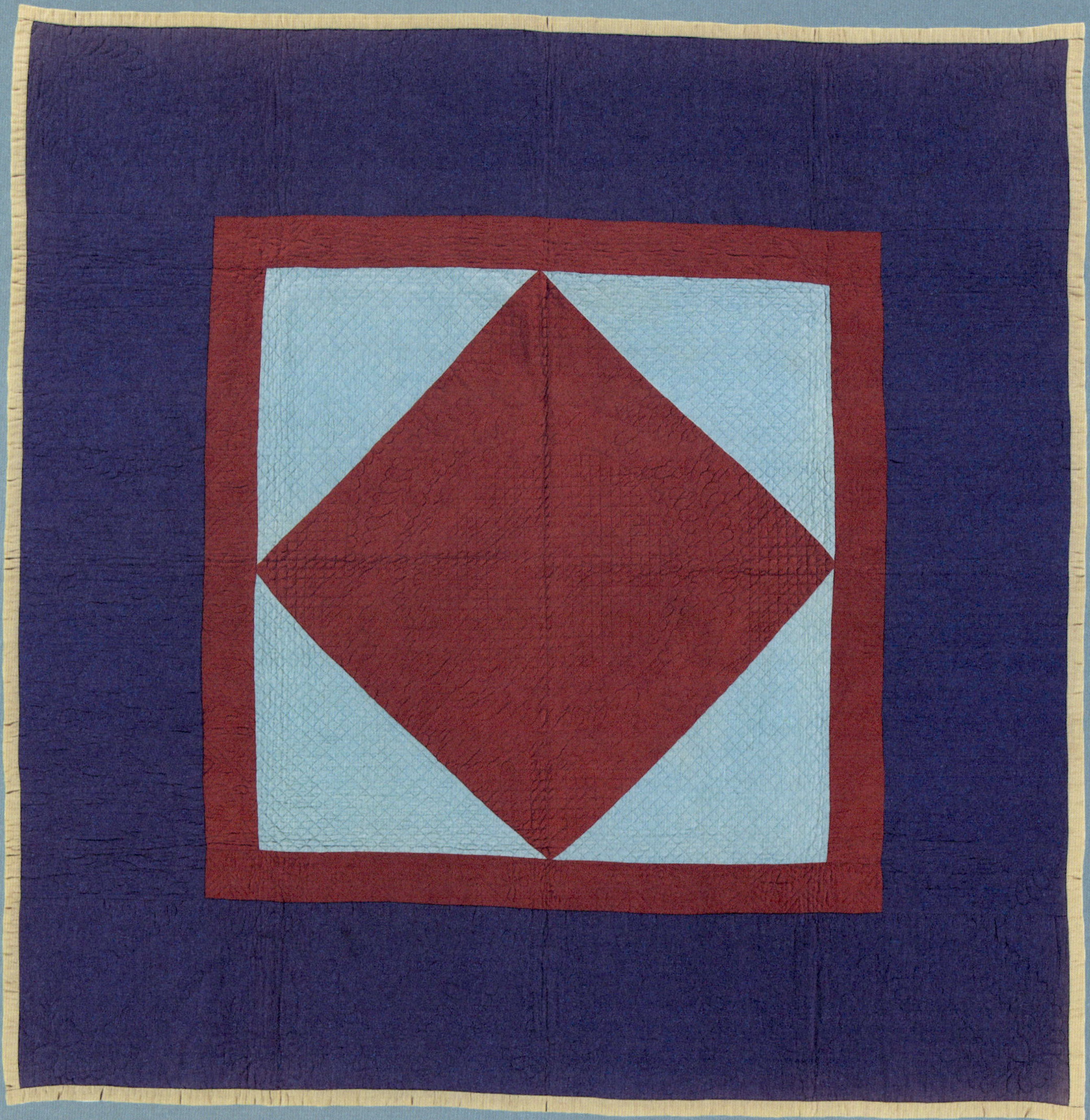

THE QUILT

AMISH CENTER DIAMOND QUILT

c. 1910–20, **Unidentified artist (Lancaster County, PA)**,
Wool, 81 × 80 in. (206 × 203 cm),
International Quilt Museum, Lincoln, Jonathan Holstein and Gail van der Hoof Collection, 2003.003.0100.

This Center Diamond quilt made by a Lancaster Amish woman around 1910, pieced from fields of gloriously saturated red, purple, and blue and stitched together with crosshatch grid patterns and a central feathered wreath, could hardly be more different from the quilts made by mainstream American women at the time.

American quilters developed regional and cultural design preferences as early as the eighteenth century. As time passed, expanded means of travel and increased exposure to the styles of others led to the cross-pollination of ideas—and to fewer differences. Deepening the fading away of regional styles was the growing availability of published designs and instruction manuals.

Historically, when the larger world "discovered" certain ethnic and religious groups of Americans, their quilts—once made for themselves—became trade goods for tourists and decorators. This monetization typically resulted in a decline in the quality of design and production. Quiltmakers in some groups, however, maintained distinct features as late as the mid-twentieth century, perhaps because of their geographic isolation, or extraordinarily strong ties to long-standing traditions within their own culture. One such group of holdouts were Amish women in Lancaster County, Pennsylvania. The Amish ultimately also succumbed to the demands of the tourist trade by the 1970s, though they were much slower than most to do so.

The Amish did not bring a quiltmaking tradition with them when they emigrated to America from Germanic Europe in the eighteenth and nineteenth centuries. Rather, starting around 1860, Amish quiltmakers developed a style that borrowed somewhat from their "English" neighbors (their term for anyone outside of their community) and, importantly, represented a central tenet of their Anabaptist beliefs: "Be in the world, but not 'of' it." Bold but unobtrusive quilting designs such as this one satisfy the Amish quiltmaker's commitment to humility, a central tenet of the Amish culture, while also suggesting a strong dedication to excellence.

When the country entered the Depression years, mainstream American quilters typically used a variety of cottons printed in colorful pastel colors, often cut from the scraps of their dressmaking. Lancaster Amish women also made quilts from fabric they purchased to make their family's clothing: dress-weight wools dyed in saturated, jewel-toned solid (and only solid) colors. But, as proficient farmers of the rich soils of Lancaster County, the Amish community there weathered the Depression better than many Americans. As a result, they more often had the luxury to create quilts with specially purchased yardage rather than scraps and the production of quilts such as this continued. Where mainstream quilters' hand quilting was done to hold the layers together and was typically simple, experienced Amish stitchers covered these expansive fields of saturated color with dense, elaborate quilting designs, blending the color of their thread into their masterwork.

Today, the Amish quilt continues to be identified with the distinctive cultural differences of that religious group—differences that the Amish quilters have retained far longer than other ethnic or regional groups in America. —JS

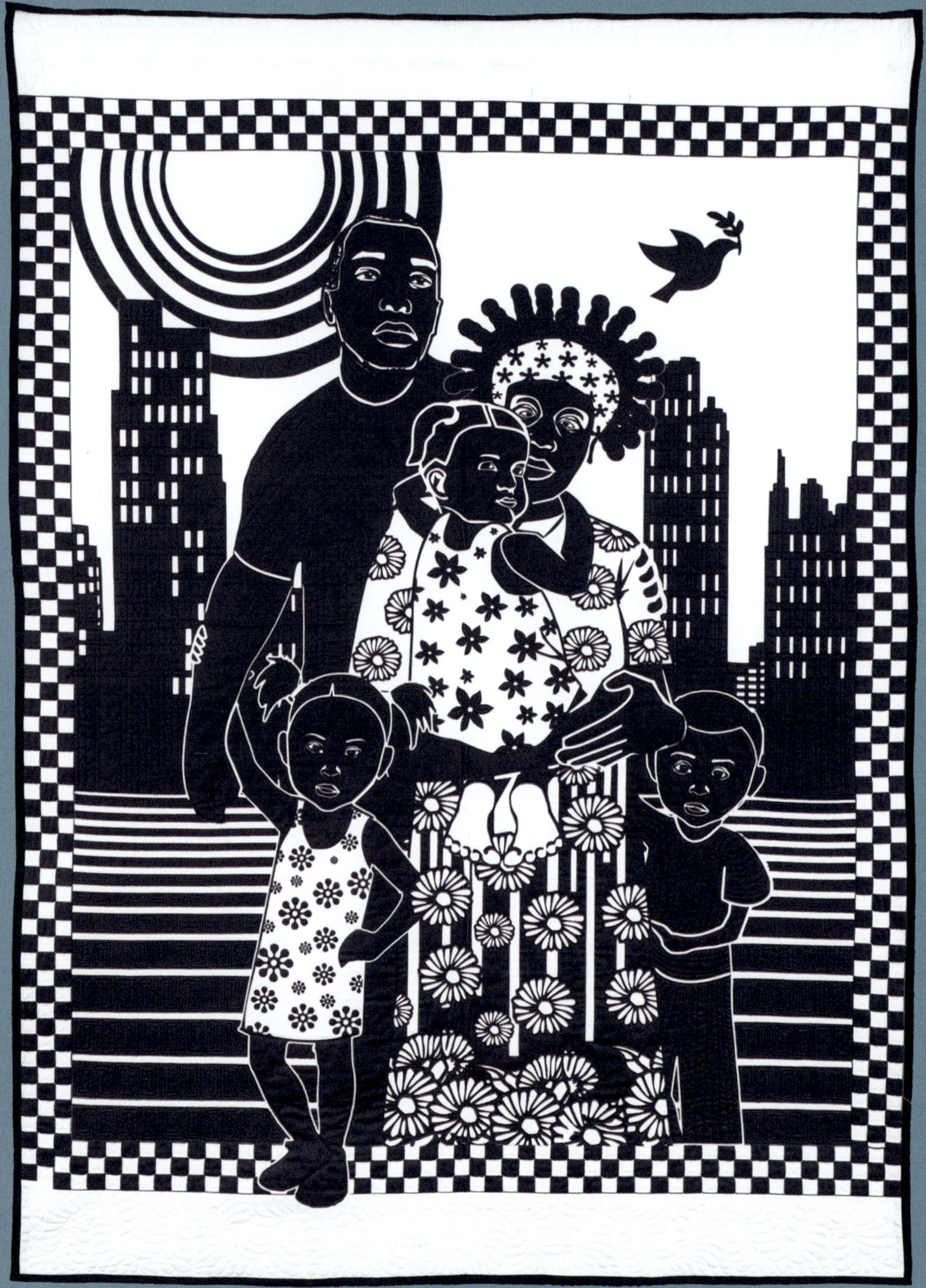

THE QUILT

SACRED UNION

1999, **Carolyn Mazloomi** (b. 1948),
Cotton, 65 × 45 in. (165.1 × 114.3 cm),
Cincinnati Art Museum, Museum Purchase: Fashion Arts and Textile Deaccession Fund, 2021.8.

In the powerful black-and-white pictorial quilt *Sacred Union*, a Black family stands against an urban skyline on a sunlit day; behind them, a bird flies high. This composition, created by Carolyn Mazloomi, a scholar, curator, founder of the Women of Color Quilters Network and maker of astounding quilts, is not only evidence of the artist's prowess in visual storytelling, but also a testament to the tenacity, love, and dedication of the Black family, which slavery sought to dismantle and destroy. Mazloomi uses the language of narrative quilts to convey untold stories from Black history that are difficult for people to hear, see, and understand. Her core palette of black and white powerfully reinforces the reality of these forgotten chapters of the past.

Quilting styles, practices, and traditions of African Americans have a long, complex history that speaks to the power of determination and a legacy equal to ancestral histories of textile traditions developed in Africa. In the era of the Middle Passage, Africans were kidnapped and brought to the Americas and Europe under vile conditions. Enslaved people arrived with no material belongings but with complex technical skills and knowledge. Fortified by their innate resilience, they formed an artistic and historical legacy vital to the foundation of this nation. African descendants who created story quilts stitched their experiences, beliefs, memories, hopes, and personal histories. Using a needle, thread, and scraps of cloth, the artists reaffirmed their intellectual, spiritual, technical, and symbolic link to their homeland—Mother Africa, the origin of all humankind. Mazloomi has advocated to expand awareness about the African American quiltmaking traditions that feed the community of contemporary quilters.

Known to Mazloomi and others as "the Mother of Quilting," Harriet Powers, most likely a first-generation African American, born into slavery in rural Georgia, created *Pictorial Quilt* in 1898. The remarkable array of story blocks Powers appliquéd into the quilt expresses both her artistic interpretations of Old and New Testament stories—such as Adam and Eve in the Garden of Eden—and environmental and astronomical events, such as the so-called Dark Day in New England, in which an unusual confluence of conditions made the day as dark as night. Each block tells its story through simple forms and flat figuration similar to the stitching traditions of Benin. The blocks are sashed together, using available cloth in an asymmetrical style typified in West African strip weaving.

Throughout the Black Atlantic diaspora, family is a driving force within communities, and intergenerational ties have been an empowering means of sharing knowledge across generations. Quilting in America, a new form of visual language spoken with a needle and thread, and its antecedent textile traditions across Africa are evidence of an endless, vibrant means of recording histories, experiences, and memories. —LKH

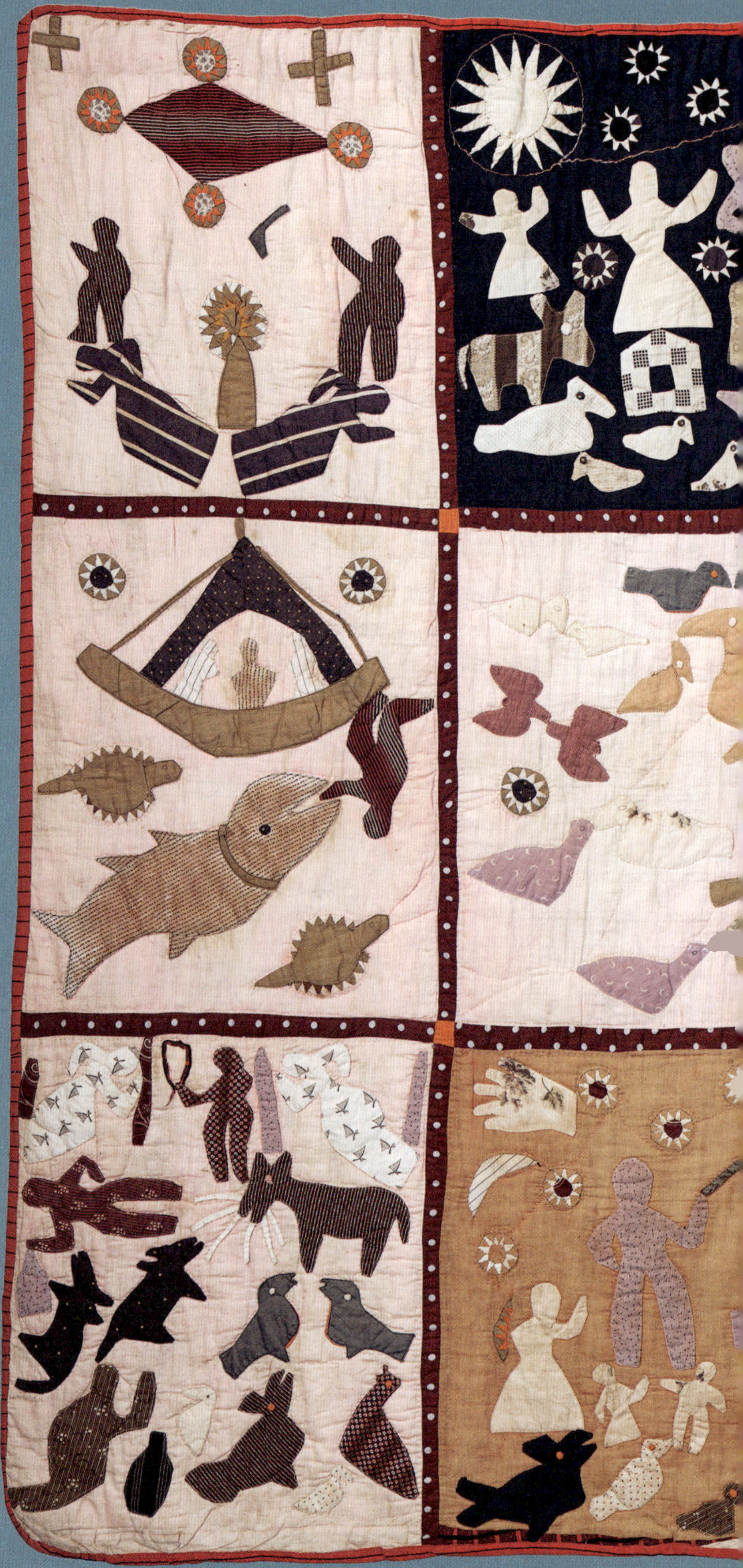

Pictorial quilt, 1895–98, **Harriet Powers** (1837–1910),
Cotton plain weave, pieced, appliquéd, embroidered, and quilted,
68⅞ × 105 in. (175 × 266.7 cm),
Museum of Fine Arts, Boston, Bequest of Maxim Karolik 64.619.

THE QUILT

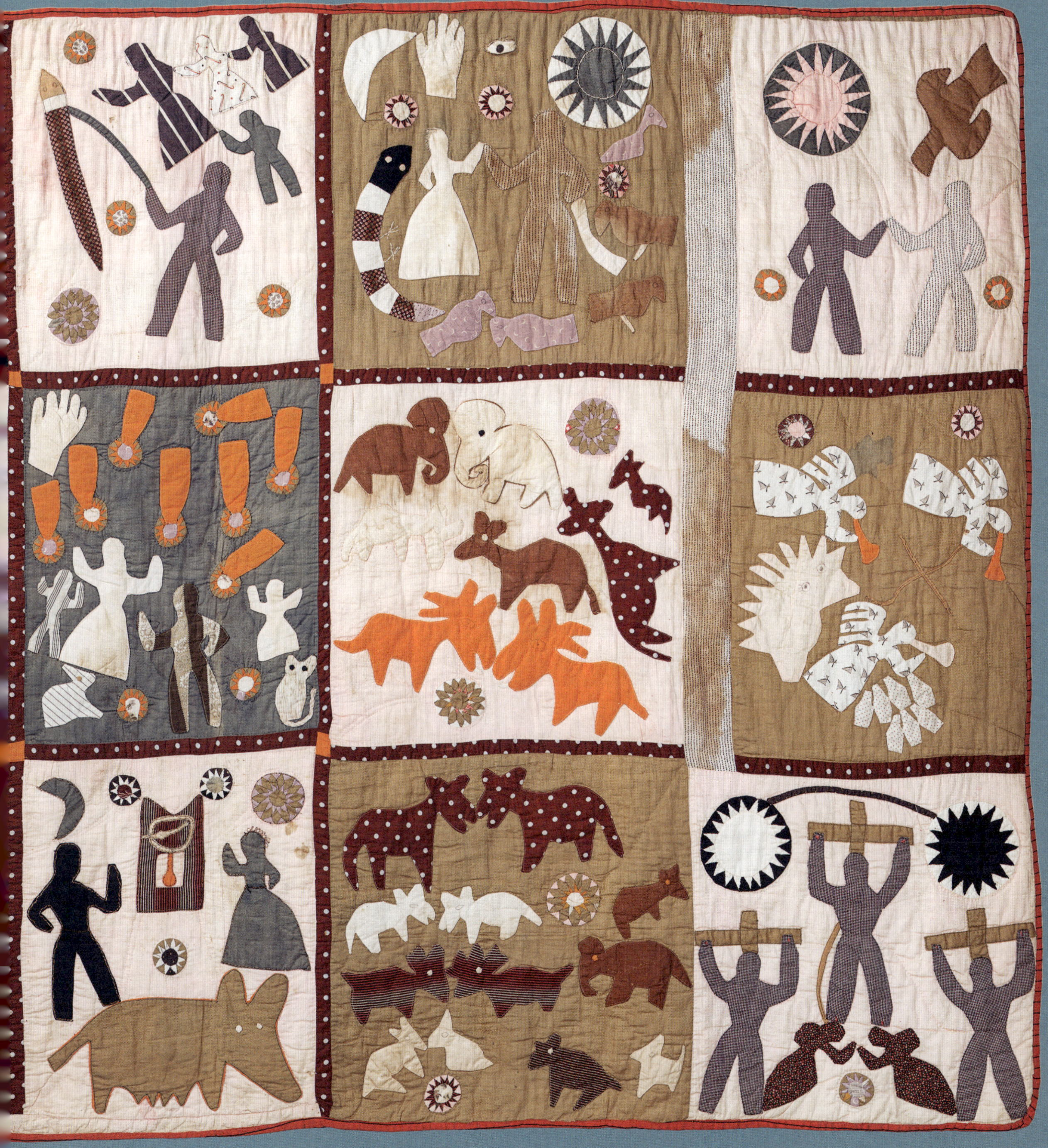

TO WARM

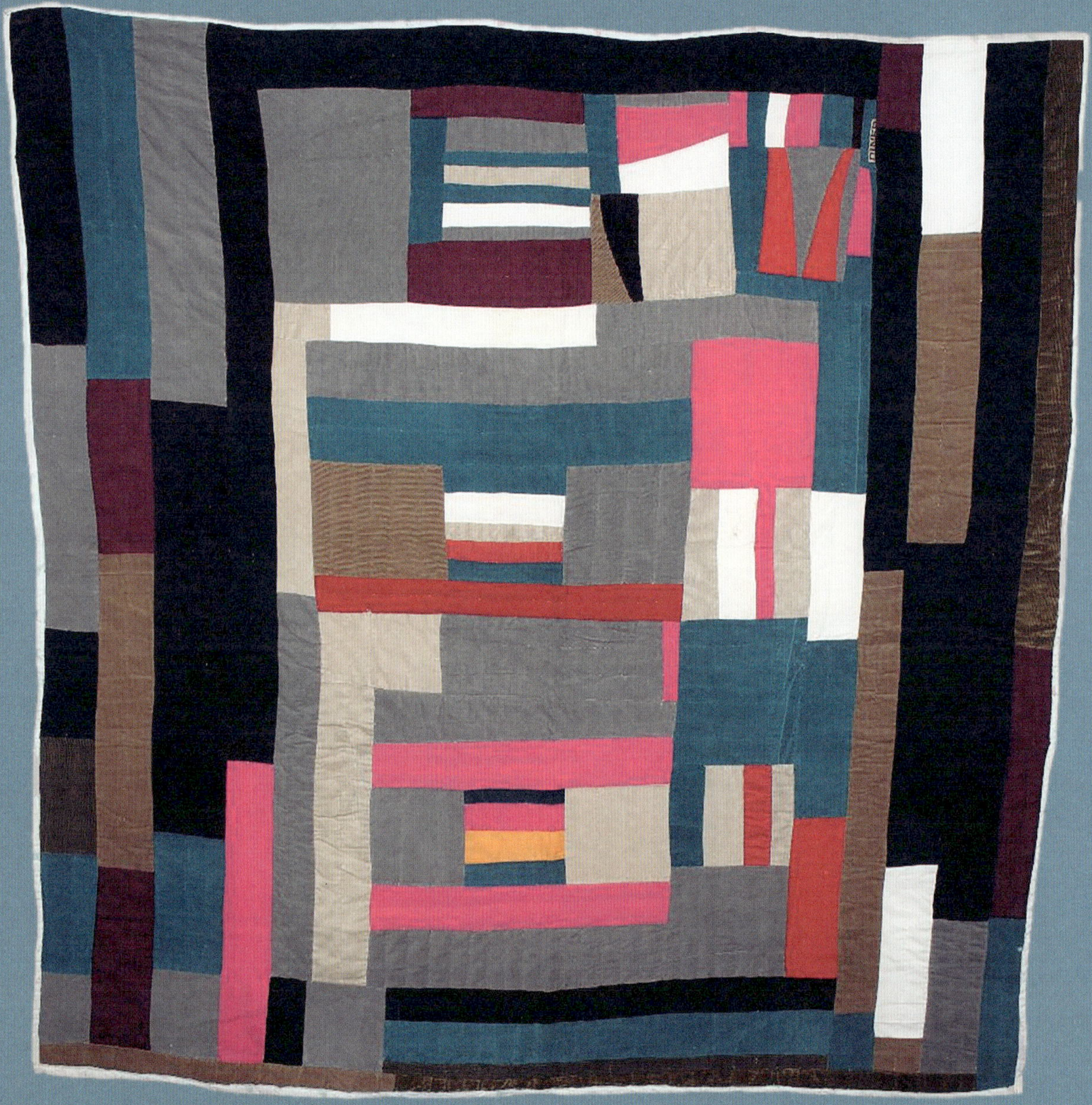

THE QUILT

DINER

2004, **Mary Lee Bendolph** (b. 1935), Corduroy and cotton, 71 × 73 in. (180.3 × 185.4 cm), The Huntington Library, Art Museum, and Botanical Gardens, San Marino, CA, purchased with funds from the Art Collectors' Council, 2021.3.2.

Through *In Search of Our Mothers' Gardens* the writer Alice Walker encourages us to consider the unexpected sites that reveal the origins of the creative traditions of Black women in America. Quilts are among these many spaces where Black women's creativity continues to flourish today, and Gee's Bend's legacy of improvisational, abstract quilt patterns is a prime example of the type of fertile landscape that Walker seemed to imagine. The artists behind these bold and vibrant housetop quilts in Gee's Bend, an isolated rural community in the Black Belt of Alabama, were inspired by the rooftops of shotgun houses of the region, reflecting both their surroundings as well as the futures they are building through repurposed fabrics and reflections of the heart.

For award-winning Gee's Bend quilter and activist Mary Lee Bendolph, quilts are a way to call attention to the lack of resources in her community and to use what she has at hand to make beauty and earn an income despite difficult circumstances. Bendolph was one of the leading quilters of the Freedom Quilting Bee, a collective that formed in 1966 of quilters in and around Gee's Bend who applied their stitching skills to create high-end home goods such as pillows and other products for retailers like Sears, Roebuck and Co. in order to provide economic opportunities.[1] Bendolph's work has often reflected the traditions and spiritual beliefs that have been passed down through generations—many of the Gee's Bend quilters tell stories of their great-grandmothers, grandmothers, and mothers as teachers of the quilting tradition—and that continue to shape everyday life within the region. Creating quilts was a means to ensure that families could keep warm; but quilts served social purposes as well: they both comforted newborn babies and loved ones at the end of their life. Even though housetop quilts exist outside of Gee's Bend, it is safe to say that a housetop quilt within Gee's Bend is a beacon of strength and survival in a town that has struggled to receive the economic support it needs.

Bendolph's 2004 work, *Diner*, is a profound example of her practice of using the scraps from her work with the Freedom Quilting Bee. Bendolph's quilt is made from corduroy, which was sourced from scraps of clothing from the apparel brand Diner (the company's label was pieced into the top right of the quilt). Bendolph uses her resourcefulness and improvisational style, with its variations on housetop-like motifs—bars and strips—to tell a story about both her journey and her community, tracing the commercial landscape of the material trade as fabrics travel in and out of the region.

Bendolph and a younger generation of quilters coming from Gee's Bend are also using their quilting to expand into other forms and mediums. In partnership with Paulson Fontaine Press in Berkeley, California, quilters translated their pieced quilt tops into fine art prints. Louisiana Bendolph, Mary Lee Bendolph's daughter-in-law, and Essie Bendolph Pettway, Mary Lee's daughter, are using the traditions that have passed down to them to create a new language of abstract patterns, including reinterpretations of the housetop quilt patterns. The tradition of Gee's Bend quiltmaking continues, as quilters apply their innovative approaches to color, fabric, and form to move forward in new directions. —LC

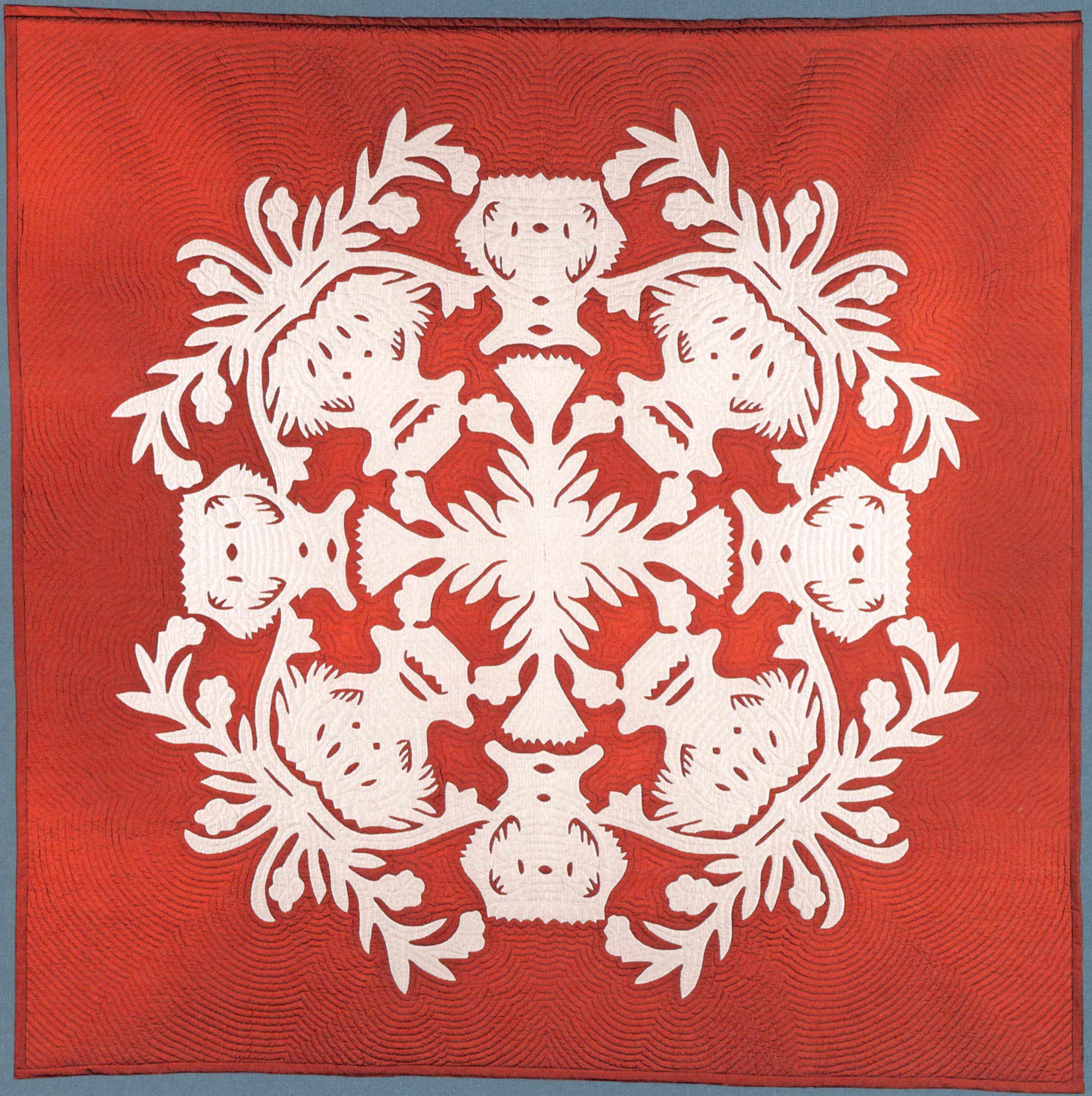

THE QUILT

UMEKE O KAMEHAMEHA

2025, **Pat Gorelangton** (b. 1952) based on a 1935 pattern by **Caroline Correa** (1884–1967), Cotton, cotton sateen, polyester, 102½ × 105½ in. (2.6 × 2.7 m), Smithsonian American Art Museum, Washington, DC, Museum purchase made possible through Federal support from the Asian Pacific American Initiatives Pool, administered by the Smithsonian Asian Pacific American Center, and in part through the Kenneth R. Trapp Acquisition Fund, 2025.28.

The iconic kapa kuiki, Hawaiian quilt, has adorned the homes of families in Hawai'i for generations. The practice of quilting was brought to Hawai'i by American Protestant missionaries in the early 1820s, and originally took the form of patchwork quilts. Over time, a distinct Hawaiian quilt style developed, integrating customary Hawaiian design aesthetics with intricate appliqué needlework and contour stitching techniques (see detail, detail, page 2). Kapa kuiki has become a significant branch of Hawai'i's textile history, building upon the art of hana kapa, bark cloth making.

Kapa kuiki draw inspiration from kapa—bark cloth—the sole textile that was produced in Hawai'i prior to Western influence and used for making clothing, bedding, and other utilitarian products. Kapa making continues to be practiced today. The cloth is commonly made from wauke (paper mulberry) fibers that are beaten on a wooden anvil to felt them together. These felted sheets can then be left unadorned or highly decorated with stamped and hand-drawn patterns. The meticulous designs used in kapa mirror the fine stitching that is present in kapa kuiki. Hana kapa motifs undoubtedly influenced the patchwork styles initially being taught by the missionaries early in the history of kapa kuiki. In turn, when kapa kuiki makers began to incorporate appliqué patterns into their construction, they inspired similar motifs to appear in hana kapa.

The appliqué patterns that became typical of kapa kuiki began as simple floral designs. Over time, these patterns became more complex, resembling elaborate snowflakes. Many patterns are inspired by local plants, flowers, and Hawaiian chiefly symbols such as feather standards and plaited fans. In the early twentieth century, a series of designs were produced that were inspired by floral arrangements in 'Iolani Palace, hotels, and private residences. This series inspired the quilt created by Pat Gorelangton, *Umeke O Kamehameha*, which honors the accomplishments and deeds of Hawai'i's first king, Kamehameha.

Kapa kuiki play a major role in telling and preserving the history of Hawai'i. In the late 1890s, a popular kapa kuiki design developed paying tribute to the Hae Hawai'i, the Hawaiian national flag. After the overthrow of the Hawaiian Kingdom on January 17, 1893, it was forbidden to fly the Hae Hawai'i in public. In protest of the overthrow, kapa kuiki makers created quilts with the flag's design and proudly displayed them in their homes over one of the most intimate spaces in a household: the bed. This act of defiance mirrored the actions taken by more than 38,000 Native Hawaiian citizens in support of Queen Lili'uokalani through their signing of petitions against annexation, also known as the Kū'ē Petitions. These signatures represented nearly every Native Hawaiian citizen in Hawai'i—undeniable proof that the Hawaiian people did not consent to the annexation.

Despite its origins in missionary teachings, the practice of kapa kuiki has transformed to become a distinctly Hawaiian art. Each design and stitch reminds us of the celebrations and struggles experienced by previous generations. The art form also lets present-day makers tell the stories of today and inspire future generations to carry on this rich heritage. —MHM

ADORN

THE VASE: TO DECORATE

THE NECKLACE: TO FRAME

THE GARMENT: TO WEAR

THE ACCESSORY: TO ENHANCE

THE SHOE: TO WALK

THE OBJECTS IN THIS CHAPTER ENHANCE our spaces and bodies. Most are wearable but not exclusively. Some of the wearables, such as the parka, the Stetson hat, and the Nike prototype track shoe, were created with function as their motivation. But in craft, practicality is merely a starting point. Adornment is the most interactive of craft categories, in social terms as well as personal. The object is designed to excel far beyond function—attracting, embellishing, providing pleasure, communicating meaning, and conveying the identity and values of the wearer.

Several objects in this chapter provide both metaphorical and physical protection. Some serve as a critical barrier from weather, disease, and even conflict. The squash blossom necklace; the chief blanket, the basis for the artwork *Contemporary Chief Set (Three Miniatures)*; the *Metabolizing the Border* suit; and the ʻahu ʻula unambiguously declare the wearer's endurance, strength, and power.

Many objects of adornment are customarily gifted from one person to another. Many are meant to be displayed for others to see and are as much about communicating with viewers as they are about the experience and sensation of the wearer. They are often our most prized possessions and the deepest material articulations of personal expression.

INTRODUCTION

Embellishment in the form of jewelry or fashion has the ability to communicate visually for the wearer. It provides cues about personality, identity, taste, status, lived experience, and personal ties. Americans have decorated themselves with the most surprising and awe-inspiring materials, from the most traditional—silver, leather, and beads—to the newest and most unconventional.

Jewelry is also the most luxurious of craft applications. This realm of craft has existed throughout time, as exemplified by the early mosaic pendant included here. People have always felt compelled to adorn themselves, and adornment has proliferated as we have gained increasing access to wealth and goods. Especially since the industrial revolution, luxury has been described as democratized. We exist in a world in which we are overwhelmingly bombarded with mass-produced goods; within this context, handmade objects are especially admired.

Adornment encompasses worlds of meaning. Objects of adornment can signify affiliation to a particular culture, religion, class, status, geography, or political group. Objects of adornment are tools used for seduction, intimidation, recognition, and the conveyance of many other unspoken messages. They have been created and exchanged as tributes of affection, as with the mourning pendant, and offerings of diplomacy, as with the wampum belt. They can be worn, used, shared—or they can simply be treasured. —EZ

INTRODUCTION

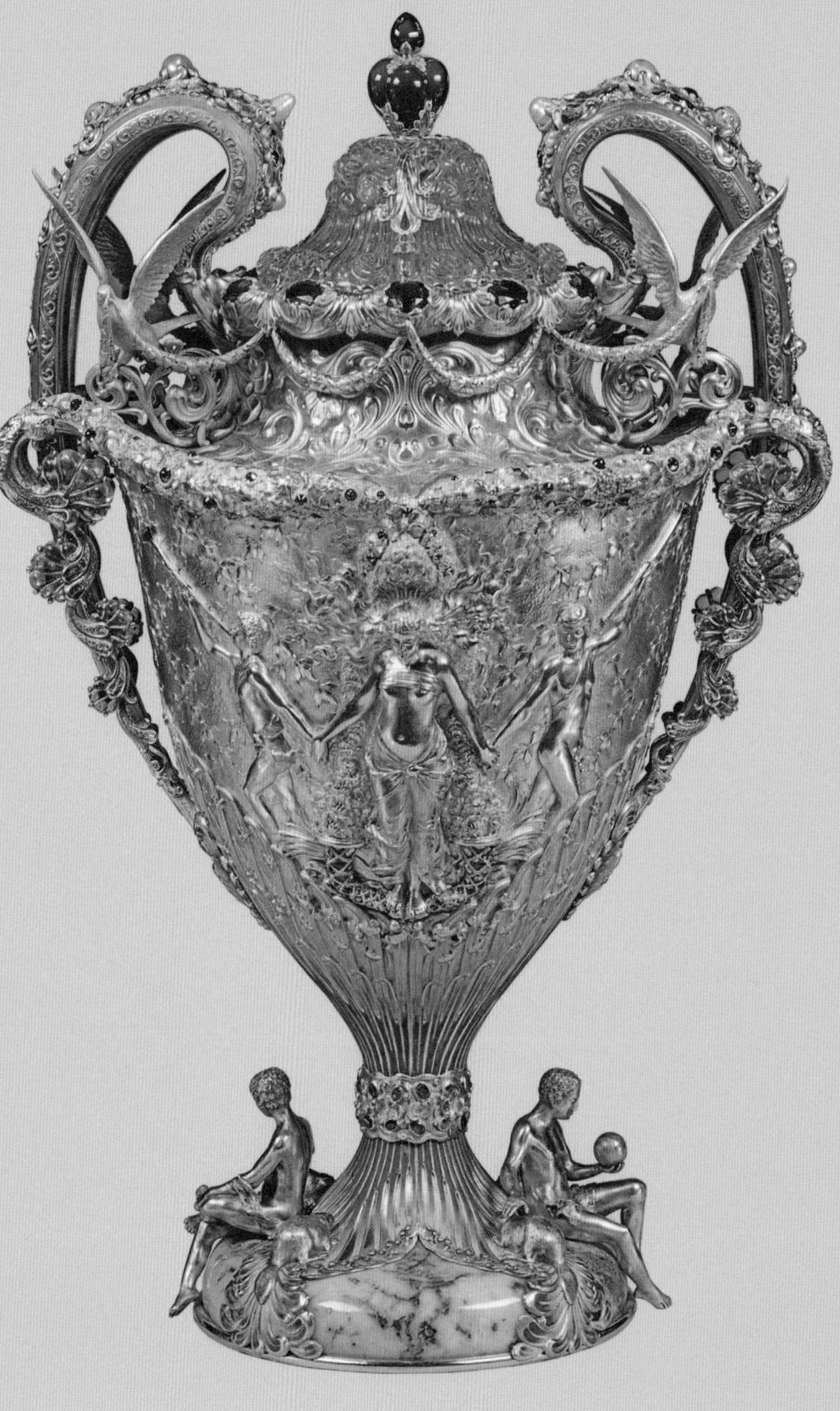

THE VASE

THE ADAMS VASE

1893–95, Designed by **George Paulding Farnham** (1859–1927) for **Tiffany & Co.** (est. 1837), Gold, amethysts, spessartites, tourmalines, freshwater pearls, quartzes, rock crystal, enamel, 19 7⁄16 × 13 × 9 1⁄4 in. (49.4 × 33 × 23.5 cm), Metropolitan Museum of Art, New York, Gift of Edward D. Adams, 1904, 04.1a-c.

Vases have been given as commemorative gifts across time. However, elaborate and ornate presentation vases such as this one became popular only during the Gilded Age, a time of incredible prosperity largely confined to the industrial elite. Formed from approximately 160 ounces of solid gold, George Paulding Farnham's dazzling *Adams Vase* is emblematic of Gilded Age design.

Created by Tiffany & Co., it was commissioned by members of the board of the American Cotton Oil Company to honor their chairman, the New York banker Edward Dean Adams. Adams was known as a shrewd power broker and was often hired to restructure failing companies, including the American Cotton Oil Company. After the Civil War, the Southern cotton industry remained dependent on Black farmers under the sharecropping system and companies such as the American Cotton Oil Company sought to diversify the market. In addition to cotton's fibers, which were central to textile production across the world, Adams helped the company to promote cottonseed oil, a by-product of cotton harvesting, touting it as a healthier cooking fat, among other applications. To reflect the company's mission in his design for the vase, Farnham studied the entire cotton plant, "the most important plant of our American industry."[1] The rock-crystal cover is engraved to mimic cotton's boll, which is crowned with a small, green precious gem to represent the cottonseed. The silhouette of the vase suggests the organic shapes of the plant.

To accompany the *Adams Vase*, Farnham published a book narrating his design intentions, the sources of the vase's materials, and the execution of the piece. For example, he reveals that he chose a green-tinted gold to suggest the palette of the cotton flower. This gold was purchased from the Ruby Gold and Gravel Mining Company in Sierra County, California. At the intersection of Nisenan, Cayuse, and Washoe homelands, this area around the Yuba River and its tributaries became an active mining region during the California Gold Rush of 1849. By the 1890s, workers for the Ruby Mine were unearthing large golden nuggets weighing as much as 201 ounces. Such an event likely caught the attention of the Tiffany & Co. designer. The vase's base is formed out of quartz with gold veining, sourced from the same Ruby Mine; it hints at the object's material origins from the same gold-rich veins beneath the earth.

The ornate *Adams Vase* is not only emblematic of the Gilded Age, but also a testament to successful collaboration across many hands. Over three years, Farnham was assisted by eighty-one specialists at Tiffany & Co.: three draftsmen, fifteen modelers, eighteen goldsmiths, twenty-one chasers, twelve finishers, four mold makers, three turners, two enamelers, three stonecutters, and two lapidary specialists. The process was as intricate as its results and involved goldsmiths raising a flat sheet of gold into a bowl and chasers forming the repoussé allegory of Modesty surrounded by two figures sounding horns of abundance. Small figures, from Atlas holding the world depicted on the base to flying birds at the top, form a pictorial narrative.[2] From its materiality to its involved construction, the *Adams Vase* speaks to the nineteenth century's vast networks of industry and specialization required to craft decorative materials. —CG

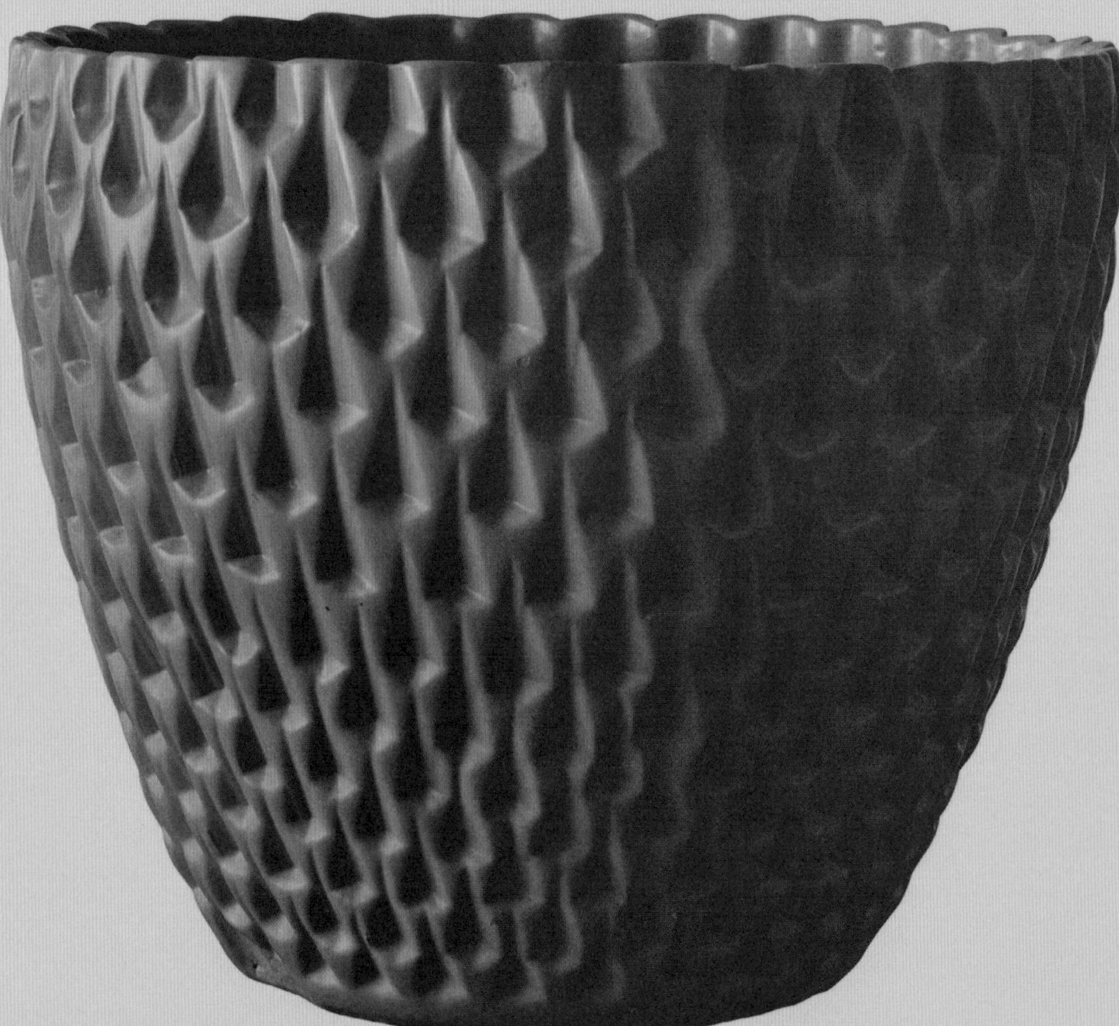

THE VASE

PHOENIX PLANTER

1966, **David Cressey** (1916–2013) for **Architectural Pottery** (active 1950–1988),
Slip-cast glazed stoneware, 20½ × 25 × 24½ in. (52 × 63.5 × 62.2 cm).

The Phoenix planter represents David Cressey's most iconic design from the Pro/Artisan studio line, manufactured by the Architectural Pottery company. Cressey masterfully created the prototype by muscling one hundred pounds of clay on a potter's wheel into a giant, gently angled cylinder. Then, while the clay remained soft and malleable, he used a carved two-by-four to create the pot's distinctive pattern of graduated indentations across the surface. The fired prototype later became the model for slip-casting production.

Unlike most of the company's catalog items assigned only model numbers, the Phoenix received its name to characterize creation and new life, according to Damon Lawrence, son of the Architectural Pottery founders Rita and Max Lawrence.[1] Literally, it nods to Cressey's transformation from studio to industrial ceramic practices; the mythical bird rising from the ashes is also figuratively suggested through the abstracted flame pattern that rises from its base—a surface design that draws the eye up and across its form.

While the Phoenix planter is a signature achievement, it represents just one facet of Cressey's distinguished career. After studying under renowned ceramists Vivika Heino at the University of Southern California and Laura Andreson at UCLA, where he earned his MFA in 1956, Cressey established himself as an educator and artist. He taught at Mount Saint Mary's College while maintaining a studio in Venice, California, where he created large-scale ceramic vessels and sculptures that earned national recognition in prestigious exhibitions. In 1961, Cressey's life changed when Rita and Max Lawrence approached him with a transformative opportunity: to leave academia and his studio practice to help launch the new Architectural Pottery factory. They recognized not only his artistic vision but also his exceptional command of large-scale ceramics and deep understanding of clay processes.

As artist-in-residence at their Manhattan Beach facility, Cressey pioneered industrial adaptations of studio techniques. He developed a special stoneware clay that could be slip-cast using industrial molds—a breakthrough that improved efficiency and consistency. He also created unique reduction-fired matte glazes and, by 1963, had designed thirty-two original stoneware pieces for the company's Artist-in-Residence catalog.

The Pro/Artisan Collection, launched in 1966, elevated Cressey's mastery of form and surface design to new heights. His innovative Flame Glazing technique created unique color variations through overlapping glazes, while his fourteen distinct textures offered unprecedented customization options. The Phoenix planter, a centerpiece of the collection, was available in either unglazed stoneware or a selection of ten glaze colors, and in two different sizes.

Cressey's collaboration with Architectural Pottery extended well beyond his initial role, yielding several innovative collections. Following the Lawrences' departure from Architectural Pottery in 1974, he continued leading the division before taking the helm as president of Earthgender Ceramics in 1976. In his final creative chapter, Cressey explored mixed-media abstract paintings, infusing them with the same mastery of texture and color that defined his ceramic work. His enduring legacy rests in transforming the garden planter from its traditional Mediterranean roots as heavily ornamented terra-cotta pots into bold, contemporary geometric forms—exemplified by the Phoenix—that perfectly complemented the era's modernist architecture. —JL

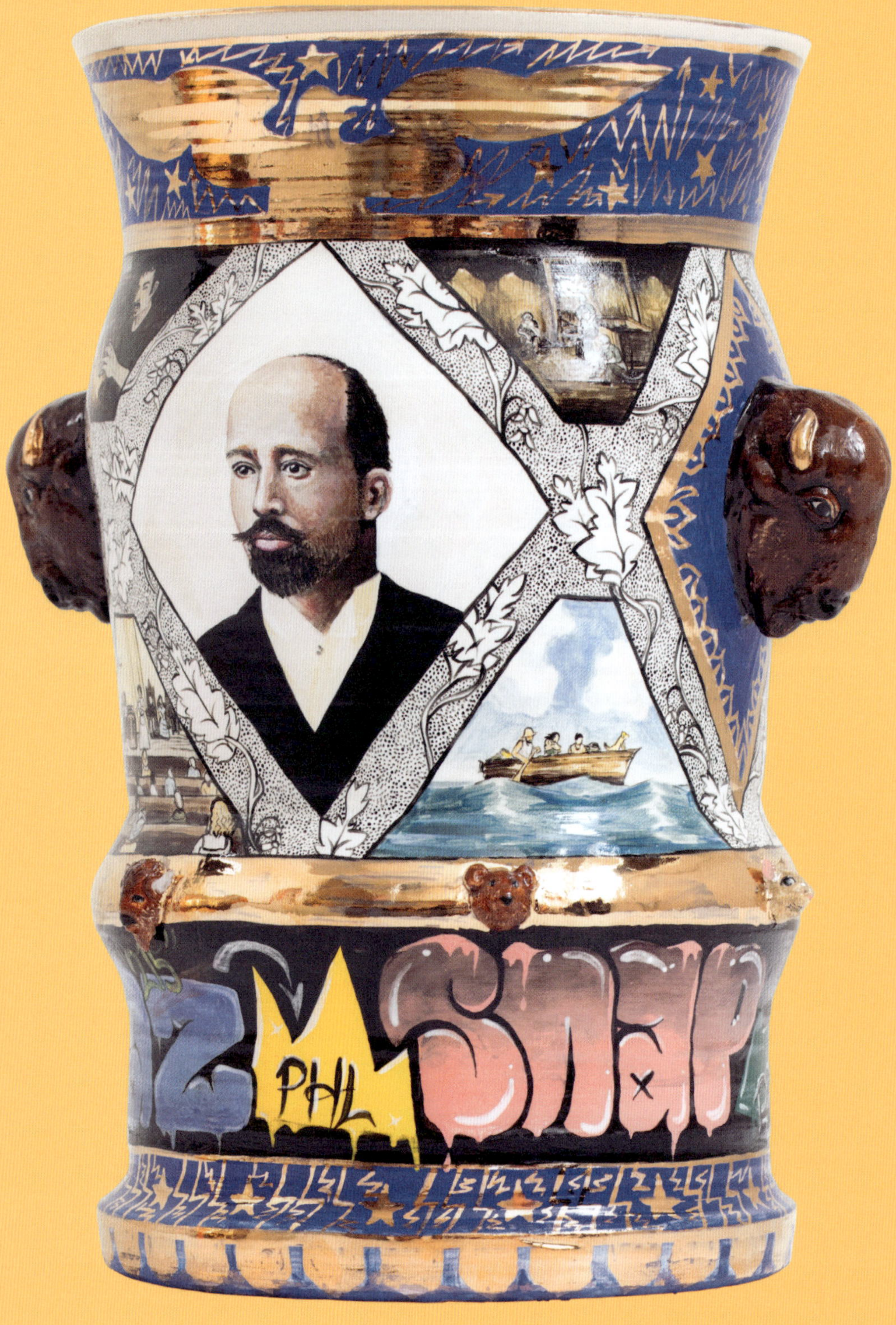

THE VASE

ROBERTO LUGO on THE VASE

A Century of Education Vase (Century Vase), 2024, **Roberto Lugo** (b. 1981),
Stoneware, enamel, luster, glaze, 15 × 10½ × 8 in. (38.1 × 26.7 × 20.3 cm), Newark Museum of Art,
Purchase 2025 The Newark Museum of Art Acquisition Bequest Fund, Catherine Viviano Fund,
Fanny H. Moore Fund, and Emma Fantone Endowment Fund, 2025.8.1.

I was first introduced to Karl L. H. Müller's *Century Vase* in my ceramics art history class at the Kansas City Art Institute, taught by Professor Michele Fricke. I was blown away by the detail of the work as well as the idea of trying to define and represent oneself through a ceramic object. The piece was made for the U.S. Centennial Exhibition in 1876 to represent America and all the innovations that had happened over the past hundred years. Imagery depicting fair trade between our founding fathers and Indigenous people adorn the work in the form of bas-relief.

Looking at it from a critical standpoint, I could see that some of the representations shown by Müller are not true for everyone, so I decided to use the century vase as a framework to talk about different subject matter. Two examples of these vases in my work are *A Century of Black Music* and *Brooklyn*. Since then, I have made dozens of works inspired by the *Century Vase*.

In my practice, I draw from the history of decorative arts. I'm attracted to its craftsmanship and excellence, but I've noticed that these works are often void of stories like mine, coming from humble beginnings. I believe ceramics give us the autonomy to represent our communities and to tell our own individual stories, and *Century Vase* has been a great way for me to accomplish this.

One way I have worked within the form and theme of the *Century Vase* is by changing the central portraits in each work from George Washington to people who relate to the often-overlooked stories I am telling. In *Brooklyn Century* I feature the Notorious B.I.G., who is from Brooklyn, and Jackie Robinson, who played for the Brooklyn Dodgers. In *Century of Education* I feature Ruby Bridges and W.E.B. Dubois, employing imagery of people overcoming adversity in order to pursue their education. From mine workers reading at lunch to my mother, who took classes for decades to get her nursing degree, these windows are opportunities to tell individual stories that add up to a whole.

Another feature of the original Müller-designed work is the inclusion of animals indigenous to America. At the forefront are bison, whose sculpted heads adorn the sides of the piece. I often use the original bison in my work in order to complete the silhouette of the piece and make an effective visual connection. But for the smaller animal heads that surround the pot further down, I substitute ram heads for animals like mice, and pit bulls, who are more commonplace in the community I come from.

The images on my vases are often painted with overglaze paint much like the original Union Porcelain Works creation. I use a quill pen dipped in a mixture of clove oil and black China paint. The pen allows me to get thin lines, as well as the stipple to create the layered effect the original work is so well-known for. My *Century Vases* are in many museums across the country and have often been displayed near originals. It is incredible to be a part of this history and to share untold stories in a medium that is as ancient as humanity itself.

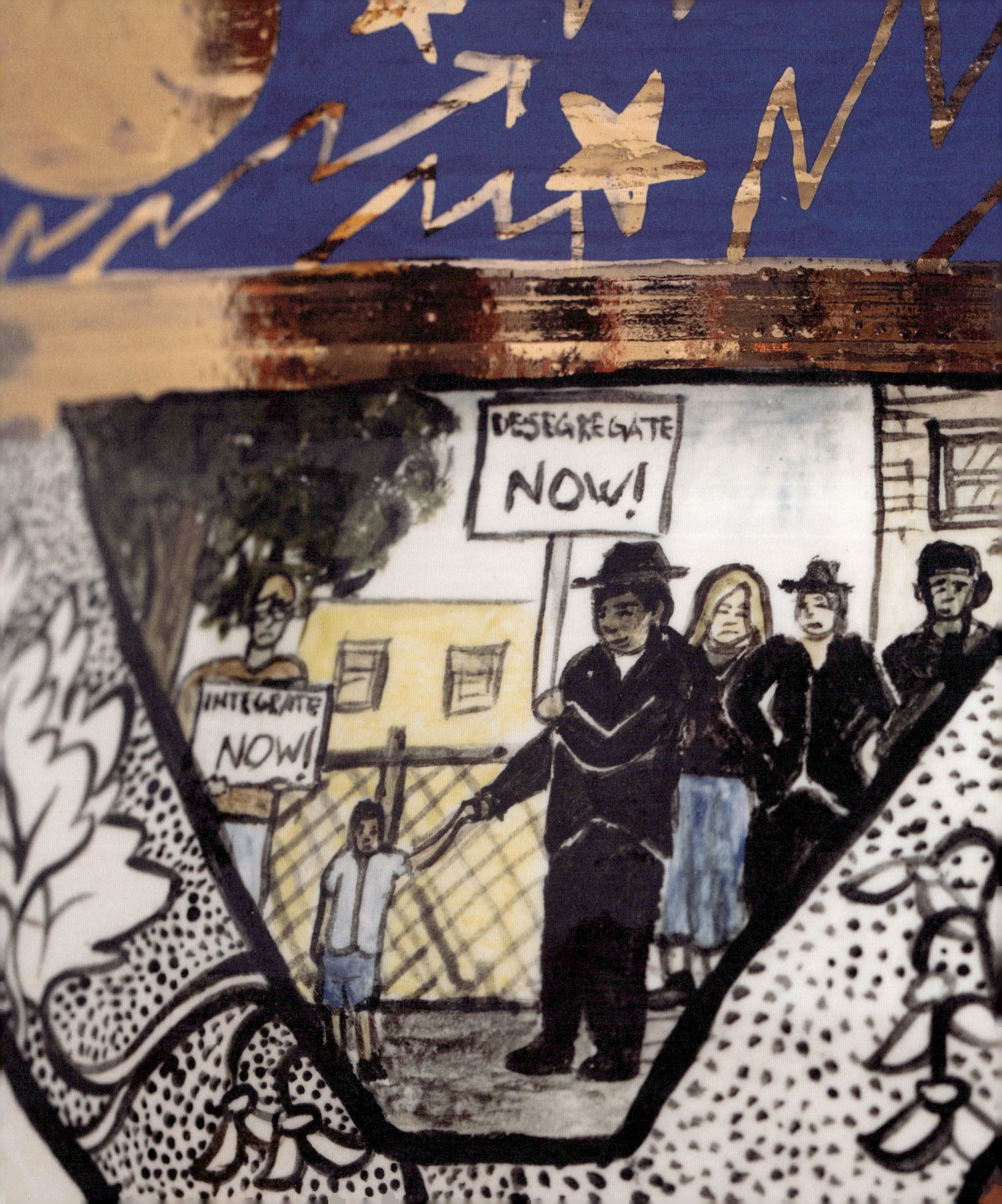
DESEGREGATE
NOW!
INTEGRATE
NOW!

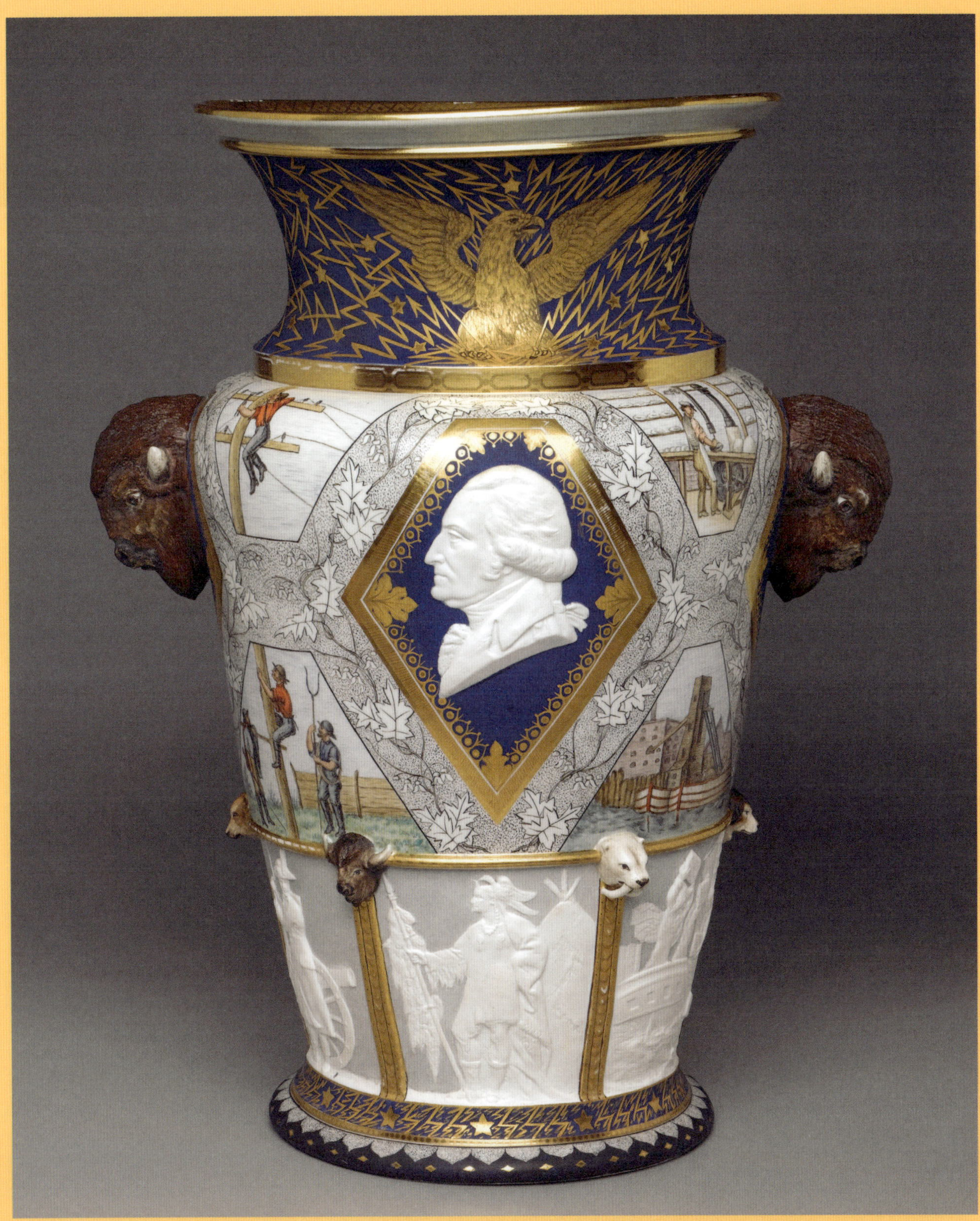

Century Vase, 1876, **Karl L. H. Müller** (1820–1887),
Porcelain, 22¼ × 10 in. diameter of base (56.5 × 25.4 cm), Brooklyn Museum,
Gift of Carll and Franklin Chace, in memory of their mother,
Pastora Forest Smith Chace, daughter of Thomas Carll Smith,
the founder of the Union Porcelain Works, 43.25.

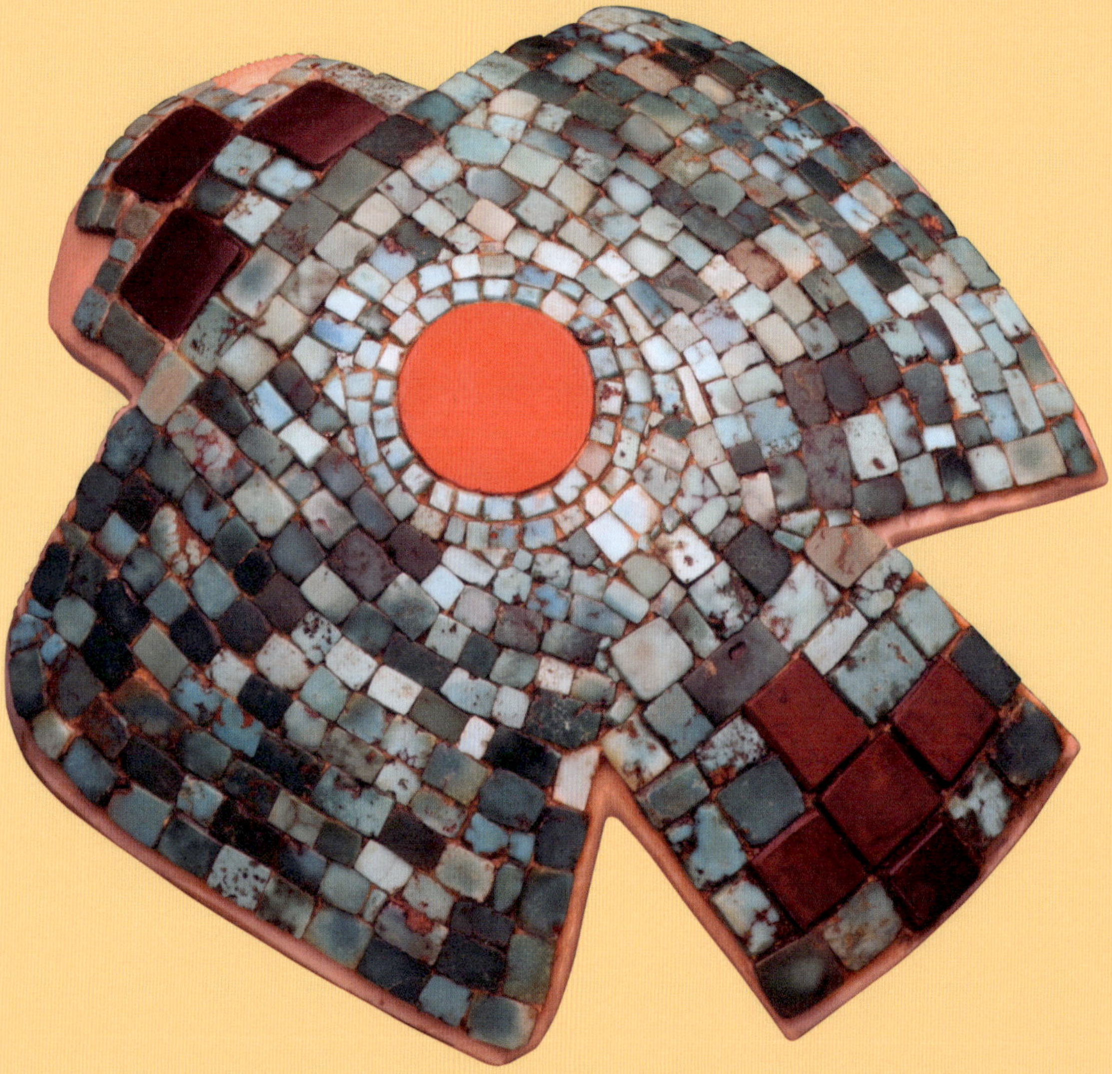

THE NECKLACE

BIRD-FORM PENDANT

c. 1200–1450, **Unidentified artist (Sinagua peoples of the Verde Valley, Arizona)**,
Overlay mosaic on spondylus shell, 3¼ in. (8.3 cm),
Pomona College Museum of Art, Claremont, CA.

The prehistoric American Southwest (primarily the states surrounding the Four Corners area) possesses the largest number of extant archaeological ruins. Many artifacts of personal adornment have been excavated from these ruins, artifacts that continue to reach deeply into contemporary Native American jewelry traditions.

Among the rarest and most beautiful of these unearthed jewelry pieces are overlay mosaic pendants. Often taking the shape of frogs and birds, both important insignias of power, these ornaments demonstrate a high level of handwork skills and techniques.[1] They also represent the influence of both local and long-distance trade with Mesoamerica, where complex ritual objects employed elaborate overlay mosaics that included turquoise traded from the Southwest. The overlay technique seen in the Southwest may have been itself adopted via this cultural exchange, coming through a Mesoamerican tradition outpost in Casas Grandes, Chihuahua.

This pendant's mosaic is overlaid on spondylus shell. Valued for millennia as a jewelry material, both in Europe and the Americas, the acquisition of this luxury shell required prehistoric Southwest peoples to travel by foot to either the Gulf of California or a slightly closer outpost where they could trade with other Southwest peoples.[2]

Not all mosaics were placed on such luxury materials. *Glycymeris,* or the bittersweet clam, was the most widely used shell in prehistoric overlay. In Montezuma Wells, Arizona, overlay mosaics were also done on wood, and there are Hopi mosaic overlay earrings on wood that date to 1900.

All prehistoric Southwestern jewelry was made without the benefit of metalsmithing tools and constructed simply by abrasion, usually stone, often the locally abundant sandstone. Despite the limitations, these craftspeople were so capable that they could make various stone tesserae (individual mosaic tiles) so small and precise that modern attempts to recreate their tiny sizes often end in failure. While the Southwest has abundant turquoise mines and a source for argillite, prehistoric jewelers were not wasteful with these valuable materials. Their thin tesserae and delicate stone mosaic tiles, adhered to shells with pine pitch, were made carefully.

The overlay mosaic technique continues to be practiced and developed by the Indigenous people of the American Southwest. Today's jewelers use epoxy, a much stronger glue, to attach much thicker pieces of tesserae onto the substrates, then grind them flat. This circumvents the huge number of hours required to shape turquoise and other stones into the hundreds of thin, individual tesserae prior to adhesion, but conserves less of the precious material. Today, the practice has culminated in virtuoso artists of the overlay mosaic's latest development: inlaid mosaics on metal, such as the intricate jewelry of the late Jesse Monongya or Carl and Irene Clark, and the overlay mosaics on wood made by Mary Lovato.[3] —**RL**

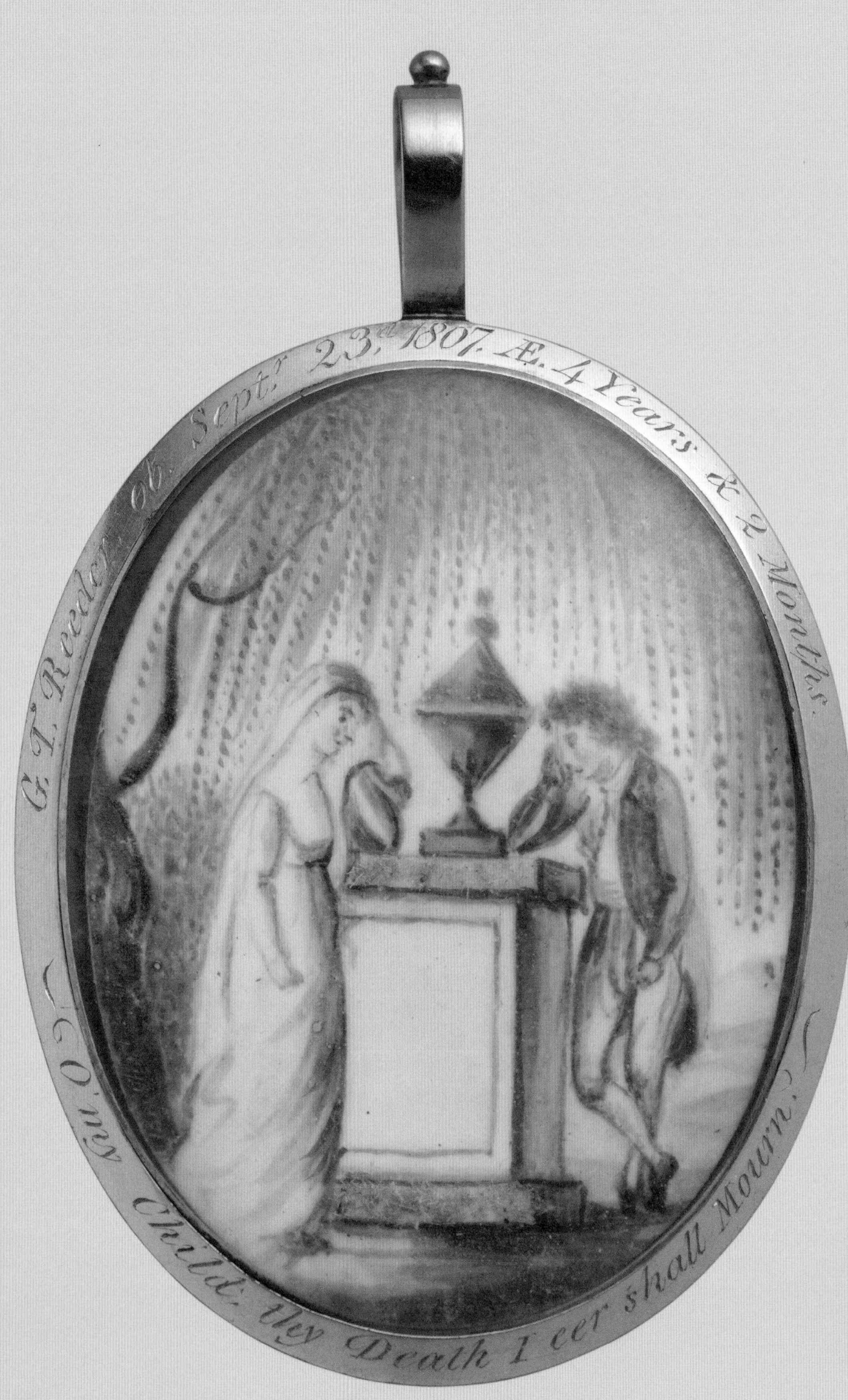
G. T. Reeder ob. Sept.r 23.d 1807. Æ. 4 Years & 2 Months.
O my Child, thy Death I e'er shall Mourn.

MOURNING PENDANT

1807, **Unidentified artist**,
Gold, ivory, hair, glass, paint. 2¾ × 1⅘ in. (7 × 4.6 cm),
Winterthur Museum, Garden, and Library, Winterthur, DE, Gift of Mr. Charles van Ravenswaay, 1974.0166.

This gold pendant, bearing an intimate scene of a mournful man and woman painted on ivory, played a part in publicly conveying grief and forming a community of shared experience among early Americans. Shrouded by the branches of a weeping willow, the bereaved pair flanks an unmarked plinth with an urn. The inscription on the surrounding frame reads: "G.T. Reeder. ob. Sep.r 23d 1807. Ae 4 years &2 months, O'my child, thy death I eer shall mourn." Encompassed in less than three inches, the couple's sorrow looms large.

From the late eighteenth century to the late nineteenth century, sentimental jewelry honoring the loved and the lost became increasingly popular. On the heels of the death of George Washington, a wave of American mourning brooches, rings, and pendants were lovingly crafted and personalized. They remain some of the earliest surviving jewelry made in colonial and early America. Memento mori (from the Latin "remember you will die") and tributes to the deceased were made across Europe and in England since at least the sixteenth century, with heightened prominence in Victorian England.[1] Funerary jewelry let the wearer be adorned by the memory of a loved one and to physically carry that bond with them.

In this pendant, and many like it, the honored spirit was represented not by imagery and inscription alone, or even by rare gems, as might be more expected in modern jewelry. Instead strands of hair, employed in a number of creative and unexpected ways, were the defining material in this jewelry genre. Here, finely cut bits of hair add color and texture that accent the tomb. Set beneath glass on the reverse side of the pendant are four neat plaits of hair; below the window is engraved: "G.Goldie, ob\t, Nov\r, 1791./ P. Goldie, ob\t July, 5th 1782./J. Goldie, ob\t August 31st 1796." The quarters of preserved hair likely came from any or all of the four noted individuals, including at least one child, perhaps the one recognized on the front.

It is easy to forget that life expectancy as well as child and infant mortality have improved drastically over the past two hundred years. Death was a much more present part of life in the 1800s and mourning a part of social interaction and identity. Wearing a token declaring your grief and loss was commonplace for those who could afford a customized piece. People then had a very different relationship with memory than today, where in the palm of a hand one can hold the casual and immediate luxury of a lifetime of digital photo albums. Hairwork jewelry was a way to physically hold on to a beloved's spirit. It became a specialized field of expertise within the jeweler's world.

Because sentimental jewelry was so popular, jewelers, miniaturists, and hair workers developed templates that could be customized with specific messages and the incorporation of locks of hair that were either ground and treated like paint pigment or braided and woven into elaborate designs. As hairwork became increasingly fashionable and elaborate during the Victorian era, women taught themselves the craft from various technical guides in what we now consider DIY craft. Then, as now, craft empowers and connects on so many levels. —EZ

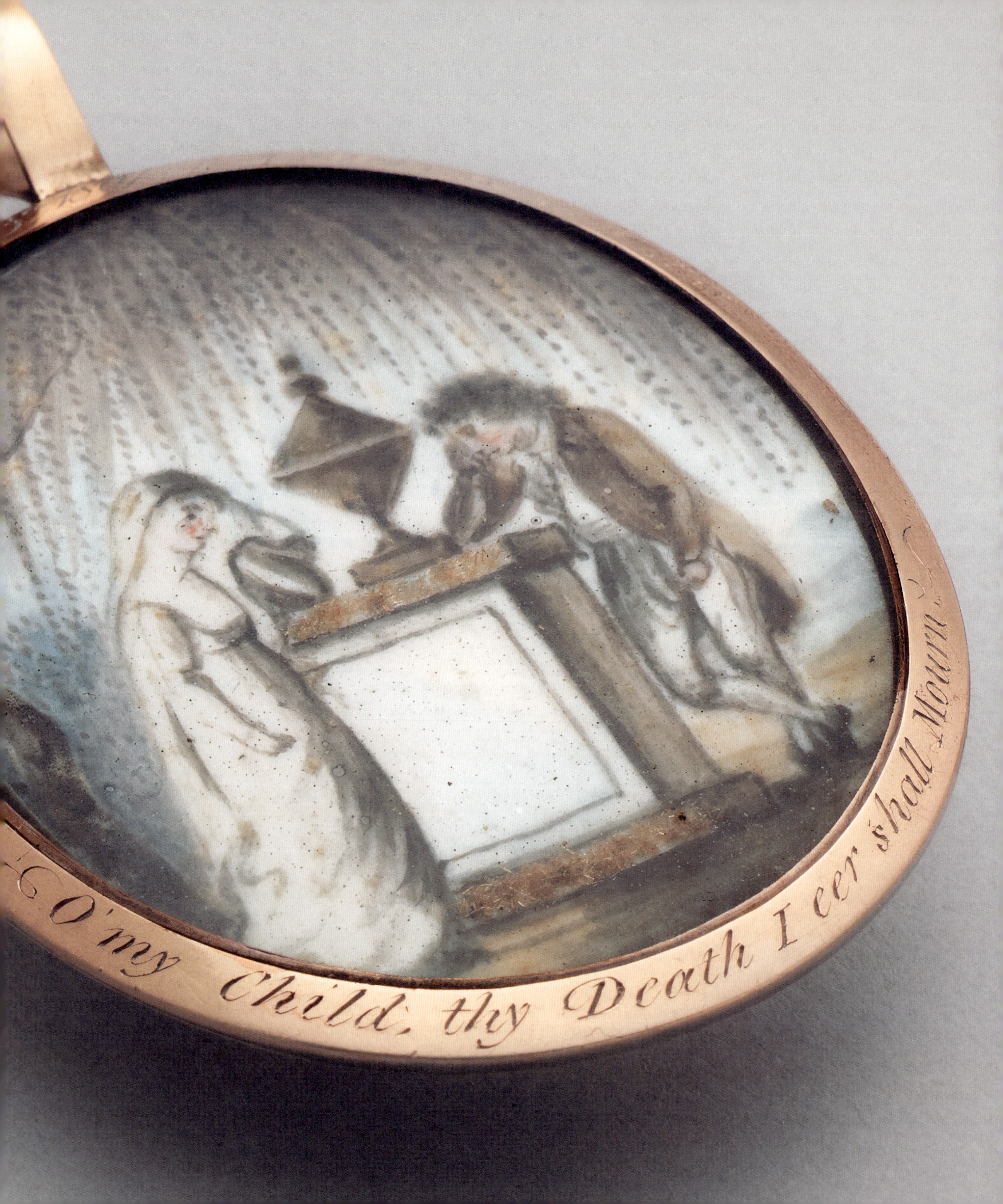
O'my Child, thy Death I eer shall Mourn

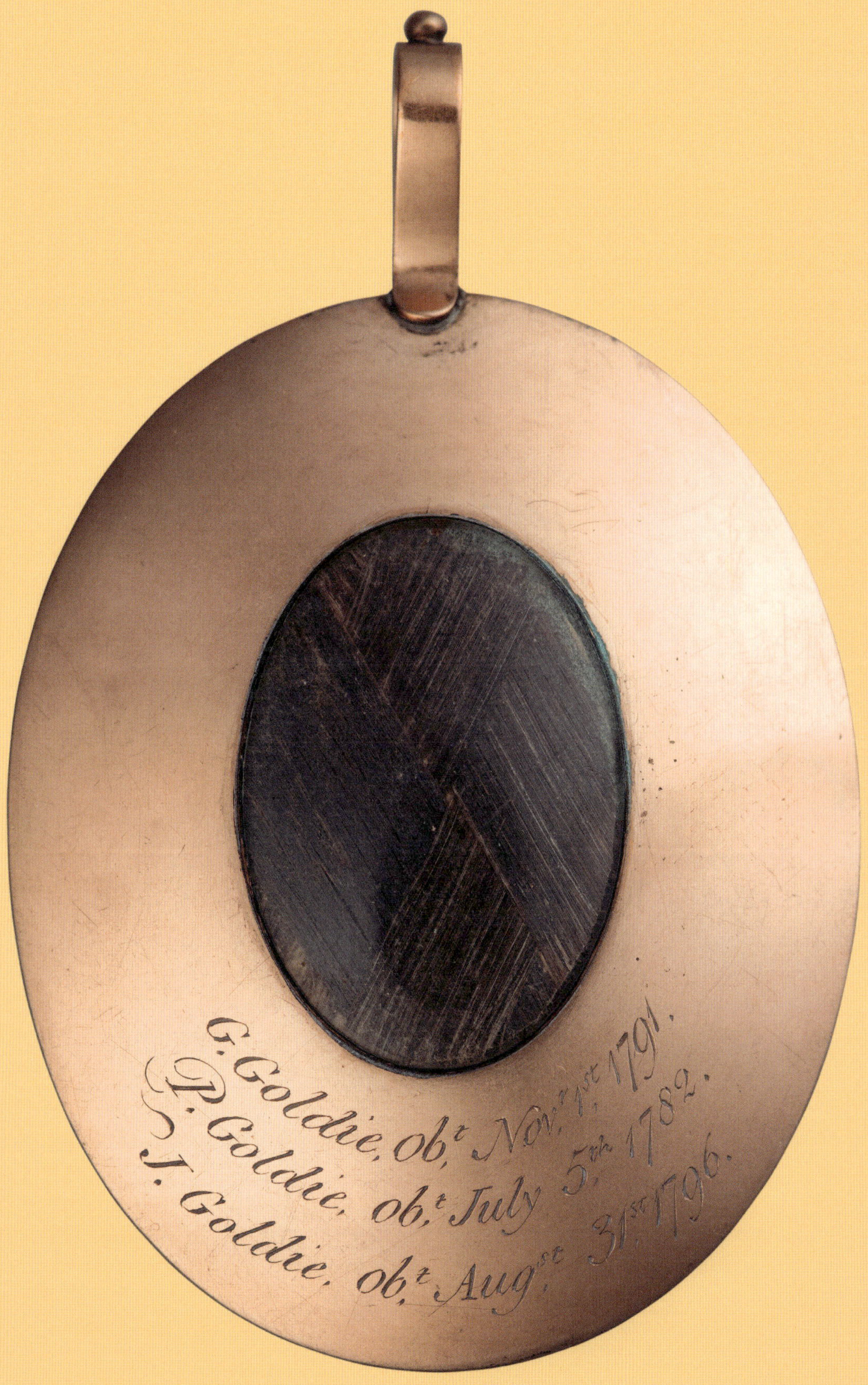
G. Goldie, obt Novr 1st 1791.
P. Goldie, obt July 5th 1782.
J. Goldie, obt Augst 31st 1796.

TO FRAME

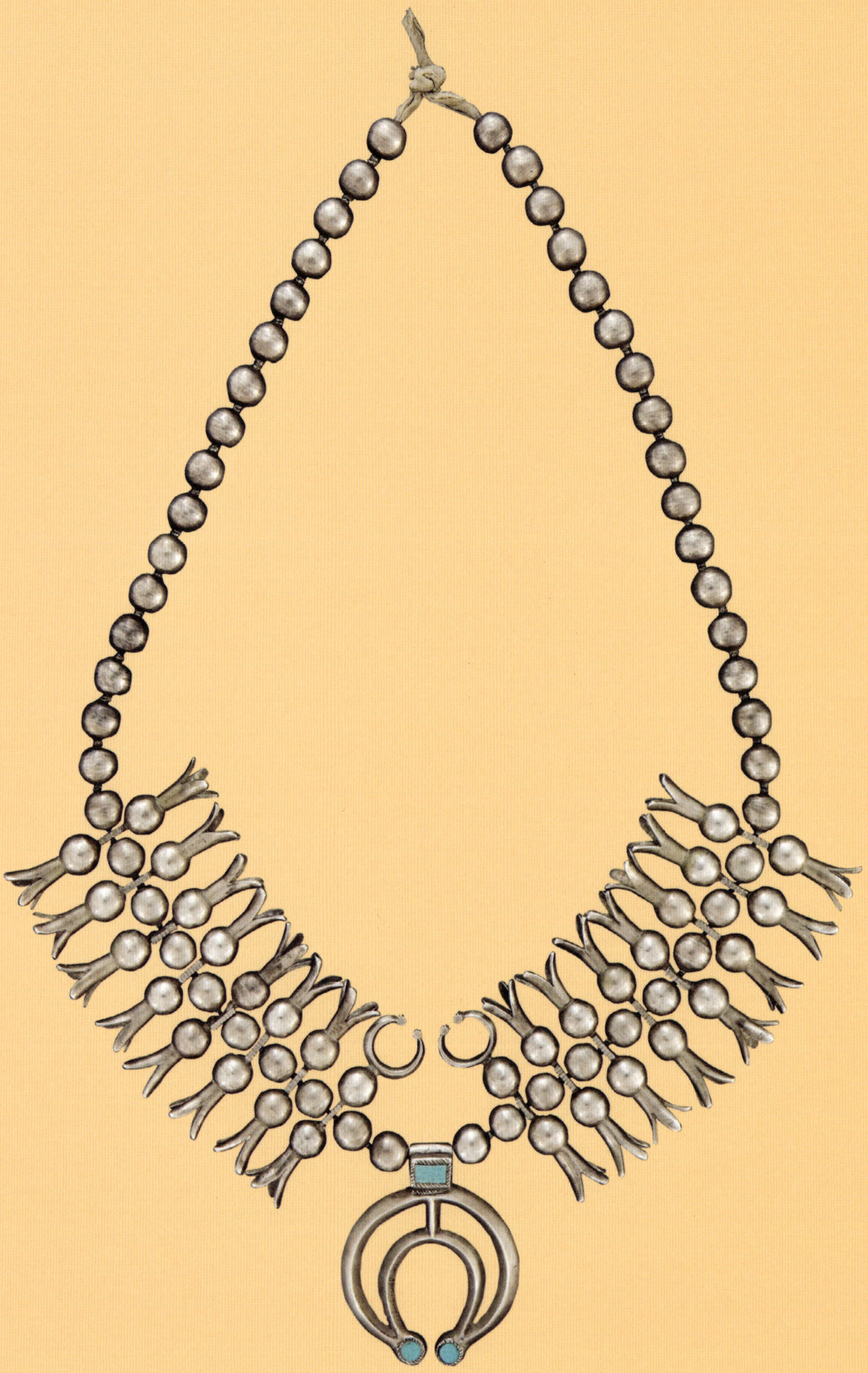

THE NECKLACE

SQUASH BLOSSOM NECKLACE

c. 1885–90, **Bééshłigai íít'íní Ałts'óózígíí (Slender Maker of Silver)** (Diné/Navajo, c. 1831–1915), Silver and turquoise, Length as worn: 17 in. (43.2 cm), Wheelwright Museum of the American Indian, Santa Fe.

The squash blossom necklace is perhaps the form of jewelry most closely linked to the American Southwest. This necklace, in particular, is a statement piece. The iconic naja pendant, or inverted crescent-shaped symbol, includes two merged bars terminating with set pieces of turquoise. Single beads are interspersed with bars joining the squash blossoms, two silver balls with stamen-like projections. Every surface of this necklace is fully polished and curved, dynamically catching and reflecting light as it moves with the wearer's body. The Diné (or Navajo) silversmith Bééshłigai íít'íní Ałts'óózígíí (also known as Slender Maker of Silver) created this necklace at the end of the nineteenth century, when silver jewelry was becoming more popular among both locals and tourists across the American Southwest.

Bééshłigai íít'íní Ałts'óózígíí emerged in the 1870s as one of the most sought-after silversmiths in the Four Corners region. He trained under the Navajo leader Atsidi Sání, who helped negotiate the Treaty of Bosque Redondo in 1868 following the Long Walk—the forced removal of the Navajo from their ancestral land and the community's incarceration by the U.S. Army outside of Fort Sumner, New Mexico—as well as Atsidi Chon, who was known for his outstanding early concho belts and bridles. From these metalsmiths, Bééshłigai íít'íní Ałts'óózígíí learned how to transform silver coins into beads and cast forms using tufa rock harvested from the region. A form of limestone, this rock is soft enough to easily carve but can only withstand a few castings before breaking under the heat of molten metal. Silversmiths used tufa to transform silver coins into ingots, belt buckles, ketohs (wrist guards), and pendants. Additionally, the turquoise stones set in the naja pendant speak to a long history of lapidary arts across the region, particularly among the Pueblos. In Diné cosmology, turquoise is connected to Tsoodził (also known as Blue Bead Mountain or Mount Taylor), which marks the southern boundary of the people's homelands. Bééshłigai íít'íní Ałts'óózígíí was one of the earliest Diné silversmiths to set stone in silver and create squash blossom beads, and, at the peak of his career, he trained many others to do the same.

Many prosperous locals and tourists sought commissions from him because of his craftsmanship and ingenuity. This necklace was commissioned by Henry Chee Dodge, the principal Navajo leader who was also co-owner of a trading post within the Navajo Nation, manager of his family's substantial flock of sheep, and on the payroll of the U.S. Army as a translator and guide. Chee Dodge worked with many American politicians, military officials, and ethnologists, some of whom also studied and commissioned Navajo silverwork, including Washington Matthews, Alexander Stephens, and James Mooney. Many of Chee Dodge's business dealings were conducted in silver coin, some of which the artist would have used to fabricate this necklace. The materiality and provenance of this necklace, stewarded by the family of Chee Dodge, helps reorient histories of early Southwestern Native silversmithing back toward an intimate network of artists and individuals. —CG

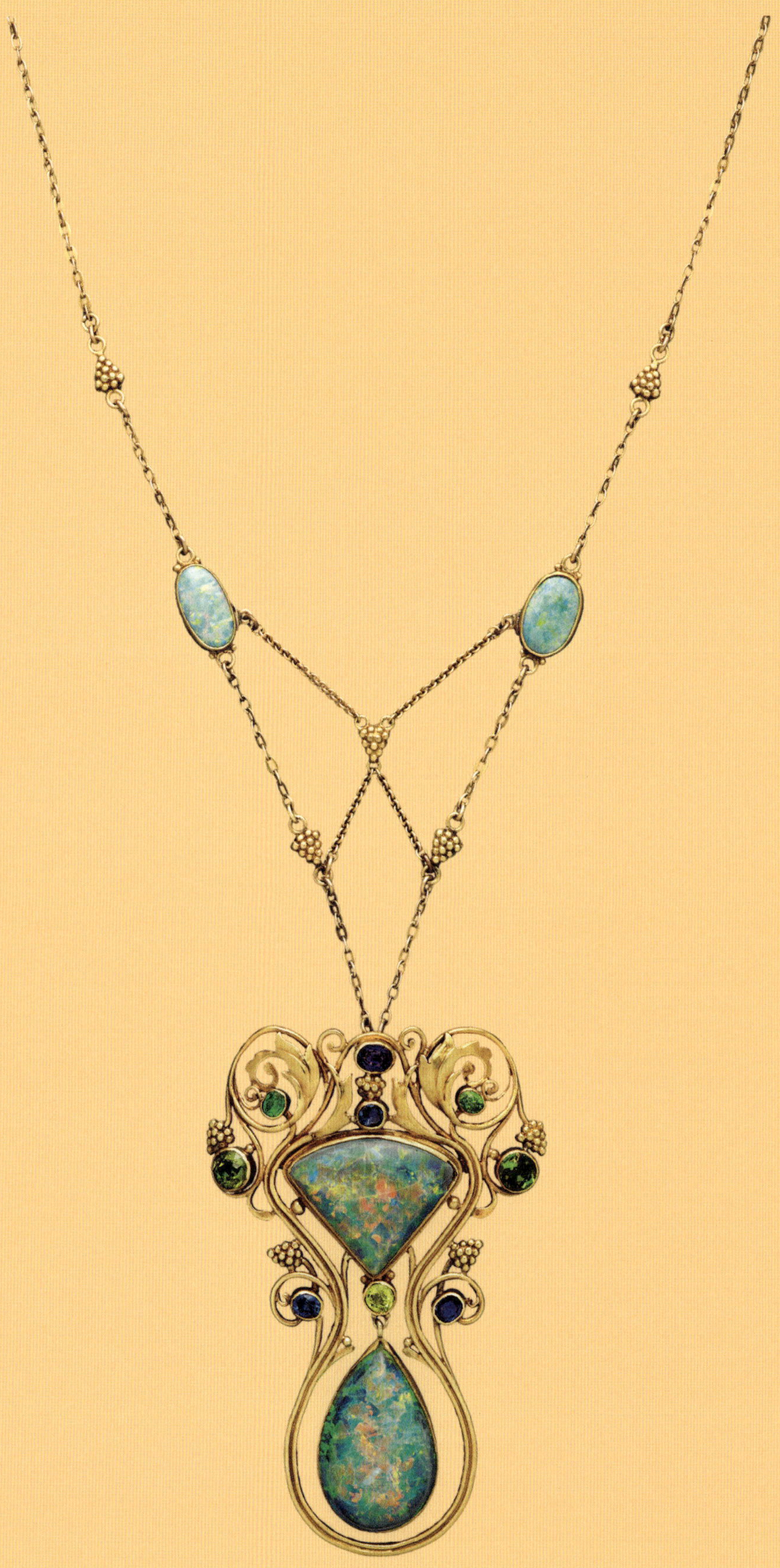

THE NECKLACE

NECKLACE

c. 1906–20, **Frank Gardner Hale** (1876–1945),
Gold, opal, green garnet, sapphire, Overall: 14⅛ in. (36 cm), Pendant: 2¾ in. (7 cm),
Museum of Fine Arts, Boston, The Susan Donald Collection.

At the turn of the twentieth century, a new style of jewelry known as "art jewelry" emerged in the United States as an alternative to the Victorian machine-manufactured wares that emphasized the value of the gemstones over the design of their settings. Art jewelry consisted of one-of-a-kind works of wearable art in which skilled craftsmanship combined with creative expression to create intricate, harmonious designs. Jewelry maker and enameler Frank Gardner Hale was a leader in Boston's distinctive style of art jewelry, which was characterized by bold color combinations of carefully selected gemstones, enamels, and less precious materials; predominantly gold settings composed of delicate scrollwork and vegetal elements; and an overall composition that extended to the chains and clasps. This elegant necklace epitomizes the look: the opal pendant is framed by scrolling gold wires and Hale's signature grape clusters, accented with sapphires and green garnets. The gold of the setting and the varying hues of green and blue gemstones enhance the iridescent tones of the fiery central opals. The grape motif is continued in the chain and clasp.

Hale and his contemporaries embraced the ideals of the Arts and Crafts movement, a design and lifestyle philosophy that promoted artistic activity and the appreciation of beauty as antidotes for life in the modern, industrialized world. The movement championed individuality and handcraftsmanship and encouraged those who were not artists to embrace a more bohemian lifestyle by becoming consumers of handmade artistic wares. At a time when more and more people were living in bustling cities, Arts and Crafts advocates encouraged people to seek respite in nature and inspiration from nostalgic visions of the past. Such ideas found a ready audience in Boston's intellectual and artisanal circles.

In 1897, these leaders established the Society of Arts and Crafts (SAC) "for the purpose of developing and encouraging higher artistic standards in the handicrafts" through promoting "mutually helpful relations" among designer, craftsman, and patron.[1] The SAC mounted juried exhibitions; promoted both craft and design training through courses, lectures, and a library; organized collaborative workshops; and maintained a shop that provided retail and exhibition space for its members.

With the support and structure of the SAC, Boston became an influential center for avant-garde jewelry making and skillful metalwork, and Hale was one of the leaders in the field. He had studied design at the School of the Museum of Fine Arts, Boston and worked for ten years as a graphic designer before learning metalsmithing and enameling at C.R. Ashbee's Guild of Handicraft in Gloucestershire, England, followed by jewelry making with Fred and May Partridge in London. Hale's skilled draftsmanship can be seen in the design drawing for this necklace, which survives in his extensive archives, held at the Museum of Fine Arts, Boston. This necklace is an exquisite example of the combination of the designer's technical ability and the Arts and Crafts sensibilities that inspired him: a vibrant, delicately worked, naturally inspired piece of art jewelry. —**NG**

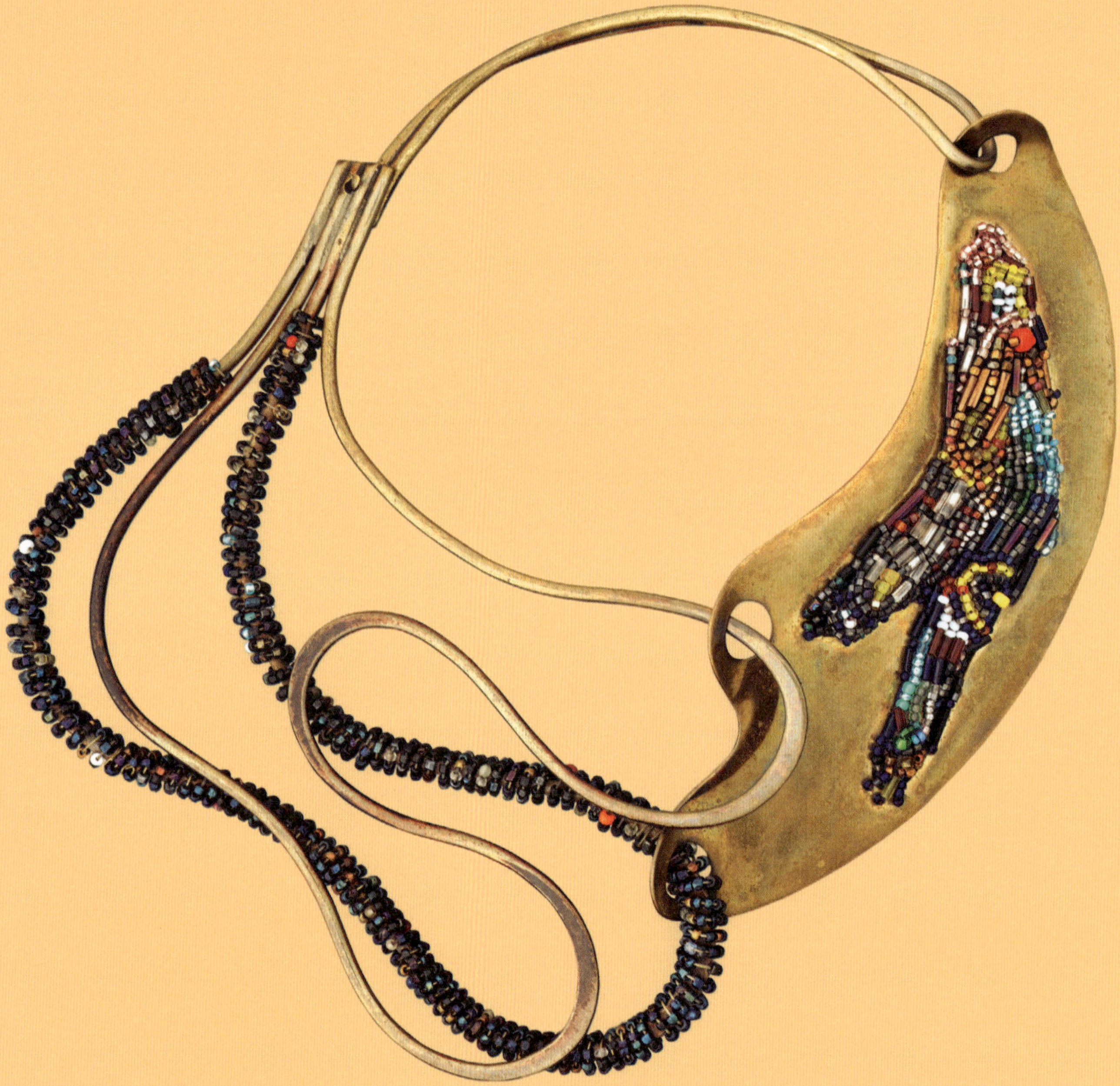

WE TWO NECKLACE

1970s or early 1980s, **Art Smith** (1917–1982)/**Joyce J. Scott** (b. 1948), Brass, glass beads, leather, 8 × 6½ in. (20.3 × 16.5 cm), Museum of Fine Arts, Boston, Gallery Instructor 50th Anniversary Fund to support of the Heritage Fund for a Diverse Collection and funds donated by Stephen Borkowski. 2016.82.

Silver Smith
Art Silver-Smith, purveyor of brass in word and deed.

Authentic Sapeur/Cubano/Jamaican, Brooklyn/HighStyle man of Mysterilisciousness.

007ing with Talley Beatty, Lena Horne and Harry B, even Eleanor Roosevelt
Conspired with Ellington, the Duke.

Tap of his hammer, OGUN percussive,
Sawing sheet music while conniving a Bluez Moan,
The torch, a flame, hot like Ella scatting.

Art Smith, unreasonably kinetic.
Deceptively glib.
Sage Alchemist, Aesthetic Engineer,
Magnanimous Metalist in word and deed.

—JS

Art Smith was an acclaimed jewelry artist whose avant-garde creations pushed the limits of modernism in the twentieth century. Smith was born in Cuba to Jamaican parents who moved to Brooklyn in 1920. He received a scholarship to the Cooper Union for the Advancement of Science and Art, where he studied architecture and commercial art and majored in sculpture. Upon graduating, he took a jewelry-making class at New York University that ultimately led to him becoming assistant to Caribbean American jewelry designer Winifred Mason. Smith opened his own shop in Greenwich Village in 1946. Within ten years his work was sold at stores across the country, from San Francisco to Dallas to Boston, and was featured in *Vogue* and *Harper's Bazaar*, among other high fashion magazines. As his artistry and reputation grew, so did his association with some of America's most prominent Black artists, including James Baldwin, composer and pianist Billy Strayhorn, Lena Horne (who wore his jewelry), and Harry Belafonte. Smith became known for creating work with a sense of movement and drama, something that was inspired in part by his circle of musicians and dancers. Much of his work was of a completely different scale than his contemporaries'. He pioneered many mid-century jewelry innovations, including bold, geometric pieces that cover and reveal the body, often fabricated from wire and large pieces of silver. —EZ

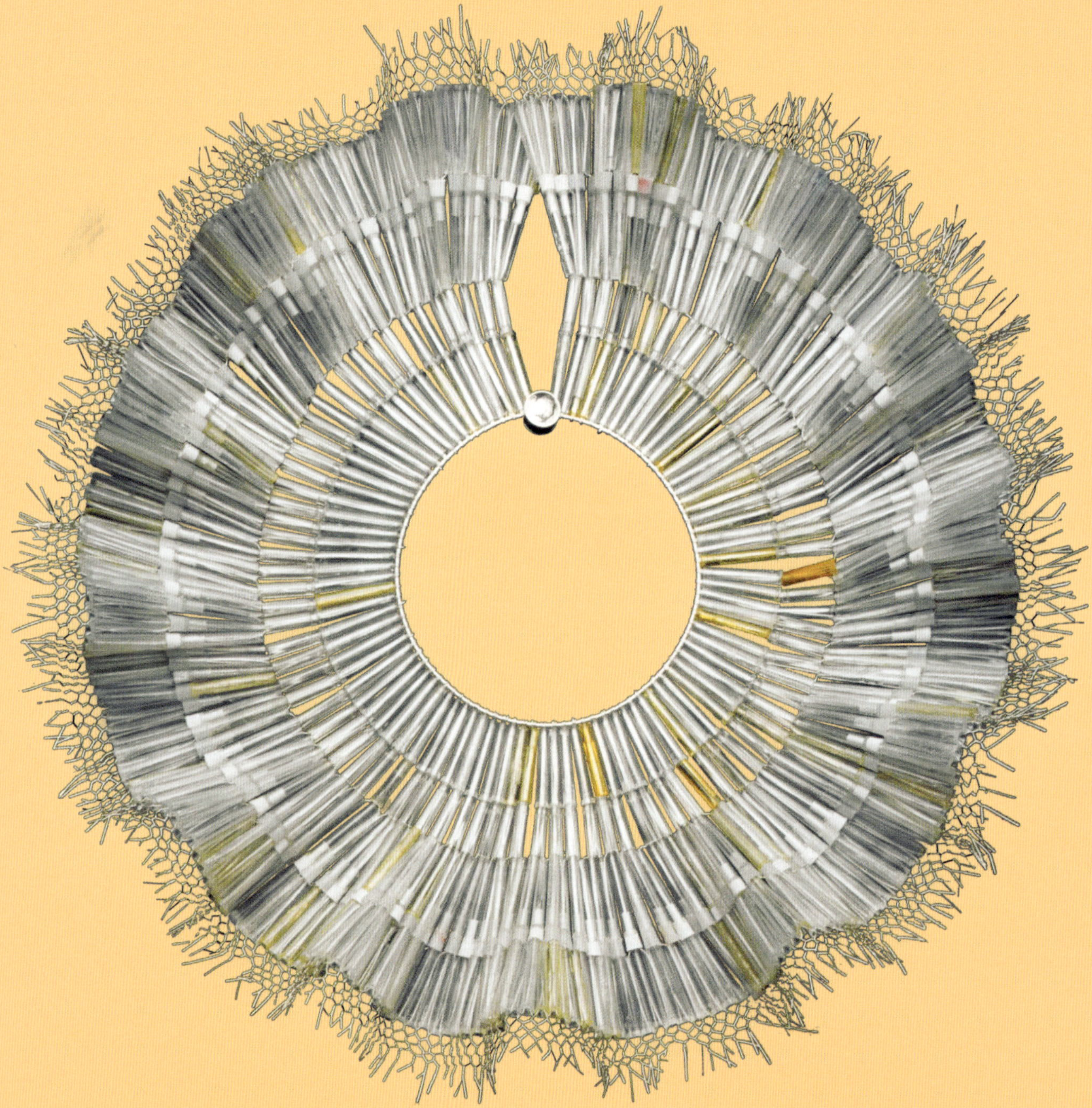

THE NECKLACE

AMERICAN RUFF, FROM THE CITY FLOTSAM SERIES

2000, **Jan Yager** (1951–2024), Crack vials, crack vial caps, sterling silver, US dime, Canadian dime, 3 × 19¾ in. (7.6 × 50.2 cm), Philadelphia Museum of Art, Purchased with funds contributed by The Women's Committee and the Craft Show Committee of the Philadelphia Museum of Art, 2003, 2003-5-2.

As a Philadelphia resident, Jan Yager saw the city's rich history and vibrant arts scene as a "visual buffet" of inspiration.[1] While she appreciated the city's flora and fauna, she was equally struck by the prevalence of crack vials, bullet casings, and syringes around her building—materials that reflected urban challenges she felt compelled to address through her art. Yager chose jewelry as a medium for its intimate scale and ability to convey both meaning and sentiment, creating pieces where "the contemporary and the ancient, the natural and the made, reality and illusion, are placed in counterpoint."[2]

Yager's work continually challenged conventional jewelry assumptions. Early in her career, a professor advised her to "draw" with her jewelry saw, advice that led to her distinctive style.[3] Her 1980s pieces avoided traditional pairings of precious gems and gold, instead employing smooth stones and silver. Growing up in Detroit during its automotive heyday influenced her initial approach to metalworking, though she eventually moved away from production techniques in favor of more thoughtful, personal creations. Her artistic philosophy always centered on authenticity. She limited herself to materials found within a block of her studio, believing this constraint would ensure her work genuinely reflected her immediate environment. Her morning routine of opening her studio door regularly revealed used crack cocaine vials, which became central to her work.

American Ruff deliberately references the elaborate pleated collars that European nobility wore in the sixteenth and seventeenth centuries—a powerful status symbol of wealth and privilege. Yet this collar necklace incorporates nearly one thousand empty crack cocaine vials and caps, all connected with sterling silver wire and arranged in a ruff pattern. By contrasting the pleated linen collar, a historical fashion accessory of elitist privilege, with materials representing modern urban poverty and drug addiction, Yager makes a strong statement on social status and inequality.

Her work often elicits complex reactions as viewers grapple with both the beauty of the pieces and the stark reality of their materials. Yager viewed her creations as documents of societal issues, exploring why her neighborhood faced such challenges and tracing them back to historical injustices that continue to impact communities centuries later. Both beautiful jewelry and compelling social commentary, her work forces viewers to confront uncomfortable truths about privilege, poverty, and the persistent echoes of historical inequality in contemporary society. —JL

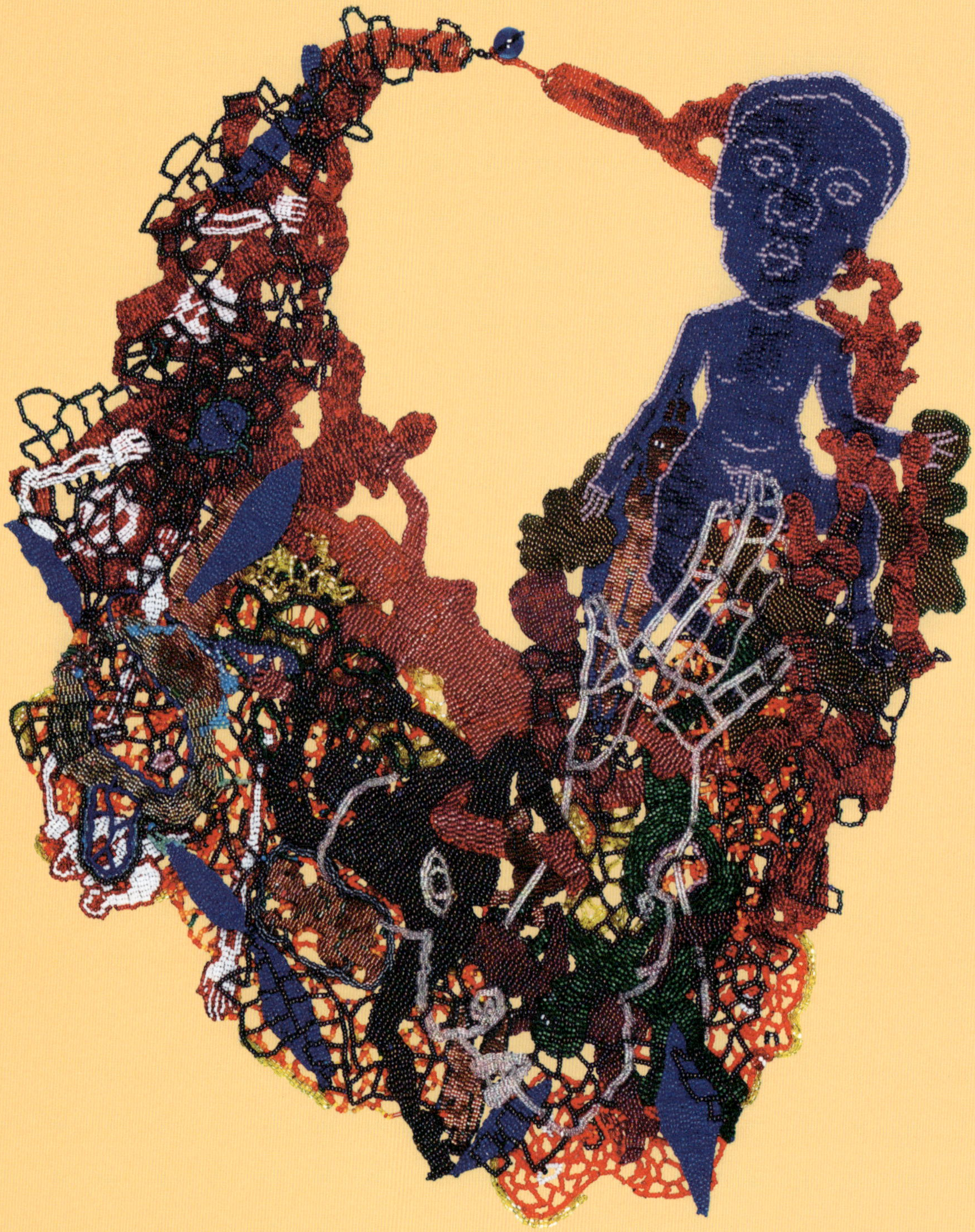

THE NECKLACE

JOYCE J. SCOTT on THE NECKLACE

War, What is it Good For, Absolutely Nothin', Say it Again, 2022, **Joyce J. Scott** (b. 1948), Peyote stitch, glass beads, thread, 17 × 15 × ½ in. (43.2 × 38.1 × 1.3 cm)

How can I be seventy-six years old? I see myself as a youngun, through the matrix of yarn, beads and thread, paint and pulp, music and performance, all laced in the web of community and in search of self. As an Artist/Craft person, an impish elucidator who perilously targets the right way, best walked roads and truest truths humans use to dismiss and diminish others, I employ ART. In reality it exploits me and my hunger for a righteous life garnered in service to the head, heart, and hands entwined. That truth is my ART.

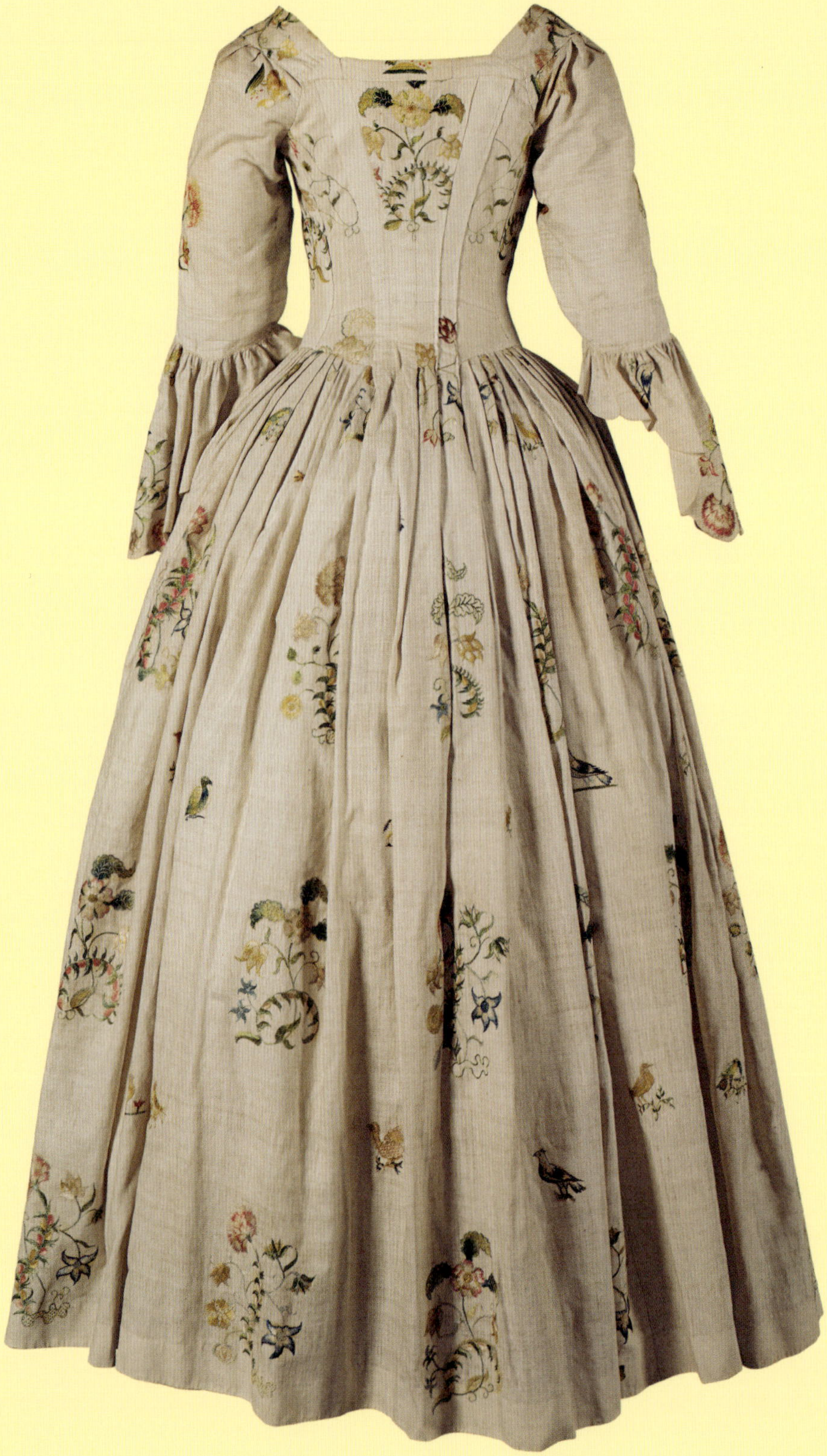

THE GARMENT

GOWN (ROBE À L'ANGLAISE)

1770–80, **Unidentified artist (Hartford)** with embroidery by **Abigail Wadsworth** (1735–1785), Linen and silk, 51 in. (129.5 cm), Wadsworth Atheneum Museum of Art, Hartford, Gift of Mrs. Frederic J. Agate, 1973.61.

According to family lore, Abigail Wadsworth stitched the motif of a horse on her dress in testament to her journey riding from Hartford to Boston to buy silk threads and embroidery patterns.[1] Eighteenth-century Boston merchants offered beautifully colored silk flosses and plied sewing threads (called "Ballendine silk" in their advertisements) alongside "worsted shades" (crewel embroidery threads) and all manner of items needed to decorate cloth or oneself.[2] Silk threads, fabrics, and even raw silk were imported to Boston from China and other countries with a sericulture industry through the British East India Company, which was established in 1600 and dominated many aspects of global trade.

The sophisticated embroidery patterns on Wadsworth's dress suggest that she may indeed have procured them from a professional pattern drawer in Boston, but a talented neighbor might also have drawn the designs, as was a common practice for similar work stitched in crewel yarns. Colonial American women adapted high-style baroque motifs of fantastic florals and foliage (which they saw in a variety of decorative arts, including furniture, gravestones, printed papers, and textiles) for their embroidery. While Wadsworth had help in producing the motifs, it would have been up to her to choose the colors, shading, and embroidery stitches. The excellence of her execution conveys her elite education, which would have emphasized accomplishments in needlework and other decorative skills.

She also exhibited her status by embroidering the flowers, birds, and horse on her linen dress with silk threads, rather than the far more typical crewels. She probably transferred her designs to the cloth by pricking the patterns with a pin along the lines of the design and pouncing powdered chalk or charcoal through the holes. Then she connected the resulting dots with a quill pen dipped in India ink.[3] Indeed, ink outlines can be seen through the embroidery stitches of the horse's tail on Abigail's dress.

The dress was constructed after the embroidery was completed, as evidenced by some motifs cut off by seams. This gown (called a "mantua" in the period), exemplifies the engineering skills and art of the professional mantua-maker. It was created by draping the cloth on Wadsworth's corseted body and pinning the pleats and seams to make the pattern. The care taken in constructing the dress is evident in the symmetrical placement of motifs and precise centering of the embroidery on the back panel.

The granddaughter of Connecticut's colonial governor, Joseph Talcott, and daughter of Daniel Wadsworth, the exceedingly wealthy minister of the First Church of Hartford, Wadsworth could afford the best mantua-maker in Hartford.[4] Her brother Jeremiah Wadsworth became commissary general of the Continental forces in the Revolutionary War, a member of the Continental Congress, and a fantastically successful businessman.[5] At only twelve years old, Abigail inherited a substantial portion of her father's estate.[6] Her silk-embroidered dress advertised her wealth and accomplishment, which certainly would have made her an attractive prospect for an ambitious young man, though she never married. Perhaps she enjoyed her economic independence. —LZB

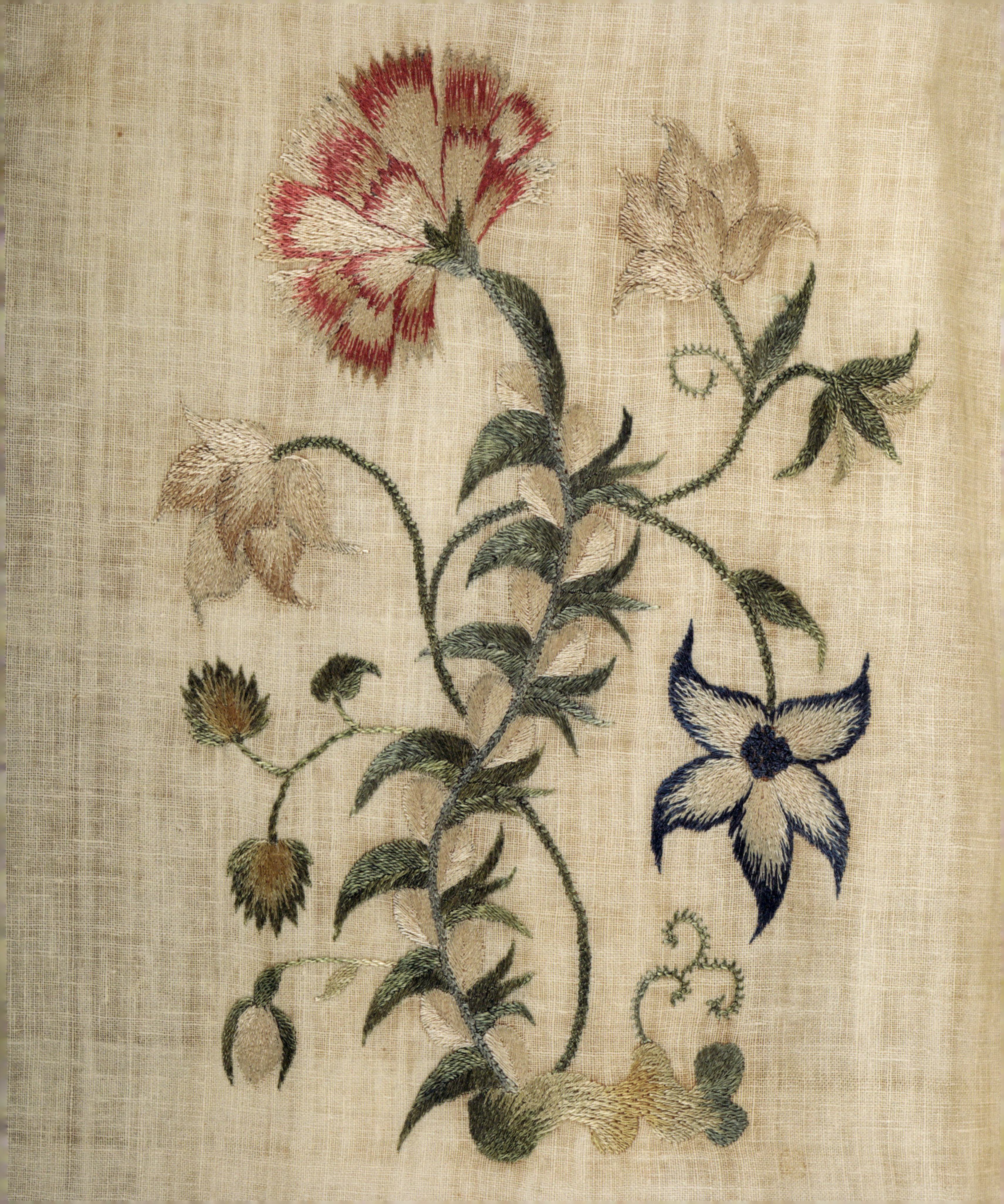

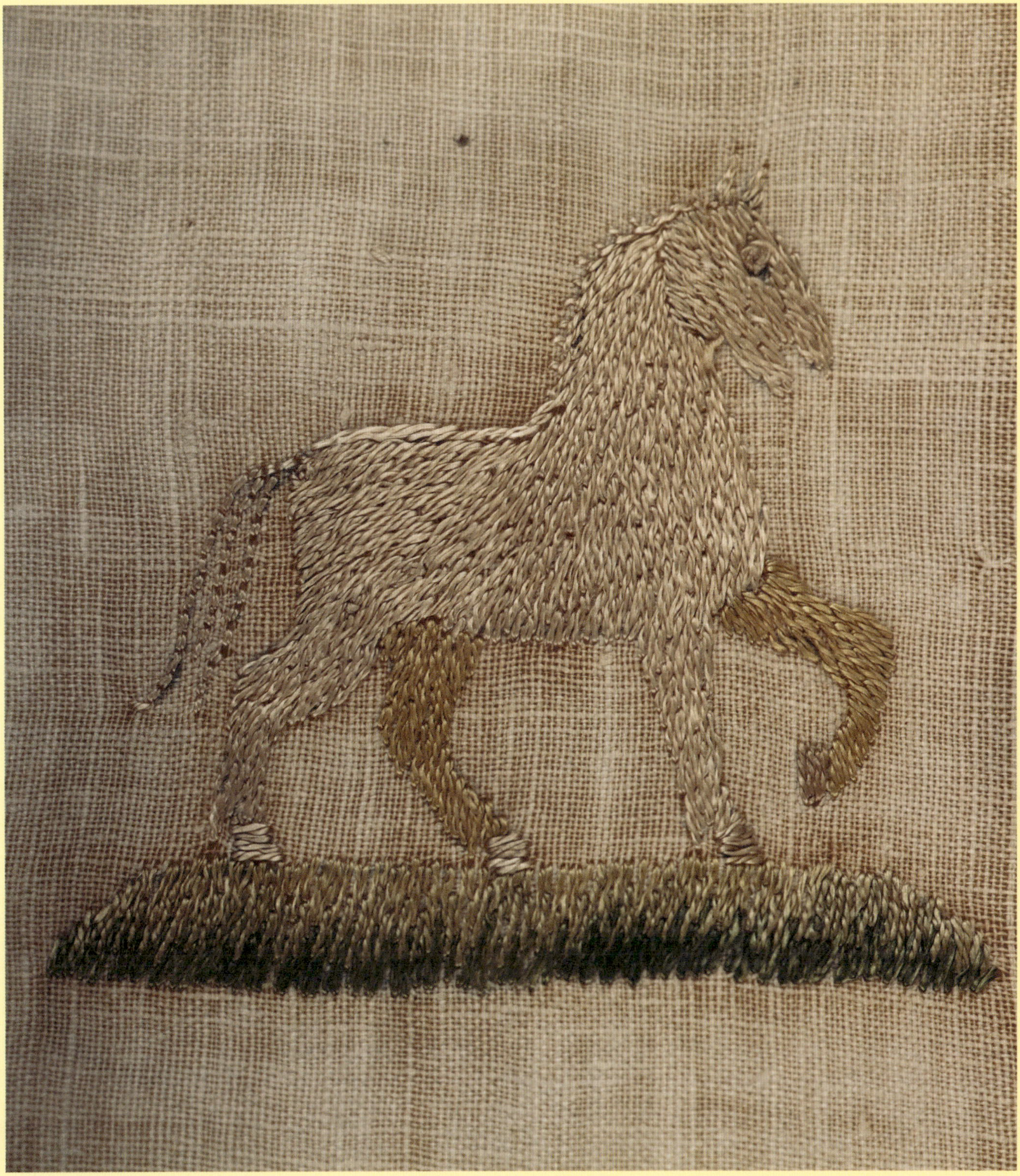

TO WEAR

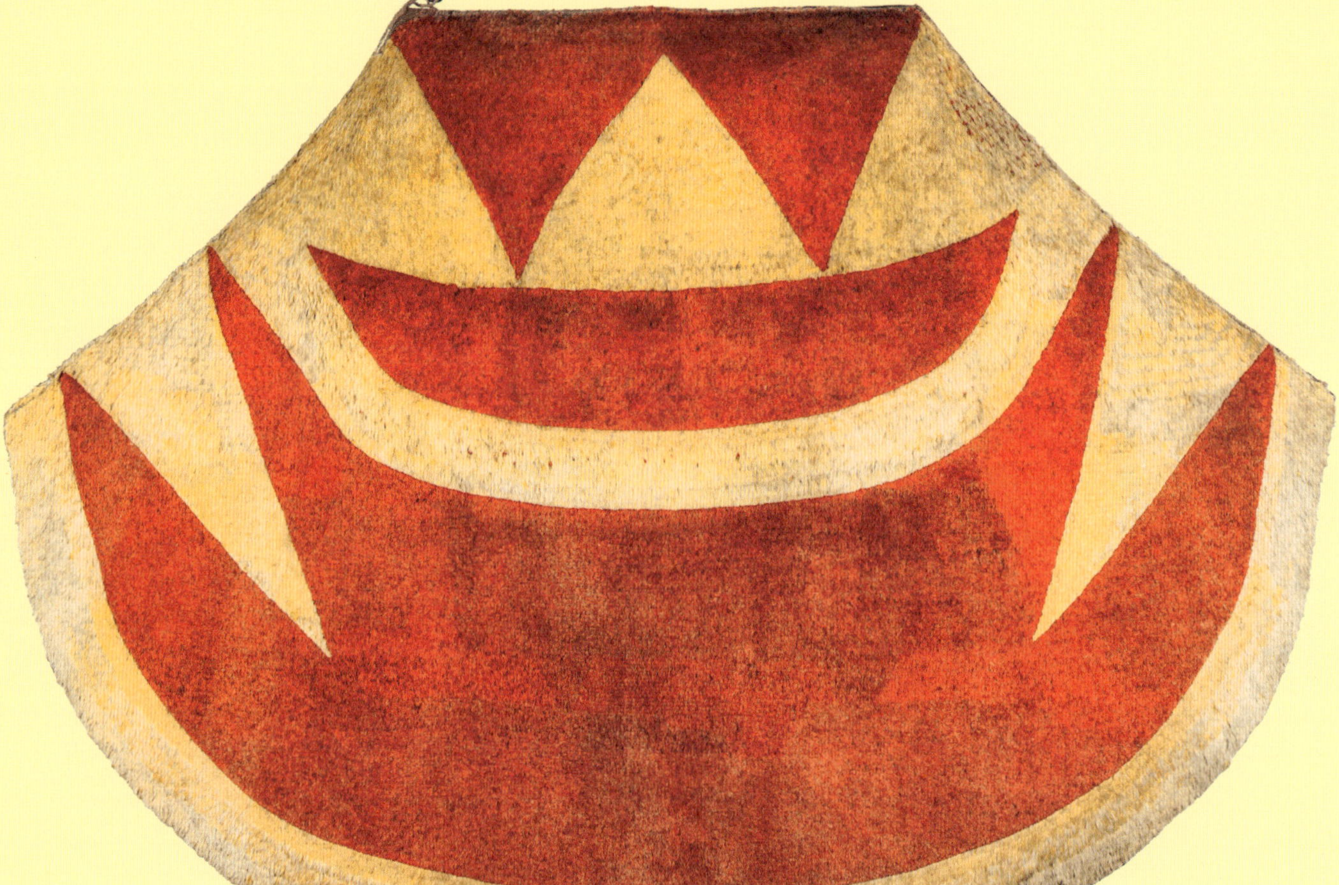

'AHU 'ULA (FEATHERED CLOAK)

1700s, **Unidentified artist (Hawai'i),**
'I'iwi (*Drepanis coccinea*), 'ō'ō (*Moho nobilis*), and mamo (*Drepanis pacifica*) feathers, olonā (*Touchardia latifolia*) fiber, 59¾ × 96½ in. (152 × 245 cm), Bishop Museum, Honolulu, Ethnology Collection, 2020.073.001.

In January 1779, high chief Kalani'ōpu'u saw two foreign ships under the command of Captain James Cook anchored off the coast of his home at Kealakekua, Hawai'i. Kalani'ōpu'u went out to greet these foreigners with his entourage and brought many provisions and gifts, including several items of Hawaiian featherwork. At one point, he removed the mahiole (chiefly helmet) and 'ahu 'ula (feather cloak) he was wearing and placed them both on Captain Cook's head and shoulders. This was a rare act; these vestments were important symbols of a chief's authority and only acquired from their community or through battle, taken from fallen foes as proof of victory.

The materials required to make 'ahu 'ula for high chiefs were difficult to acquire and labor-intensive to produce. The foundation of a traditional 'ahu 'ula is a fine mesh net made from the plied fibers of olonā (*Touchardia latifolia*), an endemic Hawaiian nettle. It is said to be one of the strongest plant fibers on earth, and was highly prized and regularly traded to Westerners who used it as rigging for their vessels. The brightly colored red and yellow feathers of this particular 'ahu 'ula were collected by kia manu, specialists trained in tracking and identifying the desired birds, capturing them through various techniques, collecting the needed feathers without harming the animals, and releasing them safely. Collecting feathers in this way takes time. It could be years or even generations until a chief acquired enough of them to create an 'ahu 'ula; it all depended on the amount of land they had stewardship over. When adequate olonā and feathers were at last acquired, they were given to a skilled artist who would assemble them. Each 'ahu 'ula was unique to its wearer, making it a means of identification in chiefly circles during times of peace or on the battlefield.

'Ahu 'ula were created for a chief by their community and became a visual representation of the resources and support a chief managed. A cloak's length often signified the size of the community and warriors that backed a chief. The color of feathers and the amounts used in an 'ahu 'ula signified the amount of material and land resources a chief oversaw—since acquiring large quantities of upland forest bird feathers required a proportionate landholding. This cloak features red and yellow featherwork. Red feathers always represented chiefly authority in Hawai'i, and few endemic species in Hawai'i had yellow feathers, making it an extremely rare commodity and highly desirable.

The visual composition of an 'ahu 'ula , especially those that included a significant quantity of yellow feathers, was both a means to intimidate opponents and to rally the community of a chief together, epitomizing their strength and resolve. The visual cues an 'ahu 'ula projects outward to those that see it also are meant to turn inward and affect its wearer. Being a chief means you have privileges and support as well as responsibilities. Chiefs' authority comes from their people bestowing that power upon them; if the community is lost, so too is that authority. These vestments serve as a chief's physical promise to protect and care for their people. —MHM

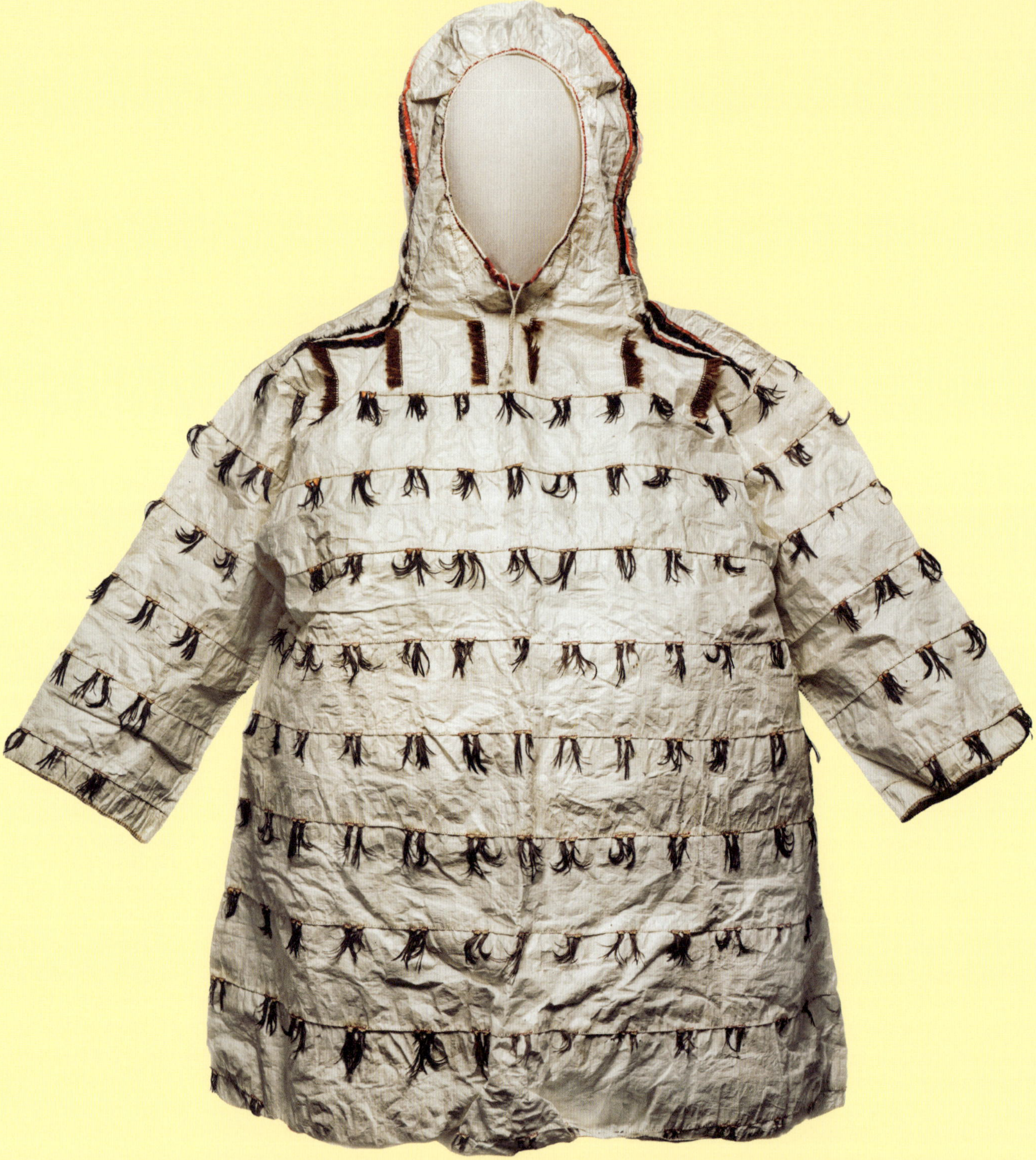

THE GARMENT

SANIGHTAAQ (CEREMONIAL GUT PARKA)

Early 20th century, **Unidentified artist (Yupik)**,
Seal gut, auklet crests, seal fur, sinew, thread, 49 × 61 in. (124.5 × 154.9 cm),
Maryhill Museum of Art, Goldendale, WA, In memory of Kathleen Anne Higgins and Thomas Menzel, 2023.17.1.

This parka was made on Saint Lawrence Island, Alaska, located in the Bering Sea to the west of mainland Alaska. Although part of the United States, it is closer to Russia and Asia than it is to North America. The island is home to two villages populated by Siberian Yupik people. The Yupik name for the landmass is Sivuqaq. The island's European name was coined by Russian cartographer Vitus Bering, who arrived there on St. Lawrence's Day in 1728. Bering's arrival represents the first European presence in Alaskan territory.

The garment's style was common until the middle of the twentieth century. The body is sewn from dried bearded seal intestines and decorated with rows of auklet crest tufts, cormorant feathers, and seal fur. The strong horizontal bands were a common design element in gut-skin clothing created throughout coastal Alaska.

Bearded seals (*Erignathus barbatus*) inhabit relatively shallow Arctic and subarctic waters. Their preferred habitat is in zones with significant quantities of sea ice, and their population moves north and south depending on the season. The seals grow up to eight feet in length, and they can attain weights of up to 800 pounds. Crested auklets (*Aethia cristatella*) are small seabirds that are abundant in the northern Pacific Ocean and the Bering Sea. Their forehead crests are composed of forward-curving feathers, like the ones incorporated into the parka decoration seen here.

The intestines of bearded seals can be up to sixty-five feet long. To turn this raw material into something that can be used for clothing, a Yupik woman, working outdoors, must unravel and inflate the intestines and then clean, scrape, and cut them. Drying them in below-freezing temperatures affects their color and leaves them in a softer state, improving the ease with which they can be worked. The intestines are then cut into long strips and rolled up for later use. These are eventually sewn together using sinew.

Parkas of this type were made to serve as windbreakers, worn over bird-skin or hide outerwear. They were ceremonial in the sense that they were not everyday clothing but were instead worn for important occasions. Gut-skin parkas throughout the region were associated with shamanic attire, dance ceremonies, and other activities. St. Lawrence Island parkas were also made and traded to neighbors living to the east—the maritime Chukchi—who similarly desired them as ceremonial attire.

Gut parkas are windproof and waterproof, and they have a long history in coastal Alaska. They continue to be made by select individuals, using intestines from sea mammal species including seals, sea lions, beluga whales, and bears. The craft is being reintroduced in some other communities in the region as well. —SG

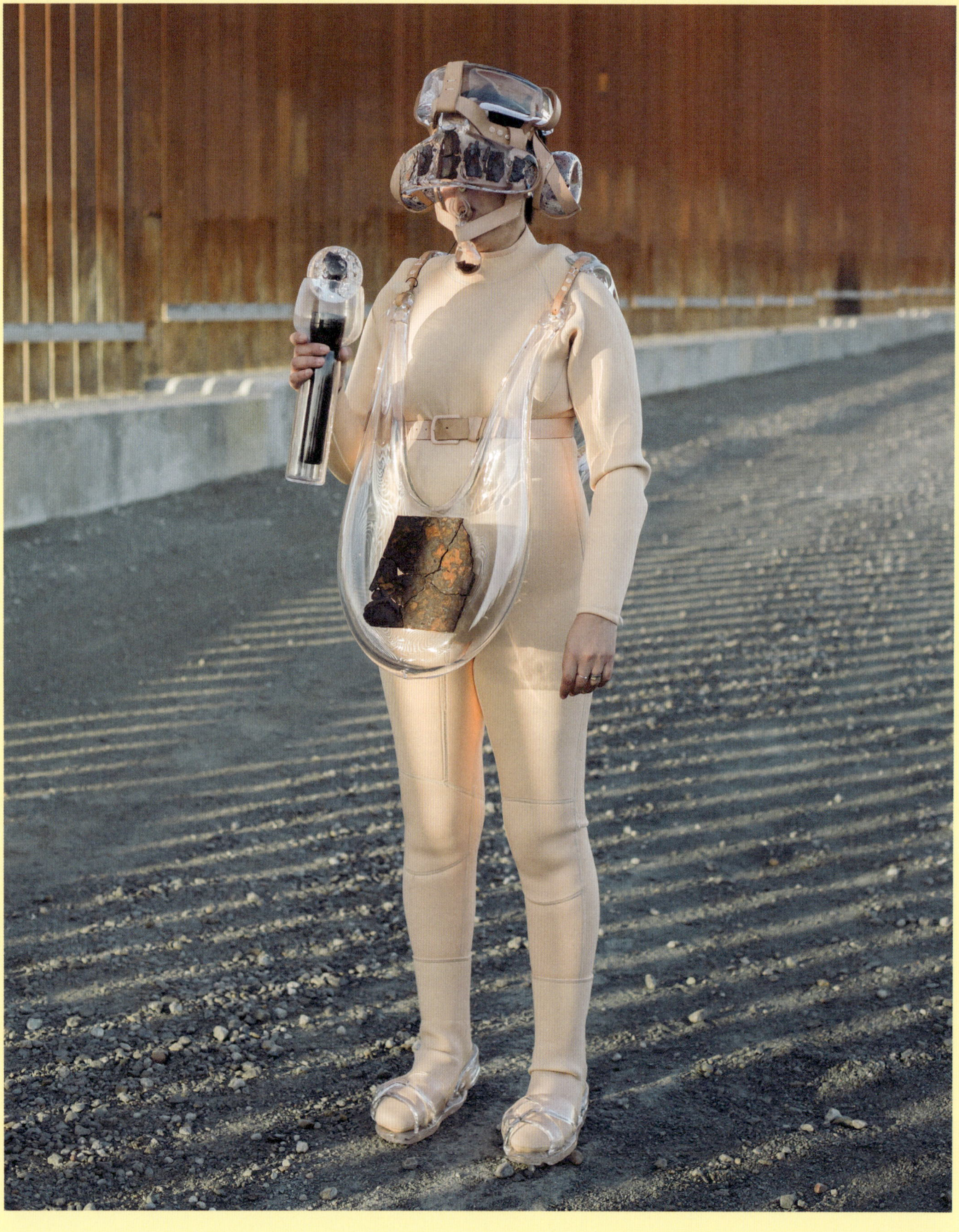

THE GARMENT

METABOLIZING THE BORDER

2018–20, **Tanya Aguiñiga** (b. 1978), Glass, neoprene, rusted metal fragments of the U.S./Mexico border fence, leather, cotton twine, flashlight, Dimensions variable, Joint museum purchase between Cooper Hewitt, Smithsonian Design Museum and Smithsonian American Art Museum through the American Women's History Initiative Acquisitions Pool, administered by the Smithsonian American Women's History Initiative.

Drawing from her experience as a Mexican American woman and mother, Tanya Aguiñiga's art practice is deeply shaped by her upbringing in the border town of Tijuana, Mexico, and her experience of crossing the border daily to attend school in San Diego, California. As a binational citizen, her work frequently advocates for transnational communities along the U.S.–Mexico border, whose stories are often overlooked and marginalized. Through her art, Aguiñiga intertwines craft and design with social activism that serves as both a form of resistance and a call for deeper understanding of the human cost of migration.

One of her most powerful projects, *Metabolizing the Border* investigates the corporeal and psychological experiences of migrants. Created during an artist residency at the Pilchuck Glass School in Washington in 2018, it consists of mixed-media "performative wearables." Each element—including a neoprene suit, headset, amplifiers, border torch, backpack filled with water, cloak, and huarache sandals—was designed to process the migrant experience through the five senses. The headpiece, modeled after a VR headset, reframes perception by combining sight, taste, and smell through an ocular lens and breath distiller while amplifying sound through ear attachments. The neoprene suit provides a layer of protection, while the water backpack serves as a crucial element for survival. The cloak, referencing the tilma of San Juan Diego, a significant Mexican spiritual and national symbol, and the glass huaraches, inspired by the tire-soled sandals worn by Indigenous and rural communities, exaggerate the sense of touch and movement. Designed to fail, the suit itself symbolizes the peril migrants endure in their search for safety and opportunity.

In 2020, Aguiñiga activated *Metabolizing the Border* by walking along the U.S.–Mexico border wall, physically engaging with the landscape that had shaped much of her work. Thirty minutes into the ninety-minute performance, the glass huaraches shattered beneath her feet, rendering visible the hardship and vulnerability of the migrant journey. She transformed the everyday act of walking into a powerful metaphor for endurance, trauma, and resilience.

The U.S.–Mexico border has long been a site of contention, with efforts to construct barriers dating back more than a century. Following the Mexican-American War and the signing of the Treaty of Guadalupe Hidalgo in 1848—which ceded nearly 55 percent of Mexico's territory to the United States—the current border was officially established. Physical barriers were minimal for decades, mainly focused on landownership or livestock control. By the early twentieth century U.S. and Mexican authorities had constructed limited fencing in urban areas, but it was not until the 1990s that large-scale fortifications were introduced. The September 11 attacks further prioritized border security, culminating in the Secure Fence Act of 2006, which authorized 700 miles of fencing along the U.S.–Mexico border.

Against this historical backdrop, Aguiñiga's work challenges the conventional understanding of craft and design, moving beyond aesthetics to engage with social and political issues. *Metabolizing the Border* not only materializes the struggles of the migrant experience but also reflects the artist's commitment to healing and regeneration within border communities. The handmade glass wearables articulate both the weight of the immigrant experience and the hope for transformation, balancing fragility, resiliency, and determination. —CDL

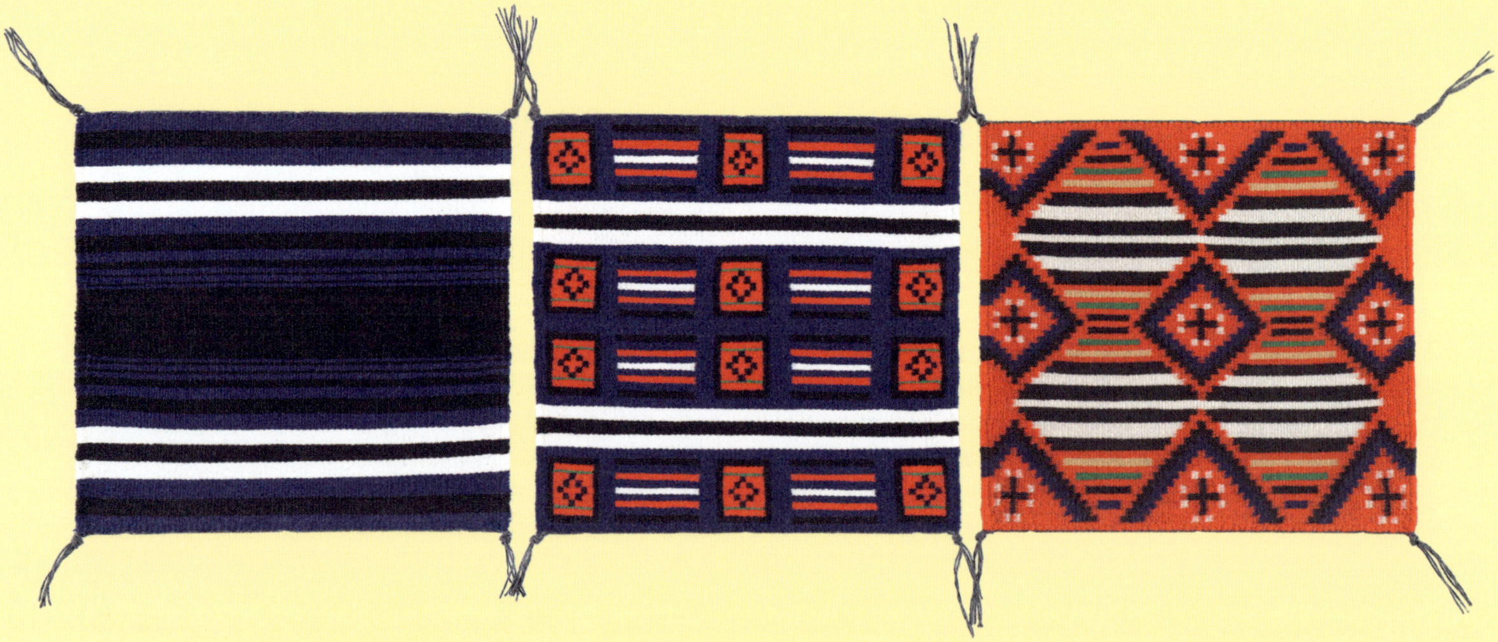

CONTEMPORARY CHIEF SET (THREE MINIATURES)

2024, **Barbara Teller Ornelas** (born to the Water's Edge Clan, Tábąąhá, born for the Water-Flows-Together Clan, Tó'aheedlíinii; Maternal grandfather born for Red Bottom People, Tł'ááshchí'í; paternal grandfather One-Walks-Around Clan, Honágháahnii, Diné, b. 1954), Wool, dovetail tapestry weave, extended selvage cord fringe. Warp: hand-carded wool and mohair, Weft: commercially processed, aniline-dyed merino wool, respun, Each approximately: 9 5⁄8 × 10 1⁄4 in. (24.5 × 26.1 cm), The Art Institute of Chicago, Don F. and Jean F. Stuck Endowment Fund, 2024.866a-c.

Barbara Teller Ornelas, a fifth-generation Diné (Navajo) master weaver, continues to preserve and transform one of the most celebrated Indigenous textile traditions in North America. Born on the Navajo Reservation near Two Grey Hills, New Mexico, she was raised in a family for whom weaving was not only a sacred practice but a vital thread of everyday life. Under the guidance of her mother and grandmother, Ornelas learned both the technical mastery and deep cultural significance that inform her work. Her weaving is deeply grounded in hózhǫ́—a concept encompassing beauty, balance, and harmony—and she approaches each piece as a means of restoring equilibrium within herself and her community.

Among her most remarkable contributions is *Contemporary Chief Set (Three Miniatures)*, a trio of small-scale Chief's blankets reimagining one of the most iconic forms in Navajo textile history. Chief's blankets, originally woven in the nineteenth century, were prestigious garments worn around the shoulders of Navajo and Plains tribal leaders. Navajo rugs were not originally made as floor coverings but as wearing blankets, woven to impart warmth, affirm status, and be used in ceremony; only later were they adapted for trade and display. Early designs, woven from Churro sheep wool, featured simple horizontal bands in white, indigo, and the natural brown of the wool itself. Over generations, these designs evolved into increasingly complex compositions with stepped motifs, crosses, and concentric diamonds—symbols rich with spiritual and cultural resonance.

The raising of Churro sheep, a species deeply intertwined with the Navajo Nation, remains a vital practice among families across the reservation, including Ornelas's kin. More than livestock, these sheep are nonhuman relatives who provide sustenance, income, and the wool essential to textile traditions. Nearly eradicated during a New Deal–era livestock reduction program, the Churro's survival represents endurance and renewal. Through community dedication and initiatives such as the Navajo Sheep Project, these sacred beings have been carefully reintroduced, restoring ecological balance and cultural continuity.

Although they measure only inches across, Ornelas's miniatures carry the same handspun wool, vegetable dyes, and intricate design decisions found in full-sized blankets. Each references a different historic style in the development of the Chief's blanket. The first weaving reflects the First Phase design, which began around 1800—a transitional period from utilitarian to more decorative weavings. The second draws on the bold geometry of a Second Phase Chief's blanket (circa 1850), characterized by greater design complexity and a central motif known as the "twelve spot" format. The third builds on the intricate, diamond-rich compositions of the Third Phase (beginning around 1860), often considered the most visually complex and symbolically rich of the classic forms. This particular blanket features stepped diamonds set against a striped background.

Executing such intricate designs at such a small scale requires unparalleled precision. More than artistic feats, these works serve as acts of cultural stewardship, preserving ancestral knowledge while expanding its contemporary relevance. Beyond her weaving, Ornelas teaches, lectures, and mentors, ensuring the matrilineal transmission of this sacred practice continues. *Contemporary Chief Set (Three Miniatures)* embodies both preservation and innovation. Ornelas's weavings celebrate the resilience of Navajo culture as a living, evolving tradition. Her loom becomes a conduit for memory and healing, transforming ancestral knowledge into art. —TL

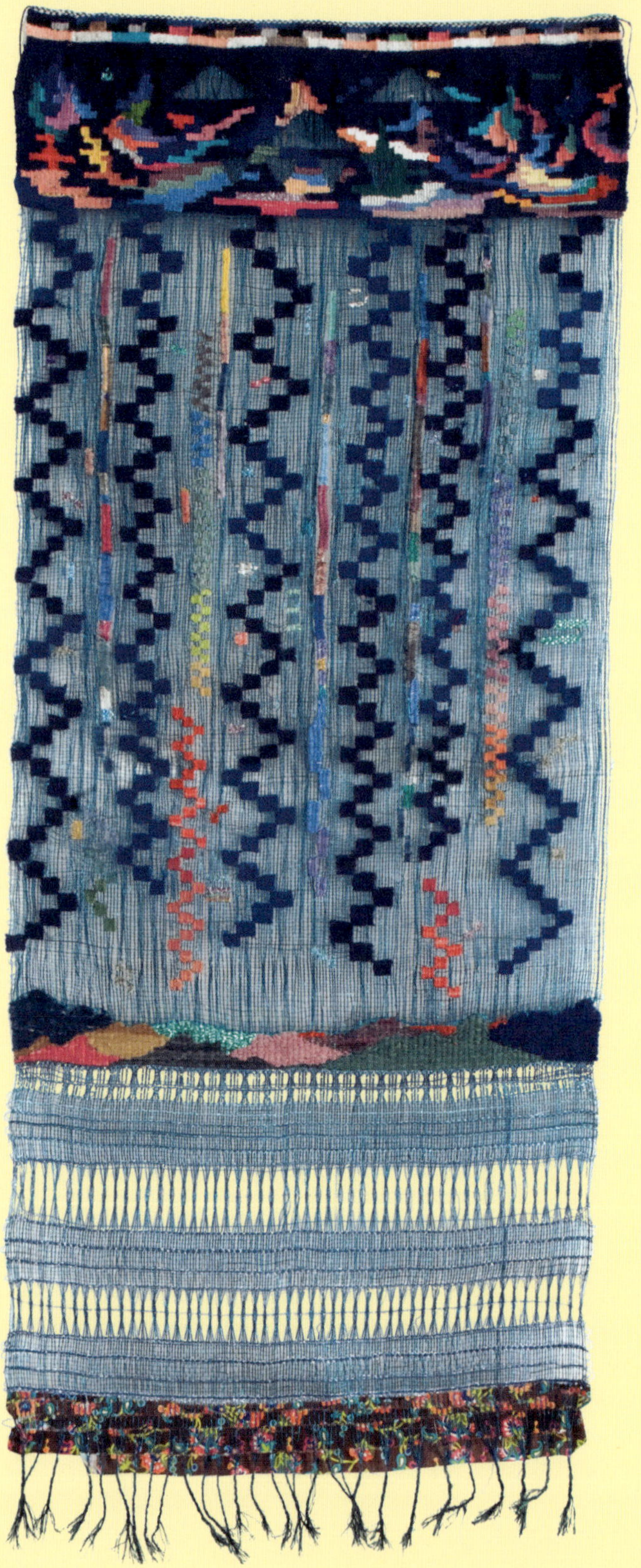

CONSUELO JIMENEZ UNDERWOOD on THE REBOZO

Inside the Rain **rebozo**, 2017, **Consuelo Jimenez Underwood** (b. 1949),
Woven linen, metallic, silk, and wool thread,
50 × 20 in. (127 × 50.8 cm).

Dysfunctionality in my familia and the hard labor that ensued made me realize early on that times were tough, but hopeful. I was young, blessed with a strong body, mind, and will. And time was on my side. I must have been five to seven years old. As we walked from Calexico to Mexicali, it seemed the city was a-hopping with commerce and activities. Quietly at a street corner or sitting up on the sidewalk, right up against the wall, were displaced Mexican indigenous women, usually with little ones in tow. *Always* they wore a rebozo—tattered, faded, worn thin. The wearer and the woven were together. I always wished I had mucho cash to give them all, enough so that they would not need to beg anymore. And I realized they had knowledge of how to create a beautiful, wearable fabric from a plant. With no electricity! How incredible! These bearers of such spectacular knowledge made me promise to myself that when I grew up, I would also learn how to weave.

I did keep my promise. As soon as I graduated, I would weave "my," "mio," "mine" rebozo—as fine as possible for "*yo*" standards. Fortunately or unfortunately, I continued "school" in the fall, this time in a full tenure track position rather than as a student. So I began "my rebozo project" that summer and completed it the following spring. When I unrolled the weaving, with intricate fringe on each end, instead of being six feet long it was nine feet! I realized my work needed to focus on length and measurement, and that I needed to avoid distraction. I resolved I would weave another one—even better, softer, and with more colors. It never happened.

Several years later, after achieving a promotion and tenure, I was running late one morning, lamenting again how there was no time, I would never be able to weave a good rebozo. As I was running out of the house, I noticed the hem on my skirt had partially fallen. With no time to sew it, I thought of the safety pin. That was the moment when my two thoughts merged and I thought, *If the old indigenous woman long ago was here now, she too would be late, but she would/could/can safety pin together her rebozo! CAUTION, if she wears it, the INS comes!*

Making the leap to rebozos was a necessary move. It was the culmination of a long desire to weave a rebozo for the Virgen de Guadalupe (VDG), but I knew that I would/could not unless I had more time. I don't remember what came first, the idea to retire or to weave the VDG her rebozo. As I began the VDG process, to draw the finished object as I perceived it to be, they came out wrong! I realized what the problem was: it was presumptuous of me to jump right in and weave a rebozo for the real main maternal icon—the VDG. I had to work up to her, and first make one for our real, natural moms—those who gave birth to us. Then I could weave a rebozo for our mothers who nurtured our world: the moon who ruled the night heavens, the ocean, the earth. These known maternal life beacons which are part of the material world, they would guide me to weave the rebozo for the VDG. By the end of the process, I began to see how to weave the VDG rebozo. Of course, by then, everything that I needed to know about how to weave the VDG rebozo—ideas, methodologies, weave structure—I knew! She made all of those natural entities that surround us and that inform me. That, in the end, is everything.

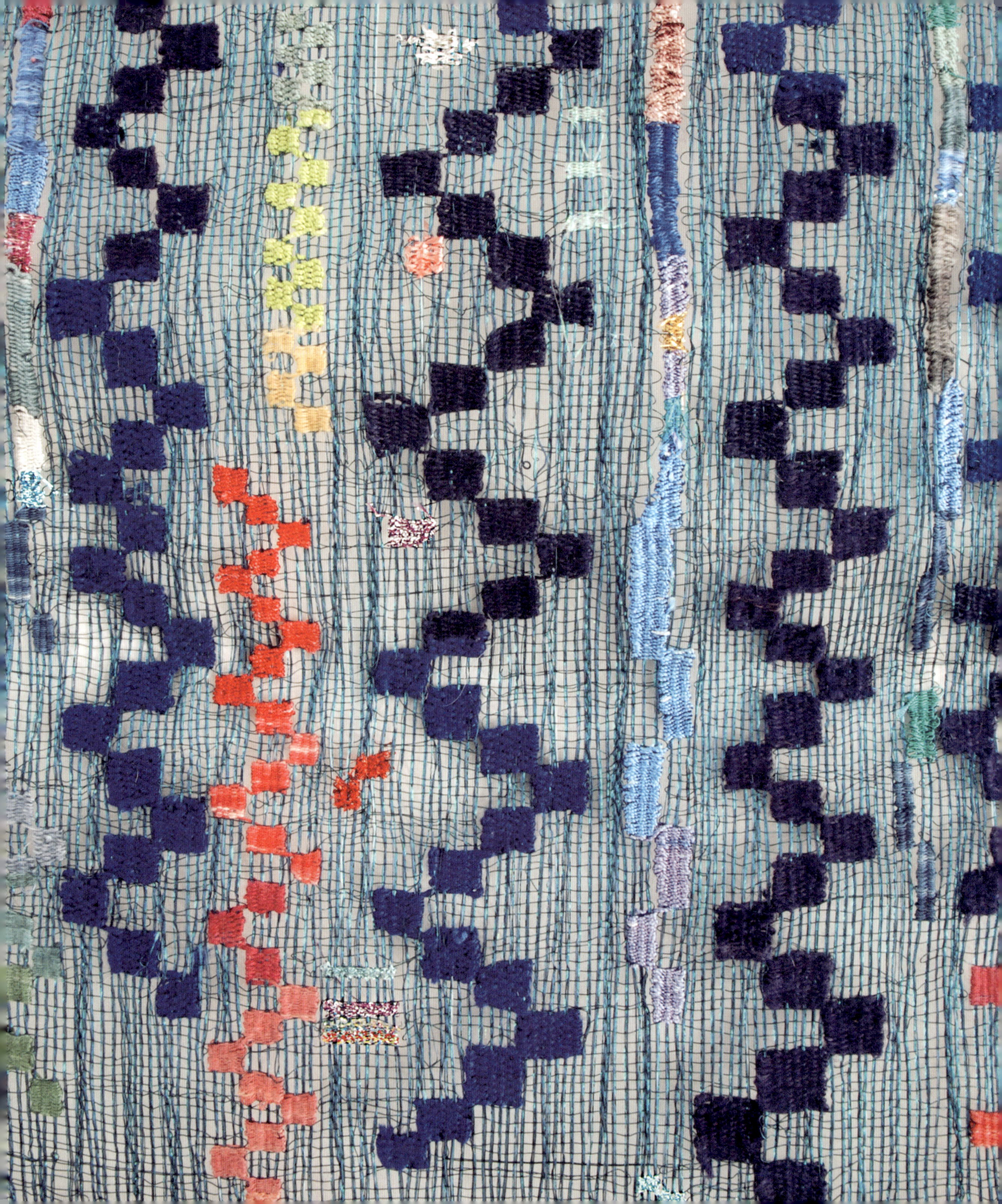

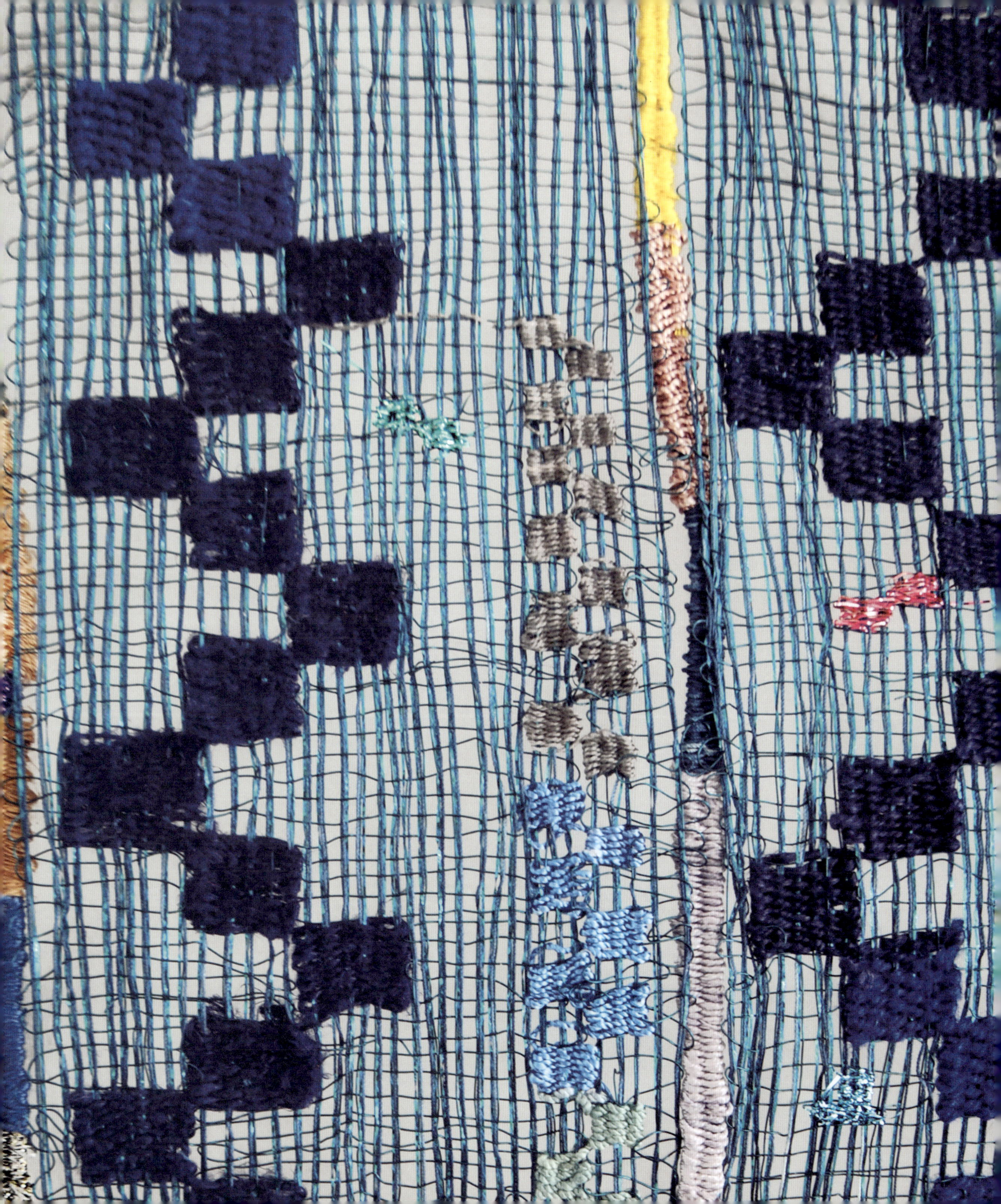

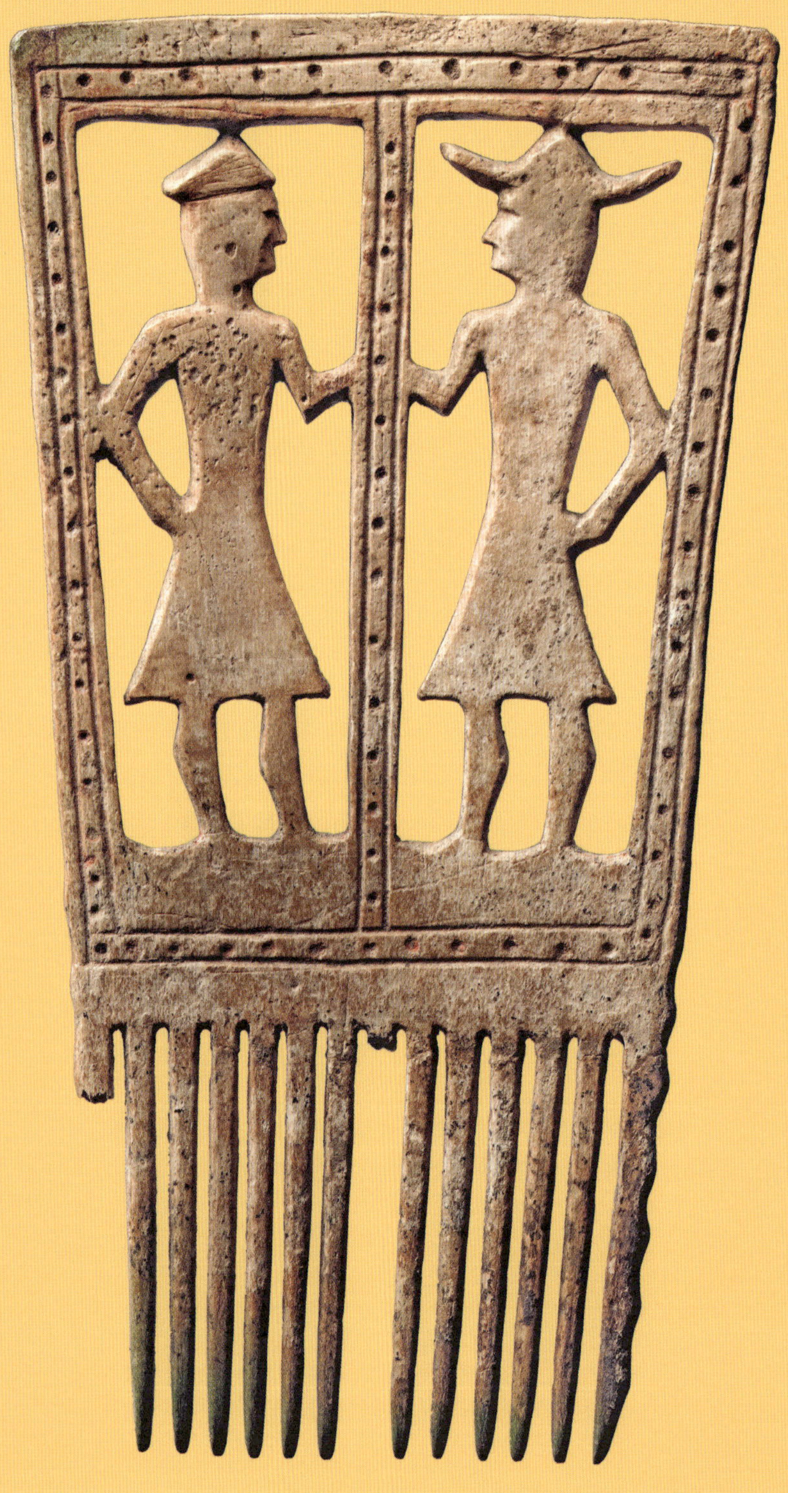

COMB

c. 1680, **Unidentified artist (Onǫda'gegá' [Seneca or Susquehannock]),**
Moose antler, 4 ¾ × 2 9⁄16 × ¼ in. (12 × 6.5 × 0.6 cm), Metropolitan Museum of Art, New York,
The Charles and Valerie Diker Collection of Native American Art, Gift of Charles and Valerie Diker, 2019, 2019.456.18.

This complexly carved comb is a compelling artifact that offers insight into the cultural, social, and political environment of its time. The comb, from the Onǫda'gegá' or Seneca Nation, features two human figures, a relatively uncommon motif. While humanoid figures have appeared on other Seneca combs, particularly from the mid-sixteenth to mid-seventeenth centuries, this example deviates from the traditional, more abstract representation of the "hocker": a squatting, humanlike form. Instead, these two individuals are portrayed in profile, with carefully recessed or notched eyes and mouths, giving them a sense of personality and presence.

The two carved figures stand below a decorative arbor, the rectangular shapes framing them. The arbor likely symbolizes a longhouse, the architectural and spiritual center of many Northeastern Indigenous communities. The figures grasp the arbor with their hands, as if physically and symbolically upholding the structure, perhaps a metaphor for supporting the community itself. It may also represent a doorway or portal, adding another layer of architectural symbolism to the frame. The overall design reflects a sort of bilateral symmetry, a common visual principle in Northeastern Indigenous art.

Despite their functionality as a grooming tool, combs also serve as a form of visual language. They traditionally depicted elements of the community in which they were made, such as oral histories or significant historical events. This particular example may communicate a complex narrative, perhaps one of alliance or treaty. The figures appear to wear frock coats and hats—clothing associated with Euro-American fashion—raising questions about their identities. Are they Native individuals adopting Euro-American dress, or are they non-Native figures depicted in a Native medium? This ambiguity may reflect the societal changes taking place at the time and possibly indicate a relationship between the wearer and another individual of cultural or political importance.

Combs such as this were used for grooming and were also worn in the hair by men, women, and children, with the carved top section exposed and the tines gripping the hairstyle. This comb originally had fourteen teeth, two of which have been lost. It is crafted from a material rich in symbolic meaning—antler, typically sourced from moose or elk. Seneca oral histories tell us that these animals were seen as omens or signs, their antlers not only valued for their durability but also imbued with meaning.

Such combs were not exclusive to the Seneca; similar forms were used throughout Northeastern tribal cultures as both regalia and practical objects. Objects like this were far more than simple tools or objects of adornment; they were expressions of cultural identity, personal relationships, and social or spiritual beliefs. As a dual-purpose item, this comb embodies the balance between utility and artistry, function and message. It visually communicates historical context, cultural values, and social dynamics, while also securing the hair of its wearer. Ultimately, this comb stands as a testament to Indigenous innovation, cultural resilience, and the ability to preserve meaning in everyday objects. —TL

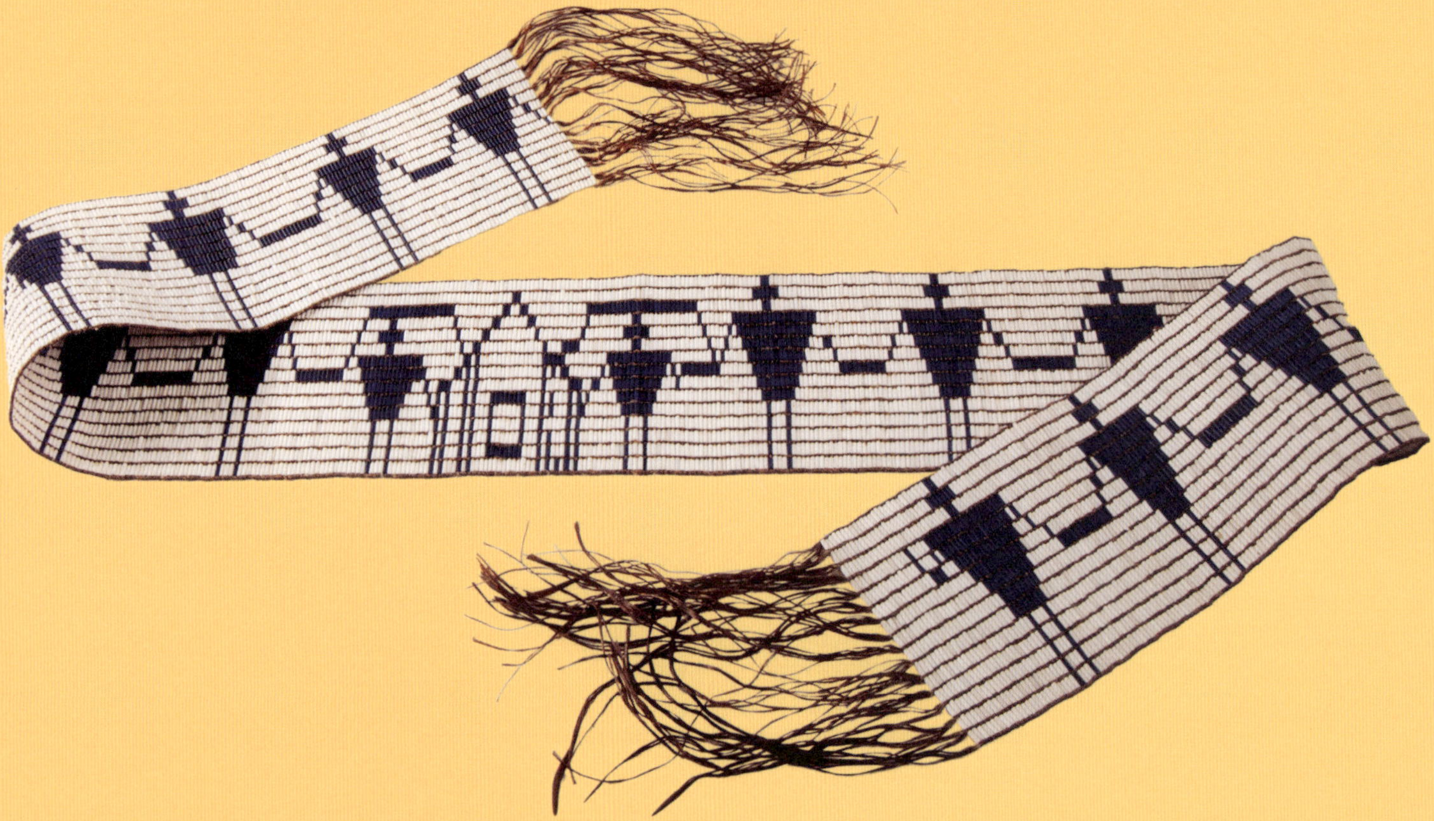

CANANDAIGUA TREATY BELT (GEORGE WASHINGTON COVENANT BELT)

Before 1794, **Unidentified artist (Onǫda'gegá')**, replica by **Yvonne Thomas (Seneca of the Snipe Clan**, b. 1944) for the Toronto Metropolitan University Libraries, Archives and Special Collections, 2020, Resin beads and animal sinew, 6.9 ft. (2.1 m).

This intricate and expressive object was constructed from purple and white pieces of quahog shell processed into beads and then woven into a belt. Quahog shells, from a mollusk residing in the coastal waters of the northeastern United States, become what is referred to as wampum when manipulated into beads or pieces of adornment. Other whelk species found along the Eastern Seaboard are also used to create white wampum. The Wampanoag word for wampum is *wampumpeak*, translating to "shell beads." Wampumpeak is used to adorn regalia and create jewelry, but is most renowned for its role in diplomacy.

Wampum belts served as powerful symbols of agreements between Indigenous nations or individuals, embodying both political and cultural significance. They were easily recognizable, allowing them to function as visual signifiers of leadership and, when worn by tribal leaders, conveyed not only authority but also wealth and status. While the material itself carried inherent value, it did not historically function as currency in the way modern monetary systems do. Instead, wampum conveyed authority and the importance of the message it carried. The intricate patterns, colors, and designs within wampum belts are not merely decorative; they carry specific meanings that visually represent the commitments made during diplomatic exchanges. They functioned as mnemonic devices, encoding history, traditions, and laws. Many wampum belts of this period varied in size, with some consisting of thousands of beads meticulously woven together to document agreements, historical events, and cultural knowledge. By interpreting these designs, knowledgeable individuals ensured that significant agreements and cultural narratives were preserved across generations.

By the seventeenth century, the exchange of wampum belts as a diplomatic practice was well established and understood, even by European colonizers. One of the best-known examples of diplomatic wampum belts is what is commonly referred to as the George Washington Belt. This belt is composed of thirteen figures holding hands, connected at the center by two smaller figures and a central longhouse. The thirteen figures represent the thirteen states of the newly formed United States of America. The two smaller figures attached to the longhouse, a traditional Onǫda'gegá' family home, symbolize Tadodaho, the spiritual leader of the Haudenosaunee, and George Washington. Their linked hands, along with the other figures, represent the peace and unity then established between the two nations. However, despite these agreements, the United States government repeatedly broke or failed to honor the treaties made with the Haudenosaunee and other Native nations. Although named after George Washington, this belt was given in honor of the 1794 Canandaigua Treaty. Signed between the Haudenosaunee Confederacy and the United States, this treaty reaffirmed land rights and sovereignty, solidifying an enduring agreement between these nations. The Canandaigua Treaty Belt remains a powerful symbol of Native diplomacy and the lasting relationships between Indigenous nations and the United States.

Contemporary Seneca elder Yvonne Thomas continues this tradition today, crafting replica wampum belts, such as the one here, that not only preserve these visual languages of diplomacy but also revitalize the cultural knowledge and techniques embedded within them. —TL

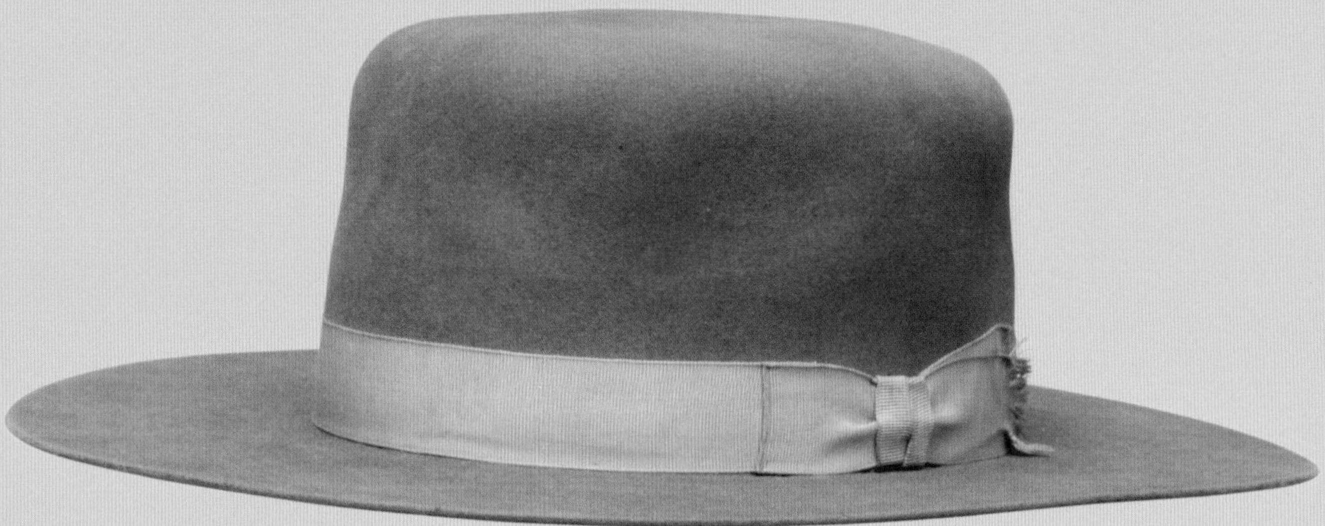

THE ACCESSORY

STETSON "BOSS OF THE PLAINS" HAT

1885, **John B. Stetson Co.** (active 1865–1970), Felt and grosgrain, 4¼ × 14¼ × 13 in. (10.8 × 36.2 × 33 cm), Dickinson Research Center, National Cowboy & Western Heritage Museum, Oklahoma City, Joe Grandee Collection, 1991.001.3057.

Known worldwide as the ultimate symbol of the West, the classic Stetson Boss of the Plains hat that became emblematic of the American cowboy actually hails from the heart of industrial Philadelphia. However, the handmade prototype for the hat was technically first fashioned on the frontier. Like many iconic American products, it began with a handcrafted solution to a need.

John B. Stetson, the man behind it all, was originally drawn to the frontier while recovering from tuberculosis and crafted this felt hat like no other to protect himself from the elements while mining in Colorado. It was inspired by what he saw Mexican cowboys wearing—practical hats with low crowns and broad brims for sun and rain coverage; some were made of felt while others were woven from light plant materials. Having grown up in his father's hat-making business in East Orange, New Jersey, Stetson had the eye of a hatter and so he decided to make his own version. According to Stetson company lore, a herder purchased that first wide-brim, tall-crown felt hat right off Stetson's head, and so it began.

Armed with an idea, Stetson brought his design back home to the East, where he set up a small one-room hat shop in the City of Brotherly Love in 1865, moving to a large building in 1872 as the business took off. He took his hats to Paris for the 1878, 1889, and 1900 Expositions, and the company boomed internationally. By Stetson's death in 1906, the company's factory was a nine-acre complex with five thousand employees. It continued to operate through 1971.[1]

Expertly crafted, designed with flair, and skillfully marketed, Stetson's signature hat became a nearly immediate success from coast to coast. The earliest hats were all entirely handcrafted, but as their popularity grew, Stetson shifted his business toward mechanization to keep up with demand. He continued to balance manufacturing with essential hand processes, ensuring the quality of the product. Hand labor employed hundreds of seamstresses, along with male fur cutters, dyers, blockers, shapers, and hatbox makers who worked with machines and by hand. Each hat took dozens of steps to create, from preparing the felt to sizing, shrinking, and shaping to banding and trimming, stitching, and finishing.[2]

The stylistic inspiration for Stetson's hats can be traced to cattle herders in Mexico, and even earlier, in Africa. In both places, woven hats kept cowboys cool and shaded, or warm when needed, and came in various crown shapes and brim sizes. The Stetson nods to the utilitarian, Mexican vaquero hat along with the pomp of charro equestrian pageantry.[3] The hat's practicality and look made it appealing to the many clients Stetson cultivated early on in the West.

The Stetson was a true product of its era: a time of national transformation on the heels of the Civil War, when the rugged open range was romanticized and intertwined with unbridled westward expansion and ideas of Manifest Destiny. The Boss of the Plains, albeit costly and less frequently worn by those doing the hard labor, embodied the wearer's readiness to face head-on whatever challenges nature would throw at them. With this ethos further popularized well into the twentieth century by writers, musicians, actors, and performers, from Annie Oakley to John Wayne, the Stetson became a wearable symbol of strength and perseverance. —EZ

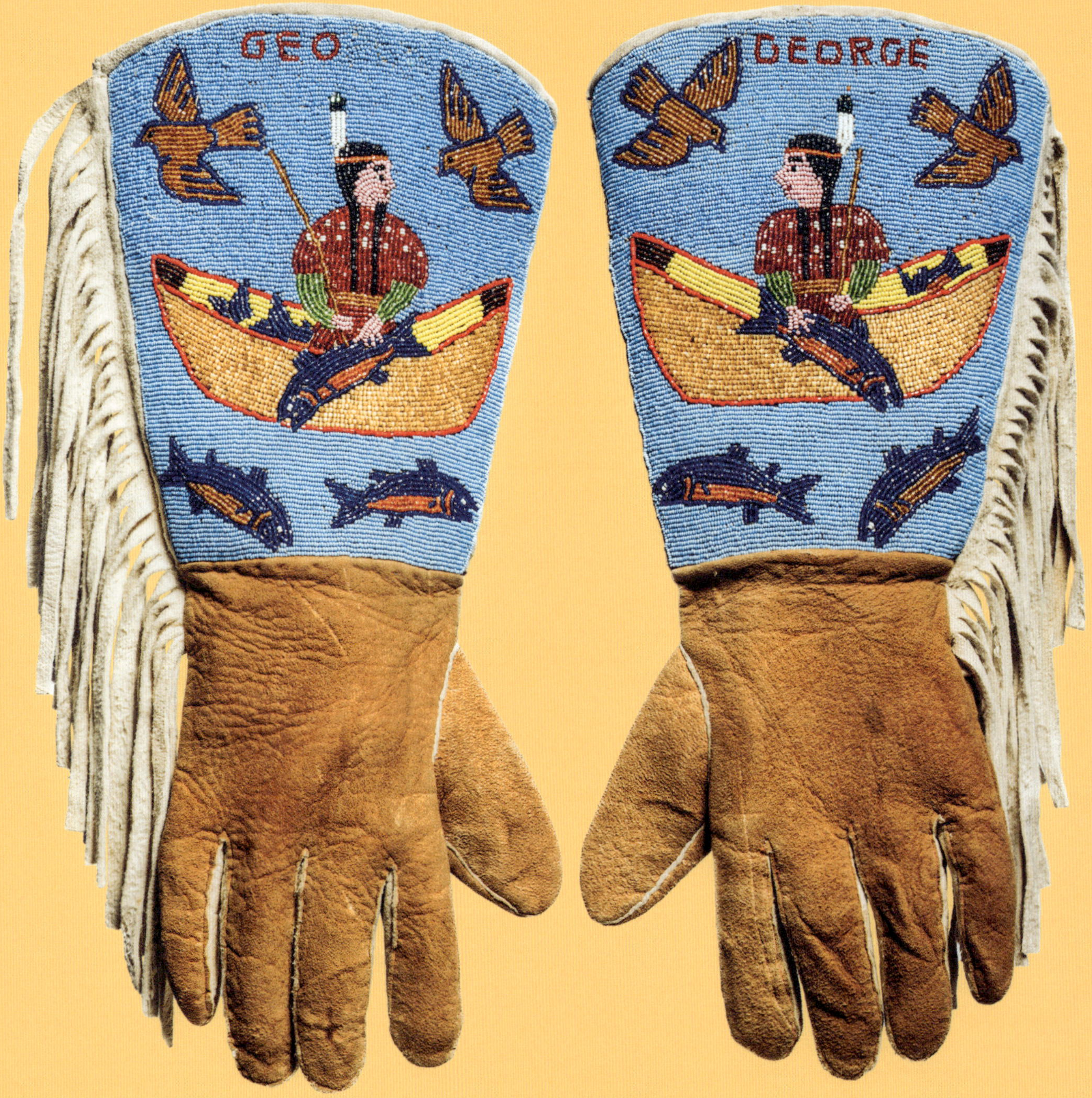
GEO
GEORGE

BEADED GAUNTLETS

c. 1950, **Attributed to Mary Gibson** (Yakama or Umatilla, active mid-20th century), Glass beads, thread, cloth, leather, 16 7/8 in. (42.9 cm), Maryhill Museum of Art, Goldendale, WA, Gift of Scott and Pam Evans and Art Dodd and Diane Plumridge, 2016.2.1a&b.

These beaded and fringed gauntlets belonged to George Gibson, a resident of northeast Oregon's Umatilla Indian Reservation. Gibson was photographed during the 1950s wearing a matching vest. His wife, Mary, may have embroidered both.

Beaded clothing and accessories are stereotypically associated with many of America's Indigenous communities. In the Pacific Northwest, glass beads first arrived during the 1770s, after coastal peoples acquired them from seagoing fur traders. Seed beads—small glass beads—became common about eighty years later. Despite the long history of beading in this region, the geneses of the resultant Columbia River Plateau beadwork styles—geometric, floral, and pictorial—are often incorrectly attributed to outside influences. Some think that Plateau geometric beadwork is based on the work of Plains-dwelling Crow (Apsáalooke) artisans. Their floral designs are sometimes said to mirror embroidery motifs borrowed from Eastern Woodlands and Great Lakes people who were employed in the Columbia River fur trade. Plateau pictorial beadwork is sometimes called "kitsch" and frequently dismissed as inauthentic, and casual observers believe that it was made for sale to outsiders. All of these evaluations and assumptions are incorrect.

Pictorial beadwork became the Columbia River Plateau's signature style even as federal and state governments waged forceful acculturation campaigns from the late nineteenth century through the mid-twentieth century. The pictorial tradition—of which these gauntlets are a part—encompasses diverse subjects: floral, equestrian, and wildlife motifs, and patriotic and religious imagery, to name a few. One unusual aspect of these gauntlets is the appearance of salmon. Despite the importance of the fish to regional economies, they seldom appear in beaded motifs. When they do, they are sometimes accompanied by birds—a possible reference to swallows returning to the Columbia River each year in concert with the initial salmon runs.

Buckskin gauntlets, frequent canvases for beadwork, have become icons of the American West. After the Civil War, soldiers continued wearing Civil War–style uniforms until the 1870s, but some officers in the West adopted unique field dress and nonstandard clothing that mimicked earlier frontier garb. In 1884, in addition to the mandated white gauntlets or gloves, leather gauntlets were authorized for enlisted men in all mounted regiments. Buckskin gauntlets remained uniform wear for both cavalry and artillery soldiers until 1912.

By the late nineteenth century, many Plains and Plateau people were making and selling both decorated gauntlets and utilitarian gloves to non-Native buyers. At the turn of the twentieth century, stars of Wild West shows such as Buffalo Bill Cody and Pawnee Bill popularized flamboyant frontier ensembles that featured intricately embroidered leather gauntlets complementing outfits of fringed buckskin. At the same time, gauntlets—until then articles of settler attire—were incorporated into Plateau men's wardrobes. Their appropriation was made complete with the addition of embroidered and beaded embellishments. Men's outfits that otherwise comprised commercially manufactured clothing were frequently completed with the addition of these highly decorated accessories. Bold representational imagery continues to be applied to gauntlets and these are proudly worn by Plateau men today. —SG

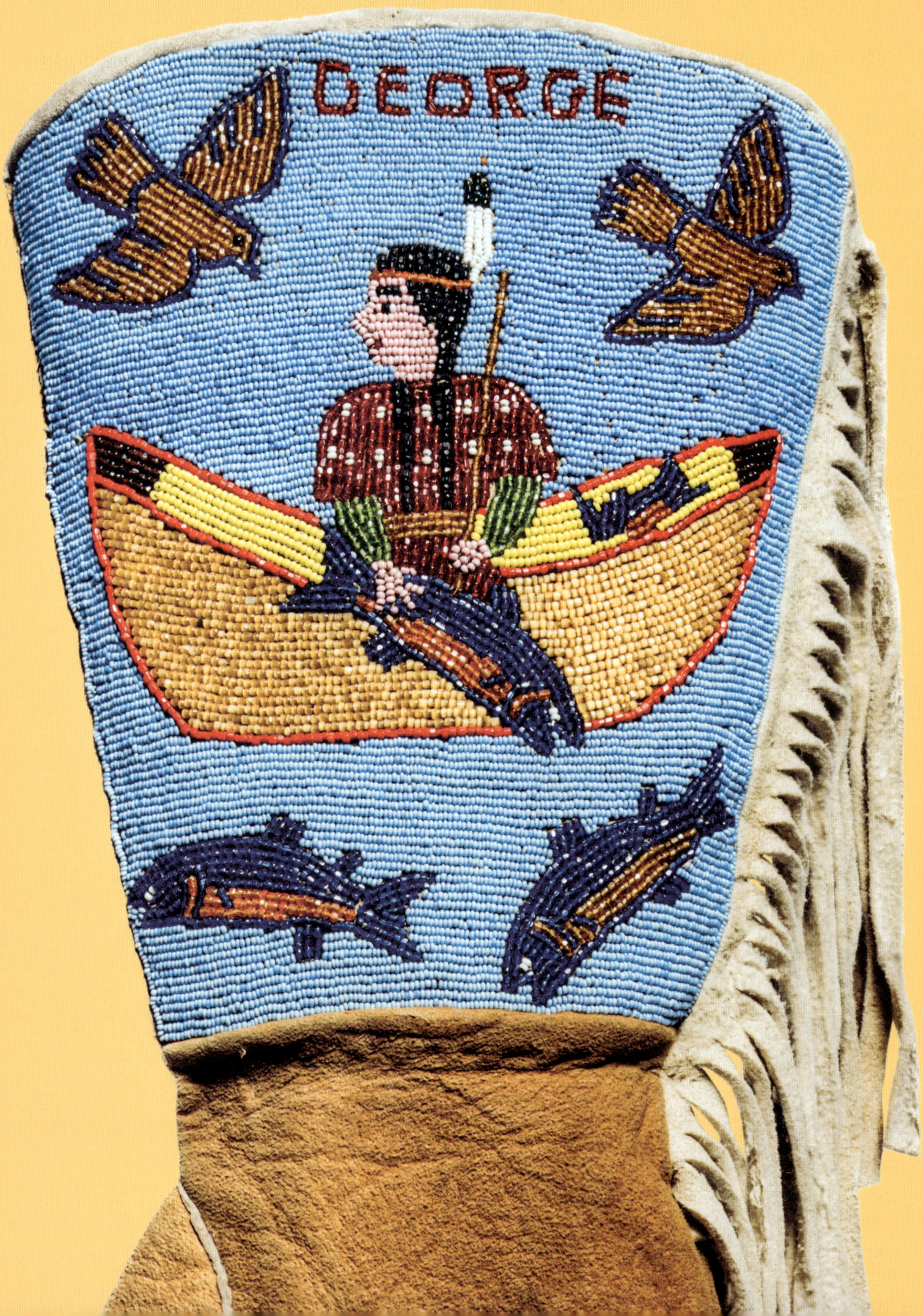
GEORGE

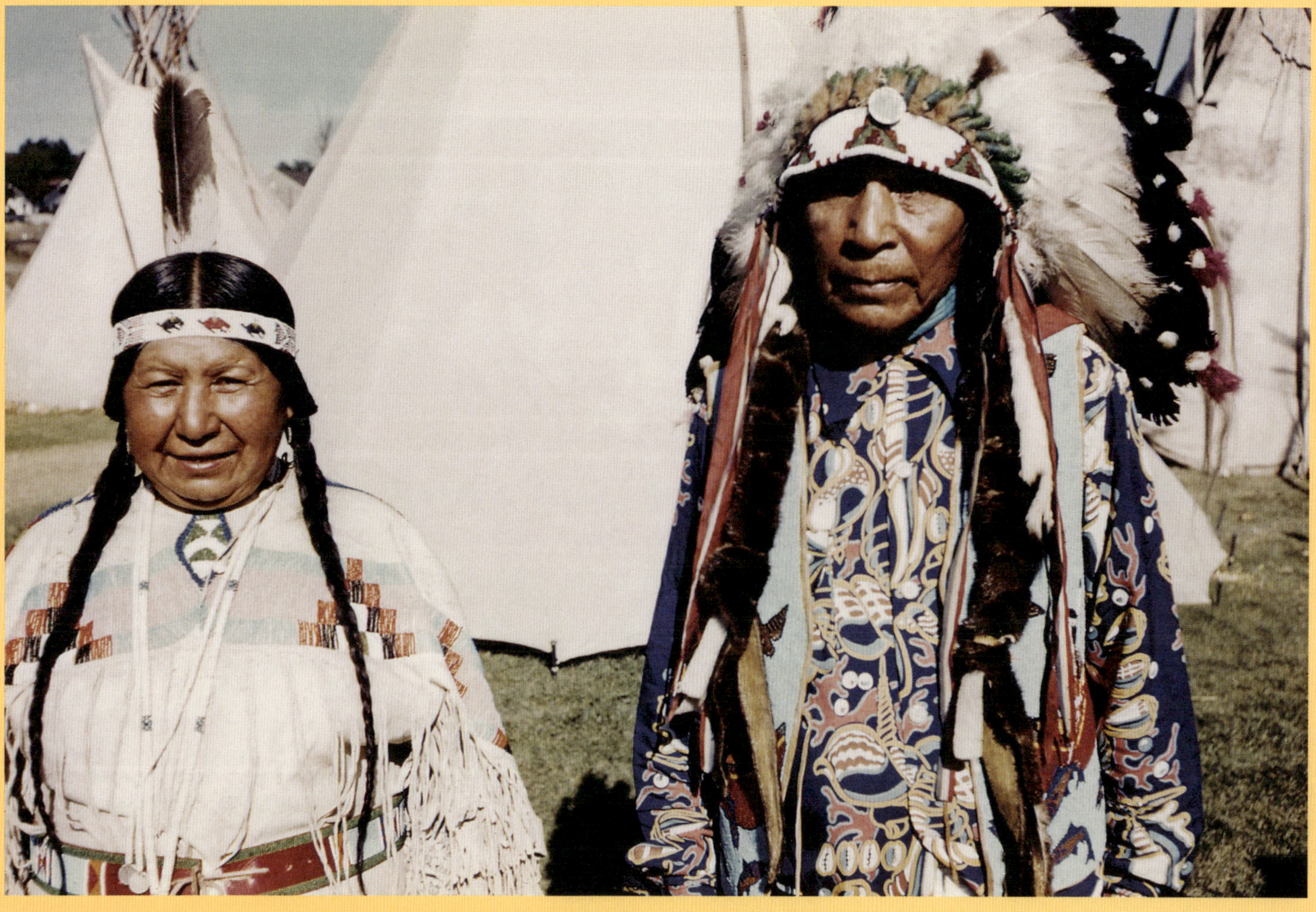

Mary Gibson and George Gibson, c. 1955,
J.W. Thompson Collection, Collection of Maryhill Museum of Art,
Goldendale, WA, 1997.10.442.

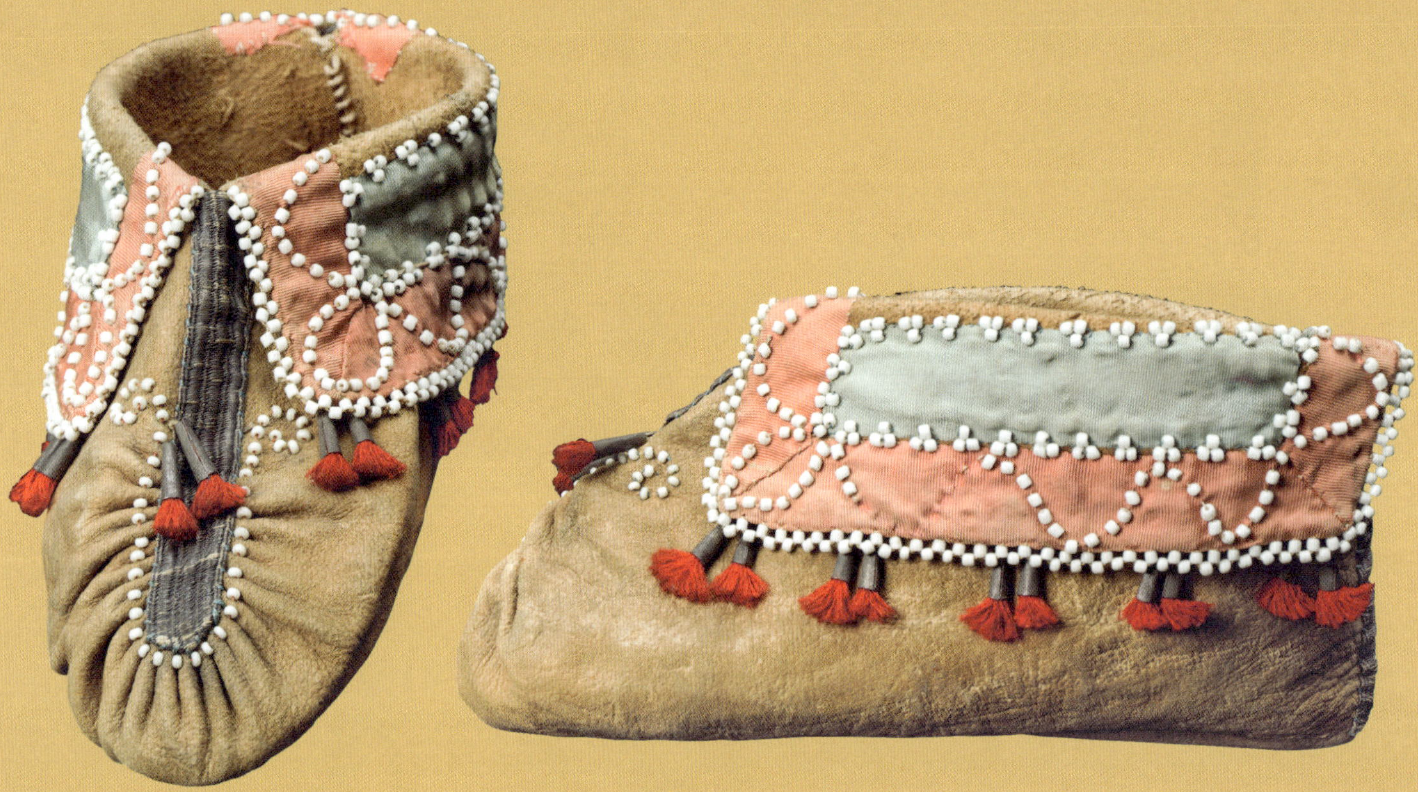

PUCKER TOE MOCCASINS

1750–80, **Unidentified artist (Eastern Woodlands or Great Lakes)**,
Deerskin leather, silk ribbon, metallic braid, glass beads, tin cones, wool yarn, linen thread,
9 in. (22.9 cm), Colonial Williamsburg, Museum Purchase, 1999-73, 1&2.

Constructed from tanned deerskin, these unique pucker toe mahkusunash (moccasins) exemplify the style of tribal communities in the Northeast and Eastern Woodlands regions of the United States. The defining feature of pucker toe moccasins is the gathered effect at the toe box, created when the sides of the shoe are sewn together. This distinctive construction technique is not only aesthetically significant but also provides durability and comfort. Embellishing the surface of these moccasins are white glass beads, silk ribbons, metallic fabric tape, and tin cones filled with worsted yarn. The careful arrangement of these elements highlights the intricate craftsmanship and artistic ability of the maker.

Historically, Native women crafted regalia not only for practical purposes but also as a means of expressing cultural identity and family lineage through intricate designs and materials. Many contemporary Indigenous artists and craftspeople carry on these traditions while incorporating modern materials and techniques.

Based on their size and provenance, these moccasins were likely made by a woman, probably for sale. These moccasins were likely made either during or shortly after the period of European contact. A distinctive Woodlands and Northeastern moccasin design appears to have been subtly altered to resemble the shape and style of English slippers that were popular at the time. This stylistic adaptation suggests an intentional transformation, one likely aimed at making items more appealing for trade. The inclusion of various trade goods in the materials used to decorate the moccasins—glass beads, silk ribbons, and tin cones—further supports the idea that this particular pair was made with commerce in mind rather than for personal use by a Native individual.

European colonization in North America brought profound changes to Indigenous material culture. French, English, Italian, and Czech colonists all engaged in trade with Native communities, introducing a variety of foreign goods, some of which became deeply integrated into Indigenous artistic and functional practices. One of the most significant trade items was glass beads, often referred to as "seed beads" due to their small size and resemblance to plant seeds. These beads became a favored material for embellishment, replacing quills as the primary medium for decoration on clothing, accessories, and regalia. Czech and English traders, as well as formal trading posts, facilitated the widespread adoption of glass beads among Native American artisans beginning in the late seventeenth century.

In addition to glass beads, silk ribbons were another prized trade good incorporated into Native material culture. First introduced by the French and English, silk ribbons became a staple of Indigenous adornment, often used to embellish garments such as shirts, dresses, skirts, and footwear. The presence of those elements on these moccasins underscores the dynamic exchange of materials and aesthetics that took place between Native communities and European traders and serves as a testament to the adaptability and creativity of Native artisans. While maintaining traditional construction methods, the maker of this pair skillfully integrated new materials and stylistic influences, demonstrating both cultural resilience and innovation. —TL

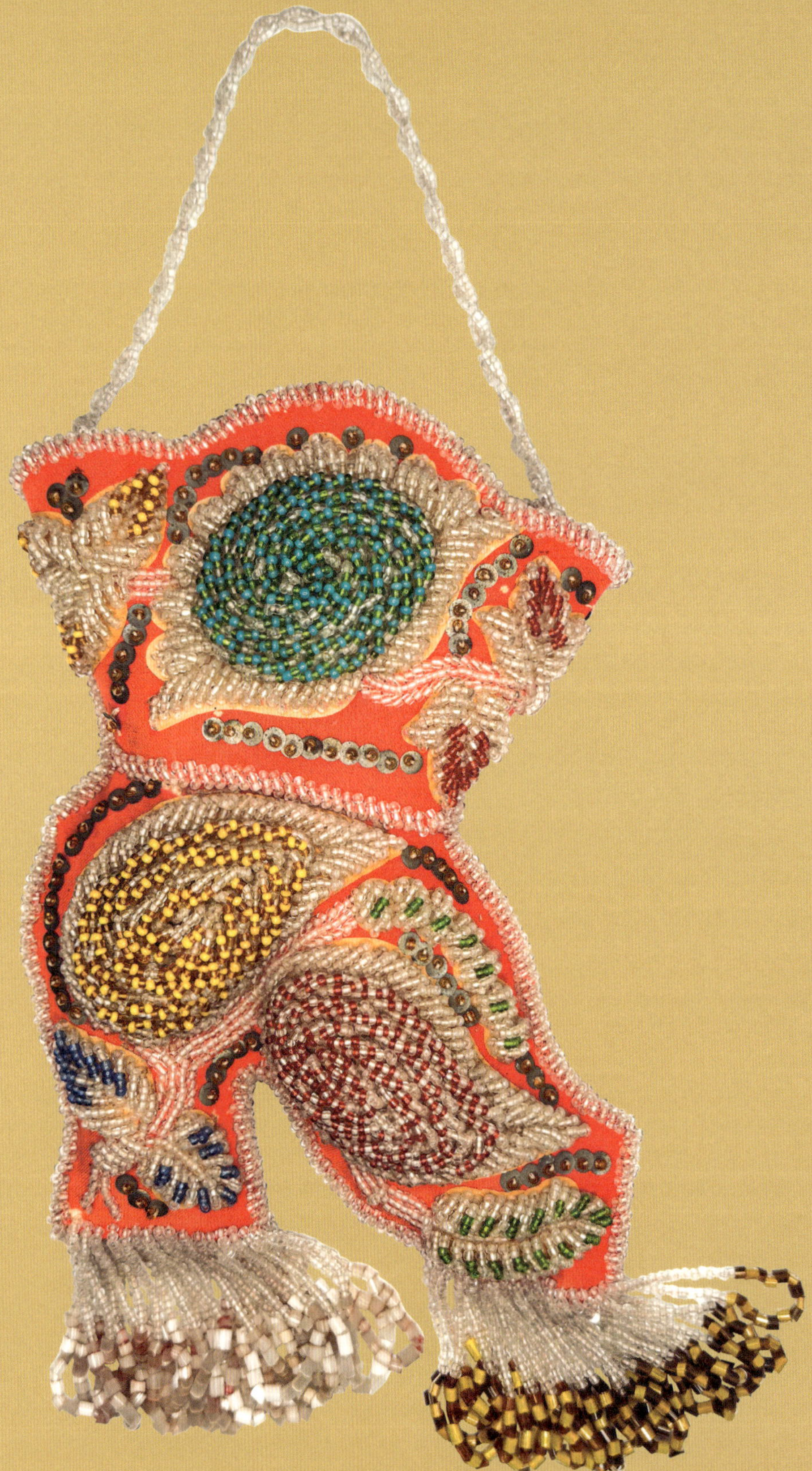

THE SHOE

SOUVENIR SHOE-SHAPED WALL POCKET

c. 1890–1905, **Unidentified artist (Kahnawake)**, Velveteen, glass beads, sequins, 9 × 12 in. (22.9 × 30.5 cm), Private collection.

Kahnawake, home to the Mohawks of Kahnawake, is located on the south shore of the St. Lawrence River, and across from Tiohtiake (Montreal). Part of our original territory extends into the Mohawk Valley of New York state, land our peoples still have ties to.

By the mid- to late 1880s in the community of Kahnawake, the women had established a cottage industry creating beaded trade goods designed for the settler audience and tourism industry. This souvenir trade would become a viable source of income for nearly a century. Women began to travel on foot to market their work on the streets and eventually to the shops in Old Montreal. The appeal and demand for their work grew to the point where their beadwork was marketed at state fairs, touring Wild West shows, circuses, and other popular attractions.

With an ever-observant eye, Kahnawake women were constantly innovating, reflecting what appealed to the settler clients of the day. A diverse array of pincushions, wall hangings, and purses were developed using a distinctive beadworking technique: raising the beads, whereby seven to nine beads were strung and placed close together to create a raised, three-dimensional effect. Made with a palette of brightly colored beads and velvet, the raised beadwork designs were quite the rage. Makers were also strategic; differing varieties were sold depending on location that best reflected the crowd to which they were being marketed. Several motifs were employed: cities, years, animals, or endearments such as Love or Dear were incorporated into the designs. It was quite rare to have work signed by an individual maker; rather specific designs and patterns were attributed to the families that produced the work.

One beautiful example of beadwork souvenirs made by the Mohawks of Kahnawake is the hanging boot—actually a wall pocket. The elaborate beadwork incorporated into this design is both distinct and pleasingly balanced. The silhouettes in these designs were heavily influenced by the Victorian era, an appealing style to the client of their time. Floral motifs, leaves, birds, and berries were hallmarks of Victorian decoration, but they were also timeless—and familiar to the women—so they often used them in their work.

Once a thriving industry, the souvenir trade saw its demise by the 1970s, as cheaply produced beadwork from overseas replaced that of the Mohawks. Beadwork continued within the community, but more for family treasures than the tourist trade. There was also a resurgence within the community to search for the old beadwork, which had been scattered around the world, and to bring it back home. —**CH**

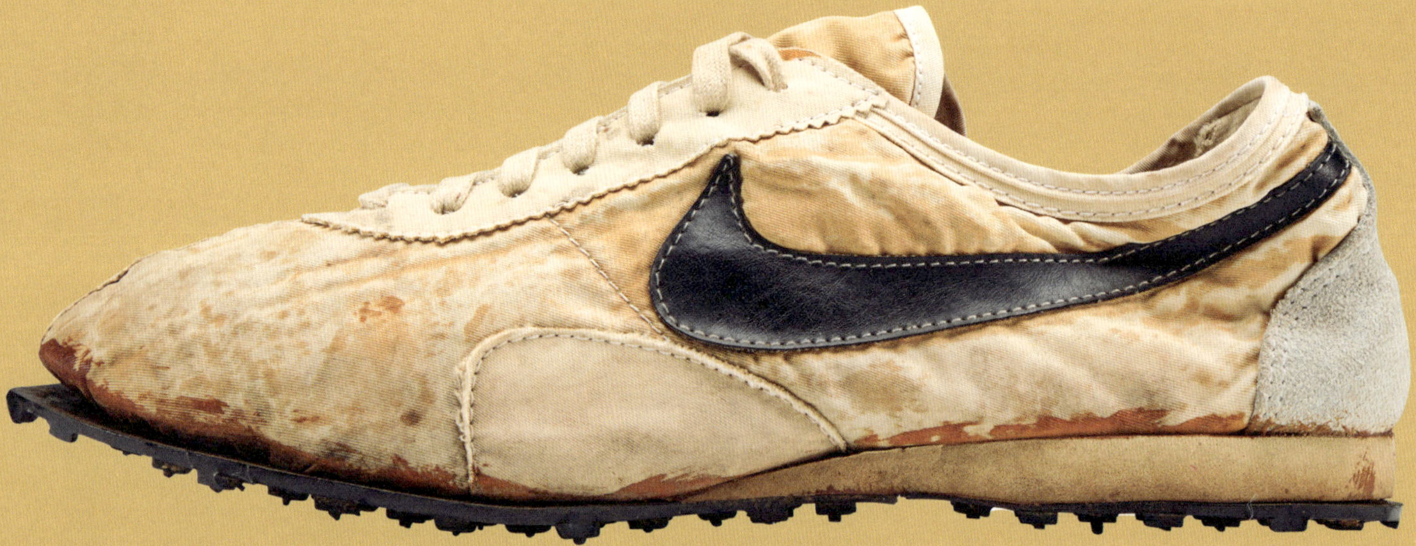

MOON SHOE

1972, **Bill Bowerman** (1911–1999) for **Nike** (est. 1964),
Nylon, rubber, cotton, leather, suede, 3¾ × 11⅓ × 3½ in. (9.5 × 28.6 × 8.9 cm).

Most humans, in most places and times in history, have made their way through life with simple footwear made from leather, cloth, and wood, perhaps with metal buckles. These shoes took all sorts of wonderful shapes, and considerable craft expertise was sometimes invested in them, but they were rarely comfortable and never entirely waterproof. Shoes of the eighteenth century were just fine when playing a harpsichord. Basketball? Not so much.

Dramatic change came to footwear in the 1950s, when Japanese and German manufacturers began experimenting with new synthetic materials. Rubber had been used for soles for a long time already, but only when paired with nylon uppers was a true performance-oriented shoe born. Sneakers produced by the Japanese brand Onitsuka Tiger were introduced to the United States by a small company in Oregon that had started out under the name Blue Ribbon Sports. By 1972, the startup was ready to go its own way, with a distinctive logo created by graphic design student Carolyn Davidson and a new name: Nike.

The company had a running start thanks to its roots in the University of Oregon track team. Bill Bowerman, the team's coach, was a cofounder of the company and remained involved in R&D for years. He is not what we usually picture when we say "craft"; aesthetics weren't of much interest to him. But he was an obsessive artisan, driven to pare away even the smallest excess weight from each shoe while maximizing strength and durability. He had the skill set of an eighteenth-century cobbler, but a totally different goal. His experimental track shoes and close collaboration with athletes set a template that Nike would follow for decades to come, including in its high-profile endorsement deals with Michael Jordan and other superstars. Nike is one of the biggest apparel brands in the world, raking in over $50 billion annually. Again—not what we normally think of when we say craft, but prototyping by hand remains vital to the company to this day.

The precipitous rise of sneaker culture and a wider shift toward informality in everyday dress has spelled trouble for traditional shoemaking in America. A craft that was practiced in every city and town as recently as the 1950s has now become a rarity. Amara Hark-Weber, a prominent spokesperson for the trade, notes that a culture of fierce secrecy didn't help: "No one was willing to teach or share what they knew, and with no apprenticeships system, there were no new makers."[1] She and her generational peers are shifting that culture, though, and proving that it's still possible to make a good living by making beautiful bespoke shoes.

Hark-Weber's own designs tend toward the classic, with little twists of color and style that feel of the moment. Other makers are blowing up the model entirely. Yohance Lacour, for example, draws on his own deep knowledge of streetwear—he grew up in Jordan-era Chicago—to make limited edition and one-off sneakers. You can see a lot of Nike in his work, but also a wide range of other influences: Italian luxury brands, hip-hop fashion, and even thoughts about the origins of shoemaking itself. After all, animal skin was once one of the few options people had to clothe themselves and protect their feet, he reasons. "The creativity was born from the hustle. That's how leather is for me. Creativity flows, and you gotta grab it when it hits."[2] —**GA**

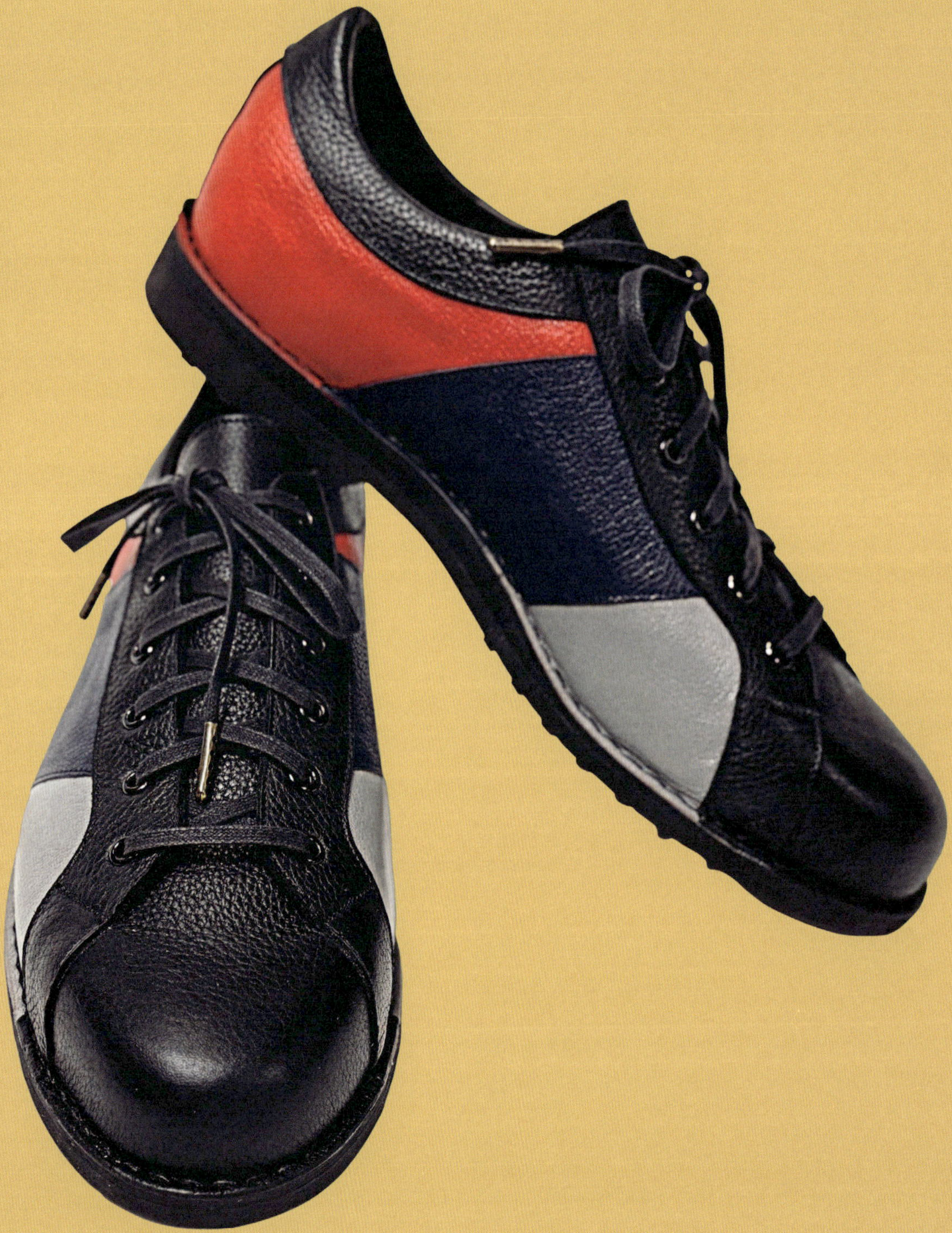

Shoes, 2025, **Amara Hark-Weber,**
Stitchdown construction with kid leather, bovine lining, and a rubber sole,
Made on commission and designed in collaboration with the client.

THE SHOE

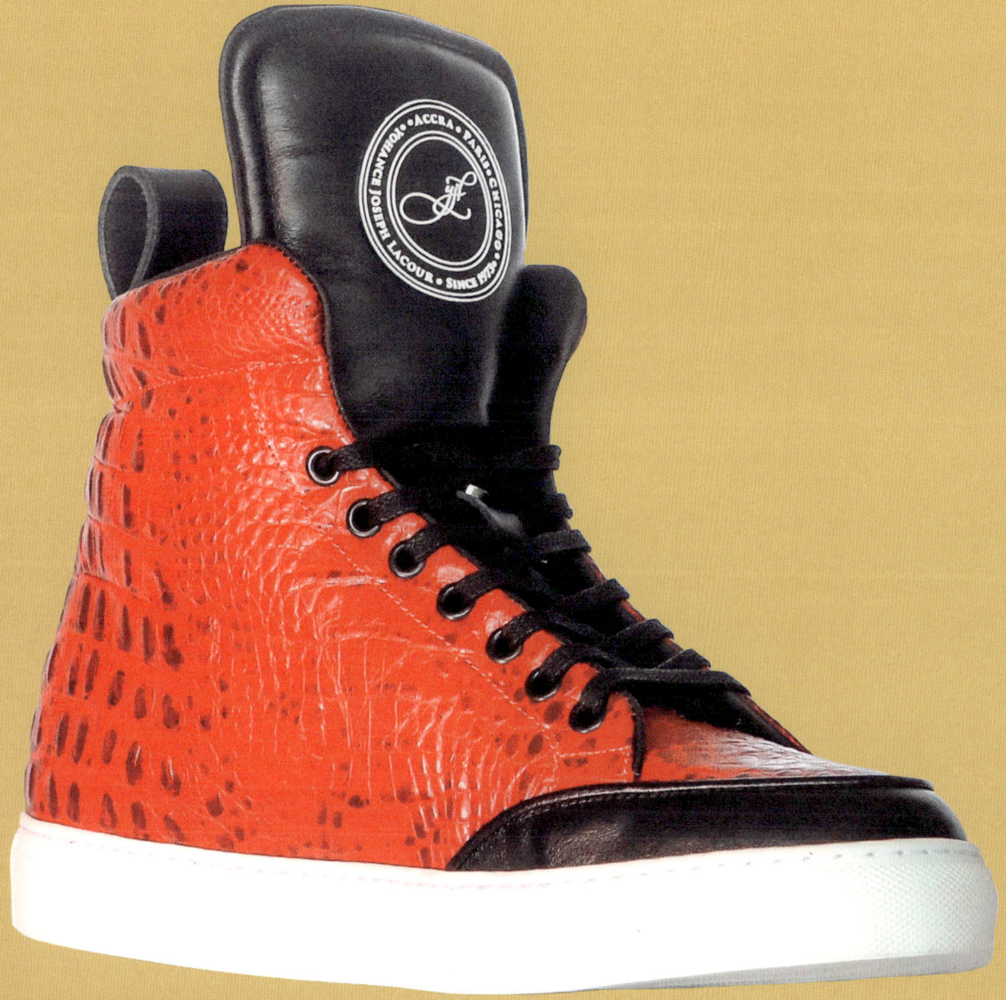

Redemption Sneaker, **2024, Yohance Lacour,**
Hand-stained lambskin leather, crocodile embossing, waxed laces.

TO WALK

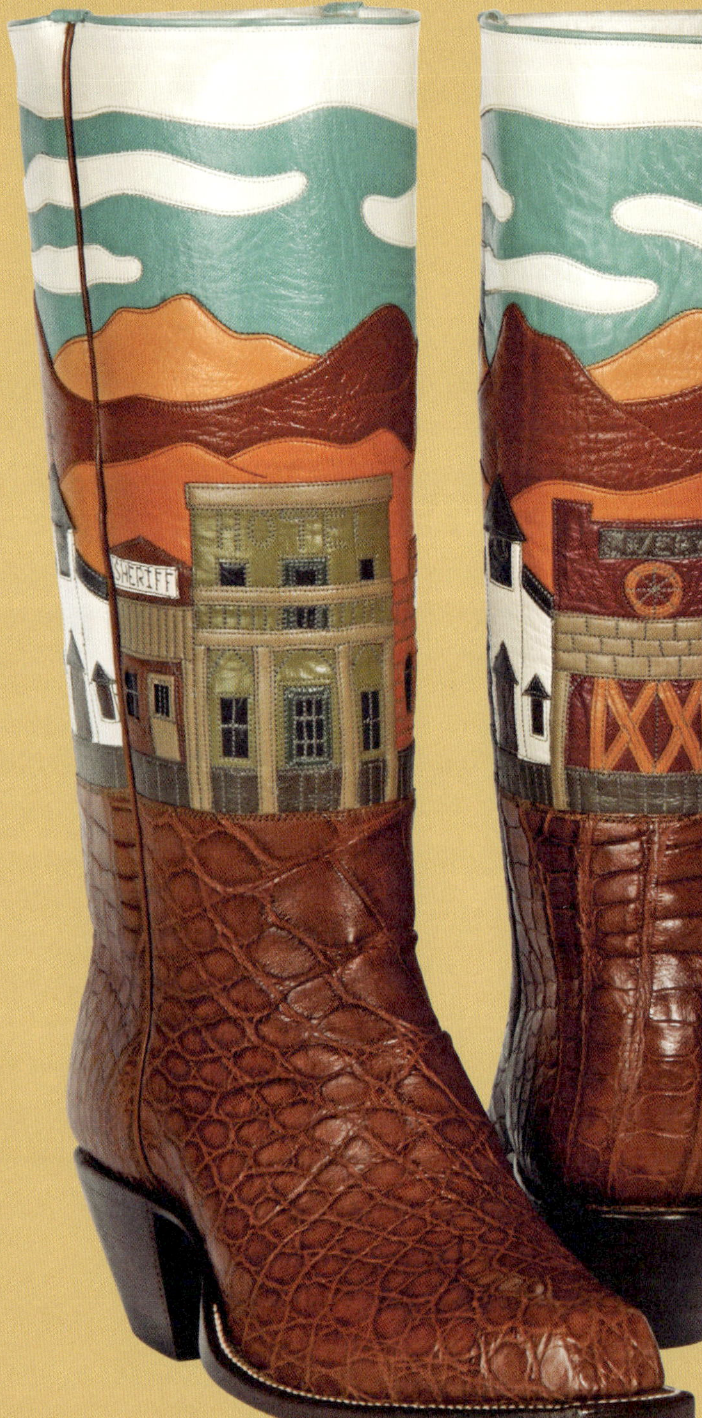
SHERIFF
HOTEL

OUT AMONG THE STARS BOOTS

2009, **Lisa Sorrell** (b. 1968), American alligator leather and kangaroo leather, 15 × 12 × 12 in. (38.1 × 30.5 × 30.5 cm).

Cowboy boots entered American fashion history in the 1800s, when former U.S. soldiers moved west to herd cattle and farm. Though quintessentially American, these boots have no sole birthplace or creator. Inspired by the Spanish vaquero-style boot of the seventeenth century, they were designed for function: the pointed toe slipped easily into stirrups; the angled heel secured the foot without trapping it; and the stitching kept the boot top upright.

Western movies of the 1940s romanticized cowboy culture down to its boots, influencing their evolution from a fully functional item to a sartorial statement. The toe became narrower and more pointed, while designs grew bolder and more ornate, featuring elaborate stitching and intricate inlays and overlays. This precise work demanded expert design and stitching skills—talents contemporary boot maker Lisa Sorrell possesses in abundance.

Before beginning this vocation, Sorrell ran a successful sewing business in Missouri making dresses for church ladies. She later moved to Guthrie, Oklahoma, with her husband, where she apprenticed with Jay Griffith, a legendary Oklahoma boot maker. After eighteen months mastering the craft, Sorrell established Sorrell Custom Boots, creating handmade boots for discerning clients.

Sorrell was drawn to boot making because it allowed her to apply her exceptional sewing skills and design sensibilities through leather inlays, overlays, and precision topstitching. She also enjoyed the challenge of creating more thought-provoking compositions than the traditional eagles, butterflies, and floral sprays that have become commonplace motifs on cowboy boots. Moreover, boot making enabled her to defy the gender roles that she had been taught through her evangelical church, where women were expected to be homemakers. As a boot maker, Sorrell could hammer, be loud, and engage in physically demanding work considered unladylike. She reflected, "It was like finding out who I'd been all along and I just hadn't known. I got to sew, be creative, and be artistic."[1]

"Cowboy boots are an American icon," Sorrell has stated. "You can show cowboy boots to almost anyone in the world and they instantly connect that with America."[2] This American identity is powerfully represented in her work *Out Among the Stars* (2009). At first glance, the boot displays a handsome leather-stitched design of a Western town with two-story buildings, a sheriff's office, and a white church set against mountains and turquoise sky.

However, this seemingly benign imagery offers deeper commentary on Manifest Destiny. As Sorrell explains, "As the settlers moved West they altered the landscapes, destroyed ecosystems, and obliterated cultures, only to attempt to recreate the way of life they left behind."[3] Through her craft, Sorrell invites us to walk the line between aesthetic appreciation and critical awareness—between romanticizing the cowboy mystique and acknowledging the cultural displacement that westward expansion wrought upon Indigenous peoples. —JL

NOTES

INTRODUCTION: THE OBJECTS THAT DEFINE US

1. A few years before he passed away, the brilliant material culture scholar Bernie Herman discussed ideas for this book with me. He talked about how the field could develop with object-driven, and not just object-centered, approaches.

2. See Sidney Mintz, *Sweetness and Power: The Place of Sugar in Modern History* (Penguin Books, 1985), xxvii.

3. For how to closely look at and juxtapose objects for a new understanding of history, see Laurel Thatcher Ulrich et al., *Tangible Things: Making History through Objects* (Oxford University Press, 2015).

4. For a nonhierarchical, interconnected way of looking at art history and the "messiness of objects," see Edward S. Cooke, Jr., *Global Objects: Toward a Connected Art History* (Princeton University Press, 2022), 256–63.

5. A similar view of object stories was taken in Richard Kurin, *The Smithsonian's History of America in 101 Objects* (Penguin Press, 2013). Kurin states, "Objects have the power to connect us in . . . ways words do not." See also Neil MacGregor, *A History of the World in 100 Objects* (Penguin Books, 2011).

6. Margaretta M. Lovell, *Art in a Season of Revolution: Painters, Artisans, and Patrons in Early America* (University of Pennsylvania Press, 2005), vii.

7. See Charles Keeler, *The Simple Home*, 1904. Reprinted, Peregrine Smith Inc., 1979, 54.

DWELL

Candelabra

1. Billie Sessions, et al., *Ripples: Marguerite Wildenhain and Her Pond Farm Students* (California State University, 2002), 5–22.

2. Marguerite Wildenhain, "Oral history interview with Marguerite Wildenhain, March 14, 1981," interview by Hazel Bray, Archives of American Art, Smithsonian Institution.

Degikup

1. Ralph T. Coe, *Sacred Circles: Two Thousand Years of Native American Art* (Nelson-Atkins Museum of Art, 1977), 211.

2. Jo Ann Nevers, *Wa She Shu: A Washo Tribal History* (Inter-Tribal Council of Nevada, 1976), 9, 18, 68–69.

Jug

1. A. Brant Zipp, "Putting Thomas Commeraw Together Again: A Brief Meditation on Two Decades of Research," *Ceramics in America 2024* (Milwaukee: Chipstone Foundation, 2024).

2. The most important resource is the Black Craftspeople Digital Archive, founded in 2019 by Tiffany Momon and codirected with Torren L. Gatson, available at blackcraftspeople.org. Alison Robinson curated an exhibition about Commeraw at the New-York Historical Society. See also Robell Awake, *A Short History of Black Craft in Ten Objects* (Princeton Architectural Press, 2025).

3. Claudia Arzeno Mooney, April L. Hynes, and Mark M. Newell, "African-American Face Vessels: History and Ritual in 19th-Century Edgefield," *Ceramics in America 2013* (Chipstone Foundation, 2013).

Doors

1. The home was designed by architect Harold Van Buren Magonigle at Fifth Avenue and East Seventy-Ninth Street and was one of Yellin's early projects. www.metmuseum.org/art/collection/search/9589.

2. See Joseph Cunningham's recent documentation. www.themagazineantiques.com/article/cradle-liberty-cradle-craft/.

3. As stated by Yellin in a lecture given in 1926; Jack Andrews, *Samuel Yellin, Metalworker* (Skip Jack Press, 2011), 71.

4. Ibid., 13.

Spinning Wheel

1. See "Spinning Wheel Makers: Marks and Information" for a list of maker's marks and information related to spinning wheel makers.

2. See Brenda Page's investigation into the J.C. mark on spinning wheels in New England. Brenda Page, "Woody Hill and Rose," Exquisite Machinery.com, exquisitemachinery.com/2022/08/25/woody-hill-and-rose/.

3. WPA-era interviews with the formerly enslaved document the stories of enslaved artisans spinning and making clothes, especially in the American South.

Tool Chest

1. Letter from Sarah Elliott Huger, New York, to Harriott Pinckney Horry, Charleston, January 4, 1816, Harriott Horry Ravenel Family Papers, 1694–1935 (1086.00), South Carolina Historical Society, Charleston.

Library Ladder

1. Information about Wharton Esherick and his practice was gleaned from Mansfield Bascom, *Wharton Esherick: The Journey of a Creative Mind* (Abrams, 2010) and Emily Zilber, ed., *The Crafted World of Wharton Esherick* (Rizzoli Electa, 2024).

2. Born in Wyncote, Pennsylvania, William Curtis Bok (1897–1962) became a common pleas court judge in Pennsylvania in 1937 and was elected as a justice of the Pennsylvania Supreme Court in 1958. He published several books dealing with aspects of law. timenote.info/en/Curtis-Bok.

3. Esherick made a variety of furniture employing parts of these wheels, most notably his Wagon Wheel Chair; the earliest known example dates to 1931. Zilber, 139. Bascom notes that this object's vertical rails are composed of "cartwheel-rim sides" and shares that its purpose was for use in a newly created law library expressly made for Judge Bok in their renovated home. Bascom, 150.

4. Esherick began work on the first-floor interiors of the Bok house in 1935 and completed the renovation in 1938. He finished Judge Bok's law library at the end of 1935. This date aligns with the library ladder, marked with a gouge on the back of the middle and bottom steps: "W.E. / MCMXXXV." Esherick placed this ladder in Bok's home law library rather than for use in other interiors he created in the Bok house that same year. When the Bok family's descendants donated the ladder to the Philadelphia Museum of Art in 2001, it was originally documented as designed for the music room before being correctly identified. For a timeline of the Bok house renovation, please consult Bascom, 142–61.

Topsy-Turvy Doll

1. Winterthur object record.

2. Felicite Wolfe, "Collections Corner: The Topsy-Turvy Doll," blog of the African American Museum of Iowa (June 7, 2019, originally published in the Summer 2017 edition of *Iowa Griot*), accessed February 2, 2025, blackiowa.org/collections-corner-the-topsy-turvy-doll/.

3. Ann Stachowski, "Black Dolls and American Children: Learning What Dark Skin Meant in Antebellum America," referenced in "Flip Dolls: A (Not So) Brief History and a Challenge to Readers," Transformative Healing Dolls (December 31, 2016), www.transformativehealingdolls.com/blog/flip-dolls-a-not-so-brief-history-and-a-challenge-to-readers.

4. Wendy Lavitt, *American Folk Dolls* (New York: Alfred A. Knopf, 1982).

5. Kimberly Wallace-Sanders, *Mammy: A Century of Race, Gender and Southern Memory* (Ann Arbor, MI: University of Michigan Press, 2008), 35.

6. Julian K. Jarboe, "The Racial Symbolism of the Topsy-Turvy Doll," *The Atlantic*, November 20, 2015. www.theatlantic.com/technology/archive/2015/11/the-racial-symbolism-of-the-topsy-turvy-doll/416985/.

Illuminated Piñata No. 21

1. Dr. Yong Chen has identified a potential link for the transmission of the piñata from China to Europe. See Yong Chen, "From the Dachunniu to the Piñata: Tracing the Alleged Chinese Origin of a Mexican Tradition," *Fudan J. Hum. Soc. Sci.* 11, 69–81 (2018). doi.org/10.1007/s40647-017-0179-6 and his presentation: www.craftinamerica.org/event/global-origins-of-the-pinata/.

Side Drum

1. John H. Johnson, "Publisher's Statement," *Ebony*, November 1975.

2. James Gleick, *The Information: A History, A Theory, A Flood* (New York: Pantheon Books, 2011), 22–27.

Kiowa Cradleboard

1. The artist's museum talk.

2. In a 2021 interview with the RISD Museum.

Skateboard

1. Located by Todd Huber and mentioned during a phone interview, April 25, 2025. The September 1913 article was donated to the Skateboarding Hall of Fame and Museum in Simi Valley, CA. See: A. Neely Hall, "The New Roller Skatemobile," *Woman's Home Companion*, September 1913, 37.

2. See Paul Stewart, "The Skateboard May Prove as Big and Giddy a Fad as the Hula Hoop," *Sports Illustrated*, May 18, 1964.

FEED

Tankard

1. Martha Gandy Fales, *Joseph Richardson and Family, Philadelphia Silversmiths*, (Wesleyan University Press for The Historical Society of Pennsylvania, 1974), 5; 267, fn. 21.

2. "Letters of William Fitzhugh," *The Virginia Magazine of History and Biography*, 1895–01, Vol. 2, 15, as cited in Barbara McLean Ward and Gerald W. R. Ward, *Silver in American Life* (American Federation of Arts, New York, 1979).

New Genesis

1. Diego Romero, Zoom interview with author, March 19, 2025.

2. Ibid.

Sons of Liberty Bowl

1. Quoted in Gerald W. R. Ward, *Paul Revere: Sons of Liberty Bowl*, MFA Spotlight (MFA Publications, Museum of Fine Arts, Boston, 2016), 17.

2. A British gill is about four fluid ounces.

Ice Bowl

1. See Unidentified artist (Iñupiaq), Harpoon rest depicting two polar bears, National Museum of the American Indian, americanindian.si.edu/collections-search/object/NMAI_102223.

Punch Bowl

1. That is, until Libbey did it again with a larger, heavier cut glass entry for the 1904 World's Fair in St. Louis (see "Art Minute: Libbey Glass Company, 'Punch Bowl and Stand,'" Toledo Museum of Art. toledomuseum.org/collection/art-minute/art-minute-libbey-glass-company-punch-bowl-and-stand).

2. The parallels between the 1890 McKinley Tariff and the Trump administration's tariffs demonstrate the cyclical patterns of economics, nationalism, and labor movements.

3. Joseph Harold Larnerd, "Decorative Cut Glass and the Working Class in America, 1876 to 1916," PhD dissertation, Stanford University, 2019, and Larnerd, "The McKinley Bowl's Services and Disservices, 1898–1901," *American Art* (Summer 2023): 108–25.

Oval Bowl

1. Otto Natzler, *Gertrud and Otto Natzler: Ceramics* (Los Angeles County Museum of Art, 1968) and Gertrud Natzler and Otto Natzler, *The Ceramic Work of Gertrud and Otto Natzler* (M. H. de Young Memorial Museum, 1971).

2. Otto Natzler, *Form and Fire: Natzler Ceramics, 1939–1972* (The Renwick Gallery of the National Collection of Fine Arts by the Smithsonian Institution Press, 1973), 26–27.

3. Natzler, *The Ceramic Work of Gertrud and Otto Natzler.*

Teapot (Bentzon)

1. Rachel Layton Elwes, "A New Addition to African American Silver," *The Silver Society Journal*, 13 (2001), 16–17.

Chocolate Pot

1. I am grateful for the guidance of Dr. Catherine Popovici and Dr. Anthony Meyer in the identification of Nahuatl and Mixtec symbols on the service, not all of which are addressed in this short essay.

2. See: William Spratling's Quetzalcóatl head brooch (Prendedor cabeza de Quetzalcóatl), LACMA, M.2013.4.11, collections.lacma.org/node/708373.

Tea Service

1. Choo's work gained international recognition through exhibitions such as *Craft Today USA*, organized by the American Craft Museum in New York (now Museum of Art + Design), which traveled to fifteen European cities between 1989 and 1993 as an official U.S. State Department cultural representation. *Tea Service* was later acquired by the Figge Art Museum in Davenport, Iowa, following its 1996 exhibition in *Forging Ahead: Contemporary Metalsmithing in Iowa.*

Swan Vessels

1. Randy Stromsoe, "Oral history interview with Randy Stromsoe, June 4–6, 2013," interview by Jo Lauria, Archives of American Art, Smithsonian Institution, http://www.aaa.si.edu/collections/interviews/oral-history-interview-randy-james-stromsoe-16093.

2. Randy Stromsoe, email exchange with the author, February 5, 2025.

Miniature Fork and Spoon Set

1. Sarah Coffin, *Feeding Desire: Design and the Tools of the Table, 1500–2005* (New York: Assouline Publishing, 2006).

2. Ibid.

3. Barbara M. Ward, "John Coney" in Patricia E. Kane, *Colonial Massachusetts Silversmiths and Jewelers* (Yale University Art Gallery, 1998), 334–51.

4. Will of Thomas Barton, Essex County, Massachusetts, Probate Records and Indexes 1638–1916, Probate Records, Vol 329–30, Book 29–30, 1749–1752, via Ancestry.com.

Sugar Tongs

1. David Barquist, *Myer Myers: Jewish Silversmith in Colonial New York* (Yale University Art Gallery, 2001), 154–60.

Pierced Truss Two

1. Bruce Pepich. "Expecting the Unexpected," Ganoksin Jewelry Making Community, January 26, 2023.

FURNISH

Rush-Bottomed Chair

1. Ludwig Christian Sprogell, a German-born dyer, owned "six red rush bottom'd chairs" when he died in 1729. Mary Martin owned nineteen when she died in 1731, including one with "elbows" (arms) and nine "old" ones, while Mary Davies owned "a rush Couch + 14 Ditto Chairs" in 1735. The shipwright Stephen Simmons died in 1744 and owned one armed rush-bottomed chair and six others in his chamber (or bedroom) and kept "a half Dozen of old rush Botomed [sic] chairs" in both his back chamber and his lower chamber.

2. Mary Attwood's 1760 inventory listed "5 pretty good rush bottom'd Chairs/ 5 very ordinary."

Armchair (United Crafts/The Craftsman Workshops)

1. Stickley's company had various names over the years. Originally called the Gustave Stickley Company, he renamed it United Crafts in 1901, then the Craftsman Workshops in 1903.

2. See Kevin Tucker, *Gustav Stickley and the American Arts & Crafts Movement* (Dallas Museum of Art, 2010), 44–47 and David Cathers, *Gustav Stickley* (Phaidon, 2003), 36.

Card Table

1. Pamela A. Parmal, *Women's Work: Embroidery in Colonial Boston* (MFA Publications, 2012), 77–97.

Devoción de Nuevo México (Devotion of New Mexico)

1. Charles M. Carrillo, "The 'Making and Breaking of New Mexican Santos,'" in *Our Saints Among Us: 400 Years of New Mexican Devotional Art*, ed. Barbe Awalt and Paul Rhetts (LPD Press, 1998), 32.

Double Chest

1. The design first appeared in 1754 as "Chest of Drawers" in the first edition of Thomas Chippendale's *Gentleman and Cabinet-Maker's Director.* George Hepplewhite essentially copied Chippendale's design in 1788 in his *Cabinet-Maker and Upholsterer's Guide.* Considered a lagging indicator of style, the 1811 *The Journeyman Cabinet and Chairmaker's Pennsylvania Book of Prices* illustrated the form with the caption "Double Chest."

2. Located east of Broad Street and south of Market Street. He operated shops at 136 Lombard and 193 South Sixth Street.

Pie Safe

1. More information about the High's pie safe may be found in Nicole Corrigan, "Pie Safe, ca. 1830–1860; Unidentified Maker, Eastern Tennessee," *Collections, Conservation, and Collaboration: A Compilation of Mellon Object-Centered Research Fellowship Papers.* link. mellonfellows.high.org/essay/pie-safe-ca-1830-1860-unidentified-maker-eastern-tennessee/.

2. J. Roderick Moore, "Wythe County, Virginia, Punched Tin: Its Influence and Imitators," *The Magazine Antiques* 126 (September 1984): 601–13.

Nail Cabinet

1. John Kelsey, "How to Be Garry Knox Bennett: The Badboy of Oakland Continues to Surprise, Annoy, and Delight." *Woodwork Magazine*, October 2001.

2. Arthur C. Danto, "Philosophizing with a Hammer: Garry Knox Bennett and Contemporary Art" in *Made in Oakland: The Furniture of Garry Knox Bennett* (American Craft Museum, 2001).

Linenfold Armoire (Perpendicular Style)

1. Gaston Bachelard, *The Poetics of Space* (Boston: Beacon Press, 1994), 78.

2. See: Linenfold paneled room, c. 1500, Museum of Fine Arts, Boston, collections.mfa.org/objects/470092/linenfold-paneled-room?ctx=56ad83da-08ee-4c34-9456-b5ccfd22f5cc&idx=1.

3. Glenn Adamson, "Critical thinking|Difficult issues: Works of Faith" in *The Magazine Antiques.* March 22, 2021. www.themagazineantiques.com/article/critical-thinkingdifficult-issues-works-of-faith/.

Lone Star Quilt

1. Lydia Maria Child, *The Little Girl's Own Book* (Boston: Carter, Hendee and Babcock, 1832), 225, and Eliza Leslie, *The House Book: or, a Manual of Domestic Economy* (Philadelphia: Carey & Hart, 1843), 311.

2. Mrs. Ann S. Stephens, "The Patch-Work Quilt," *Graham's Lady's and Gentleman's Magazine*, vol. 24, Jan.-June 1844 (Philadelphia), 27.

3. The quilt is owned by the Delaware Division of Historical and Cultural Affairs, acc. no. 99.49. See: The Quilt Index.

4. Marsha L. MacDowell and C. Kurt Dewhurst, *To Honor and Comfort: Native Quilting Traditions* (Santa Fe: Museum of New Mexico Press and Michigan State University, 1997).

Diner
1. Bendolph was also active in the Civil Rights Movement of the 1950s and '60s and advocated for the reopening of the ferry in Gee's Bend to allow greater access for economic and material commerce in the region.

ADORN

The Adams Vase
1. George Paulding Farnham, "The Adams Gold Vase" (Tiffany & Co., 1896), 14.

2. Ibid., 30.

Phoenix Planter
1. Damon Lawrence, email exchange with the author, February 8, 2025.

Bird-Form Pendant
1. Liu, R.K., "Spondylus in Precolumbian, Historic and Contemporary Southwest Jewelry," *Ornament* 28, 3): 60–66; Liu, R.K., "Prehistoric Mosaic Jewelry of the American Southwest," *Ornament* 30, 2: 54–59; Liu, R.K., "Prehistoric Southwest Jewelry and Their Sites," *Ornament* 34, 4: 64–69.

2. Dubin, L.S., "Jesse Monongya: Crafting the Jewels," *Ornament* 26, 1: 48–53.

3. P. R. Benesh-Liu., "Undivided Ancestry: The Jewelry of Carl & Irene Clark," *Ornament* no. 44 (2023) 1: 36–44.

Mourning Pendant
1. Martha Gandy Fales, *Jewelry in America 1600–1900* (Woodbridge, Suffolk: Antique Collectors' Club, 1995).

Necklace
1. Society of Arts and Crafts, Boston, founding documents; transcripts available in SAC archive, Boston Public Library.

***American Ruff*, from the *City Flotsam* Series**
1. *Craft in America*, "Jan Yager," www.craftinamerica.org/artist/jan-yager.

2. Marian Pritchard, "Jan Yager: October 9, 1951–August 14, 2024 - Art Jewelry Forum," Art Jewelry Forum, September 23, 2024. www.artjewelryforum.org/articles/jan-yager-natl-us_auth-marian-pritchard_natl-us_9-23-2024/.

3. Ibid.

Gown (Robe à l'Anglaise)
1. J. Herbert Callister, *Dress from Three Centuries: Wadsworth Atheneum* (Hartford, Connecticut: Wadsworth Atheneum, 1976), 10.

2. See, for example, the advertisement of Robert Jenkins, "on the North Side of the Town House in King-street," *Boston News-Letter*, May 17–May 24, 1739.

3. Charles Germain de Saint-Aubin, trans. Nikki Scheuer, *Art of the Embroiderer* (Boston: David R. Godine, Publisher, in association with the Los Angeles County Museum of Art, 1983), 20–21.

4. Daniel Wadsworth's probate inventory is available at: www.ancestry.com/search/collections/9049/records/2654954?tid=&pid=&queryId=8bac322d-50f4-4589-a306-fa2010871b58&_phsrc=AIO529&_phstart=successSource.

5. Joel Lang, "Jeremiah Wadsworth, 'foremost in every enterprise'," connecticuthistory.org/jeremiah-wadsworth/.

6. The will of Daniel Wadsworth (1704–1747) is available here: www.ancestry.com/search/collections/9049/records/2654954?tid=&pid=&queryId=6934eda1-b707-4964-a668-2aa2171dee0e&_phsrc=AIO532&_phstart=successSource.

Stetson "Boss of the Plains" Hat
1. See Jeffrey B. Snyder, *Stetson Hats and the John B. Stetson Hat Company 1865–1970* (Schiffer Publishing, 1997), 48–82.

2. Fredric M. Miller, *Still Philadelphia: A Photographic History 1890–1940* (Temple University Press, 2011).

3. Michael Grauer, "Sombreros Texanas and Bosses of the Plains: The Evolution of the Cowboy Hat," August 28, 2023, video, 55 min. 51 sec. www.youtube.com/watch?v=S_UsLQCLAY8.

Sneaker
1. Amara Hark-Weber, "Voices of Contemporary Shoemakers," *American Craft Inquiry* 1, no. 2 (October 2017), 30–41.

2. Yohance Lacour, "Luxury Leather," *Material Intelligence 7: Leather* (Sept. 2023), 69.

Boots
1. *Craft in America*. "Lisa Sorrell." www.craftinamerica.org/artist/lisa-sorrell.

2. Ibid.

3. Sorrell's statement about her boot designs, submitted to the author in January 2020.

SELECTED BIBLIOGRAPHY

Adamson, Glenn. *Craft: An American History.* Bloomsbury Publishing, 2021.

Adamson, Glenn, ed. *The Craft Reader.* Berg, 2010.

Anderson, Clay, et al. *The Craftsman in America.* National Geographic Society, 1975.

Anderson Galleries. *Early American Hooked Rugs. Gathered by Mrs. Edward O. Schernikow of New York City.* Forgotten Books, 2018.

Anderson Galleries. *Early New England Hooked Rugs: An Important Collection Containing Some Very Fine Examples to Be Sold by Auction Thursday Afternoon, May Twenty-Second at Two-Thirty O'clock.* Forgotten Books, 2018.

Andrews, Jack. *Samuel Yellin, Metalworker.* Skip Jack Press, 2011.

Arnett, William, et al. *Gee's Bend: The Women and Their Quilts.* Tinwood Books, 2003.

Arnett, William, Joanne Cubbs, and E. W. Metcalf. *Gee's Bend: The Architecture of the Quilt.* Tinwood Books, 2021.

Arnow, Jan. *By Southern Hands: A Celebration of Craft Traditions in the South.* Roundtable Press, 1987.

Arzeno Mooney, Claudia, April L. Hynes, and Mark M. Newell, "African-American Face Vessels: History and Ritual in 19th-Century Edgefield," *Ceramics in America 2013* (Milwaukee: Chipstone Foundation, 2013).

Awake, Robell. *A Short History of Black Craft in Ten Objects* (Princeton Architectural Press, 2025.

Bachelard, Gaston. *The Poetics of Space.* Beacon Press, 1994

Bally, Boris. "Oral history interview with Boris Bally, 2009 May 26–27." Interview by Mija Riedel. *Archives of American Art, Smithsonian Institution.* www.aaa.si.edu/collections/interviews/oral-history-interview-boris-bally-15682.

Barker, Garry. *The Handcraft Revival in Southern Appalachia, 1930–1990.* University of Tennessee Press, 1991.

Barquist, David L. *Myer Myers: Jewish Silversmith in Colonial New York.* Yale University Press, 2001.

Bascom, Mansfield. *Wharton Esherick: The Journey of a Creative Mind.* Abrams, 2010.

Batchelder, Martha. *The Art of Hooked-Rug Making.* The Manual Arts Press, 1947.

Beckert, Sven. *Empire of Cotton: A Global History.* Knopf, 2014.

Benesh-Liu, P.R. "Undivided Ancestry: The Jewelry of Carl & Irene Clark." *Ornament* 44 (2023) no. 1: 36–44.

Bergey, Barry, and Tom Pich. *Folk Masters: A Portrait of America.* Indiana University Press, 2017.

Bernstein, Bruce. *The Language of Native American Baskets: From the Weavers' View.* National Museum of the American Indian, 2003.

Bibbey, Brian, ed. *The Fine Art of California Indian Basketry.* Heyday Books, 1996.

Black Craftspeople Digital Archive, founded in 2019 by Tiffany Momon and codirected with Torren L. Gatson. Available at archive.blackcraftspeople.org.

Bowman, Leslie Greene. *American Arts & Crafts: Virtue in Design.* Los Angeles County Museum of Art, Bullfinch Press/Little Brown, 1990.

Bowman, Leslie Greene. "Arts & Crafts Silversmiths: Friedell and Blanchard in Southern California" in Edgar Morse, ed. *Silver in the Golden State: Images and Essays Celebrating the History and Art of Silver in California*, Oakland Museum History Department, 1986.

Bronner, Simon. *Making Tradition: On Craft in American Consciousness.* University Press of Kentucky, 2011.

Buck, Peter Henry. *Arts and Crafts of Hawaii.* Bishop Museum Press, 1957.

Burrison, John. *Brothers in Clay: The Story of Georgia Folk Pottery.* University of Georgia Press, 2008.

Callister, J. Herbert. *Dress from Three Centuries: Wadsworth Atheneum.* Wadsworth Atheneum, 1976.

Caplan, Allison. "Locking Eyes with the Sun: Perception, Landscape, and the Fame of Greenstone in a Sixteenth-Century Nahuatl Narrative." *MAVCOR* 5, no. 1: 2021. 10.22332/mav.ess.2021.3.

Carey, Celia. *The Quiltmakers of Gee's Bend.* Alabama Public Television. 2004. DVD.

Carrillo, Charles M. "The 'Making and Breaking of New Mexican Santos.'" in *Our Saints Among Us: 400 Years of New Mexican Devotional Art*, edited by Barbe Awalt and Paul Rhetts. LPD Press, 1998.

Cartaxo, Joseph, Pauline Holdsworth, and Alan Jalowitz. "Stetson: The Eastern Hat That Tamed the West." Pennsylvania Center for the Book. Spring 2011. pabook.libraries.psu.edu/literary-cultural-heritage-map-pa/feature-articles/stetson-eastern-hat-tamed-west.

Cash, Marie Romero. *Santos: Enduring Images of Northern New Mexican Village Churches.* University Press of Colorado, 1999.

Cathers, David. *Gustav Stickley.* Phaidon, 2003.

Chavkin, Dan, et al. *Architectural Pottery: Ceramics for a Modern Landscape.* Monacelli, 2024.

Chen, Yong. "From the Dachunniu to the Piñata: Tracing the Alleged Chinese Origin of a Mexican Tradition," *Fudan J. Hum. Soc. Sci.* 11 (2018): 69–81.

Coe, Ralph T. *Sacred Circles: Two Thousand Years of Native American Art.* Nelson-Atkins Museum of Art, 1977.

Coffin, Sarah, Ellen Lupton, and Darra Goldstein. *Feeding Desire: Design and the Tools of the Table, 1500–2005.* Assouline in association with Cooper-Hewitt, National Design Museum, 2006.

Cohodas, Marvin. "Louisa Keyser and the Cohns: Mythmaking and Basket Making in the American West," in *The Early Years of Native American Art History,* edited by Janet Catherine Berlo. University of Washington Press, 1992.

Collins, Lisa Gail. *Stitching Love and Loss: A Gee's Bend Quilt.* University of Washington Press, 2023.

Cooke, Edward S. *Global Objects: Toward a Connected Art History.* Princeton University Press, 2022.

Cooper, Wendy. *An American Vision: Henry Francis du Pont's Winterthur Museum.* National Gallery of Art, 2002.

Craft in America. "Jan Yager." www.craftinamerica.org/artist/jan-yager.

Craft in America. "Joan Baez on activism, Vietnam, and her Guitar." www.craftinamerica.org/short/joan-baez-on-activism-vietnam-and-the-guitar.

Craft in America. "Lisa Sorrell." www.craftinamerica.org/artist/lisa-sorrell.

Craft in America. "Philip Simmons." www.craftinamerica.org/artist/philip-simmons/.

Craft in America. "Rihannon Giddens." www.craftinamerica.org/artist/rhiannon-giddens.

Cross, Lauren, Solomon Cross, and Loretta Ausbie, prod. *The Skin Quilt Project.* Mae's House Productions, 2010. DVD.

Danto, Arthur C. "Philosophizing with a Hammer: Garry Knox Bennett and Contemporary Art." In *Made in Oakland: The Furniture of Garry Knox Bennett.* American Craft Museum, 2001.

Deas, Alston. *The Early Ironwork of Charleston.* Bostick & Thornley, 1941.

Diaz, RoseMary. "Avanyu: Spirit of Water in Pueblo Life and Art." *Santa Fe New Mexican,* May 16, 2014.

Dubin, L. S. "Jesse Monongya. Crafting the Jewels." *Ornament* 26 (2002) no. 1: 48–53.

Elwes, Rachel Layton. "A New Addition to African American Silver." *The Silver Society Journal,* 13 (2001).

Elwes, Rachel Layton. "Race, Authenticity and Colonialism: A 'Mustice' Silversmith in Philadelphia and St. Croix, 1783–1850." In *Colonialism and the Object: Empire, Material Culture, and the Museum,* edited by Tim Barringer and Tom Flynn. Routledge, 1998.

Fair, Susan G. *Alaska Native Art: Traditions, Innovation, Continuity.* University of Alaska Press, 2006.

Fales, Martha Gandy. *Jewelry in America, 1600–1900.* Antique Collectors' Club, 1995.

Farnham, Paulding. "The Adams Gold Vase." Tiffany & Co., 1896. Collections of the Huntington Library, 426337.

Fennimore, Donald L. *Eye For Excellence: Masterworks from Winterthur.* Winterthur Museum, 1994.

Fennimore, Donald L. *Metalwork in Early America: Copper and Its Alloys from the Winterthur Collection.* Winterthur Museum, 1996.

Ferris, William. *Afro-American Folk Art and Crafts.* University Press of Mississippi, 1986.

Fowler, Catherine, and Darla Garey-Sage. "Traditional Washoe Basketry: Art in Natural Fibers." In *Tahoe: A Visual History,* edited by Ann Wolfe. Skira Rizzoli Publications, 2015.

Garvan, Beatrice B., and David L. Barquist. *American Silver at the Philadelphia Museum of Art, Vol. 1, Makers A-F.* Philadelphia Museum of Art, 2018.

Glassie, Henry. *Daniel Johnston: A Portrait of the Artist as a Potter in North Carolina.* Indiana University Press, 2020.

Glassie, Henry. *The Spirit of Folk Art: The Girard Collection at the Museum of International Folk Art.* Museum of New Mexico Press, 1992.

Gleick, James. *The Information: A History, A Theory, A Flood.* New York: Pantheon Books, 2011.

Glisson, James, ed. *Becoming America: Highlights From the Jonathan and Karin Fielding Collection of Folk Art.* The Huntington Library, Art Museum, and Botanical Gardens, 2020.

Goldberg, Arthur, and James Witkowski. "Beneath His Magic Touch: The Dated Vessels of the African-American Slave Potter Dave." *Ceramics in America 2006* (Chipstone Foundation).

Gray, Stephen, and Robert Edwards. *Collected Works of Gustav Stickley.* Turn of the Century Editions, 1989

Hampton, Karen. "African American Women: Plantation Textile Production From 1750 to 1830." Textile Society of America Symposium Proceedings (2000). digitalcommons.unl.edu/tsaconf/770.

Hark-Weber, Amara. "Voices of Contemporary Shoemakers." *American Craft Inquiry* 1/2 (Oct. 2017).

Hewitt, Mark, and Nancy Sweezy. *The Potter's Eye: Art and Tradition in North Carolina Pottery.* University of North Carolina Press, 2005.

Hough, Samuel J. "The Class of 1870 Gorham Sterling Ice Bowls." *Silver* 22, no. 5 (September–October 1989): 30–32.

Hutchinson, Elizabeth. *The Indian Craze: Primitivism, Modernism, and Transculturation in American Art, 1890–1915.* Duke University Press, 2009.

Ingle, Marjorie. *The Mayan Revival Style: Art Deco Mayan Fantasy.* Peregrine Smith Books, 1993.

Johnson, Christy. *Common Ground: Ceramics in Southern California, 1945–1975.* American Museum of Ceramic Art, 2012.

Johnson, Geraldine. *Weaving Rag Rugs: A Women's Craft in Western Maryland.* University of Tennessee Press, 1985.

Jones, Michael Owen. *The Hand Made Object and Its Maker.* University of California Press, 1975.

Joseph, J.W. "'. . . All of Cross'—African Potters, Marks, and Meanings in the Folk Pottery of the Edgefield District, South Carolina." *Historical Archaeology* 45 no. 2 (2011): 134–55.

Kane, Patricia E. *Colonial Massachusetts Silversmiths and Jewelers: A Biographical Dictionary Based on the Notes of Francis Hill Bigelow & John Marshall Phillips* (University of New England Press, 1998.

Kaplan, Wendy. *The Arts and Crafts Movement in Europe and America.* Los Angeles County Museum of Art and Thames & Hudson, 2004.

Kaplan, Wendy, et al. *"The Art That is Life": The Arts and Crafts Movement in America, 1875–1920.* Bulfinch Press with Museum of Fine Arts, Boston. 1987.

Kay, Jon, ed. *The Expressive Lives of Elders: Folklore, Art, and Aging.* Indiana University Press, 2018.

Keawe, Lia O'Neill, and Marsha McDowell. *'Ike Ulana Lau Hala: The Vitality and Vibrancy of Lau Hala Weaving Traditions in Hawai'i.* University of Hawaii Press, 2014.

Kelsey, John. "How to Be Garry Knox Bennett: The Badboy of Oakland Continues to Surprise, Annoy, and Delight." *Woodwork Magazine,* October 2001.

Kent, William Winthrop. *The Hooked Rug: A Record of Its Ancient Origin, Modern Development, Methods of Making, Sources of Design, Value as a Handicraft, the Growth of Collections, Probable Future in America, and Other Data.* Tudor Publishing. Co, 1937.

Ketchum, William C. *All-American Folk Arts and Crafts.* Rizzoli, 1986.

Klein, Cecelia F. "The Ideology of Autosacrifice at the Templo Mayor." In *The Aztec Templo*

Mayor, edited by Elizabeth Boone. Dumbarton Oaks Research Library and Collection, 1987.

Klein, Dan. *Glass: A Contemporary Art*. Rizzoli, 1989.

Koplos, Janet. *Gertrud and Otto Natzler: Collaboration/Solitude*, American Craft Museum, 1993.

Kopp, Joel, and Kate Kopp. *American Hooked and Sewn Rugs: Folk Art Underfoot*. University of New Mexico Press, 1995.

Kurin, Richard. *The Smithsonian's History of America in 101 Objects*. The Penguin Press, 2013.

Lacour, Yohance. "Luxury Leather." *Material Intelligence 7: Leather* (Sept. 2023).

Larnerd, Joseph Harold. "Decorative Cut Glass and the Working Class in America, 1876 to 1916." PhD dissertation, Stanford University, 2019.

Larnerd, Joseph Harold. "The McKinley Bowl's Services and Disservices, 1898–1901." *American Art* (Summer 2023).

Lasser, Ethan W. "Selling Silver: The Business of Copley's Paul Revere." *American Art* 26, no. 3 (September 2012): 26–43.

Law, Rachel Nash. *Appalachian White Oak Basketmaking: Handing Down the Basket*. University of Tennessee Press, 1991.

Lehigh University. "Challenge VII DysFUNctional." Brochure. 2009. preserve.lehigh.edu/digital-special-collections/lehigh-university-art-galleries-luag/challenge-vii-dysfunctional.

Lerner, Jesse. *The Maya of Modernism: Art, Architecture, Film*. University of New Mexico, 2011.

Levin, Elaine, Dora De Larios, and the Los Angeles Craft and Folk Art Museum. *Sueños/Yume: Fifty Years of the Art of Dora De Larios*. Los Angeles Craft and Folk Art Museum, 2009.

Liu, R. K. "Prehistoric Mosaic Jewelry of the American Southwest." *Ornament* 30 (2006) no. 2: 54–59.

Liu, R. K. "Prehistoric Southwest Jewelry and Their Sites." *Ornament* 34 (2011) no. 4: 64–69.

Liu, R. K. "Spondylus in Precolumbian, Historic and Contemporary Southwest Jewelry." *Ornament* 28 (2005) no. 3: 60–66.

Lowcountry Digital History Initiative. "Keeper of the Gate: Philip Simmons Ironwork in Charleston, South Carolina." Lowcountry Digital Library and Philip Simmons Foundation, 2014. ldhi.library.cofc.edu/exhibits/show/philip_simmons.

MacKey, William. *American Bird Decoys*. Dutton, 1987.

Madison, Mary. *Plantation Slave Weavers Remember: An Oral History*. 2015.

Martin, Terry. "The Spoonish Sculptures of Norm Sartorius." *Woodwork Magazine*, 2006.

McChesney, Lea S. "'Carrying On': Gender and Innovation in Historic Pueblo Pottery,Nampeyo, Maria Martinez, and Arroh-A-Och." In *Hearts of the People: Native Women Artists*, edited by Jill Ahlberg Yohe and Terri Greeves. University of Washington Press, 2019.

Miller, Fredric M. *Still Philadelphia: A Photographic History 1890–1940*. Temple University Press, 2011.

Miller, Marla R. *Entangled Lives: Labor, Livelihood and Landscapes of Change in Rural Massachusetts*. Johns Hopkins University Press, 2019.

Miller, Marla R. "Postcards from an Imagined Early America." The Porter-Phelps-Huntington House Museum. www.pphmuseum.org/marla-miller.

Milosch, Jane. *Chunghi Choo and Her Students: Contemporary Art and New Forms in Metal*. Arnoldsche, 2022.

Miranda, Carolina A. "Dora De Larios, an Innovative Artist Known for Creating Ceramic Work That Reflected L.A., Dies at 84." *Los Angeles Times*, January 30, 2018.

Mooney, Claudia Arzeno, April L. Hynes, and Mark M. Newell. "African-American Face Vessels: History and Ritual in 19th-Century Edgefield." *Ceramics in America 2013* (Chipstone Foundation).

Moore, J. Roderick. "Wythe County, Virginia, Punched Tin: Its Influence and Imitators." *The Magazine Antiques* 126 (September 1984).

Morrill, Penny C. *William Spratling and the Mexican Silver Renaissance: Maestros de Plata*. Harry N. Abrams, 2002.

National Cowboy and Western History Museum. "History of the Cowboy Hat." nationalcowboymuseum.org/explore/history-of-the-cowboy-hat/.

National Ranching Heritage Society. "How Stetsons Became the Cowboy Hat Icon of the American West." October 7, 2022. ranchingheritage.org/stetson-cowboy-hat-icon-american-west/.

Natzler, Gertrud, and Otto Natzler. *The Ceramic Work of Gertrud and Otto Natzler*. M. H. de Young Memorial Museum, 1971.

Natzler, Otto. *Form and Fire: Natzler Ceramics, 1939–1972*. The Renwick Gallery of the National Collection of Fine Arts by the Smithsonian Institution Press, 1973.

Natzler, Otto. *Gertrud and Otto Natzler: Ceramics*. Los Angeles County Museum of Art, 1968.

Nevers, Jo Ann. *Wa She Shu: A Washo Tribal History*. Inter-Tribal Council of Nevada, 1976.

Parmal, Pamela A. *Women's Work: Embroidery in Colonial Boston*. MFA Publications, 2012.

Peck, Robert McCracken. "Icy Embellishments: Arctic Imagery and the Decorative Arts." *Antiques* 171, no. 2 (February 2007): 72–79.

Pennington, David, and Michael Taylor. *A Pictorial Guide to American Spinning Wheels*. The Shaker Press, 1975.

Pennington, David, and Michael Taylor. *Spinning Wheels & Accessories*. Schiffer Publishing, 2004.

Pepich, Bruce. "Expecting the Unexpected." Ganoksin Jewelry Making Resources. January 26, 2023. www.ganoksin.com/article/expecting-unexpected/.

Pettit, Michael. *Artists of New Mexico Tradition: The National Heritage Fellows*. Museum of New Mexico Press, 2012.

Philadelphia Art Museum. "Man's Cowboy Hat." philamuseum.org/collection/object/90747.

Pierotti, Makenna. "Stirring the Soul: Magic in the Art of Spoon Carving." *WV Living*, (Winter 2014): 50.

Pristo, Larry J. *Martelé: Gorham's Art Nouveau Silver*. Phoenix Publishing Group, 2002.

Pritchard, Marian. "Jan Yager: October 9, 1951–August 14, 2024." *Art Jewelry Forum*. September 23, 2024. www.artjewelryforum.org/articles/jan-yager-natl-us_auth-marian-pritchard_natl-us_9-23-2024/.

Risatti, Howard. *A Theory of Craft: Function and Aesthetic Expression*. University of North Carolina Press, 2007.

Rockman, Seth. *Plantation Goods: A Material History of American Slavery*. University of Chicago Press, 2024.

Rosengarten, Dale. *Row upon Row: Seagrass Baskets of South Carolina Lowcountry*. McKissick Museum, 1986.

Rosengarten, Dale, Theodore Rosengarten, and Enid Schildkraut. *Grass Roots: African Origins of an American Art*. Museum of African Art, 2008.

SELECTED BIBLIOGRAPHY

Saint-Aubin, Charles Germain de. *Art of the Embroiderer*. Translated by Nikki Scheuer. David R. Godine, Publisher, in association with the Los Angeles County Museum of Art, 1983.

Sartorius, Norm. Artist's website. www.normsartorious.com.

Sartorius, Norm. "Gallery Talk for 'Spoons to Stir the Soul' with Norm Sartorius." Museum for Art in Wood. YouTube, May 25, 2022. 1 hour, 25 min. www.youtube.com/watch?v=LF9bfaigL5w.

Sessions, Billie, et al. *Ripples: Marguerite Wildenhain and Her Pond Farm Students*. California State University, 2002.

Severson, Don R., Michael D. Horikawa, and Jennifer Saville. *Finding Paradise: Island Art in Private Collections*. Honolulu Academy of Arts, University of Hawaii Press, 2002.

Seymour, John. *The Forgotten Crafts*. Portland House, 1984.

Sid Richardson Museum. "The Evolution of the Cowboy Hat." October 18, 2023. sidrichardsonmuseum.org/the-evolution-of-the-cowboy-hat/.

Sid Richardson Museum. "Sombreros, Texanas, and Bosses of the Plains: The Evolution of the Cowboy Hat." Lecture by Michael Grauer. August 28, 2023. www.youtube.com/watch?app=desktop&v=S_UsLQCLAY8&t=1661s.

Siporin, Steve. *American Folk Masters: The National Heritage Fellows*. Harry N. Abrams, 1992.

Smith-Ferri, Sherrie. "Weaving a Tradition: Pomo Indian Baskets from 1850 Through 1996." Diss., University of Washington, 1998.

Snyder, Jeffrey B. *Stetson Hats and the John B. Stetson Company: 1865–1970*. Schiffer, 1997.

Stapleton, Constance. *Crafts of America*. Harper & Row, 1988.

Steele, Thomas J. *Santos and Saints: The Religious Folk Art of Hispanic New Mexico*. Ancient City Press, 1982.

Stetson. "Man of Many Hats: The Story of John B. Stetson" blog.stetson.com/the-story-of-john-b-stetson/.

Stevens, Benjamin. *The Silver Punchbowl made by Paul Revere to Commemorate a vote of the Honorable House of Representatives of the Massachusetts Bay in 1768*. Nathan Sawyer & Son, 1895.

Stromsoe, Randy. "Oral history interview with Randy James Stromsoe, 2012 June 4–7." Interview by Jo Lauria. Archives of American Art, Smithsonian Institution. www.aaa.si.edu/collections/interviews/oral-history-interview-randy-james-stromse-16093.

Sweezy, Nancy. *Raised in Clay: The Southern Pottery Tradition*. University of North Carolina Press, 1994.

Todd, Leonard. *Carolina Clay: The Life and Legend of the Slave Potter Dave*. W.W. Norton & Company, 2008.

Toussaint, Corbett. "Edgefield District Stoneware: The Potter's Legacy." *Journal of Early Southern Decorative Arts* 41 (2020).

Tracy, Berry B., Marilynn Johnson, Marvin D. Schwartz, and Suzanne Boorsch. *19th-Century America: Furniture and Other Decorative Arts*. Metropolitan Museum of Art, 1970.

Trapp, Kenneth R., et al. *The Arts & Crafts Movement in California: Living the Good Life*. Oakland Museum, Abbeville Press, 1993.

Ulrich, Laurel Thatcher. *The Age of Homespun: Objects and Stories in the Creation of An American Myth*. Vintage Books, 2002.

Ulrich, Laurel Thatcher, et al. *Tangible Things: Making History through Objects*. Oxford University Press, 2015.

Venable, Charles L. *China and Glass in America, 1880–1980: From Tabletop to TV Tray*. Dallas Museum of Art, 2000.

Vlach, John. *The Afro-American Tradition in Decorative Arts*. Cleveland Museum of Fine Arts, 1978.

Vlach, John Michael. *Charleston Blacksmith: The Work of Philip Simmons*. University of South Carolina Press, 1992.

Wagley, Catherine. "Dora De Larios at Beta Main." *Contemporary Art Review*, March 7, 2018.

Walker, Alice, *In Search of Our Mothers' Gardens: Womanist Prose*. Harcourt Brace Jovanovich, 1983.

Ward, Barbara M. "John Coney." In *Colonial Massachusetts Silversmiths and Jewelers*, edited by Patricia E. Kane, et al. Yale University Art Gallery, 1998.

Ward, Gerald W. R. *Paul Revere: Sons of Liberty Bowl*. MFA Publications, Museum of Fine Arts, Boston, 2016.

Ward, Gerald, et al. *MFA Highlights: American Decorative Arts and Sculpture*. MFA Publications, 2006.

White Hawk, Dyani. "In Focus: Maria, Rose, Empowerment, and Indigenous Women Rollin' Hard: A Conversation with Rose B. Simpson." In *Hearts of the People: Native Women Artists*, edited by Jill Ahlberg Yohe et al. Minneapolis Institute of Art in association with the University of Washington Press, 2019.

Wildenhain, Marguerite. "Oral history interview with Marguerite Wildenhain, March 14, 1981." Interview by Hazel Bray. *Archives of American Art, Smithsonian Institution*.

Williams, Elizabeth, ed. *Gorham Silver: Designing Brilliance, 1850–1970*. Rizzoli Electa, 2019.

Williams, Elizabeth. "The Long Road Home: The Gorham Writing Table and Chair." RISD Museum, January 15, 2014.

Zapata, Janet. "The Rediscovery of Paulding Farnham, Tiffany's Designer Extraordinaire. Part I: Jewelry." *The Magazine Antiques* 139, no. 3. (1991): 558.

Zilber, Emily, ed. *The Crafted World of Wharton Esherick*. Rizzoli Electa, 2024.

Zipp, A. Brant. "Putting Thomas Commeraw Together Again: A Brief Meditation on Two Decades of Research." *Ceramics in America* 2024 (Chipstone Foundation).

Zug, Charles G. *Turners and Burners: The Folk Potters of North Carolina*. University of North Carolina Press, 1986.

CONTRIBUTORS

Emily Zaiden is director and curator of the Craft in America Center in Los Angeles, where she has organized over eighty multidisciplinary contemporary art, craft, and design exhibitions for the center and partner museum venues. Zaiden oversees public programs, a K-12 education initiative, and digital projects, including the creation of the online Craft Video Dictionary. Her research focuses on craft processes, materiality, functional design, and cultural art, particularly from a historical lens. She worked at the Los Angeles County Museum of Art and *Architectural Digest* before joining Craft in America. Zaiden earned an MA from the Winterthur Program in American Material Culture.

Glenn Adamson is a curator, writer, and historian who was previously director of the Museum of Arts and Design and head of research at the V&A. Dr. Adamson's publications include *Thinking Through Craft* (2007), *The Invention of Craft* (2013), and *Craft: An American History* (2021).

Elisabeth Agro is a cofounder of *The Craft Chronicle* and curator of modern and contemporary craft and decorative arts at the Philadelphia Museum of Art, where she works toward craft's inclusion in the ever-changing global landscape of contemporary art. Her recent exhibitions with accompanying publications include *The Shape of Time: Korean Art after 1989* (2023) and *Boom: Art & Design in the 1940s* (2025).

Barry Bergey retired as director of folk and traditional arts at the National Endowment for the Arts after a career of thirty years at the agency. Bergey coauthored *Folk Masters: A Portrait of America* (2018) with photographer Tom Pich.

Alexandra Cade is the assistant curator at the Museum of the American Revolution and a PhD candidate in the history of American civilization at the University of Delaware. A historian and violist, she is a scholar of music, tourism, and the senses.

Lauren Cross is the Gail-Oxford Associate Curator of American Decorative Arts at the Huntington Library, where she works to grow previously underrepresented areas of the collection. She directed and produced the documentary *The Skin Quilt Project* and curated the traveling exhibition *The Skin Quilt Project: Uplifting Our Culture, Celebrating Tradition*. She has curated recent exhibitions highlighting African American traditions in textiles, silhouettes, and ceramics, including an exhibition on modern ceramist Doyle Lane.

Christina L. De León is Cooper Hewitt's acting deputy director of curatorial and its inaugural associate curator of Latino design. She has grown the museum's collection of U.S. Latino and Latin American design, while also organizing exhibitions and public programs. De León produced the museum's first feature-length documentary film, *Mud Frontier: Architecture at the Borderlands*.

Jeannine Falino is a curator whose wide-ranging exhibitions, books, and projects explore virtually every era of American craft, design, and culture. Formerly curator at the Museum of Fine Arts, Boston, she now works with private and institutional clients on exhibitions, catalogs, and books.

Nonie Gadsden is the Katharine Lane Weems Senior Curator of American Decorative Arts and Sculpture at the Museum of Fine Arts, Boston, where she is responsible for a wide range of artwork including decorative arts and sculpture from North, Central, and South America, from ancient times through the twentieth century.

Christine Garnier is assistant professor of art history at the University of California, Santa Barbara. She specializes in the histories of materials and environments in the nineteenth-century United States.

Steven L. Grafe is curator of art at Maryhill Museum and previously curated collections at the National Cowboy & Western Heritage Museum and Southwest Museum. His publications include *Peoples of the Plateau: The Indian Photographs of Lee Moorhouse, 1898–1915* (2005) and *Plateau Pictorial Beadwork: The Fred L. Mitchell Collection* (2021).

Katherine Gray is an artist who has written about glass, curated and juried multiple exhibitions, and taught workshops around the world. She lives in Los Angeles and is a professor of art at California State University, San Bernardino. She can also be seen in the Netflix series *Blown Away*.

Carla Hemlock is a textile and multimedia artist whose work addresses environmental, historical, and societal issues. Her work is in private, corporate, and public collections including the Metropolitan Museum of Art; Smithsonian American Art Museum; Smithsonian National Museum of the American Indian; Museum of Fine Arts, Boston; Royal Ontario Museum; and the Montreal Museum of Contemporary Arts.

Suzanne Isken is former executive director of Craft Contemporary in Los Angeles. Prior to that, she served as the director of education at the Museum of Contemporary Art, Los Angeles.

Leslie King Hammond is an art historian, cultural innovator and artist, professor emerita, and founding director of the Center for Race and Culture at Maryland Institute College of Art. Publications and exhibitions include *Witnessing Humanity: The Art of John Wilson*, *The Global Africa Project*, and *Art as a Verb*, in New York, Boston, and Baltimore museums and galleries.

Mary Jackson is a basket maker living in Charleston. Her practice is both innovative and deeply rooted in ancestral traditions originating in West Africa, brought to America by slaves, and evolving in the communities of Charleston and Mt. Pleasant. Her baskets are represented in collections such as the Renwick Gallery of the Smithsonian American Art Museum; the Museum of Arts and Design; the Museum of Fine Arts, Boston; and the Museum of African American History, Detroit.

Alexandra Alevizatos Kirtley has been a curator in American Art at the Philadelphia Museum of Art since 2001. She has been an appointee of the U.S. Senate's Commission on Art since 2003 and serves on the boards of the Decorative Arts Trust (officer), the Andalusia Foundation, and the Museum of Early Southern Decorative Arts.

Debra Utacia Krol, Indigenous affairs reporter at the *Arizona Republic*, is an award-winning journalist with an emphasis on Native environmental and science issues. She is an enrolled member of the Xolon Salinan Tribe from the Central California coastal ranges and has contributed articles and photos to *First Families: A Photographic History of California Indians* (2007) and *Seaweed, Salmon, and Manzanita Cider: A California Indian Feast* (2008).

CONTRIBUTORS

Jo Lauria is a curator, educator, and the author of numerous publications, including *Craft in America: Celebrating Two Centuries of Artists and Objects* (2007), which was accompanied by a traveling exhibition for which she served as chief curator. She received the 2016 American Ceramic Circle Book Award for *Ralph Bacerra: Exquisite Beauty* (2015). Her most recent publication, also complemented by an exhibition at the American Museum of Ceramic Art, is *Architectural Pottery: Ceramics for the Modern Landscape* (2024).

Colette Lemmon has worked with Haudenosaunee art and artists for three decades. Currently an independent consultant, she was curator of exhibitions at the Iroquois Museum (Howes Cave, NY) from 2012 to 2024 and guest curator and writer for the New York State Museum (Albany, NY), Museum of Contemporary Native Arts (Santa Fe, NM), Ottawa Art Gallery (Canada), Seneca-Iroquois National Museum (Seneca Nation Territory), and other facilities.

Robert K. Liu, PhD, has written extensively on ancient, ethnic, and contemporary jewelry and personal adornment. He is the author of *Collectible Beads: A Universal Adornment* and *The Photography of Personal Adornment* as well as more than 800 articles and publications. He is the coeditor of *Ornament Magazine*.

Roberto Lugo is a Philadelphia-based artist, activist, poet, and educator. He utilizes traditional ceramic techniques in conjunction with surface design reminiscent of hip-hop culture to highlight themes of poverty, inequality, and racial injustice. His work is in the collections of the Metropolitan Museum of Art; Philadelphia Museum of Art; Museum of Fine Arts, Boston; Brooklyn Museum, and many more.

Tess Lukey (Aquinnah Wampanoag) is associate curator of Native American art at the Trustees of Reservations, where she advances Indigenous-led interpretation and community-driven curation. A practicing artist in ceramics and basketry, she holds degrees from the University of New Mexico and MassArt. She was also the curator for the 2025 Boston Public Art Triennial.

Wendy Maruyama is professor emeritus at San Diego State University, where she has taught furniture design and woodworking since 1989. Trained as a furniture maker, she has used her skills to extend beyond the traditions of woodworking and into sculptural and narrative works.

Marques Hanalei Marzan is a Hawaiian visual artist and culture bearer as well as cultural advisor and the Wayne Pitluck and Judith Pyle Curator for Cultural Resilience at Bishop Museum in Honolulu, Hawai‘i. Marzan is committed to his culture and defines his work through cultural vibrancy and strengthened community engagements.

Jane Milosch is visiting professorial fellow in provenance and curatorial studies, School of Culture and Creative Arts, at the University of Glasgow and former chief curator of the Renwick Gallery, Smithsonian American Art Museum. She is the editor of *Chunghi Choo and Her Students: Contemporary Art and New Forms in Metal* (2022).

Mira Nakashima is a designer and head of George Nakashima Woodworkers. She worked with her father for many years as a colleague and designer. Since her father's death in 1990, she has been the creative director of the studio, where she continues to produce her father's classic furniture designs and to design and produce her own work as well.

Monica Obniski is curator of decorative arts and design at the High Museum. Obniski has edited and contributed to many publications. She lectures widely, has taught art and design history, and has received grants from the Terra Foundation for American Art and the Center for Craft, among other institutions.

Carol Sauvion is the creator of the Peabody Award–winning PBS series *Craft in America*. The documentary series celebrates American craft and the artists who bring it to life. She was also the executive director of Craft in America, a nonprofit dedicated to promoting and advancing original handcrafted work through educational programs in all media. Craft is Sauvion's lifelong passion. For over forty-five years she was the director of Freehand, her Los Angeles gallery specializing in functional craft. Prior to opening Freehand, Sauvion was a professional potter for ten years. Sauvion has her degree in art history from Manhattanville College in Purchase, New York. She has served on the boards of the Craft Emergency Relief Fund and the American Craft Council and on the Planning Committee for *Handwork: Celebrating American Craft 2026*.

Joyce J. Scott is known for her work in jewelry, beadwork, and glass. Her art reflects her perspective on American popular culture, her ancestry, and her community. Her work is in the collections of the Baltimore Museum of Art, Mint Museum of Craft + Design, and the Smithsonian American Art Museum. She has been named a MacArthur Fellow.

Julie Silber is a nationally known quilt expert, lecturer, and curator, as well as producer of the film *Hearts and Hands* and a coauthor of a book of the same name.

Lowery Stokes Sims is an independent curator and art historian who worked for the Metropolitan Museum of Art, the Studio Museum in Harlem, and the Museum of Arts and Design. She is an avid collector of Black dolls and memorabilia.

Therman Statom is a glass artist best known for his painted ladders, houses, chairs, and other objects that are constructed out of plate glass, blown glass objects, plywood, and found objects. Statom has taught at Pilchuck and the University of California, Los Angeles. He has also received commissions for countless permanent large-scale installations.

Matthew A. Thurlow is executive director of the Decorative Arts Trust. He has lectured widely on topics relating to late eighteenth- and early nineteenth-century furniture. He has published as editor and contributing author of *American Classical Furniture, 1810–40: Regional Identities in the Schrimsher Collection* (2025), and was a coauthor of the Metropolitan Museum of Art's exhibition catalog *Duncan Phyfe: Master Cabinetmaker in New York*.

Ehren Tool has made and given away more than 26,500 cups since 2001. He is a Marine Corps veteran of the 1991 Gulf War. Tool received his BFA from USC in 2000 and his MFA from UC Berkeley in 2005, where he has worked as a senior mechanician since graduation.

Einar and Jamex de la Torre live and work on both sides of the border: the Guadalupe Valley in Baja California, Mexico, and San Diego. Their signature style features mixed media work with blown-glass sculpture and installation art. In recent years, they have also created lenticular prints and photo murals.

Consuelo Jimenez Underwood is a fiber artist, weaver, and professor emerita at San José State University. Her artistic expression is deeply tied to traditional Huichol weaving, a heritage she incorporates into her large mixed-media textiles. Her work is in the Smithsonian American Art Museum and the Oakland Museum of Art.

Lynne Zacek Bassett is an independent scholar of historic fashion and textiles who has undertaken award-winning exhibitions and publications. She was curator of textiles and fine arts at Old Sturbridge Village in Sturbridge, Massachusetts. Her scholarly contributions have been recognized by the American Antiquarian Society and the International Quilt Study Center, among other organizations.

Zac Zetterberg serves as the curator of art of the Center for American Decoys at the Peoria Riverfront Museum in Peoria, Illinois. Under his leadership, the center has emerged as a nationally recognized destination, celebrating the rich history of American waterfowling and elevating the artistry of the decoy as a unique form of American folk art.

CREDITS

Front endpapers, 54, 154, 214, 224, 226–27: Courtesy of the Huntington Art Museum, San Marino, California
Opposite half title, 210: Courtesy of Sarah Myerscough Gallery
2, 36, 238: Courtesy of the Smithsonian American Art Museum
4, 180: Courtesy of Crab Tree Farm, © 2010, Dallas Museum of Art, Photo by Brad Flowers.
6, 142, 144, 202: Courtesy of the High Museum of Art, Atlanta
8, 58, 60, 114, 116, 126, 128, 174, 198, 200: Courtesy of the Philadelphia Museum of Art
10, 46, 48–49: Courtesy of Forrest L. Merrill. Photo by M. Lee Fatherree. Art by Kay Sekimachi © 2025 Kay Sekimachi / Artists Rights Society (ARS), New York
24: Photo by M. Lee Fatherree, Courtesy of Forrest L. Merrill
20, 118, 160, 164, 184, 186–87, 234–35, 260, 262: © 2026 Museum of Fine Arts, Boston
22: © Virginia Museum of Fine Arts, Photo by Katherine Wetzel.
26, 28–29: Courtesy of McNay Art Museum, and Einar & Jamex de la Torre Brothers
30: Courtesy of the Santa Barbara Museum of Natural History Image: TRE-009, Photo by Dovida Treiman
32: Courtesy of Philbrook Museum of Art, Tulsa, Oklahoma
34, 120, 204, 296: Photo by Madison Metro, Craft in America
36: © 2019 Jeremy Frey
38: Courtesy of the Gibbes Museum of Art/ Carolina Art Association
40, 56: Photography © The New York Historical
42: Courtesy of SFO Museum
43: © Woody De Othello, Courtesy of the High Museum of Art, Atlanta
44: The Middleton Place Foundation, Charleston, South Carolina
50, 244, 284: © The Metropolitan Museum of Art / Art Resource, NY
52: Courtesy of the South Carolina State Museum
60: Courtesy of the Philadelphia Museum of Art © Wharton H. Esherick
62: Courtesy of Toledo Museum © Therman Statom
64: Photo by Jesse W. Stephen, Bishop Museum Archives
66: Photo by Kathy Tarantola/PEM
68–69: Courtesy of studio e, Seattle, Photo by Mario Gallucci
70: Courtesy of Peoria Riverfront Museum
72, 130, 152: Courtesy of the Smithsonian Institution
74, 254, 256, 257: Courtesy of the Winterthur Museum, Garden & Library
76: Courtesy of the Dora De Larios Estate, Photo by Dale Strumpell
78: Photo by Hayden Haynes
80, 82–83: Courtesy of Roberto Benavidez © Roberto Benavidez
84,164: Courtesy of The Metropolitan Museum of Art, NY
86, 87: Photo by M. Cooper. Courtesy of the Ivy Brown Gallery
88, 90–91: Courtesy of the Museum of Early Southern Decorative Arts
92: Photo provided by the Bruce Springsteen Center for American Music
94: Photo by Russ Fill
96: Courtesy of Heard Museum, Photo by Craig Smith
98, 218–19, 272: Photo by David Franzen, Bishop Museum Archives
100: Alpha Historica / Alamy
101: Prints and Photographs Division, Library of Congress, Washington, D.C. LC-DIG-pcrd-1d08372
102, 105: Courtesy of Oregon Historical Society, Photo by Robert Warren
104: Courtesy of National Cowboy & Western Heritage Museum
106, 108, 109: Courtesy Todd Huber, Skateboarding Hall of Fame
122: © Kazuki Takizawa. Photo by Robert Wedemeyer
124: Courtesy Ehren Tool
132–33: © Kate Russell, Courtesy of Rose B. Simpson and Kate Russell
134: Courtesy of Smithsonian American Art Museum, Photo by Lucia RM Martino
146: Courtesy of Forrest L. Merrill
148: Courtesy of Fredrik Nilsen Studio
156: Courtesy of arnoldsche Art Publishers. Photo by Peter Krumhardt © Chunghi Choo
158: Photo by Ron Bez. Adapted from the original.
162: Album / Alamy
166: Courtesy Boris Bally, Photo by J.W. Johnson
168: Courtesy Norm Sartorious, Photo by Jim Osborn
176: Courtesy Chipstone Foundation, Photo by Gavin Ashworth.
178: Courtesy of the Schrimsher Foundation
182: Image courtesy of Rago/Wright. Used by permission of the Sam and Alfreda Maloof Foundation for Arts and Crafts
188, 190, 191: Courtesy of the Rhode Island School of Design, Providence
192: Courtesy of Smithsonian American Art Museum, © 1998, Charles M. Carrillo
194, back endpapers: Courtesy Friedman Benda and Misha Kahn, Photo by Daniel Kukla
196: Courtesy of the Museum of Arts and Crafts, St. Petersburg. Photo by George Erml. © George and Mira Nakashima
206, 208, 209: Courtesy of the Garry and Sylvia Bennett Estate
212: Courtesy of Wendy Maruyama
216: Photo by Noel Kenny, Bishop Museum Archives
220: Photo by Lori Bentley Law, Creative Director, Affeldt Mion Properties
222: Old Trails_Winslow Historical Society. Image courtesy of Lori Bentley Law, Creative Director Affeldt Mion Properties
223: Herb and Dorothy McLaughlin Collection, Arizona State University Library, CP MCL 9569. Courtesy of Lori Bentley Law, Creative Director Affeldt Mion Properties, on behalf of the Affeldt Mion Museum
228: Courtesy of Julie Silber
230, opposite copyright page: International Quilt Museum, University of Nebraska-Lincoln
232: Used by permission of the artist
236: © Mary Lee Bendolph, Courtesy of the Nicelle Beauchene Gallery
246: Faire du Vert/ Paul Anderson
248, 250: Courtesy the artist and R & Company, Photo by Logan Jackson
251: Courtesy of the Brooklyn Museum
252: Courtesy of the Pomona College Museum of Art, Photo by Robert K. Liu
258: Courtesy of the Wheelwright Museum of the American Indian, Santa Fe
264: Courtesy of the Philadelphia Museum of Art © Jan Yager
266: Photo by Michael Koryta. Courtesy of Mobilia Gallery © Joyce Scott.
268, 270, 271: Allen Phillips/Wadsworth Atheneum
274, 290, 292, 293: Courtesy of the Maryhill Museum of Art
276: Courtesy the artist, Photo by Gina Clyne
278: The Art Institute of Chicago / Art Resource, NY
280, 282, 283: Photo by Madison Metro, Craft in America, © Consuelo Jimenez Underwood
286: Courtesy of the Toronto Metropolitan University Libraries, Archives & Special Collections
294: Courtesy of the Colonial Williamsburg Foundation
298: © Vitra Design Museum, Photo by Unruh Jones. From *Nike: Form Follows Motion.*
300: Courtesy of Amara Hark-Weber
301: Courtesy Yohance Lacour, Photo by Ryan Beshel
302: © Lisa Sorrell

INDEX

Page numbers in italics indicate illustrations.

abstract expressionism, *77*, 147
Adams, Edward Dean, 245
Adams, Samuel, 139
African Americans. *See* Black artisans; slavery and enslaved people
African cultures and crafts: banjo's antecedents, 95; basketry, 39; drum, 85; hats, 289; story quilts, 233
Aguiñiga, Tanya, *276*, 277
Albert Bruckner's Sons, *74*, 75
American China Manufactory, *126*, 127
Amish Center Diamond quilt, *230*, 231
Anasazi pottery, 135
Andreson, Laura, 247
Aquinnah Wampanoag, *66*, 67
Architectural Pottery, *246*, 247
Art Nouveau crafts, 189
Arts and Crafts movement, 33, 51, 119, 155, 159, 181, 189, 261
Ashley's sack, *44*, 45
Assiniboine crafts, 225
Aztec: Quetzalcóatl head brooch, 155

Bacerra, Ralph, 121
Bachelard, Gaston, 211
Baez, Joan, *92*, 93
Baldwin, James, 263
Bally, Boris, *166*, 167
banjo, *94*, 95
baroque style, 21, 27, 199, 269
Barozzio, M. Jacopo, 199
Bartlam, John, 117
Barton, Thomas Drummond, 161
baskets: Chumash basket (Sitmelelene), *30*, 31; degikups (Keyser), *32*, 33; double pie basket (Curry), *34*, 35; Jackson on South Carolina basketry, *38*, 39; urchin basket (Frey), *36*, 37
Baudouin/Bowdoin, Pierre, 21
Bauhaus, 25
beaded clothing and accessories: Canandaigua Treaty Belt (wampum belt, artist unknown), *286*, 287; Gibson (attrib.), *290*, 291, *292–93*
Benavidez, Roberto, *80*, 81, *82–83*
Bendolph, Louisiana, 237
Bendolph, Mary Lee, *236*, 237, 306n1 (Diner)
Bennett, Garry Knox, *206*, 207, *208–9*
Bentzon, Peter, *152*, 153
Bering, Vitus, 275
Bertoia, Harry, 197
Black, Matthew, 201
Black artisans: ceramics, 41; metalworking, 53, 153, 201; music and musical instruments, 95; sewing and quilting, 41, 75, 85, 233, 237; spinning, 55; unearthing contributions of, 41; woodworking, 41, 201
black-on-black pottery, *130*, 131
Blanchard, Porter and George Porter, 159
Block, Matilda "Tillie," *118*, 119
Boelen, Jacob, *150*, 151
Bok, William Curtis and Nellie Lee, 61, 304nn2–3 (Library ladder)
Bonnin, Gousse, 127
Bowerman, Bill, *298*, 299
Bowers, Jacob, and Bowers family, 203
bowls: ice bowl (Gorham Manufacturing Company), *6*, *143*, 144; *Marriage in Form* (Stocksdale & Sekimachi), 47, *48–49*; Mimbres Valley bowl with rabbits (artist unknown), *136*, 137; oval bowl with fractured appearance (Natzler), *146*, 147; punch bowl (Marrett for Libbey Glass Company), *144*, 145; Sons of Liberty bowl (Revere), *138*, 139, *140–41*; *Spectral Bowl* (Gray), *148*, 149
boxes. *See* cabinets, chests, and boxes
Bragdon, Claude, 181
Branson, William, 115
Bridges, Ruby, 249
Brigham, Charles, 73
Brinckerhoff, Abraham, 163
Briscoe, Pearl Gilliland Knapp, 155
British East India Company, 269
Brown, Edith, 119

cabinets, chests, and boxes: clothes press (Kleiderschrank, artist unknown), *14*, *198*, 199; double chest (Gross), *200*, 201; *Fractured* (Maruyama), *212*, 213; *Georgy Girl* chest (Weir-Quiton), *204*, 205; *Linenfold Armoire (Perpendicular Style)* (Kurtz), *210*, 211; Maruyama on casework design, *212*, 213; *Nail Cabinet* (Bennett), *206*, 207, *208–9*; *Paired Box* (Sekimachi), *8*, *46*, 51; pie safe (artist unknown), *202*, 203; tool chest (Phyfe), *56*, 57
California Design X exhibition (1968), 205
California roundover style, 207
Campeachy chairs, *176*, 177
candelabra, *24*, 25
carriers and transportation: cradleboard (artist unknown), *96*, 97; El Camino (*Maria*, Simpson), 131, *132–33*; saddle (Hamley & Company), *102*, 103, *105*; skateboard (artist unknown), *106*, 107, *108–9*; surfboard (Kahanamoku), *98*, 99, *100–101*
Carrillo, Charles M., *192*, 193
Centennial Exposition (Philadelphia, 1876), 145, 249
ceramics: *Apocalypto* vessel (Romero), 135; bowl with two rabbits (artist unknown), *136*, 137; charger (*New Genesis*, Romero), *134*, 135; dish (Hübner), *128*, 129; pickle stand (American China Manufactory), *126*, 127; plate with Avanyu design (Martinez), *130*, 131. *See also* containers; cups; porcelain
chairs: armchair (United Crafts/The Craftsman Workshops), *4*, *180*, 181; armchair (Thomas Constantine & Co.), *178*, 179; Butaca (campeachy chair, Hemmings), *176*, 177; *Georgy Girl* (Weir-Quiton), *204*, 205; Martelé writing table and chair, *188*, 189, *190–91*; rocker (Maloof), *182*, 183; rush-bottomed chair (Fussell or Savery, attrib.), *174*, 175
chandelier, *26*, *27*, *28–29*
Chee Dodge, Henry, 259
Cherokee nations, 117
Chicago Roller Skate Company, 107
China and Chinese crafts, 77, 117, 121, 151, 269
Chippendale, Thomas, 306n1 (Double chest)
Chon, Atsidi, 259
Choo, Chunghi, *156*, 157, 305n1 (Tea service)
Chumash basketry, *30*, 31
Church, Frederic Edwin, 143
Cisco, Samuel, 73
Cisco, Sarah Marie Arnold, *72*, 73
Clark, Carl and Irene, 253
clothing. *See* beaded clothing; garments
Coates, Mary, 153
Cochiti Pueblo, 135
Codman, William Christmas, *188*, 189, *190–91*
Cody, Buffalo Bill, 291
coffee set, 163, *164–65*
coffee table, *194*, 195
Cohn, Abe and Amy, 33
coin basket, *30*, 31

Collins, Catharine, 225
colonial revival style, 195
Columbian Exposition (World's Fair, 1893), 23
Columbia River Plateau beadwork styles, *290*, 291, *292–93*
comb, *284*, 285
Commeraw, Thomas W., *40*, 41
Committee of One Hundred, 163
Coney, John, *160*, 161
Congress, US, furnishings of, 179
Constantine, Thomas, 179
containers: Ashley's Sack (Middleton), *44*, 45; jug (Commeraw), *40*, 41; *Secrets Safe* (De Othello), 41, *43*; storage jar (Drake), *42*. *See also* bowls; cabinets, chests, and boxes
Cook, James, 273
Cornelius, Eli, 79
Correa, Caroline, *238*, 239
Correll, Sophia, 89
COVID-19 pandemic, 211
cradleboard, *96*, 97
crazy quilt, *228*, 229
Cressey, David, *246*, 247
cups: mug (Block), *118*, 119; *one of thousands* (porcelain cup, Tool), *124*, 125; *Ruby Stripe, Container* Series (Takizawa), *122*, 123; silver tankard (Richardson), *114*, 115; *SUVs, Tipping Point* Series (Takayama-Ogawa), *120*, 121; teabowl (John Bartlam Manufactory), *116*, 117; Tool on therapy of making, 125
Curry, Roger and Betty, *34*, 35
Cushing, Thomas, 139

Dalí, Salvador, 205
Daughters of Liberty, 55
Davidson, Carolyn, 299
Dawson, Robert and Rebecca, 153
Day, Thomas, 41
degikup, *32*, 33
De la Cruz, José, 31
De Larios, Dora, *76*, 77
De la Torre, Einar and Jamex, *26*, 27, *28–29*
De Othello, Woody, 41, *43*
Derryberry, Melinda and Bob, 35
De Solá, Pablo Vicente, 31
dolls: McCall's Upside Down Doll, 75; Northeastern Native male doll (Cisco), *72*, 73; Topsy-Turvy doll (Albert Bruckner's Sons), *74*, 75
doors, *50*, 51, 304n1 (Doors)
double chest, *200*, 201, 306n1 (Double chest)
double pie basket, *34*, 35
Drake, David, 41, *42*
Driscoll, Clara, *22*, 23
drums, *84*, 85, *86–87*
Dubois, W.E.B., 249
Dummer, Jeremiah, 21
Dutch crafts, 151, 203

El Camino customization, 131, *132–33*
Ellis, Harvey, *180*, 181
embroidery, 45, 185, 229, *268*, 269, 291
Erickson, Michelle, 127
Esherick, Wharton H., *60*, 61, 304n3 (Library ladder)
Exposition Universelle (Paris, 1900), 23

Farnham, George Paulding, *244*, 245
Feddersen, Carly and Joe, 67, *68–69*
fishing. *See* lures
Fitzhugh, William, 115
Flame Glazing technique, 247
flatware: miniature fork and spoon (Coney), *160*, 161; *Pierced Truss Two* (Bally), *166*, 167; spoon (*Old and In the Way*, Sartorius), *168*, 169
folk art: decoy (Schoenheider), *70*, 71; hooked rug making, 215
forks. *See* flatware
Frankl, Paul, 195
Franklin, Benjamin, 117
Freedom Quilting Bee (Gee's Bend), 237
French, Joe, 71
Frey, Francis "Gal," 37
Frey, Jeremy, *36*, 37
Fricke, Michele, 249
Friedell, Clemens, *154*, 155
furnishings. *See* cabinets, chests, and boxes; chairs; household goods, tools, and utensils; rugs; tables
Fussell, Solomon, *174*, 175
Gallup Inter-Tribal Indian Ceremonial (1939), 221
garments: feathered cloak (artist unknown), *272*, 273; gown (robe à l'anglaise) (artist unknown), *268*, 269; *Metabolizing the Border* (performative wearables, Aguiñiga), *276*, 277; Navajo blankets (*Contemporary Chief Set (Three Miniatures)*, Ornelas), *278*, 279; parka (artist unknown), *274*, 275; rebozo (Underwood), *280*, 281, *282–83*; Stetson hat, *288*, 289. *See also* beaded clothing and accessories; shoes and footwear
gate, wrought iron, *52*, 53
Gee's Bend (AL), 237, 306n1 (Diner)
George Washington Covenant Belt, *286*, 287
German Americans. *See* Pennsylvanian Germans
Ghiselin, Cesar, 115
Gibson, Christopher Columbus "Lum," 35
Gibson, George, 291, *293*
Gibson, Mary, *290*, 291, *292–93*
Giddens, Rhiannon, *94*, 95
Gilded Age, 245
Gimby, Harry Arnold and Lucy, 73
Gladwell, Malcolm, 121
glass: beads, *96*, 97, *290*, 291; *Fish Trap: Coyote Frees the Salmon* (Feddersen), 66, *67*; huaraches (Aguiñiga), *276*, 277; *Pink Ladder* (Statom), *62*, 63; punch bowl (Marrett for Libbey Glass Company), *144*, 145; *Ruby Stripe, Container* Series (Takizawa), *122*, 123; *Spectral Bowl* (Gray), *148*, 149; Venetian glassware, 123. *See also* lighting and lamps
Goldschmied, Alexander Schaffner, 167
Gorelangton, Pat, *238*, 239
Gorham Manufacturing Company, *142*, 143; Martelé line, 155, *188*, 189, *190–91*
Gothic style, 211
Gray, Katherine, *148*, 149
Great Depression, 61, 221, 231
Griffith, Jay, 303
Gropius, Walter, 25
Gross, Thomas, Jr., 41, *200*, 201
Guerrier, Edith, 119
guitar, *92*, 93
Gullah Geechee culture, 53
Hale, Frank Gardner, *260*, 261
Hamley, John James "J. J.," 103
Hamley & Company, *102*, 103, *105*
Hamlin, Hannibal, 179
Hancock, John, 139
Hark-Weber, Amara, 299, *300*
Hartel, James J., *94*, 95
Hassanamisco Nipmuc community, *72*, 73
Haudenosaunee Confederacy, 79, 287
Hawaiian culture and crafts: feathered cloak, *272*, 273; fishhook, *64*, 65; makaloa mat, *216*, 217, *218–19*; quilt, *2*, *238*, 239; surfboard, *98*, 99, *100–101*
Heino, Vivika, 247
Hemings, John, *176*, 177
Hepplewhite, George, 306n1 (Double chest)
Herr, Jane and Gordon, 25
Hill, Julia Joe, *220*, 221, *222–23*
hooked rug, *214*, 215
Hope, Thomas, 179
Hopi crafts, 135, 253
household goods, tools, and utensils: butter print (artist unknown), *58*, 59; chocolate pot (Friedell), *154*, 155; clothes press (artist unknown), *198*, 199; glass ladder (Statom), *62*, 63; library ladder (Esherick), *60*, 61; spinning wheel (artist unknown), *54*, 55; tongs (Myers, attrib.), *162*, 163. *See also* cabinets, chests, and boxes; ceramics; flatware; lighting and lamps; teapots and tea service
Hubbell, Lorenzo, Jr., 221
Hubbell Trading Post, 221, *223*
Huber, Georg and Jonas, 199
Hübner, Georg, *128*, 129
Huff, Koltin, 79
hunting. *See* lures

Imperial Furniture Company (Grand Rapids), 195
Indian Arts and Crafts Board, 131
Iñupiaq homelands and art, 143
ironwork, *50*, 51, *52*, 53

Jackson, Mary, *38*, 39
Jacques, Alfred, *78*, 79
Japanese Americans, 47, *77*, 213
Japanese culture and crafts, *77*, 121, 123, 197, 213, 299
Jarboe, Julian K., 75
Jasper, Benjamin, 201
Jefferson, Thomas, 177, 213
Jennings, Vanessa, 97
jewelry. *See* necklaces
Jewish artisans, 163, *164*
Joe, Julia, *220*, 221, *222–23*
Joe, Sam, 221
John Bartlam Manufactory, *116*, 117
Johnson, Andrew, 143
Jordan, Michael, 299
jug (Commeraw), *40*, 41

Kahanamoku, Duke, *98*, 99, *100–101*
Kahn, Misha, *194*, 195
Kahnawake crafts, *296*, 297
Kalaiokamalino, *216*, 217, *218–19*
Kamehameha dynasty (HI), 217, 239
kaolin. *See* porcelain
Keckley, Elizabeth, 41
Keyser, Louisa (Dat So La Lee), *32*, 33
Kiowa cradleboards, *96*, 97
knives. *See* flatware
Knoll, Hans and Florence, 197
KT Glassworks, 123
Kurtz, Christopher, *210*, 211

Lacour, Yohance, 299, *301*
lacrosse stick, *78*, 79
Lakota crafts, 225
lamps. *See* lighting and lamps
Lancaster Amish (PA), 231
Latrobe, Benjamin Henry, 179
Lawrence, Damon, Rita and Max, 247
Libbey Glass, *144*, 145, 305n1 (Punch Bowl)
lighting and lamps: candelabra (Wildenhain), *24*, 25; candlesticks (Noyes), *20*, 21; cobweb lamp (Driscoll for Tiffany lamps), *22*, 23; *Le Point de Bascule (The Tipping Point)* (De la Torre Brothers' chandelier), *26*, 27, *28–29*
linenfold carving, 211
Loloma, Otellie, 135
Lone Star quilt, *224*, 225, *226–27*
Louisiana Purchase Exhibition (St. Louis, 1904), 189
Lovato, Mary, 253
Lugo, Roberto, *248*, 249, *251*
Lunalilo, William, 217
lures and traps (fishing and hunting): fishhook (Hawaiian artist unknown), *64*, 65; fish and eel trap (artist unknown), *66*, 67; *Fish Trap: Coyote Frees the Salmon* (Feddersen), 67, *68–69*; goose decoy (Schoenheider), *70*, 71
Luttrell Psalter, 81

Magonigle, H. Van Buren, *44*, 45 304n1 (Doors)
Maine Indian Basketmaker Alliance (MIBA), 37
mākau, *64*, 65
Maloof, Sam, *182*, 183
Manifest Destiny, 135, 289, 303
Marco Polo, 81
Marrett, William, *144*, 145
Martelé line (Gorham Manufacturing Company), 155, *188*, 189, *190–91*
Martinez, Julian, 131
Martinez, Maria Poveka and Santana Roybal, *130*, 131
Martin Guitars, *92*, 93
Maruyama, Wendy, *212*, 213
Mason, Winifred, 263
Matthews, Washington, 259
Mayan or Aztec revival style, 155
Mazloomi, Carolyn, *232*, 233
McIlhiney, Parker, 23
McKinley, William, 145
McNair, Elvira Brokaw, 51
McNay Art Museum (San Antonio), 27
Mesoamerica, 253
Mexico and Mexican crafts, 77, 81, 151, 155, 177, 277, 281, 289
Middle Atlantic silver, 115
Middleton, Ruth, *44*, 45
Migratory Bird Treaty Act (1918), 71
Mimbres pottery (New Mexico), 135, *136*, 137
missionaries, 31, 81, 135, 193, 239
moccasins, *294*, 295
modernism, 77, 147, 181, 195, 247, 263
moena pāwehe (makaloa mat), *216*, 217, *218–19*
Mohawks and tourist trade, *296*, 297
Monongya, Jesse, 253
Mooney, James, 259
Moore, Eudorah, 205
Moore, Fred "Moose," 37
Morris, George Anthony, 127
Morris, William, 181
mosaics, *252*, 253
Müller, Karl L. H., 249, *250*
musical instruments: banjo (Hartel), *94*, 95; guitar (Martin Guitars), *92*, 93; piano (Prichard), *88*, 89, *90–91*; side drum (Prentiss), *84*, 85; *World History I (Drum)* (Riley), 85, *86–87*
Myers, Myer, *162*, 163, *164–65*

Nakashima, George, *196*, 197
Nasworthy, Frank, 107
Native Americans: hunting decoys, 69. *See also* beaded clothing and accessories; Southwestern culture and crafts; *specific indigenous groups/crafts*
Natzler, Gertrud and Otto, *146*, 147
Navajo (Diné) culture and crafts, *220*, 221, *222–23*, *258*, 259, *278*, 279
necklaces: *American Ruff, City Flotsam* Series (Yager), *264*, 265; art jewelry (Hale), *260*, 261; bird-form pendant (artist unknown), *252*, 253; mourning pendant (artist unknown), *254*, 255, *256–57*; squash blossom necklace (Béésh łigai íít'íní Ałts'óózígíí), *258*, 259; *War, What is it Good For, Absolutely Nothin', Say it Again* (Scott), *266*, 267; We Two Necklace (Smith & Scott), *262*, 263
Nez Perce, Wallowa Band, 103
Nike shoe, *298*, 299
Northrop, Agnes, 23
Noyes, John, *20*, 21
Nys, Johannis, 115

Olympic sports, 99, 107
Onitsuka Tiger sneakers, 299
Onondaga Nation lacrosse, 79
Ornelas, Barbara Teller, *278*, 279

Pairpoint, Thomas J., 143
Panama-Pacific International Exposition (San Francisco, 1915), 189
papa he'enalu. *See* surfboards
Partridge, Fred and May, 261
Passamaquoddy basketry, *36*, 37
Paulson Fontaine Press, 237
Pawnee Bill, 291
Peatson, Robert, *164–65*
pendants. *See* necklaces
Pendleton Oregon Round-Up rodeo (1916), *102*, 103, *104–5*
Penn, William, 115
Pennsylvanian Germans, *58*, 59, *128*, 129, *198*, 199, 203
Perpendicular style, 211
Pettway, Essie Bendolph, 237
Philipse, Frederick and Eva, 151
Phoenix planter, *246*, 247
Phyfe, Duncan, *56*, 57
Phyfe, James D., 57
piano, *88*, 89, *90–91*
pickle stand, *126*, 127
pie basket, *34*, 35
pie safe, *202*, 203
piñata, *80*, 81, *82–83*, 305n1 (Piñata)
plates and serving pieces. *See* ceramics; teapots and tea service
porcelain, 77, *116*, 117, 121, *124*, *126*, 127, 129, 249, *250*
Potter and Company, *188*, 189, *190–91*
Powers, Harriet, 41, 233, *234–35*
Powers, Richard, 183
Prentiss, Henry H., *84*, 85
Prichard, David, *88*, 89, *90–91*
Pringle, Joseph, 53
Printer, Moses, 73
Pro/Artisan studio line, 247
Proctor, Alexander Phimister, 103
Pueblo culture and pottery, 131, 137
punched-tin panels, 203
Puritans, 161, 185

quilts, *2*, 85; Amish Center Diamond quilt, *230*, 231; crazy quilt (artist unknown), *228*, 229; *Diner* (Bendolph), *236*, 237; Lone Star quilt (artist unknown), *224*, 225, *226–27*; pictorial quilt (Powers), 233, *234–35*; *Sacred Union* (Mazloomi), *232*, 233; *Umeke O Kamehameha* (Hawaiian quilt, Gorelangton), *238*, 239

religious items: altarpiece: *Devoción de Nuevo México (Devotion of New Mexico*, Carrillo), *192*, 193; enslaved people and, 233; Torah finials (Myers), 163, *164*
Remsen, Dorothy, 163
Revere, Paul, Jr., *138*, 139, *140–41*
revivalist architecture, 51
Revolutionary War, 139, 269

Rich, Fleming K., 203
Richards, Bill, 107
Richardson, Francis, Sr., *114*, 115
Riley, Cheryl, 85, *86–87*
Rivera, Diego, 155
Robinson, Jackie, 249
Robsjohn-Gibbings, T. H., 195
rococo design, 163
Roller Derby Skateboard, 107
Romero, Diego, *134*, 135
Rothko, Mark, 147
rugs: *Contemporary Chief Set (Three Miniatures)* (Ornelas), *278*, 279; *Diyogí Tsoh (The Big Rug)* (Joe & Hill), *220*, 221, *222–23*; hooked rug (artist unknown), *214*, 215; makaloa mat (moena pāwehe, Kalaiokamalino), *216*, 217, *218–19*
Rush, Benjamin, 117
Ruskin, John, 181

saddle, *102*, 103, *105*
Sání, Atsidi, 259
San Ildefonso Pueblo pottery, 131
Santa Fe Indian Market, 37
Sartorius, Norm, *168*, 169
Saturday Evening Girls club, 119
Savery, William, *174*, 175
Schoenheider, Charles, Sr., *70*, 71
Scott, Joyce J., *262*, *266*, 267
Secord, Theresa, 37
Secure Fence Act (2006), 277
Sekimachi, Kay, *46*, 47, *48–49*
Seneca (Onǫda'gegá') crafts, *284*, 285, *286*, 287
Senska, Frances, 7
Sewall, Samuel, 21
Seward, William H., 143
shoes and footwear: bespoke shoes (Hark-Weber), 299, *300*; boots (Sorrell), *302*, 303; moccasins (artist unknown), *294*, 295; *Redemption Sneaker* (Lacour), 299, *301*; souvenir shoe-shaped wall pocket (artist unknown), *296*, 297; track shoe (Moon shoe prototype for Nike, Bowerman), *298*, 299
silversmiths, 21, 41, 115, 139, 151, 153, 155, 159, 161, 163–64, 167, 189, 259
Simmons, Carlton, 53
Simmons, Peter, 53
Simmons, Philip, *52*, 53
Simpson, Rose B., 131, *132–33*
Sinagua crafts, *252*, 253
Sitmelelene, Juana Basilia, *30*, 31
skateboards, *106*, 107, *108–9*
slavery and enslaved people: basketry, 39; ceramics, 117, 135; metalworking, 41, 53; sewing and quilting, 45, 75, 85, 233; spinning, 55, 304n3 (Spinning Wheel); woodworking, 177, 201, 213
Smith, Art, *262*, 263
Society of Arts and Crafts (SAC), 261
Sons of Liberty bowl, *138*, 139, *140–41*
Sorrell, Lisa, *302*, 303
South Carolina State Museum, 53
Southwestern culture and crafts, *136*, 137, *192*, 193, *220*, 221, *222–23*, *252*, 253, *258*, 259
souvenir shoe-shaped wall pocket, *296*, 297
spinning wheel, *54*, 55
spoons. *See* flatware
Spratling, William, 155
squash blossom necklace, *258*, 259
Statom, Therman, *62*, 63
Stephens, Alexander, 259
Stetson, John B., *288*, 289
Stevenson, Larry, 107
Stickley, Gustav, 181
Stocksdale, Bob, 47, *48–49*
Storrow, Helen Osborne, 119
Stowe, Harriet Beecher, 75
Straker, Joseph Edward, *188*, 189, *190–91*
Strayhorn, Billy, 263
Stromsoe, Randy, *158*, 159
Studio Craft movement, 25, 157, 181
sugar tongs and bowl, *162*, 163, *164–65*
Sundown, Jackson, 103, *104*
surfboards, *98*, 99, *100–101*
Susquehannock crafts, *284*, 285

tables: Arlyn table (Nakashima), *196*, 197; card table (artist unknown), *184*, 185, *186–87*; coffee table (*Enhancing Self Trust*, Kahn), *194*, 195; *Devoción de Nuevo México* altarpiece (Carrillo), *192*, 193; Martelé writing table and chair, *188*, 189, *190–91*; tea tables, 195
Takayama-Ogawa, Joan, *120*, 121
Takizawa, Kazuki, *122*, 123
tariffs, 55, 145, 305n2 (Punch Bowl)
teapots and tea service: engraved teapot (Boelen), *150*, 151; teabowl (John Bartlam Manufactory), *116*, 117; teapot and creamer (*Swan Vessels*, Stromsoe), *158*, 159; teapot with wooden handle (Bentzon), *152*, 153; *Tea Service* (Choo), *156*, 157
tea tables, 195
Thomas Constantine & Co., *178*, 179
Tiffany, Louis Comfort, 23
Tiffany & Co., *244*, 245
Tiffany Girls, 23
Tiffany Glass and Decorating Company, *22*, 23
Tool, Ehren, *124*, 125
tools. *See* household goods, tools, and utensils
Torah finials (Myers), 163, *164*
Townshend Acts (England, 1767), 139
toys: chess set (De Larios), *76*, *77*; lacrosse stick (Jacques), *78*, 79; piñata (Benavidez), *80*, 81, *82–83*. *See also* dolls
Traditional Ecological Knowledge, 33
transportation. *See* carriers and transportation
traps. *See* lures and traps
Trist, Elizabeth House, 177
Tudor, Frederic, 143

Umatilla crafts, *290*, 291, *292–93*
Underwood, Consuelo Jimenez, *280*, 281, *282–83*
Union Porcelain Works, 249

van Cortlandt, Jacobus, 151
vases: *Adams Vase* (Farnham), *244*, 245; *Brooklyn* (Lugo), 249; *A Century of Black Music* (Lugo), 249; *A Century of Education Vase* (Lugo), *248*, 249, *251*; *Century Vase* (Müller), 249, *250*; Phoenix planter (Cressey), *246*, 247
Victorian era, 181, 255, 261, 297
Vorhees, Daniel W., 71

Wabanaki basketry, *36*, 37
Wadsworth, Abigail, *268*, 269
Wadsworth, Jeremiah, 269
Walker, Alice, 237
wampum belt, *286*, 287
Warner, LaMont A., 181, (Armchair (United Crafts/The Craftsman Workshops))
War of 1812, 179
Washington, George, 255, 287
Washoe basketry, *32*, 33
weaving. *See* baskets; rugs
Weir-Quiton, Pamela, *204*, 205
Whistler, James, 71
Wildenhain, Marguerite, *24*, 25
Wilkes, John, 139
Willoughby, Mary, 161
Winthrop, John, 161
women artisans: basketry, 39; butter making, 59; ceramics, 119; embroidery, 45, 185; glassworking, 23; hairworking, 255; quilting, 225, 229, 231, 237; spinning, 55; weaving and hand-sewing, 39, 97, 215, 269, 295, 297; woodworking, 97, 205
World War II, 25, 47, 147, 181, 213

Yager, Jan, *264*, 265
Yellin, Samuel, *50*, 51, 304n1 (Doors)
Yupik culture and crafts, *274*, 275

Ziegler, Franz, *188*, 189, *190–91*

This book is part of Handwork 2026, Craft in America's nationwide semiquincentennial collaboration showcasing the importance of the handmade and celebrating the diversity of craft that defines America.

HANDWORK
Celebrating American Craft 2026

Support for this publication provided by various individuals and

The Americana Foundation

PHAIDON PRESS LIMITED
2 Cooperage Yard
London E15 2QR

MONACELLI
A Phaidon Company
111 Broadway
New York, NY 10006

PHAIDON SARL
55, rue Traversière
75012 Paris

phaidon.com/monacelli

First published 2026

ISBN 978-1-58093-727-6

Library of Congress Control Number: 2026930434

EDITORS: Jenny Florence and Jenny Mutch
PRODUCTION: Michael Vagnetti
DESIGN: Jessica Fleischmann with Lauren Cramer/ Still Room

Printed in China

OPPOSITE: Detail, Amish Center Diamond quilt, c. 1910–20, see pages 230–231.

FRONT ENDPAPERS: Detail, Hooked rug, late 19th century, see pages 214-215; Detail, *Linenfold Armoire (Perpendicular Style)*, 2020, see pages 210-211.
BACK ENDPAPERS: Detail, *Enhancing Self Trust*, 2022, see pages 194–195.

COVER: Butter print, 1800–1840, see pages 58–59; Beaded gauntlets, c. 1950, see pages 290–91; *A Century of Education Vase (Century Vase)*, 2024, see pages 248–50.
BACK COVER: *Ruby Stripe*, 2022, see pages 122–23; Rocker, 1990, see pages 182–83.

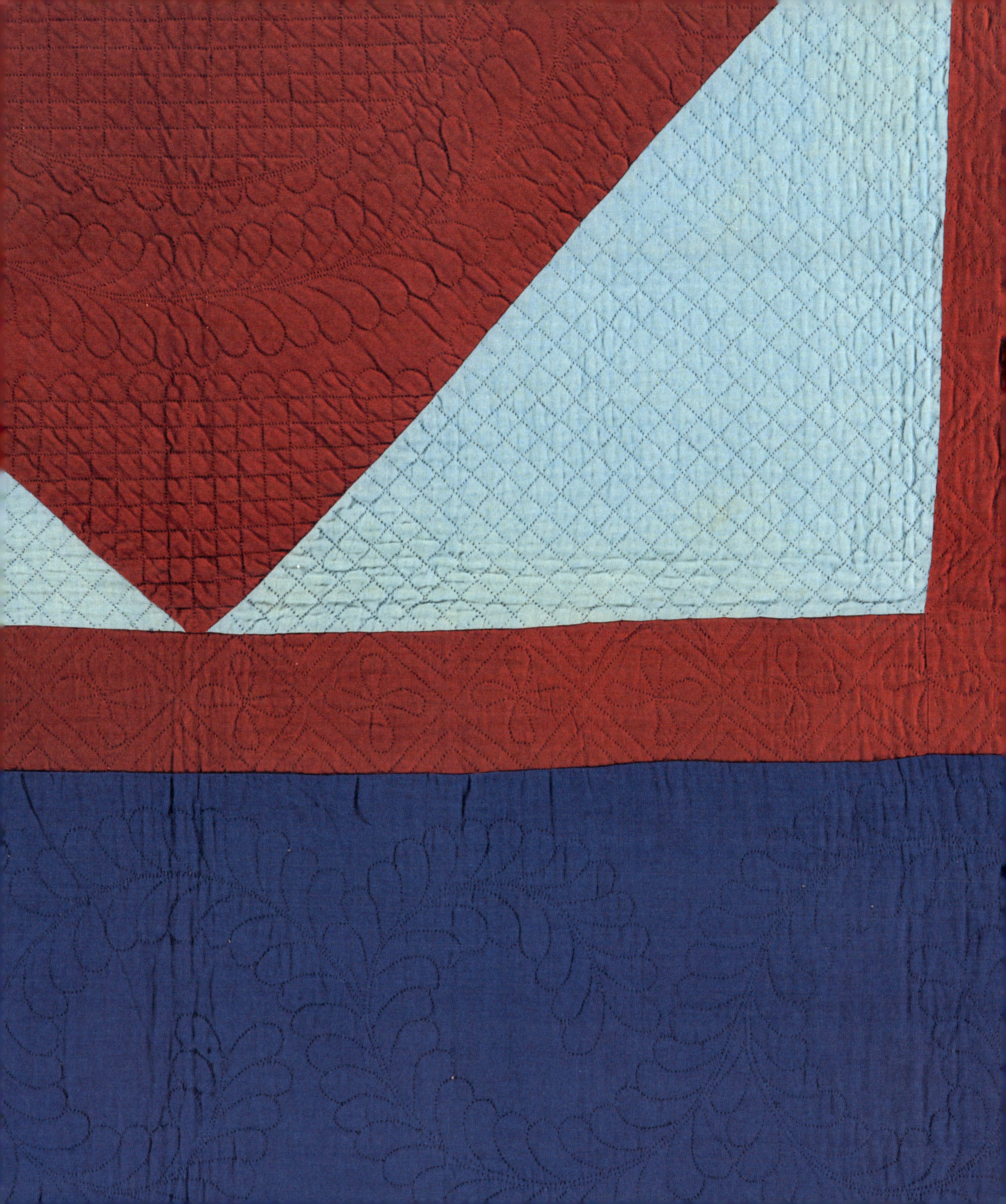

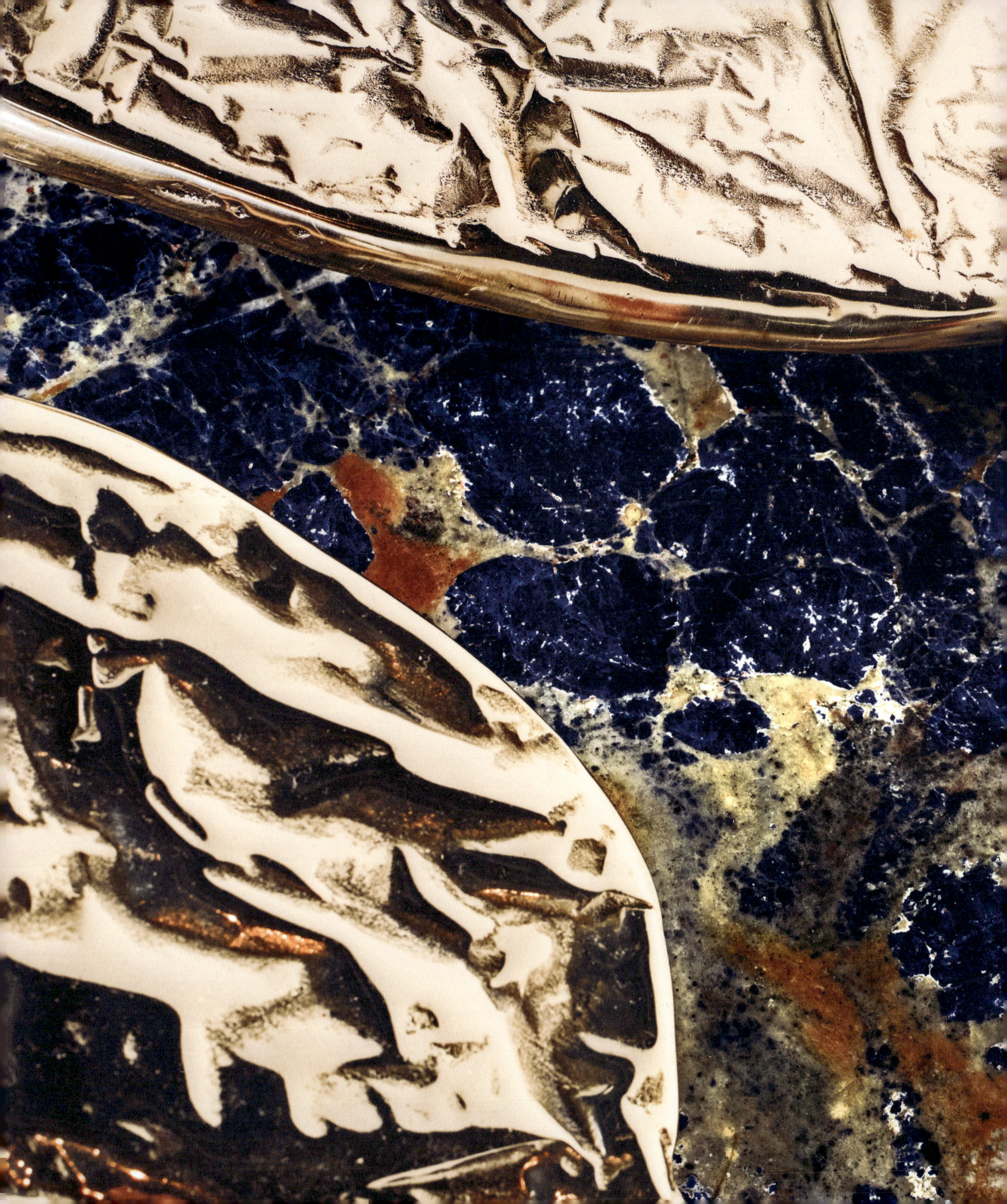